Chartered Instit
Management Accoun

How to access your on-line resources

Kaplan Financial students will have a MyKaplan account and these extra resources will be available to you online. You do not need to register again, as this process was completed when you enrolled. If you are having problems accessing online materials, please ask your course administrator.

If you are not studying with Kaplan and did not purchase your book via a Kaplan website, to unlock your extra online resources please go to www.en-gage.co.uk (even if you have set up an account and registered books previously). You will then need to enter the ISBN number (on the title page and back cover) and the unique pass key number contained in the scratch panel below to gain access.

You will also be required to enter additional information during this process to set up or confirm your account details.

If you purchased through Kaplan Flexible Learning or via the Kaplan Publishing website you will automatically receive an e-mail invitation to register your details and gain access to your content. If you do not receive the e-mail or book content, please contact Kaplan Publishing.

Your code and information

This code can only be used once for the registration of one book online. This registration and your online content will expire when the final sittings for the examinations covered by this book have taken place. Please allow one hour from the time you submit your book details for us to process your request.

Please scratch the film to access your unique code.

Please be aware that this code is case-sensitive and you will need to include the dashes within the passcode, but not when entering the ISBN.

CIMA

Paper P3

Risk Management

Study Text

Published by: Kaplan Publishing UK

Unit 2 The Business Centre, Molly Millars Lane, Wokingham, Berkshire RG41 2QZ

Acknowledgements

We are grateful to the CIMA for permission to reproduce past examination questions. The answers to CIMA Exams have been prepared by Kaplan Publishing, except in the case of the CIMA November 2010 and subsequent CIMA Exam answers where the official CIMA answers have been reproduced.

Notice

The text in this material and any others made available by any Kaplan Group company does not amount to advice on a particular matter and should not be taken as such. No reliance should be placed on the content as the basis for any investment or other decision or in connection with any advice given to third parties. Please consult your appropriate professional adviser as necessary. Kaplan Publishing Limited and all other Kaplan group companies expressly disclaim all liability to any person in respect of any losses or other claims, whether direct, indirect, incidental, consequential or otherwise arising in relation to the use of such materials.

Kaplan is not responsible for the content of external websites. The inclusion of a link to a third party website in this text should not be taken as an endorsement.

British Library Cataloguing in Publication Data

A catalogue record for this book is available from the British Library.

ISBN: 978-1-78415-925-2

Printed and bound in Great Britain.

Contents

		Page
Chapter 1	Risk	1
Chapter 2	Risk management	43
Chapter 3	Internal control	139
Chapter 4	Risk and control of information systems	207
Chapter 5	Information strategy	257
Chapter 6	Management control systems	321
Chapter 7	Fraud	391
Chapter 8	Ethics	427
Chapter 9	Corporate governance	475
Chapter 10	Audit	551
Chapter 11	Financial risk	639
Chapter 12	Currency risk management	677
Chapter 13	Interest rate risk management	775
Chapter 14	Cost of capital and capital investment decisions	825
Chapter 15	Investment implementation and review	893

Introduction

How to use the materials

These official CIMA learning materials have been carefully designed to make your learning experience as easy as possible and to give you the best chances of success in your Objective Test Examination.

The product range contains a number of features to help you in the study process. They include:

- a detailed explanation of all syllabus areas;
- extensive 'practical' materials;
- generous question practice, together with full solutions.

This Study Text has been designed with the needs of home study and distance learning candidates in mind. Such students require very full coverage of the syllabus topics, and also the facility to undertake extensive question practice. However, the Study Text is also ideal for fully taught courses.

The main body of the text is divided into a number of chapters, each of which is organised on the following pattern:

- **Detailed learning outcomes.** These describe the knowledge expected after your studies of the chapter are complete. You should assimilate these before beginning detailed work on the chapter, so that you can appreciate where your studies are leading.
- **Step-by-step topic coverage.** This is the heart of each chapter, containing detailed explanatory text supported where appropriate by worked examples and exercises. You should work carefully through this section, ensuring that you understand the material being explained and can tackle the examples and exercises successfully. Remember that in many cases knowledge is cumulative: if you fail to digest earlier material thoroughly, you may struggle to understand later chapters.
- **Activities.** Some chapters are illustrated by more practical elements, such as comments and questions designed to stimulate discussion.
- **Question practice.** The text contains three styles of question:
  - Exam-style objective test questions (OTQs)
  - "Integration" questions – these test your ability to understand topics within a wider context. This is particularly important with calculations where OTQs may focus on just one element but an integration question tackles the full calculation, just as you would be expected to do in the workplace.

– ‘Case’ style questions – these test your ability to analyse and discuss issues in greater depth, particularly focusing on scenarios that are less clear cut than in the Objective Test Examination, and thus provide excellent practice for developing the skills needed for success in the Strategic Level Case Study Examination.

- **Solutions.** Avoid the temptation merely to ‘audit’ the solutions provided. It is an illusion to think that this provides the same benefits as you would gain from a serious attempt of your own. However, if you are struggling to get started on a question you should read the introductory guidance provided at the beginning of the solution, where provided, and then make your own attempt before referring back to the full solution.

If you work conscientiously through this Official CIMA Study Text according to the guidelines above you will be giving yourself an excellent chance of success in your Objective Test Examination. Good luck with your studies!

Quality and accuracy are of the utmost importance to us so if you spot an error in any of our products, please send an email to mykaplanreporting@kaplan.com with full details, or follow the link to the feedback form in MyKaplan.

Our Quality Co-ordinator will work with our technical team to verify the error and take action to ensure it is corrected in future editions.

Icon Explanations

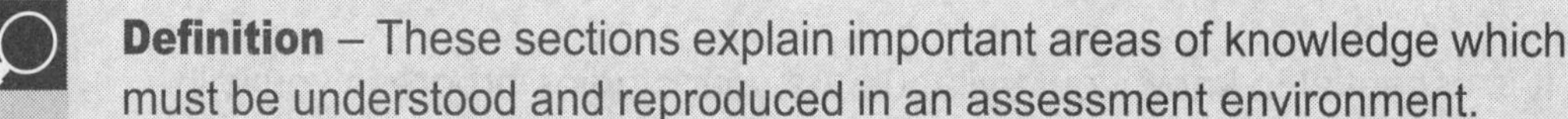

Definition – These sections explain important areas of knowledge which must be understood and reproduced in an assessment environment.

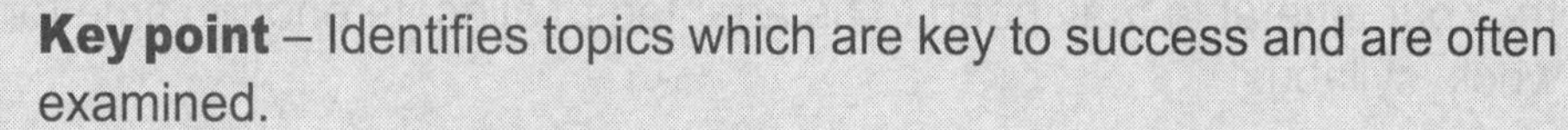

Key point – Identifies topics which are key to success and are often examined.

Supplementary reading – These sections will help to provide a deeper understanding of core areas. The supplementary reading is **NOT** optional reading. It is vital to provide you with the breadth of knowledge you will need to address the wide range of topics within your syllabus that could feature in an assessment question. **Reference to this text is vital when self studying**.

Test your understanding – Following key points and definitions are exercises which give the opportunity to assess the understanding of these core areas.

Illustration – To help develop an understanding of particular topics. The illustrative examples are useful in preparing for the Test your understanding exercises.

Exclamation mark – This symbol signifies a topic which can be more difficult to understand. When reviewing these areas, care should be taken.

New – Identifies topics that are brand new in subjects that build on, and therefore also contain, learning covered in earlier subjects.

Study technique

Passing exams is partly a matter of intellectual ability, but however accomplished you are in that respect you can improve your chances significantly by the use of appropriate study and revision techniques. In this section we briefly outline some tips for effective study during the earlier stages of your approach to the Objective Test Examination. We also mention some techniques that you will find useful at the revision stage.

Planning

To begin with, formal planning is essential to get the best return from the time you spend studying. Estimate how much time in total you are going to need for each subject you are studying. Remember that you need to allow time for revision as well as for initial study of the material.

With your study material before you, decide which chapters you are going to study in each week, and which weeks you will devote to revision and final question practice.

Prepare a written schedule summarising the above and stick to it!

It is essential to know your syllabus. As your studies progress you will become more familiar with how long it takes to cover topics in sufficient depth. Your timetable may need to be adapted to allocate enough time for the whole syllabus.

Students are advised to refer to the notice of examinable legislation published regularly in CIMA's magazine (Financial Management), the students e-newsletter (Velocity) and on the CIMA website, to ensure they are up-to-date.

The amount of space allocated to a topic in the Study Text is not a very good guide as to how long it will take you. The syllabus weighting is the better guide as to how long you should spend on a syllabus topic.

Tips for effective studying

(1) Aim to find a quiet and undisturbed location for your study, and plan as far as possible to use the same period of time each day. Getting into a routine helps to avoid wasting time. Make sure that you have all the materials you need before you begin so as to minimise interruptions.

(2) Store all your materials in one place, so that you do not waste time searching for items every time you want to begin studying. If you have to pack everything away after each study period, keep your study materials in a box, or even a suitcase, which will not be disturbed until the next time.

(3) Limit distractions. To make the most effective use of your study periods you should be able to apply total concentration, so turn off all entertainment equipment, set your phones to message mode, and put up your 'do not disturb' sign.

(4) Your timetable will tell you which topic to study. However, before diving in and becoming engrossed in the finer points, make sure you have an overall picture of all the areas that need to be covered by the end of that session. After an hour, allow yourself a short break and move away from your Study Text. With experience, you will learn to assess the pace you need to work at. Each study session should focus on component learning outcomes – the basis for all questions.

(5) Work carefully through a chapter, making notes as you go. When you have covered a suitable amount of material, vary the pattern by attempting a practice question. When you have finished your attempt, make notes of any mistakes you made, or any areas that you failed to cover or covered more briefly. Be aware that all component learning outcomes will be tested in each examination.

(6) Make notes as you study, and discover the techniques that work best for you. Your notes may be in the form of lists, bullet points, diagrams, summaries, 'mind maps', or the written word, but remember that you will need to refer back to them at a later date, so they must be intelligible. If you are on a taught course, make sure you highlight any issues you would like to follow up with your lecturer.

(7) Organise your notes. Make sure that all your notes, calculations etc. can be effectively filed and easily retrieved later.

Objective Test

Objective Test questions require you to choose or provide a response to a question whose correct answer is predetermined.

The most common types of Objective Test question you will see are:

- Multiple choice, where you have to choose the correct answer(s) from a list of possible answers. This could either be numbers or text.
- Multiple choice with more choices and answers, for example, choosing two correct answers from a list of eight possible answers. This could either be numbers or text.
- Single numeric entry, where you give your numeric answer, for example, profit is $10,000.
- Multiple entry, where you give several numeric answers.

- True/false questions, where you state whether a statement is true or false.
- Matching pairs of text, for example, matching a technical term with the correct definition.
- Other types could be matching text with graphs and labelling graphs/diagrams.

In every chapter of this Study Text we have introduced these types of questions, but obviously we have had to label answers A, B, C etc rather than using click boxes. For convenience we have retained quite a few questions where an initial scenario leads to a number of sub-questions. There will be questions of this type in the Objective Test Examination but they will rarely have more than three sub-questions.

Guidance re CIMA on-screen calculator

As part of the CIMA Objective Test software, candidates are now provided with a calculator. This calculator is on-screen and is available for the duration of the assessment. The calculator is available in each of the Objective Test Examinations and is accessed by clicking the calculator button in the top left hand corner of the screen at any time during the assessment.

All candidates must complete a 15-minute tutorial before the assessment begins and will have the opportunity to familiarise themselves with the calculator and practise using it.

Candidates may practise using the calculator by downloading and installing the practice exam at http://www.vue.com/athena/. The calculator can be accessed from the fourth sample question (of 12).

Please note that the practice exam and tutorial provided by Pearson VUE at http://www.vue.com/athena/ is not specific to CIMA and includes the full range of question types the Pearson VUE software supports, some of which CIMA does not currently use.

Fundamentals of Objective Tests

The Objective Tests are 90-minute assessments comprising 60 compulsory questions, with one or more parts. There will be no choice and all questions should be attempted.

Structure of subjects and learning outcomes

Each subject within the syllabus is divided into a number of broad syllabus topics. The topics contain one or more lead learning outcomes, related component learning outcomes and indicative knowledge content.

A learning outcome has two main purposes:

(a) To define the skill or ability that a well prepared candidate should be able to exhibit in the examination.

(b) To demonstrate the approach likely to be taken in examination questions.

The learning outcomes are part of a hierarchy of learning objectives. The verbs used at the beginning of each learning outcome relate to a specific learning objective, e.g.

Calculate the break-even point, profit target, margin of safety and profit/volume ratio for a single product or service.

The verb '**calculate**' indicates a level three learning objective. The following tables list the verbs that appear in the syllabus learning outcomes and examination questions.

CIMA VERB HIERARCHY

CIMA place great importance on the definition of verbs in structuring Objective Test Examinations. It is therefore crucial that you understand the verbs in order to appreciate the depth and breadth of a topic and the level of skill required. The Objective Tests will focus on levels one, two and three of the CIMA hierarchy of verbs. However they will also test levels four and five, especially at the management and strategic levels. You can therefore expect to be tested on knowledge, comprehension, application, analysis and evaluation in these examinations.

Level 1: KNOWLEDGE

What you are expected to know.

VERBS USED	DEFINITION
List	Make a list of.
State	Express, fully or clearly, the details of/facts of.
Define	Give the exact meaning of.

For example you could be asked to make a list of the advantages of a particular information system by selecting all options that apply from a given set of possibilities. Or you could be required to define relationship marketing by selecting the most appropriate option from a list.

Level 2: COMPREHENSION

What you are expected to understand.

VERBS USED	DEFINITION
Describe	Communicate the key features of.
Distinguish	Highlight the differences between.
Explain	Make clear or intelligible/state the meaning or purpose of.
Identify	Recognise, establish or select after consideration.
Illustrate	Use an example to describe or explain something.

For example you may be asked to distinguish between different aspects of the global business environment by dragging external factors and dropping into a PEST analysis.

Level 3: APPLICATION

How you are expected to apply your knowledge.

VERBS USED	DEFINITION
Apply	Put to practical use.
Calculate	Ascertain or reckon mathematically.
Demonstrate	Prove with certainty or exhibit by practical means.
Prepare	Make or get ready for use.
Reconcile	Make or prove consistent/compatible.
Solve	Find an answer to.
Tabulate	Arrange in a table.

For example you may need to calculate the projected revenue or costs for a given set of circumstances.

Level 4: ANALYSIS

How you are expected to analyse the detail of what you have learned.

VERBS USED	**DEFINITION**
Analyse	Examine in detail the structure of.
Categorise	Place into a defined class or division.
Compare/ contrast	Show the similarities and/or differences between.
Construct	Build up or compile.
Discuss	Examine in detail by argument.
Interpret	Translate into intelligible or familiar terms.
Prioritise	Place in order of priority or sequence for action.
Produce	Create or bring into existence.

For example you may be required to interpret an inventory ratio by selecting the most appropriate statement for a given set of circumstances and data.

Level 5: EVALUATION

How you are expected to use your learning to evaluate, make decisions or recommendations.

VERBS USED	**DEFINITION**
Advise	Counsel, inform or notify.
Evaluate	Appraise or assess the value of.
Recommend	Propose a course of action.

For example you may be asked to recommend and select an appropriate course of action based on a short scenario.

Information concerning formulae and tables will be provided via the CIMA website, www.cimaglobal.com, and your EN-gage login.

P3
RISK MANAGEMENT

Syllabus overview

P3 shows how to identify, evaluate and manage various risks that could adversely affect the implementation of the organisation's strategy. It provides the competencies required to analyse, evaluate and apply the techniques, processes and internal control systems required to manage risk. This insight is then used to manage the risks associated with both cash flows and capital investment decisions – two important areas of organisational life for which the finance function is responsible.

Summary of syllabus

Weight	Syllabus topic
20%	**A.** Identification, classification and evaluation of risk
20%	**B.** Responses to strategic risk
20%	**C.** Internal controls to manage risk
20%	**D.** Managing risks associated with cash flows
20%	**E.** Managing risks associated with capital investment decisions

P3 – A. IDENTIFICATION, CLASSIFICATION AND EVALUATION OF RISK (20%)

Learning outcomes On completion of their studies, students should be able to:		**Indicative syllabus content**
Lead	**Component**	
1 evaluate the types of risk facing an organisation and recommend appropriate responses.	(a) identify the types of risk facing an organisation	• Upside and downside risks arising from internal and external sources and from different managerial decisions. • Risks arising from international operations, such as cultural differences and differences between legal systems. **Note:** No specific real country will be tested. • Strategic and operational risks.
	(b) evaluate the organisation's ability to bear identified risks	• Quantification of risk exposures (impact if an adverse event occurs) and their expected values, taking account of likelihood. • Risk map representation of risk exposures as a basis for reporting and analysing risks.
	(c) recommend responses to identified risks.	• Enterprise Risk Management and its components. • Risk mitigation including TARA – transfer, avoid, reduce, accept. • Gross and net risks. • Assurance mapping and similar techniques for describing risks and their associated responses.
2 evaluate senior management's responsibility for the implementation of risk management strategies and internal controls.	(a) recommend techniques that will enable the board to discharge its responsibilities with respect to managing risks	• The control environment. • Internal control. • Risk register.
	(b) advise the board on its responsibilities for reporting risks to shareholders and other stakeholders.	• Risk reports and stakeholder responses.
3 evaluate the ethical impact of risk.	(a) evaluate ethical, social and environmental issues arising from risk management.	• The identification of ethical dilemmas associated with risk management. • Reputational risks associated with social and environmental impacts.

P3 – B. RESPONSES TO STRATEGIC RISK (20%)

Learning outcomes On completion of their studies, students should be able to:		**Indicative syllabus content**
Lead	**Component**	
1 **evaluate the tools and processes required for strategy implementation.**	(a) recommend appropriate measures for the strategic control and direction of various types of organisations	• Business unit performance and appraisal, including transfer pricing and taxation, reward systems and incentives. • Non-financial measures and their interaction with financial measures. • Risks of performance measurement, including the Balanced Scorecard (BSC). • Lean systems. • Cost of quality. • Big Data as a strategic resource.
	(b) recommend solutions for the risks of dysfunctional behaviour arising from the associated models of performance measurement	• Dysfunctional behaviour associated with measures of control and direction.
	(c) advise managers of the risks in the development of strategies for information systems that support the organisation's strategic requirements.	• The purpose and contents of information systems strategies, and the need for strategy complementary to the corporate and individual business strategies.
2 **evaluate ethical issues facing an organisation and its employees.**	(a) evaluate the risks of unethical behaviour.	• Ethical issues identified in the CIMA Code of Ethics for Professional Accountants. • Application of the CIMA Code of Ethics for Professional Accountants. • The board's responsibilities for the management of stakeholders' interests.
3 **evaluate the risks associated with corporate governance.**	(a) evaluate the risks associated with poor governance structures.	• The separation of the roles of CEO and chairman. • The role of non-executive directors. • The roles of audit committee, remuneration committee, risk committee and nominations committee. • Directors' remuneration. • The agency implications of salaries, bonuses, performance-related pay, executive share options and benefits in kind.

P3 – C. INTERNAL CONTROLS TO MANAGE RISK (20%)

Learning outcomes On completion of their studies, students should be able to:		Indicative syllabus content
Lead	**Component**	
1 evaluate control systems for organisational activities and resources.	(a) evaluate the appropriateness of control systems for the management of an organisation.	• Application of control systems and related theory to the design of management accounting control systems and information systems in general. • Control systems within functional areas of a business including HR, sales, purchases, treasury, distribution, IT. • Identification of appropriate responsibility and control centres within the organisation. • Performance target setting. • Performance appraisal and feedback. • Cost of quality applied to the management accounting function and 'getting things right first time'. • Responses to risks in control systems for management.
2 evaluate risk management strategies and internal controls.	(a) evaluate the essential features of internal control systems for identifying, assessing and managing risks.	• Minimising the risk of fraud: fraud policy statements, effective recruitment policies and good internal controls, such as approval procedures and separation of functions. • The risk manager role as distinct from that of internal auditor. • Purposes of internal control: the achievement of an entity's objectives, effectiveness and efficiency of operations. • Identifying and evaluating control weaknesses. • Identifying and evaluating compliance failures. • Operational features of internal control systems, including embedding such systems in a company's operations, responsiveness to evolving risks and timely reporting to management.

Learning outcomes On completion of their studies, students should be able to:		**Indicative syllabus content**
Lead	**Component**	
		• The pervasive nature of internal control and the need for employee training. • Costs and benefits of maintaining the internal control system. • Disaster recovery.
3 evaluate the purposes and process of audit in the context of internal control systems.	(a) evaluate the effective planning and management of internal audit and internal audit investigations.	• Forms of internal audit: compliance audit, fraud investigation, value for money audit/management audit, social and environmental audit. • Operation of internal audit, the assessment of audit risk and the process of analytical review, including different types of benchmarking, their use and limitations. • Effective internal audit: independence, staffing and resourcing, organisational remit. • The preparation and interpretation of the internal audit report.

P3 – D. MANAGING RISKS ASSOCIATED WITH CASH FLOW S (20%)

Learning outcomes On completion of their studies, students should be able to:		**Indicative syllabus content**
Lead	**Component**	
1 evaluate financial risks facing an organisation.	(a) evaluate financial risks facing an organisation.	• Sources of financial risk associated with international operations. • Transaction, translation, economic and political risk. • Quantification of risk exposures, their sensitivities to changes in external conditions and their expected values. • Exposure to interest rate risks.
2 evaluate alternative risk management tools.	(a) advise on the effects of economic factors that affect future cash flows from international operations	• Exchange rate theory and the impact of differential inflation rates on forecast exchange rates. • Theory and forecasting of exchange rates (e.g. interest rate parity, purchasing power parity and the Fisher effect). • Value at risk.
	(b) evaluate appropriate methods for the identification and management of financial risks associated with international operations	• Minimising political risk. • Responses to economic transaction and translation risks. • Operation and features of the more common instruments for managing currency risk: swaps, forward contracts, money market hedges, • futures and options. **Note:** The Black Scholes option pricing model will not be tested numerically. However, an understanding of the variables which will influence the value of an option will be assumed. • Techniques for combining options in order to achieve a specific risk profile: caps, collars and floors. • Internal hedging techniques.
	(c) evaluate appropriate methods for the identification and management of financial risks associated with debt finance.	• Operation and features of the more common instruments for managing interest rate risk: swaps, forward rate agreements, futures and options.

P3 – E. MANAGING RISKS ASSOCIATED WITH CAPITAL INVESTMENT DECISIONS (20%)

Learning outcomes On completion of their studies, students should be able to:		**Indicative syllabus content**
Lead	**Component**	
1 evaluate the risks arising from changes in the environment for capital investment appraisal.	(a) evaluate investment projects	• Cost of capital and risk. • Recognising risk using the certainty equivalent method (when given a risk free rate and certainty equivalent values). • Adjusted present value. **Note:** The two step method may be tested for debt introduced permanently and debt in place for the duration of the project.
	(b) evaluate conflicts that may arise from capital investment decisions	• Managing conflicts between different stakeholder groups (profit maximisation versus wealth maximisation). • Managing conflicts arising from performance indicators.
	(c) evaluate the outcomes of projects post implementation and post completion.	• Monitoring the implementation of plans. • Post completion audit.

hapter

1

Risk

Chapter learning objectives

Lead	Component
A1. Evaluate the types of risk facing an organisation and recommend appropriate responses.	(a) Identify the types of risk facing an organisation.
A3. Evaluate the ethical impact of risk.	(a) Evaluate ethical, social and environmental issues arising from risk management.

Indicative syllabus content

- Upside and downside risks arising from internal and external sources and from different managerial decisions.
- Risks arising from international operations, such as cultural differences and differences between legal systems. Note: No specific real country will be tested.
- Strategic and operational risks.
- Reputational risks associated with social and environmental impacts.

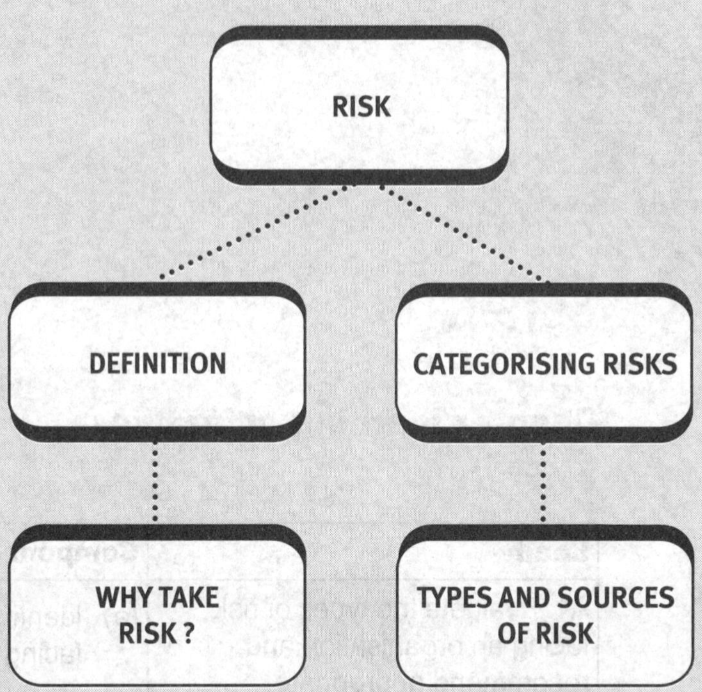

1 What is risk?

There are many different ways of defining risk, including the following:

- Risk is a condition in which there exists a quantifiable dispersion in the possible outcomes from any activity. (CIMA official terminology)
- Risk can be defined as the combination of the probability of an event and its consequences (ISO Guide 73)
- Risk in business is the chance that future events or results may not be as expected.

Risk is often thought of as purely bad (pure or '**downside**' risk), but it must be considered that risk can also be good – the results may be better than expected as well as worse (speculative or '**upside**' risk).

Businesses must be able to identify the principal sources of risk if they are to be able to assess and measure the risks that the organisation faces. Risks facing an organisation are those that affect the achievement of its overall objectives, which should be reflected in its strategic aims. Risk should be managed and there should be strategies for dealing with risk.

Risk and uncertainty

The term 'risk' is often associated with the chance of something 'bad' happening, and that a future outcome will be adverse. This type of risk is called '**downside**' **risk** or **pure risk**, which is a risk involving the possibility of loss, with no chance of gain.

Examples of pure risk are the risk of disruption to business from a severe power cut, or the risk of losses from theft or fraud, the risk of damage to assets from a fire or accident, and risks to the health and safety of employees at work.

Not all risks are pure risks or down-side risks. In many cases, risk is two-way, and actual outcomes might be either better or worse than expected. **Two-way risk** is sometimes called **speculative risk**. For many business decisions, there is an element of speculative risk and management are aware that actual results could be better or worse than forecast.

For example, a new product launch might be more or less successful than planned, and the savings from an investment in labour-saving equipment might be higher or lower than anticipated.

Risk is inherent in a situation whenever an outcome is not inevitable. **Uncertainty**, in contrast, arises from ignorance and a lack of information. By definition, the future cannot be predicted under conditions of uncertainty because there is insufficient information about what the future outcomes might be or their probabilities of occurrence.

In business, uncertainty might be an element in decision-making. For example, there might be uncertainty about how consumers might respond to a new product or a new technology, or how shareholders might react to a cut in the annual dividend. Uncertainty is reduced by obtaining as much information as possible before making any decision.

Why incur risk ?

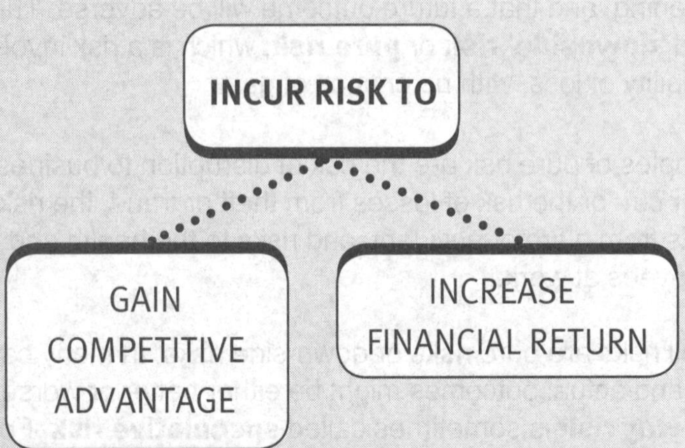

It is generally the case that firms must be willing to take higher risks if they want to achieve higher returns:

- To generate higher returns a business may have to take more risk in order to be competitive.
- Conversely, not accepting risk tends to make a business less dynamic, and implies a 'follow the leader' strategy.
- Incurring risk also implies that the returns from different activities will be higher – 'benefit' being the return for accepting risk.
- Benefits can be financial – decreased costs, or intangible – better quality information.
- In both cases, these will lead to the business being able to gain competitive advantage.

For some risks there is a market rate of return e.g. quoted equity – where a shareholder invests in a company with the expectation of a certain level of dividend and capital growth. However, for other risks there may not be a market rate of return e.g. technology risk – where a company invests in new software in the hope that it will make their invoice processing more efficient. The important distinction here is that the market compensates for the former type of risk, but might not for the latter.

Benefits of taking risks

Consider the following grid in terms of the risks a business can incur and the benefits from undertaking different activities.

		Activity risk	
		Low	High
Ability to gain competitive advantage	Low	2 Routine	4 Avoid
	High	1 Identify and develop	3 Examine carefully

Focusing on low-risk activities can easily result in a low ability to obtain competitive advantage – although where there is low risk there is also only a limited amount of competitive advantage to be obtained. For example, a mobile telephone operator may produce its phones in a wide range of colours. There is little or no risk of the technology failing, but the move may provide limited competitive advantage where customers are attracted to a particular colour of phone.

Some low-risk activities, however, will provide higher competitive advantage – when these can be identified. If these can be identified, then the activity should be undertaken because of the higher reward. For example, the mobile phone operator may find a way of easily amending mobile phones to make them safer regarding the electrical emissions generated. Given that customers are concerned about this element of mobile phone use, there is significant potential to obtain competitive advantage. However, these opportunities are few and far between.

High-risk activities can similarly generate low or high competitive advantage. Activities with low competitive advantage will generally be avoided. There remains the risk that the activity will not work, and that the small amount of competitive advantage that would be generated is not worth that risk.

Other high-risk activities may generate significant amounts of competitive advantage. These activities are worth investigating because of the high returns that can be generated. For example, a new type of mobile phone providing, say, GPS features for use while travelling, may provide significant competitive advantage for the company; the risk of investing in the phone is worthwhile in terms of the benefit that could be achieved.

The point is, therefore, that if a business does not take some risk, it will normally be limited to activities providing little or no competitive advantage, which will limit its ability to grow and provide returns to its shareholders.

2 CIMA's risk management cycle

Risk management should be a proactive process that is an integral part of strategic management.

This perspective is summarised in **CIMA's risk management cycle**, illustrated below:

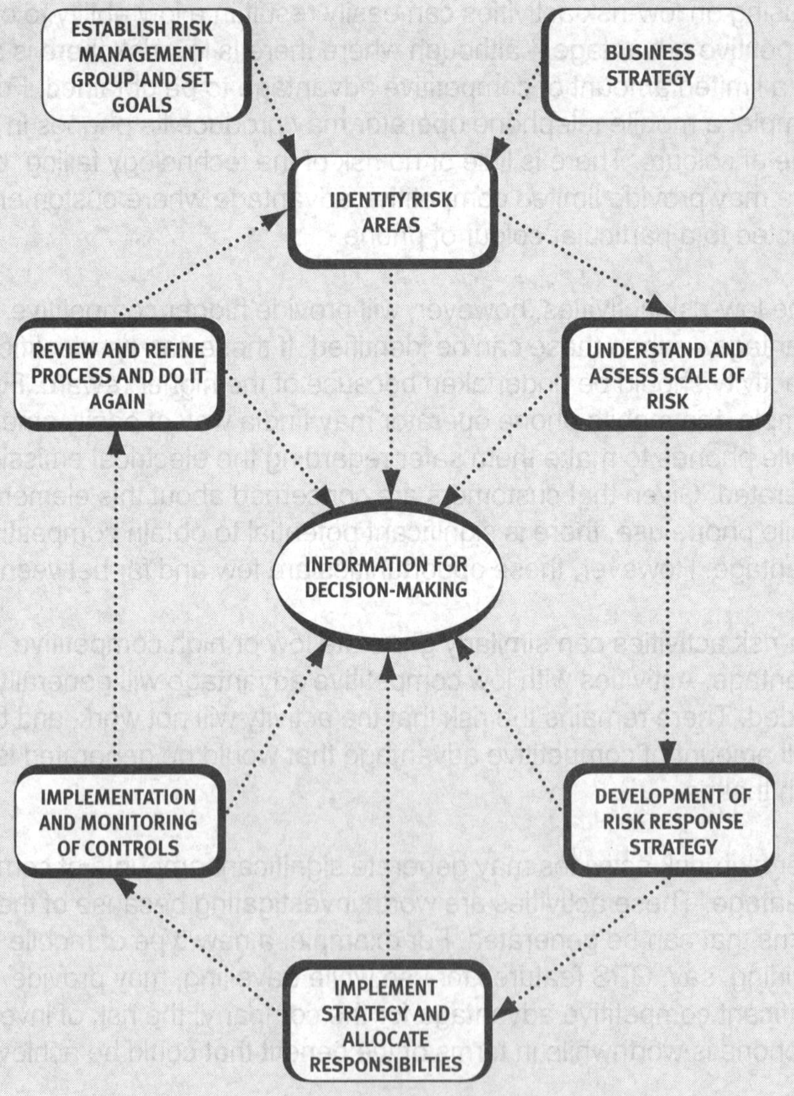

Source: Chartered Institute of Management Accountants (2002), Risk Management: A Guide to Good Practice, CIMA.

The risk management cycle is a very important tool for your exam.

Test your understanding 1

CIMA's Risk Management Cycle identifies various activities that should be undertaken during risk management.

Which of the following options shows the steps in the correct order?

A Identify risk areas; Develop risk response strategy; Allocate responsibilities; Establish risk management group.

B Establish risk management group; Identify risk areas; Allocate responsibilities; Develop risk response strategy.

C Allocate responsibilities; Identify risk areas; Develop risk response strategy; Establish risk management group.

D Establish risk management group; Identify risk areas; Develop risk response strategy; Allocate responsibilities.

3 Types and sources of risk for business organisations

Identifying and categorising risks

- Many organisations categorise risks into different types of risk. The use of risk categories can help with the process of risk identification and assessment.
- There is no single system of risk categories. The risk categories used by companies and other organisations differ according to circumstances. Some of the more commonly-used risk categories are described below.

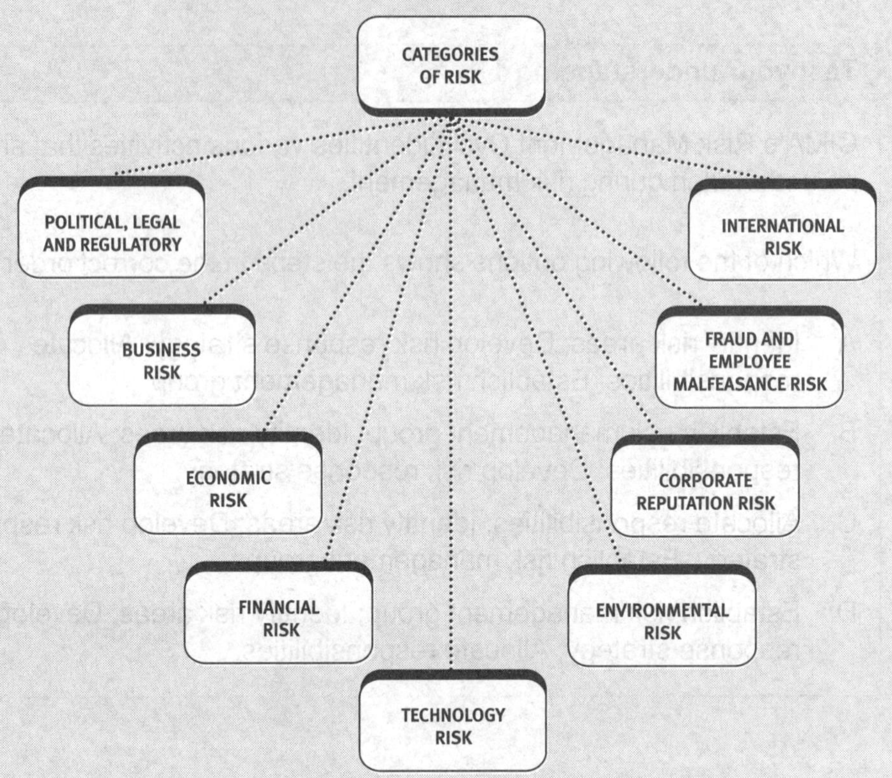

Political, legal and regulatory

These are the risks that businesses face because of the regulatory regime that they operate in. Some businesses may be subject to very strict regulations, for example companies that could cause pollution, but even companies that do not appear to be in a highly regulated industry have some regulatory risk. For example, all companies are subject to the risk of employment legislation changing or customers bringing litigation.

This risk can be broken up into different types:

Political risk	Risk due to political instability. Generally considered to be external to the business.
Legal/litigation risk	Risk that litigation will be brought against the business.
Regulatory risk	Risk of changes in regulation affecting the business.
Compliance risk	Risk of non-compliance with the law resulting in fines/penalties, etc.

More on political, legal and regulatory risks

Political risk depends to a large extent on the political stability in the country or countries in which an organisation operates, and the political institutions. A change of government can sometimes result in dramatic changes for businesses. In an extreme case, for example, an incoming government might nationalise all foreign businesses operating in the country. Even in countries with a stable political system, political change can be significant. For example, an incoming new government might be elected on a platform of higher taxation (or lower taxation).

Legal risk or **litigation risk** arises from the possibility of legal action being taken against an organisation. For many organisations, this risk can be high. For example, hospitals and hospital workers might be exposed to risks of legal action for negligence. Tobacco companies have been exposed to legal action for compensation from cancer victims. Companies manufacturing or providing food and drink are also aware of litigation risk from customers claiming that a product has damaged their health.

Regulatory risk arises from the possibility that regulations will affect the way an organisation has to operate. Regulations might apply to businesses generally (for example, competition laws and anti-monopoly regulations) or to specific industries.

Compliance risk is the risk of losses, possibly fines, resulting from non-compliance with laws or regulations. Measures to ensure compliance with rules and regulations should be an integral part of an organisation's internal control system.

Business risk

Business risk is the risk businesses face due to the nature of their operations and products. Some businesses for instance are reliant on a single product or small range of products, or they could be reliant on a small key group of staff. The risks can be considered in different categories:

Strategic risk	Risk that business strategies (e.g. acquisitions/product launches) will fail.
Product risk	Risk of failure of new product launches/loss of interest in existing products.
Commodity price risk	Risk of a rise in commodity prices (e.g. oil).
Product reputation risk	Risk of change in product's reputation or image.
Operational risk	Risk that business operations may be inefficient or business processes may fail.

Contractual inadequacy risk	Risk that the terms of a contract do not fully cover a business against all potential outcomes.
Fraud and employee malfeasance	Considered separately later.

More on business risks

Business risks for a company are risks arising from the nature of its business and operations. Some businesses are inherently more risky than others.

- **Strategic risks** are risks arising from the possible consequences of strategic decisions taken by the organisation. For example, one company might pursue a strategy of growth by acquisitions, whilst another might seek slower, organic growth. Growth by acquisition is likely to be much more high-risk than organic growth, although the potential returns might also be much higher. Strategic risks should be identified and assessed at senior management and board of director level.
- **Product risk** is the risk that customers will not buy new products (or services) provided by the organisation, or that the sales demand for current products and services will decline unexpectedly. A new product launched on to the market might fail to achieve the expected volume of sales, or the take-up will be much slower than expected. For example, the demand for 'third generation' (3G) mobile communications services has been much slower to build up than expected by the mobile telephone service providers, due partly to the slower-than-expected development of suitable mobile phone handsets.
- **Commodity price risk.** Businesses might be exposed to risks from unexpected increases (or falls) in the price of a key commodity. Businesses providing commodities, such as oil companies and commodity farmers, are directly affected by price changes. Equally, companies that rely on the use of commodities could be exposed to risks from price changes. For example, airlines are exposed to the risk of increases in fuel prices, particularly when market demand for flights is weak, and so increases in ticket prices for flights are not possible.
- **Product reputation risk.** Some companies rely heavily on brand image and product reputation, and an adverse event could put its reputation (and so future sales) at risk. Risk to a product's reputation could arise from adverse public attitudes to a product or from adverse publicity: this has been evident in Europe with widespread hostility to genetically-modified (GM) foods. There could also be a risk from changes in customer perceptions about the quality of a product. For example, if a car manufacturer announces that it is recalling all new models of a car to rectify a design defect, the reputation of the product and future sales could be affected.

- **Operational risk** refers to potential losses that might arise in business operations. It has been defined broadly as 'the risk of losses resulting from inadequate or failed internal processes, people and systems, or external events' (Basel Committee on Banking Supervision). Operational risks include risks of fraud or employee malfeasance, which are explained in more detail later. Organisations have internal control systems to manage operational risks.
- **Contractual inadequacy risk** may arise where a business has negotiated contracts and other business transactions without adequate consideration of what may happen if things don't go according to plan. For example, a builder may have a fixed completion date to complete the construction of a house. If he does not complete on time, he may have to pay compensation to the house purchaser. Similarly, there is also a risk that the purchaser does not have the funds when payment is due. This risk may be mitigated by having terms in the contract as to what rights he will have in such circumstances. Clearly, if the builder does not consider either or both of these possibilities when agreeing to build the house, then there is an unidentified and unquantified risk of loss.

Test your understanding 2

Which of the following would normally be classified as an operational risk? (Select all that apply.)

A The risk that a new product will fail

B The risk of competitors cutting costs by manufacturing overseas

C The loss of an experienced supervisor

D Raw materials being wasted during the production process due to untrained staff

Test your understanding 3

Which of the following would normally be classified as a strategic risk?

A Human error

B Information technology failure

C Fraud

D Stricter health and safety legislation

Test your understanding 4

Company Q assembles circuit boards for mobile telephones and relies on suppliers to manufacture one of their key components. This component contains a highly toxic, expensive chemical which is currently in scarce supply across the world.

Company Q has one main supplier of the component. This supplier is based in a developing country with low labour costs. The supplier has developed a great deal of expertise in handling the toxic chemical and keeping waste to a minimum. However, there have been allegations that rivers local to the supplier have been polluted with toxic waste from the chemical. There are also rumours that the supplier does not provide adequate safety equipment for staff working with the chemical. The supplier has informed Company Q that price rises may occur since safe storage of the chemical is becoming more expensive.

Which of the following represent strategic risks to Company Q? Select **all** that apply.

A Risk that the supplier's employees are injured through unsafe handling of toxic chemicals.

B Risk that pollution from local rivers is proved to be the result of the supplier's processes and waste.

C Risk that the supplier is unable to source adequate quantities of chemical.

D Risk that the supplier's storage facilities become more expensive.

E Risk that the developing country in which the supplier is based introduces a minimum wage.

Economic risk

This is the risk that changes in the economy might affect the business. Those changes could be inflation, unemployment rates, international trade relations or fiscal policy decisions by government. Again, this risk is considered to be external to the business.

The 'credit crunch'

In 2008 there was global banking crisis which then led to what has since been called a 'credit crunch' and, for some countries, recession. This section looks at the causes of the banking crisis and its knock-on effects.

Contributory factor 1: US sub-prime mortgage lending

In 2001 the US faced recession, due partly to the events of 9/11 and the Dot com bubble bursting, so the US government was keen to stimulate growth. As part of this in 2003 the Federal Reserve responded by cutting interest rates to 1% – their lowest level for a long time.

Low interest rates encouraged people to buy a house backed by a mortgage, resulting in house prices rising due to the increased demand for housing. As house prices began to rise, mortgage companies relaxed their lending criteria and tried to capitalise on the booming property market. This boom in credit was also fuelled by US government pressure on lenders to grant mortgages to people who, under normal banking criteria, presented a very high risk of default. These were the so called 'sub-prime mortgages', with many borrowers taking out adjustable rate mortgages that were affordable for the first two years.

This 'sub-prime market' expanded very quickly and by 2005, one in five mortgages in the US were sub-prime. Banks felt protected because house prices were continuing to rise so if someone defaulted the bank would recover its loan.

In 2006 inflationary pressures in the US caused interest rates to rise to 4%. Normally 4% interest rates are not particularly high but, because many had taken out large mortgages, this increase made the mortgage payments unaffordable. Also many homeowners were coming to the end of their 'introductory offers' and faced much higher payments. This led to an increase in mortgage defaults.

As mortgage defaults increased the boom in house prices came to an end and house prices started falling. In some areas the problem was even worse as there had been a boom in the building of new homes, which occurred right up until 2007. It meant that demand fell as supply was increasing causing prices to collapse. Banks were no longer able to recover their loans when borrowers defaulted. In many cases they only ended up with a fraction of the house value.

Contributory factor 2: 'Collateralised debt obligations' or CDOs

Normally if a borrower defaults it is the lending bank or building society that suffers the loss. As a result they are very diligent to verify the credit worthiness of potential borrowers and whether they have the income and security to repay loans. However, in the US, mortgage lenders were able to sell on mortgage debt in the form of CDOs to other banks and financial institutions. This was a kind of insurance for the mortgage companies. It meant that other banks and financial institutions shared the risk of these sub-prime mortgages.

Using the income from their mortgage book as security, banks sold CDO bonds with a three-tier structure:

(1) Tier 1 was "senior" or "investment grade" and supposed to be very low risk but with a low return.

(2) Tier 2 was the "mezzanine tranche" and had medium risk and medium return

(3) Tier 3 was the "equity tranche" and had highest risk and return.

As money was received on mortgages, it was used to pay the Tier 1 bond holders their interest first, then Tier 2 and finally Tier 3, so if borrowers defaulted, then Tier 3 holders would suffer first and so on, like a waterfall effect.

Unfortunately losses were so great that Tier 3 and Tier 2 and in some cases Tier 1 investors were affected. At the very least, the value of Tier 1 bonds fell due to the perceived risks.

Contributory factor 3: Debt rating organisations

The CDO bonds were credit-rated for risk, just like any other bond issues. Maybe because these sub-prime mortgage debts were bought by 'responsible' banks like Morgan Stanley and Lehman Brothers, or maybe because they didn't fully understand the CDO structures, risk agencies gave risky Tier 1 debt bundles AAA safety ratings. Normally AAA would denote extremely low risk investments.

This encouraged many banks and financial institutions to buy them, not realising how risky their financial position was. The trillions of dollars of sub-prime mortgages issued in the US had thus become distributed across the global markets ending up as CDOs on the balance sheets of many banks around the world.

Many commentators have seen this factor as an example of regulatory failure within the financial system.

Contributory factor 4: Banks' financial structure

Unlike most other commercial enterprises, banks are very highly geared with typically less than 10% of their asset value covered by equity. A drastic loss of asset value can soon wipe out a bank's equity account and it was this risk which led some banks to start selling their asset–backed securities on to the market.

However, the sellers in this restricted market could not find buyers; as a result, the values at which these "toxic assets" could be sold fell and many banks around the world found themselves in a position with negative equity.

Contributory factor 5: Credit default swaps

As an alternative (or in addition) to using CDOs, the mortgage lenders could buy insurance on sub-prime debt through credit default swaps or CDSs.

For example, AIG wrote $440 billion and Lehman Brothers more than $700 billion-worth of CDSs. These were the first institutions to suffer when the level of defaults started to increase.

Warren Buffett called them "financial weapons of mass destruction".

Contributory factor 6: Risk-takers

There is a school of thought that the risk-takers were taking risks they didn't understand. Some risks can be easily understood, however, others are far more complicated.

Implication 1: the collapse of major financial institutions

Some very large financial institutions went bust and others got into serious trouble and needed to be rescued. For example,

- In September 2008 Lehman Brothers went bust. This was the biggest bankruptcy in corporate history. It was 10 times the size of Enron and the tipping point into the global crash, provoking panic in an already battered financial system, freezing short-term lending, and marking the start of the liquidity crisis.
- Also in September 2008 the US government put together a bail out package for AIG. The initial loan was for $85bn but the total value of this package has been estimated at between 150 and 182 billion dollars.
- In the UK the Bank of England lent Northern Rock £27 billion after its collapse in 2007.

Implication 2: the credit crunch

Banks usually rely on lending to each other to conduct every day business. But, after the first wave of credit losses, banks could no longer raise sufficient finance.

For example, in the UK, Northern Rock was particularly exposed to money markets. It had relied on borrowing money on the money markets to fund its daily business. In 2007, it simply couldn't raise enough money on the financial markets and eventually had to be nationalised by the UK government.

In addition to bad debts, the other problem was one of confidence. Because many banks had lost money and had a deterioration in their balance sheets, they couldn't afford to lend to other banks. Even banks that had stayed free of the problem began to suspect the credit worthiness of other banks and, as a result, became reluctant to lend on the interbank market.

The knock on effect was that banks became reluctant to lend to anyone, causing a shortage of liquidity in money markets. This made it difficult for firms to borrow to finance expansion plans as well as hitting the housing market.

Many companies use short-term finance rather than long-term. For example, rather than borrowing for, say, 10 years a company might take out a two year loan, with a view to taking out another two year loan to replace the first, and so on. The main reason for using this system of "revolving credit" is that it should be cheaper – shorter-term interest rates are generally lower than longer-term. The credit crunch meant that these firms could not refinance their loans causing major problems.

Implication 3: government intervention

Many governments felt compelled to intervene, not just to prop up major institutions (e.g. Northern Rock and AIG mentioned above) but also to inject funds into the money markets to stimulate liquidity.

Efforts to save major institutions involved a mixture of loans, guarantees and the purchase of equity.

Usually, central banks try to raise the amount of lending and activity in the economy indirectly, by cutting interest rates. Lower interest rates encourage people to spend, not save. But when interest rates can go no lower, a central bank's only option is to pump money into the economy directly. That is quantitative easing (QE). The way the central bank does this is by buying assets – usually financial assets such as government and corporate bonds – using money it has simply created out of thin air. The institutions selling those assets (either commercial banks or other financial businesses such as insurance companies) will then have "new" money in their accounts, which then boosts the money supply.

In February 2010 the Bank of England announced that the UK quantitative easing programme, that had cost £200bn, was to be put on hold.

The end result was that many governments found themselves with huge levels of debt with the corresponding need to repay high levels of interest as well as repay the debt.

Implication 4: recession and "austerity measures"

The events described above resulted in a recession in many countries. Despite the falling tax revenues that accompany this, some governments would normally try to increase government spending as one measure to boost aggregate demand to stimulate the economy.

However, the high levels of national debt have resulted in governments doing the opposite and making major cuts in public spending.

Implication 5: problems refinancing government debt

In 2010/2011 some countries tried to refinance national debt by issuing bonds:

- A problem facing the Spanish government at the end of 2010/2011 was the need to raise new borrowing as other government debt reached maturity. Spain successfully sold new bonds totalling nearly €3 billion on 12/1/11 in what was seen as a major test of Europe's chances of containing the debt crisis gripping parts of the region. This was in addition to the Spanish government cutting spending by tens of billions of euros, including cuts in public sector salaries, public investment and social spending, along with tax hikes and a pension freeze.
- The problem of refinancing is more severe for countries whose national debt has a short average redemption period (Greece is about 4 yrs) but much less of a problem where the debt is long dated (e.g. the UK where the average maturity is about 14 yrs).

For others they needed help from other countries and the International Monetary Fund (IMF).

- Greece received a €110 billion rescue package in May 2010.
- At the end of 2010 Ireland received a bailout from the EU, the UK and the IMF. The total cost is still being debated but could be as high as €85 billion.

Financial risk

Financial risk is a major risk that affects businesses and this risk is studied in much more depth in later chapters of this text.

Financial risk is the risk of a change in a financial condition such as an exchange rate, interest rate, credit rating of a customer, or price of a good.

The main types of financial risk are:

Credit risk	Risk of non-payment by customers.
Political risk	Risk arising from actions taken by a government that affect financial aspects of the business.
Currency risk	Risk of fluctuations in the exchange rate.
Interest rate risk	Risk that interest rates change.
Gearing risk	Risk in the way a business is financed (debt vs. equity) (sometimes this is considered part of interest rate risk).

More on financial risks

Financial risks relate to the possibility of changes in financial conditions and circumstances. There are several types of financial risk. More will be seen on these risks in chapter 11.

- **Credit risk.** Credit risk is the possibility of losses due to non-payment by debtors. The exposure of a company to credit risks depends on factors such as:
  - the total volume of credit sales
  - the organisation's credit policy
  - credit terms offered (credit limits for individual customers and the time allowed to pay)

- the credit risk 'quality' of customers: some types of customer are a greater credit risk than others
- credit vetting and assessment procedures
- debt collection procedures.

- **Currency risk.** Currency risk, or foreign exchange risk, arises from the possibility of movements in foreign exchange rates, and the value of one currency in relation to another.
- **Interest rate risk.** Interest rate risk is the risk of unexpected gains or losses arising as a consequence of a rise or fall in interest rates. Exposures to interest rate risk arise from:
  - borrowing
  - investing (to earn interest) or depositing cash.
- **Gearing risk.** Gearing risk for non-bank companies is the risk arising from exposures to high financial gearing and large amounts of borrowing.

Technology risk

Technology risk is the risk that technology changes will occur that either present new opportunities to businesses, or on the down-side make their existing processes obsolete or inefficient.

More on technology risk

Technology risk arises from the possibility that technological change will occur. Like many other categories of risk, technology risk is a two-way risk, and technological change creates both threats and opportunities for organisations.

There are risks in failing to respond to new technology, but there can also be risks in adopting new technology. An example of over-investing in new technology was the so-called 'dot.com boom' in the late 1990s and early 2000s. For a time, there was speculation that Internet-based companies would take over the markets of established 'bricks and mortar' companies.

To varying degrees, established companies invested in Internet technology, partly as a protective measure and partly in order to speculate on the growth of Internet commerce. (Whereas most established companies survived the collapse of the 'dot.com bubble' in 2001 – 2002, many 'dot.com' companies suffered financial collapse.)

Environmental risk

Environmental risk is the risk that arises from changes in the environment such as climate change or natural disasters. Some businesses may perceive this risk to be low, but for others, for example insurance companies, it can be more significant. Insurance companies have to take environmental risks into account when deciding policy premiums, and unusual environmental circumstances can severely alter the results of insurance businesses.

More on environmental risk

Environmental risk arises from changes to the environment:

- over which an organisation has no direct control, such as global warming
- for which the organisation might be responsible, such as oil spillages and other pollution.

To ensure their long-term survival, some companies should consider the sustainability of their businesses. When raw materials are consumed, consideration should be given to ensuring future supplies of the raw material. For example, companies that consume wood and paper should perhaps show concern for tree planting programmes, and deep-sea fishing businesses should consider the preservation of fishing stocks.

The Japanese tsunami

The Japanese tsunami of 2011 illustrates very well the fact that some risks can be understood and others are far more complicated.

The Japanese have some of the best flood defence systems in the world, being on the edge of a plate system and regularly experiencing tremors. However, even the best defence system is built with a risk factor included – using probabilities and modelling by water engineers.

While it is not possible to prevent a tsunami, in some particularly tsunami-prone countries some measures have been taken to reduce the damage caused on shore. Japan has implemented an extensive programme of building tsunami walls of up to 4.5 m (13.5 ft) high in front of populated coastal areas. Other localities have built floodgates and channels to redirect the water from incoming tsunami. However, their effectiveness has been questioned, as tsunami are often higher than the barriers. For instance, the Okushiri, Hokkaidō tsunami which struck Okushiri Island of Hokkaidō within two to five minutes of the earthquake on July 12, 1993 created waves as much as 30 m (100 ft) tall – as high as a 10-story building. The port town of Aonae was completely surrounded by a tsunami wall, but the waves washed right over the wall and destroyed all the wood-framed structures in the area. The wall may have succeeded in slowing down and moderating the height of the tsunami, but it did not prevent major destruction and loss of life.

On 11 March, 2011 a 10-meter tsunami slammed into the Japanese city of Sendai killing hundreds and sweeping away everything in its wake. The wall of water was triggered by the country's biggest ever earthquake. Cars, lorries and boats bobbed like toys as a wave of debris spread over huge swathes of north-eastern Japan.

An after effect of the tsunami was the malfunctioning of a nuclear plant in Fukushima, north of Tokyo, where the reactor's cooling system overheated. Other nuclear power plants and oil refineries had been shut down following the 8.9 magnitude quake. Engineers opted to cover the plant in concrete, the technique used at Chernobyl 25 years ago, however this failed and experts have since tried to plug the leak using an absorbent polymer. An exclusion zone of 30 kilometres has been advised by the Japanese government, which will be long-term. It is thought the crack in reactor number two is one source of leaks that have caused radiation levels in the sea to rise to more than 4000 times the legal limit. Food products and water supplies have been affected.

Scientists in Europe are convinced this scenario could happen closer to home. They have been working on an early warning system for countries surrounding the Mediterranean Sea. The region along the Turkish coast in the Eastern Mediterranean is considered the most vulnerable.

In these scenarios, engineers have tried to learn from the past and estimate what might happen in the future. However, with the best will in the world it is sometimes impossible to ascertain all the implications of a single event, such as a tsunami.

Fraud risk

Fraud risk (a type of operational business risk) is the vulnerability of an organisation to fraud. Some businesses are more vulnerable than others to fraud and as a result have to have stronger controls over fraud. Fraud risk is a risk that is considered controllable by most businesses.

More on fraud risk

Fraud risk is the vulnerability of an organisation to fraud. The size of fraud risk for any organisation is a factor of:

- the probability of fraud occurring, and
- the size of the losses if fraud does occur.

For example, a bank will be subject to much higher fraud risk than a property investment company due to the desirability of money and the potential value that theft could achieve; it is unlikely that someone will steal a building from an investment company.

Fraud risk should be managed, by:

- fraud prevention: ensuring that the opportunities to commit fraud are minimised
- fraud detection and deterrence: detection measures are designed to identify fraud after it has occurred. If employees fear that the risk of detection is high, they will be deterred from trying to commit fraud.

The management of fraud risk should be an element of an organisation's internal control system.

Corporate reputation risk

Reputation risk is for many organisations a down-side risk as the better the reputation of the business the more risk there is of losing that reputation. A good reputation can be very quickly eroded if companies suffer adverse media comments or are perceived to be untrustworthy.

This could arise from:

- environmental performance
- social performance
- health & safety performance.

More on corporate reputation risk

Many large organisations are aware of the potential damage to their business from events affecting their 'reputation' in the opinion of the general public or more specific groups (such as existing customers or suppliers).

Some organisations succeed in being perceived as 'environmental-friendly', and use public relations and advertising to promote this image.

For many organisations, however, reputation risk is a down-side risk. The risk can be particularly significant for companies that sell products or services to consumer markets. There have been cases where a company's reputation has been significantly affected by:

- employing child labour in under-developed countries or operating 'sweat shops' in which employees work long hours in poor conditions for low pay
- causing environmental damage and pollution
- public suspicions about the damage to health from using the company's products
- investing heavily in countries with an unpopular or tyrannical government
- involvement in business 'scandals' such as mis-selling products
- management announcements about the quality of the product a company produces.

Managing reputation risk can be complicated by the fact that many of these factors lie outside the control of the organisation. For example, many companies outsource production to third parties who operate in countries where labour costs are cheaper. Such arrangements can work well, although major multinational corporations have had their reputations tarnished by being associated with third parties who used dubious employment or environmental policies in order to keep costs down.

Test your understanding 5

During their work on Worldcom and Enron, Arthur Anderson (chartered accountants and registered auditors) failed to identify serious irregularities in these companies. This led to their demise. This was mainly due to (pick ONE answer):

A Business risk

B Political risk

C Environmental risk

D Reputation risk

Employee malfeasance risk

Malfeasance means doing wrong or committing an offence. Organisations might be exposed to risks of actions by employees that result in an offence or crime (other than fraud). This, like fraud risk, is a type of operational business risk.

More on employee malfeasance

Examples of employee malfeasance are:

- deliberately making false representations about a product or service in order to win a customer order, exposing the organisation to the risk of compensation claims for mis-selling
- committing a criminal offence by failing to comply with statutory requirements, such as taking proper measures for the safety and protection of employees or customers.

Risks from illegal activities by employees should be controlled by suitable internal controls, to ensure that employees comply with established policies and procedures.

Risks in international operations

International businesses are subject to all the risks above but also have to consider extra risk factors, which could be due to the following:

Culture	A UK business may fail in a venture overseas because it does not adapt to the overseas culture. Good knowledge of local culture can, however, give companies an advantage.
Litigation	There is a greater danger of litigation risk in overseas operations as the parent company management may not understand the legislation well and therefore have more risk of breaching it.
Credit	There is often a greater difficulty in controlling credit risk on overseas sales. Chasing debts is more difficult and expensive.
Items in transit	There is a greater risk of losses or damage in transit if companies are transporting goods great distances
Financial risks	These include foreign exchange risks, and will be considered in more detail in a later chapter.

More on risks in international operations

Companies that engage in international operations could face substantial risks in addition to country risk.

- There could be significant **cultural differences** between the various countries in which the company operates. There could be a risk that products, services and business practices that are acceptable in one country will be unacceptable in another. Failure to understand a national or local culture could mean that a company will fail to succeed in establishing its business.
- A lack of understanding of local legislation could expose an organisation to **litigation risk**. When legal action is initiated in a different country, a company has to appoint lawyers to represent them and rely on their advice on the appropriate and necessary steps to take.
- When a company exports goods to other countries, there could be **risks that the goods will be held up or lost in transit**, and the loss might not always be covered by insurance. For example, goods might be held up in customs due to inadequate import documentation.

- When a customer in another country buys goods on credit, the exporter is exposed to credit risk. However, the **credit risk is often greater**, because in the event of non-payment by the customer, legal action might be more difficult to arrange (and more expensive) and the prospects of obtaining payment might be much lower.

Test your understanding 6

A company has performed a SWOT analysis and has identified two main threats:

- new legislation covering one of their products; and
- the bank asking for their loan to be repaid immediately since the company failed to pay their most recent instalment after the interest rate rose.

Which categories of risk are they best described by? (Select all that apply.)

A Financial risk

B Political risk

C Reputation risk

D Economic risk

Test your understanding 7

Risk identification and management are the responsibility of: (Select all that apply.)

A The Board

B The risk manager

C The audit committee

D Non-executive directors

Test your understanding 8

Miney plc ("Miney") is a global company, incorporated in the USA, that extracts valuable minerals from the earth.

Mining is a risky business with a death toll averaging 100 deaths per annum in the USA alone. Miney has recently had a coal mine collapse killing two men and trapping four others for three days. The accident made the national news each day and Miney became a household name. Miney is financed purely by equity and has a large cash balance and no debt. It has come to the attention of the Board that the future price of coal is forecast to fall, as renewable energy sources becomes more reliable.

Which THREE of the following risks would you identify as **most** critical for Miney to assess?

A Financial risk

B Project risk

C Reputation risk

D Production risk

E Health and safety risk

F Commodity price risk

Test your understanding 9

AW company is expanding geographically and has just appointed Miss X as divisional manager of their new branch in Country B. AW has never operated in Country B before but has a history of successful divisional expansion in other countries.

Which of the following could help Miss X minimise the risks facing AW Company relating to cultural and legal differences between Country B and AW's current working practices.

Select **all** that apply.

A Recruitment of local staff.

B Employing a local firm of solicitors to advise Miss X on local legislation and working practices.

C Replication of previous divisional expansion plans.

D A marketing campaign to introduce Country B to AW Company.

E Secondment of staff from within AW who are experienced in setting up new divisions.

Test your understanding 10

Historically, X has done business with several non-democratic or repressive governments.

In the light of this, which TWO of the following risks should the directors of X be most concerned with?

A Technology risk.

B Corporate reputation risk.

C Economic risk.

D Fraud risk

E Business risk

F Financial risk.

Test your understanding 11

You are a management accountant working on proposals to build a dam in a developing country in order to generate hydro-electric power and enable many homes to have electricity for the first time. The dam is being financed by international aid, the total amount of which is currently uncertain.

You have been made aware of a pressure group which disagrees with the proposals since construction of the dam will damage the local eco system. The pressure group have vowed to disrupt the project directly through protests.

You are also aware of negative media coverage of the dam which accusing the company you work for of making excessive profits from the project. In addition the bank financing the initial stages of the project has contacted the directors to ask that their involvement in the project not be publicised as they believe it will damage their reputation.

Your company's directors have asked you to present a briefing on the project at their next board meeting. Which of the following should you include as risks to the project's progression in your briefing to the board?

Select **all** that apply.

A Risk the international aid is not received or inadequate to fund the project.

B Risk of negative media coverage for the company.

C Threats from the pressure group to disrupt the project directly.

D Risks that the local eco system will be damaged.

E Threat that the bank will pull out due to risks to their reputation.

Test your understanding 12 – ZXC (Case Study)

Scenario

The ZXC company manufactures aircraft. The company is based in Europe and currently produces a range of four different aircraft. ZXC's aircraft are reliable with low maintenance costs, giving ZXC a good reputation, both to airlines who purchase from ZXC and to airlines' customers who fly in the aircraft.

Trigger

ZXC is currently developing the 'next generation' of passenger aircraft, with the selling name of the ZXLiner. New developments in ZXLiner include the following:

- Two decks along the entire aircraft (not just part as in the Boeing 747 series) enabling faster loading and unloading of passengers from both decks at the same time. However, this will mean that airport gates must be improved to facilitate dual loading at considerable expense.
- 20% decrease in fuel requirements and falls in noise and pollution levels.
- Use of new alloys to decrease maintenance costs, increase safety and specifically the use of Zitnim (a new lightweight conducting alloy) rather than standard wiring to enable the 'fly-by-wire' features of the aircraft. Zitnim only has one supplier worldwide.

Many component suppliers are based in Europe although ZXC does obtain about 25% of the sub-contracted components from companies in the USA. ZXC also maintains a significant R&D department working on the ZXLiner and other new products such as alternative environmentally friendly fuel for aircraft.

Although the ZXLiner is yet to fly or be granted airworthiness certificates, ZXC does have orders for 25 aircraft from the HTS company. However, on current testing schedules the ZXLiner will be delivered late.

ZXC currently has about €4 billion of loans from various banks and last year made a loss of €2.3 billion.

Task

Write a report to the directors of ZXC identifying the sources of risk that could affect ZXC, and evaluating the impact of the risk on the company.

(30 minutes)

Test your understanding 13 – Smart meters (Case study)

Scenario

E is an electricity company that has a large number of customers. All customers' homes have electricity meters that have mechanical dials that turn to record the consumption of electricity. Most homes have their meters indoors. Customers have to provide E with regular readings from their meters in order to ensure that they are billed properly for their electricity consumption. Customers can log into their accounts online to input their readings or they can telephone E's call centre to give an operator a reading.

E has a policy that customers must allow an inspector to read their electricity meters at least once per year. This inspection has two purposes. The first is to ensure that the customer has not been consistently understating the figures in order to underpay for their electricity and the second is to ensure that the meter has not been tampered with in order to reduce the readings according to the dials. The meters are designed so that they are difficult to dismantle without causing obvious damage and they also have a seal that is made out of soft metal that will be broken if the meter is ever opened.

E's inspectors generally visit all the homes within a particular area in the course of an evening. Most customers are at home then and so that is an efficient way to conduct the annual checks. If a customer is not at home then the inspector leaves a card to request an opportunity to inspect the meter. If the customer does not respond to the card within seven days E will send up to four weekly reminders. Almost all customers comply with these requests but a very small minority do not respond and E can apply to the courts for the right to force entry when that happens.

Trigger

E is considering the replacement of its electricity meters with new "smart meters" which will be located in customers' homes. These will record consumption electronically rather than mechanically. The information will be stored on the meter. The same wires that carry electricity can be used to transmit data to and from the meters and E's IT system will send coded messages to meters to request readings as and when required. It is envisaged that these electronic readings will normally be once every three months, but there is very little to prevent E from reading some meters far more often.

Each meter will be fitted with a chip that will transmit a warning if it is tampered with either physically or electronically. The memory on the meters is not affected by power cuts and the meters can restart themselves without losing any data if a power cut occurs.

Task

Write a report to the Board of E which:

(a) Discusses the potential benefits for E that may come about from the introduction of smart meters; and

(b) Evaluates FOUR risks that might arise from the introduction of smart meters. Suggest how each risk might be dealt with.

(45 minutes)

4 Chapter summary

RISK
DEFINITION
• Chance that future events/results may not be as expected
• Downside or upside
WHY TAKE RISK ?
• Gain competitive advantage
• Increase returns
CATEGORISING RISKS
TYPES AND SOURCES OF RISK
• Political, legal and regulatory
• Business
• Economic
• Financial
• Technology
• Environmental
• Corporate reputation
• Fraud
• Employee malfeasance
• International operations

Test your understanding answers

Test your understanding 1

The correct answer is D – Per CIMA's risk management cycle, a risk management group should be formed, risks identified, understand their scale, develop a strategy, implement and allocate responsibility, control and review.

Test your understanding 2

The correct answers are C and D – A and B are strategic level risks.

Test your understanding 3

The correct answer is D – A, B and C are operational risks.

Test your understanding 4

A, B and C

- Option A: If publicised, poor treatment of employees at Company Q's main supplier could greatly increase reputation risk to Company Q. This may influence Q's performance over a long period of time since it may lose support from customers, shareholders and employees. The fact that Q Company may not be able to meet it strategic objectives as a result makes this a strategic risk.
- Option B: See explanation above, Company Q will be associated with the pollution and held responsible for it.
- Option C: Would almost certainly compromise Company Q's ability to meet its' strategic objectives.
- Option D: Would not affect Company Q's performance over a long period of time. It may lead to a reduction in profit margins but only if the supplier successfully negotiates a price increase.
- Option E: See explanation for Option D above.

Test your understanding 5

The correct answer is D – Arthur Anderson consequently lost their reputation as being the number one accountancy firm in the world and consequently many of their customers.

Test your understanding 6

The correct answers are A and B – New legislation is covered within political risk. The repayment of the loan is covered within financial risk.

Test your understanding 7

The correct answers are A, B, C and D – All staff in an organisation are responsible for risk.

Test your understanding 8

C, E and F

A Financial risk – low risk due to lack of debt finance

B Project risk – large one off projects are not a major aspect of the company's business model

C Reputation risk – high due to accident

D Production risk – despite the accidents, there is not a high risk of production shortages

E Health and safety risk – high due to accident and potential for injury in the industry

F Commodity price risk – high due to threat from renewable sources

Test your understanding 9

A and B only

- Options A and B will help Miss X understand local practices.
- Option C – Previous divisional expansion plans are likely to be culturally appropriate to other countries and not Country B.
- Option D – a marketing campaign may cause more cultural issues.
- Option E – see explanation for option 3 above.

Test your understanding 10

B and D

- X should be concerned with their reputation but also the risk of fraud and corruption when dealing with non-democratic governments is greater (option D).

Test your understanding 11

A, C and E

- Options A, C and E will disrupt or halt the project directly.
- Option B is a risk to the company and not the project.
- Option D is not a risk to the project's progression although it may end up causing reputation risk for the company.

Test your understanding 12 – ZXC (Case Study)

To: The directors of ZXC

From: A.N. Accountant

Date: Today

Subject: Sources and evaluation of risk at ZXC

This report covers the identification of risk at ZXC and evaluates each risk in turn. Recommendations for risk reduction are not given at this time.

Product/market risk

This is the risk that customers will not buy new products (or services) provided by the organisation, or that the sales demand for current products and services will decline unexpectedly.

For ZXC, there is the risk that demand for the new aircraft will be less than expected, either due to customers purchasing the rival airplane or because airports will not be adapted to take the new ZXLiner.

Commodity price risk

Businesses might be exposed to risks from unexpected increases (or falls) in the price of a key commodity.

Part of the control systems of the ZXLiner rely on the availability of the new lightweight conducting alloy Zitnim. As there is only one supplier of this alloy, then there is the danger of the monopolist increasing the price or even denying supply. Increase in price would increase the overall cost of the (already expensive) ZXLiner, while denial of supply would further delay delivery of the aircraft.

Product reputation risk

Some companies rely heavily on brand image and product reputation, and an adverse event could put its reputation (and so future sales) at risk.

While the reputation of ZXC appears good at present, reputation will suffer if the ZXLiner is delayed significantly or it does not perform well in test flights (which have still to be arranged). Airline customers, and also their customers (travellers) are unlikely to feel comfortable flying in an aircraft that is inherently unstable.

Currency risk

Currency risk, or foreign exchange risk, arises from the possibility of movements in foreign exchange rates, and the value of one currency in relation to another.

ZXC is currently based in Europe although it obtains a significant number of parts from the USA. If the €/$ exchange rate became worse, then the cost of imported goods for ZXC (and all other companies) would increase. At present, the relatively weak US$ is in ZXC's favour and so this risk is currently negligible.

Interest rate risk

Interest rate risk is the risk of unexpected gains or losses arising as a consequence of a rise or fall in interest rates. Exposures to interest rate risk arise from borrowing and investing.

As ZXC do have significant bank loans, then the company is very exposed to this risk.

Gearing risk

Gearing risk for non-bank companies is the risk arising from exposures to high financial gearing and large amounts of borrowing.

Again, ZXC has significant amounts of bank loans. This increases the amount of interest that must be repaid each year.

Political risk

Political risk depends to a large extent on the political stability in the countries in which an organisation operates, the political institutions within that country and the government's attitude towards protectionism.

As ZXC operates in a politically stable country this risk is negligible.

Legal risk or litigation risk

The risk arises from the possibility of legal action being taken against an organisation.

At present this risk does not appear to be a threat for ZXC. However, if the ZXLiner is delayed any further there is a risk for breach of contract for late delivery to the HTS company.

Regulatory risk

This is the possibility that regulations will affect the way an organisation has to operate.

In terms of aircraft, regulation generally affects noise and pollution levels. As the ZXLiner is designed to have lower noise and pollution levels than existing aircraft then this risk does not appear to be a threat to ZXC.

Technology risk

Technology risk arises from the possibility that technological change will occur or that new technology will not work.

Given that ZXC is effectively producing a new product (the ZXLiner) that has not actually been tested yet, there is some technology risk. At worse, the ZXLiner may not fly at all or not obtain the necessary flying certificates.

Economic risk

This risk refers to the risks facing organisations from changes in economic conditions, such as economic growth or recession, government spending policy and taxation policy, unemployment levels and international trading conditions.

Demand for air travel is forecast to increase for the foreseeable future, so in that sense there is a demand for aircraft which ZXC will benefit from. The risk of product failure is more significant than economic risk.

Environmental risk

This risk arises from changes to the environment over which an organisation has no direct control, such as global warming, to those for which the organisation might be responsible, such as oil spillages and other pollution.

ZXC is subject to this risk – and there is significant debate concerning the impact of air travel on global warming. At the extreme, there is a threat that air travel could be banned, or made very expensive by international taxation agreements, although this appears unlikely at present.

Conclusion

ZXC will suffer from many risks which will impact on the company. The likelihood and impact of each varies, by risk and over time. ZXC should implement reduction strategies where possible.

Test your understanding 13 – Smart meters (Case study)

To: The Board of E

From: A.N. Accountant

Date: Today

Subject: Smart meters and risk

Introduction

This report discusses the benefits of introducing Smart Meters at E, and then evaluates four risks arising from this action. Recommendations are then made to reduce the risks identified.

(a) **The introduction of Smart Meters**

Smart meters will offer the potential to dramatically reduce operating expenses. E will not require meter inspectors to visit customers' homes. There will be far fewer transactions involving call centre staff and so numbers can be reduced there too.

The new meters may reduce customer fraud and so enhance revenues. The fact that they are electronic and not mechanical will make it far harder to tamper with readings.

E will be able to gather a great deal of information about individual customers. At present, E can tell how much electricity is being drawn from the grid, but it cannot identify the specific customers who are using it. The new meters will make it possible to identify customers whose demand changes in response to, say, a major sporting event. That may make it easier for E to predict demand in advance of such events and so plan more easily.

E may also be able to gather valuable marketing information. For example, some customers will have larger increases in consumption when the weather is cold. E could target such customers with offers of alternative pricing plans or discounts on home insulation.

(b) **Risks**

Customer fraud

If customers learn how to interfere with the meters then E may lose significant amounts of revenue. The new meters may be more difficult to manipulate, but history suggests that electronic safeguards can be defeated. For example, mobile phones can be unlocked and dvds can be pirated despite safeguards.

E could compare patterns of energy consumption within neighbourhoods and could identify customers whose readings seem low. Those customers' meters could be inspected for any modification. E should publicise any criminal prosecutions as a deterrent to other customers.

Installation

The installation of these new meters will be a significant undertaking. E will have to arrange access to every customer's home in order to fit the new meters. The logistics of this will be complicated because of customers' work patterns and availability because of work and so on. The old system will have to operate in parallel with the new while this work is being undertaken and so staff will be stretched.

E may offer discounts or rebates to customers who offer access at convenient times. The discounts should be self-financing if they are funded out of the cost savings of managing a customer's account once the smart meter has been installed.

IT issues

It will be difficult for E to fully test this system before installation. There will be large numbers of smart meters in the system and they will be communicating over long distances. There could be unforeseen problems with data being corrupted or lost. If that happens then the original meters will have been removed and there will be no effective way to put the system back.

It would be ideal if E could select a system that has already been used successfully by another electricity company. It would be preferable to apply a proven system even if there are more up to date versions of the technology that might offer enhancements.

Financial cost

There will have to be a significant investment in this new system and the anticipated benefits may not be realised. The shareholders and other stakeholders may be concerned that E is taking a reckless risk by making a substantial investment in a new technology. An adverse outcome could mean lower profits or higher prices for consumers.

E could possibly transfer some of the risk by paying a third party to design and implement the new system. The contract could specify penalties for any shortcomings in the operation of the new system.

Conclusions

E would appear to benefit from the introduction of Smart Meters. However, several risks may arise with their introduction. These risks can be reduced, in part, by the measures suggested in this report.

chapter

2

Risk management

Chapter learning objectives

Lead	Component
A1. Evaluate the types of risk facing an organisation and recommend appropriate responses.	(b) Evaluate the organisation's ability to bear identified risks. (c) Recommend responses to identified risks.
A2. Evaluate senior management's responsibility for the implementation of risk management strategies and internal controls.	(a) Recommend techniques that will enable the board to discharge its responsibilities with respect to managing risks (b) Advise the board on its responsibilities for reporting risks to shareholders and other stakeholders.
D1. Evaluate financial risks facing an organisation.	(a) Evaluate financial risks facing an organisation.
D2. Evaluate alternative risk management tools.	(a) Advise on the effects of economic factors that affect future cash flows from international operations.

Indicative syllabus content

- Quantification of risk exposures (impact if an adverse event occurs) and their expected values, taking account of likelihood.
- Risk map representation of risk exposures as a basis of reporting and analysing risks.
- Enterprise risk management and its components.
- Risk mitigation including TARA – transfer, avoid, reduce, accept.
- Gross and net risks.
- Assurance mapping and similar techniques for describing risks and their associated responses.
- Risk register.
- Risk reports and stakeholder responses.
- Quantification of risk exposures, their sensitivities to changes in external conditions and their expected values.
- Value at risk.

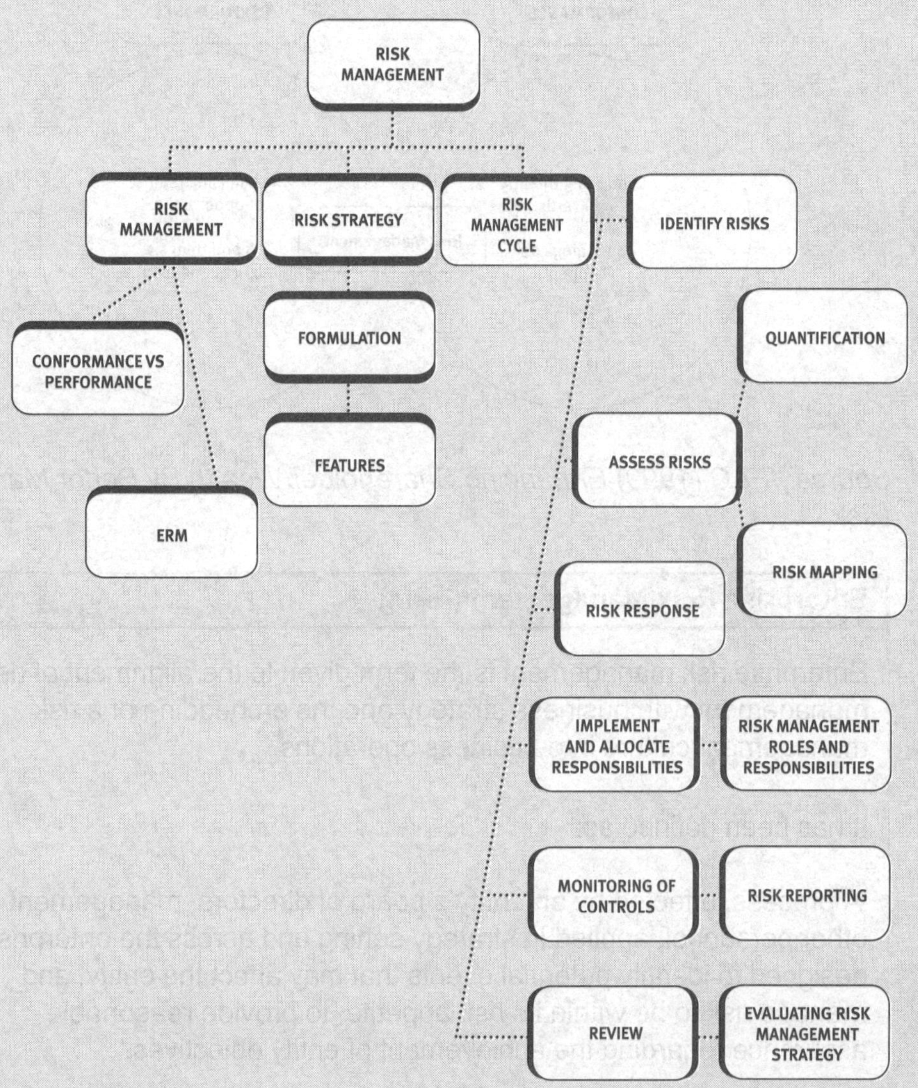

1 Risk management

Risk management is defined as:

'the process of understanding and managing the risks that the organisation is inevitably subject to in attempting to achieve its corporate objectives'

CIMA Official Terminology

- The traditional view of risk management has been one of protecting the organisation from loss through conformance procedures and hedging techniques – this is about avoiding the **downside** risk.
- The new approach to risk management is about taking advantage of the opportunities to increase overall returns within a business – benefiting from the **upside** risk.
- The following diagram shows how risk management can reconcile the two perspectives of conformance and performance (as discussed previously in chapter 1).

Source: IFAC (1999) Enhancing Shareholder Wealth By Better Managing Risk

Enterprise Risk Management (ERM)

Enterprise risk management is the term given to the alignment of risk management with business strategy and the embedding of a risk management culture into business operations.

It has been defined as:

'A process, effected by an entity's board of directors, management and other personnel, applied in strategy setting and across the enterprise, designed to identify potential events that may affect the entity, and manage risk to be within its risk appetite, to provide reasonable assurance regarding the achievement of entity objectives.'

Committee of Sponsoring Organisations of the Treadway Commission (COSO) (2003)

Risk management has transformed from a 'department focused' approach to a holistic, co-ordinated and integrated process which manages risk throughout the organisation.

The key principles of ERM include:

- consideration of risk management in the context of business strategy
- risk management is everyone's responsibility, with the tone set from the top
- the creation of a risk aware culture

- a comprehensive and holistic approach to risk management
- consideration of a broad range of risks (strategic, financial, operational and compliance)
- a focused risk management strategy, led by the board (embedding risk within an organisation's culture).

The COSO ERM Framework is represented as a three dimensional matrix in the form of a cube which reflects the relationships between objectives, components and different organisational levels.

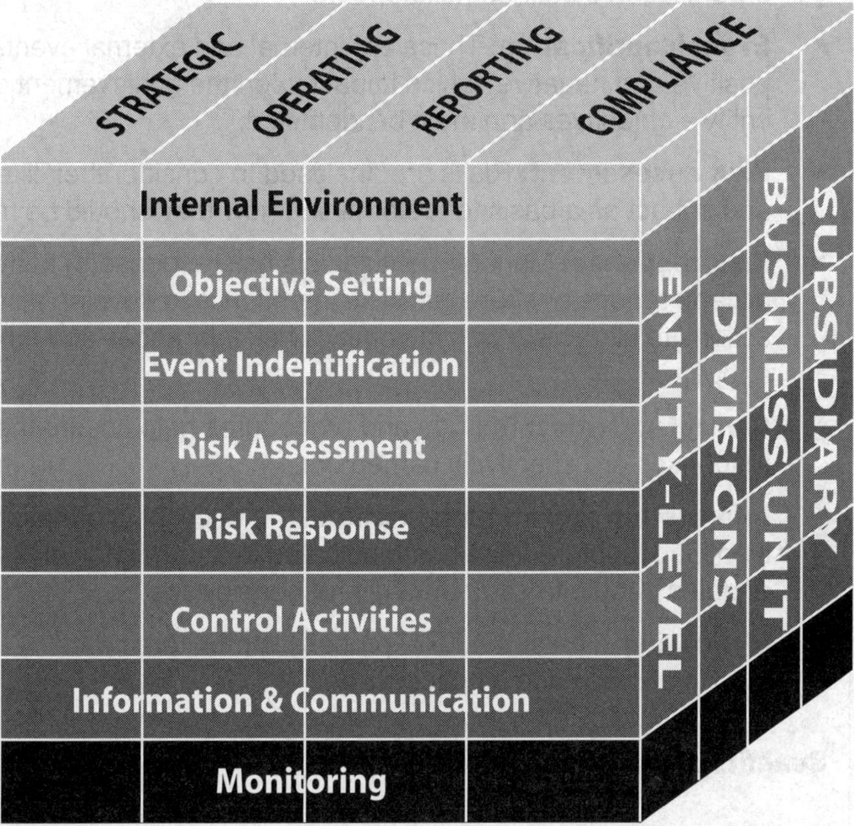

- The four objectives (strategic, operations, reporting and compliance) reflect the responsibility of different executives across the entity and address different needs.
- The four organisational levels (subsidiary, business unit, division and entity) emphasise the importance of managing risks across the enterprise as a whole.
- The eight components must function effectively for risk management to be successful.

The eight components are closely aligned to the risk management process addressed previously, and also reflect elements from the COSO view of an effective internal control system:

- **Internal environment:** This is the tone of the organisation, including the risk management philosophy and risk appetite (see later in this chapter).
- **Objective setting:** Objectives should be aligned with the organisation's mission and need to be consistent with the organisation's defined risk appetite.
- **Event identification:** These are internal and external events (both positive and negative) which impact upon the achievement of an entity's objectives and must be identified.
- **Risk assessment:** Risks are analysed to consider their likelihood and impact as a basis for determining how they should be managed.
- **Risk response:** Management selects risk response(s) to avoid, accept, reduce or share risk. The intention is to develop a set of actions to align risks with the entity's risk tolerances and risk appetite.
- **Control activities:** Policies and procedures help ensure the risk responses are effectively carried out.
- **Information and communication:** The relevant information is identified, captured and communicated in a form and timeframe that enables people to carry out their responsibilities.
- **Monitoring:** The entire ERM process is monitored and modifications made as necessary.

Benefits of effective ERM include:

- enhanced decision-making by integrating risks
- the resultant improvement in investor confidence, and hence shareholder value
- focus of management attention on the most significant risks
- a common language of risk management which is understood throughout the organisation
- reduced cost of finance through effective management of risk.

Risk management and shareholder value

Ernst and Young (2001) have developed a model of shareholder value in which

Shareholder value = Static NPV of existing business model + Value of future growth options

which more simply put is 'the sum of the value of what a company does now and the value of what they could possibly do in the future'.

Good risk management allows businesses to exploit opportunities for future growth while protecting the value already created. By aligning risk management activity to what the shareholders consider vital to the success of the business, the shareholders are assured that what they value is protected. Ernst and Young identify four stages:

(a) Establish what shareholders value about the company – through talking with the investment community and linking value creation processes to key performance indicators.

(b) Identify the risks around the key shareholder value drivers – the investment community can identify those factors that will influence their valuation of the company. All other risks will also be considered, even if not known by investors.

(c) Determine the preferred treatment for the risks – the investment community can give their views on what actions they would like management to take in relation to the risks. The risk/reward trade-off can be quantified by estimating the change in a company's market valuation if a particular risk treatment was implemented.

(d) Communicate risk treatments to shareholders – shareholders need to be well informed, as a shared vision is important in relation to the inter-related concepts of risk management and shareholder value.

Test your understanding 1

IFAC highlighted two aspects of risk management which link risk aversion and risk seeking activities. They are:

A Compliance and strategy

B Conformance and performance

C Compliance and conformance

D Performance and strategy

Test your understanding 2

The Committee of Sponsoring Organisations (COSO) outlined six key principles of Enterprise Risk Management (ERM). Identify which of the following is/are included. (Select ALL correct answers).

A Consideration of risk management in the context of business strategy

B The creation of a risk aware culture

C Consideration of a narrow range of risks, mainly financial

D Risk management is the responsibility of the Risk Committee

E A comprehensive and holistic approach to risk management

2 Risk management strategy

Formulation of a risk strategy

- For many businesses the specific formulation of a risk strategy has been a recent development.
- In the past a formal strategy for managing risks would not be made but rather it would be left to individual managers to make assessments of the risks the business faced and exercise judgement on what was a reasonable level of risk.
- This has now changed: failure to properly identify and control risks has been identified as a major cause of business failure (take Barings Bank as an example).

A framework for board consideration of risk is shown below:

Formulating a risk management strategy

A risk management strategy needs to be developed to ensure that the risk exposures of the organisation are consistent with its risk appetite. At the very least, the risk management capability within the organisation should be sufficient to:

- review its internal control system, at least annually (and whether it is adequate),
- ensure that controls are properly implemented, and
- monitor the implementation and effectiveness of controls.

However, the investment by the organisation in risk strategy should be largely determined by the performance requirements of its business objectives and strategy.

- **Risk appetite** can be defined as the amount of risk an organisation is willing to accept in pursuit of value. This may be explicit in strategies, policies and procedures, or it may be implicit. It is determined by:
  - **risk capacity** – the amount of risk that the organisation can bear, and
  - **risk attitude** – the overall approach to risk, in terms of the board being risk averse or risk seeking.
- The way that the organisation documents and determines the specific parts of its risk strategy will have to link to the business strategy and objectives.

- Overall the risk management strategy is concerned with trying to achieve the required business objectives with the lowest possible chance of failure. The tougher the business objectives, however, the more risks will have to be taken to achieve them.
- **Residual risk** is the risk a business faces after its controls have been considered (see later in this chapter for more details).

More on risk appetite

To bring risk management into line with strategic management, an organisation should define the amount of risk it is prepared to take in the pursuit of its objectives. This willingness to accept risk can be stated in a mixture of quantitative and qualitative terms. For example:

- The board of directors might state how much capital they would be prepared to invest in the pursuit of a business objective and how much loss they would be willing to face in the event that results turn out badly.
- Risk can also be stated qualitatively, for example in relation to the organisation's reputation.

In practice, in a large organisation, there will be different levels of risk appetite for different operations or different profit centres/investment centres within the business.

Risk appetite factors

The factors, or business strategies, which could affect the risk appetite of the board of a company include:

Nature of product being manufactured	A high risk of product failure in certain products (e.g. aircraft) must be avoided due to the serious consequences of such an event. This will, out of necessity, limit the risk appetite of the board with regard to these specific products. For other products the risk of failure will be less (e.g. a fizzy drink having small changes from the normal ingredients – customers may not even notice the difference). Additionally if a business is taking significant risks with part of its product range it may be limited in the risk it can take with other products.
The need to increase sales	The strategic need to move into a new market will result in the business accepting a higher degree of risk than trying to increase sales or market share in an existing market. At that stage the business will appear to have a higher risk appetite.

The background of the board	Some board members may accept increased risk personally and this may be reflected in the way they manage the company.
Amount of change in the market	Operating in a market place with significant change (e.g. mobile telephones) will mean that the board have to accept a higher degree of risk. For example, new models of phone have to be available quickly.
Reputation of the company	If the company has a good reputation then the board will accept less risk – as they will not want to lose that good reputation.

Test your understanding 3

The amount of risk an organisation is willing to accept in the pursuit of value is known as their:

A Risk map

B Risk appetite

C Risk culture

D Risk thermostat

Features of a risk management strategy

In a CIMA and IFAC (International Federation of Accountants) joint report in 2004 – Enterprise Governance – the following key features of a risk management strategy were identified:

- Statement of the organisation's attitude to risk – the balance between risk and the need to achieve objectives.
- The risk appetite of the organisation.
- The objectives of the risk management strategy.
- Culture of the organisation in relation to risk (and the behaviour the organisation expects from individuals with regard to risk-taking).
- Responsibilities of managers for the application of risk management strategy.
- Reference should be made to the risk management systems the company uses (i.e. its internal control systems).
- Performance criteria should be defined so that the effectiveness of risk management can be evaluated.

An alternative risk management process

The Institute of Risk Management (IRM) developed a risk management process containing three elements:

(1) **Risk assessment** is composed of the analysis and evaluation of risk through the process of identification, description and estimation.

The purpose of risk assessment is to undertake risk evaluation. Risk evaluation is used to make decisions about the significance of risks to the organisation and whether each specific risk should be accepted or treated.

(2) **Risk reporting** is concerned with regular reports to the board and to stakeholders setting out the organisation's policies in relation to risk and enabling the effective monitoring of those policies.

(3) **Risk treatment** (risk response) is the process of selecting and implementing measures to modify the risk.

Following risk treatment therefore will be residual risk reporting.

3 Identifying, measuring and assessing risks

Chapter 1 examined the different types of risks faced by an organisation. It is key, however, that businesses can identify the risks they face and evaluate the effect of the risks on the business. Some risks will be relatively easily borne by businesses, but others will be more difficult and more serious in their implications.

Risk identification

- The risk identification process will often be controlled by a **risk committee** or risk management specialists (see later in this chapter).
- The risks identified in the process should be recorded in a **risk register**, which is simply a list of the risks that have been identified, and the measures (if any) that have been taken to control each of them.
- There are a variety of methods that can be used by businesses to identify the risks that they face:

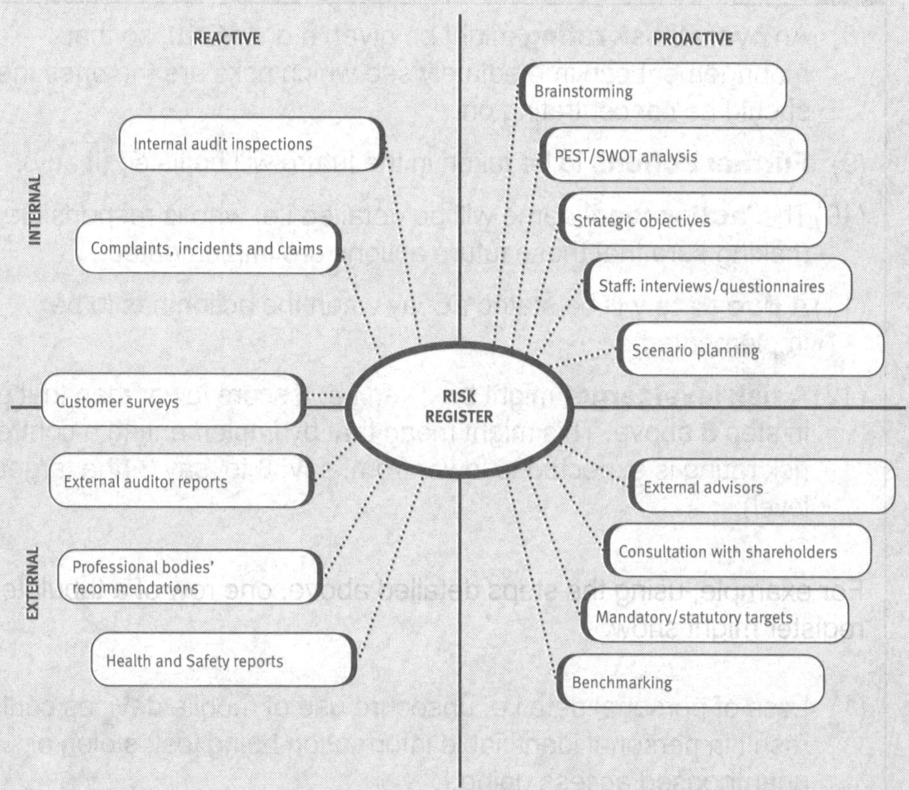

The risk register

The risk register is a very important and practical risk management tool that all companies should have these days. It takes several days, if not weeks, to produce, and needs to be reviewed and updated regularly – mainly annually (in conjunction with corporate governance guidelines).

The risk register is often laid out in the form of a tabular document with various headings:

(1) The **risk title** – stating what the risk might be.

(2) The **likelihood** of the risk – possibly measured numerically if a scale has been set e.g. 1 is unlikely, 5 is highly likely.

(3) The **impact** of the risk should it arise. Again this might be graded from, say, 1 (low impact) to 5 (high impact).

(4) The **risk owners** name will be given – usually a manager or director.

(5) The **date** the risk was identified will be detailed.

(6) The date the risk was last considered will be given.

(7) **Mitigation actions** should be listed i.e. what the company has done so far to reduce the risk. This might include training, insurance, further controls added to the system, etc.

(8) An **overall risk rating** might be given e.g. 1â€“10, so that management can immediately see which risks are the ones they should be concentrating on.

(9) **Further actions** to be taken in the future will be listed (if any).

(10) The **'action lead'** name will be detailed i.e. who is responsible for making sure that these future actions are implemented.

(11) A **due date** will be stated â€“ by when the action has to be implemented.

(12) A **risk level target** might be given i.e. a score lower than that given in step 8 above. This might mean that by implementing a control, the risk rating is expected to lower from, say, 8 to, say 2 (the target risk level).

For example, using the steps detailed above, one row of a tabulated risk register might show:

(1) Loss of personal data i.e. unsecure use of mobile devices could result in personal identifiable information being lost, stolen or unauthorised access gained.

(2) Likelihood = 3

(3) Impact = 5

(4) Risk owner = Mike Smith (IT manager)

(5) 1.1.12

(6) 2.2.14

(7) Staff receive training every 2 years which highlights the risks. All laptops are encrypted. Regular audits are undertaken. Any incidents are reported to the Audit Committee.

(8) Overall risk rating = 7

(9) Encryption technology to be implemented which meets industry standard.

(10) Mike Smith

(11) 31.7.14

(12) Risk level target = 3

Test your understanding 4

Risk registers would normally detail which of the following: (Select all that apply.)

A Risk level before controls are implemented

B Risk level after controls are implemented

C Responsibility for managing risks

D The total cost of a control being implemented

More on risk identification

Some of the common methods of risk identification include:

PEST/SWOT analysis	PEST (Political, Economic, Social, Technological) and SWOT (Strengths, Weaknesses, Opportunities, Threats) are very well known and familiar business analysis tools. These models can be used to assess risks by providing a framework to identify and think about the risks in the organisation.
External advisors	Companies may employ external risk consultants who will advise on key risks and processes that can be used to limit and control those risks. Consultants have access to other businesses and as a result may have pools of knowledge not available internally.
Interviews/questionnaires	The company may conduct interviews or send questionnaires to key business managers asking them to indicate principal risks.
Internal audit	One of the functions of internal audit should be to provide recommendations on controlling risk. As part of their work therefore, internal audit assess where the organisation faces risk.

Brainstorming The business may decide to use more informal brainstorming meetings to assess the risks they face. These meetings have the advantage of accessing many different viewpoints.

Any of these methods identify risks but at the end of the process it is important that the organisation determines what its principal risks are. These principal risks will then determine the controls that need to be put in place and the systems that have to be introduced to control and manage the risks.

Quantification of risk exposures

Quantification of risk is important in understanding the extent and significance of the exposure. This can be done by measuring the impact of the risk factor (such as exchange rates) on the total value of the company, or on any individual item such as cash flow or costs.

- Risks that are identified should be measured and assessed. The extent to which this can be done depends on the information available to the risk manager.
- In some companies, particularly in the banking and insurance industries, many risks can be measured statistically, on the basis of historical information.
- In many other situations, the measurement and assessment of risk depends on management judgement.

Some quantitative techniques include:

- expected values and standard deviation
- volatility
- value at risk (VaR)
- regression analysis
- simulation analysis

Expected values and standard deviation

- Some risks can be measured by the use of expected values.

  Expected value = Σ prob X

  where prob = probability, X = outcome

Expected value of risk

When statistical estimates are available for the probabilities of different outcomes, and the value of each outcome, risk can be measured as an expected value of loss or gain.

Expected value of loss = p × L

Where:

p is the probability that the outcome will occur

L is the loss in the event that the outcome does occur.

Example

The finance director of a company has to prepare an assessment of credit risk for a report to the board. The company has annual credit sales of $12 million, and customers are given 60 days, (two months,) credit. Experience shows that:

- irrecoverable debts written off amount to 1.5% of total annual credit sales
- 10% of irrecoverable debts written off are subsequently recovered by legal action.

Required:

(a) What is the credit risk exposure of the company?

(b) What is the expected loss each year due to credit risk?

Solution

(a) The total exposure to credit risk can be expressed either as the total annual credit sales ($12 million) or the exposure to unpaid debts at any point in time ($12 million × 2/12 = $2 million).

(b) For a full year the expected value of loss is = $12 million × 1.5% × 90% = $162,000.

The standard deviation is a measure of the dispersion of the possible values of a given factor, such as cash flow, from the expected value or mean. Thus the standard deviation provides a measure of volatility – the greater the standard deviation, the greater the risk involved.

Volatility

- Another way of assessing risk might be looking at potential volatility. For example, a company might calculate an expected value based on a range of probabilities but also assess the potential variation from that expected outcome (range or standard deviation).

Test your understanding 5 – Volatility (Integration)

The following are the forecast purchases of raw materials in a future month:

£200,000	30% probability
£250,000	50% probability
£300,000	20% probability

Calculate the upside and downside volatility from expected purchases.

Value at risk

Value at Risk (VaR) allows investors to assess the scale of the likely loss in their portfolio at a defined level of probability. It is becoming the most widely used measure of financial risk and is also enshrined in both financial and accounting regulations.

VaR is based on the assumption that investors care mainly about the probability of a large loss. The VaR of a portfolio is the maximum loss on a portfolio occurring within a given period of time with a given probability (usually small).

- Calculating VaR involves using three components: a time period, a confidence level and a loss amount or percentage loss.
- Statistical methods are used to calculate a standard deviation for the possible variations in the value of the total portfolio of assets over a specific period of time.
- Making an assumption that possible variations in total market value of the portfolio are normally distributed, it is then possible to predict at a given level of probability the maximum loss that the bank might suffer on its portfolio in the time period.
- A bank can try to control the risk in its asset portfolio by setting target maximum limits for value at risk over different time periods (one day, one week, one month, three months, and so on).
- VaR may be calculated as standard deviation × Z-score (where the Z-score can be found from the normal distribution tables).

Normal distribution

Normal distributions can be found when we measure things such as:

- Exam results
- Staff performance gradings
- The heights of a group of people etc

A normal distribution has the following characteristics:

The mean is shown in the centre of the diagram and the curve is symmetrical about the mean. This means that 50% of the values will be below the mean and 50% of the values will be above the mean.

Note: The mean, median and mode will all be the same for a normal distribution.

How far the values spread out from the mean is the standard deviation.

This can be seen in the following diagram:

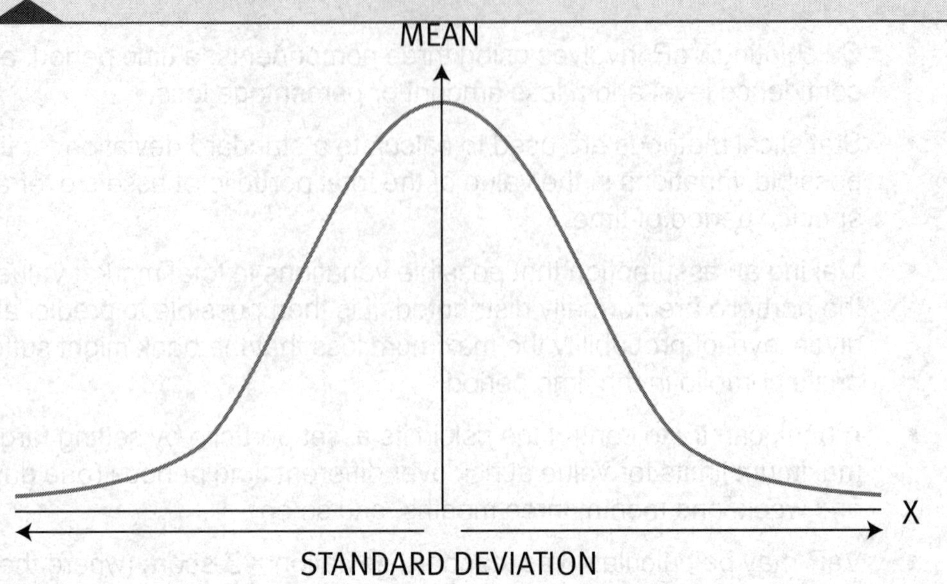

The total area under the curve is equal to 1.

If we can think of a standard normal distribution curve with three standard deviations as follows:

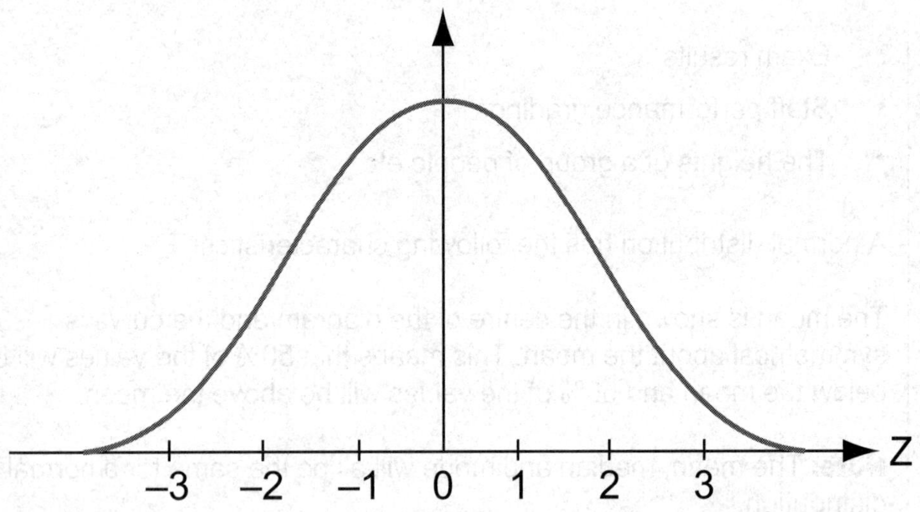

In general 68% of values are within one deviation (between -1 and 1), 95% of values are within two standard deviations (between -2 and 2) and 99.7% of values are within three standard deviations (between -3 and 3).

From this we can see that if we look at a set of data which fits a normal distribution the majority of values will occur closer to the mean, with fewer and fewer occurring the further from the mean we move.

A standard normal distribution has:

a mean of 0

a standard deviation of 1.

This special distribution is denoted by z and can be calculated as:

$$z = \frac{x - \mu}{\sigma}$$

Where:

z is the score

x is the value being considered

μ is the mean

σ is the standard deviation

This calculation is used to convert any value to standard normal distribution.

Looking up the normal distribution tables

Once we have calculated our 'z score' we can look this up on the normal distribution table to find the area under the curve, which equates to the percentage chance (probability) of that value occurring.

So if we calculated a z score of 1.00. From the table the value is 0.3413.

This means that (0.3413 ÷ 1.0) or 34.13% is the area shown from 0 - 1 on the diagram.

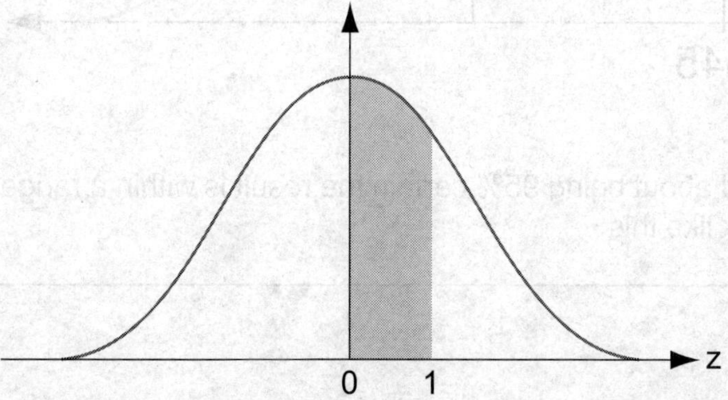

From this we can deduce that 34.13% would be the area shown from 0 - 1 on the diagram. So we can say that 68.26% of values will fall within one standard deviation (-1 to 1).

VaR calculation

For VaR , there are two types of calculation to consider:

1) The confidence level that the result will be above a particular figure – this is referred to as a **one tail test**.
2) The confidence level that a figure will be within a particular range – this is referred to as a **two tail test**.

In both cases we are working backwards from the percentage to find the value of x.

One tail test

If you are asked to calculate the 95% VaR, this is a one tail test. As we are looking at risk, it is usually about being 95% certain that the outcome will be above a particular value.

50% of the distribution is on one side of the mean, within the tables we are looking for as close to 0.4500.

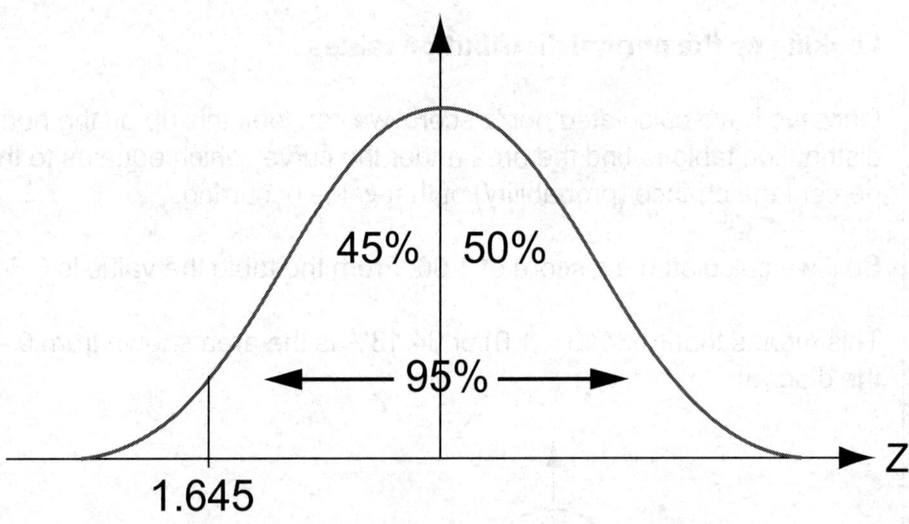

Two tail test

If you are asked about being 95% certain the result is within a range, the area would look like this:

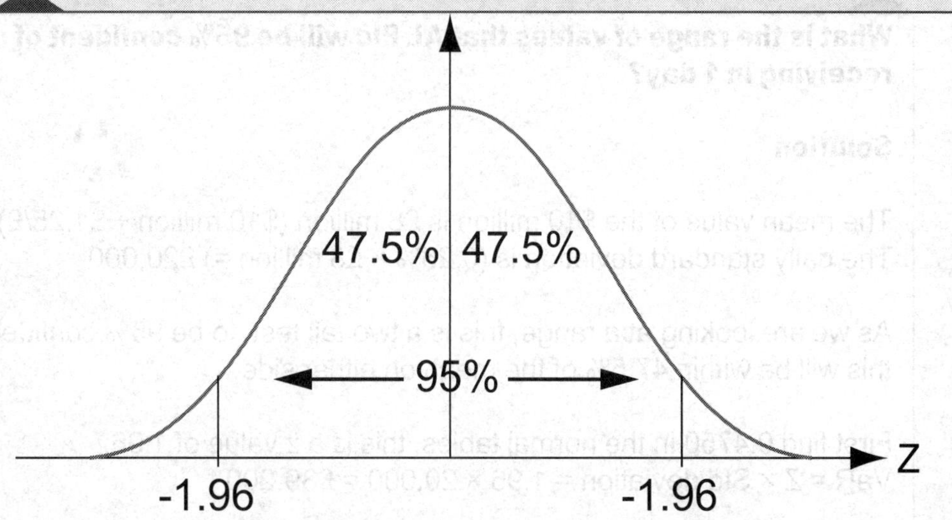

We would be looking for 0.4750 in the tables, 47.5% above and below the mean.

One tail test

Z is a bank. The management accountant of Z has estimated that the value of its asset portfolio at year end will be $1,500 million, with a standard deviation of $300 million.

Calculate the value at risk of the portfolio, at a 97.5% confidence level. (Express your answer in $, rounded to the nearest million.)

Solution

The Z value for a one-tail 97.5% confidence level is 1.96 (from the Normal Distribution tables).
VaR = standard deviation × Z value, so the
VaR = USD 300 million × 1.96 = USD 588 million

This means there is a 2.5% chance that the value of the portfolio will be (1,500 - 588) $912 million or below.

Two tail test

AL Plc , a UK based company are expecting to receive $10 million from a US customer. The value in pounds is dependant on the exchange rate between the dollar and pound.

The mean exchange rate is $1.25/£ and the daily volatility of the pound/dollar exchange rate is 0.25%.

What is the range of values that AL Plc will be 95% confident of receiving in 1 day?

Solution

The mean value of the $10 million is £8 million ($10 million ÷ $1.25/£)
The daily standard deviation is (0.25% × £8 million =) £20,000

As we are looking at a range, this is a two tail test, to be 95% confident this will be within 47.5% of the mean on either side.

First find 0.4750 in the normal tables, this is a z value of 1.96.
VaR = Z × Std deviation = 1.96 × 20,000 = £39,200

This means that AL Plc is 95% confident that the value will be within £39,200 of the mean.

Therefore AL plc is 95% confident the sterling amount will be between £7,960,800 & £8,039,200.

Given the 1-day VaR, we can easily calculate the VaR for longer holding periods as:

n day Var = 1 day Var × $\sqrt{n}$

The VaR increases with the holding period. Thus, the longer the holding period, the greater the VaR.

Example of VaR

Suppose a UK company expects to receive $14 million from a US customer. The value in pounds to the UK company will depend on the exchange rate between the dollar and pounds resulting in gains or losses as the exchange rate changes. Assume that the exchange rate today is $1.75/£ and that the daily volatility of the pound/dollar exchange rate is 0.5%.

Calculate the

(a) 1-day 95% VaR

(b) 1-day 99% VaR.

The value of the $14 million today is £8 million ($14 million ÷ $1.75/£) with a daily standard deviation of £40,000 (0.5% × £8 million).

(a) The standard normal value (Z) associated with the one-tail 95% confidence level is 1.645 (see Normal Distribution tables). Hence, the 1-day 95% VaR is 1.645 × £40,000 = £65,800. This means that we are 95% confident that the maximum daily loss will not exceed £65,800. Alternatively, we could also say that there is a 5% (1 out of 20) chance that the loss would exceed £65,800.

(b) The standard normal value (Z) associated with the one-tail 99% confidence level is 2.33 (see Normal Distribution tables). Hence, the 1-day 99% VaR is 2.33 × £40,000 = £93,200. Thus, there is a 1% (1 out of 100) chance that the loss would exceed £93,200.

If we wanted to calculate the VaR for longer period, say 5 days, at the 95% level the calculation would be:

5 day 95% VaR = 1 day 95% VaR × $\sqrt{5}$ = £65,800 × 2.236 = £147,133

There is a 5% chance that the company's foreign exchange loss would exceed £147,133 over the next 5 days.

Similarly, the 30-day 99% VaR would be:

1 day 99% VaR × $\sqrt{30}$ = £93,200 × 5.477 = £510,477

This illustrates the longer the holding period, the greater the VaR.

More on value at risk (VaR)

The Basel committee established international standards for banking laws and regulations aimed at protecting the international financial system from the results of the collapse of major banks. Basel II established rigorous risk and capital management requirements to ensure each bank holds reserves sufficient to guard against its risk exposure given its lending and investment practices. Regulators require banks to measure their market risk using a risk measurement model which is used to calculate the Value at Risk (VaR).

However, the global financial crisis has identified substantial problems with banks governance procedures in terms of understanding operational risk and applying risk measurement models like VaR. This has been emphasised by the number of banks that have failed or required government support – Northern Rock and Bradford and Bingley in the UK; Bear Sterns and Washington Mutual in the US amongst others.

Test your understanding 6

A company expects to receive $10 million from a US customer. The value in £ will depend on the exchange rate changing. Assume that the exchange rate today is $1.6667 / £ and that the daily volatility of the £/$ exchange rate is 0.5%.

Required:

What is the 10 day 95% VaR?

Test your understanding 7 – Value at risk (Integration)

A bank has estimated that the expected value of its portfolio in two weeks' time will be $50 million, with a standard deviation of $4.85 million.

Required:

Calculate and comment upon the value at risk of the portfolio, assuming a 95% confidence level.

Regression analysis

This can be used to measure a company's exposure to various risk factors at the same time. This is done by regressing changes in the company's cash flows against the risk factors (changes in interest rates, exchange rates, prices of key commodities such as oil). The regression coefficients will indicate the sensitivities of the company's cash flow to these risk factors.

The drawback with this technique is that the analysis is based on historical factors which may no longer be predictors of the company in the future.

Simulation analysis

This is used to evaluate the sensitivity of the value of the company, or its cash flows, to a variety of risk factors. These risk factors will be given various simulated values based on probability distributions, and the procedure is repeated a number of times to obtain the range of results that can be achieved.

The mean and standard deviation are then calculated from these results to give an expected value and measure of the risk.

This technique can be complex and time-consuming to carry out, and is limited by the assumptions of the probability distributions.

Other methods of measuring or assessing the severity of an identified risk include:

- scenario planning – forecasting various outcomes of an event;
- decision trees – use of probability to estimate an outcome;
- sensitivity analysis – used to ask 'what-if?' questions to test the robustness of a plan. Altering one variable at a time identifies the impact of that variable.

Drawbacks of the quantification of risk

Once a risk has been quantified, there is a problem – whether anyone really knows what it means. Unless you are a trainee or qualified accountant (or similar) this is unlikely, hence risks are often left unquantified.

Risk or assurance mapping

A common qualitative way of assessing the significance of risk is to produce a '**risk map**' or sometimes called an **'assurance map'**.

- The Board, the Risk Committee, the Audit Committee and senior management from various departments will all be involved in the preparation of the map.
- The map identifies whether a risk will have a significant impact on the organisation and links that into the likelihood of the risk occurring.
- The approach can provide a framework for prioritising risks in the business.
- Risks with a significant impact and a high likelihood of occurrence need more urgent attention than risks with a low impact and low likelihood of occurrence.
- A well-structured risk map will highlight where there are gaps in assurances over significant risk areas.
- Also, duplicated or potentially burdensome assurance processes may be identified.
- Risks can be plotted on a diagram, as shown below.

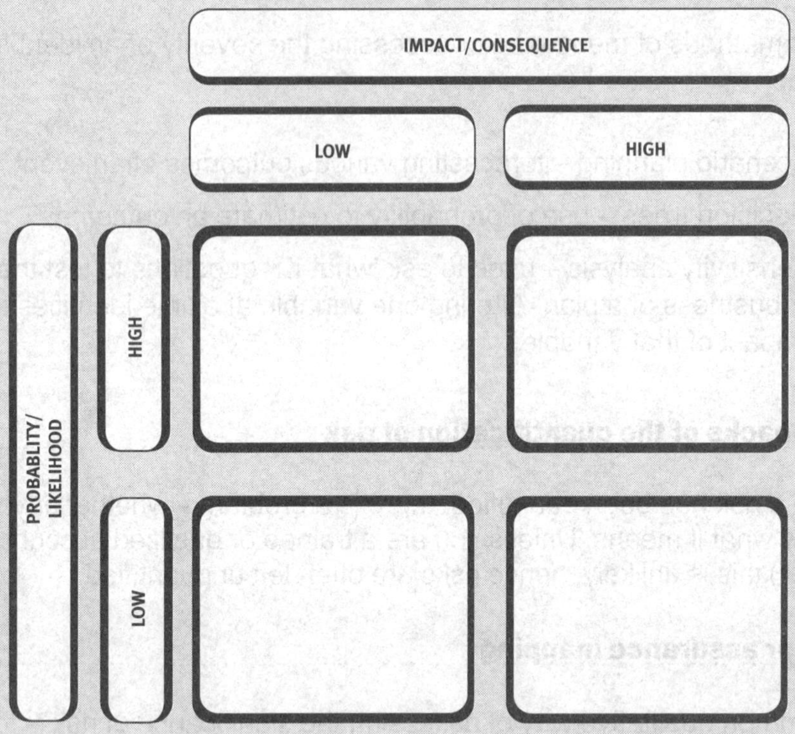

More on risk mapping

The potential loss from an adverse outcome is a function of:

- the probability or likelihood that the adverse outcome will occur, and
- the impact of the outcome if it does occur.

When an initial review is carried out to identify and assess risks, the assessment of both probabilities and impact might be based on judgement and experience rather than on a detailed statistical and numerical analysis.

- In an initial analysis, it might be sufficient to categorise the probability of an adverse outcome as 'high', 'medium' or 'low', or even more simply as 'high' or 'low'.
- Similarly, it might be sufficient for the purpose of an initial analysis to assess the consequences or impact of an adverse outcome as 'severe' or 'not severe'.

Each risk can then be plotted on a risk map. A risk map is simply a 2 × 2 table or chart, showing the probabilities for each risk and their potential impact.

Example

The following simple risk map might be prepared for a firm of auditors:

		Impact/consequences Low	Impact/consequences High
Probability/likelihood	**High**	New audit regulations for the profession	Loss of non-audit work from existing clients
	Low	Increases in salaries above the general rate of inflation	Loss of audit clients within the next two years.

Using a risk map

A risk map immediately indicates which risks should be given the highest priority.

- High-probability, high-impact risks should be.given the highest priority for management, whether by monitoring or by taking steps to mitigate the risk.
- Low-probability, low-impact risks can probably be accepted by the organisation as within the limits of acceptability.
- High-probability, low-impact risks and low-probability, high-impact risks might be analysed further with a view to deciding the most appropriate strategy for their management.

For each high-probability, high-impact risk, further analysis should be carried out, with a view to:

- estimating the probability of an adverse (or favourable) outcome more accurately, and
- assessing the impact on the organisation of an adverse outcome. This is an area in which the management accountant should be able to contribute by providing suitable and relevant financial information.

An alternative layout from a risk map being in the cruciform style so far might be that of a tabular format. Here the table might have the following columns:

(1) The risk name e.g. fraud.

(2) The likelihood of that risk arising e.g. medium.

(3) The impact of the risk if it does arise e.g. high.

(4) Controls already in place.

(5) The risk owner i.e. the name of a manger or director who watches out for this risk arising.

(6) Whether assurance is sufficient. This might be given a score out of, say, 10, or a yes/no type response.

(7) Controls to be implemented in the future.

Test your understanding 8 – Restaurant (Integration)

Suggest a risk that could be included in each quadrant for a restaurant.

Test your understanding 9

The loss of lower-level staff would best fit which category of a risk map?

A Low likelihood; low consequence

B High likelihood; low consequence

C Low likelihood; high consequence

D High likelihood; high consequence

Test your understanding 10

The axes of a risk map include: (Select all that may apply.)

A Likelihood

B Volatility

C Consequences

D Certainty

Test your understanding 11

HH Ltd is a private rehabilitation centre which provides services for people recovering from debilitating injuries. These services include a supported re-introduction to living at home through independent living units where clients can 'practice' living alone but with medical support on hand should they need it.

The managers of HH are aware they operate in a high risk industry. Clients are often prescribed strong medications which must be administered correctly by HH staff and there are two ongoing legal disputes over injuries that have occurred to clients in HH's independent living units. Some of HH's managers believe these risks are simply part of their business model and unavoidable whereas others are of the opinion that a formal risk management policy should be devised.

The directors have suggested the managers get together to carry out a risk mapping exercise.

Which of the following are benefits from a risk mapping exercise? Select **all** that apply.

A Managers will reach a consensus on which are the key risks facing HH and will be able to target the most significant.

B Managers can use the existence of the risk map to prove they have not been negligent in the legal disputes concerning injured clients.

C The risk of medication being wrongly administered can be assessed and a policy devised to reduce it going forward.

D The risk of injury to clients accessing the independent living units can be assessed and prioritised and a policy devised to reduce it going forwards.

E The existence of a risk map may prevent managers wasting time dealing with trivial risks.

4 Risk response strategy

So far we have considered the types of risk a company could be exposed to and the way it may choose to assess, measure and bear those risks. The next area is to look at the formulation of a strategy to respond to those risks, the general methods that can be used to treat risks and the implementation of such strategy.

The management of risks involves trying to ensure that:

- Exposure to severe risks is minimised.
- Unnecessary risks are avoided.
- Appropriate measures of control are taken.
- The balance between risk and return is appropriate.

The estimate of the potential loss for each risk should be compared with the acceptable risk limit for the company. If the risk is greater than the acceptable limit, the next stage in risk management is to consider how the risk should be managed or controlled, to bring it down in size.

Risk treatment (management) methods

Assuming that the business does want to manage its risks in some way a number of methods can be used. These methods will limit the risks, and the overall risk management strategy may define how the risks will be managed and the way these methods will interact.

Avoid risk

- A company may decide that some activities are so risky that they should be avoided.
- This will always work but is impossible to apply to all risks in commercial organisations as risks have to be taken to make profits.

Transfer risk

- In some circumstances, risk can be transferred wholly or in part to a third party.
- A common example of this is insurance. It does reduce/eliminate risks but premiums have to be paid.

Pool risks

- Risks from many different transactions can be pooled together: each individual transaction/item has its potential upside and its downside. The risks tend to cancel each other out, and are lower for the pool as a whole than for each item individually.
- For example, it is common in large group structures for financial risk to be managed centrally.

Diversification

- Diversification is a similar concept to pooling but usually relates to different industries or countries.
- The idea is that the risk in one area can be reduced by investing in another area where the risks are different or ideally opposite.
- A correlation coefficient with a value close to –1 is essential if risk is to be nullified.

Managing risk by diversification

The syllabus refers specifically to the principle of diversifying risk, but states that numerical questions will not be set. It will therefore be useful to look in more detail at the effect of diversification on risk.

- Risk can be reduced by diversifying into operations in different areas, such as into Industry X and Industry Y, or into Country P and Country Q.
- Poor performance in one area will be offset by good performance in another area, so diversification will reduce total risk.
- Diversification is based on the idea of 'spreading the risk'; the total risk should be reduced as the portfolio of diversified businesses gets larger.
- Diversification works best where returns from different businesses are negatively correlated (i.e. move in different ways). It will, however, still work as long as the correlation is less than +1.0.
- Example of poor diversification – swimming costumes and ice cream – both reliant on sunny weather for sales.
- Spreading risk relates to portfolio management as an investor or company spreads product and market risks.
- The most common form of diversification attempts to spread risk according to the **portfolio** of companies held within a group based more on links within the supply chain.

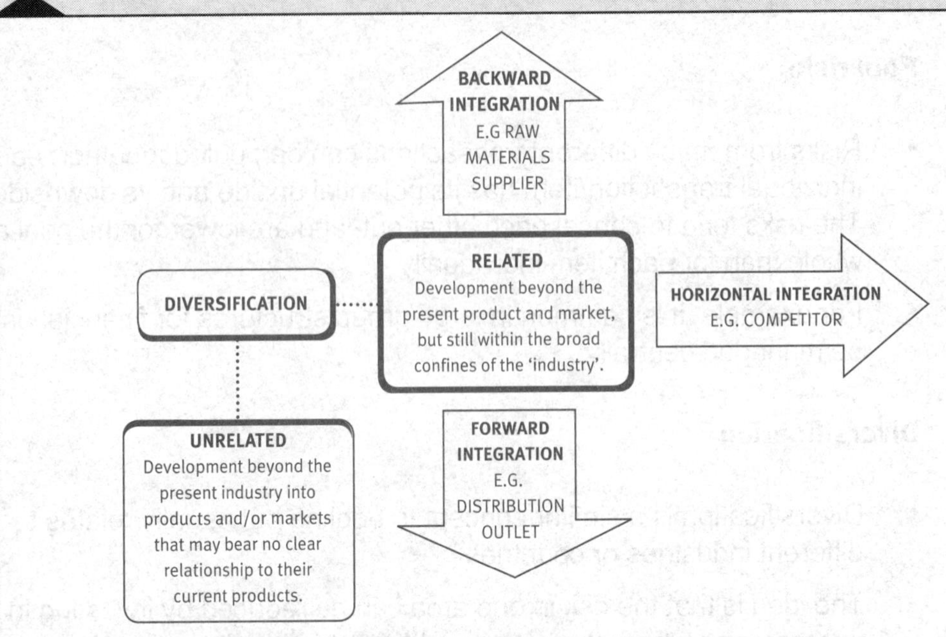

Spreading risk by portfolio management

Within an organisation, risk can be spread by expanding the portfolio of companies held. The portfolio can be expanded by integration – linking with other companies in the supply chain, or diversification into other areas.

This is development beyond the present product and market, but still within the broad confines of the 'industry'.

- **Backward integration** refers to development concerned with the inputs into the organisation, e.g. raw materials, machinery and labour.
- **Forward integration** refers to development into activities that are concerned with the organisation's outputs such as distribution, transport, servicing and repairs.
- **Horizontal integration** refers to development into activities that compete with, or directly complement, an organisation's present activities. An example of this is a travel agent selling other related products such as travel insurance and currency exchange services.

Unrelated diversification

This is development beyond the present industry into products and/or markets that may bear no clear relationship to their present portfolio. Where appropriate an organisation may want to enter into a completely different market to spread its risk.

Problems with diversification:

- If diversification reduces risk, why are there relatively few conglomerate industrial and commercial groups with a broad spread of business in their portfolio?
- Many businesses compete by specialising, and they compete successfully in those areas where they excel.
- Therefore, it is difficult for companies to excel in a wide range of diversified businesses. There is a possible risk that by diversifying too much, an organisation might become much more difficult to manage. Risks could therefore increase with diversification, due to loss of efficiency and problems of management.
- Many organisations diversify their operations, both in order to grow and to reduce risks, but they do so into related areas, such as similar industries (e.g. banking and insurance, film and television production, and so on) or the same industry but in different parts of the world.
- Relatively little advantage accrues to the shareholders from diversification. There is nothing to prevent investors from diversifying for themselves by holding a portfolio of stocks and shares from different industries and in different parts of the world.

Test your understanding 12

Risk reduction can be achieved using which of the following theories?

A Management theory

B Systems theory

C Portfolio theory

D Contingency theory

Test your understanding 13 – Diversification (Integration)

Evaluate whether it is always a good business strategy for a listed company to diversify to reduce risk.

Risk reduction

- Even if a company cannot totally eliminate its risks, it may reduce them to a more acceptable level by a form of internal control.
- The internal control would reduce either the likelihood of an adverse outcome occurring or the size of a potential loss.
- The costs of the control measures should justify the benefits from the reduced risk.
- More will be seen on internal controls in chapter 5.

Hedging risks

- Hedging will be considered in detail when financial risk is examined in later chapters.
- The concept of hedging is reducing risks by entering into transactions with opposite risk profiles to deliberately reduce the overall risks in a business operation or transaction.

Risk sharing

- A company could reduce risk in a new business operation by sharing the risk with another party.
- This can be a motivation for entering into a joint venture.

Risk management using TARA

An alternative way of remembering risk management methods is via the mnemonic '**TARA**':

Transference. In some circumstances, risk can be transferred wholly or in part to a third party, so that if an adverse event occurs, the third party suffers all or most of the loss. A common example of risk transfer is insurance. Businesses arrange a wide range of insurance policies for protection against possible losses. This strategy is also sometimes referred to as **sharing**.

Avoidance. An organisation might choose to avoid a risk altogether. However, since risks are unavoidable in business ventures, they can be avoided only by not investing (or withdrawing from the business area completely). The same applies to not-for-profit organisations: risk is unavoidable in the activities they undertake.

Reduction/mitigation. A third strategy is to reduce the risk, either by limiting exposure in a particular area or attempting to decrease the adverse effects should that risk actually crystallise.

Acceptance. The final strategy is to simply accept that the risk may occur and decide to deal with the consequences in that particularly situation. The strategy is appropriate normally where the adverse effect is minimal. For example, there is nearly always a risk of rain; unless the business activity cannot take place when it rains then the risk of rain occurring is not normally insured against.

Risk mapping and risk responses

Risk maps can provide a useful framework to determine an appropriate risk response:

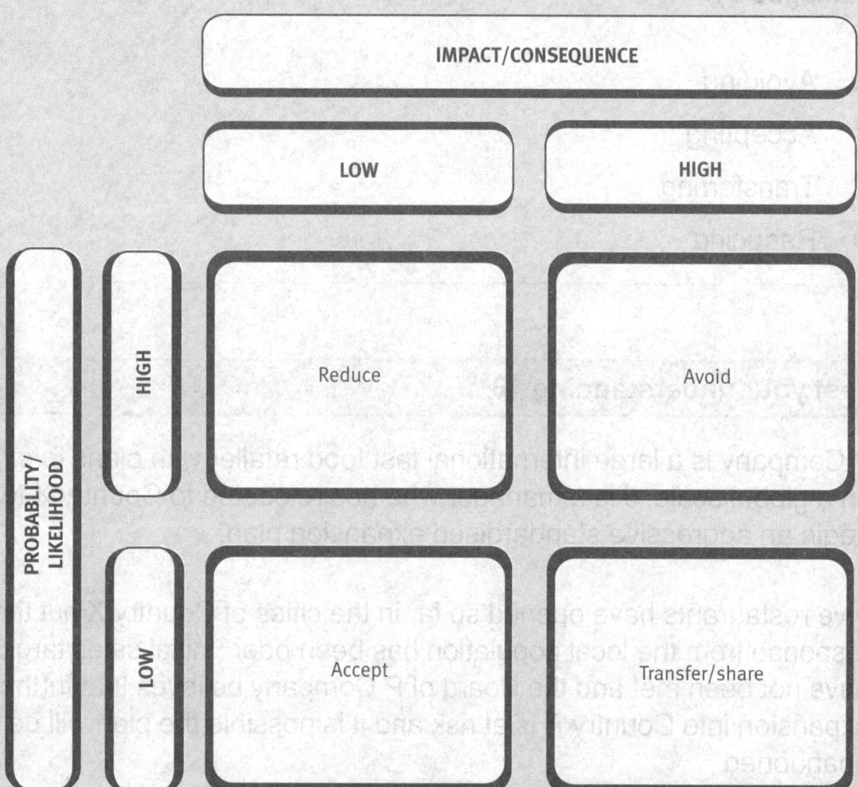

Test your understanding 14

The death of, or serious injury to, a member of staff at work would best fit which category on a risk map?

A Low likelihood; low consequence

B High likelihood; low consequence

C Low likelihood; high consequence

D High likelihood; high consequence

Test your understanding 15

A risk identified as having a low frequency and a high severity should be managed by:

A Avoiding

B Accepting

C Transferring

D Reducing

Test your understanding 16

P Company is a large international fast food retailer with plans to expand on a global scale. J is a manager who has relocated to Country X to begin an aggressive standardised expansion plan.

Five restaurants have opened so far in the cities of Country X but the response from the local population has been poor. Initial sales targets have not been met and the Board of P Company believes that further expansion into Country P is at risk and it is possible the plan will be abandoned.

J believes that the restaurants have not been immediately successful because the population of Country X, although affluent and well educated, are not used to the concept of 'fast food'. Restaurants in Country X are typically expensive and serve fresh food to order.

Which of the following are appropriate risk management responses for J to discuss with The Board? Select **all** that apply.

A P Company should embark on a marketing campaign within Country X.

B The menus of restaurants in Country X should be modified to reflect local tastes with more fresh food included.

C P Company should stop expansion plans in Country P and choose a more appropriate location.

D P Company should replace J as the manager of expansion in Country X.

E P Company should abandon their standardised plan in Country X and instead tailor their branding and products to be in line with successful local restaurants.

5 The risk cube

Another way of considering risk and its management is to use the risk cube.

Risk equals the volume of the cube.

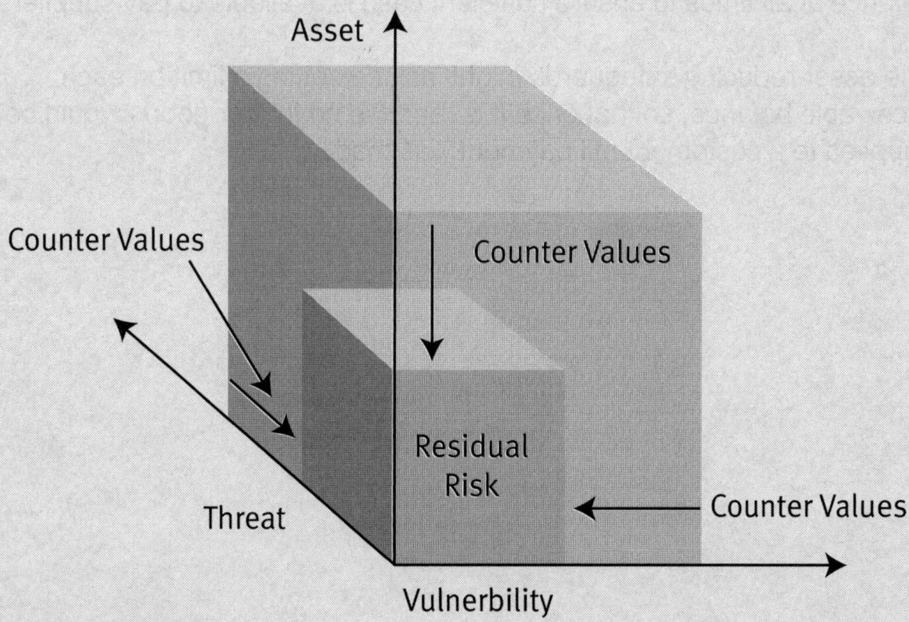

Risk is seen as some combination of a **threat**, exploiting some **vulnerability**, that could cause harm to an **asset**.

Residual risk is the combined function of:

- a threat less the effect of threat-reducing safeguards;
- a vulnerability less the effect of vulnerability-reducing safeguards; and
- an asset less the effect of asset value-reducing safeguards.

Managing the risk can be undertaken by reducing the threat, reducing the vulnerability and/or reducing the asset value.

For example, imagine a company sells machine parts on credit to industrial customers.

The threat might be that the customer doesn't pay for their machine parts.

The vulnerability might be that the selling company has a low cash balance and therefore could do with the funds to pay its own suppliers.

The asset is the receivable due in.

The threat-reducing safeguards might include performing a credit check on all customers.

The vulnerability-reducing safeguards might include holding a minimum cash balance at all times to ensure sufficient cash is available to pay suppliers.

The asset-reducing safeguards might include setting a limit on each receivable balance, so that once it is reached no further goods would be supplied to a customer until payment was made.

Test your understanding 17 – Twinkletoes (Case study)

Scenario

You are the management accountant of a large private company, Twinkletoes. Twinkletoes manufactures a high volume of reasonably priced shoes for elderly people. The company has a trade receivables ledger that is material to the financial statements containing four different categories of account. The categories of account, and the risks associated with them, are as follows:

(i) small retail shoe shops. These accounts represent nearly two thirds of the accounts on the ledger by number, and one third of the receivables by value. Some of these customers pay promptly, others are very slow;

(ii) large retail shoe shops (including a number of overseas accounts) that sell a wide range of shoes. Some of these accounts are large and overdue;

(iii) chains of discount shoe shops that buy their inventory centrally. These accounts are mostly well-established `high street' chains. Again, some of these accounts are large and overdue; and

(iv) mail order companies who sell the company's shoes. There have been a number of large new accounts in this category, although there is no history of irrecoverable debts in this category.

Receivables listed under (ii) to (iv) are roughly evenly split by both value and number. All receivables are dealt with by the same managers and staff and the same internal controls are applied to each category of receivables. You do not consider that using the same managers and staff, and the same controls, is necessarily the best method of managing the receivables ledger.

Trigger

Twinkletoes has suffered an increasing level of irrecoverable debts and slow payers in recent years, mostly as a result of small shoe shops becoming insolvent. The company has also lost several overseas accounts because of a requirement for them to pay in advance. Management wishes to expand the overseas market and has decided that overseas customers will in future be allowed credit terms.

Task

Management has asked you to classify the risks associated with the receivables ledger in order to manage trade receivables as a whole more efficiently. You have been asked to classify accounts as high, medium or low risk.

Write an email to the finance director:

(a) Classifying the risks relating to the four categories of trade receivables as high, medium or low and explain your classification (Note: More than one risk classification may be appropriate within each account category.)

(b) Describing the internal controls that you would recommend to Twinkletoes to manage the risks associated with the receivables ledger under the headings: all customers, slow paying customers, larger accounts, and overseas customers.

(30 minutes)

6 Risk reporting

Risk reports now form part of UK annual reports. It is an important disclosure requirement. (Examples of these are available on larger companies websites. Candidates are encouraged to read some.)

Managers of a business, and external stakeholders, will require information regarding the risks facing the business. A risk reporting system would include:

- A systematic review of the risk forecast (at least annually).
- A review of the risk strategy and responses to significant risks.
- A monitoring and feedback loop on action taken and assessments of significant risks.
- A system indicating material change to business circumstances, to provide an 'early warning'.
- The incorporation of audit work as part of the monitoring and information gathering process.

Marks and Spencer plc – Risk report extract

Within Marks and Spencer's annual report for 2013 there is a risk report section. This has been duplicated in part below.

It states their approach to risk management and key areas of focus:

What is our approach to risk management?

The Board has overall accountability for ensuring that risk is effectively managed across the Group and, on behalf of the Board, the Audit Committee reviews the effectiveness of the Group Risk Process.

Risks are reviewed by all business areas on a half-yearly basis and measured against a defined set of likelihood and impact criteria. This is captured in consistent reporting formats, enabling Group Risk to consolidate the risk information and summarise the key risks in the form of the Group Risk Profile.

Our Executive Board discusses the Group Risk Profile ahead of it being submitted to the Group Board for final approval.

To ensure our risk process drives improvement across the business, the Executive Board monitors the ongoing status and progress of action plans against key risks on a quarterly basis.

Risk remains an important consideration in all strategic decision-making at Board level, including debate on risk tolerance and appetite.

Key areas of focus

During the year we have focused on a number of key areas:

(1) Evolving risk descriptions

As time progresses, the nature of some Group risks is evolving. To ensure we continue to address the most important risks facing the Group at this point in time we have updated a number of risk titles and descriptions. New titles are assigned to GM product (2012: Our customers) and Food safety and integrity (2012: Food safety). New descriptions are in place for International and Our people.

(2) Action plans for key risks

We continue to assess whether sufficient additional mitigating activities are underway to reduce the net risk position of the Group's key risks. By considering net risk on both a one year and three year horizon, we are able to identify when mitigating activities will result in a tangible risk reduction. We also continue to review the ongoing appropriateness of actions to ensure they are as relevant, timely and measurable as possible.

(3) Influence of risk tolerance

Risk tolerance and appetite are important considerations in strategic decision-making at Board level. We also recognise the value in applying the concept of risk tolerance in discussions across all levels of the organisation. It is especially beneficial when determining the nature of mitigating activities and their role in addressing risk likelihood or impact.

Our principle risks and uncertainties

As with any business, we face risks and uncertainties on a daily basis. It is the effective management of these that places us in a better position to be able to achieve our strategic objectives and to embrace opportunities as they arise.

To achieve a holistic view of the risks facing our business, both now and in the future, we consider those that are:

- external to our business;
- core to our day-to-day operation;
- related to business change activity; and
- those that could emerge in the future.

Overleaf are details of our principal risks and the mitigating activities in place to address them. It is recognised that the Group is exposed to a number of risks, wider than those listed.

However, a conscious effort has been made to disclose those of greatest importance to the business at this moment in time and those that have been the subject of debate at recent Board or Audit Committee meetings.

(Two of the many principle risks and mitigating actions are detailed below.)

Economic outlook

Economic conditions worsen or do not improve, impacting our ability to deliver the plan

As consumers' disposable incomes come under pressure from price inflation and government austerity measures, trading conditions continue to remain a challenge for our business.

Mitigating activities:

- Proactive management of costs
- Regular review of customer feedback and marketplace positioning
- Continued focus on value proposition in the context of a balanced product offer, including market leading innovation
- Ongoing monitoring of pricing and promotional strategies
- Regular commercial review of product performance

Food safety and integrity

A food safety or integrity related incident occurs or is not effectively managed

As a leading retailer of fine quality fresh food, it is of paramount importance that we manage the safety and integrity of our products and supply chain, especially in light of the business' greater operational complexity and the heightened risk of fraudulent behaviour in the supply chain.

Mitigating activities:

- Dedicated team responsible for ensuring that all products are safe for consumption through rigorous controls and processes
- Continuous focus on quality
- Proactive horizon scanning including focus on fraud and adulteration
- Established supplier and depot auditing programme

(The risk report continues for several pages covering many other risks.)

The Group Risk Profile reflects the most important risks facing the business at this point in time; these risks receive specific attention by the Board to ensure that sufficient mitigating activity is in place to reduce net risk to an acceptable level. The Group Risk Profile will evolve as these mitigating activities succeed in reducing the residual risk over time, or new risks emerge. As such, we have removed a number of risks from our Group Risk Profile since the prior year:

Last year we included Business continuity on the Group Risk Profile in response to the heightened level of risk driven by the UK's summer 2012 events. With the risk now returning to a normal level it has been removed, recognising the strength of our controls in this area

Financial position, Corporate reputation, New store format, Key supplier failure and IT security have also been removed in recognition of the actions taken to reduce the net risk position.

The above risks remain important and they continue to be monitored as part of 'business as usual' activities; however, we consider that they do not represent key risks to our business at this time and they have therefore been removed from the Group Risk Profile.

Risk interconnectivity

We continue to recognise the significant interdependency between our key risks, which is in part a product of our heavily interconnected business environment (both in terms of systems and processes). The following diagrams are based on our current Group Risk Profile. Both are designed to highlight how changes to one risk could impact on those connected to it, and therefore on the profile as a whole. We have incorporated a number of potential emerging risks which do not feature on our Group Risk Profile at this point in time, but could influence our business in the longer term, illustrating how emerging risk is considered by the Board.

Test your understanding 18

A recent SWOT analysis carried out within Y Company showed that the organisation is now subject to more diverse threats than previously documented. This is mainly due to deregulation of Y Company's industry and consequently many new entrants. These new entrants, often from other countries, are able to undercut Y Company on price and so gain market share.

The directors believe they have appropriate measures in place to identify and manage the new risks that Y Company faces but are concerned that Y Company's stakeholders should be able to access information relating to company's most up to date risks. Y Company's risk profile has evolved since the prior year.

They wish to convey, via an annual risk report that risk remains a key consideration in all strategic decision making.

Which of the following should be included in Company Y's risk reporting system?

Select **all** that apply.

A A detailed review of Y Company's risk strategy and responses to risks it faces.

B A monitoring and feedback loop on action taken and assessments of significant risks such as those resulting from new entrants.

C A system indicating material change to Y Company's industry circumstances, to provide an 'early warning'.

D The incorporation of audit work as part of the monitoring and information gathering process.

E A systematic review of the risk forecast (at least quarterly).

7 Gross and net risk

Risk reports should show:

- the **gross risk** = an assessment of risk **before** the application of any controls, transfer or management responses, and
- the **net risk** (or **residual risk**) = an assessment of risk, taking into account the controls, transfer and management responses i.e **after** any controls have been implemented,

to facilitate a review of the effectiveness of risk responses.

An example of gross and net risk assessments, utilising the risk map (impact/likelihood matrix) is shown below:

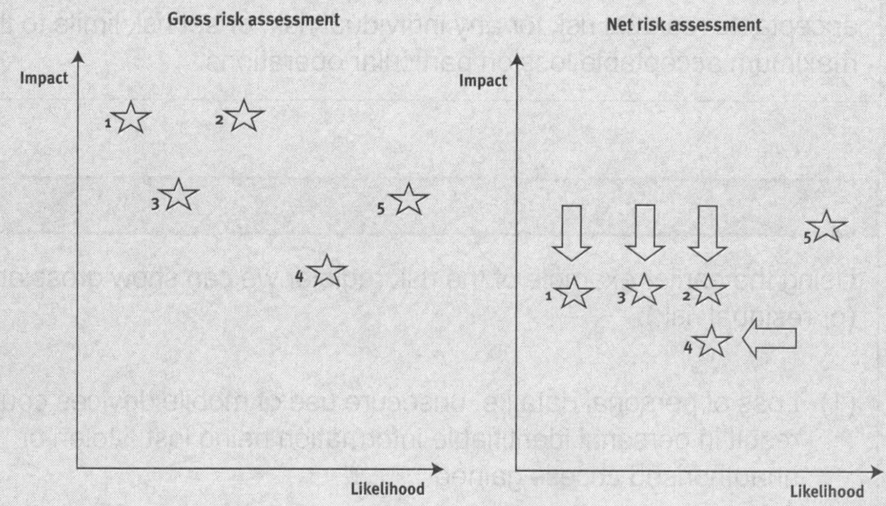

If the residual risk is considered to be too great then the company will need to:

- not expose itself to the risk situation; or
- put in place better controls over the risk.

The amount of residual risk a company can bear is ultimately a management decision.

- It is possible to measure that residual risk, possibly as a proportion of profit/capital/turnover, in order to help management make that judgement.

Ability to bear risk

One approach to assessing the ability to bear a risk is to consider the financial consequences of the risk, in relation to:

- the organisation's profits
- return on capital employed
- the organisation's expenditure budget (not-for-profit organisations).

For example, suppose that the financial consequences of a particular risk have been estimated as a potential loss of $200,000. For an organisation making annual profits of, say, $200 million, this might seem relatively insignificant. On the other hand, for an organisation with annual profits of just $250,000, say, the risk would be much more significant.

An organisation might establish policy guidelines as to the maximum acceptable residual risk for any individual risk, or set risk limits to the maximum acceptable loss on particular operations.

Gross and net risk example

Using the earlier example of the risk register we can show gross and net (or residual risk):

(1) Loss of personal data i.e. unsecure use of mobile devices could result in personal identifiable information being lost, stolen or unauthorised access gained.

(2) Likelihood = 3

(3) Impact = 5

(4) Risk owner = Mike Smith (IT manager)

(5) 1.1.12

(6) 2.2.14

(7) Staff receive training every 2 years which highlights the risks. All laptops are encrypted. Regular audits are undertaken. Any incidents are reported to the Audit Committee.

(8) Overall risk rating = 7 **(Gross risk)**

(9) Encryption technology is implemented which meets industry standard.

(10) Mike Smith

(11) 31.7.14

(12) Risk level = 3 **(Net or residual risk)**

By implementing the encryption technology the risk has reduced from a score of 7 to a score of 3. This means that there is still some risk but far less than there was. Management will have to consider whether a level 3 risk is acceptable or whether further controls need to be implemented to achieve a lower score, but at what cost.

Test your understanding 19

TGDW are assessing a new contract to provide maintenance services for a prestigious office complex. Should the complex be unable to function for more than 5 hours due an error or omission by TGDW they will face a fine of sufficient magnitude to cause the company severe financial difficulty. The directors assessed the gross risk as high impact and due to the complexity of the systems maintained there is high probability of an error occurring. The client is unwilling to reduce the penalty or to change the criteria and TGDW's internal controls are already at a high level.

Using TARA what action should TGDW take?

A Transfer

B Avoid

C Reduce

D Accept

8 Evaluating risk management strategy

Once the company has established its risk strategy and decided in what areas it will reduce its risks and the methods it will use to achieve the desired reductions, the strategy should be evaluated.

The purpose of the evaluation is two-fold, as shown below:

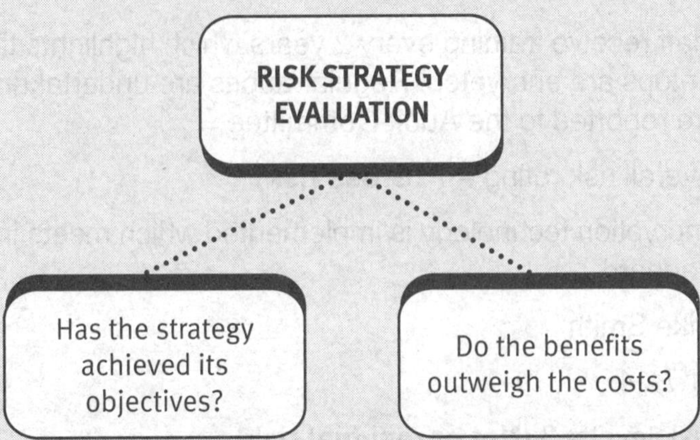

Has the strategy been successful?

Within the risk management strategy, targets should be included to enable the company to assess whether the risk strategy objectives have been achieved. For example, a company might set a target for risk of faulty products at a set number or percentage level and then formulate a risk strategy to achieve that level. In order to assess this a control mechanism will need to be set up. The basic control idea is that the company compares the actual results with a required target, and assesses whether the target has been achieved. If not, the reasons must be investigated and action taken, including possibly a re-assessment of the risk strategy.

Do benefits outweigh costs?

- The costs and benefits of risk measures such as internal controls can be evaluated, and a cost-benefit comparison carried out.
- The benefits from risk controls should preferably be measured and quantified, although some benefits (such as protecting the company's reputation) might have to be assessed qualitatively.
- The evaluation process should be based on the principle that the costs of a control measure should not exceed the benefits that it provides.
  - For example, a company could be very concerned about theft of petty cash and therefore introduce controls limiting the cash held to £25 and also requiring daily reconciliations of the cash balance by the financial controller, with observation by a member of the internal audit department.
  - This control would probably reduce theft, but would be very expensive for the company to operate and as a result the costs would exceed the benefits. The controls set up must be proportionate to the potential losses that could occur if the risk results in losses.

Cost-benefit example

A manufacturing company is concerned about the rate of rejected items from a particular process. The current rejection rate is 5% of items input, and it has been estimated that each rejected item results in a loss to the company of $10.600 items go through the process each day.

It is estimated that by introducing some inspection to the process, the rejection rate could be reduced fairly quickly to 3%. However, inspections would result in an increase of costs of $70 per day.

Required:

How should this control through inspection be evaluated?

Solution

The example is a simple one, but it is useful for suggesting an approach to risk management and control evaluation.

What is the objective of the control?

Answer: To reduce losses from rejected items from the process, initially from 5% to 3% of input.

What is the expected benefit?

Answer: A reduction in rejects by 2% of input, from 5% to 3%. The reduction in rejects each day is (2% × 600) 12. Since each reject costs $10, the total daily saving is $120.

What is the expected cost of the control?

Answer: $70 per day. Therefore the control appears to be worthwhile in achieving the objective.

Is the control effective?

Answer: This should be established by monitoring actual results. For example, if the control costs $70 each day, but succeeds in reducing the rejection rate from 5% to just 4% (a reduction of 1%), the benefits would be only $60 each day and the control would not be cost-effective (unless the savings are more than $10 per unit).

9 Risk management roles and responsibilities

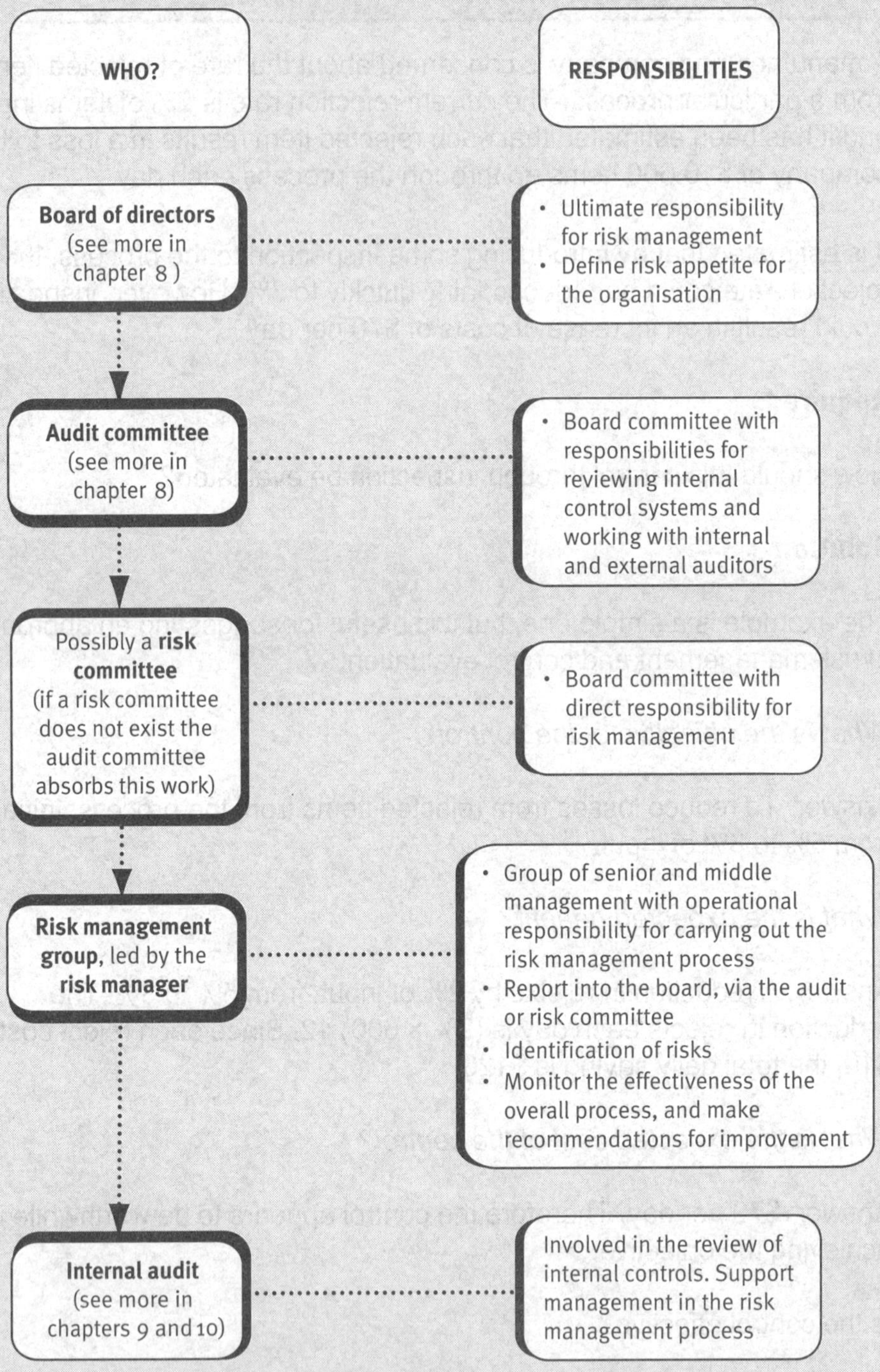

WHO?	RESPONSIBILITIES
Board of directors (see more in chapter 8)	• Ultimate responsibility for risk management • Define risk appetite for the organisation
Audit committee (see more in chapter 8)	• Board committee with responsibilities for reviewing internal control systems and working with internal and external auditors
Possibly a **risk committee** (if a risk committee does not exist the audit committee absorbs this work)	• Board committee with direct responsibility for risk management
Risk management group, led by the **risk manager**	• Group of senior and middle management with operational responsibility for carrying out the risk management process • Report into the board, via the audit or risk committee • Identification of risks • Monitor the effectiveness of the overall process, and make recommendations for improvement
Internal audit (see more in chapters 9 and 10)	Involved in the review of internal controls. Support management in the risk management process

If the company being considered is divisional there may be a **risk officer** for each division who will help to identify and manage tactical and operational level risks.

All **employees** have a role and responsibility for risk too. You should be **aware** of possible risks (through policies issued and training given) and you should be **audible** if you believe a risk needs to be managed (by reporting it to your manager or by whistleblowing).

Roles of the risk committee

In broad terms, the risk (management) committee within an organisation has the following main aims:

- Raising risk awareness and ensuring appropriate risk management within the organisation.
- Establishing policies for risk management.
- Ensuring that adequate and efficient processes are in place to identify, report and monitor risks.
- Updating the company's risk profile, reporting to the board and making recommendations on the risk appetite of the company.

Supporting these objectives of the risk (management) committee, there are many secondary objectives. These objectives may also be contained in the terms of reference of the risk (management) committee.

- Advising the board on the risk profile and appetite of the company and as part of this process overseeing the risk assurance process within the company.
- Acting on behalf of the board, to ensure that appropriate mechanisms are in place with respect to risk identification, risk assessment, risk assurance and overall risk management.
- Continual review of the company's risk management policy including making recommendations for amendment of that policy to the board.
- Ensuring that there is appropriate communication of risks, policies and controls within the company to employees at all management levels.
- Ensuring that there are adequate training arrangements in place so management at all levels are aware of their responsibilities for risk management.
- Where necessary, obtaining appropriate external advice to ensure that risk management processes are up to date and appropriate to the circumstances of the company.
- Ensuring that best practices in risk management are used by the company, including obtaining and implementing external advice where necessary.

Risk manager activities

Typical activities carried out by a risk manager include:

- Provision of overall leadership for risk management team.
- Identification and evaluation of the risks affecting an organisation from that organisation's business, operations and policies.
- Implementation of risk mitigation strategies including appropriate internal controls to manage identified risks.
- Seeking opportunities to improve risk management methodologies and practices within the organisation.
- Monitoring the status of risk mitigation strategies and internal audits, and ensuring that all recommendations are acted upon.
- Developing, implementing and managing risk management programmes and initiatives including establishment of risk management awareness programmes within the organisation.
- Maintaining good working relationships with the board and the risk management committee.
- Ensuring compliance with any laws and regulations affecting the business.
- Implementing a set of risk indicators and reports, including losses, incidents, key risk exposures and early warning indicators.
- Liaising with insurance companies, particularly with regards to claims, conditions and cover available.
- Depending on specific laws of the jurisdiction in which the organisation is based, working with the external auditors to provide assurance and assistance in their work in appraising risks and controls within the organisation.
- Again, depending on the jurisdiction, producing reports on risk management, including any statutory reports (e.g. Sarbanes-Oxley (SOX) reports in the US).

Northern Rock

A failure of risk management

Perhaps the most interesting example of risk and control was the case of Northern Rock. In September 2007 Northern Rock plc was a top five UK mortgage lender, on the FTSE 100 index with over £100 billion in assets. Northern Rock raised over 70% of the money it used in its growing mortgage lending business from banks and other financial institutions. Following the global credit crunch that resulted from the crisis in the US sub-prime (high risk) mortgage sector, banks stopped lending to each other and Northern Rock could not raise sufficient cash to cover its liabilities.

A bank run (the first on a UK bank for 150 years) on Northern Rock by its customers led to the government providing 'lender of last resort' funding and guarantees for the bank's depositors totalling about £20 billion. The result has been a 90% fall in the bank's share price, a deteriorating credit rating and a loss of reputation. The CEO has resigned and several directors have also left the board.

Northern Rock had a formal approach to risk management, including liquidity, credit, operational and market risk, fully described in its Securities and Exchange Commission filings. Northern Rock's assets were sound so there was no significant credit risk. Market risk was also well managed in terms of interest rate and foreign exchange exposure. However, despite formal procedures and a demonstrated compliance with regulations, there was an assumption by managers that access to funds would continue unimpeded. The US sub-prime crisis led to liquidity risk materialising, causing the Northern Rock problems. The consequence was also the loss of reputation that followed press reports which blamed the bank's management for not having a contingency plan to cover the possibility of disruption to its funding, an operational risk. It is likely that the board of Northern Rock failed in both monitoring liquidity risk and in monitoring the effectiveness of the existing controls.

The lesson of Northern Rock is that we need to move beyond the tick-box approach to compliance and that good governance requires a more insightful approach to risk management and internal control.

Risk in a retail chain

The group has 480 stores and sales of £1.5 billion. Risk management was part of the internal audit function. The internal auditor/risk manager said that the motivation for risk management was to 'establish best practice in corporate governance'. However, he commented that the business recently had 'problems with its fundamental controls' when 'senior management were looking at refinancing so took their eye off the ball'.

The process commenced with a brainstorming by the internal audit team of 'risk drivers' to identify what could go wrong and what controls could be put in place to address risks. The internal audit team held interviews with all managers to determine a measure of the effectiveness of these controls on a scale from 1 to 5. The threat of the control gap was identified and recommendations were made. This list looked like a risk register, although the group did not call it that. The internal auditor/risk manager did not see value in a risk register but rather saw risk management as high level.

The Risk Management Committee (RMC) meets every 2 months, comprising all business (executive) directors. The list given by the internal audit team to RMC showed the monetary value of a 'fundamental control breakdown', from which was deducted the monetary value arising from controls implemented to give a 'residual risk' (i.e. the risk after controls) to which was assigned a probability. These values were admittedly subjective. The RMC consider the risk maps, which showed the percentage probability of a threat arising and the residual monetary risk after taking account of controls. The whole process has been centrally driven, with a concern for 'high level' risks. The big risks identified through this process were: supply chain, suppliers, people management, rebates, cost base, key processes, property management, market share, product offering and pricing, brand management, strategic management, integration and change, systems and business continuity.

The most recent development is a Key Control Improvement Plan (KCIP) that provides recommendations to address the risks. It summarises each risk (the example of supply chain failure was given) and the 'mitigating factors' (i.e. controls) and what still needs to be done.

The Audit Committee (AC) of the Board has four non-executive directors, the external auditors, the finance director and the internal auditor/risk manager and monitors progress in relation to the risk maps. The risk maps also drive the audit plan which is agreed on by the AC, business directors and RMC.

The 'big nasties' are picked off, for example, purchase ordering and goods received, new stores, margins. Results are provided to the RMC and AC where the value of the report is greater than £250,000. Internal audit now had more exposure to decision-makers, as the risk management role had given them a high profile. In the future, the internal auditor/risk manager wants to implement a Risk Intelligence Report to provide early warning of risks, by looking at key performance indicators to identify what the business should be concerned with. He also wanted to introduce a Risk Management Marketing Plan to help communicate risk and to pass on the responsibility to other managers with senior managers making presentations to RMC. The internal auditor/risk manager expects it to take another 2 years to establish risk management in the organisation. More 'bottom up' controls need to be introduced and risk management needs to be embedded at the cultural level.

Risk in an engineering consultancy

This organisation is privately owned with 3,500 employees. A review of its financial performance had revealed that the estimated cost of project over-runs, non-productive time and contractual penalties incurred was about 2% of annual turnover. This represented an opportunity loss of about £3 million per annum against reported profits of about £5 million.

However, the main driver behind risk management was to address the rapidly increasing premium for professional indemnity that had increased premiums to several million pounds and had seen its excess increase from £5,000 to £500,000 per annum over the last few years. The organisation had appointed a risk manager; adopted an offshore 'captive' insurer and implemented a management development programme to improve the skills of all its managers. This had included a substantial content on risk awareness.

One of the ways in which it was helping its managers to understand risk was to undertake risk assessments as part of every project bid and to reflect each risk in pricing. During contract negotiations, each risk could be discussed between the lead consultant and the client when the value of the risk could be discussed in terms of the control devices that could be put in place by the client to reduce the risk and hence reduce that component of the project price that reflected the risk.

It was anticipated that this collaboration between consultant and client would reduce risk and lead to a more profitable outcome for both parties.

Test your understanding 20 – L tinned foods (Case study)

Scenario

L manufactures a range of very high quality tinned foods. The company was established eight years ago and it has grown steadily by selling to independent grocers in prosperous areas. Most consumers associate tinned food with poor quality and are unwilling to pay high prices. However, the consumers who buy L's products are willing to pay a premium for higher quality.

L's only large customer is H, a major supermarket chain that has a reputation for selling high-quality produce. L began sales to H just under a year ago, with H purchasing small quantities of L's most popular product in order to assess demand. After a successful period of test marketing, H started to place larger orders with L. Now H accounts for 20% of L's sales by volume.

Trigger

L has traditionally had a functional organisational structure. There is a director in charge of each of sales, production, finance and human resources. Each director has a team of senior managers who support their function. The hierarchy for organising and supervising staff is generally based on this functional structure. The only exception to this has been the result of the appointment of Peter, who is the Account Manager in charge of L's dealings with H. H insisted on the appointment of a designated account manager as a condition of placing regular, large orders with the company. Peter is the designated point of contact on all matters between L and H.

Peter's job description states that he is responsible for all decisions, including pricing, relating to L's relationship with H and that he is expected to base all such decisions on the promotion of L's commercial interests.

There have been a number of complaints from L's managers since Peter's appointment. These include several occasions when staff have received contradictory instructions. For example, Peter has ordered the production department to give priority to H's requests for large deliveries, even though that has led to regular orders to other customers being delayed. Peter has also told the staff in the credit control department not to press H for payment even though the company had several overdue invoices.

L's Sales Director believes that the company could sell even greater quantities to H and that other large supermarket chains will start placing orders in the near future once H has demonstrated that there is a demand for high quality tinned food. She has warned L's Chief Executive that additional account managers will have to be employed in the event that L starts to supply further supermarket chains.

Task

Write a report to the Board of L which:

(a) Evaluates the potential risks that might arise from L's appointment of an account manager to deal with H's business; and

(b) Recommends, stating reasons, the changes that L's board should introduce in order to minimise the threats arising from having an autonomous account manager.

(40 minutes)

Test your understanding 21 – Dental practice (Case study)

Scenario

D is a dental practice that was established eight years ago. The practice was founded by six dentists, each of whom has an equal share.

Trigger

The six dentists have decided that they should undertake a formal evaluation of the risks affecting their business. To that end, they have engaged a consultant to act as a facilitator.

The facilitator began with a brainstorming session. The dentists were provided with a flipchart and they were asked to list as many risks as they could think of. Then the risks were transferred to a risk map based on the TARA framework. A simplified version of the risk map is shown below:

Probability/likelihood		Impact/consequence Low	High
	High	Reduce	Avoid
		Negligence claims arising from failed dental implants	Cross infection
	Low	Accept	Transfer/share
		Spiral staircase	Unknown allergies

All six dentists agreed that each of these risks is worth classifying, but there was considerable debate as to where each should appear on the risk map. The facilitator has used the opinion of the dentist who identified the risk as a starting point and has asked for some discussion as to how best to classify each.

Dental implants

Dental implants are false teeth that are rooted in the patient's jaw using titanium screws. Fitting an implant is a very time-consuming and expensive procedure that costs the patient in excess of GBP 2,000. The patient's bone structure usually accepts the implant and fuses with it to form a very strong bond. In 3-5% of cases the implant causes an adverse reaction and has to be removed. The practice warns patients of this possibility and does not offer any refund in this event because the failure is beyond the dentist's control. Some patients who suffer an adverse reaction do seek compensation despite these warnings, alleging negligence on the part of the dentist.

Cross infection

Cross infection can occur when patients pass infections on to the dental staff (and vice versa) or when dental instruments transmit infections between patients. Apart from the need to work in close proximity to the patient, dental procedures always involve contact with the patient's saliva and can sometimes involve contact with blood if a tooth is extracted or the patient's gums bleed.

Spiral staircase

The dental surgery is located one floor up from street level. Patients enter via a narrow hallway and climb to the reception using a narrow spiral staircase. The building cannot be remodelled to accept a lift or a more suitable staircase.

Unknown allergies

The dentists are often required to prescribe antibiotics and other drugs in order to treat gum infections. These can cause severe allergic reactions that are impossible to foresee unless the patient has been prescribed that drug in the past and has notified the practice of this allergy.

Task

(a) Discuss the benefits that the dental practice may obtain from the risk mapping exercise described above.

(b) Critically evaluate the placing of each of the identified risks in the risk map, stating with reasons whether or not you agree with the placement.

(30 minutes)

Test your understanding 22 – B bank (Case study)

Scenario

The B Bank is a large international bank. It employs 6,000 staff in 250 branches and has approximately 500,000 borrowers and over 1,500,000 savers. The bank, which was founded in 1856, has an excellent reputation for good customer service. The bank's share price has increased, on average, by 12% in each of the last 10 years.

Trigger

There has been much adverse media coverage in many countries, including B Bank's home country, about the alleged excessive bonuses received by the directors of banks. A meeting of central bank governors from many nations failed to reach agreement on how to limit the size of directors' bonuses. The governor of the central bank in B Bank's home country is particularly concerned about this issue, and consequently put forward the following proposal:

"Directors of banks will be asked to pay a fee to the bank for the privilege of being a director. This fee will be set by the remuneration committee of each bank. Directors will be paid a bonus based solely on appropriate profit and growth indicators. The more the bank succeeds, the higher will be the bonus. This proposal directly links performance of the bank to directors' pay. I see this as a more realistic option than simply limiting salaries or bonuses by statute as proposed at the recent central bank governors' conference."

B Bank board and strategy

The constitution of the board of B Bank is in accordance with the internationally agreed code of corporate governance.

Overall board strategy has been to set targets based on previous (profitable) experience, with increased emphasis on those areas where higher potential profits can be made such as mortgage lending (this is discussed below). The bank's executive information systems are able to compute relative product profitability, which supports this strategy. This strategy generated substantial profits in recent years. The last major strategy review took place four years ago. Non-executive directors do not normally query the decisions of the executive directors.

In recent years, the profile of the major shareholders of the bank has moved. Traditionally the major shareholders were pension funds and other longer term investors but now these are overshadowed by hedge funds seeking to improve their short-term financial returns.

One of the major sources of revenue for the bank is interest obtained on lending money against securities such as houses (termed a "mortgage" in many countries) with repayments being due over periods varying between 15 and 25 years. Partly as a result of intense competition in the mortgage market, the values of the mortgages advanced by B Bank regularly exceed the value of the properties, for example B Bank has made advances of up to 125% of a property's value. Internal reports to the board estimate that property prices will reverse recent trends and will rise by 7% per annum for at least the next 10 years, with general and wage inflation at 2%. B Bank intends to continue to obtain finance to support new mortgages with loans from the short-term money-markets.

Task

Write a report to the Board:

(a) Evaluating the proposal made by the governor of the central bank; and

(b) Evaluating the risk management strategy in B Bank (except for consideration of directors' remuneration). Your evaluation should include recommendations for changes that will lower the bank's exposure to risk.

(45 minutes)

Test your understanding 23 – W consumer (Case study)

Scenario

W is a leading manufacturer of consumer electronics devices. The company has a significant share of the markets for mobile phone and personal music players ("mp3 players").W's main areas of expertise are in design and marketing. The company has a reputation for developing innovative products that set the trend for the market as a whole. New product launches attract a great deal of press interest and consequently W spends very little on advertising. Most of its promotional budget is spent on maintaining contact with leading technology journalists and editors.

Manufacturing and supply

W does not have a significant manufacturing capacity. New products are designed at the company's research laboratory, which has a small factory unit that can manufacture prototypes in sufficient quantity to produce demonstration models for test and publicity purposes. When a product's design has been finalised W pays a number of independent factories to manufacture parts and to assemble products, although W retains control of the manufacturing process.

W purchases parts from a large number of suppliers but some parts are highly specialised and can only be produced by a small number of companies. Other parts are standard components that can be ordered from a large number of sources. W chooses suppliers on the basis of price and reliability.

All assembly work is undertaken by independent companies. Assembly work is not particularly skilled, but it is time consuming and so labour can cost almost as much as parts.

- W has a large procurement department that organises the manufacturing process. A typical cycle for the manufacture of a batch of products is as follows:
- W's procurement department orders the necessary parts from parts suppliers and schedules assembly work in the electronics factories.
- The parts are ordered by W but are delivered to the factories where the assembly will take place.
- The finished goods are delivered directly to the customer.

This is a complicated process because each of W's products has at least 100 components and these can be purchased from several different countries.

Supplier communications

W insists on communicating with its suppliers via electronic data interchange (EDI) for placing orders and also for accounting processes such as invoicing and making payment. This is necessary because of the degree of coordination required for some transactions. For example, W may have to order parts from one supplier that have to be delivered to another so that the other supplier can carry out some assembly work. Both suppliers have to be given clear and realistic deadlines so that the resulting assemblies are delivered on time to enable W to meet its own deadlines.

Trigger

W recently launched a new range of mp3 players. The launch of the first batches of players attracted a great deal of adverse publicity:

The supplier which produces the unique memory chips used in the mp3 player was unable to meet the delivery deadlines and that delayed the launch. The supplier owns the patent for the design of these memory chips.

Supplies of the memory chip are now available. The assembly factories have been asked to increase their rates of production to shorten the timescale now that the memory chips have become available.

Task

Write a report to W's finance director:

(a) Evaluating THREE operational risks associated with the manufacture of W's products including an explanation of how each of these risks could be managed; and

(b) Evaluating the risks associated with the use of EDI for managing W's ordering and accounting processes.

(45 minutes)

Test your understanding 24 – SPM (Case study)

Scenario

SPM is a manufacturer and distributor of printed stationery products that are sold in a wide variety of retail stores around the country. There are two divisions: Manufacturing and Distribution. A very large inventory is held in the distribution warehouse to cope with orders from retailers who expect delivery within 48 hours of placing an order.

SPM's management accountant for the Manufacturing division charges the Distribution division for all goods transferred at the standard cost of manufacture which is agreed by each division during the annual budget cycle. The Manufacturing division makes a 10% profit on the cost of production but absorbs all production variances. The goods transferred to Distribution are therefore at a known cost and physically checked by both the Manufacturing and the Distribution division staff at the time of transfer.

Trigger

The customer order process for SPM's Distribution division is as follows:

- SPM's customer service centre receives orders by telephone, post, fax, email and through a new on-line Internet ordering facility (a similar system to that used by Amazon). The customer service centre checks the creditworthiness of customers and bundles up orders several times each day to go to the despatch department.
- All orders received by the despatch department are input to SPM's computer system which checks stock availability and produces an invoice for the goods.
- Internet orders have been credit checked automatically and stock has been reserved as part of the order entry process carried out by the customer. Internet orders automatically result in an invoice being printed without additional input.
- The despatch department uses a copy of the invoice to select goods from the warehouse, which are then assembled in the loading dock for delivery using SPM's own fleet of delivery vehicles.
- When SPM's drivers deliver the goods to the customer, the customer signs for the receipt and the signed copy of the invoice is returned to the despatch office and then to the accounts department.

- SPM's management accountant for the Distribution division produces monthly management reports based on the selling price of the goods less the standard cost of manufacture. The standard cost of manufacture is deducted from the inventory control total which is increased by the value of inventory transferred from the manufacturing division. The control total for inventory is compared with the monthly inventory valuation report and while there are differences, these are mainly the result of write-offs of damaged or obsolete stock, which are recorded on journal entry forms by the despatch department and sent to the accounts department.

Due to the size of inventory held, a physical stocktake is only taken once per annum by Distribution staff, at the end of the financial year. This has always revealed some stock losses, although these have been at an acceptable level. Both internal and external auditors are present during the stocktake and check selected items of stock with the despatch department staff. Due to the range of products held in the warehouse, the auditors rely on the despatch department staff to identify many of the products held.

Task

(a) Evaluate any weaknesses in the risk management approach taken by SPM's Distribution division and how this might affect reported profitability.

(30 minutes)

(b) Recommend internal control improvements that would reduce the likelihood of risk.

(15 minutes)

Test your understanding 25 – ABC (Case study)

Scenario

The operations division of ABC, a listed company, has responsibility to maintain and support the sophisticated computer systems used for call centres and customer database management which the organisation's retail customers rely on as much of their sales are dependent on access to these systems, which are accessed over the Internet.

Although there is no risk management department as such, ABC has a large number of staff in the operations division devoted to disaster recovery. Contingency plans are in operation and data are backed up regularly and stored off-site. However, pressures for short-term profits and cash flow have meant that there has been a continuing under-investment in capital equipment, which one manager was heard to comment as being 'a little like Railtrack'.

Trigger

A review of disaster recovery found that although data were backed up there was a real risk that a severe catastrophe such as fire or flood would have wiped out computer hardware and although data back-up was off-site, there was no proven hardware facility the company could use. While managers have relied on consequential loss insurance, they appear to have overlooked the need to carry out actions themselves to avoid or mitigate any possible loss.

Task

Write a report to the Board:

(a) Advising on the main business issue for ABC and the most significant risks that ABC faces;

(10 minutes)

(b) Advising them on their responsibilities for risk management and recommending a risk management system for ABC that would more effectively manage the risks of losing business continuity.

(30 minutes)

(c) Evaluating the likely benefits for ABC of an effective risk management system for business continuity.

(5 minutes)

10 The exam

The models and frameworks detailed in this chapter are a starting point for the exam, however, candidates need to be able to use their common sense in order to relate this material to exam questions.

11 Chapter summary

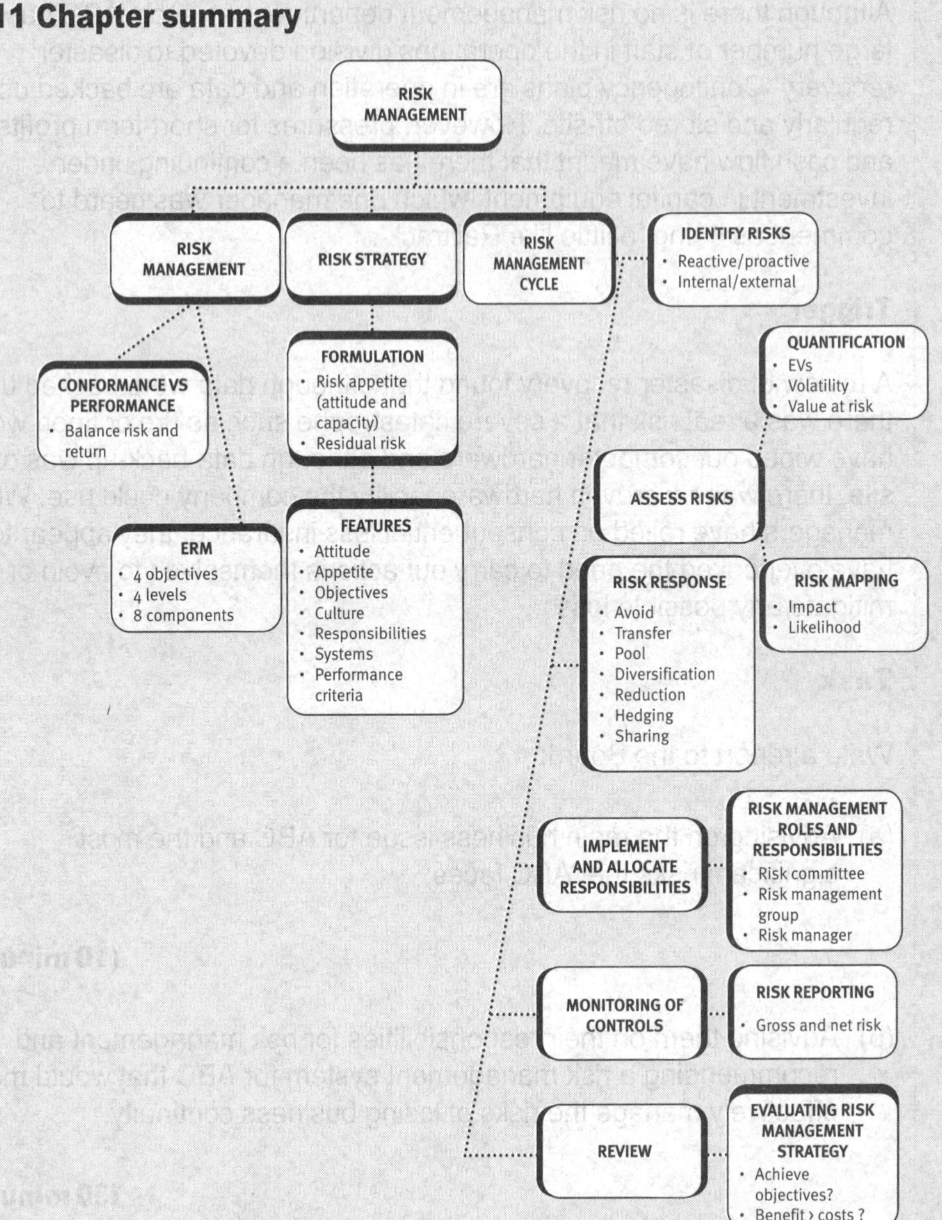
RISK MANAGEMENT
RISK MANAGEMENT
RISK STRATEGY
RISK MANAGEMENT CYCLE
IDENTIFY RISKS
• Reactive/proactive
• Internal/external
QUANTIFICATION
• EVs
• Volatility
• Value at risk
CONFORMANCE VS PERFORMANCE
• Balance risk and return
FORMULATION
• Risk appetite (attitude and capacity)
• Residual risk
ASSESS RISKS
ERM
• 4 objectives
• 4 levels
• 8 components
FEATURES
• Attitude
• Appetite
• Objectives
• Culture
• Responsibilities
• Systems
• Performance criteria
RISK RESPONSE
• Avoid
• Transfer
• Pool
• Diversification
• Reduction
• Hedging
• Sharing
RISK MAPPING
• Impact
• Likelihood
IMPLEMENT AND ALLOCATE RESPONSIBILITIES
RISK MANAGEMENT ROLES AND RESPONSIBILITIES
• Risk committee
• Risk management group
• Risk manager
MONITORING OF CONTROLS
RISK REPORTING
• Gross and net risk
REVIEW
EVALUATING RISK MANAGEMENT STRATEGY
• Achieve objectives?
• Benefit › costs ?

Test your understanding answers

Test your understanding 1

The correct answer is B – By definition.

Test your understanding 2

A, B and E

COSO considers a WIDE range of risks, and is the responsibility of EVERYONE.

Test your understanding 3

The correct answer is B – A risk map assesses an organisation's risks on the basis of likelihood and consequence.

Risk culture is the set of shared attitudes, values and practices that characterise how an entity considers risk in its day-to-day activities.

Risk thermostat is the notion that everyone has a propensity to take risks. This varies by person and is influenced by potential rewards and any previous 'accidents'.

Test your understanding 4

The correct answers are A, B and C – The total cost of a control is not normally detailed on the risk register.

Test your understanding 5 – Volatility (Integration)

The expected value of purchases is:

	£
£200,000 × 0.3	60,000
£250,000 × 0.5	125,000
£300,000 × 0.2	60,000
	245,000

The volatility therefore is:

Downside (£300,000 – £245,000)	£55,000
Upside (£245,000 – £200,000)	£45,000

The volatility is the possible amount away from the expected value.

Test your understanding 6

The value of $10 million today is £6 million ($10 m/$1.6667) with a standard deviation of £30,000 (0.5% × £6 million).

The one-tail 95% confidence level is 1.645.

Hence a five day 95% VaR is 1.645 × £30,000 × √10 = £156,058

Test your understanding 7 – Value at risk (Integration)

At the 95% confidence level the value at risk = 1.645 × 4.85 = $8 million (1.645 is the normal distribution value for a one-tailed 5% probability level – this can be taken from the normal distribution tables).

As the information is for the 2 week period, and not a daily mean or standard deviation, there is no need to use the n day VaR adjustment.

There is thus a 5% probability that the portfolio value will fall to $42 million or below.

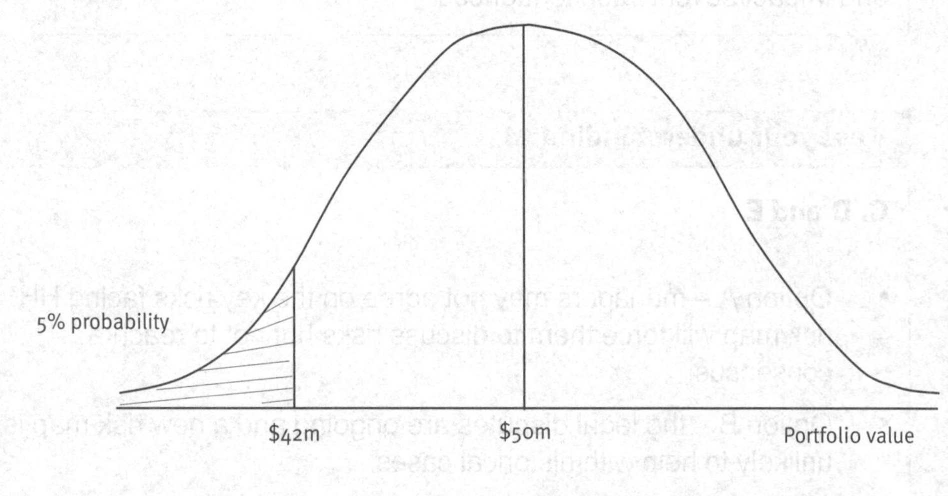

Test your understanding 8 – Restaurant (Integration)

For a restaurant:

		Impact/consequences	
		Low	**High**
Probability/likelihood	**High**	A staff member is taken ill and cannot work	Head chef resigns
	Low	Ingredient prices rise sharply	Several customers suffer from food poisoning

Each suggestion could arguably be in a different quadrant, depending on the restaurant. These are just suggestions.

Test your understanding 9

The correct answer is B – Low-level staff frequently change jobs in order to progress. The severity is low as they are unlikely to be well-trained/highly skilled and could be replaced fairly quickly and easily.

Test your understanding 10

The correct answers are A and C – The axes are likelihood/probability and impact/severity/consequences.

Test your understanding 11

C, D and E

- Option A – managers may not agree on the key risks facing HH. The risk map will force them to discuss risks but not to reach a consensus.
- Option B – the legal disputes are ongoing and a new risk map is unlikely to help with historical cases.
- Options C, D and E are benefits.

Test your understanding 12

The correct answer is C – Portfolio theory seeks to diversify the company's activities which can reduce risk (by not putting all your eggs in one basket).

Test your understanding 13 – Diversification (Integration)

Arguments for and against diversification:

For

- Reduces risks and enables company to give more predictable return to investors.
- Attracts investors who want low risk investments.

Against

- Management may not understand all the businesses that the company operates in – increases the risk.
- It is not necessary to diversify for investors – they can diversify themselves by investing in a number of different companies.
- New business areas can attract risks – for instance going into a new country may increase the risk of not understanding a company culture.

Test your understanding 14

The correct answer is C – The likelihood of this event would hopefully be low as several controls preventing this should be in place. Staff would refuse to work otherwise. The consequence of such an event would be high as it would likely lead to an investigation, legal proceedings, compensation and reputational risk.

Test your understanding 15

The correct answer is C – Low frequency/high severity risks are often transferred, by using insurance for example.

Test your understanding 16

A and B only

- Option A: Is appropriate since the population of Country X are not familiar with fast food.
- Option B: Often organisations need to adapt their standardised products because of cultural differences.
- Option C: Significant investment is likely to have already occurred in Country X and simply pulling out before embarking on other risk response plans is unlikely to be appropriate at this point. In addition, the entire strategy of P Company is based around geographical expansion. It will be more difficult in some countries to establish the brand.
- Option D: The poor performance of restaurants in Country P is unlikely to be J's fault rather it is due to rolling out standardised products in culturally diverse locations. In fact, since J has now built up some experience in Country X, he should be retained to continue expansion.
- Option E: The global brand of P Company is based on uniformity and although small tweaks to this make sense to enable the restaurants to 'fit' with the local culture, the brand needs to be consistent with values applied globally.

Test your understanding 17 – Twinkletoes (Case study)

To: The Finance Director

From: The Management Accountant

Date: Today

Subject: Risk management at Twinkletoes

Dear Finance Director,

Please find attached my classification of risks for receivables and a recommendation for internal controls.

(a) **Classification of risks for receivables**

(i) **Small retail shoe shops**

Despite the fact that individual accounts in this category have small balances, the category as a whole is significant to Twinkletoes because of the total amounts owed (one-third of total receivables), the rising level of irrecoverable debts and the adverse effect of slow payers on cash flow. It is likely that most of these accounts individually are low risk because customers pay promptly and the amounts are small. Accounts that are significantly overdue may be classified as medium risk, but probably only if they are substantial accounts because all entities must expect to experience a small number of small irrecoverable debts. If, however, a large number of accounts are significantly overdue, they may be classified as high risk.

(ii) **Large retail shoe shops**

Some of these accounts are large and overdue and may therefore be classified as medium or high risk. However, as the total value of such accounts is around 22% of total receivables and the total value of the overdue accounts may be small in relation to total receivables, the classification should probably only be medium risk. The classification for accounts that are not overdue may be low risk

Overseas accounts. Whilst these might at first appear to be at risk because the accounts are being lost, they represent a small proportion of accounts by both number and value (customers currently pay in advance). This means that they may be viewed as low risk.

(iii) **Chains of shoe shops**

As with the large shoe shops, large and overdue accounts might be classified as medium or high risk. However, 'high street' chains of well-established shops are less likely to become insolvent than less well-established entities and therefore represent a lower risk. This means that the classification may be low risk, even for accounts that are large and overdue.

(iv) **Mail order companies**

New accounts generally represent an increased risk of irrecoverable debts and a large number of new accounts increases this risk. However, there is no history of irrecoverable debts in this category at all so the new accounts may therefore be classified as medium risk. Existing accounts within this category may be classified as low risk because there is no history of irrecoverable debts.

(b) **Internal controls**

(i) **All customers**

I would recommend that:

- credit checks be performed when new customers seek credit, and that cash in advance or on delivery is required where large orders are placed by new customers;
- credit limits be set for all customers based on the length of the relationship with the customer, the volume of sales and their payment history;
- payment terms be set (say, 30 days for local customers, 45 days for overseas customers);
- insurance be taken out against the risk of irrecoverable debts.

These controls will help ensure that accounts do not become overdue, damaging the company's cash flow and increasing the risk of irrecoverable debts.

(ii) Slow paying customers

I would recommend that:

- dedicated staff are assigned to chase slow payers regularly for outstanding amounts and to ensure that a `stop' is put on accounts that are significantly overdue;
- legal action is taken against those customers owing large amounts for long periods for which there are no good reasons.

(iii) Larger accounts – large shops, chains of shops and mail order companies

I would recommend that:

- dedicated staff are assigned to manage the relationship with larger customers, particularly the mail order companies.

(iv) **Overseas customers**

I would recommend that:

- overseas customers be allowed a credit period of say, 45 days in order to permit the required bank transfers to take place;
- overseas customers be required to pay in the currency used by Twinkletoes (except perhaps for large orders which may be backed by government guarantees) or in a stable currency which does not fluctuate significantly against the currency used by Twinkletoes.

If you have any queries, please do not hesitate to ask.

Best wishes

Management Accountant

Test your understanding 18

B, C and D

- Option A – responses to significant risks only.
- Option E – such a review should be carried out at least annually.

Test your understanding 19

B – avoid

It would appear that the gross risk cannot be reduced since the client will not renegotiate the level of the penalty then the impact remains high and as TGDW's internal controls are already at a high level it is unlikely that the likelihood can be reduced.

As the likelihood is high then it is unlikely that TGDW will able to get insurance against this event occurring so transference is not possible.

Acceptance is unthinkable in this case and there appears to be no further scope for reduction.

Therefore unless TGDW are an exceptionally risk seeking organisation they will need to avoid this risk.

Test your understanding 20 – L tinned foods (Case study)

To: The Board of L

From: A.N. Accountant

Date: Today

Subject: Risks and recommendations regarding account managers

Introduction

This report evaluates the potential risks that might arise from L's appointment of an account manager to deal with H's business. It then goes on to recommend the changes that L's board should introduce in order to minimise the threats arising from having an autonomous account manager.

(a) **The risks of appointing an account manager**

L has effectively introduced a matrix management structure with respect to its dealings with H. This has the potential for a number of upside risks. In particular, it means that H's interests will be kept under constant review by a designated manager. Thus, there is less risk that H's business will be lost because of an oversight or a breakdown in communications. If any of the decision makers at H require anything then they know to contact Peter and he will then be responsible for dealing with their request.

There are a number of downside risks arising from this arrangement. The most obvious of these is that there may be a conflict between Peter's role as an account manager and the roles of the other functional managers within L. H is an important customer, but it accounts for only 20% of sales by volume and so it could be argued that the smaller customers are, collectively, far more important than H. Presumably, H is capable of negotiating significant trade discounts and so the additional volume of business is unlikely to be particularly profitable.

Peter's role may be important, but there is a danger that it will lead to dysfunctional behaviour on his part. He will be motivated to retain H's business because that is the whole point of his employment. H will be aware of that and may start to pressure him into granting further discounts, extensions of credit and other concessions.

Peter has already disrupted transactions involving existing customers with whom L has an established relationship. The most immediate threat is that those customers may cease trade with L. It is also possible that such behaviour will lead to conflict between Peter and the functional managers, which will waste time. The functional managers may also become demotivated if their efforts are thwarted by Peter.

Junior staff will also be confused by contradictory instructions. If they are unsure whether to obey Peter or their usual functional managers then they may delay acting in order to seek clarification. Once they start to question instructions from their superiors then the overall control environment may be undermined.

(b) **Recommendations for change to reduce the threat of autonomous account managers**

Firstly, there has to be clear communication between the account manager and the functional managers. It should be made clear that any conflict should be discussed and, if possible, resolved by compromise. If, for example, H wishes to place a large and urgent order then it may be possible to ask the production manager to increase output so that all potential sales can be made without disappointing existing customers. That will reduce the threat of disagreement between the account manager and the functional managers.

It should be made clear that any conflict that cannot be resolved by compromise should be dealt with in a manner that is in L's overall best interests. It should be made clear that any dysfunctional behaviour will be regarded as a disciplinary matter. That will reduce the threat that the account manager will be tempted to act in H's best interests rather than L's.

Subordinate staff should be free to state that any instruction contradicts policy or a previous request. It should then be the functional or account manager's responsibility to seek a compromise so that subordinate staff have an agreed instruction. That will avoid the stress and confusion that will arise for junior staff if they are caught between competing managers.

Ideally, the account manager should have been appointed from within L and it should be made clear that the appointee's continued employment is not conditional on retaining H as a customer. An internal appointee will, hopefully, have a more immediate loyalty to L than to H. The assurance of continuing employment will reduce the extent to which H might pressure the account manager.

There should be a clear policy for resolving conflicts between managers. It may be that the appropriate functional manager should make the final decision, on the basis that the business from H is worth only 20% of the company's sales by volume, and those may be subject to a substantial discount because H is the company's largest customer. That should lead to a consistent response to any conflicts between managers.

Conclusion

There are several risks arising from the appointment of an account manager, however, these risks can be reduced by improving communication, having a clear policy for conflict resolution and implementing disciplinary action if necessary.

Test your understanding 21 – Dental practice (Case study)

(a) The risk-mapping exercise is not an objective process and so the resulting diagram is not an objective or "correct" representation of the risks faced by the practice. The dentists should not risk relying too heavily on the map itself to determine their overall risk-management strategies.

The main benefit to be had from this exercise is that the dentists will have the opportunity to discuss the risks facing the practice.

This communication will mean that each of the dentists is made aware of the threats that have been identified by each of the others. That should mean that each of them will have a more comprehensive understanding of the risks faced by the practice as a whole.

The discussion will also ensure that there is an opportunity to address colleagues' understanding of identified risks. It may be that some dentists are devoting too much time and effort to managing trivial risks. Conversely, potentially serious risks could be misunderstood and overlooked. The discussion will enable the dentists to reach some agreement as to the most appropriate response to each risk. A consensus opinion is more likely to be balanced and logical than any individual view.

The fact that the risks have been identified and discussed can be recorded for future reference. In the event that the practice is ever accused of negligence then the fact that a risk was discussed and a response put in place may enable the dentists to argue that they acted with reasonable skill and care. That, of course, implies that an appropriate response has been put in place for any identified risks.

2 **Dental implants**

It is logical to state that the probability of occurrence is high if this is a relatively common procedure. Presumably the failures are caused by random factors that are out of the dentist's control, such as the patient's overall health or dental hygiene and so the laws of probability will mean that failures will occur from time to time.

It is natural for a patient who has spent a significant amount of money on a procedure to be aggrieved if that procedure fails and so the practice may be accused of malpractice. Patients may discount the risk of failure when agreeing to the implant because the probability seems reasonably remote when looking ahead and making plans.

The impact of a claim will be low because it is a known risk that the patient has agreed to accept. It will be both difficult and expensive for a patient to pursue any formal claim for a refund or a repeat procedure.

Cross infection

It is important to be clear about whether the likelihood is expressed in terms of gross risk or net. Every dental procedure puts the dental staff in close proximity to the patient and will involve contact with body fluids. The gross risks are, therefore, high. The net risks of cross infection can, however, be minimised through good hygiene, such as the dentist and the nurse wearing disposable gloves that are changed between patients and also face masks to reduce the risk of transmitting respiratory infections.

The impact of causing an infection will be high. This is a preventable problem and so there is a risk that any failure will constitute medical malpractice. In the event that a patient complains to the health authorities or the dentists' professional body there could be a significant penalty. There could also be a serious threat of adverse publicity, with patients choosing to use another dental practice.

Spiral staircase

The staircase could prevent disabled or infirm patients from obtaining access to the practice. It may be that a potential patient will choose to make this a matter of principle and complain that the practice has not made adequate provision for the disabled. Legally, the practice is not under any obligation to do more than make reasonable provision for access and there is no practical solution that could be offered.

It is unlikely that the impact will be significant. The practice is already well established, so it has already attracted a viable number of patients who can cope with this access problem. Any complaints can be addressed by a polite comment to the effect that the practice is located in a building that cannot accommodate a lift or a conventional staircase.

Given that there is no viable response to this risk, it really has to be accepted in almost any case. Dealing with it would require an extreme and potentially disproportionate response, such as moving to new premises.

Allergies

The probability that a patient will suffer an allergic reaction is low. Pharmaceutical products are tested to ensure that they do not generally cause reactions. Patients will, hopefully, be aware of most allergies that they suffer from and the dental practice can record those in patient files.

The impact of an allergic reaction is probably not high for the practice, despite the fact that it could be a serious matter for the patient. Provided the dentist has prescribed the antibiotic in good faith there is very little risk that the practice will be in trouble for prescribing a relevant drug to treat an infection. The dentist should always check that the patient's medical history is up to date in order to ensure that there is no reason to avoid any particular medication. Provided that has been done, any reaction will be viewed as an unfortunate accident rather than medical negligence.

Test your understanding 22 – B bank (Case study)

To: The Board of B Bank

From: A.N. Accountant

Date: Today

Subject: Directors bonuses and risk management

Introduction

This report covers an evaluation of the governors suggestion and an evaluation of B banks risk management strategy.

(a) **Evaluate the proposal made by the governor**

The governor of the central bank in B Bank's country has suggested that directors of banks pay a fee, and that the bonuses will be based on profit and growth indicators.

Director's viewpoint

From the view point of the banks directors this will not be a welcome solution. The amount of the fee will be questioned – will it be the same for all directors? What will the fee be used for? Will it be returned when a director retires? It is likely that there will be much unrest and argument before this proposal is accepted.

The remuneration committee is to set the fee. Presumably the committee should be an independent one consisting of non-executive directors (NEDs). The NEDs should not be included under the heading of 'directors' and need not pay a fee.

The target of 'appropriate profit and growth indicators' is very vague. What is appropriate to one person e.g. a director may not be appropriate to an investor.

However, the idea of linking profits and bonuses is a better idea than simply paying out large bonuses with little justification (even when a bank has made a loss).

The linking of bonuses with profit may, however, encourage the directors to take excessive risks in order to boost their bonuses.

Staff viewpoint

The staff of B Bank may not be happy with this proposal since there is no mention of them receiving a bonus. They may fear that all profits are paid out to the directors when they feel that they have worked hard.

The directors may not be accepting of this proposal either if they consider the fact that many external factors out of their control can affect the bank's profits. They may work extremely hard and still make a loss in extreme circumstances due to, say, a fall in the demand for mortgages.

Central bank's viewpoint

Finally, the proposal may go against any future decision by the governors of the central banks in other nations.

However, on the plus side, at least the governor in B Bank's home country is trying to alleviate the adverse media coverage by doing something rather than delaying the issue.

(b) **Evaluation of the risk management strategy**

In the past a formal strategy for managing risks would not be made but rather it would be left to individual managers to make assessments of the risks the business faced and exercise judgement on what was a reasonable level of risk.

This has now changed: failure to properly identify and control risks has been identified as a major cause of business failure e.g. Barings Bank.

Risk management strategy

CIMA identified the following key features of a risk management strategy:

A statement of the organisation's attitude to risk – the balance between risk and the need to meet objectives

The risk appetite of the organisation

The objectives of the risk management strategy

The culture of the organisation in relation to risk

The responsibility of managers for the application of risk management strategy

Reference should be made to the risk management systems the company uses. i.e. its internal control systems

Performance criteria should be defined so that the effectiveness of risk management can be evaluated

B Bank meets only a few of these criteria.

B Bank's risk management strategy

A statement of B Bank's attitude to risk and risk appetite is not mentioned in the scenario. However it can probably be assumed that they are risk takers by being able to achieve an increase in share price of 12% per annum, and also by attracting hedge funds as investors. In this way, from the view point of the investors, B Bank's risk management strategy is good.

The culture of B Banks managers will probably be one of risk seeking in order to provide the high returns mentioned. (A risk averse manager would feel very uncomfortable in these surroundings.) The staff at B Bank may or may not like the risk management strategy. If it provides them with high salaries then they are probably happy. However, these high salaries may be short-term if an incorrect decision is made in the future and the bank hits hard times or goes bust. Then the staff may have been happier with lower salaries and job security.

Since a risk management strategy is not formally mentioned it is difficult to say whether managers have been allocated responsibility for the application of risk management. That said, for the bank to have traded successfully for over 150 years, some risk management must take place, however, once again this should be formalised.

The risk management systems will include the bank's executive information system (EIS). It is able to compute product profitability which supports the targets set on previous profitable experience. On the plus side, having an EIS is an advantage for B Bank; however, it is not being used to its full potential. (See recommendations below.)

Also, B Bank has non-executive directors (NEDs) but they are a poor internal control since they do not question the decisions of the executive directors.

Performance criteria to assess the effectiveness of the risk management strategy are not mentioned in the scenario, other than the targets set on previous experience. It seems that while B Bank is successful the targets will just roll forward without any reference to what is happening in the external environment of B Bank.

Evaluation of the risk management strategy in B Bank is two-fold:

Has the strategy achieved its objectives? This is hard to say since no formal strategy has been set.

Do the benefits outweigh the costs? Most certainly yes. Since the setting of the strategy cost nothing (no strategy was set) and large returns have been achieved, then the benefits have far outweighed the costs.

Conclusions and recommendations

Overall, the current risk management strategy in B Bank is not good enough. In order to lower the bank's exposure to risk the following recommendations are made:

A major strategy review needs to be performed as soon as possible since the last one was four years ago and much has changed since then. The management appear to be adopting an incremental approach to planning ahead (using previous profitable experiences as the basis for their targets). The past is not always a good indicator of the future and this could be a very dangerous philosophy. B Banks directors need to formally identify the banks attitude to risk, set up a risk committee, and communicate their risk attitude and appetite to its management and investors. They also need to perform an environmental analysis in order to prepare themselves for events that may affect them in the future. E.g. a further fall in house prices.

More effective NEDs need to be appointed who will query the decisions of the executive directors. They may also be able to provide further experience and insight into the banking industry and its environment that the executive directors don't have, or don't have the time to consider.

The property price trend into the future needs to be corroborated with external information, not just internal reports. B Bank should obtain independent, external advice on this in case their internal department is wrong in its prediction.

Currently B Bank is obtaining finance to support new mortgages with loans from the short-term money-markets. This is a very dangerous practice should the source of finance dry up. The principle of 'matching' should be adopted whereby long-term assets (mortgages) are matched with long-term loans (liabilities). This will secure the finance required for the duration of the mortgage and avoid 'renewal risk'.

B Bank may wish to seek new investors. The current investors – hedge funds, may be driving B Bank down a risky road in order to provide them with short-term financial returns. B Bank was founded in 1856 and presumably has the objective of continuing in business into the future. Taking high risks to provide high returns may prevent this objective from being met.

Conclusion

There appear to be more negative viewpoints than positive viewpoints regarding the governor's proposal and B Bank's risk management strategy could be significantly improved.

Test your understanding 23 – W consumer (Case study)

To: The finance Director

From: A.N. Accountant

Date: Today

Subject: Evaluation of operational risk and the use of EDI at W

Introduction

This report covers the evaluation of operational risks at W and suggests management techniques to reduce those risks. It then goes on to consider the risks in using EDI.

(a) **Operational risks**

W is dependent upon a small number of third parties for the manufacture of critical components. If a supplier defaults on a delivery then W may run out of product to sell. The likelihood of this is impossible to predict, but it is a risk that is not under W's direct control. The best safeguard against such problems would be to have more than one potential supplier for any given item. W should make sure that it owns the patents for any components or processes that it relies on or that it has a licence in place just in case it needs to move to an alternative supplier. Penalty clauses will not mitigate losses in the event of any disruption, but they may concentrate the attention of its suppliers.

W has no direct control over the quality of its products, which may lead to customer dissatisfaction. Parts are sourced from many different suppliers and so it will be difficult for W to ensure that every component is manufactured to the required tolerances. Manufacturing staff at the component and assembly factories will not feel that they are part of W and they may resent the fact that they do not enjoy the security of working for a large organisation. The owners and managers of the factories may not feel that there is a huge incentive to do much more than meet the minimum standards for quality and delivery because they may be replaced at the conclusion of their contract. W can control that risk by introducing quality checks on both components and finished goods. W could request samples on a random basis and check these thoroughly. W could also have a policy of rewarding reliable suppliers by retaining them and giving them as much work as possible so that they have an incentive to exceed expectations.

The global nature of W's manufacturing process creates logistical problems for manufacturing. Manufacturing may be disrupted by delays in delivery, which could be outside the control of W and its suppliers. For example, electronic components are frequently transported by air freight, which can be affected by weather or industrial action. Goods crossing international borders can be delayed by customs inspections. One way round this would be to localise sources as much as possible, with suppliers for minor parts such as screws and plastic cases chosen for proximity to the assembly factories even if they are not necessarily the cheapest. W might use a specialist logistics company to manage the transport of parts and assemblies so that there is clarity as to who is responsible for any logistical problems. W might also have a policy of keeping safety stocks of all but the most expensive parts and assemblies to cover any disruption.

(b) **EDI**

EDI is potentially more efficient than more traditional methods of communication. W has a very complicated manufacturing process and EDI makes it possible to break the task of ordering and paying for a batch of completed mp3 players much simpler. In theory, this system will reduce W's staffing costs considerably. The system will place orders and will keep track of inventory as it is received. The bookkeeping will be done automatically because invoices will be received, recorded and passed for payment electronically.

The problem with W is that it does not really have a long-term relationship with all of its suppliers. It is possible that many of the suppliers it uses will be replaced in the medium or even the short term if a cheaper source becomes available. For example, a shift in currencies could make an alternative source of labour for fabrication tasks cheaper than the present supplier. Potential suppliers might not be prepared to install the necessary technology and that could restrict W's sources.

Another problem is that W might find it difficult to manage the processing of invoices and payments. A supplier could invoice W for parts or fabrication work on sub-assemblies that are delivered to another third party. W will have no way of verifying that the goods being invoiced were, in fact, delivered in good order and so the system will not be able to make payment. Suppliers could be reluctant to accept orders unless they are likely to be paid for promptly and efficiently.

On a related matter, the lack of human interaction could complicate the manufacturing process. Suppliers of even small parts could delay the completion of finished products if their IT systems accept electronic orders without any consideration of whether the requested delivery dates are feasible. A manager in the sales office could review incoming orders and ensure that the necessary capacity is available.

Conclusions

There are several risks identified in this report and risk management recommendations made. Although EDI would help W, there are many issues which need to be resolved first before EDI could be implemented.

Test your understanding 24 – SPM (Case study)

(a) Risk management is the process by which organisations systematically identify and treat upside and downside risks across the portfolio of all activities with the goal of achieving organisational objectives. Risk management increases the probability of success, reduces both the probability of failure and the uncertainty of achieving the organisation's objectives. The goal of risk management is to manage, rather than eliminate risk. This is most effectively done through embedding a risk culture into the organisation.

For SPM's Distribution division, there is a risk of stock losses through theft, largely due to the lack of separation of duties. This lack of separation occurs because the Distribution Division:

- enters all orders to the computer;
- selects all stock from the warehouse;
- despatches all goods to customers;
- receives the signed paperwork evidencing delivery;
- writes off stock losses due to damage and obsolescence;
- carries out and to a large extent controls the annual physical stocktake.

This lack of separation of duties could result in stock losses or theft that is not identified or not recorded and any stock losses or theft may be disguised during the stocktake due to the expertise of the Distribution division which the auditors appear to rely on.

These stock losses or theft may not be accurately recorded and the reported profits of SPM may overstate profits if physical inventory does not match that shown in the accounting records. Stock of stationery is easy to dispose of and losses can easily happen due to error or carelessness, for instance through water damage, dropping and so on. The possibility of theft of stock which can readily be sold in retail stores is also high and the consequences of not identifying stock losses or theft might be severe over a period of time. There is a risk that inventory records may substantially overstate the physical stock. There is a serious limitation of accounting here as it relies on computer records and a stocktake process that may be severely impaired and hence there may be hidden losses not reflected in SPM's reported financial statements.

Fraud is dishonestly obtaining an advantage, avoiding an obligation or causing a loss to another party. Those committing fraud may be managers, employees or third parties, including customers and suppliers. There are three conditions for fraud to occur: dishonesty, opportunity and motive. If stock theft is occurring, the weakness in systems due to the lack of separation of duties provides an opportunity. Personnel policies and supervision may influence dishonesty and employment or social conditions among the workforce may influence motive.

As for all other risks, a risk management strategy needs to be developed for fraud. This strategy should include fraud prevention; the identification and detection of fraud and responses to fraud.

Existing risk treatment does not appear to be adequate due to the lack of separation of duties, the possibility of fraud and the reliance of internal and external auditors on the Distribution division's staff.

(b) The main recommendation is for the separation of duties in SPM's distribution division. The customer service centre should process all customer orders, even though this may mean transferring staff from the despatch department. It may be more effective to use a document imaging system to reduce paperwork by the conversion of orders into electronic files that are capable of being read by computer programs and transferred to the despatch department. Further separation can be carried out by signed paperwork evidencing delivery being sent to the accounts department and for all write offs of stock losses due to damage or obsolescence to be carried out by the accounts department. Finally, the reliance on Distribution staff for stocktaking needs to be reduced and accountants and internal auditors need to play a more prominent role in physical counting and reconciling to computer records.

The second recommendation is for greater emphasis on controls to prevent dishonesty. These include pre-employment checks, scrutiny of staff by effective supervision, severe discipline for offenders and strong moral leadership. Motive can be influenced by providing good employment conditions, a sympathetic complaints procedure, but dismissing staff instantaneously where it is warranted.

Test your understanding 25 – ABC (Case study)

To: The Board

From: A.N. Accountant

Date: Today

Subject: Risk management

Introduction

This report covers:

(a) The main business issue for ABC and the most significant risks that ABC faces;

(b) The Board's responsibilities for risk management and recommending a risk management system for ABC that would more effectively manage the risks of losing business continuity;

(c) An evaluation of the likely benefits for ABC of an effective risk management system for business continuity.

Risks

(a) A review of disaster recovery had identified a lack of hardware back-up as costs had been continually deferred from year to year to maintain current profits. This has an effect on business continuity for both ABC and its retail customers. Insurance is only one type of risk treatment and ABC has overlooked the need to address business continuity more proactively and comprehensively.

The pressure on short-term profits and cash flow is important to recognise but the short-term view may lead to medium- and long-term problems if under-investment continues. This needs to be the focus of a risk management exercise to properly assess, evaluate, report and treat the business continuity risk.

Although a severe catastrophe may have a small likelihood of occurrence, the impact will be severe and insurance cover is unlikely to be adequate as ABC will not have taken adequate steps to mitigate the loss. Customer awareness of the risk is likely to result in customers moving their business elsewhere. Public disclosure or a severe catastrophe will have a major impact on the reputation of ABC and on ABC's share price.

(b) **Board responsibilities**

The board is responsible for maintaining a sound system of internal control to safeguard shareholders' investment and the company's assets. When reviewing management reports on internal control, the board should consider the significant risks and assess how they have been identified, evaluated and managed; assess the effectiveness of internal controls in managing the significant risks, having regard to any significant weaknesses in internal control; consider whether necessary actions are being taken promptly to remedy any weaknesses and consider whether the findings indicate a need for more exhaustive monitoring of the system of internal control.

Risk management is the process by which organisations systematically identify and treat upside and downside risks with the goal of achieving organisational objectives. The goal of risk management is to manage, rather than eliminate risk. Initially, there needs to be a commitment from the board and top management in relation to risk management generally and business continuity in particular, even if this means a short-term detrimental impact on profitability. The board of ABC, through the audit committee, needs to be more involved in the risk management process. Individual responsibilities for risk management need to be assigned and sufficient resources need to be allocated to fund effective risk management for business continuity.

ABC needs to identify its appetite for risk, and a risk management policy needs to be formulated and agreed by the board. The risk management process needs to identify and define risk, which needs to be assessed in terms of both likelihood and impact. For ABC, the risks have been clearly defined: a loss of business continuity caused by a major catastrophe and the consequent loss of reputation this would involve.

The likelihood of fire, flood, terrorist or criminal activity and so on needs to be assessed, particularly in terms of the risk avoidance processes that are already in place. For example, ABC needs to evaluate whether there has been flooding in the area before, whether water pipes run near the computer facility, whether fire prevention measures are in place, whether firewalls are in place and have been tested so as to reduce the likelihood of attack via the Internet. An assessment of probability of these and other catastrophes should be made. Although these may be low probability events, the impact on the business of any such catastrophe will be severe.

Risk evaluation determines the significance of risks to the organisation and whether each specific risk should be accepted or treated. It should be emphasised that these risks cannot be accepted but do need to be treated. Risk treatment (or risk response) is the process of selecting and implementing measures to reduce or limit the risk. The existing contingency plans need to be examined in detail. While data appear to be backed up regularly and stored off-site, there seems to be inadequate back-up for hardware. Risk treatment will involve deciding the most cost-effective method by which to manage the risk. A preferred solution given the reliance of ABC's customers on the system is to have a remote site equipped with a second system that data can be restored onto. While this is the most expensive option there may be business benefits in having two sites. A second solution may be to outsource the back-up facility so that ABC contracts with a third party to have a system available if one is needed. A third option is to negotiate with suppliers as to the availability of other sites and the replacement of equipment on a short notice basis. Finally, insurance coverage needs to be reviewed and the mitigation decided in consultation with ABC's insurers. The present method of risk management that relies only on off-site data back-up is inadequate to assure business continuity.

As business continuity is so important, the board and audit committee need to be involved in the decision-making process about risk treatment. There needs to be regular risk management reporting to assess the control systems in place to reduce risk; the processes used to identify and respond to risks; the methods used to manage significant risks and the monitoring and review system itself. Reporting should take place to business units, senior management, internal audit, the board and the audit committee.

(c) **The benefits of effective risk management**

For ABC, the benefits include the maintenance of profitability in the medium- and longer-term and the avoidance of sudden losses if business continuity is impeded. The major benefit for ABC in such a case is the avoidance of profit warnings and major exceptional items. Additional benefits may include more cost-effective insurance cover and reduced premium cost. If the recommendations are adopted, despite the increased costs that will almost necessarily be incurred, the board of ABC will have greater degree of assurance that business continuity will be safeguarded in the event of a catastrophe, will continue to satisfy its customers and will maintain its reputation with customers, the public and investors.

Conclusions

The main risk for ABC is the lack of a disaster recovery plan as this has an effect on business continuity.

The board is responsible for maintaining a sound system of internal control to safeguard shareholders' investment and the company's assets.

The benefits of effective risk management outweigh the costs.

hapter

3

Internal control

Chapter learning objectives

Lead	Component
A2. Evaluate senior management's responsibility for the implementation of risk management strategies and internal controls.	(a) Recommend techniques that will enable the board to discharge its responsibilities with respect to managing risks.
C2. Evaluate risk management strategies and internal controls.	(a) Evaluate the essential features of internal control systems for identifying, assessing and managing risks.

Indicative syllabus content

- The control environment.
- Internal control.
- Purposes of internal control: the achievement of an entity's objectives, effectiveness and efficiency of operations.
- Identifying and evaluating control weaknesses.
- Identifying and evaluating compliance failures.
- Operational features of control systems, including embedding in company's operations, responsiveness to evolving risks and timely reporting to management.
- The pervasive nature of internal control and the need for employee training.
- Costs and benefits of maintaining the internal control system.

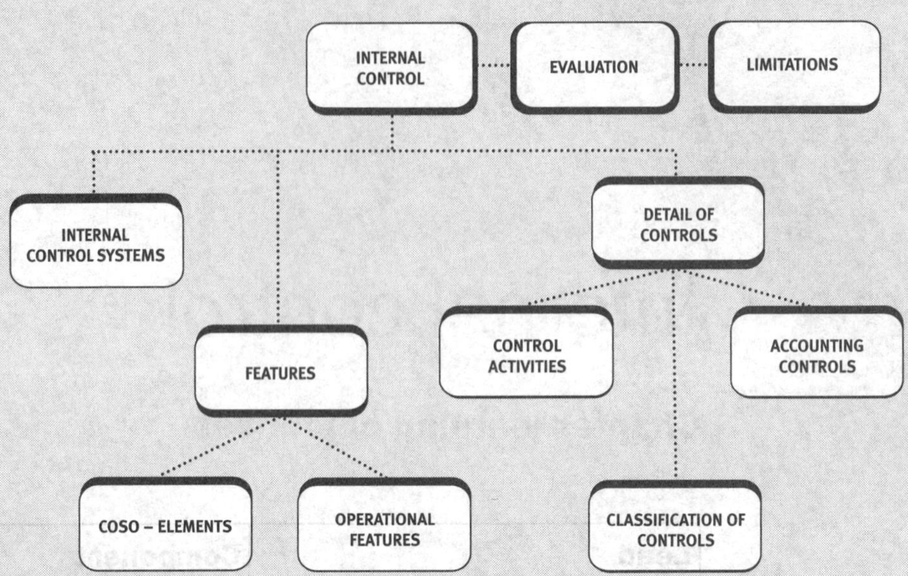

1 Internal control systems

- In order to manage their risks, businesses need to set up internal control systems.
- These internal controls apply across all parts and activities of a business.

Definition

There are a number of different definitions of internal control systems, but all have similar features. One definition is:

> 'The whole system of controls, financial and otherwise, established by the management in order to carry out the business of the enterprise in an orderly and efficient manner, ensure adherence to management policies, safeguard the assets, prevent and detect fraud and error and secure as far as possible the completeness and accuracy of the records.'

An internal control system can be thought of as a *system for management to control certain risks and therefore help businesses achieve their objectives*.

Internal controls and risk management

- Internal controls can be considered as part of the risk reduction method of responding to risk.
- The need for a robust system of internal control and risk management is seen as a major element of good corporate governance.
- In the UK for example, the Corporate Governance Code requires the board of directors to review the system of internal control in their organisation, and satisfy themselves that a suitable system is in place.

Objectives of internal control

A definition of an internal control system included:

Definition	Commentary
...the orderly and efficient conduct of its business, including adherence to internal policies'	There will be systems in place to ensure that all transactions are recorded (so the business is conducted in an orderly manner) through to following policies such as provision of good customer service.
...the safeguarding of assets'	Assets in this case include buildings, cars, cash, etc. (e.g. those things that can be touched) through to other assets including the intellectual property of the company (e.g. those things which cannot be touched but are still an asset of the business).
...the prevention and detection of fraud and error'	This will include fraud an error at the operational level through to the strategic level (e.g. off balance sheet finance or the adoption of incorrect or suspect accounting policies (think of Enron).
...the accuracy and completeness of the accounting records and ...'	Again, ensuring that all transactions are recorded – so liabilities are not 'hidden' and assets are not overstated.
...the timely preparation of financial information.'	Reporting deadlines in many jurisdictions are quite strict (60 days in the US for some reports) hence the need to ensure information is available to produce those reports in a timely fashion.

The main point to note here is that the internal control system encompasses the **whole business**, not simply the financial records.

2 The Turnbull Report

In October 2005, the Financial Reporting Council issued 'Internal Control - Revised Guidance for Directors on the Combined Code', known more commonly as the Turnbull Report (originally published in 1999). The report covered the importance of internal control in companies. An extract is detailed below.

The importance of internal control and risk management

(1) A company's system of internal control has a key role in the management of risks that are significant to the fulfilment of its business objectives. A sound system of internal control contributes to safeguarding the shareholders' investment and the company's assets.

(2) Internal control facilitates the effectiveness and efficiency of operations, helps ensure the reliability of internal and external reporting and assists compliance with laws and regulations.

(3) Effective financial controls, including the maintenance of proper accounting records, are an important element of internal control. They help ensure that the company is not unnecessarily exposed to avoidable financial risks and that financial information used within the business and for publication is reliable. They also contribute to the safeguarding of assets, including the prevention and detection of fraud.

(4) A company's objectives, its internal organisation and the environment in which it operates are continually evolving and, as a result, the risks it faces are continually changing. A sound system of internal control therefore depends on a thorough and regular evaluation of the nature and extent of the risks to which the company is exposed. Since profits are, in part, the reward for successful risk-taking in business, the purpose of internal control is to help manage and control risk appropriately rather than to eliminate it......

Responsibilities

(15) The board of directors is responsible for the company's system of internal control. It should set appropriate policies on internal control and seek regular reassurance that will enable it to satisfy itself that the system is functioning effectively. The board must further ensure that the system of internal control is effective in managing those risks in the manner which it has approved...

(16) All employees have some responsibility for internal control as part of their accountability for achieving objectives. They, collectively, should have the necessary knowledge, skills, information, and authority to establish, operate and monitor the system of internal control. This will require an understanding of the company, its objectives, the industries and markets in which it operates, and the risks it faces.

Elements of a sound system of internal control

(19) An internal control system encompasses the policies, processes, tasks, behaviours and other aspects of a company that, taken together:

- facilitate its effective and efficient operation by enabling it to respond appropriately to significant business, operational, financial, compliance and other risks to achieving the company's objectives. This includes the safeguarding of assets from inappropriate use or from loss and fraud and ensuring that liabilities are identified and managed;
- help ensure the quality of internal and external reporting. This requires the maintenance of proper records and processes that generate a flow of timely, relevant and reliable information from within and outside the organisation;
- help ensure compliance with applicable laws and regulations, and also with internal policies with respect to the conduct of business.

(20) A company's system of internal control will reflect its control environment which encompasses its organisational structure. The system will include:

- control activities;
- information and communications processes; and
- processes for monitoring the continuing effectiveness of the system of internal control.

(21) The system of internal control should:

- be embedded in the operations of the company and form part of its culture;
- be capable of responding quickly to evolving risks to the business arising from factors within the company and to changes in the business environment; and
- include procedures for reporting immediately to appropriate levels of management any significant control failings or weaknesses that are identified together with details of corrective action being undertaken.

(22) A sound system of internal control reduces, but cannot eliminate, the possibility of poor judgement in decision-making; human error; control processes being deliberately circumvented by employees and others; management overriding controls; and the occurrence of unforeseeable circumstances.

(23) A sound system of internal control therefore provides reasonable, but not absolute, assurance that a company will not be hindered in achieving its business objectives, or in the orderly and legitimate conduct of its business, by circumstances which may reasonably be foreseen. A system of internal control cannot, however, provide protection with certainty against a company failing to meet its business objectives or all material errors, losses, fraud, or breaches of laws or regulations.

('Internal Control – Revised Guidance for Directors on the Combined Code' – Financial Reporting Council – October 2005)

3 Features of internal control systems

COSO model of internal control

In 1992 COSO (Committee of Sponsoring Organisations) stated that effective internal control systems consist of five integrated elements.

Control environment

The control environment can be thought of as management's **attitude**, **actions** and **awareness** of the need for internal controls.

If senior management do not care about internal controls and feel that it is not worthwhile introducing internal controls then the control system will be weak.

Management can try to summarise their commitment to controls in a number of ways:

- Behave with integrity and ethics (corporate governance will be considered in the next session).
- Maintain an appropriate culture in the organisation.
- Set up a good structure – for example, an independent internal audit function, and have segregation of duties.
- Set proper authorisation limits.
- Employ appropriately qualified staff and conduct staff training.

When auditors assess the control systems of business for the audit, if the environment is poor they will place no reliance on any detailed control procedures.

Risk assessment

Risk assessment (as discussed in chapter 3) feeds directly into the internal control system. A risk assessment must be performed and should identify:

- **Controllable risks** – for these risks internal control procedures can be established.
- **Uncontrollable risks** – for these risks the company may be able to minimise the risk in other ways outside the internal control environment. Uncontrollable risks could be risks that are caused by the external environment that the company operates in. For example, the best internal control processes in the world cannot reduce the risk of inflation or the economy going into recession.

Control activities

Once controllable risks have been identified, actual specific control activities can be undertaken to reduce those risks. There is a huge variety of control activities that companies can adopt at all levels of management and in all parts of the organisation.

Due to the need to adapt and change control systems, most companies use a variety of different control processes to ensure that the business achieves its objectives.

The typical processes that could be used are:

- having a defined **organisation structure.** All staff need to understand how their role fits in with the rest of the organisation to aid their understanding of the job. They need to know who to report to on a daily basis and also points of contact when they need to deal with other departments or divisions;
- having **contracts of employment** with individuals at all levels. Contracts of employment guide an employees behaviour. Typically they include hours of work, job title, salary and pension entitlements, holiday, data protection rules through to codes of dress. A major control within the contract of employment is the section on disciplinary action where it is outlined what constitutes a disciplinary procedure and the resulting event which will usually include dismissal;
- establishing **policies**, and subsequently procedures to ensure the policies are followed. Organisations typically have policies on health and safety, travel expenses, dignity at work, etc. Procedures might include the setting up of an audit department to ensure that the policies are adhered to;

- setting up a suitable **discipline and reward system**. Discipline has already been mentioned, however, rewards can also control an individuals behaviour. If an employee knows that there is a month-end bonus for meeting a particular sales target then most if not all of their actions will be focussed on that outcome. The objective is performance and conformance. However, if rewards are not structured correctly they can lead to 'dysfunctional behaviour' which is covered later in the chapter;
- ensuring a system of **performance appraisal and feedback**. Appraisals are usually at least an annual event (perhaps more often whilst an employee is being trained). During the appraisal the manager and employee should have an opportunity to discuss whether the job is being performed satisfactorily, whether previous objectives have been met, and what any future objectives are. An employees behaviour is controlled via an appraisal since they know that their manager will be watching their work in order that a discussion can be held. It is an opportunity for the manager and employee to feedback on any issues that concern them or activities which may have been performed well.

Information and communication

In order for managers to operate the internal controls, they need information and therefore a good information system must be set up. The information provided to managers must be:

- Timely.
- Accurate (and therefore reliable).
- Understandable.
- Relevant to the actions being taken.

Computer systems have led to increased quality of information being provided to managers but the systems must be integrated into the business strategies if they are to provide what managers need.

Information systems and information management are a specific part of this syllabus because they are so important to the successful running and control of business. These topics are covered in more detail in other chapters.

Monitoring

The company may have produced a very good internal control system but it must be monitored. If the system is not monitored it will be very difficult to assess whether it is out of control and needs amendment. Internal control systems are also dynamic in that they need to evolve over time as the business evolves.

The internal audit function is often the key monitor of the internal control system. Internal auditors will examine the controls and control system, identify where controls have failed so that the failures can be rectified, and also make recommendations to management for new and improved systems. More will be seen in later chapters on internal audit.

Elements of an internal control system

COSO identify five elements of an effective control system.

(1) **Control environment**

This is sometimes referred to as the 'tone at the top' of the organisation. It describes the ethics and culture of the organisation, which provide a framework within which other aspects of internal control operate. The control environment is set by the tone of management, its philosophy and management style, the way in which authority is delegated, the way in which staff are organised and developed, and the commitment of the board of directors.

The control environment has been defined by the Institute of Internal Auditors as: 'The attitude and actions of the board and management regarding the significance of control within the organisation. The control environment provides the discipline and structure for the achievement of the primary objectives of the system of internal control.

The control environment includes the following elements:

- Management's philosophy and operating style.
- Organisational structure.
- Assignment of authority and responsibility.
- Human resource policies and practices.
- Competence of personnel.

(2) **Risk assessment**

There is a connection between the objectives of an organisation and the risks to which it is exposed. In order to make an assessment of risks, objectives for the organisation must be established. Having established the objectives, the risks involved in achieving those objectives should be identified and assessed, and this assessment should form the basis for deciding how the risks should be managed.

The risk assessment should be conducted for each business within the organisation, and should consider, for example:

- **internal factors,** such as the complexity of the organisation, organisational changes, staff turnover levels, and the quality of staff
- **external factors,** such as changes in the industry and economic conditions, technological changes, and so on.

The risk assessment process should also distinguish between:

- **risks that are controllable:** management should decide whether to accept the risk, or to take measures to control or reduce the risk
- **risks that are not controllable:** management should decide whether to accept the risk, or whether to withdraw partially or entirely from the business activity, so as to avoid the risk.

(3) **Control activities**

These are policies and procedures that ensure that the decisions and instructions of management are carried out. Control activities occur at all levels within an organisation, and include authorisations, verifications, reconciliations, approvals, segregation of duties, performance reviews and asset security measures. These control activities are commonly referred to as internal controls.

(4) **Information and communication**

An organisation must gather information and communicate it to the right people so that they can carry out their responsibilities. Managers need both internal and external information to make informed business decisions and to report externally. The quality of information systems is a key factor in this aspect of internal control.

(5) **Monitoring**

The internal control system must be monitored. This element of an internal control system is associated with internal audit, as well as general supervision. It is important that deficiencies in the internal control system should be identified and reported up to senior management and the board of directors.

COSO model applied to fraud prevention

The main elements of an internal control system should be in place for dealing with fraud. In general terms, managing the risks of fraud is similar to the management of other types of risk and consists of the following elements:

- **Control environment.** Management should show an active interest in the prevention and detection of fraud. There should also be a fraud policy statement on how to respond to suspicions of fraud, to ensure that timely and effective action is taken in a consistent manner, and that management responsibilities are clear. For example, should initial suspicions be reported to the line manager in whose area of operations the suspected fraud is taking place, or should the matter be reported to senior accounts management for investigation?
- **Risk recognition and assessment**
  - Identify risk areas. Management should identify those areas that are vulnerable to fraud risk.
  - Activities where the risks might be high include cash handling and payments, purchasing and payroll.
- **Assess the scale of the risk.** The scale of the risk depends on the probability of fraud and the size of potential losses if fraud occurs. It also depends on the measures that are already in place to prevent fraud, and their apparent effectiveness. The scale of the risk to be considered is the 'residual risk' after allowing for the existing control measures.
- **Control activities and procedures.** The responsibility for the management of each risk to specific individuals. Specific controls are suggested below.

- **Information: monitoring and reporting.** Information should be provided regularly to management so that they can monitor performance with respect to efficiency and effectiveness in achieving targets, economy and quality. Effective monitoring can detect certain types of fraudulent activity. A company might use internal auditors to investigate a problem, after line management have established the basic facts. Any risk of continuing fraud should be dealt with if possible, for example by halting further payments or changing operating procedures until the matter is resolved.
- **Monitoring activities and correcting deficiencies**
  - Identify the need for revised controls. The adequacy of existing controls should be evaluated. Where appropriate, the need for specific additional controls should be identified, to reduce or eliminate the risk of fraud.
  - Implement the revised controls.
  - Monitor the implementation of the revised controls, to assess their effectiveness. One way of doing this is to carry out an internal audit investigation.

'The risk management cycle should be treated as an iterative process. If the implementation of revised controls is not sufficient to eliminate the threat of fraud, then the cycle must begin again' (HM Treasury).

Test your understanding 1

In 1992 COSO stated that effective internal control systems consist of five integrated elements. These included: (Select all that apply.)

A Risk

B Control activities

C Control environment

D Monitoring

E Information and communication

Test your understanding 2

COSO categorises objective setting into four categories. These do include: (Select all that apply.)

A Strategic

B Management

C Operational

D Reporting

Test your understanding 3

Five elements make up an effective internal control system. Which of the following is regarded as the most important?

A Risk assessment

B Monitoring

C Information and communication

D Control environment

Operational features of internal control systems

There are considered to be three features of a sound internal control system:

EMBEDDED WITHIN OPERATIONS AND NOT TREATED AS A SEPARATE EXERCISE.
ABLE TO RESPOND TO CHANGING RISKS WITHIN AND OUTSIDE THE COMPANY.
SOUND INTERNAL CONTROL SYSTEM
INCLUDES PROCEDURES FOR REPORTING CONTROL FAILINGS OR WEAKNESSES

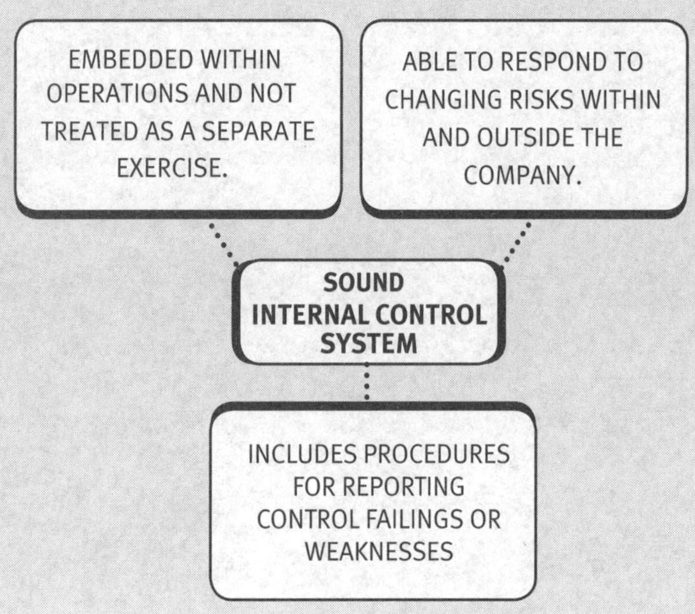

More on sound internal control systems

The Turnbull guidance described three features of a sound internal control system:

- Firstly, the principles of internal control should be **embedded** within the organisation's structures, procedures and culture. Internal control should not be seen as a stand-alone set of activities and by embedding it into the fabric of the organisation's infrastructure, awareness of internal control issues becomes everybody's business and this contributes to effectiveness.
- Secondly, internal control systems should be capable of **responding quickly** to evolving risks to the business arising from factors within the company and to changes in the business environment. The speed of reaction is an important feature of almost all control systems. Any change in the risk profile or environment of the organisation will necessitate a change in the system and a failure or slowness to respond may increase the vulnerability to internal or external trauma.
- Thirdly, sound internal control systems include **procedures for reporting** immediately to appropriate levels of management any significant control failings or weaknesses that are identified, together with details of corrective action being undertaken. Information flows to relevant levels of management capable and empowered to act on the information are essential in internal control systems. Any failure, frustration, distortion or obfuscation of information flows can compromise the system. For this reason, formal and relatively rigorous information channels are often instituted in organisations seeking to maximise the effectiveness of their internal control systems.

Test your understanding 4

J Company is suffering from working capital problems and the directors wish to make several changes to internal controls over purchases, inventory and sales in order to try and improve cash flow. They feel that currently there is no real commitment or belief in the internal controls system. The sales director keeps high levels of finished goods on site to give customers plenty of choice and the purchasing manager keeps high levels of raw materials as he is afraid of shortages. Each blames the other for J Company's current problems. Suppliers are paid within 25 days despite agreed terms being 30 days because the CEO wishes to maintain good relationships with them. Customers are encouraged to take credit with J Company in order to increase sales. Staff are generally well paid (with sales related bonuses) and staff turnover is low. J Company is seen as a good place to work and management are respected.

Which of the following are likely to be reasons that embedding the principles of internal controls in J's culture will be difficult?

Select **all** that apply.

A There is a blame culture with the sales and purchasing managers each feeling the other is responsible for cash flow problems.

B Senior management are not fully committed to solving the working capital problems.

C Sales related bonuses encourage staff to think of increasing sales rather than whether the debt is recoverable.

D Staff turnover is low meaning staff will be set in their ways.

E Staff are well paid and happy in the workplace.

4 The detail of controls

As discussed in the COSO model of internal control, specific control activities will be undertaken to reduce risks. Some examples of organisational controls include:

Segregation of duties

Most accounting transactions can be broken down into three separate duties: authorisation or initiation of the transaction, the handling of the asset that is the subject of the transaction, and the recording of the transaction. This reduces the risk of fraud and the risk of error.

For example, in the purchases system, the same individual should not have responsibility for:

- Making a purchase;
- Making the payment;
- Recording the purchase and payment in the accounts.

If one individual had responsibility for all of these activities they could record fictitious purchases (for personal use) and pay themselves for transactions that had not occurred, which is fraudulent.

Also segregation of duties makes it easier to spot unintentional mistakes.

Physical controls

Physical controls are measures and procedures to protect physical assets against theft or unauthorised access and use. They include:

- using a safe to hold cash and valuable documents;
- using a secure entry system to buildings or areas within;
- dual custody of valuable assets, so that two people are required to obtain access;
- periodic inventory checks;
- hiring security guards and using closed-circuit TV cameras.

Authorisation and approval

Authorisation and approval controls are established to ensure that a transaction must not proceed unless an authorised individual has given his approval, possibly in writing.

For **spending transactions**, an organisation might establish **authorisation limits**, whereby an individual manager is authorised to approve certain types of transaction up to a certain maximum value.

Management control

Controls are exercised by management on the basis of information they receive.

- **Top level reviews.** The board of directors or senior management might call for a performance report on the progress of the organisation towards its goals. For example, senior management might review a report on the progress of the organisation toward achieving its budget targets. Questions should be asked by senior management, prompting responses at lower management levels. In this way, top level reviews are a control activity.
- **Activity controls**. At departmental or divisional level, management should receive reports that review performance or highlight exceptions. Functional reviews should be more frequent than top-level reviews, on a daily, weekly or monthly basis. As with top-level reviews, questions should be asked by management that initiate control activity. An example of control by management is the provision of regular performance reports, such as variance reports, comparing actual results with a target or budget.

Supervision

Supervision is oversight of the work of other individuals, by someone in a position of responsibility. Supervisory controls help to ensure that individuals do the tasks they are required to and perform them properly.

Organisation

Organisation controls refer to the controls provided by the organisation's structure, such as:

- the separation of an organisation's activities and operations into departments or responsibility centres, with a clear division of responsibilities
- delegating authority within the organisation
- establishing reporting lines within the organisation
- co-ordinating the activities of different departments or groups, e.g. by setting up committees or project teams.

Arithmetic and accounting

Controls are provided by:

- recording transactions properly in the accounting system
- being able to trace each individual transaction through the accounting records
- checking arithmetical calculations, such as double-checking the figures in an invoice before sending it to a customer (sales invoice) or approving it for payment (purchase invoice) to make sure that they are correct.

Personnel controls

Controls should be applied to the selection and training of employees, to make sure that: suitable individuals are appointed to positions within the organisation; individuals should have the appropriate personal qualities, experience and qualifications where required; individuals are given **suitable induction and training**, to ensure that they carry out their tasks efficiently and effectively.

Staff should also be given **training** in the purpose of controls and the need to apply them. Specific training about controls should help to increase employee awareness and understanding of the risks of failing to apply them properly.

Remember that any controls recommended in the exam should **cost less than the benefits** they bring. For example, you would not recommend the hiring of a security guard at £35,000 per annum to watch over the petty cash tin which held £100.

Test your understanding 5 – Types of control (Integration)

Recommend the types of control that a company could put in place for the following risks:

(1) Shoplifting from a retail business.

(2) Goods being sent to customers but not invoiced.

(3) Poor quality supplies being purchased.

(4) Incorrect prices being charged.

Test your understanding 6

The internal control whereby an accounting transaction is broken into three separate tasks – initiation, handling and reporting, and dealt with by three different staff, is called:

A Authorisation and approval

B Supervision

C Segregation of duties

D Arithmetic and accounting

Test your understanding 7

The risk that orders could be taken from a customer that is unable to pay or unlikely to pay for a long time could be controlled by:

A Checking that all goods delivered notes are matched to an invoice

B All new customers being subject to a credit check

C Picking goods for despatch by using a copy of the customer's order

D Customer statements being sent out

Test your understanding 8

X plc has been criticised for its apparent lack of internal control. Staff behaviour is considered to be unprofessional, management don't appear to reprimand staff for this (often because their allocated staff changes frequently) and there is no annual assessment or feedback on staff. Which of the following controls should help to reduce these problems? (Select all that apply.)

A Organisation structure

B Contracts of employment

C Policies and procedures

D Discipline and rewards

E Performance appraisals

Test your understanding 9

The COSO framework consists of 8 interrelated components which include: (Select all that apply.)

A External environment

B Risk assessment

C Control activities

D Monitoring

Classification of controls

Controls can be understood as falling within three broad categories:

- Financial controls;
- Non-financial quantitative controls;
- Non-financial qualitative controls.

Financial controls

- These controls express financial targets and spending limits.
- Examples include
  - budgetary control
  - controls over sales, purchases, payroll and inventory cycles.

Sales cycle

Objectives of controls

The objectives of controls in the sales cycle are to ensure that:

- sales are made to valid customers
- sales are recorded accurately
- all sales are recorded
- cash is collected within a reasonable period.

Below is a summary of the sales cycle, showing examples of possible risks and the related controls:

Process	**Risks**	**Control procedures**
Receive an order.	Orders may be taken from customers that are unable to pay or unlikely to pay for a long time.	All new customers subject to credit check.
Goods are despatched to customer.	Incorrect goods may be sent to customers leading to loss of goodwill.	Pick goods using a copy of the customer's order.
Invoice is raised.	Invoices may be missed, incorrectly raised or sent to the wrong customer.	Checked that all goods delivered notes (GDNs) match an invoice.
Sale is recorded.	Invoiced sales may be inaccurately recorded.	Customer statements sent out (customers let you know if error).
Cash received.	Customer may not pay for goods.	Review aged debt listing and investigate (customer underpaid).
Cash recorded.	Cash received may be stolen.	Regular banking/physical security over cash (i.e. a safe).
Receive an order.	Orders may not be recorded accurately.	Confirm order back to customer (or) get all orders in writing.
	Orders may be taken from customers that are unable to pay or unlikely to pay for a long time = financial loss.	All new customers subject to credit check. Perform regular credit checks on existing customers. Credit limit check before order is accepted.
	Orders cannot be fulfilled and therefore customer goodwill is lost (and possibly the customer).	Check inventory system before issuing order. Automatic re-ordering system linked to customer order system.

Goods are despatched to customer.	Goods may not be despatched for orders made. Incorrect goods may be sent to customers leading to loss of goodwill or goods may not be in inventory.	Use sequentially numbered customer order pads. Send a copy to the warehouse where they are filed numerically and sequence is checked to ensure that all are there (none missing). Pick goods using a copy of the customer's order. Get the copy signed by the picker as correct. When GDN is raised check it matches with the customer order (staple together and file). Get the customer to sign a copy of the GDN and return to the company. Use sequentially numbered GDNs, file a copy numerically and check that they are all there.
Invoice is raised.	Invoices may be missed, incorrectly raised or sent to the wrong customer. Credit notes may be raised incorrectly, missed or to cover cash being mis-appropriated.	Copy of sequentially numbered GDN sent to invoicing dept, stapled to copy of the invoice, checked all GDNs are there and having invoice to match. On copy of the invoice sign as agreed to original order and GDN, signed as agreed to customer price list, signed as agreed it adds up properly. Credit notes to be allocated to invoice it relates. Authorised by manager and sequence check done on a regular basis.

Sale is recorded.	Invoiced sales may be inaccurately recorded, missed or recorded for the wrong customer.	Review receivables ledger for credit balances (paid for goods but no debtor recorded). Perform a receivables ledger reconciliation (check info in individual ledger matches that in nominal). Computer controls. Double check back to invoice. Perform receivables ledger control account reconciliation. Customer statements sent out (customers let you know if error).
Cash received.	Incorrect amounts may be received.	Agree cash receipt back to the invoice.
	Customer may not pay for goods.	Review receivables ledger for credit balances (customer overpaid). Review aged debt listing and investigate (customer underpaid). Review aged debt listing regularly, phone when overdue by 30 days, another letter at 45 days final letter threatening legal action at 60 days. Refer receivable to solicitor.
Cash recorded.	Cash maybe incorrectly recorded or recorded against the wrong customer account.	Customer statements. Perform a bank reconciliation. Customer statements.
	Cash received may be stolen.	Regular banking/physical security over cash (i.e. a safe). Reconciliation of banking to cash receipts records. Segregation of duties.

The **purchases cycle** is similar to the sales cycle but concentrates upon the risk of staff ordering goods for themselves, more goods being ordered than necessary (leading to obsolescence or theft), payments being made to fictitious suppliers (theft), and goods being overpriced by the supplier.

Controls might include segregation of duties so that one staff member cannot order goods for themselves or payments be made to a fictitious supplier. Recruitment and training procedures in addition to a fraud policy statement might help. Agreeing a supplier invoice to a supplier quote or price list and recomputing the invoice for quantity, price and tax will ensure that the correct amount enters the financial statements.

Bank and cash controls

Bank and cash

Objectives of controls

The objectives of controls over bank and cash are to ensure that:

- cash balances are safeguarded
- cash balances are kept to a minimum
- money can only be extracted from bank accounts for authorised purposes.

Below is a summary showing examples of possible risks to cash and bank accounts and the related controls:

Risk	Control
Cash is stolen from the premises.	Safes/strongroom/locked cashbox with restricted access. Tills emptied regularly.
Money is taken from bank accounts for unauthorised purposes (i.e. stolen).	Restricted list of cheque signatories. Regular bank reconciliations reviewed by person with suitable level of authority.

Risks	Control procedures
Cash is stolen from the premises.	• Safes/strongroom/locked cashbox with restricted access. • Security locks. • Swipe card access. • Key access to tills. • Night safes. • Imprest system. • Use of security services for large cash movements. • People making bankings vary routes and timings. • Tills emptied regularly. • Frequent bankings of cash and cheques received.
Money is taken from bank accounts for unauthorised purposes (i.e. stolen).	• Restricted list of cheque signatories. • Dual signatures for large amounts. • Similar controls over bank transfers and on-line banking, e.g. secure passwords and pin numbers. • Cheque books and cheque stationery locked away. • Regular bank reconciliations reviewed by person with suitable level of authority.

Controls in other departments

Controls over **human resources** i.e. employees, managers and directors might include:

- Recruitment policies including the completion of an application form and the checking of any relevant qualifications to independent documentation. e.g. certificates;
- References being taken up prior to appointment;
- Continuous training;
- Eligibility to work in the country (visa);
- Contract of employment.

Controls over the **distribution department** might include:

- The human resources controls listed above;
- Signed goods received and goods despatched notes;
- Regular inventory counts;
- Monitored CCTV cameras around the distribution depot;
- Security guards at exits;
- Bag searches when staff leave their shift.

Test your understanding 10

B has a chain of service stations across motorways in Country X. These service stations sell fuel, confectionary and newspapers and also have a café offering hot food.

The directors of B are concerned that there have been incidences of fraud in the café's in several service stations and they have linked this to poor recruitment policies. The HR department insists that they carry out rigorous checks before offering positions in the service stations but the directors wish extra controls to be implemented. Since staff turnover in the service stations is so high, it is expected that new controls should make a difference quickly.

Which of the following controls over HR should be implemented to make fraud less likely in the café's at the service stations?

Select **all** that apply.

A Include induction training for each new member of staff.

B Only candidates with recent experience of working in a café or restaurant should be recruited.

C Each new staff member should provide two recent character references before they are offered a job at B.

D New staff members should be asked to work a six week probationary period before they are given a contract to ensure their suitability for the job.

E Shift patterns and teams should be varied so that no staff member works alone in the café or with the same team members on a regular basis.

Test your understanding 11

B is a training college offering courses in professional qualifications. Each course has a tutor who lectures from the front of the room and passes around a class register at the start of the day which students sign to confirm attendance. The register is systems generated and any student whose name does not appear on it due to late enrolment is asked to add their name and signature to the bottom so that B can invoice them for the course.

On day one of the course, text books and notes are available at the front of the classroom for students to collect on their way into the room. A separate materials register is left at the front of the room for students to sign to acknowledge they have received materials.

Recently B's management has received reports of students attending class for the first session and then not returning after morning break. In addition, there have been cases of students being observed simply passing the class register on instead of signing or adding their name to it. B is concerned that it may be losing revenue if these incidents are occurring on a larger scale.

Which of the following control procedures could help prevent revenue loss in B?

Select **all** that apply.

A Class registers to be taken around the room by and signed under tutor supervision.

B Class register taken later in the day rather than first thing.

C Material to be given or sent to students on enrolment rather than left at the front of the room.

D Tutor to carry out head count to ensure the number of signatures on the register matches the number of people in the room. Discrepancies checked immediately.

E Only students enrolled and whose names appear on the register should be allowed to attend the course.

Non-financial quantitative controls

- These controls focus on targets against which performance can be measured and monitored.
- Examples include
  - balanced scorecard targets
  - TQM quality measures

- It is important that a feedback loop exists:
  - performance target (standard) set
  - actual result recorded
  - compared with target
  - control action taken (if required).

Non-financial qualitative controls

- These form the day-to-day controls over most employees in organisations.
- Examples include
  - employee training
  - management control methods (such as organisation structure, contracts of employment)
  - physical controls
  - project management.

The Bribery Act

The Bribery Act is a type of non-financial control. It came in to force in the UK on 1st July 2011 and it is designed to bring the UK in line with international norms on anti-corruption legislation. It will make it a criminal offence to give or receive a bribe. It will also introduce a corporate offence of failing to prevent bribery.

The Serious Fraud Office will be able to prosecute both domestic and foreign companies, providing they have some presence in the UK. Bribes committed in the UK and abroad could be prosecuted under the Act.

Some experts have argued the new law could put British companies at a disadvantage as it goes further than similar legislation in other jurisdictions.

Individuals will face up to 10 years in prison and an unlimited fine if found guilty of committing bribery.

For example, a former court worker became the first person to be convicted under the Bribery Act 2010. He was jailed for six years having been convicted of bribery and misconduct in a public office after admitting that he received a bribe in his role as an administrative officer at a Magistrates' Court. The administrative officer pleaded guilty for requesting and receiving a £500 bribe to "get rid" of a speeding charge and to misconduct in public office for other similar offences. He was sentenced to three years for bribery and six years for misconduct in a public office, to be served concurrently.

Test your understanding 12

If found guilty of committing bribery, the UK Bribery Act states that individuals will face:

A Up to 5 years in prison and an unlimited fine

B Up to 10 years in prison and an unlimited fine

C Up to 5 years in prison and a £10,000 fine

D Up to 10 years in prison and a £10,000 fine

5 Evaluation of an internal control system

Developing an adequate control system

The first step in designing an adequate control system is to ascertain the objectives of the system in question. For example, the system may be human resources and their objectives are many, but include sourcing, recruiting, training and retaining quality staff.

Secondly, research should be conducted regarding the current systems in place (if any) and communication with employees (questionnaires and interviews for example) would help to collate useful information.

Inputs to the process should be identified to check whether they meet the intended objective (or create the desired output). For example, the objective of retaining quality staff will not be met if, say, an appraisal process is not carried out whereby well-trained but unhappy staff repeatedly leave the company.

In order to work out whether the system currently works, the company should have a comparator set up, for example, a target labour turnover indicator. If this is met or surpassed then action should be taken since it demonstrates that the current system, in say HR, of retaining a certain level of staff, is not working.

In this example, the control system appears to work – it has identified a problem with labour turnover, however, it has also identified a problem in the HR process. This now needs to be resolved.

New controls can be implemented, such as regular appraisals – giving an employee a forum to discuss their job satisfaction, or setting up a new policy on staff welfare which might include an open-door policy, a whistleblowing policy or even just a suggestion box.

These new processes now also need controls putting in place. Again indicators that will be acted on are required. Appraisals need to be done for all staff on, say, a yearly basis. The number of suggestions put in the suggestion box needs to be logged and a record kept of the number which have been actioned.

A responsible individual then needs to ascertain whether these extra controls have led to a reduction in the number of leavers and whether this is now at a satisfactory level. If not, then further corrective action needs to be taken.

Costs v benefits

The internal control system of the business is no different to other business activities – the benefits of maintaining the system must outweigh the costs of operating it. As part of the monitoring process therefore management must consider the costs and benefits.

However, it can be difficult to quantify those costs and benefits as they are often not direct cash costs.

Costs of an internal control system will include:

- time of management involved in the design of the system
- implementation:
  - costs of IT consultants to implement new software
  - training all staff in new procedures
- maintenance of system:
  - software upgrades
  - monitoring and review.

Benefits are to be found in the reduction of the risks and achievement of business objectives.

Limitations of internal control systems

Warnings should be given regarding over-reliance on any system, noting in particular that:

- A good internal control system cannot turn a poor manager into a good one.
- The system can only provide reasonable assurance regarding the achievement of objectives – all internal control systems are at risk from mistakes or errors.
- Internal control systems can be by-passed by collusion and management override.
- Controls are only designed to cope with routine transactions and events.
- There are resource constraints in provision of internal control systems, limiting their effectiveness.

To protect employees health and safety whilst at work a statement might be issued that all staff are supposed to follow. This statement might include:

The company aims to protect the health, safety and welfare of people at work, and to safeguard others, mainly members of the public, who may be exposed to risks from the way work is carried out...

HSE believes in firm but fair enforcement of health and safety law. This should be informed by the principles of proportionality in applying the law and securing compliance; consistency of approach; targeting of enforcement action; transparency about how the regulator operates and what those regulated may expect; and accountability for the regulator's actions...

Those whom the law protects and those on whom it places duties (dutyholders) expect that action taken by enforcing authorities to achieve compliance or bring dutyholders to account for non-compliance should be proportionate to any risks to health and safety, or to the seriousness of any breach...

...making sure that contacts are targeted primarily on those whose activities give rise to the most serious risks or where the hazards are least well controlled; and that action is focused on the dutyholders who are responsible for the risk and who are best placed to control it – whether employers, manufacturers, suppliers, or others...

Decisions on enforcement action are discretionary, involving judgement by the enforcer. All enforcing authorities should have arrangements in place to promote consistency in the exercise of discretion, including effective arrangements for liaison with other enforcing authorities...

Transparency

Transparency means helping dutyholders to understand what is expected of them and what they should expect from the enforcing authorities...

Investigations are undertaken in order to determine:

- causes;
- whether action has been taken or needs to be taken to prevent a recurrence and to secure compliance with the law;
- lessons to be learnt and to influence the law and guidance;
- what response is appropriate to a breach of the law...

While the primary purpose of the enforcing authorities is to ensure that dutyholders manage and control risks effectively, thus preventing harm, prosecution is an essential part of enforcement...

Prosecution of individuals

Subject to the above, enforcing authorities should identify and prosecute or recommend prosecution of individuals if they consider that a prosecution is warranted. In particular, they should consider the management chain and the role played by individual directors and managers, and should take action against them where the inspection or investigation reveals that the offence was committed with their consent or connivance or to have been attributable to neglect on their part and where it would be appropriate to do so in accordance with this policy. Where appropriate, enforcing authorities should seek disqualification of directors under the Company Directors Disqualification Act 1986.

Publicity

Enforcing authorities should make arrangements for the publication annually of the names of all the companies and individuals who have been convicted in the previous 12 months of breaking health and safety law...

Action by the courts

Health and safety law gives the courts considerable scope to punish offenders and to deter others, including imprisonment for some offences. Unlimited fines may be imposed by higher courts.

Death at work

Where there has been a breach of the law leading to a work-related death, enforcing authorities need to consider whether the circumstances of the case might justify a charge of manslaughter or corporate manslaughter...If in the course of their health and safety investigation, the enforcing authorities find evidence suggesting manslaughter or corporate manslaughter, they should pass it on to the police.

An example of compliance failure could include the death of an employee several years ago.

The employee was clearing a dyke bank of green waste material using a mechanical digger. The employee was trained to be wearing a lifejacket in the event that the digger should slip down the dyke bank into the water, or if the employee fell out of the cab into the dyke water.

The employee found the lifejacket cumbersome to wear and so, despite his training, he chose not to wear it. Unfortunately the digger did slip down the bank into the water, and the employee died from drowning. Several compliance issues were raised during an investigation:

(1) Had the employee been sufficiently trained to know that the wearing of the lifejacket was compulsory? When was the last time he was trained?

(2) Was the lifejacket operational? (The canisters blowing up the lifejacket have a finite life.)

(3) The employee was trapped by the digger, so would the lifejacket have helped?

(4) Should there have been a second employee assisting the first, so in the event of an accident he could have tried to save the employees life or report the accident to the emergency services?

(5) Should 'second' employees be advised to assist a drowning colleague?

Many more questions were asked during the investigation, but the employee had ultimately failed to comply with company rules by not wearing the lifejacket. And the company had failed to implement sufficient controls to prevent such an accident.

This compliance failure would be allocated a 'serious' rating due to a 'death at work' and post-investigation many new controls would be implemented to prevent any future occurrence. Employee training would probably feature heavily within any new controls.

Test your understanding 13

Theft of the petty cash tin occurred at Y plc. This was the second time it had happened in three years. The tin held £750 in the first instance and £7,500 in the second instance (due to a new van being paid for later in the day). Normally the tin would only hold around £100.

Controls that should be in place to prevent these thefts are: (Select all that apply.)

A Insurance

B Maximum limits on the value of cash held

C Confidentiality

D Keeping the tin locked when unused

Test your understanding 14

A new member of staff has started working in the receivables department of ABC Ltd. She previously worked in the sales department at ABC's main competitor. Which controls should be implemented to ensure that the new staff member operates in the correct manner at ABC? (Select all that apply.)

A Employment contract

B Confidentiality clause

C Training

D Supervision

Test your understanding 15

Examples of non-financial quantitative controls include: (Select all that apply.)

A An organisation structure

B Physical controls

C The number of faulty goods returned

D The percentage of staff attending training courses each year

Test your understanding 16

The risk that money could be stolen from PQ's bank account could be reduced by: (Select all that apply.)

A Having a restricted list of dual cheque signatories

B Locking away cheque books

C Annual bank reconciliations

D Having secure passwords and PIN numbers

Test your understanding 17

A sole trader, Yu Yang, owns a new consultancy business employing ten highly-skilled, autonomous staff.

Yu yang has just attended a new business education lunch, run by a government advisory committee, set up to help new business. The topic of discussion at lunch was internal control systems. Yu yang has come back to the office enthused by the lunch and looking to start the implementation of new controls.

Advise Yu Yang which THREE of the following are limitations to the effectiveness of internal controls within his consultancy business.

A An employees could ignore the internal control

B Internal control systems will only target manufacturing companies

C Additional control could negatively affect employee motivation

D Internal controls can slow down the companies' response time to market

E There likelihood of a major accident is low given the work of Yu Yang's business, therefore internal control is not necessary

F Internal controls are only needed if the company is a limited company

Test your understanding 18

TT is a passenger ferry operator which operates several vessels between busy ports in countries A and B.

One of TT's larger ships was damaged in high winds during a crossing. The damage led to multiple passenger injuries and compensation claims against TT which the company was not adequately insured for. It was acknowledged that TT should not have operated the particular ferry service due to the weather conditions and that control failures were largely responsible for the incident and injuries.

TT has a history of control weakness and the internal audit team have listed the main weaknesses which were in evidence on the day of the incident. The management of TT now wish to establish which control weaknesses contributed to the incident.

Which of the following weaknesses would have made the incident more likely to occur?

Select **all** that apply..

A Passengers not being provided with suitable safety equipment to use in an emergency.

B Crew members failing to secure the ship adequately against the weather on departure due to time constraints.

C TT's internal procedures lacking routine weather checks and instead relying on each ship's captain to decide locally on safety to operate the service.

D Inadequate checks on the relevance and extent of insurance over incidents involving weather damage.

E The captain overriding speed controls in order to meet the scheduled arrival time.

Test your understanding 19 – G Manufacturing (Case study)

Scenario

G is a manufacturing company that employs 800 production staff and 90 administrative staff. The company operates from a single site.

Trigger

A new Chief Executive was appointed in July. She was recruited from a much larger manufacturing company that is an indirect competitor of G, where she was the Marketing Director.

Since her appointment the Chief Executive has focussed on learning as much as she possibly can about the company's culture. She spent the whole of August meeting representatives from all levels of staff from within the company and other stakeholders such as customers and suppliers. She has called a board meeting to discuss her findings.

Her findings are as follows:

- The company manufactures high quality products that are popular with customers. All members of G's staff are proud to be associated with the manufacture of the products.
- G's managers and supervisors take a very relaxed approach when working with subordinates. Staff are empowered to make decisions on their own without consulting their superiors if they are confident that they are acting in the company's best interests.
- The relaxed management style has harmed the control environment immensely. Only a minority of the company's staff take the budgetary control system seriously and hardly any of them pay serious attention to variance reports. In contrast to all other departments, morale in the accounts department is very low because the members of the accounts staff feel that they waste a significant amount of time every month chasing heads of departments for reports and for other important information.
- These attitudes are echoed by external stakeholders. Customers are delighted with the quality of G's products, but often find that G's invoices and monthly statements contain errors. Suppliers claim that invoices submitted to G are settled very promptly 90% of the time, but the remainder have to be chased because G's accounts staff do not always receive accurate and complete records of orders placed and goods received.

The Chief Executive has warned the board that the control environment must be improved as a matter of priority. She proposes to send an email to all staff congratulating them on their achievements on product quality, but stating that the rather lax attitude towards management and record keeping will have to stop. Over time, she plans to impose disciplinary measures on staff who are responsible for bookkeeping errors or delays. She also proposes that G should create an internal audit department to monitor compliance with formal processes and procedures.

The Production Director has argued that the Chief Executive's proposals are counter-productive and that most of the delays and omissions are due to employees giving priority to the creation of an excellent product.

Task:

Write a report to the Board:

(a) Explaining why it is necessary to improve G's control environment; and

(b) Evaluating the Chief Executive's proposal to impose disciplinary measures on staff who are responsible for bookkeeping errors or delays.

(30 minutes)

Test your understanding 20 – U internet (Case study)

Scenario

U is an internet-based company that sells books, DVDs and CDs to consumers. U's customers are required to create an account, to which they register their name, address and credit card details. The customers must also create a password, which they must use whenever they wish to log into their account in order to update their details or place an order. Registered customers can log in and place orders very easily because all of their delivery and payment details are already on file. That feature is one of the main factors behind U's success. The other main factor is that U's software tracks each customer's purchases and uses that information to email recommendations based on past orders. Many customers buy recommended products and the proportion is growing because U's tracking software becomes increasingly accurate as more data is gathered.

Trigger

U has recently suffered a security breach involving 2,000 of its highest spending customers. One of U's analysts had been asked to write a report about those customers' buying habits. The report was required urgently and so the analyst copied the customers' files onto a memory stick, which he took home to analyse on his home PC over the weekend. He copied the final report onto the same memory stick, but lost the stick during the train journey into work.

The analyst had one of his flatmates email him a copy of the report, which was still on the hard drive of his home PC, so the report's deadline was met. The analyst did not report the loss of the memory stick because he did not wish to get into trouble for losing the data. He hoped that anybody who found the stick would simply erase the files.

Over the next two weeks, U started to receive complaints from customers that orders were being placed without the account holders' permission. U's policy in these circumstances is to seek clarification from the account holder and suggest that the order could have been placed by a family member who knew the account password. The volume of complaints was higher than usual and the analyst was asked to investigate them to determine whether there was a security problem. The analyst quickly realised that many of the complaints were from the 2,000 customers whose files were on his memory stick and that the person who had found the stick was abusing that information. He admitted the loss of the memory stick and was suspended.

U's customer services department wrote to all of those customers whose accounts had been compromised and offered to cancel any disputed charges on their accounts. The customers were also advised to contact their credit card providers and to study their card statements carefully in case the thief had used that information to defraud them. Several of these customers complained to a national newspaper and U received many further complaints concerning disputed charges, mainly from customers whose details had not been copied by the analyst.

Task:

Write a report to U's Board which:

(a) Advises on the weaknesses in both the control environment and the internal controls that led to this loss of data;

(b) Recommends, stating reasons, actions that U's board should take:

(i) to restore the confidence of its existing and potential customers;

(ii) to prevent similar problems occurring in the future.

(45 minutes)

Test your understanding 21 – College (Case study)

Scenario

A large college has several sites and employs hundreds of teaching staff.

Trigger

The college has recently discovered a serious fraud involving false billings for part-time teaching.

The fraud involved two members of staff. M is a clerk in the payroll office who is responsible for processing payments to part-time teaching staff. P is the head of the Business Studies department at the N campus. Part-time lecturers are required to complete a monthly claim form which lists the classes taught and the total hours claimed. These forms must be signed by their head of department, who sends all signed forms to M. M checks that the class codes on the claim forms are valid, that hours have been budgeted for those classes and inputs the information into the college's payroll package.

The college has a separate personnel department that is responsible for maintaining all personnel files. Additions to the payroll must be made by a supervisor in the personnel office. The payroll package is programmed to reject any claims for payment to employees whose personnel files are not present in the system.

M had gained access to the personnel department supervisor's office by asking the college security officer for the loan of a pass key because he had forgotten the key to his own office. M knew that the office would be unoccupied that day because the supervisor was attending a wedding. M logged onto the supervisor's computer terminal by guessing her password, which turned out to be the registration number of the supervisor's car. M then added a fictitious part-time employee, who was allocated to the N campus Business Studies department.

P then began making claims on behalf of the fictitious staff member and submitting them to M. M signed off the forms and input them as normal. The claims resulted in a steady series of payments to a bank account that had been opened by P. The proceeds of the fraud were shared equally between M and P.

The fraud was only discovered when the college wrote to every member of staff with a formal invitation to the college's centenary celebration. The letter addressed to the fictitious lecturer was returned as undeliverable and the personnel department became suspicious when they tried to contact this person in order to update his contact details. By then M and P had been claiming for non-existent teaching for three years.

The government department responsible for funding the college conducted an investigation and concluded that the college's management had relied excessively on the application controls programmed into administrative software and had paid too little attention to the human resources aspects of the system.

Task

Write a letter to the Dean of the college which:

(a) Advises on the weaknesses in the college's systems and procedures; and

(b) Discusses the suggestion that the human elements of control systems are frequently more important than the software elements in ensuring that records are correct.

(30 minutes)

Test your understanding 22 – V (Case study)

Scenario

V is a quoted company. Its board comprises an equal number of both executive and non-executive directors. The company has a remuneration committee, comprised entirely of non-executives.

Trigger

A major institutional investor in V has written to the chair of the remuneration committee to raise some concerns about the manner in which the performance of V's executive directors is controlled and rewarded.

At present, each of the executive directors receives a fairly substantial fixed annual salary combined with options granted under an executive share option scheme ("ESOS"). The ESOS is designed in order to align the directors' interests with those of the shareholders:

The remuneration committee reviews each director's performance during the financial year and grants a number of share options in accordance with performance.

The options are issued "at the money" (that is, the exercise price is the same as the market price) so that the directors have an incentive to increase the share price.

The options can only be exercised on a specified date that falls three years after their issue.

If a director leaves the company then any outstanding options will lapse without compensation.

The institutional investor has expressed concern about the ESOS arrangement because of the underlying financial implications of the scheme. V first introduced ESOSs in order to motivate the executive directors to act in the shareholders' interests. If the directors work towards maximising V's share price then the options will provide higher returns if they are in the money when they come due for exercise. In addition, V's directors are much less likely to reject positive net present value investment opportunities if they hold options. Normally the directors are more risk averse than the shareholders when it comes to project appraisal, but holding options makes risk-taking more appealing.

The institutional investor is concerned that the options may have encouraged dysfunctional behaviour by the directors, although it is difficult to be certain that that has arisen because of the limited information that is available to the shareholders.

The institutional investor has suggested that the executive directors should be rewarded with a simpler scheme, such as an annual profit-related bonus. At present, it is unclear whether the reward system in place provides the executive directors with meaningful feedback on their performance. As a shareholder, the investor wishes to see a clearer link between the directors' performance and their remuneration.

Task

Write a letter to the institutional investor which:

(i) Explains why the introduction of ESOSs could motivate V's executive directors to accept positive net present value (NPV) projects;

(ii) Explains how an ESOS scheme could affect the actions taken by the directors (other than the project appraisal decision).

(30 minutes)

Write a memorandum to the remuneration committee which evaluates the advantages AND disadvantages of rewarding executive directors by paying a bonus based on a simple and transparent measure such as profit.

(15 minutes)

Test your understanding 23 – Cliff (Integration)

Day-to-day internal controls are important for all businesses to maximise the efficient use of resources and profitability. Your firm has recently been appointed as auditor to Cliff, a private company that runs a chain of small supermarkets selling fresh and frozen food, and canned and dry food. Cliff has very few controls over inventory because the company trusts local managers to make good decisions regarding the purchase, sale and control of inventory, all of which is done locally. Pricing is generally performed on a costplus basis.

Each supermarket has a standalone computer system on which monthly accounts are prepared. These accounts are mailed to head office every quarter. There is no integrated inventory control, sale or purchasing system and no regular system for inventory counting. Management accounts are produced twice a year.

Trade at the supermarkets has increased in recent years and the number of supermarkets has increased. However, the quality of staff that has been recruited has fallen. Senior management at Cliff are now prepared to invest in more up-to-date systems.

Required:

(a) Describe the problems that you might expect to find at Cliff resulting from poor internal controls.

(15 minutes)

(b) Make FOUR recommendations to the senior management of Cliff for the improvement of internal controls, and explain the advantages and disadvantages of each recommendation.

(30 minutes)

Test your understanding 24 – SPD (Integration)

SPD has been approached by Q, a specialist manufacturer of extremely expensive high performance cars. Q is in the process of developing a new car that will be one of the fastest in the world. The car will be designed to be driven on public roads, but the owners of such cars often take them to private race tracks where they can be driven at very high speeds.

Q has designed an electronics system to enable an average driver to drive the car safely at high speed. The system will monitor the engine, brakes and steering and will compensate for errors that could cause a crash. The system will, for example, sense that the car is about to skid and will compensate for that. The electronics system will be based on a circuit board that Q wishes to have built by SPD.

Building Q's circuit board will pose a number of challenges for SPD. The circuit board will be subject to a great deal of vibration when the car is driven at speed. The cars are expected to last for a very long time and so there could be problems if the circuit boards deteriorate with age. The circuit board will be installed in an inaccessible part of the car where it will be difficult to inspect or maintain.

Many of the components on the board will be manufactured by SPD, but some crucial components will be supplied by a third party that has already been selected by Q.

Required:

Discuss controls that should be in place to reduce the risks faced by SPD if they accept an order from Q.

(15 minutes)

Test your understanding 25 – Rhapsody Company (Integration)

Rhapsody Co supplies a wide range of garden and agricultural products to trade and domestic customers. The company has 11 divisions, with each division specialising in the sale of specific products, for example, seeds, garden furniture, agricultural fertilizers. The company has an internal audit department which provides audit reports to the audit committee on each division on a rotational basis.

Products in the seed division are offered for sale to domestic customers via an Internet site. Customers review the product list on the Internet and place orders for packets of seeds using specific product codes, along with their credit card details, onto Rhapsody Co's secure server. Order quantities are normally between one and three packets for each type of seed. Order details are transferred manually onto the company's internal inventory control and sales system and a two part packing list is printed in the seed warehouse. Each order and packing list is given in a random alphabetical code based on the name of the employee inputting the order, the date and the products being ordered.

In the seed warehouse, the packets of seeds for each order are taken from specific bins and despatched to the customer with one copy of the packing list. The second copy of the packing list is sent to the accounts department where the inventory and sales computer is updated to show that the order has been despatched. The customer's credit card is then charged by the inventory control and sales computer. Irrecoverable debts in Rhapsody are currently 3% of the total sales.

Finally, the computer system checks that for each charge made to a customer's credit card account, the order details are on file to prove that the charge was made correctly. The order file is marked as completed confirming that the order has been despatched and payment obtained.

Required:

In respect of sales in the seeds division of Rhapsody Co

(a) identify and evaluate weaknesses in the sales system.

(25 minutes)

(b) provide a recommendation to alleviate each weakness.

(20 minutes)

Test your understanding 26 – Bassoon Ltd (Integration)

Bassoon Ltd runs a chain of shops selling electrical goods all of which are located within the same country.

It has a head office that deals with purchasing, distribution and administration. The payroll for the whole company is administered at head office.

There are 20 staff at head office and 200 staff in the company's 20 shops located in high streets and shopping malls all over the country.

Head office staff (including directors) are all salaried and paid by direct transfer to their bank accounts.

The majority of the staff at the company's shops are also paid through the central salary system, monthly in arrears. However, some students and part time staff are paid cash out of the till.

Recruitment of head office staff is initiated by the department needing the staff who generally conduct interviews and agree the terms and conditions of employment. Bassoon has an HR manager who liaises with recruitment agencies, places job adverts and maintains staff files with contracts of employment, etc.

Shop managers recruit their own staff.

Shop staff receive a basic salary based on the hours worked and commission based on sales made.

The company has a fairly sophisticated EPOS (electronic point of sale) till system at all shops that communicates directly with the head office accounting system.

All staff when making a sale have to log on with a swipe card which identifies them to the system, and means that the sales for which they are responsible are analysed by the system and commissions calculated.

Store managers have a few 'guest cards' for temporary and part time staff, who generally do not receive commissions.

Store managers and regional supervisors are paid commissions based on the performance of their store or region. Directors and other head office staff usually receive a bonus at Christmas, depending on the company's performance. This is decided on by the board in consultation with departmental managers and put through the system by the payroll manager.

The payroll manager is responsible for adding joiners to the payroll and deleting leavers as well as for implementing changes in pay rates, tax coding and other deductions and for making sure that the list of monthly transfers is communicated to the bank.

The computerised payroll system is a standard proprietary system which is sophisticated enough to incorporate the commission calculations mentioned above which are fed in directly from the EPOS system.

The company employs an IT manager who is responsible for the maintenance of all IT systems and installing new hardware and software.

Required:

Identify the risks inherent in the payroll system at Bassoon Ltd and recommend any changes which you think are appropriate.

(30 minutes)

6 Chapter summary

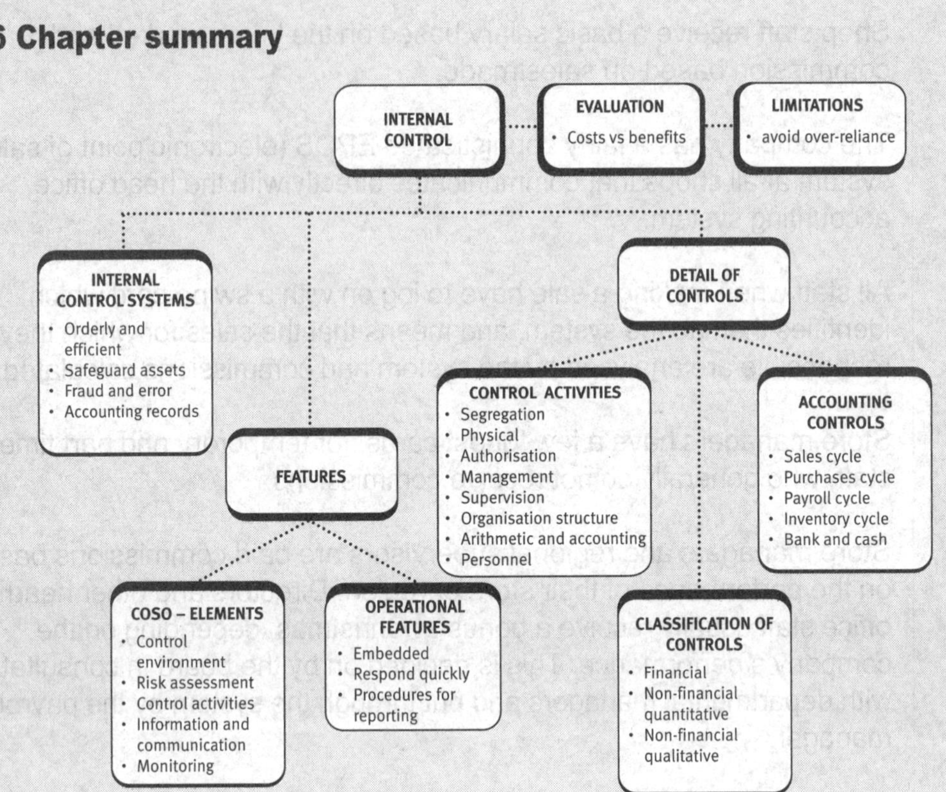
INTERNAL CONTROL
EVALUATION
• Costs vs benefits
LIMITATIONS
• avoid over-reliance
INTERNAL CONTROL SYSTEMS
• Orderly and efficient
• Safeguard assets
• Fraud and error
• Accounting records
DETAIL OF CONTROLS
FEATURES
CONTROL ACTIVITIES
• Segregation
• Physical
• Authorisation
• Management
• Supervision
• Organisation structure
• Arithmetic and accounting
• Personnel
ACCOUNTING CONTROLS
• Sales cycle
• Purchases cycle
• Payroll cycle
• Inventory cycle
• Bank and cash
COSO – ELEMENTS
• Control environment
• Risk assessment
• Control activities
• Information and communication
• Monitoring
OPERATIONAL FEATURES
• Embedded
• Respond quickly
• Procedures for reporting
CLASSIFICATION OF CONTROLS
• Financial
• Non-financial quantitative
• Non-financial qualitative

Test your understanding answers

Test your understanding 1

The correct answers are B, C, D and E – The five elements were control environment, risk assessment, control activities, information and communication and monitoring.

Test your understanding 2

The correct answers are A, C and D – The four categories of objective setting are strategic, operational, reporting and compliance.

Test your understanding 3

D

Control environment refers to the attitudes of management and in particular directors towards controls. An organisation may have all of the other five aspects of internal control in place but they cannot be relied upon if management and directors do not regard them as important. Their actions may override or disregard control failures. A poor control environment therefore can undermine an otherwise sound internal control system.

Test your understanding 4

A and B only

- Option A: A blame culture means it is unlikely that staff will integrate controls into their jobs for fear of being blamed if problems are uncovered.
- Option B: The CEO's attitude towards suppliers shows he is not committed to solving the problems as do the views of the sales director and purchasing manager.
- Option C: This may be true but it would not prevent internal controls principles being embedded within J.
- Option D: Similarly, staff who have worked in J Company for a long term may actually be more committed to solving its' problems and happy to incorporate internal controls as part of their jobs.
- Option E: Well-paid happy staff may be complacent but they may also be willing to adapt to change with minimal fuss, especially if they have respect for management.

Test your understanding 5 – Types of control (Integration)

(1) **Shoplifting**

- CCTV cameras in the shop.
- Security tagging of products.
- Stock reconciliations to detect theft.
- Employment of security guards.

(2) **Goods not invoiced**

- Reconcile goods despatch notes to invoices.
- Check sequences of goods despatch notes and invoices.
- Segregation of duties between despatch and invoicing.
- Reconcile stock movement and sales figures.

(3) **Poor quality supplies**

- Inspection of all goods when received.
- Approval of suppliers who can supply high quality.

(4) **Incorrect prices**

- Arithmetic checks on invoices.
- Computer system control to ensure that every invoice is priced on current price levels.
- Authorisation of staff who can change price levels.

Test your understanding 6

The correct answer is C – By definition.

Test your understanding 7

The correct answer is B – By definition. A ensures that all deliveries have been invoiced. C ensures the correct goods are despatched. D will remind the customer to pay but if they are unable to pay it will not help.

Test your understanding 8

The correct answers are A, B, C, D and E – All of the controls should help to some extent.

Test your understanding 9

The correct answers are B, C and D – The COSO framework does not mention the external environment, but does mention the internal environment.

Test your understanding 10

C and E only

- Option A may help staff learn about B and its operations but not guard against fraud.
- Option B may make the café run more smoothly but not guard against dishonesty.
- Option C may ensure only trustworthy staff are recruited.
- Option D may ensure suitability for the job but any dishonest recruit could just wait six weeks before perpetrating a fraud.
- Option E is not a HR control, rather an operational control.

Test your understanding 11

A, C and D

- Option A: This would ensure every student present signs the register and so is invoiced for the course.
- Option B: This would prevent students turning up, signing in and leaving but it would not pick up those students who do not sign the register at all and so do not get charged.
- Option C: This would prevent theft of material from students not enrolled however may not be practical unless students enrol early.
- Option D: This would ensure that all students signed in and could be invoiced for the course.
- Option E: This may cause a loss in revenue since provided there is room in the class students who turn up on the day should be allowed to attend. They can be invoiced later as long as their details are recorded by B.

Test your understanding 12

The correct answer is B – By definition.

Test your understanding 13

The correct answers are B, C and D – Insurance does not prevent theft. Amounts over £100 should be dealt with by cheque or bank transfer, and not through petty cash. Transactions should be kept confidential – it would appear that someone knew when to steal the tin, while large amounts were held.

Test your understanding 14

The correct answers are A, B, C and D – All of the controls should help.

Test your understanding 15

The correct answers are C and D – A and B are non-financial qualitative controls.

Test your understanding 16

The correct answers are A, B and D – Annual bank reconciliations will not be often enough to spot a fraud.

Test your understanding 17

A, C and D

Note:

- B – internal control systems can be applied to service organisations as well
- E – internal controls address more than just major accidents
- F – internal controls are needed for all types of organisation

Test your understanding 18

B, C and E

- Option A may have contributed to more injuries but not made the incident more likely to occur.
- Option D would have caused monetary loss to TT but not made the incident more likely to occur.

Test your understanding 19 – G Manufacturing (Case study)

To: The Board

From: A.N. Accountant

Date: Today

Subject: The control environment at G

Introduction

This report covers an explanation of why it is necessary to improve G's control environment and evaluates the Chief Executive's proposal to impose disciplinary measures on staff who are responsible for bookkeeping errors or delays.

(a) **The control environment**

The control environment is essentially a reflection of the attitudes of senior management towards the operation of the system. If management is seen to condone control weaknesses and compliance failures then the staff at more junior levels will tend to interpret that as an indication that controls do not matter.

It is clear that G's senior management has tolerated a situation in which the staff are concerned only with the technical success of the production process. That has led to problems with the bookkeeping and administrative arrangements, which could prove very costly to the company. The delays and errors in those areas could disrupt cash flows and irritate customers. The fact that the accounts staff are demotivated means that there is a risk that they will leave and so time and energy will have to be invested in appointing replacements.

(b) **Disciplinary measures**

G has been successful because its staff have tended to focus on the quality of the product and the customer satisfaction with the product itself is evidence of that. It may be that the relaxed working relationships mean that staff can focus on product innovation and quality management and that has enhanced the company's reputation. Any changes that are introduced will have to be undertaken with some sensitivity in case they lead to staff becoming demotivated in the process and so it may not be constructive to use the threat of disciplinary action in the first instance. The fact that the new Chief Executive is keen to improve the administrative side of the company could be communicated to all staff as a positive step that will make the company more secure and efficient. The company will be unable to function, and to provide employment in the process, if it is unable to pay for materials or to bill customers properly because of accounting errors or lost documentation. It should be possible to communicate a positive attitude and encourage staff to view the accounting aspects of the company's operations as an extension of the whole organisation. The same attitude could be taken towards budgets and variance reports because they can help to ensure the smooth and efficient running of the organisation. The threat of disciplinary action may help to demonstrate that the Chief Executive takes these matters seriously and should send a clear message to staff. The problem is that the workforce is motivated and hardworking and so it may be counter-productive to make that threat unless other approaches have been tried and failed. Quite apart from damaging relations with the workforce, if G threatens to discipline staff and does not carry out that threat then the impression that errors and delays are acceptable will be reinforced.

The threat of swift and decisive action may motivate and encourage the bookkeeping staff. The fact that the Chief Executive is prepared to take action against employees who make their jobs more difficult could make the bookkeeping staff feel valued and reassured that there will be a change for the better.

Conclusion

In summary, the control environment at G is very important and should be improved. Disciplinary action, where threatened, must be carried out to prevent a future culture of carelessness.

Test your understanding 20 – U internet (Case study)

To: The Board

From: A.N. Accountant

Date: Today

Subject: U's control environment and recommended improvements

Introduction

This report covers the weaknesses in both the control environment and the internal controls that led to this loss of data. It goes on to recommend actions that should be taken to restore the confidence of existing and potential customers, and to prevent similar problems occurring in the future.

The control environment

There appear to be major shortcomings within U's control environment. The analyst's behaviour suggests that staff may be overworked, which will lead to errors and possibly short-cuts such as taking files home. The fact that the analyst was afraid to admit to the loss of the files adds to the sense that the environment is unsupportive and punitive.

Staff should have been trained on the sensitivity of personal details in a company such as U. The information that has been lost may be very personal in nature and could lead to losses because of identity theft and related fraud. Such training should have reduced the risk of a member of staff leaving a file of customer records on an unsecure PC.

Staff should not be permitted to connect personal disk drives to U's computers. There is a danger that these will carry viruses or other malware. Ideally, staff PCs should not have open USB sockets to reduce the risk of this occurring. Any files that need to be shared with colleagues can be transferred over the firm's network.

The files themselves should not be accessible in their entirety. Only accounts staff need details of credit card numbers and so access to those should be restricted to them. Fields within files should be made available to U's staff on a strictly "need to know" basis. The analyst did not need to know customers' names and full postal addresses. It would have been sufficient to have identified customers by a user number and provided the analyst with a buying history for each.

(a) **Recommendations**

(i) The first priority is to make a public announcement that all affected customers have been informed about the loss of their records. That will reduce the speculation about the loss and may reduce the number of claims from customers who have not been affected by the loss.

U should close all affected accounts and assist customers to create replacements. That will prevent customers' claims that they are having unauthorised charges to their accounts.

U should offer to assist customers who open replacement credit card accounts in order to prevent fraudulent charges. U should reimburse any fees or charges and should also offer a discount or a voucher as a goodwill gesture for the inconvenience.

U should take steps to remedy the control weaknesses and should announce the fact that security has been improved. The fact that sensitive data could be compromised in this way will be a concern to all customers, particularly given that U initially refused to assist affected account holders.

U should quietly change its policy of denying all responsibility for claims of fraudulent charges. Care will have to be taken in case customers attempt to deny liability for genuine purchases in the hope that U will cancel their balance. It is hardly acceptable for U to claim that customers are mistaken about false charges when the company has been responsible for the loss of data.

(ii) The company should make it very clear that the removal of files without authorisation is a serious breach of company rules and that any offenders will be dealt with. The threat should hopefully deter any recurrence and will also ensure that there is no doubt that files cannot be taken home.

If it is ever necessary for files to be taken home there should be a provision made for secure custody of the data. Files could be encrypted and staff could be issued with a company laptop that is password protected and equipped with all relevant antivirus and firewall software.

Conclusion

There appear to be major shortcomings within U's control environment which need to be improved. Several recommendations have been made including a public announcement, closure of all affected accounts, reimbursement of fees and the improvement of future security measures.

Test your understanding 21 – College (Case study)

Address

Date

Dear Sir,

I am writing in answer to your request to advise on the weaknesses in the college's systems and procedures. I also cover the suggestion that the human elements of control systems are frequently more important than the software elements in ensuring that records are correct.

Weaknesses

(a) Additions to the payroll should require further authorisation than just the head of the department in which he or she would be teaching. That is not just to prevent fraud and error, but also to ensure that those appointed are competent and well qualified.

Teaching time should be budgeted and allocated to specific classes. That should be part of the normal planning and budgeting process. Again, that is largely about ensuring that the college obtains value for money from teaching rather than merely trying to prevent fraud and error. This budgeting should be conducted, or at least reviewed in detail, by a dean of faculty or an assistant principal rather than the heads of individual departments.

Pass keys should not be issued to anybody other than designated security and cleaning staff. If a member of staff requires a door to be unlocked then the security guard should open the door personally rather than making a loan of a pass key. Computer passwords should be issued to staff so that they cannot invent their own, easily guessable passwords. The college should have a policy of holding staff responsible for all input made using their electronic identities – regardless of whether they were actually involved – so that they are motivated to take care over logging out of systems and protecting access.

Human controls

(b) It could be argued that the most important aspect of any secure system is authorisation.

Software can compare entries in different files and highlight discrepancies, but it cannot make meaningful decisions about whether a transaction should be processed. For example, a bookkeeping package will process any transaction that is input by a user with access rights, regardless of whether that entry makes sense. The physical security of any system is dependent on the behaviour of the people who operate it. It is, for example, common for security to break down because staff are careless over locking doors or restricting access to authorised personnel. The most important changes that are made, such as amendments to standing data, often require some judgement on the part of the person responsible for authorising the change.

If that person is not careful in agreeing to make the change then the fact that the software is programmed to ensure that the change has been authorised will be almost pointless. Most fraud involving computers tends to be relatively low-tech. For example, the input of fictitious purchase invoices in the hope that this leads to a payment that can be intercepted. Such fraud is more easily detected by a human being than a computer programme.

I hope you have found my advice and suggestions useful. However, if you have any further queries, please do not hesitate to contact me.

Yours faithfully,

A.N. Accountant

Test your understanding 22 – V (Case study)

Address

Date

Dear institutional investor,

I write regarding your recent concerns over director's remuneration at V. This letter should explain why the introduction of ESOSs could motivate V's executive directors to accept positive net present value (NPV) projects, and how an ESOS scheme could affect the actions taken by the directors.

Motivation to accept positive NPV projects

(i) There is a difference between the risk profiles of shareholders and executive directors. Shareholders should hold diversified portfolios, in which case they are subject only to systematic risk. Directors cannot diversify in the same way because each director has only one career and can generally only be an executive director of one company at a time and so the directors are subject to total risk.

A director who is offered an investment that has a positive NPV at the shareholder's required rate of return may implicitly evaluate that investment at a higher rate that reflects total risk and so may reject it.

If the directors hold options then the value of those options is directly related to the total risk of the underlying security and so the directors could be motivated to accept riskier securities in order to increase the value of their options. There is a huge potential gain if the option is in the money when it is time to exercise it, but there is no symmetry because there is no specific loss other than the expiry of the options if it is out of the money. This means that there is effectively only an upside risk to the directors with respect to their options and that may make them less risk averse in project evaluation.

Director's actions

(ii) The most obvious advantage of V's ESOS is that the options only have value if the share price rises. Increasing the share price is one aspect of maximising shareholders' wealth. Certainly, the directors will have a clear incentive to increase the share price through hard work and initiative.

The fact that the options will take three years before they can be exercised means that the directors will be forced to think in terms of the medium term future rather than simply short term gain.

The ESOS will deter directors from leaving because they will have at least two years' worth of options that will lapse under their terms of employment. That should encourage a degree of continuity of senior management and make it more expensive for another company to poach board members.

ESOS options can only be exercised on a specific date, which means that the directors are motivated to deliver sustained increases in the share price. A sustained growth will mean that the options are more likely to be in the money when the decision has to be taken as to whether they are exercised or allowed to lapse.

There is a risk that the directors may be motivated to withhold dividends because the payment of a dividend will always reduce the share price when the shares become ex-dividend. Retaining earnings may not maximise shareholder wealth, but it could increase the share price to the directors' advantage.

I hope these points alleviate any concerns you may have. Please do not hesitate to contact me should you have any further concerns.

Yours faithfully,

Management Accountant

Memorandum

To: The remuneration committee

From: A. N. Accountant

Date: Today

Subject: Executive directors pay

This memorandum evaluates the advantages AND disadvantages of rewarding executive directors by paying a bonus based on a simple and transparent measure such as profit.

Any form of feedback-based control system is designed to ensure that positive impacts are encouraged and reinforced and negative impacts are discouraged and penalised. Feedback measures and controls performance by referring to actual outcomes. From the shareholders' point of view, that suggests that the directors are incentivised to work towards producing regular progress towards a specific goal such as increasing profit or share price.

The simplicity of such a scheme makes it easier to understand the directors' motives. A more complicated appraisal and performance scheme may simply create more opportunity for the directors to indulge in dysfunctional behaviour or otherwise play games in order to maximise their rewards at the shareholders' expense.

From the shareholders' point of view, it may be that maximising reported earnings is suboptimal and that a more complicated set of benchmarks would be preferable. On the other hand, a simple benchmark does have the advantage of making the directors accountable for a specific aspect of performance. A simple control and feedback mechanism may be more effective simply because it has the potential to work.

There is a risk that linking pay to reported earnings will simply lead to creative accounting and the overstatement of earnings figures.

Reported earnings is also a relatively short term indicator for most entities. The directors are being encouraged to adopt a planning horizon of twelve months which could mean that longer term cycles, such as the development of new products or the acceptance of longer term projects will be overlooked because a high NPV project may be a short term loss maker. The shareholders will have to ensure that they look out for evidence of such actions rather than simply taking the reported figures at face value.

Test your understanding 23 – Cliff (Integration)

(a) Problems expected at Cliff: poor internal control

(i) I would expect the company to experience some level of over-ordering, leading to reduced profitability as a result of inventory going past its `best before' date.

(ii) Inventory that is not well-controlled in a supermarket may result in a breach of health and safety regulations which may result in fines or even closure of the supermarkets.

(iii) I would expect there to be stock-outs leading to the potential loss of business to other supermarkets.

(iv) I would expect there to be inefficiencies as a result of a lack of central ordering system resulting from quantity discounts not being obtained.

(v) All of the problems noted above are likely to be exacerbated where local managers or staff are either inexperienced or possibly dishonest – the question states that poorer quality staff have been recruited recently.

(vi) Supermarket inventory is very easily pilfered either by staff or customers even where it is well-controlled. The lack of regular inventory counts in particular means that pilferage is very easy to hide.

(vii) I would expect there to be a lack of understanding in the business as a whole as to the availability of new products, products with high margins or other areas in which profitability might be improved.

(b) Four recommendations, explanation of advantages and disadvantages: improvements to internal control

Recommendation 1: that an integrated system be introduced across all supermarkets that links sales, purchases and inventory records.

Advantages

This would provide the company with an overall view of what inventory is held at any particular time, enable it to order centrally and reduce the scope for pilferage. It would result in reduced stock-outs and reduced inventory obsolescence.

Disadvantages

This would require considerable capital investment in hardware, software and training. It would also take control away from local managers which would almost certainly cause resentment.

Recommendation 2: the imposition of regular, or continuous inventory counting procedures together with the prompt update of inventory records for discrepancies found and investigation of the reason for the discrepancies.

Advantages

This would further reduce the possibility of stock-outs and provide evidence of over-ordering, which would enable purchasing patterns to be refined.

Disadvantages

There are costs in terms of staff time and, again, a certain level of resentment among staff who may feel that they are being `spied on', or that they are no longer trusted. Training would also be required and additional administrative work would need to be undertaken by local managers

Recommendation 3: that management accounts are produced on at least a quarterly basis, that figures relating to each supermarket are provided to head office on a monthly basis, and that an analysis is undertaken by head office on the performance of individual supermarkets and inventory lines.

Advantages

This would enable the company to determine which supermarkets are performing better than others. It would also enable the company to identify those inventory lines that sell well and those that are profitable.

Disadvantages

The production of more regular and detailed information will be time consuming. Local managers may feel that they are unable to service the particular needs of their customers if decisions are made on a global basis; customers may feel the same way.

Recommendation 4: that sales price decisions are made by head office.

Advantages

This would enable the company to experiment with the use of `loss leaders', for example, and to impose a degree of consistency across supermarkets to prevent inappropriate pricing decisions being taken by local managers.

Disadvantages

Again, loss of control at a local level is likely to result in resentment and the possible loss of good staff. What sells well in one supermarket may not do so in another. To the extent that head office have less experience of local conditions than local staff, it is possible that inappropriate pricing decisions may be made by head office.

Test your understanding 24 – SPD (Integration)

Reputation risk could be managed by actively warning drivers of the system's limitations. That could involve insisting that Q signs an acknowledgement that the system cannot prevent all crashes. This document should be kept in a safe place at SPD for future reference if need be. The warning could be repeated in the owner's handbook which should be signed for by the driver, and, again, a copy should be kept at SPD.

Any promotional material published by Q should stress that the system is designed to enable drivers to be even safer when driving within their limits but that responsibility for any failure cannot be accepted by SPD.

SPD could insist that the circuit board is designed to "fail safe" conditions. It could have a diagnostic routine programmed into it which will check that it is functioning correctly whenever it is switched on. In the event that this routine fails the circuit board will immobilise the engine. A contract drawn up by their solicitors would be required to absolve SPD of any blame for failure.

SPD should ask Q to accept responsibility for the work done by the third party and get this put in writing. Again a solicitor would need to deal with this. Any lost business due to delays or failures to meet delivery deadlines should be compensated. SPD will also have to insist on its own quality control procedures over this component. That may involve having the right to request details of the technical specification of the part and the subsequent testing of it on a regular basis.

Test your understanding 25 – Rhapsody Company (Integration)

Tutorial note: It is not recommended that you lay out answers to examination questions in a tabular format such as that shown below. Full sentences and paragraphs will ensure that you explain points in enough detail to earn full marks.

Weakness	**Evaluation of weakness**	**Recommendation**
Recording of orders		
Orders placed on the Internet site are transferred manually into the inventory and sales system. Manual transfer of order details may result in information being transferred incompletely or incorrectly, for example, order quantities may be incorrect or the wrong product code recorded.	Customers will be sent incorrect goods resulting in increased customer complaints.	The computer systems are amended so that order details are transferred directly between the two computer systems. This will remove manual transfer of details limiting the possibility of human error.
Control over orders and packing lists		
Each order/packing list is given a random alphabetical code. While this is useful, using this type of code makes it difficult to check completeness of orders at any stage in the despatch and invoicing process.	Packing lists can be lost resulting either in goods not being despatched to the customer (if the list is lost prior to goods being despatched) or the customer's credit card not being charged (if lost after goods despatched but prior to the list being received in the accounts department).	Orders/packing lists are controlled with a numeric sequence. At the end of each day, gaps in the sequence of packing lists returned to accounts are investigated.

Obtaining payment		
The customer's credit card is charged after despatch of goods to the customer, meaning that goods are already sent to the customer before payment is authorised.	Rhapsody Co will not be paid for the goods despatched where the credit company rejects the payment request. Given that customers are unlikely to return seeds, Rhapsody Co will automatically incur a bad debt.	Authorisation to charge the customer's credit card is obtained prior to despatch of goods to ensure Rhapsody Co is paid for all goods despatched.
Completeness of orders		
The computer system correctly ensures that order details are available for all charges to customer credit cards. However, there is no overall check that all orders recorded on the inventory and sales system have actually been invoiced.	Entire orders may be overlooked and consequently sales and profit understated.	The computer is programmed to review the order file and orders where there is no corresponding invoice for an order, these should be flagged for subsequent investigation.

Test your understanding 26 – Bassoon Ltd (Integration)

Tutorial note: It is not recommended that you lay out answers to examination questions in a tabular format such as that shown below. Full sentences and paragraphs will ensure that you explain points in enough detail to earn full marks.

Risks	Recommendation
Cash paid to part time staff (easier to misappropriate cash).	Apply the payroll system to all employees.
No control over the appointment of head office staff the HR Manager deals with (may recruit unnecessary staff).	Head office staff should be approved by the board.
No control over shop staff, the shop manager recruits own staff.	Should be approved by head office.
Guest cards, could be anybody and they could steal a card to access till at a later date to steal money.	A control system to monitor guest cards so management know who has a specific card.
Lack of segregation of duties, the payroll manager is responsible for all processing.	Split the responsibilities up, maybe get a manager to review the payroll manager's work.
In the question it states the IT manager is responsible for systems, but doesn't state there is restricted access.	Place passwords on the system and change them on a regular basis.

chapter

4

Risk and control of information systems

Chapter learning objectives

Lead	Component
C1. Evaluate risk management strategies.	(a) Evaluate the essential features of internal control systems for identifying, assessing and managing risks.
B1. Evaluate the tools and processes required for strategy implementation.	(c) Advice managers of the risks in the development of strategies for information systems that support the organisation's strategic requirements.

Indicative syllabus content

- Disaster recovery.
- The purpose and contents of information system strategies, and the need for strategy complementary to the corporate and individual business strategies.

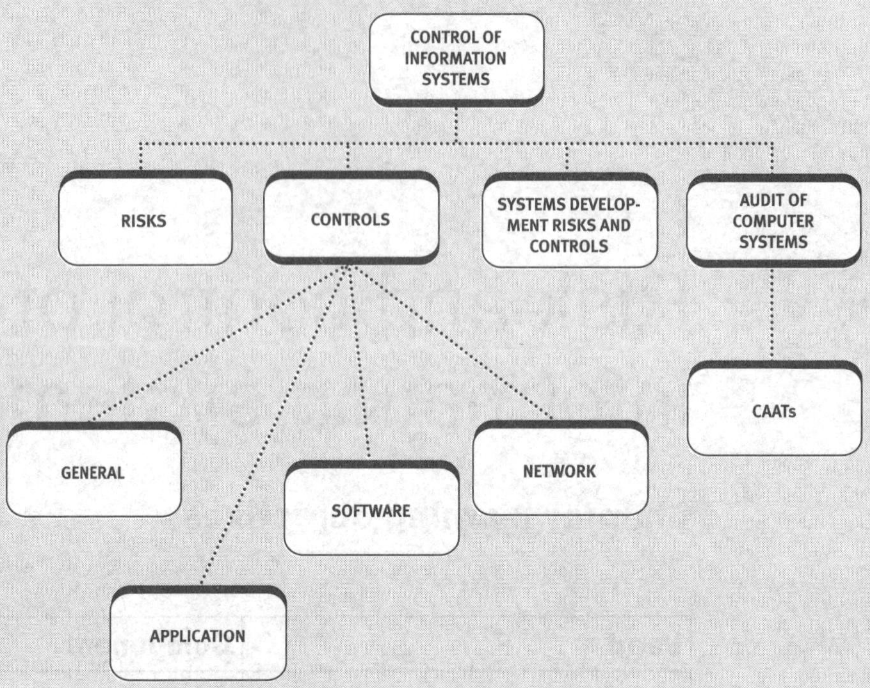

1 Risks

Computer systems have unique risk and control issues that need to be addressed by business. As with any risk factor the company needs to make an assessment of the risks and decide on the appropriate level of control to reduce the risks to an acceptable level.

Risks to a computer system

A risk to a computer system could be anything that prevents the managers getting the information they need from the system at the time that they need it.

Risks to information processing facilities may arise from:

- Dissatisfied employees might deliberately modify or destroy information in the system.
- A hacker or industrial spy might break into the system.
- Viruses or malicious software could be introduced.
- Accidental mistakes could be made on input to the system.
- Inadequate security of the hardware or data.
- Faults in the hardware system.

Such risks result in the loss of information (or the loss of its integrity or confidentiality), business disruption and a loss of time and money.

Further detail on risks

Information security

Risks to information security can be categorised as follows:

Risks	Description
Risk of hardware theft	This risk might seem fairly obvious, but the theft of computer hardware is common.
Physical damage to hardware and computer media (disks, etc)	Physical damage can be caused by: • malicious damage • poor operating conditions causing damage to equipment and magnetic files • natural disasters, such as fire and flooding.
Damage to data	Data can be damaged by hackers into the system, viruses, program faults in the software and faults in the hardware or data storage media. Software, particularly purpose-written software, can become corrupted. Programs might be altered by a hacker or computer fraudster. Alternatively, a new version of a program might be written and introduced, but contain a serious error that results in the corruption or loss of data on file.
Operational mistakes	Unintentional mistakes can cause damage to data or loss of data; for example, using the wrong version of computer program, or the wrong version of a data file, or deleting data that is still of value.
Fraud and industrial espionage	This can lead to the loss of confidentiality of sensitive information, or the criminal creation of false data and false transactions, or the manipulation of data for personal gain.

Data protection legislation

Some countries give individuals the right to seek compensation against an organisation that holds personal data about them, if they suffer loss through the improper use of that data. In the UK, for example, rights are given to 'data subjects' by the Data Protection Act. There could be a risk that an organisation will improperly use or communicate personal data about individuals, in breach of the legislation.

Erroneous input

Many information systems, especially those based on transaction processing systems and with large volumes of input transactions, are vulnerable to mistakes in the input data.

- Some input items might be overlooked and omitted. Other transactions might be entered twice.
- There might be errors in the input data, particularly where the data is input by humans rather than by electronic data transfer. For example, in a system relying on input via keyboard and mouse, data accuracy depends on the ability of the operator to input the data without making a mistake.

Where input errors are high, the integrity of the data and information becomes doubtful.

Hacking

Hacking is the gaining of unauthorised access to a computer system. It might be a deliberate attempt to gain access to an organisation's systems and files, to obtain information or to alter data (perhaps fraudulently).

Once hackers have gained access to the system, there are several damaging options available to them. For example, they may:

- gain access to the file that holds all the user ID codes, passwords and authorisations
- discover the method used for generating/authorising passwords
- interfere with the access control system, to provide the hacker with open access to the system
- obtain information which is of potential use to a competitor organisation
- obtain, enter or alter data for a fraudulent purpose
- cause data corruption by the introduction of unauthorised computer programs and processing on to the system (computer viruses)
- alter or delete files.

Viruses

A virus is a piece of software that seeks to infest a computer system, hiding and automatically spreading to other systems if given the opportunity. Most computer viruses have three functions – avoiding detection, reproducing themselves and causing damage. Viruses might be introduced into a computer system directly, or by disk or e-mail attachment.

Viruses include:

- trojans – whilst carrying on one program, secretly carry on another
- ransomware – blocks access to files and threatens to delete or publish unless a fee is paid
- worms – these replicate themselves within the systems
- trap doors – undocumented entry points to systems allowing normal controls to be by-passed
- logic bombs – triggered on the occurrence of a certain event
- time bombs – which are triggered on a certain date.

Information security risks

There are examples of these information security risks and breaches around us all the time. Here are two notables ones.

In 2014 there was a high profile breach of a major cloud service provider in which private details, calendars, phone call logs and photographs were stolen. This was possible due to a control issue that allowed the hackers to make unlimited attempts at guessing the users passwords.

In 2017 there was a global issue from a ransomeware attack called WannaCry that infected organisations worldwide, including parts of the NHS in the United Kingdom. This was possible as many organisations were using older operating systems that were no longer supported by the service provider.

Risks and benefits of internet and intranet use

Many organisations have intranet systems or use the Internet directly. Using an intranet or the Internet has obvious advantages, but also creates substantial risks.

The advantages of intranets and the Internet

- Employees have ready access to vast sources of external data that would not otherwise be available. Using external information can help to improve the quality of decision making.
- Organisations can advertise their goods and services on a website, and provide other information that helps to promote their image.
- Organisations can use the Internet to purchase goods or supplies, saving time and money. For example, the Internet is used regularly by businesses to purchase standard items such as stationery, and to reserve hotel rooms and purchase travel tickets.
- The Internet/intranet provides a means of operating an e-mail system. Communication by e-mail is fast and should remove the requirement for excessive quantities of paper. Using e-mails might also reduce the non-productive time spent by employees on the telephone.
- Intranets create the opportunity for more flexible organisation of work. For example, employees who are away from the office can access the organisation's IT systems and files through the Internet. Similarly, employees can work from their home but have full access to the organisation's systems.

The disadvantages of intranets and the internet

There are disadvantages with using intranets and the Internet.

- E-mail systems can become inefficient if too many messages are sent and users have to look through large amounts of 'junk mail' to find messages of value.
- E-mails can be disruptive, especially if a prompt appears on an individual's computer screen whenever a new message is received.
- Senders of e-mails often expect an immediate reply to their messages, and a delay in responding can create bad feelings and ill-will.
- Employees might waste too much time looking for information on the Internet, when the value of the information is not worth the time spent looking for it.

- Without suitable controls, employees might spend large amounts of time on the Internet or exchanging e-mails for their personal benefit, rather than in carrying out their work responsibilities.

The greatest problem with using intranets and the Internet, however, is the vulnerability of the organisation's IT systems to:

- unauthorised access by hackers, including industrial spies
- the import of viruses in attachments to e-mail messages and other malicious software.

2 Controls in an information systems environment

To combat the types of risks discussed above companies will put in place control procedures. These must be assessed for cost effectiveness and should reduce risk to an acceptable level.

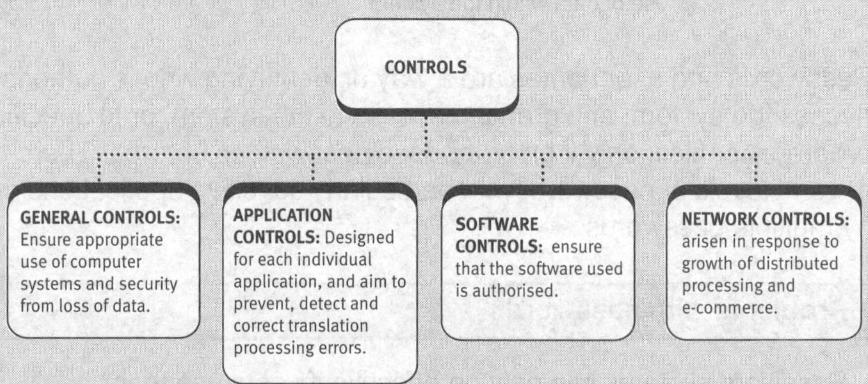

CONTROLS
GENERAL CONTROLS: Ensure appropriate use of computer systems and security from loss of data.
APPLICATION CONTROLS: Designed for each individual application, and aim to prevent, detect and correct translation processing errors.
SOFTWARE CONTROLS: ensure that the software used is authorised.
NETWORK CONTROLS: arisen in response to growth of distributed processing and e-commerce.

Alternative control classification

There are a number of different ways in which controls can be classified in an IT environment.

An alternative to the classification described above is:

- **Security controls:** controls designed to ensure the prevention of unauthorised access, modification or destruction of stored data.
- **Integrity controls:** controls to ensure that the data are accurate, consistent and free from accidental corruption.
- **Contingency controls:** in the event that security or integrity controls fail there must be a back-up facility and a contingency plan to restore business operations as quickly as possible.

3 General controls

Personnel controls

Recruitment, training and supervision needs to be in place to ensure the competency of those responsible for programming and data entry.

Logical access controls

Security over access is often based on a logical access system. This is illustrated by the following diagram:

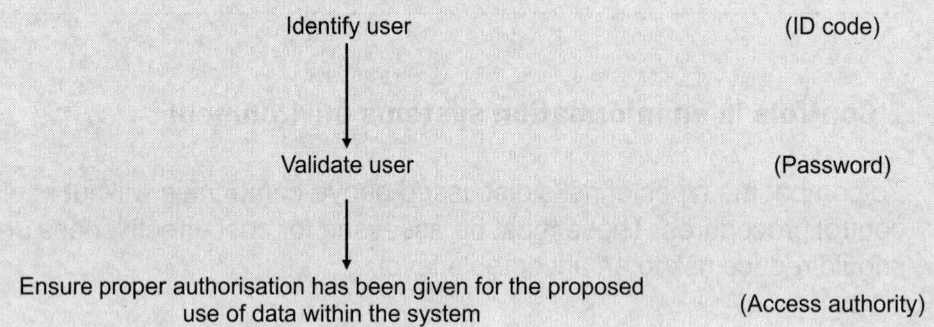

Passwords and user names are a way of identifying who is authorised to access the system, and granting access to the system, or to specific programs or files, only if an authorised password is entered. There may be several levels of password, with particularly sensitive applications protected by multiple passwords.

Problems with passwords

Password systems can only be effective if users use them conscientiously. There are several inherent problems with a password system:

- Authorised users may divulge their password to a colleague.
- Many passwords may have associations with the user so that a hacker can discover them by experimentation.
- Passwords are often written down close to the computer (e.g. pinned to the notice board inside the office) and so easily discovered.

To protect passwords and user numbers against discovery, a number of precautions should be adopted:

- Users should be required to change their passwords regularly.
- Passwords should be memorable but not obviously related to a user's private life.
- Users should be encouraged never to write down their passwords.

- There should be strict controls over passwords – they should never be 'lent' or written down where they can be easily seen.
- There should be automatic sentinel or watchdog programs to identify when a password has been keyed incorrectly.

Access logging

The system will produce regular reports including a system access report and various pre-determined exception reports. The effectiveness of these reports is determined by:

- The frequency of report production.
- The follow up of detected breaches in security.

Audit trail

An audit trail consists of a record or series of records that allows the processing of a transaction or an amendment by a computer or clerical system to be identified accurately, as well as verifying the authenticity of the transaction or amendment, including the identity of the individuals who initiated and authorised it.

Audit trails are also used to record customer activity in e-commerce on a company's website. The audit trail records the customer's initial access to the website, and then each subsequent activity (purchasing and payment, confirmation of order and delivery of the product). The audit trail can be used to deal with any subsequent enquiry or complaint from the customer. In some cases, 'audit trails' can be used to track down hackers into a system. A hacker might sometimes unknowingly leave a trail of where he came from, for example through records in the activity log of the hacker's Internet service provider.

Facility controls

Physical access

There are various basic categories of controlling access to sensitive areas. These include:

- security guards in buildings
- working areas to which access is through a locked door or a door with an ID card entry system or entry system requiring the user to enter a personal identification code (PIN number)
- using safes and lockable filing cabinets

- closed circuit TV used to monitor what is happening in a particular part of a building – this may be backed up by security video cameras
- doors automatically locked in the event of a security alarm.

Additionally, procedural controls to protect files and output include:

- disks should not be left lying around on desks and working surfaces
- computer printout and disks should be shredded or otherwise destroyed before being thrown away.

Location of IT facilities

It is imperative that the location of the system is considered, and hence all equipment is located so as to protect against:

- Fire
- Flood
- Smoke
- Food
- Drinks
- Power failure
- Environment.

Business continuity

Business continuity planning (**disaster recovery planning**) takes place in order to recover information systems from business critical events after they have happened. It involves:

- Making a risk assessment
- Developing a contingency plan to address those risks.

More on disaster recovery plans

An unexpected disaster can put an entire computer system out of action. For large organisations, a disaster might involve damage from a terrorist attack. There could also be threats from fire and flood damage. A disaster might simply be a software or hardware breakdown within a system.

Disaster recovery planning involves assessing what disasters might occur that would pose a serious threat to the organisation, and trying to ensure that alternative arrangements are available in the event that a disaster occurs.

In the case of a computer system for a clearing bank, this would mean having an entire back-up computer system in place that could be brought into operation if a disaster puts the main system out of action.

Not all organisations have extensive disaster recovery plans. Certainly, however, back-up copies of major data files should be kept, so that in the event that the main files are destroyed, the data can be re-created with the back-up files.

System back-ups

All files containing important information should be backed up on a regular basis. Backing up provides protection against the loss or corruption of data due to:

- faults in the hardware (e.g. hard disk)
- the accidental deletion of a file by a computer operator
- damage to a data file by a hacker.

A back-up is simply a copy of the file. If the original file is lost or becomes corrupt, the back-up can be substituted in its place, and the master file can be re-created.

There will be some loss of data if the input to the system since the most recent back-up copy of the file was made.

- However, if back-ups are made regularly, the loss of data should be limited. If there are paper records of input transactions since the most recent back-up copy was made, the file can be brought up to date by re-inputting the data.
- Some systems provide back-up copies of both master files and transaction data files, and copies of these files can be used to re-create an up-to-date master file if the original master file is lost or corrupted.

Back-up copies might be stored on the same physical computer file as the original file, but this is risky, since damage to the physical file will result in the loss of the back-up as well as the main file.

Back-up files might be created by copying them on to a disk or tape. Where security is important, any such back-up copies should be held in a secure place, such as a safe.

To counter the risk of damage to a file due to a fire or similar disaster at the premises where the IT system is located, a back-up copy might be taken off-site and held somewhere else.

The need for robust disaster recovery plans

In May 2017 British Airways had an issue with the power supply to business critical IT systems which led to BA's check in systems, call centre and website all going off line.

The company has been criticised for failure to have an appropriate disaster recovery plan for systems critical to their core operation. Questions have been raised as to why an uninterruptible power supply was not used, why there was no back-up power supply to automatically start up if the uninterruptible power supply was compromised, or why there was no back-up server running alongside the main system.

The impact of this was still being felt by passengers 3 days later and is expected to cost the company a significant amount in compensation payments, with some estimating £100 million.

Test your understanding 1

An oil company uses an IT server for a major system and the management believe that it is essential that the continuity of processing must be assured at all times. Which of the following risk control measures is the most appropriate for ensuring that this happens?

A A secure password protection system

B A standby server

C Surplus capacity in the memory of the operational server

D Fire safety measures

4 Application controls

These are controls to ensure that data are correctly input, processed and correctly maintained, and only distributed to authorised personnel.

Application controls are specific to each application, but can be grouped as follows:

Input controls:

- Checking and authorising source documents manually.
- The use of batch controls.
- Pre-numbered forms.

Processing controls:

- Computer verification and validation checks.
- Error detection controls such as
  - control totals
  - balancing.

Output controls:

- Monitoring of control logs.
- Physical checking of output.

More on input controls

Some controls over the completeness and accuracy of the data to the system can be written into the system design as controls by the program.

Software controls might be applied to:

- ensure the completeness of input data
- improve the accuracy/correctness of input data.

Controls over the completeness of input. This is only possible if there is a way of checking how many transactions should be processed, or whether a transaction has been omitted. Within accounting systems, examples of completeness checks might be:

- in a payroll system, checking that the number of payroll transactions processed is exactly equal to the number of employees on the payroll file
- in a sales invoicing system, where all invoices are numbered sequentially, to ensure that no invoices have been omitted from processing. (Altering an invoice should be dealt with by raising a credit note to reverse the original invoice and issuing a new invoice.)

Controls over the accuracy of input: In computer systems, software validation checks might be written into the software to identify logical errors in the input. Examples of data validation checks might be:

- Existence checks: if a particular item of data must have a code 1, 2 or 3, a data validation check can be carried out on the input to make sure that the value entered is 1, 2 or 3, and if any other value is entered, the input will not be accepted.
- Reasonableness check or range check: this is a logical check to ensure that the value of an item input to the system is a reasonable value. For example, a system might carry out a reasonableness check that the value of a sales order is not in excess of, say, $50,000.
- Check digit verification: Some codes used in a computer system, such as customer identity codes or inventory codes, include a check digit. A check digit allows the program to check that the entire code is valid, and that there is no error in the input digits for the code.
- Controls over the authorisation of input: Manual controls include requiring the signature of an authorised individual on the authorisation document (e.g. a document giving approval to make a payment). Within a computer system, authorisation is granted by the input of an appropriate user name/password.

5 Software controls

Software control prevents making or installing unauthorised copies of software. Illegal software is more likely to fail, comes without warranties or support, can place systems at risk of viruses and the use of illegal software can result in significant financial penalties.

Software can be controlled by:

- Buying only from reputable dealers.
- Ensuring that the original disks come with the software.
- Ensuring that licences are received for all software.
- Retaining all original disks and documentation.

6 Network controls

Risks on networks

The increase in popularity of the LAN (local area network) has brought concerns in relation to system security. A LAN allows for many more breaches of security than does a single computer.

The main areas of concern are:

- Tapping into cables.
- Unauthorised log in.
- Computer viruses.
- File copying.
- File server security.

Controls

Controls must exist to prevent unauthorised access to data transmitted over networks and to secure the integrity of data.

Methods include:

- Firewalls.
- Flow.
- Data encryption.
- Virus protection.

More on network controls

Firewalls: A firewall will consist of a combination of hardware and software located between the company's intranet (private network) and the public network (Internet). A set of control procedures will be established to allow public access to some parts of the organisation's computer system (outside the firewall) whilst restricting access to other parts (inside the firewall).

Flow: This regulates movement of data from one file to another. Channels are specified along which information is allowed to flow, i.e. confidential/non-confidential, and these are linked by authority levels.

Data encryption: Encryption is a technique of disguising information to preserve its confidentiality. It is disguised during processing/storage. In essence it is a method of scrambling the data in a message or file so that it is unintelligible unless it is unscrambled (or decrypted).

Virus protection: It is extremely difficult to protect systems against the introduction of computer viruses. Preventative steps may include:

- control on the use of external software (e.g. checked for viruses before using new software)
- using anti-virus software, regularly updated, to detect and deal with viruses

- educating employees to be watchful for viruses being imported as attachment files to e-mail messages.

Legislation surrounding information systems

Data Protection Act (DPA)

The DPA was needed to protect individuals against the misuse of personal data. This was necessary due to:

- Easy interrogation of large files.
- Speed of response (less control).
- Interrogation from outside.
- Entire files can be copied or transmitted in seconds.
- Computer systems can be cross-linked to obtain personal profiles.
- Individuals' records can be selected easily through the search facilities.

Registration

All users of computers who are intending to hold personal data are required to register and supply the following details:

- Name and address of data user.
- Description of, and purpose for which, data are held.
- Description of source data.
- Identification of persons to whom it is disclosed.
- Names and non-UK countries to which transmission is desired.
- Name of persons responsible for dealing with data subject enquiries.

If an organisation fails to register, this is a criminal offence, although compensation is through a civil action.

Key principles

The DPA has the following key principles:

- Personal information shall be obtained and processed fairly and lawfully.
- Personal data shall be held and used only for specified purposes.
- Personal data shall be adequate, relevant and not excessive in relation to those specified purposes.
- Personal data shall not be used or disclosed in a manner incompatible with those specified purposes.
- Personal data shall be accurate and kept up to date.
- Personal data should not be kept for longer than is necessary.
- A data subject is entitled to be informed and is:
  - entitled to access
  - entitled to have data corrected or erased.
- A data user is responsible for the security and protection of data held against unauthorised access, alteration, destruction, disclosure or accidental loss.

Exemptions to the Act

Data subjects are not entitled to see their personal data if it is held for:

- Law enforcement purposes.
- Revenue purposes.
- Statistical and research purposes.
- Regulating provision of financial service (covered by Consumer Credit Act 1974).
- Legally privileged reasons.
- Back-up security reasons.
- Social work.
- Medical purposes.

The following are exempt from the provisions of the Act:

- Manual records.
- Payroll, pension, test preparation, etc.

- Data held which is crucial to the interests of the state:
  - Crime
  - Tax
  - National security.
- Data held relating to personal household.

Computer Misuse Act 1990

Computer crime is defined as 'any fraudulent behaviour connected with computerisation by which someone attempts to gain dishonest advantage' (Audit Commission). Computer crime was enshrined within the Computer Misuse Act 1990.

Objectives

The key objective of the Act was to make crimes of 'hacking' and the theft of data.

Unfortunately the Act does not provide a definition of:

- Computer.
- Program.
- Data.

Criminal offences

The Act created three new criminal offences:

- Unauthorised access, e.g. by employee who exceeds authority – minor offence (Magistrates Court) – penalty six months imprisonment/fine/both.
- Unauthorised access with intent to commit and then facilitate the commission of a further offence, e.g. divert funds – serious offence – penalty five years imprisonment/fine/both.
- Knowingly causing an unauthorised modification of the contents of any computer with the intention of interfering with the operation of that computer, preventing access to a program or data, or interfering with the operation of the program or the reliability of the data – includes introducing a virus to a system – penalty five years imprisonment/fine/both.

Test your understanding 2

Which of the following are application controls? (Select all that apply.)

A Pre-numbered forms

B Validation checks

C Buying software from reputable dealers

D Renewing licences

E Firewalls

F Access logging

Test your understanding 3

YY plc is a large manufacturer in electrical components, which was established as a family hardware store 20 years ago and has grown rapidly since. The newly-appointed IT manager has just completed the implementation of a new integrated IT system, including new hardware and software. All staff have completed 2 hours of training in the new systems.

Identify the THREE main risks to the information systems at YY plc from the following list.

A A hacker might break into the system

B Viruses or malicious software could be introduced into the system

C Newly trained staff may make unintentional mistakes can which cause damage to data

D The computer hardware could be stolen

E The employees may not like the new system

F The system is the first of many ideas the new IT manager wishes to implement

7 Systems development

The systems development life cycle SDLC)

The systems development life cycle is assumed knowledge at this level. However, there were six stages within the SDLC, with several activities involved:

- Planning – project initiation document, project quality plan, work breakdown structure, budget;
- Analysis – get to the root of the problem via user involvement in the form of interviews and questionnaires, complaints review;
- Design – prototyping;
- Development – build the system which has been agreed on;
- Implementation – staff training, file conversion, documentation, testing;
- Review – post completion audit/review on quality, cost, timescale.

Systems development risks

The development of new computer systems, designed and written for a specific user organisation, is a high-risk venture. It is widely recognised that many new purpose-written systems fail, for several reasons:

- They fail to satisfy the user's real requirements: the system was specified incorrectly.
- They do not provide the data processing or information for which they were designed, or to the quality expected.
- The system was therefore designed and programmed incorrectly.
- They cost much more to develop and run than expected. The system is therefore less efficient than expected.

8 Controls

Controls

Controls should be built into the system development process to reduce these risks. These controls should be implemented at all stages of the systems development life cycle (SDLC).

Examples of systems development controls

Control	**Comments**
Approval of an outline system specification by the user/IT steering committee.	The proposed system must be specified in terms of what it is expected to provide to the user, in terms of data processing and information quality, and should evaluate the expected costs and benefits. A system should not progress to detailed system design without formal authorisation. By giving formal approval to the system design, the user confirms the objectives of the system.
System designed in detail, using system design standards. The system is fully documented. A detailed system design is produced.	The documentation provides a source for checking in the event of problems with the system. By giving approval to the detailed system design, the user confirms that the programming work should begin.
Programs written using programming standards. All programs fully documented.	The documentation provides a source for checking in the event of problems with the system.
Systems and program testing.	The systems analysts and programmers should carry out their own tests on the programs and the system as a whole, to satisfy themselves that the system objectives have been met.
User testing.	Before the system 'goes live', it should be tested by the user. Before accepting the system for implementation, the user must be satisfied that it meets the planned objectives.
Development timetable and cost control.	The project development should be completed on time and within the budgeted cost. A management/project team should be given the responsibility for monitoring the progress of the project (e.g. using critical path analysis techniques) and its costs.

Control over implementation.	The implementation of the new system should be carefully planned and monitored. There are three methods of implementing a new system: • To introduce the system initially in one area or department, as a pilot test. Implement the system universally if the pilot test is successful, and after initial 'teething troubles' have been identified and resolved. • To introduce the new system by running it in parallel with the old system, until the new system is operating successfully. Parallel running can be expensive, because it involves running two systems at the same time. However, it should be less risky than an immediate changeover. • To make the changeover from old system to new system immediately and in full, without pilot testing or parallel running.
Monitoring the new system: audit of new systems.	A new system should be monitored, with a view to checking that it has been successful and has achieved its objectives. The success of a system should also be assessed in terms of: • user satisfaction levels and level of system use • actual costs and benefits.

Test your understanding 4

The system development lifecycle has six stages. The correct order of four of the stages is:

A Analysis; Development; Design; Review

B Analysis; Design; Development; Implementation

C Planning; Analysis; Development; Design

D Planning; Design; Analysis; Review

Test your understanding 5

CP Ltd are implementing a new, bespoke computer system to replace an existing system. The stages they have gone through so far include the purchase and installation of the hardware, software development, system testing, staff training and the production of system documentation. This will be followed by:

A File conversion, database creation and changeover

B File conversion, database creation and review

C Changeover and review

D Changeover and maintenance

Changeover methods

- **Direct changeover** – This is where the old system is switched off and the new system is switched on. This is appropriate when the two systems are very different or it is too expensive to run two systems. Although this method is cheap, it is also risky since if the new system doesn't work properly then the company might be unable to revert to their old system quickly. (Also, staff trust of the new system would be lost.)
- **Parallel running** – The old and new systems are run together for a period of time, until it feels safe to switch the old system off. This method will be costly (inputting data twice and possibly employing more staff to do this), however, it will be less risky than direct changeover.
- **Pilot changeover** – This is where one part of the business changes over first. When the system operates correctly there, the rest of the business will changeover. The pilot department or division could be using direct or parallel changeover. Again, this is a safer method of changeover as only one part of the business will be affected if anything goes wrong. However, when the system is rolled out across the rest of the company there may be different problems in each location and the IT teams resources will be stretched.
- **Phased changeover** – This involves bringing in the new system one part of the business at a time, say, by department or division. It differs from pilot changeover in that all departments or divisions are staggered with respect to receiving the new system. The downside of this is that this method is time-consuming. However, this method is less risky as should there be a problem in any particular department or division, the IT staff are able to deal with the problems one at a time.

Test your understanding 6

The most risky changeover method is:

A Phased changeover

B Pilot changeover

C Parallel changeover

D Direct changeover

Test your understanding 7

A large company has five separate divisions. They all use different computer systems and software for financial reporting purposes. A new and very expensive software package is to be used from the beginning of the next financial year. The new software package has been bespoke-written for the company and is to be implemented in all five divisions. It is currently still being tested. Several bugs have been found and implementation may be delayed. Costs have escalated to a level where management are saying that costs elsewhere in the IT budget will need to be reduced to compensate.

Which ONE of the following changeover methods would be most appropriate?

A Direct changeover

B Parallel changeover

C Phased changeover

D Pilot changeover

Test your understanding 8

X is a multi-site retail organisation, formed by the recent merger of four independent retailers. You were previously Management Accountant of one of the retail companies, and have recently been appointed Systems Accountant for the merged organisation.

Each of the merged companies currently uses a different information system for the recording and processing of inventory. It is planned to replace these systems with one new system that will be common to every site. You have been talking to the Finance Director about the need to standardise systems, and he has expressed concern regarding the disruption that will be caused by the changeover.

Advise the Finance Director which of the following system changeover methods can be used. (Select ALL correct answers)

A Direct

B Parallel

C Pilot

D Phased

Post-implementation review

A post-implementation review should establish whether the objectives of a project have been met.

When appraising a new system after changeover, comparison should be made between predicted and actual performance (variance analysis). This might include:

- Throughput speeds;
- Number of errors or queries;
- Cost of processing;
- Amount of downtime.

The review would also need to cover whether users' needs had been met.

The review should not be performed too soon after the new system goes live, or 'teething problems' and lack of user familiarity will distort the results.

Recommendations should be made where appropriate to improve the system's future performance.

The review should also make wider recommendations on improving systems development and project planning and management processes.

Criminal records bureau

The objective of the Criminal Records Bureau (CRB) is to widen access to criminal records so that employers could make better informed recruitment decisions, especially in relation to the protection of children and vulnerable adults. The CRB is a Public Private Partnership with Capita plc which operates a call centre, inputs applications for checking, collects fees, develops and maintains the IT infrastructure and issues disclosures. Planning for the CRB commenced in 1999 and live access began in March 2002, seven months later than planned caused by problems in business and technical development and the decision to conduct more extensive testing prior to live operations.

There were weaknesses in the business assumptions made by Capita. In particular, the assumption that 70–85 per cent of people would apply by telephone to a call centre or on-line was incorrect and not based on adequate research with potential users, 80 per cent of whom preferred paper applications. However, data entry screens had been designed for input from a telephone call, not from paper forms, and Optical Character Recognition (OCR) systems did not have the capacity to handle the volume of paper applications. Also, systems had been designed around receipt of individual applications and could not cope when batched applications were received. The processes were also unable to cope with the volume of errors and exceptions on paper applications.

Since June 2003 the CRB has met service standards in terms of turnaround times and backlogs have been eliminated. A House of Commons Report concluded that 'the key to running a complex, Greenfield operation with a private sector partner is to work together as a team to solve operational problems'.

Source: House of Commons, Criminal Records Bureau: Delivering Safer Recruitment? (HC266), 2004

Test your understanding 9 – C bank (Case study)

Scenario

C Bank provides traditional banking services to individual customers and small businesses. It is a small bank that has 14 branches within a region of its home country. The bank has 48,000 customers. Each customer has at least one bank account and many customers have several accounts.

The bank maintains detailed, computerised records of every account. These are maintained on a database that can be queried in a variety of ways. The database shows all transactions on every account going back to 2003, when the database was first established. The database records are very detailed, showing the time and date of every transaction and the identity of the member of staff who processed the transaction.

Trigger

The bank received a letter in January 2014 from a lawyer who is dealing with the estate of a customer who died in 2009. The customer was an elderly person who did not have any close relatives. It had taken almost five years for a distant relative, R, to claim the estate. R had obtained correspondence that showed that the deceased customer had held a savings account with C Bank that had a substantial balance. When R contacted the bank in order to claim this balance the bank replied that the account had been closed by the account holder in 2013 and all funds had been withdrawn in cash. R took legal advice and the lawyer wrote to C Bank to point out that the cash could not have been withdrawn by the account holder, enclosing a copy of the account holder's death certificate.

The bank's internal audit department conducted an investigation. C Bank has a policy of requiring the branch manager to authorise withdrawals of more than GBP 500. Starting in June 2013 there had been a daily withdrawal of GBP 495 from the account that had continued until the funds had been exhausted. All of the withdrawals had been processed by H, a bank clerk employed in the Westown branch.

The Head of Internal Audit believes that H knew that the customer had died in 2009 and had checked that the account had been dormant since that time. H then appears to have acted on the assumption that he could withdraw the funds without getting caught because the customer's relatives did not appear to be aware of the account.

H was interviewed and was formally warned that the internal audit department was investigating his behaviour with a view to determining whether he had defrauded the bank. H denied the suggestion that he had acted fraudulently and he claimed that it was purely a coincidence that he had processed all of those transactions. H claims that the cash must have been withdrawn by a third party who came to the bank with forged credentials.

The Head of Internal Audit does not believe that there is sufficient evidence to report H to the police or even to take disciplinary action against H. C Bank's Head Computer Programmer has been asked to assist by using the database to determine whether H has processed any similar transactions involving other accounts.

The Head of Internal Audit is also concerned that these events have highlighted a potential loophole in the bank's control system. The system allows bank staff to withdraw cash from dormant accounts without attracting suspicion, provided the account holder is not monitoring the account balance. C Bank has many dormant accounts.

(A dormant account is a bank account showing no activity (other than posting interest) for some specified period, usually several years.)

Task 1

(a) Write a email to the Head Computer Programmer discussing the factors that should be taken into account in designing database queries to assist the internal audit department investigate the clerk's suspicious behaviour.

(20 minutes)

Task 2

Write a report to the Board:

(i) Evaluating whether there is a need for C Bank to determine if additional controls to prevent unauthorised withdrawals are necessary; and

(10 minutes)

(ii) Recommending, stating reasons, control procedures that C Bank should introduce in order to deter unauthorised withdrawals from dormant accounts if it is established that there is a need for such controls.

(15 minutes)

Test your understanding 10 – H training company (Case study)

Scenario

H is a training company that provides executive training in management subjects. H provides short courses that range from a single day to five days. H has five offices and each office has between ten and twenty full-time trainers.

H's courses are very expensive. Delegates are senior managers and company directors. All courses are paid for by employers who are keen to equip their staff with new skills or to update existing knowledge. Many courses are taught in H's offices to small groups of delegates, each of whom has come from a different company. These courses are advertised on H's website and some, like "finance for non-financial managers", are taught frequently throughout the year. H will also adapt an existing course or even write a new course from scratch and offer it in-house for a client company. Trainers often have to travel away from home and stay in hotels in order to present in-house courses at clients' offices.

Each course delegate receives a printed copy of the course materials and an electronic copy on a memory stick. Feedback indicates that delegates like to refer to the paper copy during the course and then take the electronic copy for ease of storage and future reference.

Courses are presented using laptops and projectors. Slides are written on an industry-standard presentation software package. H has provided each trainer with a laptop and all of the company's training rooms are equipped with projectors. Client companies also have projectors that are available for presentations.

Each course has a very specific syllabus and the course materials are written to a very high standard. A master copy of the material used on each course, including client-specific "in-house courses" is stored on a PC at H's head office and updated copies are backed up to a server at another office. Courses are reviewed regularly and updated when required. The company- specific courses are held so that they can be adapted if necessary for other companies or to become a general offering.

Trigger

'Image' is very important and H's trainers all take great pride in their personal appearance. They all take care to ensure that they are well dressed. That pride also extends to being seen to have the latest technology. Many of H's trainers have bought themselves tablet computers that they can use instead of their laptops. There are different operating systems for these machines, but all can run the software required to edit and present course materials and all of the trainers have purchased models that can work with standard projectors. The trainers feel that these tablets look more impressive and that they are lighter to pack when they have to work away from home on in-house courses. The tablets have also been used to go online and access H's systems.

H's Head of IT is concerned that there could be problems associated with the trainers using their own tablet computers in this way.

Task

As a senior employee in the IT department write a memorandum to the IT director of H which:

(a) Discusses the risks associated with H's staff using their own equipment (for example tablets) instead of the laptops provided by H; and

(b) Recommends, with explanations, the policies and procedures that H should adopt for the use and purchase of laptops and other devices used by the trainers.

(45 minutes)

Test your understanding 11 – H legal firm (Case study)

Scenario

H is a legal firm that specialises in pursuing small claims for compensation for personal injuries that its clients have suffered. The company advertises its services on television and guarantees that its clients do not have to pay any legal fees even if they lose the case. The losing side is normally liable for the other party's legal fees and so H's fee is paid by the negligent party who caused the injury, provided H wins the case for its client.

H has to take great care when evaluating applications from potential clients. If H loses the case it will not be paid for any of the work it has done on the case and H will also be liable for the other side's legal fees. To reduce the risk of taking on cases that it might subsequently lose, H uses highly trained legal staff to conduct telephone interviews with applicants. These staff work in a telephone call centre and ask each potential client a series of questions to establish the likelihood of winning that case. This procedure has proven to be very reliable: H has won more than 80% of the cases that it has accepted. Unfortunately, this system is expensive because H has to pay high salaries in order to recruit suitably qualified legal staff.

Trigger

H's Head of Information Technology (IT) has suggested that the legal staff in the call centre could be replaced by an 'expert system'.

Such a system could be manned by operators who would not require a great deal of training or expertise. The expert system will be an interactive software package that will provide call centre staff with a series of questions to ask potential clients. The call centre operators will be trained to explain the meaning of the questions if necessary and to input the responses into the system in a consistent way. The expert system will choose the questions that are asked to reflect information that has already been input. For example, if a case involves a road traffic accident then there will be different questions depending on whether the police were involved in the incident and whether either party has been charged with a motoring offence. Once all of the questions have been answered the software will provide the operator with a recommendation as to whether the case should be accepted, rejected or referred to a lawyer in H's legal department for further consideration.

H's Head of IT believes that a well-designed expert system will be as reliable as the legal staff who are presently employed. It will be expensive to develop, but it will save a great deal of money in the long term because the call centre operators will be cheaper to employ.

The expert system would be developed by an external consultant who would act as a "knowledge engineer". The knowledge engineer would work with the senior lawyers in H's legal department to identify the logic that runs through the evaluation of a potential client's case and codify that logic using a standard expert system package. H's senior lawyers would then have to assist in testing the expert system. Finally, call centre staff will have to be trained in the operation of the expert system.

Task

Write a report to the Board which:

- Advises H's directors on the risks of using an expert system instead of legal staff at the call centre; and
- Recommends, giving reasons, the procedures that should be in place to ensure the successful design and testing of the expert system.

(45 minutes)

Test your understanding 12 – H travel agent (Case study)

Scenario

H is a major travel agent that specialises in holiday travel. H's sales are all made either online or through a call centre.

H's primary data processing centre is located in a large office building close to a major city centre. This data processing centre houses the computers and the staff who operate and maintain the website that enables customers to make online bookings. The data processing centre also houses the call centre that handles bookings made by telephone.

The website operates continuously. The call centre operates six days per week from 8.00 in the morning until 10.00 at night. There are 120 call centre operators who work on a two shift basis. The call centre staff work at terminals that are linked through a local network to the same data servers that provide the online service. H's system runs on the standard software package that is used across the travel industry to enable travel agents, airlines and hotels to communicate with one another. All holiday sales are recorded in real-time to prevent overbooking.

Data processing is a key part of H's operations. Consequently H has two data processing sites one central and one remote. The primary site is in the city centre and employs 60 systems staff, who operate a three shift system to ensure that the website is always available and up to date.

The remote site is located in an industrial estate 40 miles away; it has the same hardware as the primary site. The two sites are linked electronically and data is backed up frequently. There is a full back up every Sunday and incremental backups occur several times every day.

The remote site has a small team of systems operators and their shift patterns ensure that there is always at least one of them onsite at all times to ensure that hardware and software are maintained and backups are secure.

Trigger

H's directors decided to test the operation of the backup site by conducting the company's first ever full-scale disaster simulation. The first Tuesday in September is usually the quietest day of the year with a low volume of activity and so that was designated as the test day. All systems and call centre staff were asked to arrive at the primary data processing centre two hours before their normal start time on the test day so that they could be taken to the remote site by chartered buses. The chartered buses would then operate a shuttle service to the city centre site to allow for shift changes and to enable staff to get home at the end of their shift.

Systems and call centre staff were warned several weeks in advance that the primary data processing centre would be taken offline at 6.00 on the morning of the test day, immediately after the scheduled incremental backup. The website would go offline at that time. That would simulate a disaster such as a major fire that had disrupted power and communications. It was planned that the systems operators at the remote site would be asked to recreate the data files at 6.30 on the morning of the test day by combining the most recent backup copy with the subsequent incremental backups. The website would be brought back online from the remote site within an hour and the call centre operated from the remote site for a full working day.

There was an unexpected 40% absenteeism rate on the day of the simulation, which made it impossible to operate a full service during the simulation. Many of the staff had been concerned that they would find it difficult to travel to and from work at the proposed times because there would be little or no public transport. Furthermore, many would find it disruptive to their childcare arrangements. Almost all of those who were absent emailed their supervisors on the day of the simulation to say that they had minor illnesses and that they would return to work next day.

Task

Write a report to the Board which:

(a) Discusses the advantages and disadvantages to H of running a disaster simulation; and

(b) Discusses the weaknesses of the planned approach taken by H to its simulation.

(30 minutes)

(c) Recommend, stating reasons, ways in which H could ensure that the remote centre would be fully staffed in the event that a genuine disaster occurs.

(15 minutes)

9 Chapter summary

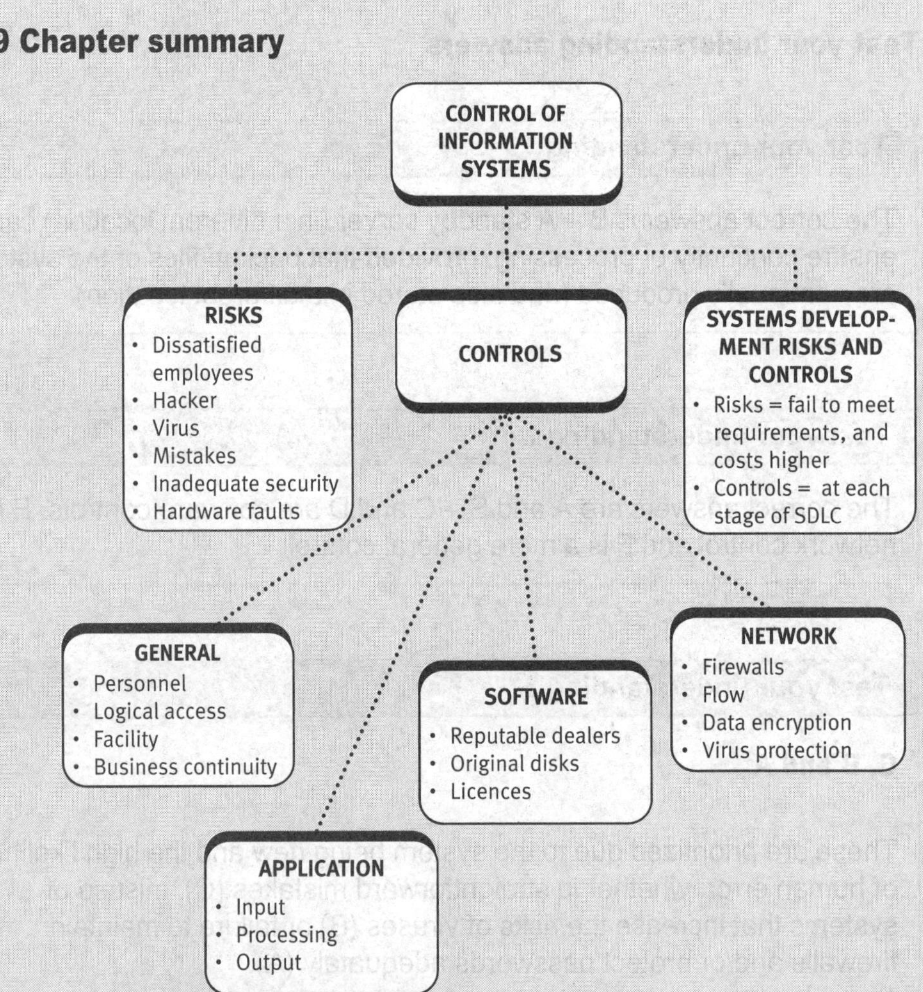
CONTROL OF INFORMATION SYSTEMS
RISKS
• Dissatisfied employees
• Hacker
• Virus
• Mistakes
• Inadequate security
• Hardware faults
CONTROLS
SYSTEMS DEVELOPMENT RISKS AND CONTROLS
• Risks = fail to meet requirements, and costs higher
• Controls = at each stage of SDLC
GENERAL
• Personnel
• Logical access
• Facility
• Business continuity
SOFTWARE
• Reputable dealers
• Original disks
• Licences
NETWORK
• Firewalls
• Flow
• Data encryption
• Virus protection
APPLICATION
• Input
• Processing
• Output

Test your understanding answers

Test your understanding 1

The correct answer is B – A standby server (in a different location) can ensure continuity of processing, provided that backup files of the system are continually produced (and also stored in a different location).

Test your understanding 2

The correct answers are A and B – C and D are software controls, E is a network control and F is a more general control.

Test your understanding 3

C, B and A

These are prioritized due to the system being new and the high likelihood of human error, whether in straightforward mistakes (C), misuse of systems that increase the risks of viruses (B) or failure to maintain firewalls and/or protect passwords adequately (A).

Test your understanding 4

The correct answer is B – the six stages in the correct order are Planning, Analysis, Design, Development, Implementation and Review.

Test your understanding 5

The correct answer is A – New files will need to be created for the new system. This will be followed by implementation, by whichever changeover method is deemed appropriate. Review and maintenance are stages after implementation.

Test your understanding 6

The correct answer is D – This is where the old system is switched off and the new system is switched on. This is only appropriate where the two systems are very different or it is too expensive to run both. This method is cheap but very risky since if the new system doesn't work then the company may be unable to revert to the old system.

Test your understanding 7

C

A is too risky – as a bespoke system that is having problems during the testing stage this method of changeover is not recommended.

B is too expensive – since costs have to be reduced elsewhere there probably isn't the budget to run two systems simultaneously.

D has limited usefulness – since each division uses a different computer system, lessons learnt at one would have limited applicability to the others.

Test your understanding 8

A, B and D

Pilot changeover cannot be used, as it assumes that any 'lessons learned' in the first changeover can be transferred to all of the other sites.

We are told that each of the merged companies currently uses a different information system, suggesting that results at one pilot would be of limited usefulness when looking at other locations.

Test your understanding 9 – C bank (Case study)

To: The head computer programmer

From: Management accountant

Date: Today

Subject: Designing database queries

Dear Sir,

I understand the database queries will take programmers' time to write. The programmers will be full-time employees, but they will be distracted from their regular duties while they are involved in this investigation. The searches should be designed carefully so that the internal auditor can draw the clearest possible conclusion without repeating the search. The searches should be designed to minimise the impact on the system. Bank customers may be affected if the system slows down for the duration of a long search. It may not be possible to avoid any impact on the system's response times when running non-standard queries, but the programmers may be able to reduce the problem by choosing search parameters that make the search more efficient.

The searches must minimise the number of false positives. It will waste the internal audit department's time if too many accounts are highlighted without good reason. The manner in which the search is conducted must take account of the laws of evidence. If the clerk is accused of a crime and details are passed to the police then the manner in which the search was conducted may be challenged by the defence. Great care will have to be taken to ensure that the very search process cannot be said to have changed the data collected so that the clerk is blamed for transactions that were actually conducted by somebody else.

Best wishes

Management accountant

Report

To: The Board

From: A.N. Accountant

Date: Today

Subject: Controls over unauthorised withdrawals

Introduction

This report covers whether there is a need for C Bank to determine if additional controls to prevent unauthorised withdrawals are necessary, and recommends control procedures that C Bank should introduce in order to deter unauthorised withdrawals from dormant accounts.

(i) **Is there a need for additional controls?**

The first step is to determine the number of dormant accounts that the bank has. If there are very few then the bank may decide that it would not be cost-effective to introduce a control. Similarly, the sizes of the balances in dormant accounts should be considered. If the total value of the funds at risk is small then it might be cheaper for the bank to compensate the victims of staff fraud.

If the potential risk is high then the bank could consider checking whether the account holders are checking their balances. The best way to do this would be to contact the account holders by telephone to ask whether they would be interested in moving to a more efficient savings strategy. If the account holder is alive and well and aware of the balance then any fraudulent withdrawal will be reported and so there is very little risk. Contacting the customers in this way will also give the bank the opportunity to earn some commission from the sale of savings products.

(ii) **Control procedures**

This will require a change to the bank's software. Every account should be tagged with the date of the most recent deposit or withdrawal. If an account has not had a transaction for, say, two years any subsequent deposit or withdrawal should be flagged. If a transaction is flagged then the clerk should be required to seek authorisation from a supervisor before proceeding. This procedure need not delay the transaction by more than a few minutes while the authorisation is sought and so the customer need not be inconvenienced.

Deposits have to be flagged in the same manner as withdrawals, otherwise a fraudulent clerk could make a small deposit in order to rid an account of its dormant status.

The software could record the number of flagged transactions processed in each branch or by each counter clerk. Large numbers of transactions occurring in any given branch or by any given member of staff could be viewed as suspicious. In that case, it would be worth following up the transaction with the customer in order to confirm its validity.

The fact that these procedures have been introduced should be publicised within the bank. This type of fraud is not difficult to design or to perpetrate. If bank staff realise that C Bank is aware of the threat and is controlling for it then they may be less inclined to risk stealing in this way.

Conclusions

Additional controls to prevent unauthorised withdrawals are necessary, and control procedures (particularly in relation to the bank's software) should be introduced in order to deter unauthorised withdrawals from dormant accounts.

Test your understanding 10 – H training company (Case study)

Memorandum

To: IT director

From: Senior IT employee

Date: Today

Subject: The use of tablets – risks, policies and procedures

(a) **Risks with the use of tablets**

The most immediate risk is that these tablets are being connected to H's servers in order to both download files and upload edited and modified versions. H has no way to ensure that these devices are free of viruses and other malware and so the systems could be corrupted. The laptops are a known quantity and H can specify the security software that must be used and kept up to date.

The files that are given to delegates are also potentially open to infection. The delegates could open their own organisations up to a threat and H could be held liable.

H's IT staff may not be able to support these devices. If a compatibility issue arises with either hardware or software then the staff will be unable to seek support from H and that could affect the smooth running of a presentation. There are several different platforms for tablet computers and so it would be difficult for H's staff to be current with all of them.

Tablets do not always run industry-standard software, but there are often simplified packages that claim to be able to edit these files. The creation or modification of a file using a "compatible" software suite may mean that it cannot be opened or that some of the formatting is lost. That could make H's presentations seem far less professional.

Tablets and similar devices may be less robust than a business laptop and so the courses could be disrupted by machines breaking down or failing.

The software running on the tablets may not be licenced and H may be open to accusations of copyright theft if its staff are using these devices using unauthorised copies.

In the event that a trainer leaves the company it will not be as easy for H to request the return of its files because they will be on the trainer's personal tablet.

There are very few upside risks, but this arrangement does mean that H's trainers will often appear to be at the forefront of technology. It also gives H the opportunity to experiment with new technology at very little direct cost to the company.

(b) **Policies and procedures over the use of tablets**

The starting point should be to insist that staff use only the hardware and software that have been provided by the company. That will give H control over the platforms that are being used to develop and deliver courses.

H should have a designated evaluation group to evaluate new technology as it becomes available. That group should comprise both IT experts and trainers, so that the new technology can be assessed from both a technical and a practical point of view. H needs to ensure that it makes the best possible use of new technology as and when it becomes available in a reliable and cost-effective product. H should avoid getting carried away by the rush to adopt new technologies that are at the "bleeding edge" because early adopters pay more and bear most of the risks.

New hardware and software should be evaluated in terms of a detailed checklist covering both security and compatibility. H has to be certain that none of its materials will be at risk of infection or corruption and that they will also be capable of being opened, edited, stored and passed onto clients. Security should be evaluated by referring to third-party reviews by security specialists because it is unlikely that H will have sufficient expertise in-house to test the firewall and anti-virus systems on a new computer platform.

When new devices require a change in software, such as a switch to a cut-down version of a package that can be run on a tablet, H should insist that the presentations are reviewed slide-by-slide to ensure that they all open and have the required format. H should consider insisting that the materials continue to be updated using industry-standard packages and that the new hardware should be used to present courses using copies of the updated files.

There should be a genuine business reason for making the change to new platforms, otherwise H will simply be exposed to the risks arising from the adoption of new technology for no better reason than trainers' preferring to use the latest "toys". That would not prevent H from agreeing to use new hardware simply for the sake of impressing clients because image is very important in this business.

Test your understanding 11 – H legal firm (Case study)

Report

To: The Board

From: A.N. Acoountant

Date: Today

Subject: Expert system

Introduction

This report advises on the risks of using an expert system instead of legal staff at the call centre; and recommends the procedures that should be in place to ensure the successful design and testing of the expert system.

(a) **Use of an expert system**

The use of an expert system has both upside and downside risks.

The expert system may prove better at identifying suitable cases than the present staff. It could do so because it should replicate the thought processes of senior members of the company's legal team, who are more experienced and better qualified than the legal advisors employed in the call centre. Furthermore, the system will be less prone to emotional factors. At present, the legal advisors may have some sympathy for the victim and that could affect their judgement. The expert system will be an impartial and objective tool to identify the probability of winning the case.

The expert system is dealing with a very complicated decision that may not lend itself to a computerised thought process. There may be matters of judgement that only a human interviewer could determine. For example, the present arrangements lend themselves to asking open-ended questions that will make it easier to identify inconsistencies in the potential client's story. The inputs into an expert system will lead to asking more closed questions that may have the effect of leading a dishonest applicant who wishes to pursue a weak case at H's expense.

The expert system will not necessarily be able to react in the same manner as a human operator. For example, the client may misunderstand the nature of a case and may describe an accident at work in terms of negligence whereas a legally-trained operator would quickly determine that the actual issue is one of employment law. The expert system may require operators to be almost as well qualified as the present staff and that may reduce the potential for salary reductions.

H is heavily exposed to any errors in the expert system. There is an opportunity cost to every rejected case that could have been won. Any weak cases that are accepted will leave H exposed to the risk of wasted billable hours and the threat of paying legal fees to successful defendants.

If there is any bias or error in the system then that will not be apparent until the system has been running for some time. H will only be aware that it is rejecting winnable cases if it is discovered that a large proportion of applicants is being rejected, in which case the clients will have made arrangements with other legal firms and the opportunity to represent them will be lost. H will only discover that it is accepting too many unwinnable cases after it has signed up to represent those clients and it may then be too late to withdraw.

The expert system may not be as easy to update as a human staff. Human operators can be briefed on developments in the law or changes in the attitude of the courts by means of a memo or a training course. The expert system will have to be reprogrammed, and that may require significant changes that will take time and expense to introduce. The new system will be far less responsive in an area that can change very quickly.

Once H makes its legally trained staff redundant then it will not be able to revert to the former system in the event that the expert system fails. The present staff will start to look for alternative employment as soon as the proposed change is announced and they are unlikely to be available if H decides to offer them their jobs back in the event that the expert system proves unreliable.

(b) **Procedures during design and testing**

A briefing document should be developed to highlight the nature of the decision that has to be coded and to reflect the lack of clear-cut decision criteria and the consultant should be asked to provide examples of similar tasks that have been undertaken.

H should ask the consultant to discuss the decision process with several people in the organisation, both senior lawyers and present members of the call centre staff. That will provide some scope for differences of opinion to be identified, particularly with respect to the possibility that senior managers may have become detached from the actual process of dealing with applications.

Testing

The system should be tested in the first instance by running a sample of past applications through it to establish the consistency of the responses. The results should be interpreted with care because it is possible that the criteria coded into the expert system will be superior to those used in practice by the call centre staff and so there should be a detailed review to determine why the differences arose. The test cases should be selected so that most (ideally all) of the branches that questioning can follow are tested – for example, if different questions are asked in cases of road traffic accidents compared with industrial accidents then examples of both should be included.

There should be a further review of a sample of cases by H's lawyers to establish that they agree with the decision that is being recommended.

The incidence of cases referred for further review should be established because too many of those will imply that the system is not sufficiently sophisticated and so it will not be a satisfactory replacement of the present system.

Operators will have to be trained carefully. The first draft of the training materials should be prepared by the consultant who designed the system, so that they are consistent with the software and the interface. The first training course should also be attended by members of H's legal team to ensure that any legal terminology is properly reflected in the materials and so will be fully understood. Any recurring requests for clarification by operators under training should be noted and either result in a revision to the software so that the questions are more precise or result in an amendment to the training materials so that future courses cover the points raised.

The proportion of cases accepted should be kept under constant review. If that changes from the proportion accepted under the previous system then the reasons should be investigated by having the decisions made by the expert system reviewed by a member of the legal department. The results from accepted cases should be kept under review anyway as a matter of course. Any deterioration in the success rate of accepted cases should be investigated in case there is a problem with the expert system.

Conclusion

Although the expert system will save money in the future it is a risky strategy due to the potential for error. The design and testing stage of the expert system is critical to ensure that it runs correctly. It will need constant monitoring post-implementation to ensure that it is operating correctly.

Test your understanding 12 – H travel agent (Case study)

Report

To: The Board

From: A.N. Accountant

Date: Today

Subject: Disaster simulation day

Introduction

This report covers the advantages and disadvantages to H of running a disaster simulation and discusses the weaknesses of the planned approach taken.

It then goes on to recommend ways in which H could ensure that the remote centre would be fully staffed in the event that a genuine disaster occurs.

(a) The advantages and disadvantages of running a disaster simulation

H must be totally confident that the backup arrangements will be available and effective if the time ever comes when they must be relied upon. An exercise that brings the system online and tests its operation will demonstrate that the hardware and software operate as expected and that staff are able to work effectively in the alternative site. It is far better to discover an unexpected problem while the primary system is still available than to wait until the primary system is taken out of operation for an extended period.

The simulation will also help to train staff and ensure that they are confident and capable of running the backup system. The call centre staff in particular must be able to deal with complex queries and transactions and must be familiar with the IT systems that underpin their work.

The most obvious disadvantage is cost. It will be expensive to bring a standby system online and to transport and accommodate staff. It is possible that the costs will not be justified if many of the tests could be conducted just as effectively without actually running a full-scale simulation. For example, the systems staff at the remote site could practise recreating the records from backups on a frequent basis and the resulting files could be compared with the files on the primary system. That would be just as valid a test as shutting down the primary system and it would be far less expensive and disruptive.

(b) Weaknesses found

Perhaps understandably, H is conducting the exercise under the simplest of conditions: the quietest day of the year and at a time when the call centre is closed anyway. Proving that the entity can cope with the simplest case may not give real reassurance that it is robust.

The staff are all being warned well in advance. It is very likely that systems staff will take the opportunity to check things more carefully than usual to prevent any problems that may reflect badly upon them. That may invalidate the results slightly if the system in operation at the time of the "disaster" is different from the usual one.

A real disaster may make it impossible for H to communicate with staff to ask them to make their way to an assembly point for transportation to the remote site. Unless H keeps a database of mobile phone numbers at the remote site so that a text can be sent to all staff, they will make their way to the primary site as usual. The logistics of dealing with a real disaster are not being tested.

The test is effectively taking the backup facility offline for the duration of the exercise. Unless there is a system in place to back the remote site up at the primary site the transactions recorded at the remote site could be lost if a disaster strikes there. H will be totally dependent upon the system for reinstating the files from the remote site and any shortcoming in that system may lead to errors being introduced into the records that will prove difficult to correct.

(c) **Ways to ensure full staffing during disaster simulation**

H should make it a condition of employment that staff agree to work at the remote site as and when circumstances dictate that it is necessary for them to do so. That may mean changing contracts of employment to ensure that the company can impose that as a duty whenever it is necessary to do so.

It should be made clear that staff will be likely to be asked to be examined by a medical professional in the event that they claim to be ill at such an inconvenient time.

H must also investigate ways of dealing with the causes of the absenteeism. H should ensure that staff become familiar with the location of the remote site and have a realistic understanding of the implications of working there. It may be possible to run training courses there or organise other functions so that staff become used to making their way to and from the site.

All staff will be reluctant to have their working day extended and so it might be necessary to compensate them with overtime pay. Call centre staff are not always particularly well paid and so paying time and a half or double time for any additional travelling time may be a worthwhile investment.

It may also be necessary to address the transportation issues faced by staff. Public transport may be more frequent during the morning and evening rush hours and so asking staff to arrive early and travel home late may cause some inconvenience. H could organise a car-share system with the driver being paid a realistic rate per mile for the journey. That could require organising parking facilities and ensuring that staff are properly insured to carry colleagues as passengers under such circumstances.

H could also attempt to deal with the childcare problem by paying for any additional carer or nursery fees or by establishing a crèche close to the remote facility. Again, that could raise liability and insurance issues and so care would have to be taken.

H will also have to ensure that there is not a deeper issue such as a lack of loyalty that discourages employees from cooperating when some flexibility is required. This may be worth investigating as a more general HR matter.

Conclusions

There are many advantages and disadvantages to H of running a disaster simulation but the advantages outweigh the disadvantages.

There were several weaknesses of the planned approach taken by H to its simulation which can be learnt from for the future.

Ways in which H could ensure that the remote centre would be fully staffed in the event that a genuine disaster occurs include making it a condition of employment, paying overtime, and addressing the transportation issue.

hapter

5

Information strategy

Chapter learning objectives

Lead	Component
B1. Evaluate the tools and processes required for strategy implementation.	(a) Advise managers of the risks in the development of strategies for information systems that support the organisation's strategic requirements.

Indicative syllabus content

- The purpose and contents of information system strategies, and the need for strategy complementary to the corporate and individual business strategies.

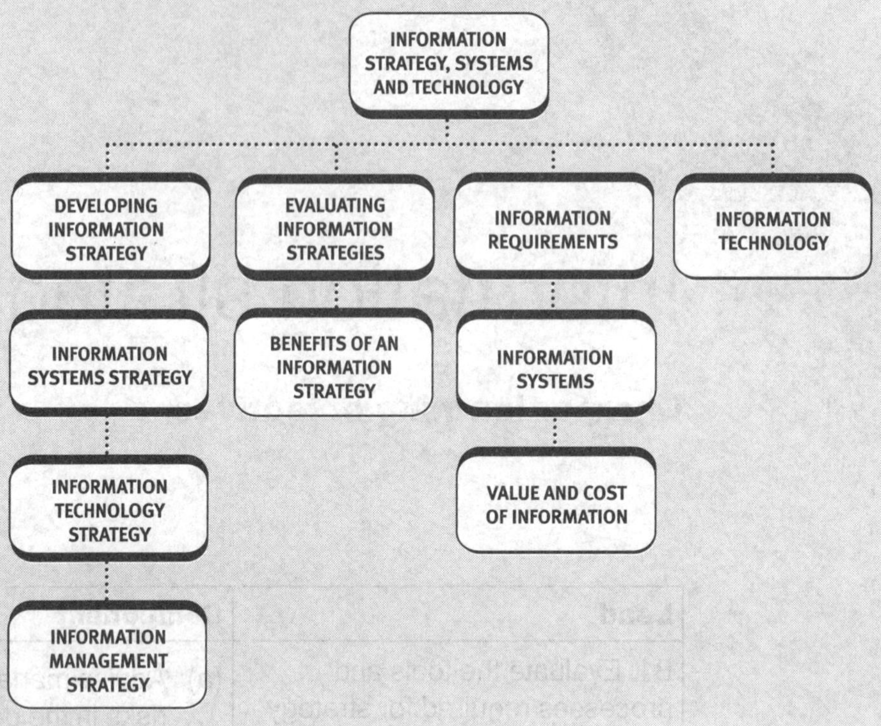

1 Developing an information strategy

A key factor in companies controlling and monitoring the risks they face is being able to provide the information to managers to run the business. Companies therefore need information systems and an information strategy.

The reason companies now refer to and talk about 'information strategy' as opposed purely to information systems is that information is being identified as a key strategic resource, arguably the most valuable resource businesses create and have. Because of its value it is worth having a good plan to structure the information provision, ensure it meets the needs of the business and secure and control it.

Information strategy

The company needs to develop a plan to link its business and information strategies, and the model below shows how this can be done.

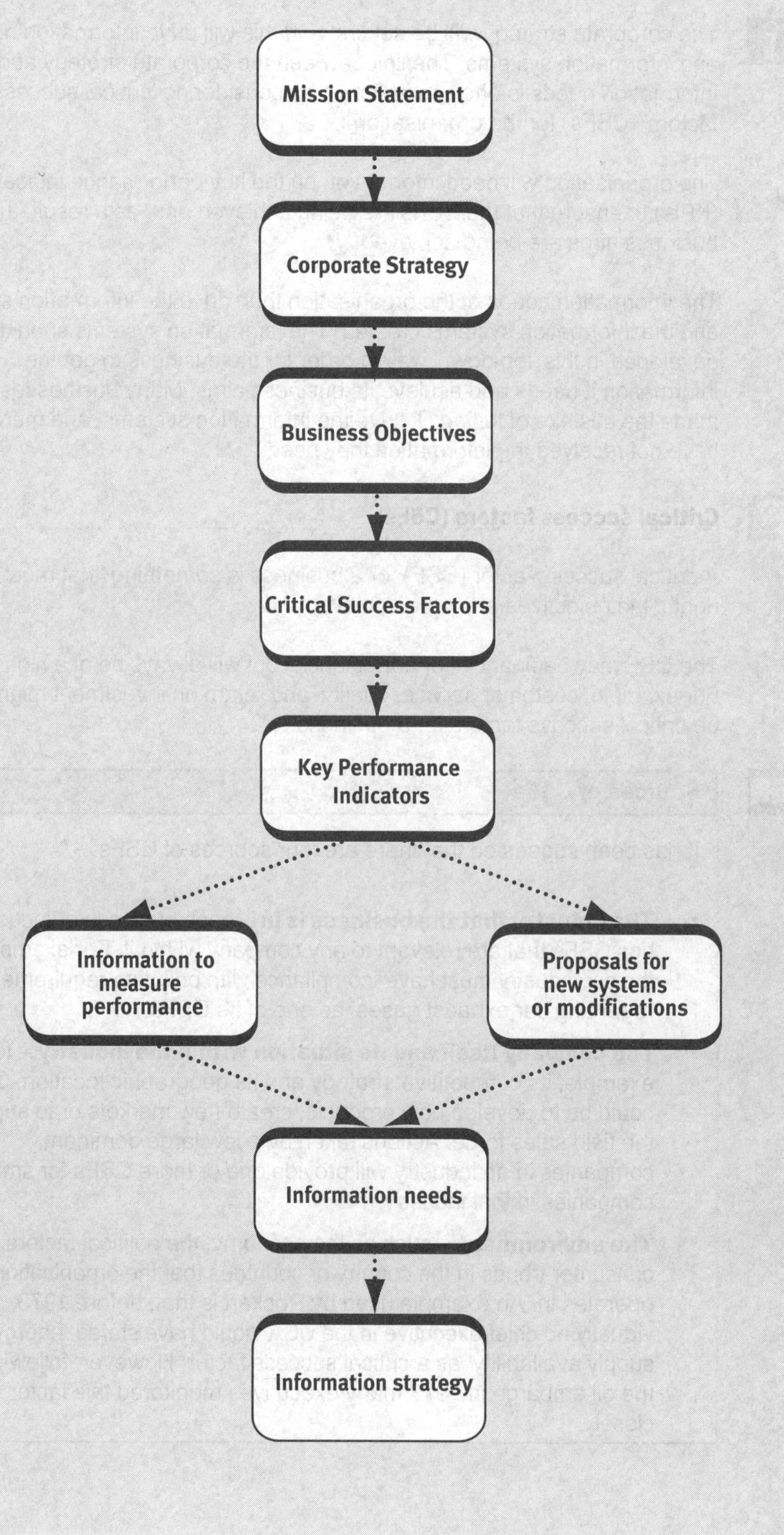
Mission Statement
Corporate Strategy
Business Objectives
Critical Success Factors
Key Performance Indicators
Information to measure performance
Proposals for new systems or modifications
Information needs
Information strategy

The corporate strategy will be set first and this will drive information needs and information systems. The link between the corporate strategy and the information needs is often established by considering 'critical success factors' (CSFs) for the organisation.

The organisation will need information on the key performance indicators (KPIs) to ensure that the CSFs are being achieved and, as a result, that the business aims are being achieved.

The information needs of the organisation then drive the information strategy and the information systems created. The information systems should be developed in this 'top down' way in order for the business to get the information it needs and achieve its business aims. Many businesses have made the mistake of letting IT drive the information systems, and managers have not received the information they need.

Critical success factors (CSFs)

A critical success factor (CSF) for a business is something 'that must go right if the objectives are to be achieved'.

The CSF may be financial or non-financial but will always be at a high level. For example, customer service, quality, and return on investment might all be critical success factors for a business.

Sources of CSFs

It has been suggested that there are four sources of CSFs:

- **The industry that the business is in** – each business or industry has CSFs that are relevant to any company within it. For example, the car industry must have 'compliance with pollution requirements regarding car exhaust gases' as one of its CSFs.
- **The company itself and its situation within the industry** – for example, its competitive strategy and its geographic location. CSFs could be to develop new products, create new markets or to support the field sales force. Actions taken by a few large dominant companies in an industry will provide one or more CSFs for small companies in that industry.
- **The environment** – such as the economy, the political factors and consumer trends in the country or countries that the organisation operates in. An example used by Rockart is that, before 1973, virtually no chief executive in the USA would have stated 'energy supply availability' as a critical success factor. However, following the oil embargo in 1973 many executives monitored this factor closely.

- **Temporal (short-term) organisational factors** – these are areas of company activity that are unusually causing concern in the short-term because they are unacceptable and need attention. For example, cases of too little or too much inventory might classify as a CSF for a short time during recession.

Many CSFs will require new systems to be developed or improvements made to existing systems. Other CSFs will require improved information to monitor performance of key indicators which measure the achievement, or otherwise, of success factors and objectives. This may require further development of information systems.

Performance indicators

A performance indicator (PI) is an objective stated in such a way that progress towards the achievement of a critical success factor can be measured.

More on PIs

The PIs should be:

Specific	Expressed clearly and precisely.
Measurable	Capable of quantification.
Achievable	Realistically achievable by the organisation.
Relevant	To the critical success factor that is being measured.
Time-constrained	By when?

Test your understanding 1

In the correct order, the stages in developing an information strategy are:

A Mission statement; Objectives; KPIs; Information strategy

B Information strategy; Objective; Mission statement; KPIs

2 Information strategy components

The information strategy is the overall plan a business has to create and develop its information systems.

Information strategy is usually broken up into three parts:

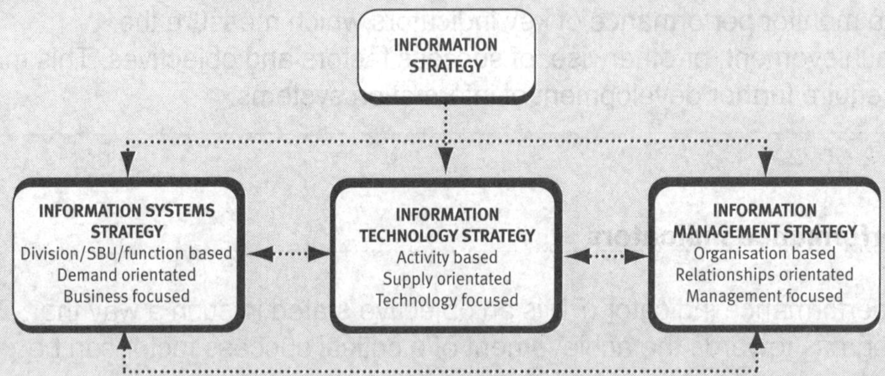

The three strategies link as shown in the diagram.

The term **information systems strategy** is normally used to cover all three.

The differences between the three components are summarised below:

- **IS strategy** looks at the way in which information systems in various parts of the organisation are organised.
- **IT strategy** looks at the technology infrastructure of the systems.
- **IM strategy** considers how the systems support management processes.

More on IS strategy

Information systems (IS) strategy is concerned with identifying the information requirements of the organisation. IS strategy must ensure that the information required by the organisation, to help it achieve its strategic objectives, is:

- acquired
- retained
- shared, and
- made available for use.

It relates to all aspects of information, and all areas of activity (financial and non-financial; strategic, tactical and operational; human resources, operations, sales and marketing, research and development; internal and external information, and so on). It is concerned with answering the questions, for all aspects of activity at all levels within the organisation:

- What information is required? and
- Where might it come from?

IS strategy should be demand-oriented, in the sense that answers to the question 'What information is required?' should focus on the demands of the business managers for information. IS strategies must also be business-driven and capable of delivering tangible benefits, for example increased productivity, enhanced profits, and perhaps a reduction in the workforce.

Traditional organisational structures that divide business functions are not suitable as a basis for IS strategy development in a 'process-oriented' business environment. Client-server technologies have the capability to integrate business functions. This results in a blurring of the divisions found in the old functional-based organisation structure and demands a different way of conceptualising organisations and their associated business processes and information requirements.

More on IT strategy

Information technology can be defined as 'the use of computers, microelectronics and telecommunications to help us produce, store, and send information in the form of pictures, words or numbers, more reliably, quickly and economically'.

Information technology (IT) strategy is concerned with what specific IT systems are needed to meet the demands for information within the organisation, in terms of:

- system networks and communication systems
- hardware, and
- software.

IT systems should be developed or adapted so that they are capable of obtaining, processing, summarising and reporting the information required by the organisation. The IT systems must also be consistent with the requirements for the storage and availability of data and information to users.

IT strategy is about the delivery of workable solutions to business problems – the practical application of information technology to the organisation. It is described as activity-based, supply-oriented and technology-focused and is seen as the technology framework or architecture that drives, shapes and controls the IT infrastructure. In other words, it considers what technologies are available, and which of these would be most suitable for meeting the information requirements of the organisation.

More on IM strategy

Information management (IM) strategy is concerned with the management of the information that is gathered by the organisation, and how it is stored and made available for access by users. It is therefore concerned with matters such as:

- the use of databases, and the type of databases used
- data warehousing
- back-up facilities for data storage
- data security issues
- archiving.

The IM strategy should ensure that information that has been provided through IT systems is made available to the individuals who need it. From an economic perspective, it should also be concerned with making the information available in the most efficient way but at the least cost. IM strategy might therefore promote the elimination of data duplication.

Information management is also concerned more broadly with:

- planning – ensuring that the IS and IT strategies are integrated with the other strategic plans and objectives of the organisation
- organisation – this involves issues such as decentralisation or centralisation of the IT function, the formation of steering committees, management education and training, IT reporting procedures and the responsibilities of IT managers
- control – control issues relate to the assessment of the performance of IT systems and controls over IT costs (and benefits). Key aspects are performance measurement and investment appraisal of IT
- technology – is related to managing the priorities for IT strategy, e.g. the design and development of new methodologies for IT, security practices and data management techniques.

Test your understanding 2

During the production of the information strategy at P plc several questions were asked regarding where the information needed would come from and what information was required. This is part of the:

A Information system strategy

B Information technology strategy

C Information management strategy

3 Benefits of an information strategy

The benefits of an information strategy include:

- Achievement of **goal congruence** between the information systems objectives and the corporate objectives. Failure of computer systems to work can result in the failure of some organisations to function at all e.g. Amazon and eBay.
- The organisation is more likely to be able to create and sustain **competitive advantage**. The company's computer system will likely impact on the customer these days, if they order over the internet or rely on order information for a delivery date.
- The high levels of expenditure on information systems will be more focused on **supporting** key aspects of the **business**.
- **Developments in IT can be exploited** at the most appropriate time – which is not always when they are first available.
- Computers are often of strategic importance in a company. Having an information strategy is a **costly** business and unmanaged development can lead to costly mistakes.
- IT affects all levels of **employees and management**. Having a plan that can be communicated to these employees should ensure that they 'buy-in' to the ideas within it and efficiency will be increased more quickly.

4 Evaluating information strategies

You could be asked about the information strategy and systems developed by a business.

The key feature of the strategy is that it should support business needs and managers and be an integral part of the overall business strategy and therefore if it does not achieve this it is a poor strategy.

A structured evaluation approach would be:

(1) Identify the objectives of the organisation and the CSFs.

(2) Identify objectives for risk management and control.

(3) Identify key information requirements of managers.

(4) Establish information currently available and assess whether information provision is adequate.

(5) Identify alternative strategies and the beneficial information they would provide.

(6) Evaluate whether the technology used by the organisation is the best and most appropriate available (IT strategy assessment).

(7) Assess whether the information is managed and controlled in the best way for the organisation (IM strategy assessment).

(8) Evaluate whether the information strategy is appropriately controlled in the organisation and ensure that there are clear lines of responsibility for it.

In the exam there is likely to be a scenario littered with IT issues in a company where the information systems are not working optimally. Think about your own place of work:

- How old is your computer system?
- Is it slow to process information?
- Is the information well laid out, superfluous, have errors in it?
- Do you have a good IT support department that can resolve any issues quickly and to your satisfaction?

There are many other issues which you could probably think of since you probably use a computer each day at work – always try to relate your own experiences to the scenario given in the exam and the options you could select.

5 Information requirements of managers

Levels of management

The various levels of management that exist within an organisation may be illustrated by Anthony's Triangle:

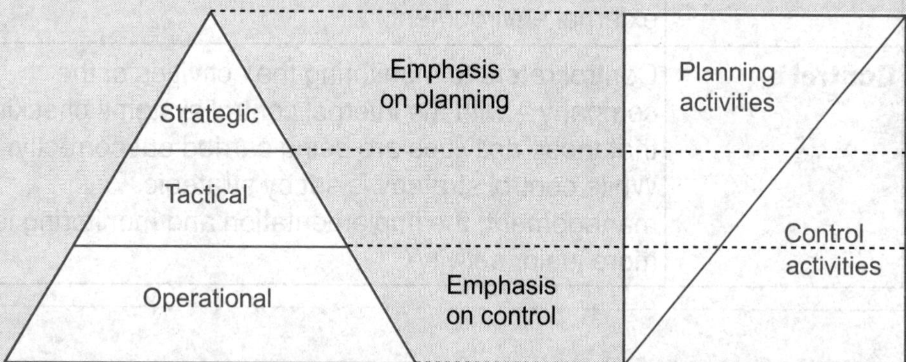

The different levels of management within an organisation will take different types of decision and will require different information to take those decisions. The information systems of the organisation must meet the information needs of all of these different levels.

More on management levels

In general terms, each level of management will be involved in specific activities:

Level	Activity
Strategic	Involved with monitoring and controlling the organisation as a whole, making decisions on areas such as opening of new shops and factories or investment in new product line.
Tactical	Responsible for implementing the decisions of strategic managers and ensuring that the different divisions or departments within the organisation are operating correctly.
Operational	Controlling the day-to-day operations of the organisation, reporting queries or problems back to tactical management for decisions as necessary.

The two key activities of management are therefore:

Planning	Planning refers to setting the strategic direction of the company. This involves a significant degree of risk as strategic decision makers are effectively determining what the company will do in the context of a risky external environment.
Control	Control refers to monitoring the activities of the company – with the internal control systems checking that those activities are being carried out correctly. While control strategy is set by strategic management, the implementation and monitoring is a more junior activity.

Good information

The information received by management needs to be of a certain standard to be useful in internal control, risk management and monitoring.

The information should meet the criteria of 'good' information:

- **A**ccurate
- **C**omplete
- **C**ost-beneficial
- **U**ser-targeted
- **R**elevant
- **A**uthoritative
- **T**imely
- **E**asy to use

Information needs of managers

Information is required to enable managers at all levels to plan and control their responsible activities. Information must be provided to enable managers to make timely and effective decisions.

Management level	Information needs
Strategic management	• Business markets • Suppliers • Customers • Competitors • Stock market • Technology • Politics • Environmental issues.
Tactical management	• Tactical planning information • Targets • Production • Plant capacity • Budgets • Purchasing • Operating expenses • Manpower levels.
Operational management	• Primary activities • Work scheduling • Work force • Immediate resources.

Information characteristics

Strategic and operational information – characteristics

Information characteristic	Strategic	Operational
Time period	Information can be both historical (enabling management to learn from what has happened in the past) and forecast.	Operational information must be actual historical information.
Timeliness	Generally speaking, the timeliness of information is not crucial as decisions are taken over a series of weeks or months. Significant changes, such as the acquisition of a competitor, will normally be reported quickly to senior management.	Information must be immediately available
Objectivity	Strategic decision making will require a mixture of objective and subjective information. Building long-term plans needs future information, which incorporates subjective forecasts of what is likely to happen.	The highly structured and programmable decisions made at the operational level need information that is both objective and quantifiable. The comparatively junior level at which decisions are made requires strict guidelines to be set and disqualifies subjective data as a basis for this level of decision.
Quantifiability	Strategic decision making needs both qualitative and quantitative information, although attempts will often be made to quantify apparently qualitative data. This enables such data to be incorporated into the kind of mathematical models often used in the building of strategic plans.	
Accuracy	There is no demand for information to be completely accurate, it will often be rounded to the nearest thousand.	Information must be accurate to the nearest £ or $ – as it relates to low level or detailed decision making.

Certainty	By its very nature, future information is subject to uncertainty. Strategic planners must be capable of adjusting to the limitations of the data.	Information will have little or no uncertainty as it relates to historical recording of actual events, e.g. individual sales.
Completeness	Strategic planners will often need to work with only partial information, using assumptions and extrapolations to try to build as complete a picture as possible.	The sort of decisions to be made at this level are highly predictable, which enables the information needed to be specified and an appropriate information system built. This will ensure that a complete set of information is available when it is needed.
Breadth	A wide variety of data are needed for strategic planning. It must cover the whole gamut of the organisation's operations and can come in various forms.	Information will be focused on the specific decisions being made – any other data are irrelevant and potentially distracting.
Detail	It is unnecessary to have a great deal of detail when building a strategic plan, and detail is likely to be distracting and confusing. Aggregated and summarised data are most commonly used by senior management.	Information will be detailed to enable the manager to make decisions about individual items, e.g. the number of items to order.

Tactical information – characteristics

Just as tactical decision making forms a link between strategic and operational management, the information it requires has some of the characteristics of each.

Forecast and historical data are both required, although historical data are not needed as immediately as it is for operational decisions. Information is largely objective and quantitative but the greater experience of middle managers making tactical decisions makes this less important than for operational information.

For each of the other information qualities – accuracy, certainty, completeness, breadth and detail – tactical information occupies the mid-point between strategic and operational information.

6 Information systems to support management

To meet their information needs, managers use information systems, of which there are a number of different types. The different types of system meet the different information needs of the different managers.

The main systems can be summarised in the following diagram:

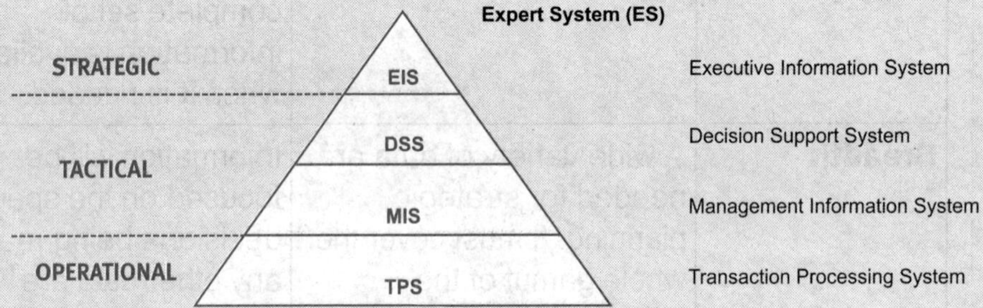

As a basic idea the systems towards the top of the tree will support the strategic decisions and they will use the data from systems in the levels below.

Definitions of information systems

Transaction Processing System (TPS)

- This is the system that records historic information and it represents the simple automation of manual systems.
- The TPS routinely captures, processes, stores and outputs the low level transaction data. This system is very important – data input incorrectly will effect every report produced using it, giving management mis-information and hence they will make poor decisions.

Management Information System (MIS)

- A management information system is defined as 'a system to convert data from internal and external sources into information, and to communicate that information in an appropriate form to managers at all levels and in all areas of the business to enable them to make timely and effective decisions'.
- MIS has evolved over time to fit with computer trends from mainframe computer systems to the modern era of cloud computing, Wi-Fi networks and applications allowing managers to access the information remotely from various mobile devices.

Decision Support System (DSS)

- A decision support system is defined as a 'computer based system which enables managers to confront ill-structured problems by direct interaction with data and problem-solving programs'.
- They are computer systems which are used as an aid in making decisions when presented with semi-structured or unstructured problems. Their aim is to provide information in a flexible way to aid decision making.

Executive Information System (EIS)/Executive Support System (ESS)

- An executive support system (ESS) or executive information system (EIS) is an interactive system that allows executives to access information for monitoring the operations of the organisation and scanning general business conditions. It gives executives ready access to key internal and external data.

Enterprise Resource Planning System (ERPS)

- An enterprise resource planning system is comprised of a commercial software package that promises the seamless integration of all the information flowing through the company – financial, accounting, human resources, supply chain and customer information.
- This is achieved by holding the data for all transaction and management information systems on a common database.

Expert Systems (ES)

- An expert system is defined as 'a computerised system that performs the role of an expert or carries out a task that requires expertise'.
- The system holds expert/specialist knowledge and allows non-experts to interrogate a computer for information, advice and recommended decisions.

Strategic Enterprise Management System (SEMS)

- A strategic enterprise management system assists management in making high-level strategic decisions.
- Tools such as activity-based management (ABM) and the balanced scorecard are applied to the data to enable the strategic goals of the organisation to be worked towards.

Test your understanding 3

You have been presented with a summary report of sales in the last month, with a breakdown of totals per product, and with variances from the corresponding monthly sales plan.

This report is an output from:

A A Transaction Processing System

B A Management Information Systems

C An Executive Information System

D None of the above

7 Value and cost of information

Cost-benefit analysis (CBA) can be used to assess the expected costs and benefits of the system design to be recommended. It is often called a method for 'system justification' – if the system is justified, then it will be recommended.

(This section does not relate solely to IT projects but to all projects a business could undertake – be prepared in the exam to deal with a cost-benefit analysis from more than an IT viewpoint.)

The **net value of information** in decision-making situations could be calculated as:

- the difference in the values of outcomes in a decision with and without the information, minus
- the cost of obtaining the information.

In other words a manager will make a decision based upon the information currently known. If additional information is available, which makes the manager take a different decision, then the value of that information is:

- the savings or profits made as a result of taking the different decision
- adjusted for the cost of obtaining the information, which may be:
  - a cost arising from preparing the information internally
  - the cost of purchasing the information from external sources
  - the cost of the delay to the decision whilst the information is prepared.

Cost of information

The cost of information could be classified under three general headings:

(a) The cost of **designing and setting** up the system that produces the information including:
- systems design
- systems testing
- capital costs of equipment (e.g. IT equipment)
- installation
- training.

(b) The **day-to-day running** costs of the system providing the information, including:
- staff salaries
- supplies (paper, disks, etc)
- other running expenses such as premises costs and security costs.

(c) **Storage** costs including:
- hardware costs
- retrieval costs
- security costs.

Cost benefit example

The Cloud

The cloud is a form of remote data storage. The data storage could be at a great distances form the access point, often on another continent. It is remote from the PC and not held on the PC's local storage.

Although using new technology and concepts, it is similar to very early computing when no-one held data locally and it was all held on a large central computer owned and run by the company, at that time known as a mainframe.

There are benefits and risks of using cloud storage.

One of the main benefits is cost:

- only paying for the storage used
- in-house staff are not required to maintain and protect the data

The costs relate to the risks involved:

remoteness can be a problem, when communications break (you cannot gain access to your data)

reliance on a third party to protect the integrity of the data

sharing storage space with others which may compromise your data.

Assessing the value and cost of information

Assessing the value of information

In order to assess the value of information, the following questions can be asked:

- What information is provided?
- What is it used for?
- Who uses it?
- How often is it used?
- What benefit is achieved by using it?
- Is it used as often as it is provided?

- What other relevant information is available that could be used instead?

Unfortunately, the value of information is not always easy to quantify in terms of benefits obtained. An alternative approach might therefore be to assess the consequences of not having the information, taking into account the quantity of the information and its availability (e.g. on-line), accuracy, level of detail and other information qualities.

Budgeting and IS/IT costs

The description of cost-benefit analysis above assumes that there are identifiable IT projects whose costs and benefits can be estimated and evaluated. In practice, although some new projects can be evaluated in this way, much spending on IT does not take the form of spending on identifiable new projects. A considerable amount of spending is incurred on maintaining, expanding and upgrading existing systems.

This type of spending, particularly IT running costs but also some capital expenditure (e.g. on new PCs and printers) is included within the normal budgeting process. Where an organisation uses an incremental approach to budgeting, annual IT spending could be agreed simply by taking spending for the previous year and adding a percentage for anticipated growth and cost inflation.

There is clearly a risk that when IT costs are budgeted in this way, they could easily grow more quickly than necessary and get out of control. For example:

- New PCs, laptops or other equipment might be purchased without due consideration to the benefits as well as the cost.
- Systems upgrades might be purchased in the same way, when an upgrade is not necessary.
- Spending on system maintenance, such as providing protection against software viruses, or 'cleaning up' systems affected by viruses, might escalate without the costs being adequately monitored and controlled.

Budgeting for IT costs might benefit from:

- a zero-based budgeting approach, although this will depend on whether the organisation uses ZBB for all its budgeting
- an activity-based budgeting approach, where the costs of IT activities (and cost drivers for those activities) are identified and used as the basis for budgeting.

The use of IT systems and services might also be controlled through a system of charging for the use of central IT systems.

8 Information technology

The system to deliver information to management must have the following attributes:

- the system must produce material in an appropriate way to enable informed decision-making.
- the system must process the required volumes of data within the required timescales, with adequate controls and efficient use of resources.
- to avoid being stuck with outdated technology and solutions, the system should be sufficiently adaptable to people's varied and changing needs and behaviour.
- the system should capitalise on the best of people and of machines to obtain the optimum mix of human intuition and machine reliability and speed.

The most common complaints levelled at information systems are the lack of decision orientation and the lack of flexibility. The unsatisfactory systems are those that deny people the access to take decisions in the way they wish to.

9 Organising the IT function

The previous sections considered the structure and development of information strategy and the types of information systems that might be available to business managers to assist them in their duties.

This section considers how the business could structure its information provision to those managers, i.e. the information management. It also looks at some of the practical issues that have to be addressed with these different solutions.

The issues are split between internal and external solutions. The **internal solutions** are:

(i) Central data processing (all computer access from one point).

(ii) End-user computing and information centres.

(iii) Databases and data warehouses.

The **external solution** discussed is outsourcing or facilities management.

Steering committees

Due to the strategic importance of IS/IT and the high level of spend that many companies make in this area, steering committees are usually established to decide on the provision of the information services.

Membership of the steering committee

A steering committee would normally be structured with the following groups represented:

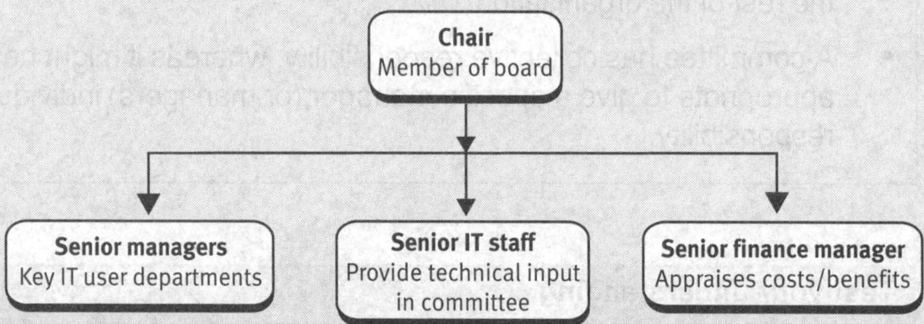

Purpose of the steering committee

The purpose of the steering committee is to:

- Plan, monitor and control IS/IT/IM strategy.
- Identify and analyse IS/IT risk.
- Consider the competitive issues raised by IT.
- Ensure that IS/IT programmes achieve their specified objectives, in line with organisational policy and objectives.
- Make resource decisions and IT funding decisions.
- Plan for future systems developments.

More on the steering committee

Other activities of the steering committee include:

- providing leadership at senior level for the exploitation and management of IT
- ensuring that resource allocation decisions are effective
- approving the terms of reference for IT project teams for new systems developments
- monitoring the progress of the various systems development projects.

The approval of new systems developments could be the responsibility of a steering committee at either corporate or divisional level within the organisation.

Several problems could arise with ensuring that steering committees are effective in fulfilling their responsibilities:

- The experience and skills of the members do not match the requirements of the committee.
- A failure in the communication process between the committee and the rest of the organisation.
- A committee has collective responsibility, whereas it might be more appropriate to give a specific manager (or managers) individual responsibility.

Test your understanding 4

ST plc are setting up their first IT steering committee to oversee the introduction of a new automated production line. They are unsure who should be appointed to the committee. Select the THREE members who would be most likely to be appointed.

A The senior manager of the production line

B The supplier of the automated production line

C The finance director of ST

D A non-executive director of ST

E The project manager overseeing the production line implementation

F A junior IT employee

Test your understanding 5

You have just been appointed Financial Controller of X, a marketing consultancy. You are in a meeting with the CEO of X, and have been discussing the need for a major upgrade of all the information systems throughout X, as they are all very old. Knowing that major change should be managed effectively, you have suggested that X should have a 'systems steering committee'.

Advise the CEO which of the following should be included in the Terms of Reference of the steering committee. (Select ALL correct answers).

A Manage projects

B Develop new systems

C Consider the competitive issues raised by IT

D Plan for new systems

E Ensure that systems projects achieve the goals of the organisation.

10 Data warehousing

Data warehousing

Data warehousing is defined as 'the concept of integrating data from disparate internal and external sources centrally within the organisation such that the database thus established can be used for flexible reporting and analysis'.

Data warehousing is a very valuable tool if an organisation wants to

- set up an effective executive information system
- introduce an enterprise resource planning system.

IT structure

An effective data warehouse will need a particular IT structure in order to operate. The structure will be set-up on the basis of a distributed (or client-server) architecture, but with a very controlled data storage system.

For data warehousing to be effective, however, all data would be stored centrally, with local branches only storing the applications that use the data. The knock-on effect of this is that communication lines between the central data store and local branches will probably need to be permanent and dedicated.

Advantages of data warehousing (as opposed to local databases):

- Lower volumes of data are held.
- Lower storage costs.
- Easy to amend data, and only one piece of data needs amendment.
- Users have confidence they are using up-to-date data.
- Data management is improved as it is practical to employ database administrators.
- Controls over data are improved.
- More consistency is achieved in decision making.

Disadvantages of data warehousing:

- Most of the departments will require new hardware and software before they can use the data warehouse.
- Almost all staff who want to use the new system will need training.
- The data will either need to be analysed and 'cleansed' before it can be integrated into a warehouse. This will not be easy, quick or cheap to achieve.
- Data needed by individual locations may not be collected and stored by the central data function, and reporting requirements may differ.
- If the database fails or is damaged then the organisation processes stop, hence effective back-up arrangements are vital.
- Response times may be slower (however, for some data items the central store will be able to respond more quickly).

Data mining

Data mining is the process of analysing data from different perspectives and summarising it into useful information – information that can be used to increase revenue, cuts costs, or both. It allows users to analyse data from many different angles, categorise it, and summarise the relationships identified. Technically, data mining is the process of finding correlations or patterns among dozens of fields of data in large, relational databases.

For some years, companies have used powerful computers to sift through large volumes of supermarket scanner data and analyse market research reports. However, continuous innovations in computer processing power, disk storage, and statistical software are dramatically increasing the accuracy of analysis while driving down the cost.

For example, one grocery chain has used the data mining capacity of Oracle software to analyse local buying patterns. They discovered that when men bought nappies on Thursdays and Saturdays, they also tended to buy beer. Further analysis showed that these shoppers typically did their weekly grocery shopping on Saturdays. On Thursdays, however, they only bought a few items. The retailer concluded that they purchased the beer to have it available for the upcoming weekend. The grocery chain could use this newly discovered information in various ways to increase revenue. For example, they could move the beer display closer to the nappy display. And, they could make sure beer and nappies were sold at full price on Thursdays.

Data mining is primarily used today by companies with a strong consumer focus - retail, financial, communication, and marketing organisations. It enables these companies to determine relationships among 'internal' factors such as price, product positioning, or staff skills, and 'external' factors such as economic indicators, competition, and customer demographics. And, it enables them to determine the impact on sales, customer satisfaction, and corporate profits. Finally, it enables them to 'drill down' into summary information to view detailed transactional data.

With data mining, a retailer could use point-of-sale records of customer purchases to send targeted promotions based on an individual's purchase history. By mining demographic data from comment or warranty cards, the retailer could develop products and promotions to appeal to specific customer segments.

For example, American Express suggest products to its cardholders based on analysis of their monthly expenditures.

Demonstrating how long data mining has been used, twenty years ago WalMart used massive data mining techniques to transform its supplier relationships. WalMart captures point-of-sale transactions from over 2,900 stores in 6 countries and continuously transmits this data to its massive 7.5 terabyte data warehouse. WalMart allows more than 3,500 suppliers, to access data on their products and perform data analyses. These suppliers use this data to identify customer buying patterns at the store display level. They use this information to manage local store inventory and identify new merchandising opportunities.

Also, years ago, Blockbuster Entertainment mined its video rental history database to recommend rentals to individual customers.

What is Big Data?

There are several definitions of Big Data, the most commonly used referring to large volumes of data beyond the normal processing, storage and analysis capacity of typical database application tools. The definition can be extended to incorporate the types of data involved. Big Data will often include much more than simply financial information and can involve other organisational data which is operational in nature along with other internal and external data which is often unstructured in form. One of the key challenges of dealing with Big Data is to identify repeatable business patterns in this unstructured data, significant quantities of which is in text format. Managing such data can lead to significant business benefits such as greater competitive advantage, improved productivity and increasing levels of innovation.

Why is Big Data so important?

Several major business benefits arise from the ability to manage Big Data successfully:

- Driving innovation by reducing time taken to answer key business questions and therefore make decisions
- Gaining competitive advantage
- Improving productivity

Risks associated with Big Data

- The availability of skills to use Big Data systems, which is compounded by the fact that many of the systems are rapidly developing and support is not always easily and readily available. There is also an increasing need to combine data analysis skills with deep understanding of industry being analysed and this need is not always recognised;
- The security of data is a major concern in the majority of organisations and if the organisation lacks the resources to manage data then there is likely to be a greater risk of leaks and losses;
- There can be a risk to the data protection of organisations as they collect a greater range of data from increasingly personal sources (e.g Facebook);
- It is important to recognise that just because something CAN be measured, this does not necessarily mean it should be. There is a risk that valuable time is spent measuring relationships that have no organisational value;
- If organisations are to effectively utilise Big Data, this will require a change in perspective to ensure that sense can be made of the information;

- There may be technical difficulties associated with integrating existing data warehousing and Hadoop systems.

(**Hadoop** is an open source programming framework which enables the processing of large data sets by utilising multiple servers simultaneously.)

Examples of how Big Data is used

Consumer facing organisations monitor social media activity to gain insight into customer behaviour and preferences. This source can also be used to identify and engage brand advocates and detractors, and assess responsiveness to advertising campaigns and promotions.

Sports teams can use data of past fixtures to track tactics, player formations, injuries and results to inform future team strategies.

Manufacturing companies can monitor data from their equipment to determine usage and wear. This allows them to predict the optimal replacement cycle.

Financial Services organisations can use data on customer activity to carefully segment their customer base and therefore accurately target individuals with relevant offers.

Health organisations can monitor patient records and admissions to identify the risk of recurring problems and to intervene to avoid further hospital involvement.

Big data in the real world

UPS uses telematics to improve performance. Delivery vehicles are equipped with sensors which monitor data on speed, direction, braking performance and other mechanical aspects of the vehicle. This information is then used to optimise maintenance schedules and improve efficiency of delivery routes saving time, money and reducing wastage.

Data from the vehicles is combined with customer data, GPS information and data concerning the normal behaviour of delivery drivers. Using this data to optimise vehicle performance and routes has resulted in several significant improvements:

- Over 15 million minutes of idling time were eliminated in one year. This saved 103,000 gallons of fuel.
- During the same year 1.7 million miles of driving was eliminated, saving 183,000 gallons of fuel.

It is widely reported that **Walmart (Asda)** tracks data on over 60% of adults in the US. Data gathered includes online and instore purchasing pattern, Twitter interactions and trends, weather reports and major events. This data, according to the company, ensures a highly personalised customer experience. Walmart detractors criticise the company's data collection as a breach of human rights and believe the company uses the data to make judgements and conclusions on personal information such as sexual orientation, political view and even intelligence levels.

Tesco plc has sophisticated sensors installed on all refrigeration units. They collected 70 million data points from the sensors and perform complex analysis to monitor performance, optimise service intervals and carry out planned preventative maintenance to achieve energy savings.

Netflix has 44 million users worldwide who watch 2 billion hours of programmes a month. The company uses information gathered from analysis of viewing habits to inform decisions on which shows to invest in. Analysing past viewing figures and understanding viewer populations and the shows they are likely to watch allows the analysts to predict likely viewing figures before a show has even aired. This can help to determine if the show is a viable investment.

Test your understanding 6

Data mining uses which technique to establish trends in data?

A Portfolio theory

B Correlation

C Risk mapping

D Probability theory

E Decision trees

F Sensitivity analysis

Test your understanding 7 – MC mobile phones (Integration)

MC is a mobile phone network provider, offering mobile phones and services on a range of different tariffs to customers across Europe. The company enjoyed financial success until three years ago but increasing competitive pressure has led to a recent decline in sales. There has also been an increase in the level of complaints regarding the customer service provided, and the company's churn rate (number of customers leaving the company within a given time frame) is at an all time high.

Required:

Discuss how Big Data could help drive the strategic direction of MC company.

Test your understanding 8 – L supermarket (Case study)

Scenario

L is a major supermarket chain, with over 500 stores spread across the country. L has three major competitors, each of which has roughly the same number of stores and a very similar geographical spread.

Trigger

L has conducted a large number of focus group meetings with customers in its stores in order to compete more effectively. These meetings established that customers regard price and convenience as the two major factors when choosing where to shop.

Loyalty cards

Two of L's competitors give their customers loyalty cards which track customers' purchases and give a $5 voucher to spend in store whenever their cumulative purchases reach $500. In addition, loyalty cardholders receive regular mailings and discount vouchers for products that might be of interest to them. Most of the people in L's focus groups admitted that these promotions saved them very little money when they shopped at L's competitors, but they admitted that even small rewards made them feel as if they were getting something in return for their custom.

Focus groups

The focus group participants tended to have a slightly mixed opinion about the convenience of shopping at L's major competitors. They felt that the competing stores were generally better laid out, with products being grouped in such a way that customers did not need to walk around the whole store in order to complete a typical shopping trip. Despite this they claimed that the competitors tended to rearrange their stores quite frequently and so they often found themselves going to the wrong part of the store for a particular product. In contrast, L's layout was not necessarily the best but the arrangement of the company's stores tended not to change and so regular shoppers were happy that they knew where everything was.

L's Sales Director has studied the report of the meetings with the focus groups. He believes that the other three supermarket chains have made much larger investments in information management than L has. L's business model is to offer good quality, branded products at the lowest possible prices. The company avoids unnecessary costs and that extends to the company's information management systems. The electronic point of sales system keeps very accurate records of cash and card sales and it updates the inventory records in real time. L's information management system is industry standard, but the company deliberately chose the cheapest and least sophisticated software to run on it.

Competition

The competing supermarket chains use powerful software that is capable of "data mining" sales information. For example, it can sift through records of individual transactions to identify patterns, such as a tendency for customers who buy cleaning products also tending to buy bottled water. That can lead to products being arranged to match buying habits that may not always be obvious. Furthermore, those competitors which issue loyalty cards can track the buying habits of individual customers over time and that may give those competitors further insights that can be used to target customers with vouchers and other promotional materials. L's Sales Director believes that L is at a commercial disadvantage to the other supermarket chains because competitors' information management systems are superior.

L's Information Technology Director has confirmed that the company's system could be upgraded to offer data mining and could also support a loyalty card scheme. This would not require any physical changes to the hardware already in place but it would require a significant investment in new software.

Task

(a) Evaluate the Sales Director's belief that L's competitors are at an advantage because of their superior information management systems.

(15 minutes)

Write a report to the Board which:

(b) (i) Advises L's directors on the difficulties associated with quantifying the potential benefits that L would gain from improved information management systems; and

(ii) Recommends actions that L could take in order to overcome the difficulties identified in your answer to (b)(i) above.

(30 minutes)

Test your understanding 9 – J (Case study)

Scenario

J rents cars and small vans to individual and business customers. The company has twelve branches located in large towns spread across J's home country.

Each of J's branches has its own computer network which stores details of all vehicles located at the branch, advanced bookings and current rentals. The only paper records held at branches are the signed rental agreements. Everything else is held electronically. Each branch has several PCs that are linked to a branch server where all of the files are stored. The files on each branch server are backed up to the head office computer system after the close of business every evening.

Customers can book rentals in advance by telephoning their local branch or by logging onto the branch web page. Customers details are initially collected on the branch network but all details including verification of identity and driver's licence are checked when the customer collects the car. Details of the vehicle, including any dents or scrapes on the bodywork or minor mechanical defects, are printed on the rental agreement form and the member of staff and the customer check the vehicle together before the customer signs the agreement.

The branch network keeps track of all vehicles that are supposed to be returned each day. If a vehicle is overdue without good reason then the police are informed that the vehicle has been stolen.

All returned vehicles are checked for damage that was not listed on the rental agreement. Customers have to pay for any damage that occurred while the vehicle was in their possession.

Trigger

The manager in charge of J's information systems (IS) at the company's head office has been asked to investigate two potential problems that occurred at the Southtown branch. A member of the IS team visited the branch in order to carry out some routine maintenance and discovered the following:

- The Branch Manager had a notebook computer plugged into the branch network. The manager explained that the notebook computer was his own personal property. He found it useful to copy branch files so that he could work on writing his monthly management reports at home.
- One of the PCs in the branch was not the standard model used throughout J. The branch manager explained that there were never sufficient PCs in the branch and so he had used part of the branch equipment budget to purchase an inexpensive PC from a local computer store. The inexpensive PC came equipped with the latest version of a standard operating system. The PCs communicate with the branch network using a specially written program. The branch staff loaded a copy of that program from a CD that had been left behind by a member of the head office IS team during an earlier visit.

J's system uses an older version of the standard operating system and the branch network software installed on the PC was not the latest version, although the Branch Manager insisted that the PC worked perfectly. It has also been useful because the other PCs in the branch were not fitted with optical drives (i.e. they cannot read CDs or DVDs) and he has found it useful to be able to use this machine to install software to other machines over the branch network in order to enhance efficiency.

Task

Write a letter to the branch manager which:

(a) Advises on the importance of adequate information systems (IS) for J.

Your answer to part (a) should NOT discuss the specific matters identified by the member of the IS team during the branch visit.

(15 minutes)

(b) Evaluates the control implications of each of the matters discovered by the member of the IS team.

(30 minutes)

Test your understanding 10 – Printing company (Integration)

Some time ago, a printing company designed and installed a Management Information System that met the business needs of a commercial environment which was characterised at that time by:

- a unitary structure with one profit centre
- central direction from senior managers
- 100% internal resourcing of ancillary services
- the employment exclusively of permanent full-time employees
- customers holding large inventories who accepted long delivery times
- most of the work concerned with long print runs for established large publishing houses.

A radical change in the business environment has resulted in the following outcomes:

- the development of a divisionalised structure with four profit centres that utilise each others services
- empowerment of team leaders and devolved decision making
- considerable outsourcing of activities
- a significant proportion of the employees work part-time and/or on temporary contracts
- customers now commonly operate JIT systems requiring immediate replenishment of inventories
- the typical customer requires specialist low volume but complex high value printing.

Required:

Recommend the significant changes in the Management Information Systems that would probably be required to meet the needs of this new situation. Explain the reasons for your recommendations.

(30 minutes)

Test your understanding 11 – HZ (Integration)

The HZ hospital has recently invested in the most up-to-date computer systems to assist its doctors in making assessments of patients' illnesses. Two of the software packages now available to doctors are:

- a Management Information System which provides information on the medical history of each patient. It includes detailed factual information on past illnesses and any recurring symptoms as well as the patient's name, address and other personal information.
- an Expert System which is used to assist in the diagnosis of current illnesses. The Expert System is linked to the MIS to obtain details on each patient's medical history. From this information, and symptoms of the current illness, the Expert System provides an initial diagnosis, which the doctor uses in making his recommendation for the treatment of the patient. The diagnosis is stated in terms of probabilities of what the illness could be, rather than giving definite conclusions. Both systems are accessed and updated via a series of on-line terminals located at key points around the hospital. All terminals are linked directly to a central file server; there are no external communications links due to the sensitive nature of the information being held.

Required:

(a) Explain the differences in the characteristics of information being provided by the two systems.

(15 minutes)

(b) Describe three general conditions, which must exist in order for an Expert System to be appropriate.

(15 minutes)

(c) Describe three advantages of using Expert Systems (other than speed and accuracy).

(10 minutes)

Test your understanding 12 – Cost benefit (Integration)

A systems analyst must be prepared to carry out both cost-benefit calculations & risk analysis as part of the proposal for a new computer system.

Required:

(a) Describe two methods for demonstrating the costs and benefits of such a system over a period of time.

(10 minutes)

(b) Explain the specific problems associated with the measurement of information systems costs and benefits.

(20 minutes)

(c) Explain the factors you would take into account when undertaking a risk analysis of the costs and benefits of a proposed computer project.

(15 minutes)

Test your understanding 13 – RBT (Integration)

RBT manufactures tractors, harvesting machinery and similar farm equipment. It operates from one integrated office and factory near the capital of the country in which it is based. Due to restricted demand and the cost of manufacture of individual items, all equipment is manufactured to specific orders from clients. No inventories of finished goods are maintained although inventories of spare parts are available for sale.

The farm equipment is sold to farm owners by one of 20 sales representatives. The general procedure for making a sale is for the representative to visit the farm owner to discuss the owner's requirements. Basic price and model specification information are obtained from printed manuals that the representative carries. The representative then telephones the RBT office and confirms with production staff that the order can be made, checks the price and receives an estimated delivery date. An order confirmation is written out and the representative moves on to the next appointment. The farmer pays for the equipment on receipt.

As the country in which RBT operates is large, representatives cannot often visit RBT's office, so their price and model specification manuals may be out of date.

The Board of RBT is considering the introduction of a new information system. Each representative will be given a portable PC. Information on such things as products and prices will be kept on an Intranet and downloaded by telephone line when needed by the representative. Access to production managers and sales representatives will also be made via the Intranet. The voice telephone system will be discontinued and e-mail is thought to be unnecessary.

Required:

(a) Evaluate the proposed use of the Intranet within the RBT Company showing whether it would provide an appropriate communication channel for the sales representatives. Suggest ways in which any problems you have identified with the new systems may be resolved.

(20 minutes)

(b) Identify and evaluate any information systems that can be used to provide clients with information on the progress of their orders with RBT while they are being manufactured.

(30 minutes)

11 Chapter summary

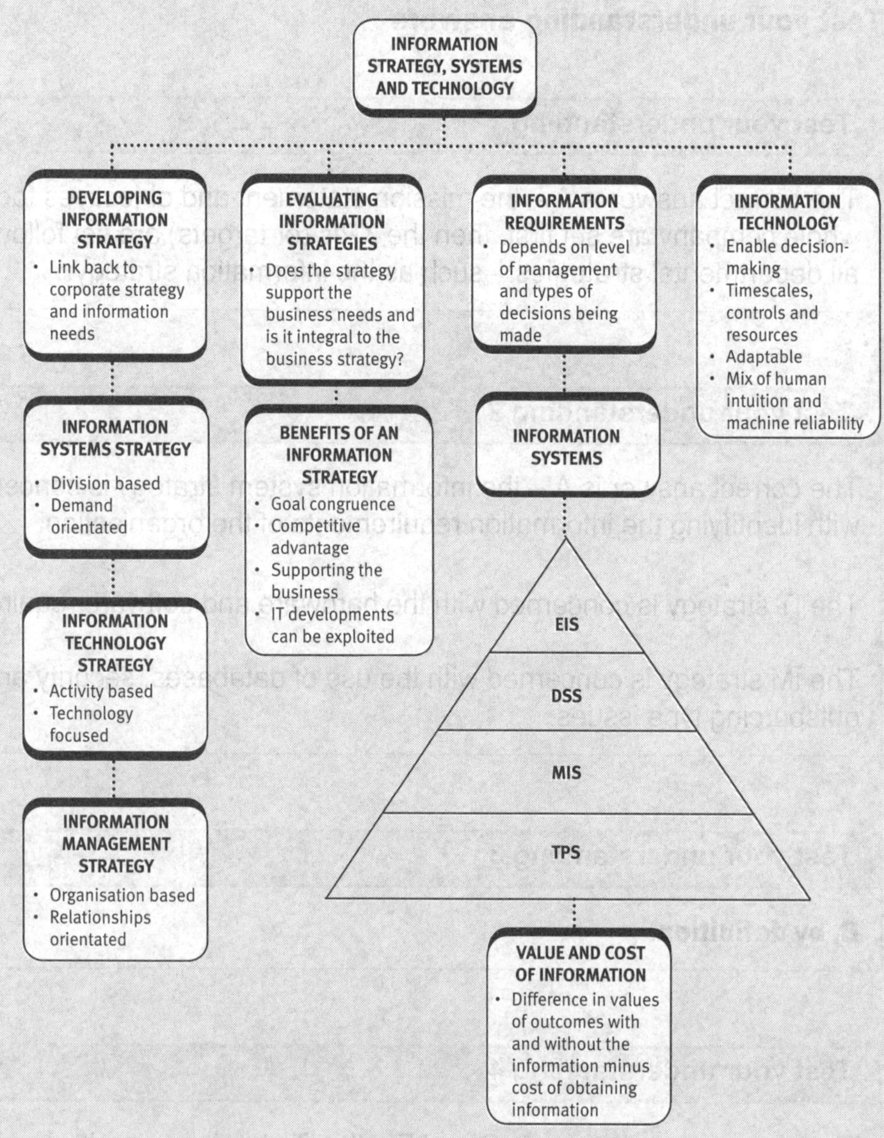

Test your understanding answers

Test your understanding 1

The correct answer is A – the mission statement and objectives for the whole company are set first, then the KPIs (or targets) are set followed by all departmental strategies – such as the information strategy.

Test your understanding 2

The correct answer is A – the information system strategy is concerned with identifying the information requirements of the organisation.

The IT strategy is concerned with the hardware and software required.

The IM strategy is concerned with the use of databases, security and outsourcing type issues.

Test your understanding 3

B, by definition.

Test your understanding 4

The correct answers are A, C and E – the IT steering committee usually has representation from senior managers, senior IT staff and senior finance staff.

The supplier, the non-executive director and the junior IT employee would not be included in any IT planning and oversight activities.

Test your understanding 5

C, D and E

Managing projects is the role of the Project Managers, while developing new systems will be the job of the project teams.

Test your understanding 6

The correct answer is B – Correlation is used to plot variables against each other e.g. the weather versus sales of televisions, to see if there is any link that could be used to further a company's sales. It may be that sales increase with hot weather. Data mining will not tell us why. We have to generate that ourselves – perhaps the television components overheat... But the company now knows that if hot weather is approaching they should have plenty of televisions in stock, and to perhaps locate them at the front of their shop.

Test your understanding 7 – MC mobile phones (Integration)

Big Data management involves using sophisticated systems to gather, store and analyse large volumes of data in a variety of structured and unstructured formats. Companies are collecting increasing volumes of data through everyday transactions and marketing activity. If managed effectively this can lead to many business benefits although there are risks involved.

A company like MC will already collect a relatively large amount of data regarding its customers, their transactions and call history. It is likely that a significant proportion of their customers are also fairly digitally engaged and therefore data can be gathered regarding preferences and complaints from social media networks. This will be particularly useful to MC as they have seen an increase in complaints and have a high churn rate so engaging with customers will be highly beneficial.

Recent competitive pressure has led to a decline in sales and so MC need to consider the strategic direction which is most appropriate for them to improve performance.

Analysing the large amounts of data available to them will inform decisions on areas such as:

- The type of handsets currently most in demand and therefore the prices required when bundling with tariffs; Main areas of complaint and therefore the areas of weakness which need to be resolved;
- Which types of communication are most popular (e.g data, call minutes, text messages) to ensure the tariffs have the right combinations;
- Usage statistics for 'pay as you go' customers, to drive the most appropriate offers and marketing activity;
- Most popular competitor offerings with reasons.

Test your understanding 8 – L supermarket (Case study)

(a) It could be argued that L's presence as a major supermarket company is evidence that it is capable of competing with the other companies in the industry. L's business model requires it to keep costs to a minimum so that it can afford to offer customers lower prices. L's present system is less expensive, it is compatible with the business model.

L's competitors can use the data gathered through their EPOS terminals to understand their customers' behaviour. They can organise merchandise so that customers who come into a store to buy a list of specific products may buy more than they intended. L's competitors can experiment with different store layouts and can track the effects on the sales of relocated products in more or less real time. The fact that this effect is potentially counter-intuitive means that customers will be unaware of the impact on their buying decisions and so it may prove highly effective.

Two of L's competitors can also gather information through their loyalty card records. For example, if one of the other supermarket chains cuts its prices or runs a new advertising campaign and previously loyal customers make smaller or less frequent purchases then the data collected from loyalty cards will pick that up. That makes it possible for them to study the effects of changes in the retail environment on the behaviour of particular groups of customers. L does not have the ability to track changes in individual buying habits in that level of detail and so the company may be a little vulnerable because it may be less well equipped to deal with competitors' actions. Having said that, its existing technology could be of some value in identifying problems. For example, the inventory control system will make it relatively easy to identify increasing wastage on perishable lines and slower sales for all lines of inventory. L can also use details gathered from credit and debit card billings as the starting point for tracking individual customers who pay by card rather than cash.

(b) **Report**

To: The Board

From: A.N. Accountant

Date: Today

Subject: Improved information management systems

Introduction

This report advises on the difficulties associated with quantifying the potential benefits that L would gain from improved information management systems and recommends actions that L could take in order to overcome the difficulties.

(i) Difficulties with quantification of potential benefits

The main problem with any investment in information management systems is that the potential benefits cannot be accurately predicted. A new software suite may equip L to increase sales, but the amount of new business will be impossible to foresee.

It is debatable whether L's competitors derive any real benefit from their more sophisticated information management systems. Feedback from the focus group meetings suggests that the competitors' merchandising policies displease customers because they cannot always find the products they want. L could obtain much of the motivational benefit of loyalty cards without any of the associated administrative costs by giving away discount vouchers at the point of sale.

Asking customers their opinions, as has already been happening through the focus groups, may prove misleading. Customers may not realise the extent to which their subconscious buying decisions are influenced by store layout or by feedback from the loyalty card systems. Furthermore, it costs them nothing to claim that they are attracted by savings from vouchers and such claims may encourage L to offer a similar incentive.

Other information sources may be equally biased. For example, the software vendor has an incentive to overstate the benefits offered by an upgrade to L's existing information management systems. The competitors may argue in public that their systems generate significant and commercially valuable information, but such claims may be rhetoric intended to impress their shareholders.

(ii) Recommended actions

One approach would be to extend L's market research to target customers who tend to shop at the competitors to establish why they do not shop at L. They could undertake market research, perhaps targeting areas close to competitors' stores to get a better understanding of why their competitor's customers tend to shop elsewhere. The results could then be linked to the types of information that could be collected from the competitors' information systems to establish whether they could be the source of some competitive advantage.

L could experiment with the benefits to be had from the strategic arrangement of products by copying the competition. L could use researchers equipped with camcorders to record the order in which goods are organised in competitors' stores. Three or four of L's stores could be reorganised in exactly the same manner in order to establish whether sales are increased. If there is a persistent increase in sales then it is realistic to argue that there is an observable and quantifiable effect to be had from observing patterns.

To a certain effect the savings associated with loyalty cards could be replicated on a smaller scale. For example, for a limited period L could give customers a £3 voucher in return for a £40 shop to see whether that increases sales volume. It would also be possible to estimate the effects of targeted vouchers by giving customers vouchers that are linked to the goods in their baskets. A customer who buys a particular brand of coffee could receive a voucher for money off their next purchase in order to see whether sales increase.

Essentially, anything that L can do to move towards the sales and promotional techniques used by the competitors should make it easier to determine whether upgrading the information management system is likely to improve sales.

Test your understanding 9 – J (Case study)

Address

Date

Dear branch manager,

I write to advise on the importance of adequate information systems (IS) for J and to evaluate the control implications of each of the matters discovered by the member of the IS team.

The importance of adequate information systems

(a) The information system at J forms part of the overall information strategy of the company. If the information system is inadequate then the information strategy will not be effective and the objectives of J will not be met.

The information system affects many stakeholders both inside (management and staff) and outside (customers) the business.

Management

Information systems are used in order that management can make informed decisions about the future of the company. If the information is inaccurate then the wrong decision will be made ultimately causing a loss of income, or an increase in costs for J.

Efficiency can be gained by the use of information systems. Information collation, interpretation and transfer can be much faster and enable good decisions to be made more quickly. This might give J a competitive advantage.

Since J holds all records electronically (other than the signed rental agreements) the information system is critical to the business. Without it J would be unable to:

- track which customer had which car or van;
- determine how much each customer should be charged for their rental;
- trace any customer who did not return the car or van. This would ultimately lead to loss of income and/or assets.

Customers

The information system is important with respect to the customer being able to make bookings on the website, increasing customer service and hence possibly increasing future sales. If competitors have this facility then so must J in order to be able to compete in this market place. It is important that the system is available at all times and is user-friendly.

The information system would be important to use in the event that a customer wanted to hire a car or van from one branch and return it to another. The sharing of the network would be of critical importance so that cars and vans were not 'lost' on the information system.

The information system must be maintained well since all records are stored on it. Loss of these records will be costly to J, in the form of difficulty in producing the accounts, being able to make decisions based on past information gathered, and customers would be angry if their bank details were lost.

Information on the system must be kept up to date and be accurate. If for example information about a return date was incorrect and J informed the police that a car or van was stolen, it would prove very embarrassing for the customer, who would not use J again and this could lead to the harm of J's reputation.

Staff

Adequate information systems will prevent staff from becoming frustrated with the system. This has been evidenced by the manager of the Southtown branch where unlicensed software has been copied and used, and an unauthorised notebook computer has been purchased for use.

Staff will have to deal with fewer complaints, by telephone or in person, if the website is available at all times, since the customer will be able to access the price lists and make their booking at their convenience.

(b) **Control implications of the matters discovered by the member of the IS team**

A notebook computer was plugged into the branch network

The notebook computer will be a useful tool for the branch manager to work on his management reports at home. In this way, J is getting more hours of work out of their manager for which they are probably not paying, so it is to J's benefit.

However, the removal of company information from the branch may be against company guidelines. The information could be lost and fall in to the wrong hands if the computer was stolen.

Hopefully customer bank details would not form part of the information stored on the notebook or this would cause further issues should that information be lost. Customers would be unhappy and J would certainly lose their future business. It would also harm J's reputation. The Data Protection Act would need to be considered and the management at J should be aware of the implications of not meeting the regulations.

Plugging an unauthorised computer into the network can cause problems. This will include viruses which may affect the rest of J's system adversely. There should be guidelines in place that all staff should be aware of that this sort of action is against company rules. Ultimately it could lose J business if their system is down at any time since customers would be unable to make bookings, and it could also corrupt other files that J's management rely on in order to make business decisions.

J's management would be advised that to overcome some of these problems they should either provide the branch managers with an authorised notebook or laptop for use at home, or they should advise the manager to stay at work and use the computer there.

Non-standard model of PC

Insufficient PCs in any branch will slow the branches work making them inefficient. Management should be made aware of this and seek to rectify the problem by acquiring enough computers for each branch. This would prevent the need to acquire the non-standard computers.

The branch equipment budget was probably not intended for the purchase of computers. Again, head office should have guidelines to cover this eventuality – advising branch managers what they can and can't buy with this part of the budget.

The manager has effectively circumvented the rules in J, which is not uncommon in many businesses. However, the rules are there for a reason and the branch manager should be reminded of this and possibly be reprimanded for his actions.

Standard operating system

The PC having the latest version of the standard operating system may cause problems when data is transferred from the PC to head office. Documents may not be able to be opened causing frustration and inefficiency for other staff.

Specially written software

The copy of the specially written software loaded on to the PC by the branch staff causes three issues:

- The staff may not have a licence to use the software and therefore could be sued by the writer of the software;
- The CD that was left by the IS team should have been known to be an error on the IS members part. The ethics of the branch staff should be questioned for using it;
- The member of the IS team has been careless in leaving the CD at the branch. There should be controls over the CDs, such as counting them out and back in before leaving, to prevent this happening.

Optical drives

The lack of optical drives on the other PCs will have been intentional so that the importing of information or the installation of other software was prevented. This would prevent viruses entering J's system and files being corrupted. Because the software has been installed on the other machines over the branch network, which is linked to the branch server, which is backed up to head office, the entire company could be affected by any problems that arose.

Having seen that there are many negative effects of the actions of Southtown branch, the head office management should investigate whether this is common place across all branches, which might indicate a shortfall in the computer facilities available to staff. Investment may be required in this area. If the branch manager believes that it improves efficiency then this should be considered. The branch manager should raise this with the senior management.

Policies and guidelines over the use of computers at J should be generated if they haven't already. Communication of these policies to staff should be ensured and training undertaken where necessary so that staff are educated in acceptable use of the information system.

Should you have any queries regarding the above, please do not hesitate to contact me.

Yours sincerely

Management accountant

Test your understanding 10 – Printing company (Integration)

The change from a unitary to a divisionalised structure

Each division or profit centre will require its own accounting information and other management information. The accounting system must therefore provide for the recognition of revenues and costs of individual divisions.

There is now a requirement to assess the performance of each division, and the management information system must therefore provide performance reports containing both quantitative and qualitative, and financial and non-financial information

Since each division is a profit centre, the system must provide for a system of transfer pricing for goods or services provided by each division to the other divisions. Ideally, the management information system will provide benchmarking data, whereby the performance of each division can be compared with the available performance data about similar printing operations in other (rival) companies.

Change from central direction to empowerment of divisional managers

The management information must be capable of providing information to the divisional managers that they need to make decisions. The system should allow each division to extract the data it requires from the company's files for analysis and reporting to management. In addition, local managers should have access to other sources of data external to the company. This might simply be internet access.

Whereas divisional managers will need access to more management information and operational data, the management at head office will need less detailed information. Reports to head office management will monitor the performance of each profit centre, and will also be more strategic in nature. Reports to head office managers will therefore need to be re-designed.

Since authority has been delegated to divisional level and below, new control systems will be required to meet the requirements of the newly-empowered team leaders, as well as the requirements of senior management.

To ensure consistency in control throughout the company, there should be some standardisation in the nature of the control systems and control information.

The change from internal sourcing of ancillary services to outsourcing

The management information system needs to identify the responsibilities for outsourcing. If outsourcing decisions are taken at divisional level, the costs must be allocated to the division concerned. If outsourcing decisions are taken at head office, individual managers at head office should be made accountable, through a control reporting system.

The information system should maintain a file of external service providers (e.g. approved contractor lists). There should also be a control reporting or monitoring system to ensure that only contractors on the approved list are used.

It will probably also be necessary to establish a system for recording both the costs and the quality and amount of services provided by external suppliers. Outsourcing reports can then be provided to show the total cost and amount of outsourcing, and the cost of individual services. Comparisons between different service providers, and comparisons over time can be reported, for costs, volumes of service and quality.

Use of part-time and temporary employees

The implications for the management information system of using part-time and temporary employees are likely to relate mainly to hours worked and the costs of labour. When all staff are full-time employees, the management information system might report costs per employee. However, when part-time staff are used, it is more appropriate to report costs per labour hour or costs per activity.

Management should also monitor the costs of the various types of employee, to ensure that inefficiencies do not occur. Management reports are therefore likely to include an employee cost report that analyses the costs of each type of employee.

Other aspects of management information might also be affected, such as information relating to the employees themselves (availability in the case of part-time staff, contract termination dates for temporary staff, training records, and so on).

Customers adopting JIT systems

When customers adopt a JIT purchasing system, the supplier becomes responsible for ensuring that customer orders can be met either immediately or very quickly. This has implications for the inventory system of the printing company, and for its production scheduling systems. The information system must be able to recognise JIT customers, and respond instantly to their orders.

This might involve maintaining inventories to meet demand, or immediate scheduling of a print run to satisfy the order.

Change from long print runs to high-value low-volume production

The change in the character of customer orders has several important implications for the company's management information systems and order processing systems. First, the order processing system must be capable of handling complex orders. Secondly, there must be a reliable system for measuring the costs of these orders: an entirely different cost and management accounting system might be necessary, based on job costing rather than batch process costing. In addition, due to the complexity of the work, it might be appropriate to analyse overheads differently, perhaps using an ABC costing system. The information system should then be able to estimate prices for customers, if a cost-plus pricing system is appropriate, and also to compare actual and expected job costs for control purposes.

It is also probable that customers for high-value printing will insist on high quality printing, and the management information system should therefore be capable of providing control information about quality standards, and also the costs of achieving those quality standards.

Test your understanding 11 – HZ (Integration)

(a) **The characteristics of information** provided by the Management Information System (MIS) and the Expert System (ES) in the HZ hospital are different in every respect. The management information system provides information on the medical history of each patient. It includes factual information on past illnesses and any recurring symptoms as well as the patient's name, address and other personal information. An expert system is used to diagnose an illness. The differences in the characteristics of the information provided by the two systems can be explained under the following five headings: accuracy, completeness, timeliness, reliability, and security and control.

(i) In terms of **accuracy** of information, the MIS should be accurate and give a true reflection of the medical history of a particular patient. It is the basic record-keeping system for the hospital's patients. It holds the records for each patient including details of past illnesses and symptoms, and has the ability to produce reports either on statistical or individual bases.

The hospital uses the MIS to automate the record-keeping and, instead of writing out patients' notes to be kept in a paper-based file, this information is input to the computer system to create an electronic file. The expert system is unlikely to be as accurate or precise as the MIS. It does not have records and data but comprises a knowledge base and an inference engine, which is a rule set from which the likelihood of illnesses can be inferred. It is used to provide several diagnoses with a range of probabilities and precision can only be increased by entering more symptoms or details about the patient or the illness.

(ii) The MIS must be **complete and up-to-date**. The system depends on inputs made to it following a patient's visit to hospital. The doctor may input information during the consultation with the patient and any medication prescribed would be recorded. The ES depends on being updated to reflect the latest research findings or expert opinion. There is a very good chance of it being incomplete and out of date and not representing a complete body of knowledge. Also, if the knowledge base was created by the hospital, i.e. the software framework purchased and the information (knowledge) input locally, then there is no guarantee that all the necessary information will be present.

(iii) **Timeliness.** The MIS produces information quickly with typical response times of a few seconds. Most MIS are record-based within a hierarchical or relational database, both types being able to display records quickly at the touch of a button. In comparison, the ES is very slow because it may need to consider many different combinations of symptoms, rules and information before it can perform a diagnosis. If the patient is showing unusual symptoms, the ES may take a lot longer relatively (i.e. minutes rather than seconds) before it can respond, particularly. This obviously depends on the sophistication of the inference engine and the speed and capacity of the processors used.

(iv) **Reliability**. MIS data is only reliable if it has been input correctly. Even if the information is incomplete, the doctor can see from the screen where the gaps are and, with the patient's help, it should be possible to obtain a good indication of their history. The MIS can therefore offer a degree of assurance that there is control over matching the patient to the information. In the case of the ES the information should never be considered 100% reliable because the doctor or consultant will not know if all the relevant information has been input.

For example, some completely different illnesses are identified by similar symptoms. It is very difficult to diagnose appendicitis because the symptoms are similar to stomach problems, constipation problems and pregnancy problems. When the ES creates its diagnostic inference, it will only pick up the information present and could therefore present a faulty diagnosis.

(v) **Security** and control procedures are much easier with the MIS than the ES. When the records are input, the operating system controls the processing and the information can be prevented from corruption by the database management system (DBMS). It is more difficult with an ES because of the potential size of its knowledge base and the complexities of its rule-based inference engine. With the hospital ES, there is also a link to the historical records within the MIS. If a link is missing, or a piece of information is incorrect, then the processing could take the completely wrong path towards its goal. The only way this could be tested is by completing every single diagnostic/symptom combination. This would not help because it would create almost an infinite number of possibilities.

General conditions for the application of an expert system

Three of the conditions that should be present if a particular domain of knowledge warrants the building of an expert system are:

(i) The expert is capable of explaining how decisions are made in all situations, and the decisions that are reached are consistent. If the expert might reach different conclusions given the same data, or the decision is taken on 'feel', then an expert system is not appropriate. It should be noted that some experts may find it difficult to explain how a decision has been made because their experience enables them to reach a conclusion automatically. An example of this would be in the diagnosis of why a car will not start. The conclusion may be reached that 'the starter motor is jammed'. Although the decision may be instant, it is the result of a series of logical thoughts and therefore is suitable for an expert system. 'The make and model of the car is XYZ, the engine makes a particular noise, the engine does not turn over, therefore the probability is high that the car has a jammed starter motor'. In the situation where the expert finds it difficult to rationalise their conclusion, a skilled knowledge engineer is required to help design the system.

(ii) The expertise that is the basis of the expert system is rare and in demand. This often manifests itself in the situation that the expert is always busy answering the questions of others and cannot do his or her own job properly. In many situations the 'users' are themselves experts in an associated field but sometimes need to augment their knowledge with specialised information. Doctors who are GPs may need to find out if a particular combination of drugs may react together to give bad side effects, or they may need to find out information about a rare speciality. Lawyers or accountants may need to consult about a complex and/or specialised category of law.

(iii) The problem must be one that is worth solving and it must cost less to develop the system than the cost of non-experts making the wrong decision. Examples include:

- when decisions are taken by non-experts ('should a customer be allocated a credit card'); or
- when the cost of making a bad decision is so horrendous that the right decision is vital (this often occurs in legal situations).

(c) **Three advantages of using expert systems**

(i) An expert system may enable a person training in a job to be immediately useful. Expert systems themselves are useful training aids, and if the trainee makes decisions based on the output from an expert system, then the manager can be assured that the right decision is reached despite the trainee's inexperience. This situation is particularly beneficial when there is a high turnover of staff in a particular job. A telephone sales operation is an example of when this benefit is important.

(ii) The expert is released from the mundane task of answering 'routine' queries to work where their expertise is of more value.

(iii) The process of building an expert system can provide significant advantages in understanding the problems to be solved. By going through the disciplines that are vital in building a knowledge base, then the expert is often able to understand their own decision making better, and sometimes to eradicate bad habits that may have crept in to their work.

Test your understanding 12 – Cost benefit (Integration)

(a) **Cost-benefit analysis techniques**

Techniques of cost-benefit analysis fall into two main categories: those that ignore the time value of money (TVM), and those that take into account the TVM. First, we will consider two techniques, which do not take into account the TVM.

Payback period – this method measures the number of years taken by the project to recoup the initial investment. Obviously, the shorter the payback period the better. Companies use this method frequently because it is easy to apply and comprehend. Use of the payback period does, however, have a number of drawbacks. The determination of the cut-off period is essentially an arbitrary decision. The payback period ignores cash flows, which occur after the cut-off date; it also ignores the timing of cash flows within the payback period itself. As a result, viable projects may easily be rejected.

In its favour, the payback period does allow for risk and uncertainty by attempting to recover the initial outlay in as short a period as possible.

Return on investment – using this method, the benefits of the project are expressed as a return on investment in terms of a rate per year.

This technique assumes that the investment is repaid over its economic life in a straight-line way. As with the payback period method, it is easy to apply and comprehend but it, too, does not take into account the time value of money. It does, however, provide a useful indicator; organisations obviously seek to invest scarce resources where they will derive the highest return.

Discounted cash flow (DCF) methods take into consideration the time value of money. We will consider the two principal DCF methods of project appraisal: Net Present Value (NPV) and Internal Rate of Return (IRR).

Net Present Value – this method takes the discounted present value of the future cash flows generated by the project, less the initial outlay. If the NPV is equal to, or greater than, zero the project should be considered as it will at least attain the required rate of return; when greater than zero it will enhance the value of the firm. When using this method to compare projects the one with the largest NPV should be selected.

Internal Rate of Return – this method identifies the rate of return, which produces an NPV of zero for the project. If the IRR of a project is greater than the firm's required rate of return (usually the cost of capital), it should proceed with the project.

(b) **Measurement of information systems costs and benefits**

Costs – some categories of costs associated with a computer system can be quite precisely ascertained, while others are less easily defined. The main costs related to information systems are those of building the system, installation costs, and operational and maintenance costs.

The costs associated with building the system include staff costs (the average salaries for all levels of staff participating in the project; lost time due to sickness, holidays etc; staff training where the use of new software or hardware is necessary, and travel expenses incurred when making associated trips to suppliers etc) and computer-related costs (computer time incurred during system development, and any new equipment which may need to be bought). Many of these costs cannot be accurately defined, but can only be estimated.

The cost of installing the system, which may include recruitment and training, commissioning and installation, conversion of files, user training, parallel running or phased implementation etc, may be easier to quantify. Operating and maintenance costs, (usually contributing to as much as 70% of the total cost of the system) would include the costs of financing the system, maintenance contracts, etc. These costs are often predetermined, and therefore their measurement is less problematic.

Benefits – tactical benefits are those, which enable the company to continue functioning in the same way, but at a lower level of costs, or with increased profits. These can be moderately straightforward to define, although the accuracy of any estimation will be determined by the effectiveness of the new system, and its ability to accomplish the required functions. Strategic benefits are those that enable the company to enter new markets, either offering a new product/service or reaching new customers, or both. These are of fundamental importance, yet are so difficult to predict, or quantify.

The improved system will enable better use to be made of information, which should enhance decision-making and the productivity of managers. Monitoring and quantifying these could present difficulties.

The information system may help in attracting new customers and retaining existing ones; and it should improve stock and credit control. Again, attempts to quantify and classify these benefits may be problematic.

(c) **Risk analysis of the costs and benefits**

The majority of investments are exposed to at least some element of risk. It may be categorised as systematic (factors that affect all organisations) or unsystematic (events that affect one project).

Most managerial decisions involve an element of uncertainty, and are therefore subject to some level of risk. Identifying, and being able to quantify, the risk factor is of great consequence.

Management want to have their vulnerable assets identified, their security requirements outlined, and protective measures delineated. The costs of safeguarding against risks can then be balanced against the estimated costs, which would be incurred if the event took place. The project may be affected by prices that are higher than anticipated.

This may be caused by:

(i) bankruptcy of hardware suppliers;

(ii) high turnover of staff on the project team;

(iii) technology not meeting expectations;

(iv) opportunity being lost;

(v) unforeseen problems with contractors, unions etc;

(vi) inadequacies in the project team;

(vii) instability in the economic environment;

(viii) unforeseen costs/overheads;

(ix) inadequate information from the users with regard to their needs of the system.

The project may equally be affected by anticipated benefits, which do not emerge:

(i) the users may experience difficulties or apprehension in adopting the new system; delays or disruption may ensue as a result;

(ii) projected increases in the market share may not occur;

(iii) the system may not be capable of performing at the level estimated, resulting in lower productivity than predicted;

(iv) the benefits derived from the information being produced by the new system may not be discernible.

Risk assessment often involves scenario-based methodologies, which may involve preparing three scenarios: worst case, best case, and expected case.

Test your understanding 13 – RBT (Integration)

(a) **Intranet**

An intranet is an internal company information system where a wide variety of internal information can be posted for access by staff members. Internal information often includes company news, telephone directories, standard forms, copies of rules and procedures, and so on. In this case of the system under consideration by RBT, the intranet would hold up-to-date information on products and prices, so that sales representatives can download this information to their laptops from customer's premises and other remote locations.

Advantages

The proposed new system has the following advantages over the old system:

(1) **More regularly updated information**
An intranet site is very easy and cheap to update, and product and price information can be kept fully up-to-date by head office. The downloaded product information will therefore be much more up-to-date than the old printed materials, and a better customer service can be provided. All the latest products would be made available to customers and customers would always be given the correct prices.

(2) **Reduced costs of producing price lists/brochures**

Regular price lists and brochures will no longer be required, and the production and printing costs of paper-based products should be reduced.

Disadvantages

The intranet site has the following disadvantages compared with the old system:

(1) **Slower communication with the production department**

Since the telephone system will be discontinued, the sales people will not have access to production staff to resolve any queries or difficulties with customers. This would be a serious weakness in the system. Good communications between sales and production staff must be maintained.

Solutions

Possible solutions to this problem include:

(i) *E-mail system*

E-mail might provide an efficient way for sales representatives to communicate directly with the production staff, although controls would need to be in place to ensure that the production staff respond promptly to e-mail queries they receive.

(ii) *Maintain telephone access*

Voice telephone access offers immediate communication. A salesperson can get in contact with a member of the production staff and get an immediate reply. Maintaining telephone access for certain queries would be a useful way of ensuring very quick communication where needed.

(iii) *Access to production scheduling system*

Allowing salespeople access to the production scheduling system over the intranet would allow them to estimate delivery date themselves thus reducing the need for direct contact between production and sales.

(2) **Less personal communication with production department**

The intranet is a very impersonal way to communicate with people. It does not allow for two-way conversation, whereas personal contact may be required to resolve difficult issues.

Solution

Both e-mail and a voice telephone system are more personal forms of communication than the intranet. The voice telephone system in particular allows a two-way conversation to take place so that more difficult issues can easily be resolved.

(3) **Rejection of new technology**

The sales people may dislike the new technology that they are required to use. At present they do not use IT significantly in their work, and so new skills may be required. Many new systems also have 'teething problems' on implementation, which may also make users dislike the new system.

Solutions

(i) *Training*

Training will be required so people know how the system works and can get the best use from it.

(ii) *Consultation*

Consulting users early in the development process is an excellent way of getting user buy-in to the new system. It will also ensure the system is practical from a day-to-day usage point of view.

(iii) *Testing*

Testing systems well prior to implementation will help avoid the teething problems which may be encountered, particularly if the end users are involved since they know better than anyone else the way the system will be used in practice.

(4) **Up-front costs**

The proposed new system will require significant up-front costs both in terms of developing the new systems and training staff. Given the relatively small number of sales representatives (just 20) the investment may not be financially justified.

Solution

A cost benefit analysis can be undertaken to ascertain whether the costs of the investment are justified.

(5) **Information systems – order progress**

Manufacturing system – order tracking

As part of the manufacturing process, progress on orders will need to be recorded. The information recorded will include work done, work still to do and the expected completion date. This information might already exist within the current system or it may need to be input into a database which can be accessed by clients.

EDI or extranet

Using electronic data interchange the customer would be able to log on to RBT's systems to directly access the production data.

An extranet is an extension of an intranet. External parties are allowed to log onto the intranet site and use it to access sections of the intranet. The intranet site would need to be connected to the manufacturing system/database so that up-to-date information was available.

Advantages

(1) Clients could access information themselves. This could save staff time and resources in RBT, since there will be fewer customer queries to deal with.

(2) An extranet would be relatively easy to provide if the manufacturing system is already linked to the intranet for the benefit of the salespeople.

(3) Other information could also be provided to customers (such as past order information, account balances and so on).

Disadvantages

(1) There would be a loss of personal contact with customers. The salesperson would not have as many opportunities to make contact with customers in order to build an ongoing relationship. As a consequence, they might identify fewer sales opportunities or find it harder to make a sale because they are less trusted by the customer.

(2) External parties would be accessing internal systems. There is a danger that hackers will get into parts of the system that are confidential, and a risk that important information is stolen or damaged. It could also increase the possibility of viruses being brought in which could damage internal systems.

Internet

Alternatively the RBT could put tracking information on a database which is connected to the company's web site. Clients would then be able to access their information through this site.

Advantages

(1) Labour cost savings, as described for an extranet.

(2) Customers will be familiar with the internet and so find it easier to use than an extranet or internal system accessed via EDI. It also means they will not have to dial in directly to the company's internal network, saving them time and effort.

(3) There is less opportunity for hackers or viruses to enter the internal systems using a web site on the internet, since they are not directly accessing internal systems.

(4) Other information could also be provided to customers on the internet site.

Disadvantage

The company may not currently have an internet site. This could be a significant extra expense, in terms of designing, creating and maintaining the site.

hapter

6

Management control systems

Chapter learning objectives

Lead	Component
B1. Evaluate the tools and processes required for strategy implementation.	(a) Recommend appropriate measures for the strategic control and direction of various types of organisations. (b) Recommend solutions for the risks of dysfunctional behaviour arising from the associated models of performance measurement.
C1. Evaluate control systems for organisational activities and resources.	(a) Evaluate the appropriateness of control systems for the management of an organisation.

Indicative syllabus content

- Business unit performance and appraisal, including transfer pricing and taxation, reward systems and incentives.
- Non-financial measures and their interaction with financial measures.
- Risks of performance measurement, including the Balanced Scorecard.
- Lean systems.
- Cost of quality.
- Big Data as a strategic resource.

- Dysfunctional behaviour associated with measures of control and direction.
- Application of control systems and related theory to the design of management accounting control systems and information systems in general.
- Control systems within functional areas of a business including human resources, sales, purchases, treasury, distribution, IT.
- Identification of appropriate responsibility and control centres within the organisation.
- Performance target setting.
- Performance appraisal and feedback.
- Cost of quality applied to the management accounting function and "getting things right first time".
- Responses to risks in control systems for management.

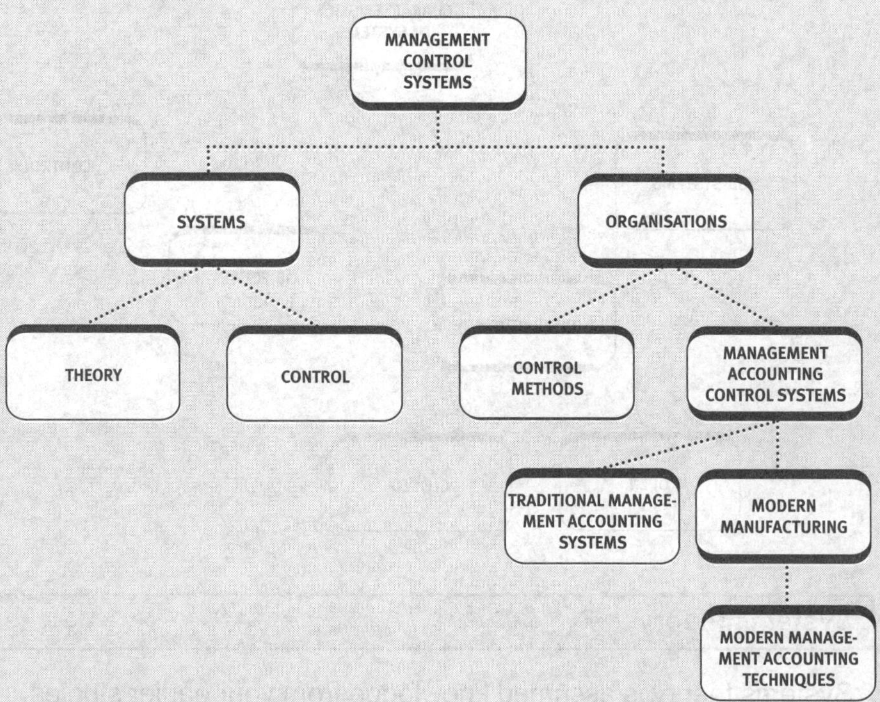

1 Organisations as systems

This section has been covered in your earlier studies and is here as a reminder.

- An organisation is a system in which people combine to carry out the purpose for which the organisation exists.
- Control makes an organisation function in a way that should enable it to meet its objectives.

Systems and their characteristics

- A system is a set of interacting components that operate together to accomplish a purpose.

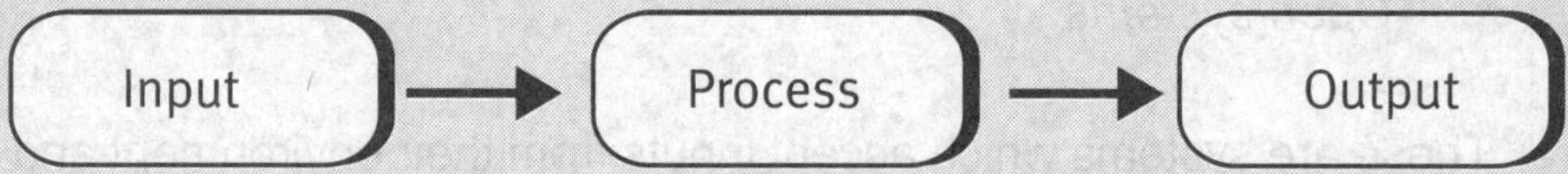

- There are inputs to a process which converts those inputs to outputs.
- All systems have these characteristics but some systems have other characteristics as well.

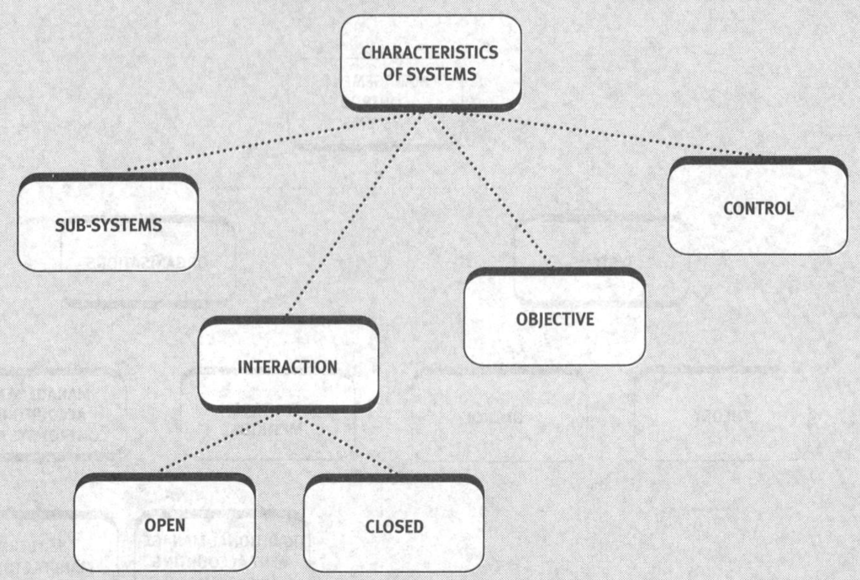

Systems theory

Systems theory is assumed knowledge from your earlier studies.

Definitions

- *Sub-systems*

Within a system there will usually be sub-systems. For example, if a company is a system, then the finance department is a sub-system. Within the finance department will be a sub-sub-system such as the management accounting system, and so on.

- *Closed systems*

These are systems that accept no input from the environment, are self-contained and cannot respond to change. These do not exist in business.

- *Open systems*

These are systems which accept inputs from their environment and provide output to the environment. They react to their environment, e.g. a company.

- *Objective*

A system must have an objective to function correctly. For example, a company's objective might be to maximise shareholder wealth. The objective allows the system to be monitored or controlled.

- *Control*

All systems should be controlled if they are not to decay over time and start to fail to meet their objectives.

- A system must be controlled to keep it stable or to allow it to change safely.
- Control is dependent on receiving and processing information. Information in the form of feedback allows us to judge how well or badly a system is performing.

Feedback control is defined as:

'The measurement of differences between planned outputs and actual outputs achieved, and the modification of subsequent action and / or plans to achieve future required results.' This is the more common type of control system.

Feedforward control is defined as:

'The forecasting of differences between actual and planned outcomes and the implementation of actions before the event to prevent such differences.'

Examples of a feedforward control system could be found in a budgeting system. A cash budget might predict that an overdraft will be required in a particular month. This could be organised in advance thereby avoiding any unauthorised overdraft charges. Or it may be that an adverse material price variance has arisen for several months in a row. Without feedforward control, this variance would continue. On investigation it may be due to the general price of the goods rising (feedback), and therefore the standard should be altered for future periods (feedforward). Therefore future prices paid are now compared to a more up to date standard. The action of changing the standard is an example of feedforward control. (Even better, the company should have anticipated the price rise and altered its standard already.)

Managers often spend more time on considering feedback. This is mainly because it is certain and can be quantified. Feedforward controls are often uncertain and accountants typically do not like dealing with the unknown. Changes will be continual and take up much management time which managers think might be better spent on other issues. Also frustrations will set in when management think they have resolved an issue only for the environment to change yet again and more time be required on the issue.

Any good manager should spend their time looking at the future of the business and consider the outside world, in conjunction with learning from aspects of the companies historic performance. Any manager who ignores feedforward control will contribute to the downfall of a company.

Primary feedback could be reported to line management in the form of control reports, comparing actual and budgeted results. If the variances are small or can be corrected easily then the information may not be fed back to anyone higher in the organisation.

Secondary feedback is where feedback is sent to a higher level in an organisation and can lead to a plan being reviewed and possibly changed; for example, the revision of a budget after large variances were discovered due to price changes over time.

Negative feedback is feedback taken to reverse a deviation from standard. This could be by amending the inputs or process so that the system reverts to a steady state; for example, a machine may need to be reset over time to its original settings.

Positive feedback is feedback taken to reinforce a deviation from standard. The inputs or process would not be altered.

Open loop systems are where there is scope within the control mechanism for outside involvement; for example, a manager might decide what action should be taken from, say, three options.

Closed loop systems are where the control action is automatic, for example, the thermostat on a central heating system.

Systems within an organisation

The company that you work for is a system incorporating many sub-systems, sub-sub-systems and so on. Materials, labour, machines and finance are inputs into a process, say food manufacture, which produces outputs, which in this case would be food.

The accounts department within this company is an example of a sub-system. The accounts department has inputs – labour, IT, etc. which process information to output the management and financial accounts amongst other things.

Within the accounts department itself there will be sub-systems. For example, there will probably be a system in place for operating the receivables ledger. Particular staff will be responsible for inputting certain data regarding sales and cash received, the computer will process it, and one of the outputs – aged receivables, might be used as an input to another process – debt collection, where that department has its own processes.

This shows that there are many, many systems within a company and all of them will be linked.

Without control a company will perform very badly. For example, if customers knew there were no controls to identify they hadn't paid (the aged receivables list), or that debt collectors wouldn't chase the debt, then customers would buy goods with no intention of payment and the company would certainly go bust. This could be said of many of the controls in all organisations – they are there to ensure that the companies objectives will be met, which is often profit maximisation.

The airline industry

British Airways (BA) promotes itself as a world leading airline, providing a quality service. It has not performed well in the past and was criticised for operating almost as a closed system.

In 1980 fuel prices for BA and its competitors increased by 70% per annum and many unprofitable routes were dropped. In 1984 the Civil Aviation Authority issued a white paper demanding a reduction in BA's routes which lead to several routes being provided by competitors. BA was accused of being reactionary to these events which appeared to take it by surprise.

The business model for airlines was fairly similar. Pricing reflected little competition and the only real differentiators between airlines were around reputation, largely a result of airline safety records. Having little competition leads to complacency and BA could be accused of this, operating as though it was almost in a closed system with little regard for what was happening in the outside world.

Around 1985 the Ryan family identified a gap in the market for a low cost European airline (Ryanair) and initially challenged BA and Aer Lingus to offer a low cost Dublin to London flight. Ryanair's passenger numbers increased from 5,000 to 82,000 in a year taking most of its custom from BA.

When applying the management control model to a conventional airline such as BA, primary control would be exercised through cost control over employment costs, fuel prices, the cost of acquiring aircraft, maintenance expenses, etc. Much of this would be performed via budgets and variance analysis which is a form of feedback control.

Secondary control can be exercised, typically through changing objectives or standards, such as varying prices, altering financial and non-financial targets. This is an example of feedforward control – where the future is considered and targets and objectives are altered so that changes in the future business environment are factored into the business model.

Amending the predictive model is a form of learning from past experience. If for example certain routes are more profitable and some less profitable or unprofitable, resources are shifted towards the more profitable routes and unprofitable ones are closed. This is what BA did - feedback had been received indicating they would not meet their objectives and so feedforward control was exercised by making changes for the future. One of these changes was when BA launched their own low cost airline 'Go' in 1998.

Ryanair and Easyjet responded by cutting their prices further, selling seats for the price of £1 plus taxes and charges, and BA decided from its feedback that they could not compete. In 2001 they sold Go due to its inability to compete with Ryanair and Easyjet on this low cost basis. (Also to some extent Go conflicted with BA's objective of being a higher quality airline and customers were confused.)

The introduction of low cost airlines such as EasyJet and Ryanair has changed the business model for airlines completely. Some of the changes introduced have been:

- Selling seats via the Internet rather than through travel agents. BA followed Ryanair's lead.
- Yield management with variable prices depending on capacity utilisation. Most airlines do this these days.
- Using lower cost, out-of-town airports. BA still differentiates by using central airports and charging for the convenience.
- No printed tickets, seat allocations, or free meals and drinks. Although many airlines offer these facilities at an extra charge.
- No exceptions policies to reduce the cost of handling exceptions (e.g. no flexibility for passengers who arrive late).
- Fast turnaround times for aircraft to improve utilisation.

These changes have reduced costs (inputs); changed processes such as turnaround times and yield management for pricing; and the predictive model (most certainly that of BA) that perceived that customers would only book through travel agents, fly from central airports, demand seat allocations and meals, etc., has been dramatically altered.

EasyJet and Ryanair have focused on the short-haul market which has grown as a result of lower prices, rather than compete head-on with the major long-haul airlines. It is the latter market segment that has been significantly affected by the reduction in international travel over recent years. Consequently, the profit declines in the major airlines are contrasted with the generally successful performance of the low cost airlines, although in the last few years even these airlines have begun to come under increasing competitive pressure from each other and Ryanair's financial performance has deteriorated.

BA has since had many other challenges to overcome – frequent strikes by their cabin crew despite being the highest paid staff in the world, reduced flyers after September 11th and increasing fuel prices. To counter this, feedforward control has been used and BA has been 're-engineered' to some extent – this has included cost cutting, consolidation of the airline industry and alliances between some of the major operators to share routes, new livery (which wasn't very successful), and cabin restructuring to offer fewer first-class seats and more World Traveller (economy) seats. It appears that BA are much more forward thinking than they used to be and are faring as well as many other major long-haul airlines in these times of recession. However, they paid a big price back in the 1980's for not assessing the outside environment, listening to their customers and missing an opportunity to become an early provider of a low cost airline. If they had spent more time using feedforward control this might have been avoided.

Test your understanding 1

Feedback reported to a high level in an organisation that can lead to the revision of a plan is called:

A Primary feedback

B Secondary feedback

C Positive feedback

D Negative feedback

Test your understanding 2

Systems that accept no input from the environment, are self-contained and cannot respond to change are called:

A Sub-systems

B Open systems

C Closed systems

D Management control systems

Test your understanding 3

The type of organisational structure where employees have two or more managers is:

A Functional

B Divisional

C Matrix

D Network

Test your understanding 4 – J television (Integration)

J is a major television broadcaster that broadcasts within its home country. J is a commercial enterprise that generates revenues by selling advertising slots in the breaks between, and during, programmes. The price of an advertising slot varies according to the anticipated number of people who will be watching J's television channel at that time. There are several other broadcasters which also sell advertising slots and therefore compete with J for advertising revenues.

J's programming department is responsible for purchasing programmes to broadcast. All of J's programmes are created by third parties. Some of the programmes are sold on the open market and J has to compete with other broadcasters for the right to show them. J also commissions a small number of programmes directly from the producers. Programmes that are commissioned by J cannot be sold to anybody else without J's permission. Commissioned programmes are usually more expensive. J sometimes recovers some of the cost of its commissioned shows by selling the rights to broadcast the programmes to broadcasters in other countries.

An independent agency conducts daily surveys to determine the performance of all of the broadcasters in J's home country. Viewers are asked to list the programmes that they watched during the previous 24 hours and to state whether they enjoyed the programmes. These surveys are used to estimate the total number of people who watched each programme and also the level of satisfaction with each programme. Both statistics are very important to advertisers and both can affect a television broadcasting company's ability to negotiate favourable rates for future advertising slots.

Once a programme has been purchased there is very little that J can do if it is unsuccessful. J will have already paid to broadcast the programme and cannot obtain a refund even if it decides not to broadcast it.

J's directors evaluate the performance of the programming department in terms of the responses from viewers. J's Head of Programming is expected to achieve an audience share of at least 20% of those watching television at any given time. Also at least 60% of those who watched a programme must state that they enjoyed it. The previous Head of Programming was replaced because he could not consistently achieve these figures. The present Head of Programming has been in place for eight months and has achieved the targets for at least 95% of the time.

J's directors are concerned that the evaluation of the programming department takes the form of negative feedback. The emphasis in a negative feedback system tends to be on the identification of failures to achieve targets, with a view to addressing the causes of such failures. The directors are now considering shifting their emphasis over to positive feedback, which tends to focus on the identification of successes, in the hope that further successes can be achieved.

Required:

(a) Discuss the potential benefits to J of considering viewers' satisfaction as well as the viewing figures themselves.

(10 minutes)

(b) Advise the directors about the potential drawbacks of their focus on negative feedback.

(15 minutes)

(c) Evaluate the potential advantages and disadvantages to J of the directors' proposal to use positive feedback.

(15 minutes)

2 Control in organisations

It is necessary to consider how management control systems operate and to ensure that businesses achieve their objectives.

- **Management control** is defined as 'the process of guiding organisations into viable patterns of activity in a changing environment'.

- **Management control systems** are defined as 'the processes by which managers attempt to ensure that their organisation adapts successfully to its changing environment'.

These definitions are both about adapting to changing environments and therefore management control systems must be a variety of open systems that change over time.

If the control systems are to be successful, management must always be monitoring the way the system operates and how the system could be changed to improve its performance.

At the highest level, one way of controlling a business is by controlling directors' remuneration.

Performance target setting

One factor within any discussion of control systems is that there must be some standards of performance if the system is to operate successfully. The standards of performance allow the feedback loops discussed earlier to work.

- An effective control system must incorporate a feedback loop such as:
  - performance target (standard) set
  - actual result recorded
  - compared with target
  - control action taken (if required).
- If managers are to be controlled successfully then the standards set must be sufficiently varied to ensure that the manager works in the best interests of the company. The standards set can be:
  - **Financial:** These would be based on information supplied by the management accounting system and are often financial ratios, but they have the problem of being historic-looking and short-term.
  - **Non-financial:** These are measures that consider other factors such as customer perception, research and development, production efficiency or staff satisfaction. These measures are very important to help managers focus on long-term future performance.

Behavioural implications of management accounting control systems

When structuring the control system, companies must take account of the behavioural aspects of setting performance targets and standards. As with any control reporting system, there is a risk of unintended behavioural consequences.

A basic assumption should be that if a manager's performance is judged according to success or failure in achieving one or more specific targets or budget figures, the main concern of the manager will be to succeed in achieving the target. Missing a specific target would be a sign of failure. The focus of managers on performance targets will be even greater if the reward system is based on achieving them.

Focusing on performance targets or the profits or return on investment for the responsibility centre might have the following consequences:

- If the manager's performance targets are budget targets, he will **concentrate on budgeted results** to the exclusion of longer-term considerations and objectives.
- If the manager's performance targets are exclusively financial targets, the manager will **ignore non-financial considerations**.
- If the manager's performance is judged exclusively by profit or return, he might be tempted to **ignore the risks**, and take high-risk decisions in the hope of boosting profits. The risk exposures from such decisions might not be justified by the size of the expected profits.
- The manager will be more concerned about the results of his own centre rather than those of the organisation as a whole. As a consequence, the manager might make decisions that are damaging to the interests of the organisation because they will improve the performance of his own centre.
- Responsibility centre managers might get into **disputes** with each other **about transfer prices**. Transfer prices for inter-divisional transactions do not affect the profits of the organisation as a whole, but do affect the profits of each of the profit centres or investment centres involved. Arguments about transfer prices could result in a refusal by profit centre managers to co-operate with each other, and decisions to sell to or buy from the external market, when its inter-divisional transactions would benefit the organisation more.
- If the targets set for responsibility centre managers are too ambitious, the control system could be **demotivating**, when it should provide an incentive or motivation to improve performance. A criticism of ideal standard costs, for example, is that they are unattainable. If ideal standard costs are set (or if budget targets are too challenging) managers might be discouraged by the adverse performance reports he receives.
- When performance targets are financial targets, there might be opportunities for a centre manager to **manipulate short-term costs or profits**, for example by recognising revenue early or deferring costs to a later period.

- When managers participate in setting their own budget for the next financial year, and they are judged according to whether they succeed in keeping expenditure within budget limits, there will be a strong temptation to build **'padding'** or **'slack'** into the budget expenditure estimates. In other words, the manager might try to budget for more expenditure than is actually needed, to that it will be much easier to meet budget targets (and be rewarded accordingly).

Management accounting control systems

- A **management accounting control system** can be defined as an information system that helps managers to make planning and control decisions.
- All management accounting control systems differ as the circumstances of businesses always differ and the systems are designed to meet the needs of the business.

Designing a management accounting control system

- Even though the systems differ between businesses there are common factors that should be considered in the design of the systems.

There are a number of things to be considered when establishing the structure of management accounting control systems:

Organisational structure

Organisations operate through a variety of organisational forms, such as:

- functional
- divisional
- matrix
- network

The form of structure that is adopted will determine the type of control processes implemented throughout the business. Each structure has its advantages and disadvantages which were covered in lower level CIMA papers and are assumed knowledge.

Responsibility accounting

- A key aspect of management accounting control systems is that the information presented must be given to the managers who are responsible for it.
- Responsibility accounting tries to ensure that managers are only held responsible for activities that are under their control. This is known as the **principle of controllability**.
- If managers are appraised on factors outside their control, they will become demotivated.

Performance measures for investment centres might be:

- return on investment (ROI)
- residual income, and
- economic value added or EVA®.

The **return on investment** (ROI) for an investment centre is similar to the return on capital employed (ROCE) for an organisation as a whole. It is calculated for a particular period as follows:

$$\text{ROI} = \frac{\text{Profit before interest and tax}}{\text{Operations management capital employed}} \times 100$$

(CIMA Official Terminology)

Residual income is a measure of the profitability of an investment centre after deducting a notional or imputed interest cost. This interest cost is a notional charge for the cost of the capital invested in the division.

Residual income = Accounting profit – Notional interest on capital

(1) Accounting profit is calculated in the same way as for ROI.

(2) Notional interest on capital = the capital employed in the division multiplied by a notional cost of capital or interest rate. The selected cost of capital could be the company's average cost of funds (cost of capital). However, other interest rates might be selected, such as the current cost of borrowing, or a target ROI.

Economic value added (EVA®) is discussed later in the chapter.

Test your understanding 5

Performance measures that could be used for investment centres, but not profit centres, include: (Select all that apply.)

A Return on investment

B Gross profit

C Residual income

D Economic value added

Test your understanding 6

Division X of Woking plc produced the following results in the last financial year.

- Net profit = $200,000
- Gross capital employed = $1,000,000

For evaluation purposes all divisional assets are valued at original cost. The division is considering a project that has a positive NPV, will increase annual net profit by $15,000, but will require average inventory levels to increase by $50,000 and non-current assets to increase by $50,000.

Woking plc imposes a 16% capital charge on its divisions.

Given these circumstances, will the evaluation criteria of return on investment (ROI) and residual income (RI) motivate division X managers to accept the project?

	ROI	RI
A	Yes	Yes
B	Yes	No
C	No	Yes
D	No	No

Traditional management accounting systems

The traditional management accounting systems that have been employed by businesses have included techniques such as:

- Standard costing, budgeting and variance analysis.
- Overhead allocation: labour hour and machine hour costing systems.
- Capital investment appraisal (such as NPV, IRR, ARR).
- Transfer pricing.
- Rewards and appraisal based on financial/management accounts.

These methods have all been considered in your earlier studies.

Criticisms of traditional management accounting systems.

Despite their continuing popularity in many businesses, all these methods have been criticised for a number of reasons:

- Systems are often too formal. They produce routine pre-set information whereas managers require more on-demand adaptable information.
- Some assumptions they make are questionable, for example treating labour costs as a variable cost when in the short-term they are really a fixed cost.
- The systems are very cumbersome (for example, budgets are time-consuming) and produce information of little value.
- Traditional systems view many costs as production costs, when in reality they are overhead costs of businesses.
- The systems may not take account of the business strategy. They tend to focus on low cost, hence not assisting a business that wants to differentiate itself and produce very high quality.

Beyond budgeting

It has been argued that the entire budgeting process is limiting and unsuitable for business planning and control, and budgeting systems should be abandoned.

The argument for abolishing budgets, referred to as **'beyond budgeting'**, was put forward by Hope and Fraser (Management Accounting, December 1997).

Their criticisms of budgeting are:

- Budgets are a **commitment**. They therefore act as a **constraint** on doing anything different. However, in a fast-changing business environment, budgets are based on assumptions that will soon become out-of-date. It would be much better to measure performance against challenging but achievable strategic targets, rather than detailed short-term targets.
- Traditional budgets are seen as a **mechanism for top-down control** by senior management. It strengthens the chain of command, when organisations should be empowering individuals in the 'front line'.
- Traditional budgets **restrict flexibility** because individuals feel they are expected to achieve the budget targets. This is a deterrent to continual improvement (and so is inconsistent with TQM).
- Budgeting **reinforces the barriers between departments**, instead of encouraging a sharing of knowledge across the organisation.
- Budgets are **bureaucratic**, **internally-focused** and **time-consuming**. What is needed is a flexible approach, with managers looking forward and at the business environment, and not wasting their time on needless formal planning exercises.

Modern manufacturing methods

Traditional manufacturing	Modern manufacturing
• standardisation of product	• globalisation
• long production runs	• competition
• 'acceptable' level of quality	• JIT and TQM
• slow product development	• 'intelligent machines'

Major impacts on manufacturing philosophy.

In recent years the impact of 'globalisation' has led to the reduction in trade barriers and the improvement of trade links. This means that competition is not only from local companies but from around the globe. In order to compete industry has had to change the manner in which it does business. The main competition has come from Japan and other East Asian economies where the approach to manufacturing was quite different. These included the use of the following techniques and philosophies such as, just-in-time (JIT), total quality management (TQM) and value analysis (economic value added (EVA)). Finally, manufacturing has been affected by the introduction of computerisation. This has had two key impacts:

(1) The introduction of 'intelligent' machines that are capable of doing a range of different jobs without constant labour supervision. This is best illustrated by considering such technological advances as Computer Aided Design (CAD), Computer Aided Manufacture (CAM), Computer Integrated Manufacture (CIM) and Flexible Manufacturing Systems (FMS). These were all covered in your earlier studies.

(2) The vastly improved ability of computers to track and record all aspects of the workplace due to faster processing and dramatically reduced cost of installation. The difficulty does not lie with how to collect data, that is now cheap and relatively easy to do. Instead the question is what data do we collect and how do we use it.

Just-in-time (JIT)

- This is a technique for the organisation of work flows, to allow rapid, high-quality, flexible production whilst minimising manufacturing waste and stock levels.
- The JIT system can be applied to both production and purchasing.

Conditions for successful JIT adoption

JIT systems were first introduced in Japan but have become more popular in the UK. They are not applicable for all businesses as a number of conditions must be present:

- Stable high volume of demand.
- Co-ordination of daily production programmes of supplier and consumer.
- Co-operation of supplier who has to be reliable on both delivery and quality.
- Suitable factory layout.
- Reliable transport system.

If these conditions are not present or cannot be created then JIT will not work. The technique has probably been most successfully employed by the motor industry, where car manufacturers have developed by finding key suppliers and locating the suppliers in very close proximity to the production facilities. They have even developed IT links to suppliers to ensure good co-ordination between the car manufacturer and the supplier.

Operational requirements of JIT

The operational requirements for JIT are as follows:

- High quality and reliability. JIT relies on getting things right first time, and preventing scrap or re-working. Hold-ups due to poor quality slow down the delivery of the product or service to the customer and reduce throughput.
- Speed of throughput. Throughput in a manufacturing operation must be fast, so that customer orders can be met by production rather than out of inventory.
- Flexibility. In order to respond immediately to customer orders ('just-in-time'), production must be flexible, and in small batch sizes. The ideal batch size is 1.
- Lower cost. Lower inventory, faster throughput and better quality will drive down costs.

The JIT philosophy and management accounting control systems

Management accounting systems within a JIT environment must be capable of producing performance and control information consistent with the JIT philosophy. Information must therefore be produced that directs management attention to the following issues.

- **Elimination of waste.** Waste occurs with any activity that does not add value. Examples of waste are:
  - Overproduction, i.e. producing more than is immediately needed by the next stage in the process.
  - Waiting time or non-productive time.
  - Movement and transport of goods. Moving items around a plant does not add value. Waste can be reduced by changing the physical layout of the factory floor to minimise the movement of materials.
  - Waste in the process. Waste and re-working of items do not add value and hold up throughput.
  - Defective finished goods are 'quality waste', and are a significant cause of waste in many operations, resulting in sales returns and customer complaints.
  - Inventory is wasteful. The target should be to reduce inventory.
- **Set-up reductions**. 'Set-up' is the collection of activities carried out between completing work on one job or batch of production and getting the process or machine ready to take the next batch. Set-up time is non-productive time. An aim in JIT is therefore to reduce set-up times, for example by pre-preparing some set-up tasks that can be done in advance, or by carrying out some tasks whilst the machines are running that were previously not done until the machines had stopped (i.e. during set-up time).
- **Continuous improvement**. The aim is to do things well, and then try to do them even better. The ideal target in JIT is to meet demand immediately with perfect quality and no waste. In practice, this ideal is never achieved. However, the JIT philosophy is that an organisation should work towards the ideal, and continuous improvement is both possible and necessary. The Japanese term for continuous improvement is 'kaizen'.

Total quality management (TQM)

TQM was covered in your earlier studies. You may remember that TQM is a business philosophy aimed at:

- minimising errors (ideally to zero) as the cost of getting things right the first time is always less than the costs of correction; and
- maximising customer satisfaction such that every customer's expectations are met or exceeded.

To achieve this philosophy a TQM firm should have an appropriately installed quality culture and very good systems that are documented and adhered to by all staff. It's fundamental features include:

- Prevention of errors before they occur;
- Continual improvement;
- Real participation by all;
- Commitment of senior management.

Costs of quality

Prevention costs: these are the costs of avoiding or reducing defects and failures. It includes the design and development of quality control equipment and the maintenance of the equipment. It could also include the cost of setting up 'quality circles' – a small group of employees who meet on a regular basis to discuss quality issues and to develop solutions to problems arising.

Appraisal costs: these are the costs of assessing the actual quality achieved. They include the costs of goods inwards inspection, and the monitoring of the production output.

Internal failure costs: these are the costs arising within the organisation when the predetermined specifications are not met. They include the cost of reworking or rectifying the product, the net cost of scrap, downtime of machinery due to quality problems.

External failure costs: these are the costs of inadequate quality that are incurred once the product has been sold. They include dealing with customer complaints, warranty claims costs of repairing or replacing returned faulty goods.

Continuous improvement

Businesses should always be looking to improve their performance. All staff should be encouraged to look for areas where improvements are possible and make those improvements. Suggestions of all staff are considered and a reward system that supports continuous improvement needs to be introduced.

Value analysis

This is the reduction of costs into value added and non-value added activities. Value added activities will increase the overall worth of a product by increasing their saleability in some way. Therefore any part of the production process is value adding to a greater or lesser extent.

Non-value added activities add no value to the product and hence the elimination of these activities will have no adverse impact on the product, but will lead to cost savings.

A success story

Corning Inc is the world leader in speciality glass and ceramics. This is partly due to a TQM approach. In 1983 the CEO announced a $1.6 billion investment in TQM. After several years of intensive training and a decade of applying the TQM approach, all of Corning's employees had bought into the quality concept. They knew what was meant by 'continual improvement', 'empowerment', 'customer focus', 'management by prevention', and they witnessed the companies profits soar.

TQM failure

British Telecom launched a TQM program in the late 1980's. This resulted in the company getting bogged down in its quality processes and bureaucracy. The company failed to focus on its customers and later decided to dismantle the TQM program. This was at great cost to the company and they have failed to make a full recovery.

Test your understanding 7

Modern manufacturing generally includes: (Select all that apply.)

A Intelligent machines

B Short production runs

C JIT

D TQM

Test your understanding 8

Features of a just-in-time system include: (Select all that apply.)

A Fluctuating demand

B Low volumes

C Reliable transport systems

D A flexible workforce

Test your understanding 9

Within total quality management, a training cost is:

A A prevention cost

B An appraisal cost

C An internal failure cost

D An external failure cost

Test your understanding 10

Techniques used in JIT and TQM environments include: (Select all that apply.)

A Throughput accounting

B Backflush accounting

C Non-financial performance indicators

D Activity based budgeting

Test your understanding 11

The philosophy of management based on cutting out waste and any unnecessary activities is:

A Throughput accounting

B Backflush accounting

C Lean accounting

D Management accounting

Test your understanding 12

JJT is a manufacturer of machinery parts for other businesses. It operates an inventory strategy designed to increase efficiency and decrease waste by receiving materials only as they are needed in the production process, thereby reducing inventory costs. It aims to finish customer orders just in time for customers to take delivery of goods.

Which of the following issues will make it difficult for JJT to operate this policy? Select all that apply.

A JJT is historically poor at forecasting demand for its products.

B JJT's suppliers are small in comparison to JJT.

C JJT's operations director prides himself on meeting changing customer needs efficiently and effectively.

D JJT's raw material prices are volatile with a tendency to increase in price suddenly.

E JJT is in the middle of a full and detailed efficiency review of every stage of production which is taking considerable time.

Test your understanding 13

T Co manufactures toy cars and train sets. Over the last year, there has been an increase in products failing final quality checks. Failed products have no value to the company as the rework costs are not economic. Over the last year, failure rates have gone from 2% to 6% resulting in lost revenues from hundreds of units of production not sold on to customers. Failure rates do now appear steady at 6%.

Management are already assessing actual quality achieved in detail by inspecting raw materials and production output. A review of the main production operation has revealed nothing that might explain the increased failure rate. The quality control department itself has not yet been reviewed.

Which of the following costs may now increase in order for T Co to find the reason for the increased failure rates?

Select all that apply.

A Prevention Costs.

B Quality Circles.

C Appraisal Costs.

D Internal Failure Costs.

E External Failure Costs.

Test your understanding 14 – G valves (Case study)

Scenario

G manufactures a range of valves that are used in the manufacture of car braking systems. G sells its components to several major car manufacturers.

It is difficult to manufacture a perfectly serviceable valve every time because the manufacturing process is complicated and involves several steps. After each step has been completed the company runs a series of quality checks and valves that fail are discarded before they go on to the next stage or are accepted into inventory. The rejection rates vary from step to step, but can be as high as 5% in some stages of the production process. Overall, G budgets for a 20% rejection rate when estimating the size of production runs.

There are substantial costs associated with quality checks and rejections. Approximately 20% of staff time is devoted to quality control. The rejected components have no scrap value and so G has to pay to dispose of them in an environmentally acceptable manner.

Staff morale appears to have a role in the determination of quality. Failure rates are higher on Friday afternoons and Monday mornings when employees are distracted by looking forward to the weekend or demotivated by the start of the working week. Also major televised sporting events broadcast late at night can lead to deterioration in the quality of the following day's output because staff have stayed up to watch the event.

The failure rate depends largely upon the care with which the manufacturing machinery has been set up and calibrated before a batch of parts is processed, although that is not the only factor. For example, a defective part may have passed through earlier quality checks unnoticed and could cause a failure at a later stage.)

Trigger

G's board is keen to enjoy the benefits associated with total quality management (TQM), but has not committed itself to a full implementation of TQM. As an initial step the board asked production supervisors to come into work an hour early once a week for a quality circle meeting. The board had intended to devote more time and effort to TQM if this initial step had proved successful, but the directors have been disappointed by the initial feedback, which can be summarised as follows:

The supervisors have proposed that the working week be reorganised so that staff can leave early on a Friday afternoon and have longer breaks on a Monday. This proposal is supported by a revised schedule that would make up for this time by having staff work longer hours in the middle of the week. G's board has rejected this proposal because there would be some additional administrative costs associated with the proposed new working arrangements.

The supervisors wish to reallocate some of the present quality control staff to production so that more staff time would be available to permit production processes to be properly set up. The supervisors believe that production staff have to work at close to 100% of their capacity and that such effort is not consistent with producing high quality work. Reducing the pressure would lead to a dramatic reduction in failed parts and so the company would need fewer quality inspectors. G's board has rejected this proposal because it believes that staff should be encouraged to work harder and not to slow down. Also, the board would expect any reduction in the quality control staff to offer the opportunity to reduce staffing and save costs.

Task

Write a report to G's Board:

(a) Advising on the shortcomings of the approach that it has taken to TQM;

(b) Recommending, stating reasons, the actions that G's board should have taken in order to successfully introduce TQM within G.

(c) Advising on the risks associated with reducing the number of quality control staff in the factory.

(45 minutes)

Economic Value Added (EVA)

Economic value added (EVA®) is a measure of performance developed by Stern Stewart, a US management consultancy firm. The basic concept of EVA is that the performance of a company as a whole, or of investment centres within a company, should be measured in terms of the value that has been added to the business during the period.

- EVA attempts to measure the true economic profit that has been earned.
- It is a measure of performance that is directly linked to the creation of shareholder wealth.
- Economic profit is defined as NOPAT – the net operating profit after tax.
- The cost of the capital employed is the economic value of the business assets multiplied by the business cost of capital = (cost of funding, both debt capital and share capital).

EVA = NOPAT minus Capital charge

Capital charge = Economic value of business assets × Cost of capital (%).

There are similarities between EVA and residual income, because both are calculated by subtracting a capital charge from a reported profit figure. Both are based on the view that management decisions will be based on increasing this net 'profit' figure in order to improve performance.

The major difference between EVA and residual income is that:

- residual income is calculated using accounting profit and an accounting value for capital employed
- EVA is calculated using an estimated value for economic profit and an estimated economic value of capital employed.

Economic profit and economic value of capital employed are estimated by making adjustments to accounting profit and accounting capital employed.

3 Transfer Pricing

In an organisation with profit centres and investment centres, there will almost certainly be some inter-connection between different centres. Some profit centres will supply goods and services to others.

When *inter-divisional* (inter-company) trading takes place between profit centres, the centre providing the goods or services to the other will want to earn income from the transfer. Unless it receives income from the transfer, it will make a loss on the transaction.

For example, if Division A provides items to Division B that cost $10 each to make, Division A must earn at least $10 from the transfer, otherwise it will make a loss. If decision making is delegated to profit centre management, the manager of Division A would refuse to supply Division B unless it is allowed to earn income of at least $10 for each unit.

Inter-divisional transfers must therefore be priced. The price of the transfer is the **transfer price**.

- The transfer is treated as an internal sale and an internal purchase within the organisation. It provides sales income to the supplying division and is a purchase cost for the receiving division.
- The sales income of one division is offset by the purchase cost of the other division. The transfer therefore affects the profits of the two divisions individually, but has no effect on the profit of the organisation as a whole.

Setting a transfer price: Inter-divisional trading policy

The transfer price for inter-divisional transactions is significant because:

- it determines how the total profit is shared between the two divisions, and
- in some circumstances, it could affect decisions by the divisional managers about whether they are willing to sell to or buy from the other division.

Both divisions must benefit from the transaction if inter-divisional sales are to take place.

- A selling division will not agree to sell items to another division unless it is profitable for the selling division to do so.
- Similarly, a buying division will not wish to purchase items from another division unless it is profitable for the division.

Transfer prices have to be established and agreed. They could be decided either centrally or locally.

- They could be imposed by head office.
- Alternatively, they could be decided by commercial negotiation between the profit centre managers.
- If decentralisation is to allow the power of decision making to profit centre managers, they should have the authority to agree transfer prices by discussion or negotiation between themselves.

Inter-divisional trading should take place within a broad company policy, that:

- for a 'selling division', given the choice between making a sale to an external customer or supplying goods or services to another division within the group, **the preference should be to sell internally**
- for a 'buying division', given the choice between purchasing from an external supplier or from another division within the company, the **preference should be to purchase internally**.

However, a division should be allowed to sell externally rather than transfer internally, or buy externally rather than internally, if it has a good commercial reason. Good commercial reasons would include an external customer offering a higher price, or an external supplier offering a lower price.

4 Objectives Of Transfer Pricing

(1) **Goal Congruence**

Within a divisionalised company, divisional managers will have responsibility for and will be judged on their division's performance. They will act independently, autonomously and selfishly in the best interests of their own division. They neither know nor care what is happening in other divisions.

It is the task of the management accounting system in general and the transfer pricing policy in particular to ensure that what is good for an individual division is good for the company as a whole.

(2) **Performance Measurement**

The transfer pricing system should result in a report of divisional profits that is a reasonable measure of the managerial performance.

(3) **Maintaining Divisional Autonomy**

One of the purposes of decentralisation is to allow managers to exercise greater autonomy. There is little point in granting additional autonomy and then imposing transfer prices that will affect the profitability of the division.

(4) **Minimising the global tax liability**

When a divisionalised company operates entirely within one tax regime the transfer pricing policy will have a minimal impact on the corporate tax bill. However multinational companies can and do use their transfer pricing policies to move profits around the world and thereby minimise their global tax liabilities.

(5) **Recording the movement of goods and services**

In practice, an extremely important function of the transfer pricing system is simply to assist in recording the movement of goods and services.

(6) **A fair allocation of profits between divisions**

Most of the advantages claimed for divisionalisation are behavioural. Insofar as transfer pricing has a material effect on divisional profit it is essential that managers perceive the allocation of corporate profit as being fair if the motivational benefits are to be retained.

Needless to say, a number of these objectives can conflict with each other, and prove difficult to achieve in practice. It is highly unlikely that any one method would meet all the firm's requirements in all circumstances the best that can be hoped for is a reasonable compromise.

Example 3 – Dual Pricing: Pool Group

Pool Group has two divisions that operate as profit centres. Each centre sells similar products, but to different segments of the market:

- Division P makes product P29 which it sells to external customers for $150. Variable costs of production are $45 per unit. The maximum annual sales demand for P29 is 5,000 units, although Division P has capacity for 7,000 units. Increasing output from 5,000 to 7,000 each year would result in additional fixed cost expenditure of $8,000.
- The manager of Division L has seen an opportunity to sell an amended version of Product P29 to its own customers, and is interested in buying 2,000 units each year to re-sell externally at $90 per unit. The costs of amending Product P29, for sale as Product L77, would be $25 per unit. However, the manager of Division L will not pay more than $40 per unit of Product P29. He argues that Division P will benefit from lower fixed costs per unit by working at full capacity. The manager of Division P refuses to sell at a price that does not cover the division's incremental costs.

Required:

Suggest a dual transfer pricing arrangement that might overcome the disagreement between the two divisional managers.

Transfer Pricing: Behavioural considerations

Transfer prices tend to vary over the product life cycle according to Cats-Baril et al. (1988). During the introductory phase, they suggest a cost plus fixed fee or cost plus a profit share. During the growth phase, they suggest a price related to the closest substitute and during maturity a price based on identical products. This is common sense to a large extent. It is probably only during the maturity stage that identical substitutes exist and during the introductory phase there may be no basis other than cost on which to base the price.

Using any actual cost or cost plus as a transfer price does not motivate the supplying division to act in the interest of the group. Standard or predetermined costs should always be used in place of actual cost. If actual cost is used, the supplying division is not encouraged to be efficient, and control costs as inefficiencies are passed on to the receiving division by way of a higher transfer price. It is even worse if a mark-up is used because the selling division is encouraged to push up the actual cost as this will increase the mark-up, and increase the division's profit. Standard costs are at least subject to scrutiny when they are set once a year and the receiving division has a chance to challenge them. If standard cost is used, the selling division has an incentive to control actual costs below that level and so increase its own profits.

It is usual to imagine transfer pricing taking place in vertically integrated manufacturing organisations. This is not the norm today. Transfer pricing takes place in many different types of organisation and it can have a profound effect on behaviour. For example, a garage carries out a number of different activities that are linked to the activities of another section. The activities include selling new cars, selling old cars, servicing cars sold, general repairs, repairing and servicing used cars accepted in part payment, providing financing and so on. A transfer price is used to transfer a used car accepted in part-payment for a new car between the new car sales and used car sales divisions. A transfer price will also have to be established for transferring the cost of servicing and repairing these cars for sale between the servicing division and the used car sales division. These prices will have considerable implications for the profitability of the different sections and on the actions of the employees when making sales deals. If performance measurement and assessment is to be fair, transfer prices need to be set carefully.

Transfer prices can also be used to deter competitors. If a vertically integrated company concentrates profits at the stage of production where there is least competition, competitors may be attracted to enter. On the other hand, competitors operating at the other stages may be disadvantaged by the low profits the vertically integrated company is taking and they may not be able to achieve a satisfactory return if they are only operating in a limited area of the value chain. Neghandhi (1987) cites cases of US oil companies and Japanese trading and manufacturing companies doing this.

Test your understanding 15

JB Ltd is a divisionalised organisation comprising a number of divisions, including divisions A and B. Division A makes a single product, which it sells on the external market at a price of $12 per unit. The variable cost of the product is $8 per unit and the fixed cost is $3 per unit. Market demand for the product considerably exceeds Division A's maximum production capacity of 10,000 units per month.

Division B would like to obtain 500 units of the product from Division A. If Division A does transfer some of its production internally rather than sell externally, then the saving in packaging costs would be $1.50 per unit.

What transfer price per unit should Division A quote in order to maximise group profit?

A $8

B $10.50

C $11

D $13.50

5 International Transfer Pricing

Transfers within an international group will often be cross-border, between divisions in different countries. With international transfers and international transfer pricing, the issues already described in this chapter still apply. In addition, other factors need to be considered.

6 Different tax rates

A multinational company will seek to minimise the group's total tax liability. One way of doing this might be to use transfer pricing to:

- reduce the profitability of its subsidiaries in high-tax countries, and
- increase the profitability of its subsidiaries in low-tax countries.

Changes in the transfer price can redistribute the pre-tax profit between subsidiaries, but the total pre-tax profit will be the same. However, if more pre-tax profit is earned in low-tax countries and less profit is earned in high-tax countries, the total tax bill will be reduced.

[In the PEG September 2010, the examiner regrets that candidates are not considering the consequences of using an inflated transfer price to reduce the overall tax burden of the company.]

Taxation and Transfer Pricing

International and intra-group trading is a very important part of business today. One-third of the UK's exports to Europe are intra-group transactions. Foreign-owned assets in Europe and the USA increased considerably during the 1980s and 1990s. During the 1980s, foreign-owned assets in the USA tripled, but the tax paid changed very little, as more than half the companies involved reported no taxable income (Pear, 1990).

International intra-group transfer pricing has its own special considerations, and so a multinational organisation will have matters other than behavioural ones to consider when it sets its transfer prices. There is a natural inclination to set transfer prices in order to minimise tax payments.

Taxation

If a group has subsidiaries that operate in different countries with different tax rates, the overall group corporation tax bill could be reduced by manipulating the transfer prices between the subsidiaries.

For example, if the taxation rate on profits in Country X is 25 per cent and in Country Y it is 60 per cent, the group could adjust the transfer price to increase the profit of the subsidiary in Country X and reduce the profit of the subsidiary in Country Y.

Thus, if the subsidiary in Country X provides goods or services to the subsidiary in Country Y, the use of a very high transfer price would maximise the profits in the lower-tax country, and minimise the profits in the higher-tax country.

There is also a temptation to set up marketing subsidiaries in countries with low corporation tax rates and transfer products to them at a relatively low transfer price. When the products are sold to the final customer, a low rate of tax will be paid on the difference between the two prices.

According to a survey by Ernst and Young (1995), more than 80 per cent of multinational companies viewed transfer pricing as a major international tax issue, and more than half of those companies saw it as the major issue. The taxation authorities in most countries monitor transfer prices in an attempt to control the situation and in order to collect the full amount of taxation due. Double taxation agreements between countries mean that companies pay tax on specific transactions in one country only. However, if the company sets an unrealistic transfer price in order to minimise tax, and the tax authority spots this, the company will pay taxation in both countries, that is, double taxation. This additional payment can amount to millions of pounds and, as a result, is quite an effective deterrent. On the other hand, the gains of avoiding taxation may be even greater.

There have been many cases of transfer price fixing for one reason or another over the years. One of the most notorious of UK transfer pricing cases was that of Hoffman La Roche, as it was then called. Hoffman La Roche had developed the drugs of Librium and Valium. The products were imported into the UK at prices of $437 and $979 per kilo, respectively. The UK tax authority accepted the prices; however, the Monopolies Commission sprang into life and questioned the prices on the grounds that the same chemical ingredients, which were unbranded, could be obtained from an Italian company for $9 and $28 per kilo. Hoffman La Roche argued on two grounds: (1) that the price was not set on cost but on what the market would bear, and (2) they had incurred the research and development costs and so had to recover those in the price. However, this was not accepted and they were fined $1.85 m in 1960.

More recently in the UK in 1992, Nissan was caught for unpaid tax of $237 m for falsely inflated invoices that were used to reduce profits. The freight charges were inflated by 40–60 per cent by a Norwegian company. The next year Nissan was required to pay $106 m in unpaid tax in the USA because the authorities felt that part of their USA marketing profits were being transferred to Japan as transfer prices on imports of cars and trucks were too high. Interestingly, the Japanese tax authorities took a different view and returned the double tax, which is a very rare occurrence.

Most countries now accept the Organisation for Economic Co-operation and Development's (OECD) 1995 guidelines. These guidelines were produced with the aim of standardising national approaches to transfer pricing as part of the OECD's charter to encourage the freedom of world trade. They provide guidance on the application of 'arm's length' principles. They state that where necessary transfer prices should be adjusted using an 'arm's length' price, that is, a price that would have been arrived at by two unrelated companies acting independently. There are three methods the tax authorities can use to determine an arm's length price.

The first is the comparable price method. This is the most widely used and involves setting the arm's length price by using the prices of similar products, that is, the market price or an approximation to one. The method is known as using comparable uncontrolled prices (CUPS) and is the preferred method wherever possible. This may seem a straightforward basis but as most international trade is carried out between related companies meaningful comparisons are hard to find. For example, in the UK in the 1980s, it was possible to use independent car distributorships to find a CUP but now that car manufacturers have developed their own dependent distributor networks, finding arm's length comparability is much more difficult.

Where a CUP cannot be found, or is inappropriate, one of two gross margin methods should be used. These involve a review of gross margins in comparable transactions between uncontrolled organisations. The resale price method is used for the transfer of goods to distributors and marketing operations where goods are sold on with little further processing. The price paid for a final product by an independent party is used and from this a suitable mark-up (to allow for the seller's expenses and profit) is deducted. The second gross margin method is the cost-plus method. Here an arm's length gross margin is established and applied to the seller's manufacturing cost.

These methods are of little help when attempting to establish an arm's length price for intangible property such as a patent right or trade name. Also, much of the data needed may not be in the public domain and so setting fair transfer prices is not easy. In the past, this did not matter so much but today it is often up to the taxpayer to 'prove' the price.

For example, the US section 482 regulations on transfer pricing cover 300 pages and the onus is on the taxpayer to support the transfer price with 'timely' documentation. If this is not done, a non-deductible penalty of up to 40 per cent of the arm's length price may be levied. In the past in the UK, it was up to the tax authorities to detect cases of inappropriate transfer pricing. This left the UK vulnerable to a certain amount of tax leakage. But now under the self-assessment regulations, the onus has switched to the taxpayer to provide correct information. Failure to demonstrate a reasonable attempt at an arm's length price in the tax return will give rise to a penalty of 100 per cent of any tax adjustment. Other European countries are also tightening their regulations in response to the USA and OECD's moves.

To safeguard the position, the taxpayer may enter into an Advanced Pricing Agreement (APA) with the relevant two tax authorities involved. This is a new approach and is done in advance to avoid any dispute and the costly penalty of double taxation and penalty fees. According to the Ernst and Young (1995) survey referred to earlier, more than 60 per cent of companies intend to do or are doing this.

7 Government action on transfer prices

Governments are aware of the effect of transfer pricing on profits, and in many countries, multinationals are required to justify the transfer prices that they charge. Multinationals could be required to apply 'arm's length' prices to transfer prices: in other words, they might be required under tax law to use market-based transfer prices, to remove the opportunities for tax avoidance.

It is also possible, on the other hand, that some countries wishing to attract business might have tax laws that are very favourable to business. A country with the status of a 'tax haven' might offer:

- a low rate of tax on profits
- a low withholding tax on dividends paid to foreign holding companies
- tax treaties with other countries
- no exchange controls
- a stable economy
- good communications with the rest of the world
- a well-developed legal framework, within which company rights are protected.

Multinationals might set up subsidiary companies in tax havens, trade through these companies, and hope to reduce their total tax liabilities.

8 Transfer pricing to manage cash flow

Some governments might place legal restrictions on dividend payments by companies to foreign parent companies.

In this situation, it would be tempting for a multinational to sell goods or services to a subsidiary in the country concerned from other divisions in other countries, and charge very high transfer prices as a means of getting cash out of the country.

This tactic is not possible, however, when the country's tax laws require that transfer prices should be set on an arm's length basis.

9 International transfer pricing and currency management

When inter-divisional transfers are between subsidiaries in different countries or currency zones, a decision has to be made about the currency to select for transfer pricing.

Exchange rates, even for strong currencies, can be very volatile and subsidiaries could make unexpected profits or losses from movements in an exchange rate.

Example: A UK subsidiary sells goods to a US subsidiary for $12.80 per unit. The exchange rate was £1 = $1.60 when the transfer price was agreed, and the cost of making each unit in the UK and shipping it to the US is £6.

When the exchange rate is $1.60, the sterling equivalent value of the $12.80 transfer price is £8, and the UK subsidiary makes a profit of £2 per unit transferred.

However, if the dollar weakened in value, and the exchange rate moved to \$2.00, the sterling value of the transfer price would fall to £6.40, and the profit per unit would fall to £0.40.

The implications for an international group of currency risk in transfer prices are as follows:

(i) With inter-divisional trading between subsidiaries in different currency zones, one subsidiary or the other (or possibly both, if the transfer price is set in a third currency) will be exposed to a risk of losses from adverse movements in the exchange rate.

(ii) When one subsidiary makes a loss on an adverse exchange rate movement, the other will make a profit.

(iii) The company as a whole should manage its exposures to currency risks. This might be the responsibility of either the profit centre managers or a treasury department.

(iv) When it is fairly certain which way an exchange rate might move in the future, a multinational company might be tempted to set transfer prices in a currency such that any currency losses arise in the subsidiary in the high-tax country, and currency profits arise in the country with the lower tax rate.

Transfer pricing at Starbucks

Starbucks – the international coffee chain, has been in the UK news over the past few years due to its Board declaring it profitable in the UK, yet reporting losses in its financial statements, and paying very little or no UK corporation tax.

Over the past three years Starbucks has reported no profit and has paid no UK tax on UK sales of £1.2 billion. (By comparison, McDonalds had a tax bill of £80 million on £3.6 billion of UK sales.)

This apparent contradiction arises from perfectly legal tax avoidance – a tactic used by many multi-nationals the world over.

Starbucks achieves this, in part, through transfer pricing. Starbucks buys coffee beans for the UK through a Switzerland based subsidiary. Before the beans reach the UK they are roasted at the subsidiary in Amsterdam. The tax authorities in the Netherlands and Switzerland require Starbucks to allocate some profits from its UK sales to its Dutch roasting and Swiss trading units.

The Dutch roasting plant declares a small operating profit, while in Switzerland the Swiss trading unit is not required to publish accounts. Corporate profits are taxed at 24% in the UK, 25% in the Netherlands, but as low as only 5% in Switzerland. In this way it minimises its UK tax bill.

Starbucks was subject to a UK customs enquiry in 2009 and 2010 due to its transfer pricing practices, but it was resolved without further action or penalties. HMRC declined to comment.

Test your understanding 16 – Multinational car manufacturer

Scenario

M is a multinational car manufacturer. M sells six models of car around the world. Each model has its own assembly factory. Each of the factories is located in a different country and each factory is incorporated as a company. Car assembly is heavily automated, using robots to assemble and weld, and so final assembly is generally in a country that is chosen for its proximity to major markets.

M has many other factories that make components. For example, one factory manufactures all of the music systems for every car sold by M and another manufactures all of the windscreens. These factories can be located in countries that offer low labour costs. For example, the music systems are built using unskilled labour in a developing country.

Each country in which M sells cars has its own M subsidiary that deals with distribution. All sales are to car dealerships and each dealership buys cars directly from its local M subsidiary.

National governments are keen to ensure that intra-group transfers are at arm's length prices and are set so that M will not pay too little tax. Therefore the transfer pricing policy in M is that transfers should be at "market price". Consequently the transfer prices that are used by M do not necessarily reflect the manufacturing costs and so some group members report very small profits. The company's reward system for its senior managers and directors is linked to the profits that are reported by their subsidiary.

M's transfer pricing arrangements take up a great deal of management time. In many cases, arm's length market prices are difficult to identify because there are no direct comparisons available. For example, the subsidiary that manufactures music systems does not sell its products to anyone other than the six assembly companies. Even if similar products can be found that are traded openly by other manufacturers, there are very specific problems with determining an objective market price. For example, there are transport costs and questions over the discounts that are granted for bulk sales. There is an even greater problem with finished cars because M sells its cars at higher prices in more prosperous markets.

Trigger

M's main board is concerned that the company may be investigated by the tax authorities in one or more of the countries where it does business. The Head of Group Internal Audit has been asked to assist the board by conducting an internal investigation in order to establish whether M should change any of its transfer pricing practices.

Task

Discuss the possibility that M's transfer pricing arrangements will cause dysfunctional behaviour.

(30 minutes)

Non-financial performance indicators

Non-financial measurement is increasingly common in most organisations. Targets are set to cover a variety of aspects of business performance. As for all systems of internal control, it is important to set targets, measure actual results, compare actual results with target and take corrective action. Performance may then be judged relative to:

- Improvements over time (i.e. trend);
- Achievement of targets;
- Benchmark comparisons with world-class organisations, competitors or industry averages.

Non-financial indicators can provide better targets and predictors for the firm's long-term profitability goals. These targets can be used effectively for control purposes, through feedback and feed forward processes. As well as monitoring target achievement, indicators can also be shown as trends, to determine whether performance is improving or deteriorating over longer time periods than is usually disclosed in financial reports. Finally, non-financial indicators can be benchmarked to internationally-recognised 'best practice', to competitor organisations and to industry averages. This is to some extent a return to the operations-based measures that were the origin of management accounting systems.

Balanced scorecard

Financial perspective	• Return on investment • Economic value added (EVA) • Profit target • Operating cash flow target • Cost reduction target • Profit target
Customer perspective	• Target for new customers • Target for retention of existing customers or repeat orders • Percentage of orders met within X days • Percentage of orders delivered on time • Market share target • Target for customer satisfaction (quantifiable measure of satisfaction)
Internal business perspective	• Percentage of tenders accepted by customers • Percentage of items produced that have to be re-worked • Production cycle time
Innovation and learning perspective	• Number of new products launched • Target for employee productivity • Percentage of total revenue coming from new products • Revenue per employee • Time from identifying a new product idea to market launch

There are dysfunctional consequences of non-financial performance measures. Berry, Broadbent and Otley identified the following problem areas for performance measurement.

- Tunnel vision: the emphasis on quantifiable data at the expense of qualitative data.
- Sub-optimisation: the pursuit of narrow local objectives at the expense of broader organisation-wide ones.
- Myopia: the short-term focus on performance may have longer term consequences.

- Measure fixation: an emphasis on measures rather than the underlying objective.
- Misrepresentation: the deliberate manipulation of data so that reported behaviour is different from actual behaviour.
- Misinterpretation: the way in which the performance measure is explained.
- Gaming: an employee can pursue a particular performance standard when that is what is expected of him/her, even though s/he knows that this is not in the organisation's best interests in terms of its strategy.
- Ossification: sometimes referred to as inflexibility, unwillingness to change the performance measurment scheme can inhibit innovation and lead to paralysis of action.

Problems with the balanced scorecard

There is a risk that when performance targets are selected for each of the four perspectives:

- the targets for the different perspectives could be contradictory and inconsistent with each other;
- non-financial performance targets could become an end in themselves, rather than a means towards the overall financial objective of maximising shareholder wealth or shareholder returns.

Test your understanding 17

Which of the following cover all four perspectives of the balanced scorecard? (Select all that apply.)

A Number of new customers; Market share; Production cycle time; Time to market

B Profit; Return on investment; Production cycle time; Time to market

C Profit; Market share; Training costs; Time to market

D Profit; Market share; Production cycle time; Time to market

Test your understanding 18

X Company is a large retailer which operates a divisional structure. The overall strategy of X Company is to develop 'greener' environmentally friendly policies across every division since this is in keeping with the company's overall mission and market research into stakeholder claims.

The directors have attempted to tie both board and divisional management performance to this overall strategy with varying results. One of the biggest issues they have is that management now receive bonuses for hitting 'green' targets regardless of whether the profit of the division or the company is below budget.

This appears to anger stakeholders who see the bonus payments as rewards for failure despite believing in the overall green strategy. The stakeholders are now questioning the performance targets set.

In addition, the directors believe that divisional managers are pursuing the 'green' targets at the expense of the more traditional measures of success like sales and profits.

Which of the following statements describe the current situation at X Company? Select all that apply.

A Non-financial performance targets have become an end in themselves, rather than a means towards the overall financial objective of maximising shareholder wealth or shareholder returns.

B The balanced scorecard approach being taken does not include the environmental perspective and so is not appropriate for X Company.

C The 'green' target is inconsistent with the more traditional profit based targets stakeholders expect X Company to have.

D The stakeholders reaction to the bonus payments shows that the board of X Company have misunderstood stakeholder claims

E The board of X Company have not communicated their priorities to the stakeholders, causing them to question the performance targets set.

Test your understanding 19

U is an organisation which has been under pressure from shareholders to demonstrate its commitment to caring for the environment. As a result, the Board of Directors has overseen the implementation of new performance measures, designed to show (via their inclusion in the annual report) not only how much U values and cares for the environment but also ongoing improvements via reductions in pollution and emissions recorded.

Management have on the whole, welcomed a chance to improve performance in a non-financial context, recognising its importance to the shareholders as well as society as a whole. Some staff however, view the non-financial measures as secondary to the financial measures and there have also been a few minor issues with lower level managers misreporting recorded emissions in the belief that 'no-one would ever know'. These managers have received training to ensure this does not happen again.

The Board is pleased with the response to the new measures although Directors have some concerns that the measures have become the focus of management's attention rather than looking at ways to decrease the organisations impact on the environment.

Which of the following are apparent in U? Select **all** that apply.

A Tunnel Vision

B Myopia

C Sub-optimisation

D Measure Fixation

E Misrepresentation

Test your understanding 20 – D cars (Case Study)

Scenario

D is currently a large business which sells cars. D was established almost 30 years ago when the founder started buying and selling used cars. The company has expanded steadily since then. It now owns 32 vehicle dealerships that are spread across the country.

All of the dealerships now sell new cars. Each dealership has a franchise from a specific motor manufacturer. The dealerships do not compete with one another. Those which sell luxury models are well distanced from one another, as are those which sell more basic models. D has at least one dealership for each of the major manufacturers.

All of the dealerships accept customers' old cars as trade-ins against the cost of their new car. Trade-in cars are resold at the dealerships if they are less than four years old and are in good condition. If they do not meet these criteria then they are sold through a third party's car auction. It is company policy that each trade-in is serviced and repaired by the dealership that accepted the car from the customer.

D's inventory of second hand cars is organised in order to maximise selling prices. Cars are often moved across the country in order to ensure that each dealership has a balanced inventory on offer. High quality luxury cars are sold through the dealerships that specialise in luxury models. Other cars are sorted according to manufacturer. Second hand cars tend to attract higher selling prices if they are sold through a dealership that sells new cars of the same make.

Trigger

The founder of the business remains in place as D's Chief Executive. He has always been closely involved in the day to day supervision of the business but he has now decided to change things. He is thinking about setting up a divisional structure, with four regional divisions for dealerships in the North, South, East and West of the country. Each division will be managed by its own divisional manager and there will be a small executive team based at D's head office to take charge of the business as a whole. The founder's intention is that the divisional managers will be left free to manage without interference from the centre, but performance will be observed and monitored closely.

Tasks

(a) The founder has decided that each of the divisional managers will be evaluated using a balanced scorecard system.

Recommend, with reasons, TWO measures that should appear under each perspective:

– Financial
– Customer
– Learning and growth
– Internal business processes

(30 minutes)

(b)

(i) Evaluate the potential for dysfunctional behaviour arising from the transfer of trade-ins between dealerships and divisions.

(ii) Explain how the problems identified in (i) might be overcome.

(15 minutes)

Strategic management accounting (SMA)

'The preparation and presentation of information for decision-making laying particular stress on external factors.'

CIMA Official Terminology

- SMA is linked with business strategy and maintaining or increasing competitive advantage. The achievement of objectives requires the 'linking' of strategic planning to short-term operational planning.
- Lord (1996) characterised SMA as:
  - Collection of competitor information (such as pricing, costs and volume).
  - Exploitation of cost reduction opportunities (a focus on continuous improvement and non-financial performance measures).
  - Matching the accounting emphasis with the firm's strategic position.

Lean organisations and lean accounting

- Lean manufacturing is a philosophy of management based on cutting out waste and unnecessary activities.
- Organisations can become 'lean and mean' if they can get rid of their unnecessary 'fat'.
- Two elements in lean manufacturing are JIT and TQM.

Lean management accounting

- Provides information to control and improve the value stream (focus on value streams rather than traditional departmental structures).
- Provides information for performance measurement and cost reporting purposes (non-financial measures, continuous improvement and techniques such as target and lifecycle costing).
- Provides relevant cost information for financial reporting purposes (only that which is required, eliminating non-value added information (via implementing techniques such as backflush accounting)).
- Ensures that management are provided with statements that are:
  - instantly accessible through an IT system, and
  - simple to read.

10 Problems with modern management accounting

Modern management accounting techniques are not perfect. All of the techniques discussed above are open to criticism. Some of the criticisms levied include:

- JIT – Some big manufacturers have been accused of holding smaller suppliers to ransom by dictating the way they operate. The big customer expects the small supplier to forego other work to undertake their order immediately. Meanwhile the prices paid for the goods supplied might be quite low, but the smaller company reluctantly accepts this in order to keep the business in the hope that they can grow on the back of it. The ethics of this relationship have been questioned.
- TQM – The idea of 'continual' improvement can be hard to ensure. Management often have other important issues to deal with and in many companies TQM is put aside for long periods of time.
- Balanced scorecard – The criticism of the balance scorecard is that management are asked to meet so many different objectives (some of which might be conflicting) that they lose all perspective. There is a risk that the maximisation of shareholder wealth might be forgotten.

Test your understanding 21 – H (Case study)

Scenario

H is a large marketing consultancy that provides a range of services including developing marketing campaigns, designing web pages, managing media relations and so on. There are approximately 300 professional staff working in departments such as advertising and media relations and 600 support staff in areas such as administration and information technology (IT). H operates from a large office block in the centre of a major city.

In common with similar agencies, H is successful because it can offer clients an integrated service for all of their marketing and public relations needs. Sometimes those needs are related. For example, advertising staff may work alongside public relations staff to ensure that a new product is advertised effectively and that any positive press publicity, such as the consumers' favourable reaction at the product's launch, can be maximised.

H has a traditional management accounting system. Each department has its own detailed management accounts, which show financial transactions and chargeable hours. Financial transactions include all revenue from billings invoiced to clients and all costs. Included in the costs are substantial amounts for overheads associated with the running costs of the office building and the business as a whole. Chargeable hours are monitored for each member of staff. The hourly charge-out rate varies according to the seniority of the staff member and is set so that all costs are recovered and a healthy profit is charged on top. Any work undertaken for another department is charged internally at the staff member's full charge-out rate.

The media buying department of H buys and sells advertising space in newspapers and airtime on radio and television. The department sells this space and time to its clients at cost plus a mark-up and also makes it available at the same price to other departments in H. This means that H can offer to plan and implement a marketing campaign from the initial design all the way through to the publication or broadcast of the finished advertisement.

Trigger

H's board is concerned that the company's traditional management accounting system is encouraging dysfunctional behaviour and causing disputes between managers.

The following examples have been debated at recent board meetings:

The public relations department is paying external web designers to design "blogs" on behalf of clients rather than using the web designers from H's web design department. The web design business has seasonal peaks and troughs and there are times when there is spare capacity, but the hourly rates charged by the web design department are more expensive than those available from third parties.

The staff coffee shop was closed to create additional work space. Since the closure the space has been empty because none of H's department heads wish to be charged with the cost of additional overheads.

Account executives within H are keen to earn as much profit for themselves from each sale. Consequently they are dealing directly with major broadcasters and newspapers and are not using the media buying department. These individual deals are taking away the bargaining power of the media buying department.

H's board is keen to consider whether the implementation of lean manufacturing and lean management accounting techniques might improve matters. In particular, the following principles have been identified as being relevant to H:

H should be managed through processes or value streams rather than traditional departmental structures. The board believes that the two value streams are the sale of professional services and the sale of media space.

The consultancy should maximise the flow of services through the value streams while eliminating waste. Lean management accounting should provide the value stream leader with performance measurement information to both control and improve the value stream.

Task

Write a report to the Board:

(i) Advising on the differences between managing value streams and managing departmental profits.

(10 minutes)

(ii) Recommending, stating reasons, the changes that H should make to its management accounting systems and policies in order to improve the management of the value streams.

(20 minutes)

(iii) Advising on the difficulties that are likely to be associated with implementing the changes that a move towards lean management accounting will create. Your advice should include recommendations as to how those difficulties might best be dealt with.

(20 minutes)

11 Chapter summary

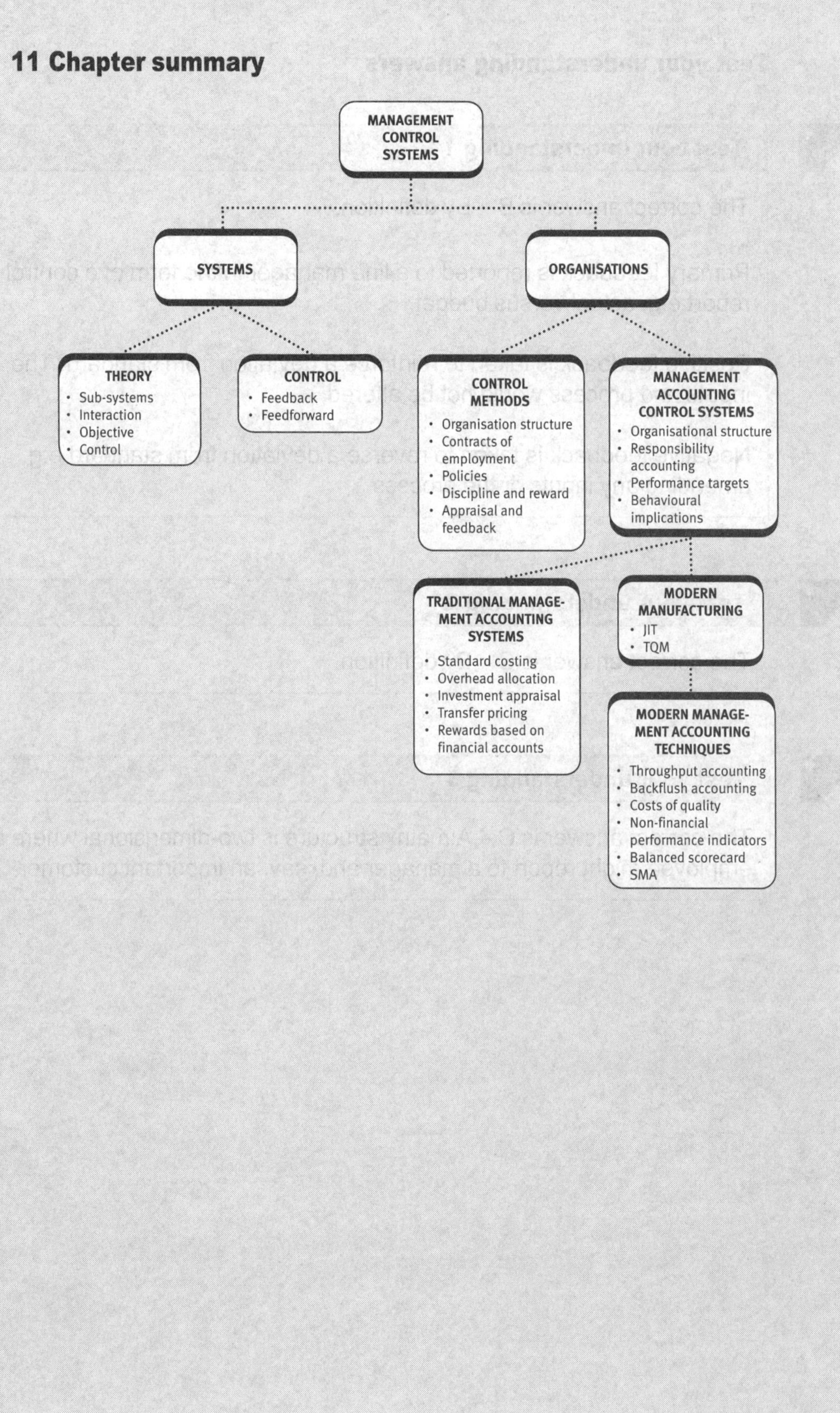
MANAGEMENT CONTROL SYSTEMS
SYSTEMS
ORGANISATIONS
THEORY
• Sub-systems
• Interaction
• Objective
• Control
CONTROL
• Feedback
• Feedforward
CONTROL METHODS
• Organisation structure
• Contracts of employment
• Policies
• Discipline and reward
• Appraisal and feedback
MANAGEMENT ACCOUNTING CONTROL SYSTEMS
• Organisational structure
• Responsibility accounting
• Performance targets
• Behavioural implications
TRADITIONAL MANAGEMENT ACCOUNTING SYSTEMS
• Standard costing
• Overhead allocation
• Investment appraisal
• Transfer pricing
• Rewards based on financial accounts
MODERN MANUFACTURING
• JIT
• TQM
MODERN MANAGEMENT ACCOUNTING TECHNIQUES
• Throughput accounting
• Backflush accounting
• Costs of quality
• Non-financial performance indicators
• Balanced scorecard
• SMA

Test your understanding answers

Test your understanding 1

The correct answer is B – By definition.

Primary feedback is reported to a line manager in the form of a control report e.g. actual versus budget.

Positive feedback is taken to reinforce a deviation from standard. The inputs and process would not be altered.

Negative feedback is taken to reverse a deviation from standard e.g. amending any inputs or the process.

Test your understanding 2

The correct answer is C – By definition.

Test your understanding 3

The correct answer is C – A matrix structure is two-dimensional where an employee might report to a manager and, say, an important customer.

Test your understanding 4 – J television (Integration)

(a) Viewers' satisfaction could reflect the extent to which their viewing decision was based on the lack of an acceptable alternative. Viewers could have watched J because the programmes being broadcast on the other channels were inferior and so J was not actually attracting anybody. If satisfaction figures are low then the audience could decline if a competitor broadcasts a superior show at that time in the future.

J should also be aware of the satisfaction figure in case viewers are starting to get bored with a particular programme. It would make little sense to buy further series once a particular show reaches the end of its run if viewers' satisfaction is declining. It may be necessary to exercise some caution. If viewing figures are acceptable then advertisers' needs are being met, which is J's most important consideration. Viewers' responses could have been motivated by embarrassment if a particular show is popular despite bad reviews from the critics.

(b) The excessive use of negative feedback could lead to dysfunctional behaviour on the part of the programming department. A series of programmes will be purchased in advance. If a new programme proves to be unpopular then it may lead to a failure to achieve targets on several evenings. Rather than risk that, the programming department might concentrate on low-risk programmes that are likely to attract an acceptable audience share without necessarily being likely to attract a substantial audience or break new ground.

The programming department might also argue that J should overpay for programmes that will definitely attract good viewing figures. However, the cost of such programming could outweigh the additional advertising revenue that it attracts.

The negative feedback could be demotivating. Viewing figures are affected by the programmes broadcast by competitors. The programming department could develop a good range of programmes that is as good as the company can afford but that might fail because competing companies could have superior shows.

The programming department could lose competent staff who are unhappy because of the blame culture. They could be open to approaches from competitors which offer a more supportive environment.

(c) The biggest advantage is that positive feedback is consistent with J's business model. If J identifies an opportunity to attract a larger audience then it may be able to offer advertisers the opportunity to reach a very high proportion of the viewing audience for at least part of a typical week.

The programming department will be focussed on attracting large numbers of viewers rather than avoiding poor viewing figures. It may be willing to take calculated risks that could lead to the discovery of very successful programmes, albeit at the risk of buying an unknown programme that turns out to be unpopular.

If the programming department is encouraged to concentrate on popular programmes then it might focus on locking in successes. For example, if a new programme has a good viewing rate then the programming department could negotiate the purchase of later series before its competitors act.

The programming department could be encouraged to be a little more creative, perhaps by commissioning shows that have the same basic format as successful programmes. J could then develop a reputation for broadcasting programmes that fall within a particular niche and so its viewers' loyalty could be strengthened. Any such successes can generate revenues from the resale of the programme to other countries.

There is still some role for negative feedback. The programming department should be permitted to make mistakes, but it should not be allowed to be complacent and so major disappointments should at least be discussed and investigated.

Test your understanding 5

The correct answers are A, C and D – For the performance measure to be related to an investment centre part of the formula must include the investment i.e. A, C and D all include either the investment or an interest charge based on it. Gross profit considers only sales and revenue costs passing through the statement of profit or loss.

Test your understanding 6

D

- ROI falls from 20% to 215/1100 = 19.55%
- RI falls from $40,000 to $39,000

Test your understanding 7

The correct answers are A, B, C and D – Long production runs were more common in traditional manufacturing where economies of scale were thought to be best. Modern thought prefers customer led production runs which could be short and specific to the customer need.

Test your understanding 8

The correct answers are C and D – A JIT system requires stable demand and high volumes to work effectively.

Test your understanding 9

The correct answer is A – Training of staff should help to prevent any quality problems.

Test your understanding 10

The correct answers are A, B and C – ABB is usually found in businesses which have large overhead costs and is not directly related to JIT or TQM. Throughput accounting tries to remove bottlenecks – a problem in JIT. Backflush accounting requires inventory levels to be low – a condition for JIT. Non-financial performance indicators are used to measure factors such as the number of rejects – which is found in TQM.

Test your understanding 11

The correct answer is C – By definition.

Test your understanding 12

A and D only

- Option A: Organisations operating Just In time strategies must be good at forecasting demand otherwise they will not have enough finished products to meet customer needs or they will be left with excess inventory.
- Option B: A smaller company is more likely to accept JJT's demands to 'drop everything' and meet their orders however unethical this may seem.
- Option C: In theory JIT should fit well with the operations director's attitude since no inventories are kept, items can be made to customer specifications without needing to clear existing inventories first.
- Option D: If raw material prices are liable to go up suddenly, there is a benefit to buying excess amounts and holding them as insurance against such increases.
- Option E: This should actually help with the JIT policy since, when it is finished there will be fewer bottlenecks and inefficiencies to hold up production and production planning will be easier.

Test your understanding 13

A and B only

- Option A: These are the costs of avoiding or reducing defects and failures. They include the redesign, development and maintenance of quality control equipment which could be at fault at T Co and causing the false detection of unsaleable units.
- Option B: This would be the cost of setting up a small group of employees who meet on a regular basis to discuss quality issues and to develop solutions to problems arising. This could be an option for T.
- Option C: These are the costs of assessing actual quality achieved. These costs are already present in T Co and therefore unlikely to rise.
- Option D: these are the costs arising within the organisation when the predetermined specifications are not met. For T Co they may include the net cost of scrap and downtime of machinery due to quality problems. They are unlikely to increase since failure rates are steady (although high).

- Option E: these are the costs of inadequate quality that are incurred once the product has been sold. They include dealing with customer complaints, warranty claims, costs of repairing or replacing returned faulty goods. It appears in T Co that defects are picked up on before products are sold so this cost is unlikely to rise.

Test your understanding 14 – G valves (Case study)

Report

To: The Board

From: A.N. Accountant

Date: Today

Subject: Quality

Introduction

This report advises on the shortcomings of the approach that G has taken to TQM, recommends the actions that should have been taken in order to successfully introduce TQM and advises on the risks associated with reducing the number of quality control staff in the factory.

(a) **Shortcomings**

G's board has not really implemented TQM; the directors have simply established a weekly meeting for production supervisors and called that a quality circle.

There is no evidence that G's board is prepared to make meaningful changes in response to the need to prevent errors and improve quality. Firstly, the initiative to promote quality must come from the very top of the organisation and permeate through the various levels of management and supervision. G has clearly got significant quality problems because one fifth of all output is scrapped and the associated manufacturing costs cannot even be offset by scrap sales.

The supervisors' first suggestion sounds like a practical means of reducing errors. G's board should have been prepared to at least experiment with rescheduling so that there was less happening at times when the workforce is less attentive. Apart from anything else, the change might give an idea of the extent to which defects are due to staff motivation rather than some other factors.

The board should not have rejected the supervisors' proposal to move staff to reduce the incidence of errors. The concept of "getting it right" is an important aspect of TQM. The supervisors appear to have a greater commitment to TQM principles than the board. The board's insistence that any improvement in quality will lead to redundancy is unlikely to capture the commitment of the workforce to making improvements.

The fact that the comments obtained from the quality circle have been ignored in this manner means that the supervisors will be discouraged and will not take the TQM process seriously in the future.

(b) **Recommendations**

Firstly, the directors should have commissioned a study to determine the failure rates at each stage in the manufacturing process. Stages that have a higher incidence of errors should be reviewed more carefully, as should stages that are later in the production process because they will have cost more to manufacture. A sample of rejected parts should be studied for each of the more costly areas and the causes of the defects identified. That will give G an insight into whether losses are caused by operator error, defective materials, or whatever.

The next step would be to review the design and manufacture of the parts. It may be possible to eliminate errors by simplifying the product or by combining or replacing some of the manufacturing stages.

The workforce should be involved in the process. The board should introduce training and publicity so that staff at all levels should be involved. There should be an incentive scheme for suggesting improvements that would reduce waste or increase quality. Ideally, there should be an overall incentive to motivate staff to eliminate errors, such as a bonus that will be payable to all staff if particular quality standards can be met.

The quality circles should be established to give production supervisors an opportunity to make suggestions. These should be properly resourced, with participants being trained in order to give them a better idea of what their role entails. The quality circles should be supported, to the extent that any recommendations are considered and only rejected if they are clearly impractical or involve significant risk.

(c) Risks of reducing the number of quality control staff

G's products form part of car braking systems. Any defects in delivered parts could cause injury or death and so there are risks of legal action and adverse publicity in the event of an accident that can be attributed to a manufacturing defect. Reducing the number of quality control staff will increase the risk that any defects in completed goods will be overlooked and the resulting items shipped to customers. There may be some compensation arising from the fact that the car manufacturers should be conducting their own quality control before using parts and before completed cars are delivered. Thus, G is not entirely responsible for any cars sold with defective brakes.

Hopefully, the new working practices will reduce the number of defects and so there will be some compensation for the reduction in inspections. One problem is that the smaller number of inspectors may not be able to detect any increase in the numbers of defects because there will be too few inspections.

If G is ever criticised because of an accident arising from one of its products then the reduction in the quality staff may be cited as evidence of negligence. The fact that any claim will be made in the aftermath of an accident will give the injured party the benefit of hindsight and that can be linked to the defective part that has been sold by G. G knows that the parts will be used for this purpose and so any damages that are awarded will be substantial.

The possibility of an accident creates risks to G's reputation because any blame arising from concerns about quality control will make the company appear to be negligent. The reduction in quality staff could be made to look as if G would rather risk customer's safety than invest in adequate quality control. G's customers may feel obliged to source these parts from another supplier if G is accused of negligence.

Conclusions

G has not really implemented TQM and should revisit the steps required to properly implement an effective programme.

Also, the risks of reducing the number of quality control staff is very high and is not recommended due to the potential reputational damage that could occur should they be found negligent.

Example 3 – Dual Pricing: Pool Group

It is in the interests of Pool Group for the additional units to be made and sold as Product L77.

The contribution per unit will be $90 – $45 – $25 = $20. The contribution from selling 2,000 units each year ($40,000) exceeds the additional fixed costs of $8,000.

To cover the incremental costs in Division P, the transfer price needs to be $45 + $(8,000/2,000 units) = $49.

Division L will not pay more than $40.

A dual transfer pricing arrangement that might win the agreement of both divisional managers is for Division P to receive $49 per unit of P29 and for Division L to pay $40. The difference of $9 per unit or $18,000 in total for the year would be a charge to head office.

Test your understanding 15

B

Division A can sell all of its output on the outside market at $12 per unit. Any internal transfer will be at the expense of external sales. However, the external sales also include a packaging cost of $1.50 per unit which is not incurred on an internal transfer and this saving can be passed on to the buying division. Therefore, the correct transfer price from a decision-making point of view is $12 (the market price) – $1.50 (the saving in packaging cost) = $10.50.

Test your understanding 16 – Multinational car manufacturer

Dysfunctional behaviour is a potential problem because transfer prices are, effectively, imposed from outside the group. A subsidiary company will not necessarily be able to recover all of its costs and generate a realistic profit when selling to a fellow group member. For example, a component manufacturer in a low-cost environment may be able to charge intra-group transfers at a higher price than the prevailing arm's-length market price. That will leave the component manufacturer with an artificially high profit, whereas the buyer may be aggrieved that the purchase from a fellow group member costs as much as, or even more than, buying the same component on the open market from a third party.

Managers will have very little control over their reported performance if these transfer prices are used. For example, a local increase in the cost of labour could coincide with a worldwide reduction in the cost of the product (e.g. electronic components) and so the subsidiary responsible for manufacturing a component could be forced to reduce transfer prices at the very time that its cost base is increasing.

These arrangements could lead to dysfunctional behaviour with subsidiary company boards attempting to reduce prices in a sub-optimal manner in order to report higher profits. For example, a subsidiary with high input prices may attempt to reduce local costs in order to boost added-value. That could result in short cuts being taken over health and safety or maintenance in order to inflate profit and such savings may prove to be uneconomic in the long run.

Management time could be wasted because of constant internal arguments about transfer pricing. Staff time could be spent tracking and monitoring market prices in order to ensure that any favourable changes are implemented immediately.

Managers may be demotivated if profit-related bonuses or staff evaluations are based on these externally imposed transfer prices.

Subsidiaries could even attempt to disrupt internal transfers of generic parts in order to justify buying from third parties from whom a discount can be negotiated.

The risk of dysfunctional behaviour could be avoided if M invests in an appropriate management accounting system. The subsidiaries could report on the basis of value added for internal management accounting purposes. The fact that alternative figures are used for external reporting to national tax authorities need have little or nothing to do with the basis upon which management teams are evaluated. Indeed, M will have to produce such information anyway in order to ensure that the company is making the correct decision with respect to make or buy.

Test your understanding 17

The correct answer is D – Financial perspective – profit; customer perspective – market share; internal business perspective – production cycle time; innovation and learning perspective – time to market.

Test your understanding 18

A only

- Option A: This is confirmed by the director's view that divisional managers are pursuing the green targets at the expense of sales and profits.
- Option B: There is no indication that X Company has adopted a balanced scorecard approach. In fact it appears that they have concentrated on one area of performance rather than developed a measurement mix.
- Option C: As part of a measurement mix, the green targets can be consistent with financial targets. In fact, through measuring impact on the environment, more customers may be attracted to buy from X Company thereby increasing sales.
- Option D: It is entirely possible for stakeholders to believe in green policies but also wish to see financial success in X Company. It appears that underperformance in financial areas is the cause of their reaction rather than green targets being met.
- Option E: There is no indication that the stakeholders are unaware of the focus on green targets, it is more the case that stakeholder expectations are that financial targets should be included in bonus calculations.

Test your understanding 19

A, D and E

- Option A: the emphasis on quantifiable data at the expense of qualitative data as shown by those staff seeing the non-financial measures as secondary to the financial measures
- Option B: the short term focus on performance may have longer term consequences. No evidence in scenario.
- Option C: the pursuit of narrow local objectives at the expense of broader organisation wide ones. No evidence in scenario.#
- Option D: an emphasis on measures rather than the underlying objectives voiced by the board's concern.
- Option E: the deliberate manipulation of data so that reported behaviour is different from actual behaviour as occurred with the lower level managers.

Test your understanding 20 – D cars (Case Study)

(a) **Balanced scorecard**

Financial

Revenue growth would be a useful means of encouraging the divisional managers to enable the business to grow through generating sales. That could be measured on a short-term basis, e.g. by measuring month-by-month sales in comparison with previous years, or longer term, e.g. by aiming for annual growth.

Return on equity would be a useful longer term measure to counter the potential for dysfunctional behaviour if sales or some other short term measure is introduced. Aiming for an increase in annual RE will give divisional managers a long-term goal for financial performance.

Customer

Repeat sales, perhaps measured in terms of sales made to customers who purchased a car from D during the previous three years, would give the divisions a long-term goal of developing a good working relationship with existing customers. Ideally, customers will buy a car from D and be encouraged to return after, say, two or three years to trade it in and buy another.

Conversion of car sales into service sales should be measured. D should aim to generate as much revenue as possible from car buyers by selling additional products such as regular servicing and maintenance. Apart from the contribution from that activity, the company will also be keeping contact with customers and may be able to target promotion more effectively, e.g. by having a member of sales staff telephone a customer whose mileage is high to point out the benefits of switching to a newer model.

Learning and growth

The development of innovative marketing and promotional techniques is vital because D's products are essentially identical to those of the other vehicle dealerships that it is competing against. Cost effective marketing strategies must be developed in order to maintain footfall through dealerships. Those strategies should not focus on price because there is little to be gained from entering a price war with competitors.

New products may be difficult to develop in this market, but that does not make innovation impossible. For example, the dealerships could offer to collect customers' cars for servicing during the working day and return them after the work has been completed. Such developments would possibly generate revenue in themselves and would also give the opportunity to correspond with customers to remind them of D's interest in their business.

Internal business processes

The number of complaints or requests for rectification of faults on new cars should be minimised (or eliminated). The dealership is responsible for preparing new cars for delivery, which would include valeting and cleaning the vehicle and checking for any manufacturing defects that were not noticed by the maker. All of this work should be done to such a high order that customers are not disappointed because of an avoidable complaint.

Sales effort should be linked to inventory availability to avoid old inventory and also to ensure that customers are committed to a purchase before a competitor has the opportunity to take their business. If supplies of popular models are running low then sales staff should be encouraged to press the possibility of an alternative from the dealership's product range or to offer a new car in place of a second hand car or vice versa.

(b) (i) **Dysfunctional behaviour**

The biggest problem is that of transfer price. If a customer offers a car of a different make as a trade-in then the dealership will be aware that it will be passed on to another dealership or division. The dealership may feel that there is no real incentive to negotiate the lowest acceptable price or the trade in with the customer if that cost will be recovered from elsewhere within D.

Vehicles are to be serviced before their sale and that will be a cost to the dealership that undertakes the work. Dealerships may underspend on servicing because of the possibility that the car will be transferred to another dealership or division. That could harm the company's reputation when the cars are subsequently sold with defects that should have been corrected. Problems with cars may take some time to appear and so it may be possible to overlook defects that will not be obvious until after the vehicle has been resold.

(ii) **Solutions**

All transfers should be valued at their market value, using the "going rate" for a model of that age and mileage. Such rates are relatively easy to determine for used cars and so there should be little cause for dispute.

All trade-ins should be serviced by the dealership that receives the cars for sale, which may not be the dealership that accepts the car as a trade-in if the car is not of the same make as the dealership's franchise. The dealership that receives the car for sale should pay full market value, but should be able to recover repair costs against that as an incentive to check the car carefully before accepting it.

If a car is subsequently transferred to another division in order to balance inventories then the receiving division should be able to recover any rectification costs from the other division, again to avoid dealerships having an incentive to leave faults uncorrected.

Test your understanding 21 – H (Case study)

Report

To: The Board

From: A.N. Accountant

Date: Today

Subject:

Introduction

This report covers three aspects of H's operations:

It advises on the differences between managing value streams and managing departmental profits;

It recommends, stating reasons, the changes that H should make to its management accounting systems and policies in order to improve the management of the value streams; It advises on the difficulties that are likely to be associated with implementing the changes that a move towards lean management accounting will create.

(i) **Managing value streams**

Managing value streams involves paying far greater attention to the ways in which H adds value. H's services are sold on the basis of an integrated service that breaks down distinctions between specialisms and so it seems illogical that the internal management process should emphasise those distinctions. Managing value streams would encourage decision makers to focus on the creation of added value rather than increasing the individual's reported contribution to that added value.

The biggest change would therefore involve rethinking the way in which H conducts business. Staff time and media capacity are both commodities that should be managed and utilised for the good of H as a whole. "Ownership" of those resources may be costly if it means that decisions are being based on irrelevant information such as sunk costs. Managers should be motivated to think in terms of opportunity costs instead.

(ii) **Changes to the management accounting system**

One major change would be to switch to a marginal costing system. Charging overheads to departments is encouraging waste and dysfunctional behaviour. The fact that H must provide an integrated service means that there is very little point in determining the notional profit provided by any given department. H will probably have to maintain a department even if it is found to contribute very little to total profit or even runs at a loss.

The consultancy operates an expensive city-centre site and it would be better to review the total fixed cost of doing so as a separate management exercise rather than spending time charging out elements of those fixed costs to departments. Ideally, those costs should be kept under review so that they can be minimised wherever possible. The management accounting system could track the use of space (in terms of, say, occupancy levels) in order to make the most efficient use of space. There should be no overt charges for the use of those facilities because that may lead to suboptimal decisions. From time to time there ought to be a review based on ABC principles to determine what drives these central costs and whether they could be reduced in any way.

The client should be the focus in terms of recording costs and revenues rather than the department. Every client should be the responsibility of a designated senior account executive who manages all of the services given to that client. Staff should log the time spent on chargeable work for billing purposes. Senior management should receive regular reports of the contribution made by each client, with supporting details such as the value of unbilled work in progress or chargeable hours that have not been billed because of client retention issues.

There should be a centralised budget for advertising purchases. Campaigns are likely to be planned well in advance and there should be a designated department that is evaluated on its ability to buy space as cheaply as possible. Any unexpected purchases should be reported separately so that the buyer is not penalised by the loss of any possible discount.

(iii) **Difficulties during implementation**

The biggest difficulty is the uncertainty that this will create in the short term for staff at all levels, particularly managers. Changing the management accounting system will change the basis on which individual contributions are assessed and reported and staff may be afraid that this will have an adverse effect on their careers.

Communication is the key to dealing with staff concern. If possible, the board should make it clear that it is not intended that the elimination of waste will involve redundancies. Hopefully, the changes will empower staff and that positive message should be stressed.

H may require new systems in order to track relevant information. It is possible that the information that is required to make the best possible decisions will be difficult to identify at an early stage and later changes may be more expensive to incorporate.

Determining information needs may require detailed discussions with functional managers in order to determine what is important. For example, it may emerge that creative professionals need sufficient free time to keep abreast of trends and to read and absorb other companies' work and that aiming for high staff utilisation rates would be inappropriate.

The reengineering of these processes may prove financially expensive. The danger is that there may not be sufficient waste or dysfunctional behaviour to justify the expense.

H's board should engage a consultant to report on whether H is a good candidate for such a process. Ideally, H should also try to gather information from similar businesses which have organised themselves in this way to establish whether there has been a net benefit.

Conclusions

Rethinking the way in which H conducts business is necessary. In particular, managers should be motivated to think in terms of opportunity costs.

Marginal costing and centralised budgets are recommended.

Staff will be unsettled by any change and communication with them is imperative.

hapter

7

Fraud

Chapter learning objectives

Lead	Component
C2. Evaluate risk management strategies and internal controls.	(a) Evaluate the essential features of internal control systems for identifying, assessing and managing risks.

Indicative syllabus content

- Minimising the risk of fraud: fraud policy statements, effective recruitment policies and good internal controls, such as approval procedures and separation of functions.
- Fraud investigation.

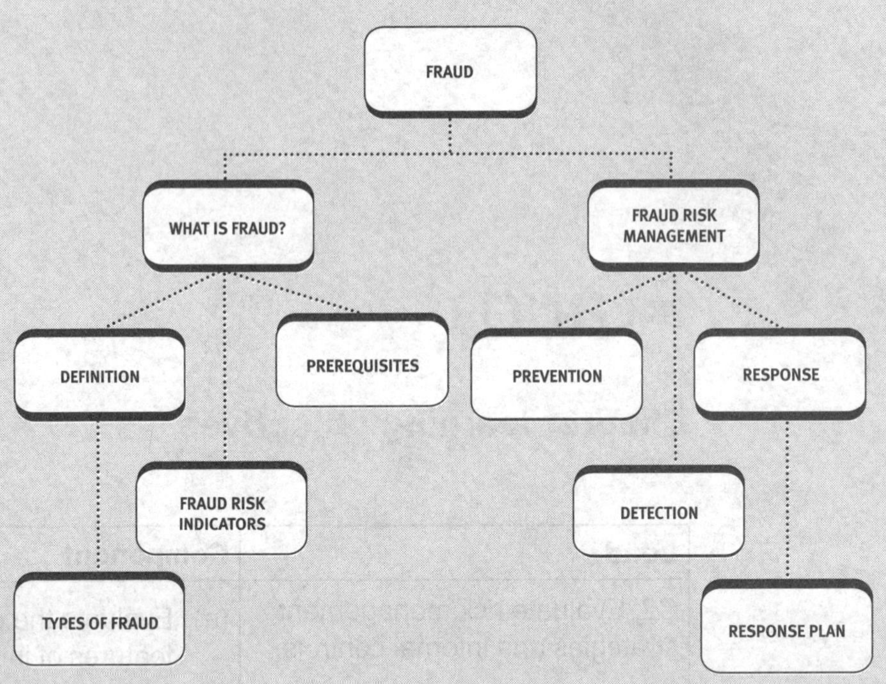

1 What is fraud ?

Fraud can be defined as:

'dishonestly obtaining an advantage, avoiding an obligation or causing a loss to another party'.

Fraud or error

Fraud is a crime, but does not have a precise legal definition. The term 'fraud' refers to an intentional act by one or more individuals among management, those charged with governance, employees or third parties, involving the use of deception to obtain an unjust or illegal advantage. (International Standard of Auditing 240 *The Auditor's Responsibility to Consider Fraud in an Audit of Financial Statements*).

A distinction is made between:

- fraud, which is deliberate falsification, and
- errors, which are unintentional mistakes.

Findings about Fraud

The CIMA publication "Fraud risk management: a guide to good practice" mentions that various surveys have highlighted the following facts about fraud:

- organisations may be losing as much as 7% of their annual turnover as a result of fraud
- corruption is estimated to cost the global economy about $1.5 trillion each year
- only a small percentage of losses from fraud are recovered by organisations
- a high percentage of frauds are committed by senior management and executives
- greed is one of the main motivators for committing fraud
- fraudsters often work in the finance function
- fraud losses are not restricted to a particular sector or country
- the prevalence of fraud is increasing in emerging markets.

Different types of fraud

Examples of fraud include:

- the theft of cash or other assets
- false accounting: this includes concealing or falsifying accounting records with a view to personal gain or providing false information that is misleading or deceptive
- crimes against consumers or clients, e.g. misrepresenting the quality of goods; pyramid trading schemes; selling counterfeit goods
- employee fraud against employers, e.g. payroll fraud; falsifying expense claims; theft of cash
- crimes against investors, consumers and employees, e.g. financial statement fraud
- crimes against financial institutions, e.g. using lost and stolen credit cards; fraudulent insurance claims
- crimes against government, e.g. social security benefit claims fraud; tax evasion
- crimes by professional criminals, e.g. money laundering; advance fee fraud

- e-crime by people using computers, e.g. spamming; copyright crimes; hacking.

Pyramid schemes

Pyramid schemes are also known as multi-level plans and network marketing plans. Although the law on these schemes varies between countries, as a general rule some pyramid schemes are legitimate and some are illegal.

The nature of a pyramid scheme is for the originator of the scheme to offer other people the opportunity to become a distributor for a product or service, which could range in size and value from vitamins to car leases. The distributor is given the opportunity to sell the product or service from home, in return for a commission.

In addition, a person who becomes a distributor is encouraged to sign up other people as distributors, and in return receives a commission for each new distributor they persuade to join the scheme.

The concept of the pyramid is that the originator of the scheme signs up a few distributors, who then sign up new distributors themselves. These new distributors in turn sign up more distributors, who then sign up more distributors.

Each new distributor signing up to the scheme is asked to make a payment, for an initial amount of products to sell, or for marketing material. Sometimes, new distributors might be persuaded to pay to go on a training course in the product or service.

If a pyramid scheme is intended primarily to sell the product or service to outside customers, it could well be legal. In the UK, for example, these schemes are legal provided they comply with certain regulations.

However, **these schemes are illegal** if their primary purpose is to sign up new distributors rather than to sell products or services to external customers.

When distributors earn money mainly by signing up more distributors, the pyramid selling scheme is illegal (in many countries) because there is a limit to the number of new distributors. At some stage, there will be no more distributors willing to sign up to the scheme. The distributors at the bottom of the pyramid will have spent money buying inventory and/or marketing material, with very little prospect of getting any money back. The scheme is then likely to be wound up, possibly with many commissions still unpaid, having made a large amount of money for its originator.

Advance fee fraud

This is a fraud in which a victim is persuaded to become involved in an apparent scheme to get money out of another country with the promise of a huge reward. Having become an accomplice in this scheme, the victim is then persuaded to make payments to overcome a series of problems that 'unexpectedly' arise in gaining access to the money.

In a typical advance fee fraud, an individual working for a company receives a letter, fax or e-mail from a person claiming to be an 'official' in a government department or government agency in another country. The letter states that the person, for a reason that is explained, would like to transfer money out of the country but cannot do so for legal reasons or because of exchange control regulations.

The fraudster asks the intended victim to help by providing blank paper with a company letterhead and personal bank details. The fraudster claims that the company stationery will be used to create an invoice for a fictitious contract, and when this invoice is paid the money will then be paid into the victim's bank account. In return for his assistance, the victim is offered a large portion of the money, typically 30% or so.

By responding to the letter and supplying headed paper and bank details, the victim is hooked. The fraudster then sends a number of official-looking documents to the victim, to testify to the authenticity of the scheme that the victim is being asked to join.

There is a sense of urgency, and having to claim the money 'now' before it is too late. The victim is also sworn to secrecy. In most cases, the victim is also asked to go to the country concerned, or to a country near it. The scheme apparently moves forward to the point when the money is with the central bank of the country concerned, waiting for final approval to transfer it abroad, into the victim's bank account.

The victim starts losing money when a problem arises with the transfer of the money. The reasons for the problem might be that:

- a transaction fee has to be paid to the bank, or
- a local tax must be paid before the money can be sent abroad, or
- a local official is demanding a payment (a bribe) before he will agree to authorise the transfer of the money, or
- legal fees have to be paid before the lawyers will sign a document for the transfer of money to go ahead.

The fraudster persuades the victim to make the payment. Being so close to getting a large amount of money in return, the victim is far too involved to refuse. Several 'problems' with transferring the money might arise, one after another, and the victim might make several payments, before the nature of the fraud finally becomes apparent.

Test your understanding 1

An originator offers others an opportunity to distribute a product in return for a fee. The distributor is then encouraged to recruit other distributors in return for a fee. Eventually the last distributors will have no one to distribute to thereby losing their investment.

This type of fraud is called:

A A distributor fraud

B An advance fee fraud

C A pyramid scheme

D False accounting

Test your understanding 2

A victim is persuaded to become involved in a scheme to get money out of another country with the promise of a reward. The victim is then persuaded to make payments to overcome a series of problems that arise in gaining access to the money. There is no transfer of monies out of the country, and the victim has simply paid monies to the fraudster.

This type of fraud is called:

A A distributor fraud

B An advance fee fraud

C A pyramid scheme

D False accounting

Fraud risk indicators

Fraud indicators fall into two categories:

Warning signs

Warning signs have been described as organisational indicators of fraud risk. Examples include the following:

- Absence of an anti-fraud policy and culture.
- Lack of management supervision of staff.
- Inadequate recruitment processes and absence of screening.
- Dissatisfied employees who have access to desirable assets.
- Lack of job segregation and independent checking of key transactions.
- Poor physical security of assets.
- Management compensation highly dependent on meeting aggressive performance targets.
- Highly competitive market conditions and decreasing profitability levels within the organisation.
- Rapid changes in information technology.

Fraud alerts

Fraud alerts have been described as specific events or red flags, which may be indicative of fraud. Examples include the following:

- Anonymous emails/letters/telephone calls.
- Emails sent at unusual times, with unnecessary attachments, or to unusual destinations.
- Discrepancy between earnings and lifestyle.
- Unusual, irrational, or inconsistent behaviour.
- Alteration of documents and records.
- Subsidiary ledgers, which do not reconcile with control accounts.
- Extensive use of 'suspense' accounts.
- Inappropriate or unusual journal entries.
- Confirmation letters not returned.

Prerequisites for fraud

- A major reason why people commit fraud is because they are allowed to do so.
- The likelihood that fraud will be committed will be decreased if the potential fraudster believes that the rewards will be modest, that they will be detected or that the potential punishment will be unacceptably high.
- Therefore, a comprehensive system of control is needed to reduce the opportunity for fraud and increase the likelihood of detection.

There are three prerequisites for fraud to occur:

- **Dishonesty** on the part of the perpetrator.
- **Opportunity** for fraud to occur.
- **Motive** for fraud.

More on prerequisites

Three conditions that are generally present when fraud exists are:

- an ability to **rationalise** the fraudulent action and hence act with **dishonesty** – virtually anyone can justify almost any dishonest or illegal action that they undertake. The idea is that many people obey the law because they believe in it and/or they are afraid of being shamed or rejected by people they care about if they are caught. However, some people may be able to rationalise fraudulent actions as:
  - necessary – especially when done for the business
  - harmless – because the victim is large enough to absorb the impact
  - justified – because 'the victim deserved it' or 'because I was mistreated.'
- a perceived **opportunity** to commit fraud – this can cover a vast range of circumstances, from the board of directors (whose position almost always gives some opportunity to publish fraudulent statements) to members of staff or the general public who think that the system might be weak.
- a **motive**, incentive or pressure to commit fraud – this can range from the members of the board wishing to maximise the value of their performance-related remuneration packages to greed on the part of a dishonest employee or third party.

All three factors generally exist within all organisations and at all levels.

Test your understanding 3

Which of the following are pre-requisites for fraud to occur: (Select all that apply.)

A Opportunity

B Dishonesty

C Detection

D Motive

2 Fraud risk management strategy

In common with any other type of risk, a risk management strategy needs to be developed for fraud. This strategy should include three key elements:

- Fraud prevention.
- Fraud detection.
- Fraud response.

Together, these should result in a fourth element - risk deterrence.

For example, fraud detection acts as a deterrent by sending a message to likely fraudsters that the organisation is actively fighting fraud and that procedures are in place to identify any illegal activity that has occurred. Similarly, the possibility of being caught will often persuade a potential perpetrator not to commit a fraud.

As well as addressing the legal aspects of fraud, this process operates within the wider context of the organisation's risk management strategy, corporate governance and ethical culture.

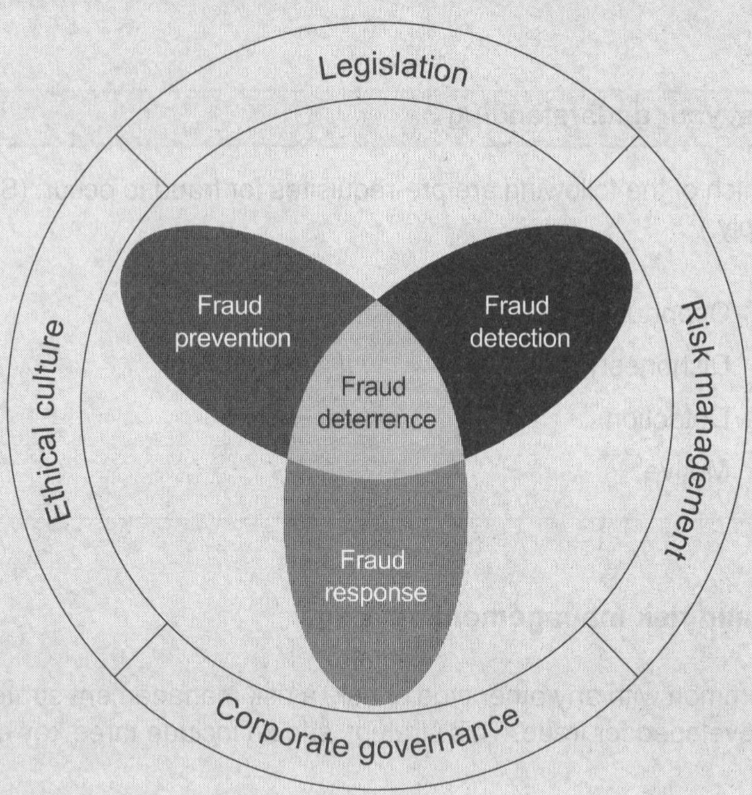

Fraud prevention

The aim of preventative controls is to reduce opportunity and remove temptation from potential offenders. Prevention techniques include the introduction of policies, procedures and controls, and activities such as training and fraud awareness to stop fraud from occurring.

Some specific examples of fraud prevention include:

- An anti-fraud culture;
- Risk awareness;
- Whistleblowing;
- Sound internal control systems.

A **fraud policy statement**, effective recruitment policies and good internal controls can minimise the risk of fraud.

Sample fraud policy statement

Introduction

(1) The group is committed to preventing, detecting and reporting fraud, and in co-operating with other organisations to reduce opportunities for fraud.

(2) The Company will manage the fraud risk by:

- defining, setting and maintaining cost effective control procedures to identify and deter fraud;
- investigating all incidences of actual, attempted or suspected fraud, and all instances of major control breakdown;
- encouraging staff to be vigilant and raising fraud-awareness at all levels;
- ensuring key controls are complied with;
- providing staff with effective confidential reporting mechanisms and encouraging their use;
- taking action against individuals and organisations perpetrating fraud against the group and seeking restitution of any asset fraudulently obtained and the recovery of costs;
- co-operating with the police and other appropriate authorities in the investigation and prosecution of those suspected of fraud.

Purpose

(3) To document clearly the Company's attitude to and stance on fraud.

(4) To demonstrate to internal and external stakeholders that the group deals with fraud in an appropriate manner.

Scope

(5) his policy applies to the Company group, and will be applied globally. It should be read inconjunction with the Group Security Policy, the Group Crisis Management Policy and the Group Malpractice Reporting Policy.

(6) The following actions are among those considered to fall within the definition of fraud:

- theft of company property, including information;
- forgery or alteration of company documents;
- willful destruction or removal of company records;
- falsification of expense claims;
- unauthorised disclosure of confidential information to outside parties;
- misappropriation or use of company assets for personal gain;
- undertaking or assisting in illegal activity (including money laundering, which is covered by the Group Anti-Money Laundering Policy);
- acceptance of bribes or gifts to favour third parties;
- unauthorised premium discounting;
- knowingly generating or paying false claims or invoices.

Underlying Philosophy

(7) Fraud risk can best be managed through preventative and detective control measures. The group is committed to the continuous improvement of fraud prevention and detection techniques.

(8) Management has a responsibility to ensure adequate anti-fraud measures and controls are present in systems. However, all staff are equally expected to be vigilant and play an active part in anti-fraud activity.

(9) The overt investigation of all actual or suspected instances of fraud and the prosecution of offenders provides an effective deterrent. Therefore, all known or suspected incidences of fraud will be thoroughly and impartially investigated.

(10) The investigation of fraud involving employees is best conducted independently – i.e, outside the control of the line management of the area in which the investigation will take place.

Corporate Objectives

(11) To develop an anti-fraud culture and define management and employee responsibilities in this area.

(12) To reduce the opportunity for fraud by introducing preventative and detective measures into systems and processes.

(13) To ensure that anti-fraud controls are considered and built into new systems and processes at the design stage.

(14) To promote an open and ethical culture within the organisation which deems unethical behaviour unacceptable.

(15) To increase the vigilance of management and staff through raising fraud risk awareness.

(16) To ensure that the directors of the group meet their statutory responsibilities towards fraud, as per the Companies Act and the Turnbull requirements for corporate governance.

(17) To learn from previous incidents and recycle lessons and experiences in fraud prevention and detection globally.

(18) To encourage management and staff to report their suspicions while guaranteeing anonymity where requested.

(19) To investigate impartially and thoroughly all cases or suspected cases of fraud, to prosecute offenders and, where appropriate, to seek to recover monies and costs through legal means.

(20) To co-operate with other organisations, such as other XXX companies and the police, in the industry-wide detection and prevention of fraud.

Corporate Principles & Practice

Fraud Prevention and Detection

(21) The group's Standards of Business Conduct will define the boundaries for acceptable conduct.

(22) HR policies include reference to recruitment and screening of new staff, an effective appraisal system and exit interviews.

(23) Fraud risk will be assessed regularly as part of the business's risk management process, and at the design stage of new systems and processes. Cost-effective controls will be introduced where appropriate.

(24) Fraud risk awareness training will be undertaken with staff in high-risk functions on a regular basis.

(25) Regular assurance will be completed on key controls to ensure their effective mitigation of the fraud risk.

(26) Data mining and data analysis will be used to proactively manage the fraud risk and identify actual and potential problems.

(27) Fraud contingency plans will be developed to ensure appropriate and timely action is taken if fraud is suspected or uncovered.

Fraud Investigation

(28) Where reasonable suspicion that fraud against the Company has taken place, the Company is entitled to investigate the matter thoroughly using recognised and legitimate investigative techniques.

(29) All investigations will be carried out objectively and confidentially, and independently of the line management for the area in which the fraud has occurred or is suspected.

(30) In the normal course of events we would look to hand over the investigation to the police, or other authorities, as soon as practical.

(31) In certain cases, third-party investigators may be employed by the director of fraud & investigations and director of group security in order to gather sufficient evidence to hand the case over to the proper authorities. Responsibility for the management of third parties rests with the director of fraud & investigations and director of group security. For non-UK business units, the head of the business unit may appoint a third-party investigator. Responsibility for the management of third parties in these cases rests with the BU head, who must take steps to ensure the investigation is conducted in an appropriate manner.

(32) Will be subject to the investigations guidelines attached as Appendix Y to this policy.

(33) The director of fraud & investigations and director of security are authorised to enter any group premises, be given access to any information requested, and have access to all staff (with reasonable notice).

(34) The rights of individuals will be respected at all times.

(35) Where members of staff are involved in a fraud against the group, whether actual or attempted, they will be subject to the group's disciplinary procedures, which may result in dismissal from the group.

(36) The Company will seek to prosecute anyone who commits fraud and will seek to recover its assets through legal means.

(37) The code of conduct adhered to by all investigators will include considerations of all relating legislation (e.g Police and Criminal Evidence Act, Data Protection Act, Public Interest Disclosure Act, European Convention on Human Rights etc in the UK and relevant local legislation overseas) and group HR policies.

(38) Lessons learnt will be shared across the group as soon as possible after an investigation is concluded.

External Reporting

(39) It is the policy of the Company to report all known criminal activity to the police for investigation by them. The timing of police involvement will be at the discretion of the director of fraud & investigations, in conjunction with the appropriate line and group directors.

(40) Similarly, the Company will report other breaches discovered in the course of investigations to the relevant authorities, including HM Customs & Excise, Inland Revenue, FSA, and the appropriate authorities overseas. The timing of such involvement will be at the discretion of the director of fraud and investigations, in conjunction with the appropriate line and group directors.

Responsibilities

(41) Group Business Risk is responsible for:

- Maintenance of this policy and the Policy for Malpractice Reporting.
- Development of a group fraud centre of excellence and group-wide fraud contingency plans.
- Provision of fraud and investigation services to UK business units, including policy development, contingency planning, and staff awareness training.
- Liaison with business unit fraud and security units, and other group functions, as appropriate.
- Investigation into all known or suspected instances of fraud by an employee in the UK.
- Assisting business units with the implementation of this policy, and regular reporting on the effectiveness of the policy globally.
- Global sharing of best practice and provision of fraud and investigation services to them on request.
- Regular reporting on the fraud risk globally.
- Management of any third parties employed and ensuring their adherence to this policy.

(42) Business Units are responsible for:

- Ensuring compliance with this policy throughout their operations. To this end a senior manager should be appointed with specific responsibility for its implementation and monitoring. In particular, business units must ensure that any third parties employed by them to investigate actual or suspected frauds comply with this policy and local laws and regulations.
- Considering their exposure to fraud risk and introducing preventative controls into new and existing systems and processes.
- Encouraging an open and ethical culture amongst staff and management.
- Developing pro-active methods of fraud detection, such as data mining and analysis.
- Reporting all suspected cases of fraud or theft by an employee to the director of fraud & investigations. For non-UK business units, this applies to cases where the employee is a senior manager or where the sums or assets involved may exceed £25,000. In all cases, where the sums or assets may exceed £500,000, the director of group security should also be advised.
- Allocating sufficient and appropriate resources to implement this policy effectively.
- Implementing initiatives that enhance fraud risk management effectiveness, including procedures that enable employees to inform management of suspected fraud, theft and wrongdoing.

(43) Staff are responsible for reporting known or suspected fraud, or instances of unethical or illegal behaviour within the company, as per the Group Malpractice Reporting Policy.

Test your understanding 4 – Causes of fraud (Integration)

Explain the major causes of fraud and discuss controls that should be in place to reduce fraud.

Fraud detection

A common misbelief is that external auditors find fraud. This is actually rarely the case – in fact their letters of engagement typically state that it is **not their responsibility** to look for fraud. Most frauds are discovered accidentally, or as a result of information received (whistleblowing).

Some methods of discovering fraud are:

- Performing regular checks, e.g. stocktaking and cash counts.
- Warning signals or fraud risk indicators (see previous section). For example:
  - Failures in internal control procedures
  - Lack of information provided to auditors
  - Unusual behaviour by individual staff members
  - Accounting difficulties.
- Whistleblowers.

Test your understanding 5

A fraud risk management strategy will normally deal with fraud in the following order:

A Prevention; response; detection

B Detection; prevention; response

C Response; detection; prevention

D Prevention; detection; response

Test your understanding 6

Fraud prevention includes: (Select all that apply.)

A An anti-fraud culture

B Risk awareness

C Whistleblowing

D A sound internal control system

More on fraud detection

The risks of fraud can be reduced by suitable internal controls, properly applied. However, the internal auditor should be on the look-out for possible fraud in carrying out audit work, and should look for evidence of suspicious circumstances.

- **Failures in internal control procedures**. The risk of fraud is high when internal controls are ignored or by-passed. For example, expenditures might be made without proper authorisation or without proper documentation. In a computer system, there might be evidence of unauthorised 'hacking' into the system. There might be an 'all-powerful' individual in the department, whose work is not checked by anyone else or who appears to over-ride some internal controls.
- **Lack of information**. The auditor might be suspicious when there is an absence of documentation, and staff are unhelpful or evasive when questioned.
- **Unusual behaviour by individual staff members**. Warning signs might be members of staff who arrive first in the morning and leave last in the evening, and do not take holidays, or members of staff who keep an area of the office for their exclusive use and do not share files with others.
- **Accounting difficulties**. The auditor might be concerned if the work of the accounts department is continually behind schedule, and there is a backlog of work waiting to be done. Within the ledger accounts themselves, there might be large balances in suspense accounts, the causes of which the accounts staff have been unable to identify.

The legal position of the whistleblower

The legal position of the whistleblower is covered within the Public Interest Disclosure Act 1998.

The Act ensures that as a whistleblower you are protected from victimisation if the you meet all the following:

- You are a worker (employee, agency worker, or training with employers)
- You are revealing information of the right type: a **'qualifying disclosure'**
- You reveal information to the right person and in the right way: this makes it a **'protected disclosure'**.

Qualifying disclosures

To be protected you need to reasonably believe that malpractice is happening, has happened, or will happen. The malpractice can take the form of:

- Criminal offences
- Failure to comply with a legal obligation
- Miscarriage of justice
- Threats to health and safety
- Damage to the environment.

Protected disclosure

For a disclosure to a prescribed person to be protected you must:

- Make the disclosure in good faith
- Reasonably believe that the information is substantially true
- Reasonably believe that you are making the disclosure to the right 'prescribed person'.

In certain circumstances disclosures can be made to others:

- To your legal adviser
- To a government minister if you are a public sector worker
- To a professional body or in extreme circumstances the media (but in this case stricter rules apply).

Fraud response

- The fraud response plan sets out the arrangements for dealing with suspected cases of fraud, theft or corruption.
- It provides procedures for evidence-gathering that will enable decision-making and that will subsequently be admissible in any legal action.
- The fraud response plan also has a deterrent value and can help to restrict damage and minimise losses to the organisation.

The organisation's response to fraud may include:

- Internal disciplinary action, in accordance with personnel policies.
- Civil litigation for the recovery of loss.
- Criminal prosecution through the police.

Responsibilities

Within the response plan responsibilities should be allocated to:

- **Managers**, who should take responsibility for detecting fraud in their area.
- **Finance Director**, who has overall responsibility for the organisational response to fraud including the investigation. This role may be delegated to a **fraud officer** or internal security officer.
- **Personnel** (Human Resources Department), who will have responsibility for disciplinary procedures and issues of employment law and practice.
- **Audit committee**, who should review the details of all frauds and receive reports of any significant events.
- **Internal auditors**, who will most likely have the task of investigating the fraud.
- **External auditors**, to obtain expertise.
- **Legal advisors**, in relation to internal disciplinary, civil or criminal responses.
- **Public relations**, if the fraud is so significantly large that it will come to public attention.
- **Police**, where it is policy to prosecute all those suspected of fraud.
- **Insurers**, where there is likely to be a claim.

Elements of a fraud response plan

Any organisation's fraud response plan should include the following:

(1) **Purpose of the fraud response plan**
   - Set out arrangements for dealing with suspected cases of fraud

(2) **Corporate policy**

(3) **Definition of fraud**

(4) **Roles and responsibilities**
   - (see above)

(5) **The response**

- Reporting suspicions
- Establishing an investigation team
- Formulating a response

(6) **The investigation**

- Preservation of evidence
- Physical evidence
- Electronic evidence
- Interviews
- Statements from witnesses and suspects

(7) **Organisation's objectives with respect to fraud**

- Internal report
- Civil response
- Criminal response

(8) **Follow up action**

- Lessons learned
- Management response

Taken from CIMA "Fraud Risk Management: A guide to good practice" (2008)

Test your understanding 7

A fraud response plan normally includes a section on:

A Possible frauds

B Corporate policy

C Roles and responsibilities

D Investigation and evidence

Test your understanding 8

K plc is a manufacturing company that has recently seen the CEO forced to tender her resignation over serious fraud allegations. The rest of the board are looking to regain shareholder confidence.

Identify the THREE main fraud prevention strategies you would recommend to the Board.

A Create a culture that is anti-fraud with an anti-fraud 'tone at the top'

B Do nothing, let the matter blow over

C Create a sound system of internal control

D Create and publish a whistle blowing policy

E Send all of the large shareholders a gift to apologise

F Dismiss any employee who directly reported to the CEO just in case they might have been involved in any wrong doing

Investigation of fraud

When a fraud comes to light, internal auditors might be asked to investigate it. The purpose of investigating a fraud should be to:

- Establish the facts.
- Establish how the fraud occurred and initially went undetected. Were the internal controls weak or inadequate? Or were the internal controls by-passed or not properly applied?
- Consider whether anyone else might have been involved in the fraud.
- Establish or estimate the size of the loss.

The investigator should look at all relevant documents and files, listen to recorded telephone conversations and read the fraudster's e-mails. Individuals working with the fraudster should be interviewed, such as colleagues, supervisor and manager.

Great care must be taken to ensure that evidence is gathered and maintained in a manner that could be used in any criminal proceedings that the company institutes. The company might also have to defend allegations of unfair dismissal or defamation by an employee who claims they have been wrongly accused.

As a result of an investigation, an auditor should make recommendations about the system. These are likely to be that, if the risk of losses is high, either:

- the existing internal controls are not sufficient to limit the risk; new controls or stronger controls should therefore be introduced, or
- the existing internal controls should be sufficient to limit the risk, but were applied inadequately or were ignored in the past; measures should therefore be taken to ensure that the controls are properly applied in the future.

Test your understanding 9

O is a multinational organisation which sells a large number of goods, including books and DVD's online to individual customers. A review of one of the IT systems which processes internet sales has revealed several transactions over the last few months which suggest there has been some 'hacking' or fraudulent access to the customer database. Each transaction resulted in a lack of payment by the customer and transactions being immediately deleted from the customer database so that sales were not recorded.

Which of the following control recommendations may help to prevent a reoccurrence of the issues outlined above?

Select **all** that apply.

A Only despatch goods where payment has been received in full.

B Monitor system access from internal sources, using a control log, to identify whether staff in the IT department are placing fraudulent orders.

C Only sell to those customers who have an account set up with O.

D Check a number of transactions at regular intervals on a daily basis to make sure they are not deleted.

E Invest in fraud insurance to cover losses resulting from unauthorised access.

Reputation risk

If a fraud becomes public knowledge it can affect a company's reputation. The control systems within the company will be considered weak which will worry investors. The share price may fall (dependent on the size of the fraud and the investors opinion of it). Future investors will be wary and it may prevent the company from raising future finance.

(In the past companies have adopted two different attitudes to the disclosure of fraud – admit to it, or hide it. Hiding fraud is unethical. Also, often the press find out and the consequences are worse than they would have been if the company had come clean in the first place.)

Litigation risk

If fraud has been identified by the company and they take the case to court, then the perpetrator may deny the accusations resulting in a long and drawn out court case which can be costly for the company. (Often companies consider settling out of court to avoid large court costs and media attention.) However the evidence may be insufficient for a court to find the perpetrator guilty and in some cases the perpetrator might counter-sue for loss of their own reputation. If the company is large and of public interest, this will probably be covered in the press, which may be detrimental to the company's reputation and share price once again.

Test your understanding 10

The ultimate responsibility for fraud detection lies with:

A The internal auditors

B The external auditors

C The directors

D The employees

Test your understanding 11

Which TWO risks can a fraud lead to:

A Litigation risk

B Political risk

C Employee risk

D Reputation risk

Test your understanding 12 – Private hospital (Integration)

A private hospital has a canteen that provides staff and visitors with subsidised meals and refreshments. The canteen's selling prices are supposed to cover running costs, so that there is no net cost to the hospital. Over the past eighteen months the canteen has been reporting losses that have been increasing steadily despite monthly sales remaining constant. The cost of purchases has grown substantially for no apparent reason. The purchasing of supplies and the choice of suppliers is the sole responsibility of the Canteen Manager. The current Canteen Manager has been in post for almost two years.

The hospital's Chief Executive asked the Head of Internal Audit to investigate why the canteen was making losses and a thorough investigation was conducted under the supervision of F, an experienced auditor and qualified accountant. The internal audit team discovered that the losses started shortly after the Canteen Manager changed suppliers. F compared the invoiced prices charged by the new supplier with those charged by the former supplier and discovered that the new supplier was significantly more expensive.

F interviewed the Canteen Manager, who claimed that he had changed suppliers because the new supplier was more reliable and provided higher quality products. F was suspicious and contacted a number of alternative suppliers. None of the potential suppliers whom F contacted would have charged as much as the canteen was paying for basic commodities such as rice and potatoes. Furthermore, the canteen's invoices showed that it was paying far more than the normal market price for branded goods, such as crisps and chocolate bars.

F was in the Canteen Manager's office one lunch time. He saw a laptop computer open at an email to the supplier and investigated further. The Canteen Manager had been using a personal email account to email the owner of the supplier on a daily basis. The emails revealed that:

- the owner had been inflating the selling prices of all goods sold to the hospital by 20%;
- the Canteen Manager passed these inflated invoices for payment; and
- the owner then paid half of the 20% that had been overcharged to the Canteen Manager in cash.

F confiscated the laptop, which was the Canteen Manager's personal property, and submitted it, along with a full report, to the Head of Internal Audit.

Two weeks later, F was asked to meet with the hospital's Chief Executive. The hospital's directors had discussed the report carefully and had interviewed the Canteen Manager and decided that they did not wish to refer the matter to the police. The Canteen Manager had been accompanied by a lawyer, who stated that the Canteen Manager denied all charges of fraud and pointed out that there was very little evidence to support F's accusations. F could have easily falsified the emails on the laptop and the owner of the food supplier had supplied the lawyer with a statement that no payments had been made to the Canteen Manager. The Chief Executive had agreed that the hospital would return the Canteen Manager's laptop and would make him a substantial payment in return for his agreement to resign quietly. The Chief Executive had also promised that the Canteen Manager would receive a positive reference. F was asked to destroy any remaining notes and documents relating to this investigation and to remain silent, not discussing the case with anyone either within the hospital or any third parties.

Required:

Discuss the difficulties associated with proving that the Canteen Manager was fraudulent.

(30 minutes)

Test your understanding 13 – Fraud and mitigation (Integration)

XYS is a company manufacturing and selling a wide range of industrial products to a large number of businesses throughout the country. XYS is a significant local employer, with 2,000 people working out of several locations around the region, all linked by a networked computer system.

XYS purchases numerous components from 500 local and regional suppliers, receiving these into a central warehouse. The company carries about 20,000 different inventory items, placing 15,000 orders with its suppliers each year.

The Accounts Payable Department of XYS has five staff who process all supplier invoices through the company's computer system and make payment to suppliers by cheque or electronic remittance.

Required:

Explain the risk of fraud in Accounts Payable for a company like XYS and how that risk can be mitigated.

(20 minutes)

Test your understanding 14 – College (Case study)

Scenario

A large college has several sites and employs hundreds of teaching staff.

Trigger

The college has recently discovered a serious fraud involving false billings for part-time teaching.

The fraud involved two members of staff. M is a clerk in the payroll office who is responsible for processing payments to part-time teaching staff. P is the head of the Business Studies department at the N campus. Part-time lecturers are required to complete a monthly claim form which lists the classes taught and the total hours claimed. These forms must be signed by their head of department, who sends all signed forms to M. M checks that the class codes on the claim forms are valid, that hours have been budgeted for those classes and inputs the information into the college's payroll package.

The college has a separate personnel department that is responsible for maintaining all personnel files. Additions to the payroll must be made by a supervisor in the personnel office. The payroll package is programmed to reject any claims for payment to employees whose personnel files are not present in the system.

M had gained access to the personnel department supervisor's office by asking the college security officer for the loan of a pass key because he had forgotten the key to his own office. M knew that the office would be unoccupied that day because the supervisor was attending a wedding. M logged onto the supervisor's computer terminal by guessing her password, which turned out to be the registration number of the supervisor's car. M then added a fictitious part-time employee, who was allocated to the N campus Business Studies department.

P then began making claims on behalf of the fictitious staff member and submitting them to M. M signed off the forms and input them as normal. The claims resulted in a steady series of payments to a bank account that had been opened by P. The proceeds of the fraud were shared equally between M and P.

The fraud was only discovered when the college wrote to every member of staff with a formal invitation to the college's centenary celebration. The letter addressed to the fictitious lecturer was returned as undeliverable and the personnel department became suspicious when they tried to contact this person in order to update his contact details. By then M and P had been claiming for non-existent teaching for three years.

The government department responsible for funding the college conducted an investigation and concluded that the college's management had relied excessively on the application controls programmed into administrative software and had paid too little attention to the human resources aspects of the system.

Task

Write a memorandum to the Board evaluating the difficulties associated with preventing and/or detecting this fraud.

(20 minutes)

3 Chapter summary

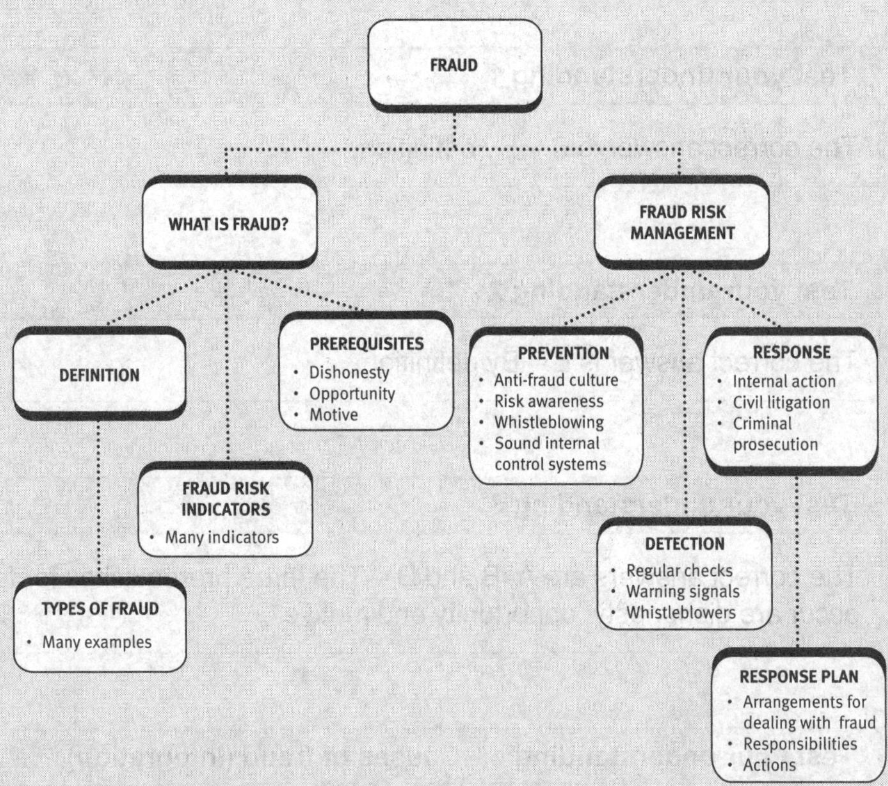

Test your understanding answers

Test your understanding 1

The correct answer is C – By definition.

Test your understanding 2

The correct answer is B – By definition.

Test your understanding 3

The correct answers are A, B and D – The three prerequisites for fraud to occur are dishonesty, opportunity and motive.

Test your understanding 4 – Causes of fraud (Integration)

Fraud is dishonestly obtaining an advantage, avoiding an obligation or causing a loss to another party. Those committing fraud may be managers, employees or third parties, including customers and suppliers.

Fraud risk arises out of errors or events in transaction processing or other business operations where those errors or events could be the result of a deliberate act designed to benefit the perpetrator.

There are three conditions for fraud to occur: dishonesty, opportunity and motive. Controls to prevent dishonesty include pre-employment checks; scrutiny of staff by effective supervision; severe discipline for offenders and strong moral leadership.

Opportunity can be reduced by the separation of duties, controls over inputs, processing and outputs and by the physical security of assets, especially cash.

Motive can be influenced by providing good employment conditions, a sympathetic complaints procedure, but dismissing staff instantaneously where it is warranted.

A major reason why people commit fraud is because they are allowed to do so. The likelihood of fraud will be decreased if the potential fraudster believes that the rewards will be modest, or that the chance of detection or punishment will be unacceptably high. Therefore, a comprehensive system of controls is needed to reduce the opportunity for fraud and increase the likelihood of detection.

Test your understanding 5

The correct answer is D – Initially a fraud is best prevented. If this cannot be done, controls to enable fraud detection should be put in place. Finally if fraud has occurred, then a company should consider their response to it.

Test your understanding 6

The correct answers are A, B, C and D – Fraud prevention should include all of these.

Test your understanding 7

The correct answers are B, C and D – The fraud response plan covers what to do when a fraud is discovered. It does not suggest what constitutes a fraud or how to perpetrate a fraud.

Test your understanding 8

A, C, D

Note:

- B will not restore shareholder confidence
- E will please shareholders but do nothing about their confidence that similar frauds will not happen again
- F is unfair to the staff concerned who should not be dismissed without following due process and without good reason.

Test your understanding 9

A and B only

- Option A: This will prevent deliveries being made without the customer being invoiced or the cash being received.
- Option B: The computer systems appear to have been accessed by third parties with the aim of obtaining goods without paying. It could be that IT staff are actually perpetrating the fraud and this control will detect if this is the case as well as act as a deterrent to staff attempting to place such orders.
- Option C: Since there is a possibility of customer accounts being hacked, this control will not remedy the weakness in the system.
- Option D: This may highlight a reoccurrence of the issue but it will not prevent it from occurring in the first place.
- Option E: This may help minimise financial losses from goods being 'given away' but will not prevent the hacking from occurring.

Test your understanding 10

The correct answer is C – The directors are ultimately responsible for detecting fraud, although all stakeholders in the business should have a fraud awareness.

A common misnomer is that the external auditors 'look' for fraud. This is not the case, however, they often come across it during their testing procedures and should report it to the Board.

Test your understanding 11

The correct answers are A and D – If a fraud becomes public knowledge it can affect a company's reputation.

If a fraud has been identified the company may choose to take the perpetrator to court.

Test your understanding 12 – Private hospital (Integration)

There is very little evidence against the manager and the law will almost certainly require the hospital to prove that the Canteen Manager was fraudulent. The material and the information that has been gathered by F is persuasive but most of it could simply be denied by the Canteen Manager.

The hospital can prove that the Canteen Manager's purchases cost more than might have been charged by another supplier, but that is not in itself proof of fraud. The manager could claim to have been careless in permitting the supplier to overcharge the hospital, but could deny any fraudulent intent. The purchases clearly did take place because the food was received and sold through the canteen. The transactions were authorised by the manager, who was empowered to authorise new suppliers and to sign for purchases. All of the documentary evidence proves that the canteen purchases were made from an authorised supplier for the purpose stated in the bookkeeping records.

The only way to prove that the manager had defrauded the hospital would be to seek a formal statement from the supplier that there had been fraudulent collusion. The supplier is owner-managed and the owner is clearly implicated in the fraud. All the owner has to do is to claim that the sales actually occurred at the recorded prices. If the owner admits to participating in the fraud then s/he will be admitting to a criminal offence and will then be open to the threat of criminal charges. The hospital might also be able to reclaim the overstatement of the prices from the owner.

The only correspondence concerning the fraud is in an electronic format. By his own admission, the internal auditor has accessed the email account and so the manager could claim that the files and messages have been tampered with. There is no direct proof that the emails were sent to and from the Canteen Manager and the owner. Anybody could have created that email account and sent and received bogus emails describing a fraud. The manager could simply deny ever having sent or received those messages.

Test your understanding 13 – Fraud and mitigation (Integration)

Computer systems provide a particular opportunity for fraud, although this requires dishonesty by employees, opportunity to commit fraud, and motive. Accounts Payable in particular presents the opportunity for unscrupulous suppliers to claim payment for goods not delivered or services not supplied, or to overcharge. It also provides the opportunity for employees to redirect payments to themselves or third parties rather than to the intended supplier, either alone or in concert with third parties.

Some controls are preventative to limit or prevent an event from occurring. This could include physical access control over the computer system, selection and training of staff, separation of duties between invoice and payment processing or authorisation levels for invoices and payments. Other controls are detective: they identify events that have already occurred, through, for example, the reconciliation of invoices to a supplier statement. Internal audit, based on risk identification and assessment procedures have an important role to play in detective controls. Finally, corrective controls correct events after they have occurred (e.g. recovering overpayments from suppliers, or seeking recompense from employees under a fraud response plan).

It is particularly important that strong controls exist over programme alterations to accounts payable software, physical and logical access controls to accounts payable systems, authorisation levels for invoices and payments and control over forms such as cheques and electronic bank remittances.

The risk of fraud can be reduced through fraud prevention, identification and response policies. Fraud prevention requires an anti-fraud culture and risk awareness which is part of the control environment; sound control systems; and an effective whistle-blowing policy.

Fraud can be identified through regular internal audit checks, warning signals such as late payments, work backlogs, untaken annual leave, and the lifestyle of staff where it is incommensurate with their salary. Fraud response should include disciplinary action under human resource policies, civil litigation for recovery and criminal prosecution.

Test your understanding 14 – College (Case study)

Memorandum

To: The Board

From: A.N. Accountant

Date: Today

Subject: Fraud mitigation

This fraud would have been extremely difficult to prevent and/or to detect.

The fraud involved collusion between two members of staff. Segregation of duties is one of the most powerful means of preventing fraud, but it can be defeated by fraudulent collusion. It would be virtually impossible to make a system effective without relying on segregation of duties.

The fact that one of the perpetrators was a senior member of staff made it more difficult to prevent. The head of an academic department in a college would be regarded as a trusted member of staff, who would not normally be expected to steal from the college.

Systems are often designed in the expectation that senior members of staff will not betray such trust.

The system was further defeated by the falsification of a record on the personnel department. There was a sound control in place that was only defeated because of a combination of human error and blatant falsification. It would be almost impossible to design any system so that it was foolproof in preventing all mistakes and in preventing fraudulent falsification.

Once the fictitious entry had been made in the personnel files the fraud would be difficult to detect because it would add only a very small amount to the overall payroll. A college would have a large number of lecturers and there would be a substantial turnover in staff.

The only people who could be expected to detect this fraud were implicated in it.

hapter

8

Ethics

Chapter learning objectives

Lead	Component
A3. Evaluate the ethical impact of risk.	(a) Evaluate ethical, social and environmental issues arising from risk management.
B2. Evaluate ethical issues facing an organisation and its employees.	(a) Evaluate the risks of unethical behaviour.

Indicative syllabus content

- The identification of ethical dilemmas associated with risk management.
- Ethical issues identified in the CIMA Code of Ethics for Professional Accountants.
- Application of the CIMA Code of Ethics for Professional Accountants.
- The Board's responsibilities for the management of stakeholder' interests.

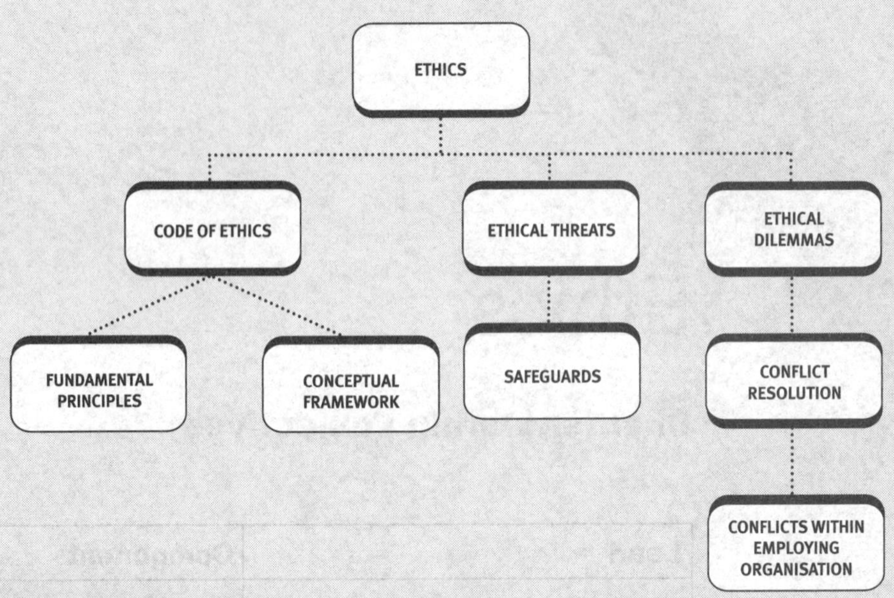

1 Code of ethics

As Chartered Management Accountants, students throughout the world have a duty to observe the highest standards of conduct and integrity, and to uphold the good standing and reputation of the profession. They must also refrain from any conduct which might discredit the profession. Members and registered students must have regard to these guidelines irrespective of their field of activity, of their contract of employment or of any other professional memberships they may hold.

The Institute promotes the highest ethical and business standards, and encourages its members to be good and responsible professionals. Good ethical behaviour may be above that required by the law. In a highly competitive, complex business world, it is essential that CIMA members sustain their integrity and remember the trust and confidence which is placed on them by whoever relies on their objectivity and professionalism. Members must avoid actions or situations which are inconsistent with their professional obligations. They should also be guided not merely by the terms but by the spirit of this Code.

CIMA members should conduct themselves with courtesy and consideration towards all with whom they have professional dealings and should not behave in a manner which could be considered offensive or discriminatory.

CIMA has adopted a code of ethics based on the IFAC (International Federation of Accountants) code of ethics which was developed with input from CIMA and the global accountancy profession. The CIMA Code of Ethics is freely available on CIMA's website – cimaglobal.com > Standards and ethics > Code of ethics.

If a member cannot resolve an ethical issue by following this code or by consulting the ethics support information on CIMA's website, he or she should seek legal advice as to both legal rights and any obligations (s)he may have.

The code of ethics is in three parts:

- Part A establishes the fundamental principles of professional ethics and provides a conceptual framework for applying those principles.
- Parts B and C illustrate how the conceptual framework is to be applied in specific situations:
  - Part B applies to professional accountants in business.
  - Part C applies to professional accountants in public practice.

Fundamental principles

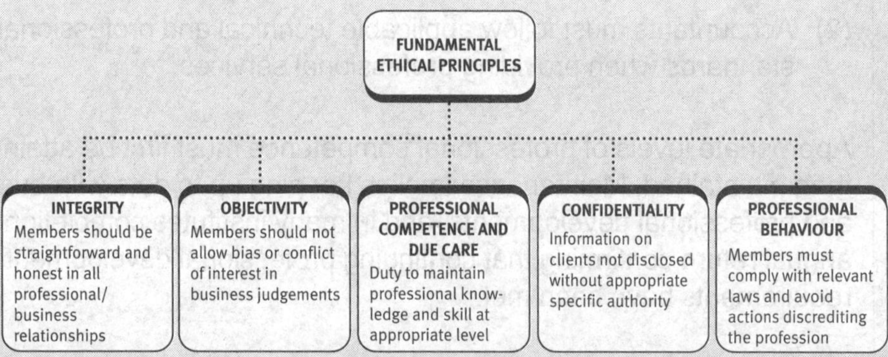

More on fundamental ethical principles

Integrity

Integrity implies fair dealing and truthfulness.

Members are also required not to be associated with any form of communication or report where the information is considered to be:

- materially false or to contain misleading statements
- provided recklessly
- incomplete such that the report or communication becomes misleading by this omission.

Objectivity

Accountants need to ensure that their business/professional judgement is not compromised because of bias or conflict of interest.

However, there are many situations where objectivity can be compromised, so a full list cannot be provided. Accountants are warned to always ensure that their objectivity is intact in any business/professional relationship.

Professional competence and due care

There are two main considerations under this heading:

(1) Accountants are required to have the necessary professional knowledge and skill to carry out work for clients.

(2) Accountants must follow applicable technical and professional standards when providing professional services.

Appropriate levels of professional competence must first be attained and then maintained. Maintenance implies keeping up to date with business and professional developments, and in many institutes completion of an annual return confirming that continuing professional development (CPD) requirements have been met.

Where provision of a professional service has inherent limitations (e.g. reliance on client information) then the client must be made aware of this.

Confidentiality

The principle of confidentiality implies two key considerations for accountants:

(1) Information obtained in a business relationship is not disclosed outside the firm unless there is a proper and specific authority or unless there is a professional right or duty to disclose.

(2) Confidential information acquired during the provision of professional services is not used to personal advantage.

The need to maintain confidentiality is normally extended to cover the accountant's social environment, information about prospective clients and employers and also where business relationships have terminated. Basically there must always be a reason for disclosure before confidential information is provided to a third party.

The main reasons for disclosure are when it is:

(1) permitted by law and authorised by the client

(2) required by law, e.g. during legal proceedings or disclosing information regarding infringements of law

(3) there is professional duty or right to disclose (when not barred by law), e.g. provision of information to the professional institute or compliance with ethical requirements.

Professional behaviour

Accountants must comply with all relevant laws and regulations.

There is also a test whereby actions suggested by a third party which would bring discredit to the profession should also be avoided.

An accountant is required to treat all people contacted in a professional capacity with courtesy and consideration. Similarly, any marketing activities should not bring the profession into disrepute.

Test your understanding 1

The fundamental ethical principles include: (Select all that apply.)

A Communication

B Objectivity

C Professional competence and due care

D Integrity

Test your understanding 2

Fair dealing and truthfulness is implied within the ethical principle of:

A Confidentiality

B Objectivity

C Professional competence and due care

D Integrity

Test your understanding 3

Compliance with all relevant laws and regulations is implied within the ethical principle of:

A Professional behaviour

B Objectivity

C Professional competence and due care

D Integrity

Test your understanding 4

John is a CIMA Member in Practice, and advises a range of individual clients and organisations.

A client has called John, asking for his annual accounts to be finalised as a matter of urgency. Apparently, one of John's staff promised that the accounts would be completed a week earlier. John asks his staff member, a part-qualified accountant, to tell him the situation relating to the Client's accounts. The staff member says that the accounts need another four or five hours' work. As it is Friday, the staff member offers to complete the accounts at home, over the weekend, and to deliver them to the Client on his way to work on Monday morning.

For John to allow this would be in breach of which fundamental ethical principle (according to CIMA's Code of Ethics)?

A Integrity

B Objectivity

C Professional competence and due care

D Confidentiality

E Professional behavior

Test your understanding 5

L is a CIMA Member in Practice, and advises a range of individuals and organisations. An owner manager of one of L's clients has contacted her to ask if she can urgently contact the bank on the client's behalf in order to give a credit reference. Without an injection of funds from the bank, the client's business will be unable to continue trading. The client, a personal friend of L's has asked for this to be done as a 'favour'. Both L and the client are aware that the business' cash flow problems are severe and a positive reference would be misleading.

For L to give the bank a positive credit rating would be in breach of which fundamental ethical principles?

Select **all** that apply.

A Integrity.

B Objectivity.

C Professional Competence and Due Care.

D Confidentiality.

E Professional Behaviour.

Conceptual framework approach

- The circumstances in which management accountants operate may give rise to specific threats to compliance with the fundamental principles.
- It is impossible to define every situation that creates such threats and specify the appropriate mitigating action.
- A conceptual framework that requires a management accountant to identify, evaluate and address threats to compliance with the fundamental principles, rather than merely comply with a set of specific rules which may be arbitrary, is, therefore, in the public interest.

Ethical threats

- The self-interest threat

  May occur due to financial or other self-interest conflict

- The self-review threat

  May occur when previous judgement needs to be re-evaluated by the member responsible for that judgement.

- The advocacy threat

  May occur when a member promotes a position or opinion to the point that subsequent objectivity may be compromised.

- The familiarity or trust threat

  May occur when, because of a close or personal relationship, a member becomes too sympathetic to the interests of others.

- The intimidation threat

  May occur when a member may be deterred from acting objectively by threats, whether real or perceived.

Test your understanding 6

John is a CIMA member, working as Financial Controller of a listed public company.

John's wife owns a large number of shares in the company, and John knows that the share price depends, to some extent, on the reported profits. John is responsible for producing the published accounts of the company.

This represents which type of ethical threat (according to CIMA's Code of Ethics)?

A self interest

B self review

C advocacy

D intimidation

E familiarity

2 Ethical issues as sources of risk

- As stated above, CIMA's code of ethics has a 'threats and safeguards' approach to resolving ethical issues.
- If identified threats are other than clearly insignificant, a management accountant should apply safeguards to eliminate the threats or reduce them to an acceptable level such that compliance with the fundamental principles is not compromised.
- Note that the ethical threat does not necessarily have to relate to personal ethics but could focus on a business decision and its possible implications.

Ethical safeguards

Safeguards

Safeguards are actions or other measures that may eliminate threats or reduce them to an acceptable level.

There are two basic types of safeguards:

- Safeguards created by the profession, legislation or regulation
  - Educational, training and experience requirements for entry into the profession.
  - CPD requirements.
  - Corporate governance regulations.
  - Professional or regulatory monitoring and disciplinary procedures.
  - External review by a legally empowered third party of the reports, returns, communications or information produced by a professional accountant
- Safeguards in the work environment
  - Firm-wide safeguards
  - Engagement-specific safeguards

Test your understanding 7

One of B Company's products, a computer printer, has been found to be at risk of setting alight if left plugged in for long periods of time. The directors of B Company are meeting to decide whether to begin a universal recall of the product or do nothing and just settle any claims for compensation as they arise.

B company's risk assessment concluded that due to safety mechanisms built in to the printer, serious injuries as a result of the fault are very unlikely and the likelihood of fire in the first place is thought to be less than 1 in 100,000.

Which of the following are likely risks to B Company if they decide not to recall the product? Select **all** that apply.

A Risk that the company's sales of other products suffer if knowledge of the fault becomes public

B Risk that the cost of compensation claims outweigh the cost of the recall

C Risk that serious injury occurs and a recall is necessary anyway

D Risk that the company's decision not to recall the product becomes public and the company is seen as unethical.

Test your understanding 8

D is an importer and processor of a product called R33, which is a material used in many household products. It is mined in some of the poorest countries where large communities rely on it for their incomes. These incomes support education, sanitation and health facilities in these countries.

Recently, independent research discovered that R33 was very harmful to human health, particularly in its' raw mined form. Some of the respiratory diseases it caused remained inactive in the body for decades. Doctors had suspected this to be the case but it had never been confirmed before.

The board of D have met to discuss a report commissioned on whether the health risk to workers could be managed with extra internal controls relating to safety measures. The report concluded that, unless expensive redesign of facilities took place and breathing apparatus was issued to all employees, this was unlikely. The report also pointed out that the workers in the poorest nations were more afraid of losing their jobs than the health implications of working with R33.

The board recognise they have an ethical dilemma associated with how they manage the risks associated with the mining of R33. Which of the following statements are correct with respect to the ethical dilemma associated with risk management in this case?

Select **all** that apply.

A The board of D has a duty towards it employees to safeguard their health and so must act on the report, regardless of whether this leads to job losses.

B D has a duty to the local communities its mines support. These communities are under threat because of the report findings.

C If the workers in the poorest developing countries are willing to take the risks to their health, D has a duty to keep providing work.

D Legally, D must provide the safety equipment and redesign the facilities regardless of cost.

E D can choose to ignore the report and continue with its existing risk management strategies.

CIMA's Financial Management magazine has a section on ethical dilemmas each month.

3 Ethical dilemmas and conflict resolution

What is an ethical dilemma ?

- A dilemma will only occur if there are two or more interests at stake, even if it is only an ethical duty to oneself.
- An ethical dilemma exists when one or more principles of the code are threatened.
- You may have discovered something unethical, illegal or fraudulent going on where you work, or perhaps you feel that you have been asked to do something that compromises your professional integrity.
- Conflicts of interest and confidentiality issues are also ethical problems.
- In general, ethical issues should be dealt with by taking actions (called safeguards) to reduce them to a level where they are no longer significant or of any consequence.

Ethical conflict resolution

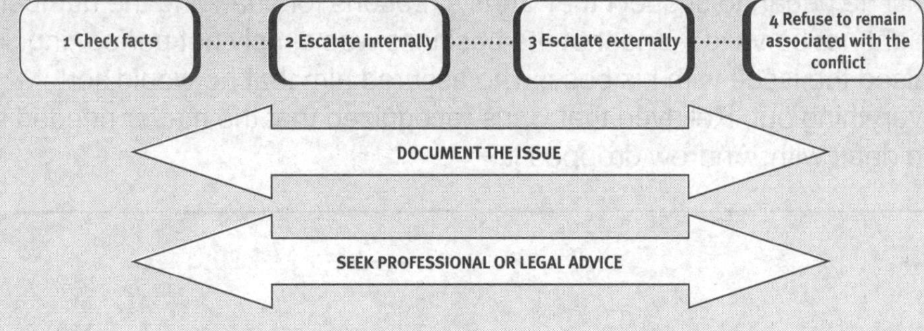

CIMA recommends the following process for addressing situations of ethical conflict:

- Gather all facts and relevant information.
- Ascertain the ethical issues involved and identify the fundamental principles related to the matter in question.
- Escalate concern internally, i.e. to direct management.
- Escalate issue further to your manager's boss, the Board or a non-executive director (following any internal grievance or whistleblowing procedure).
- Seek advice from CIMA.
- Report externally to auditors or relevant trade/regulatory body.
- Remove yourself from the situation.

Throughout the process, document the steps you take to resolve the issue. For example, raise your concern in writing and keep copies of relevant correspondence. This will allow you to demonstrate how you dealt with the problem should you ever need to do so.

Ethics and CIMA

Going downhill fast

Danielle Cohen shares the true story of a CIMA member who contacted the institute's ethics helpline for advice. His problem stemmed from allowing what seemed, on the face of it, a minor issue to snowball into a job-threatening situation.

Andrew was the management accountant of a small firm that was part of a plc. His boss, Chris, was the firm's CEO. Several months ago Chris has approached him with a query about the month-end figures that Andrew has produced, saying that they must be wrong. At the time there was a certain amount of confusion, because their firm had just taken over another small company, so Andrew adjusted them as instructed.

Next month Chris questioned the numbers again, and Andrew duly changed them once more. This happened at several more month-ends until he began to suspect that Chris's reasons for changing the numbers might not be valid – and that the business was simply not performing. He raised the issue with his boss, who assured him that he would sort everything out. Relieved that Chris recognized that the matter needed to be dealt with, Andrew dropped it.

At the end of the firm's financial year, Chris announced that he had, as promised, found a solution to the problem of the ongoing adjustments. Unfortunately, this was very different from what Andrew was expecting. Chris proposed that he own up to the discrepancies, admit that they were the result of a simple error and then resign to prevent any further questions from being asked. In return for carrying the can, Andrew would receive a glowing reference – on the understanding, of course, that he kept quiet about the whole affair.

Shocked and unsure about what to do, Andrew contacted CIMA's ethics helpline. He had gone from accepting a small month-end adjustment to his figures to finding himself about to lose a job. Our guidance to Andrew was that he should consider taking the problem to more senior people in the group, since raising it with Chris wasn't an option. Andrew had some concerns about the possible repercussions of doing this, particularly because Chris was well respected in the group, and he was worried that his version of events would not be believed. The lack of an internal grievance or whistle blowing procedure made it hard for him to predict how his case would be handled.

Given all these factors, Andrew questioned whether quitting was an acceptable solution. A good reference had been promised, but was this pledge worth anything coming from Chris? And how would he explain to any future employer why he had left? And what would happen if a colleague were to complain to CIMA about his lack of competence? If this were to happen, he could potentially lose his membership. Even worse, lying to accept responsibility that wasn't his would be another breach of CIMA's code of ethics. If discovered, this would also have consequences for his membership.

After further discussion, Andrew identified a potential ally (a financial controller) at group level. He arranged a meeting through a trusted colleague in order to minimize the chances of discovery by Chris.

We suggested that Andrew should speak to the institute's legal advice line for expert guidance on his legal obligations and employment rights, and also to the whistle-blowing advice line for free, confidential, independent advice on raising his concerns.

Andrew spoke to the financial controller and Chris was eventually forced to resign. But Andrew's ongoing compliance with his boss's wishes was enough to have tarnished his reputation. A few months later he resigned of his own accord.

Andrew's case is a reminder of how crucial it is to use your professional judgment, heed the warning signs and establish the facts at the first sign of an ethical dilemma. Armed with these and CIMA's code of ethics, you can decide whether or not you need to act and, if so, what that action should be.

So how exactly do you know when an ethical dilemma is an ethical dilemma? As Oscar Wilde observed: 'Morality, like art, means drawing a line someplace.' When the amount of money is not material, the report is only for internal purposes or when no one else seems to think there's an issue, how can you be sure where that line is?

Taking time to consider the situation from all angles will help you to know for sure. In the code of ethics, the line is where a threat to our fundamental principles is anything more than trivial. Although the changes that Andrew made to the numbers in that first month might not have been material, the pattern that they established was. If he had stood up to Chris the first time he was asked to adjust the figures, the situation might never have developed.

Danielle Cohen is CIMA's ethics manager.
This article appeared in Financial Management, November 2007.

Test your understanding 9

The procedure for ethical conflict solution is:

A To check the facts; escalate internally; escalate externally; dissociate with the conflict

B To check the facts; escalate externally; escalate internally; dissociate with the conflict

C To check the facts; dissociate with the conflict; escalate internally; escalate externally

D Escalate internally; escalate externally; check the facts; dissociate with the conflict

Test your understanding 10

JJ is the management accountant at D Co, a small family company run by a board of three directors who are husband, wife and son. There are no other managers within the organisation.

The son also owns another company with his wife and JJ is aware that he has been selling D Co's products to this company at prices below cost. This has caused the profit margin in D Co to fall considerably. The son has now asked JJ to alter the figures in the management accounts before signing them off as he would prefer to explain the transactions to his parents at a later date.

JJ is certain that the other directors know nothing about the sales and realises that disclosure of the situation will have long term implications for the future of D Co including JJ's job.

Which of the following courses of action appear reasonable for JJ at this stage?

Select **all** that apply.

A Alter the figures since a professional accountant in business should support the objectives established by their employer.

B Report the correct figures directly to the board of directors.

C Obtain advice on the best course of action from other managers within D Co.

D Seek legal advice.

E Follow the formal dispute resolution process within D Co.

F Ask the son to speak to his parents immediately since changing the figures is not possible.

4 Case study – Nike

Nike is one of the famous franchises in the world that sells sportswear for all ages. But is mostly famous for their athlete shoes and apparel and Nike is also one of the major manufacturers of sport equipment as well. The slogan for Nike is "Just Do It". Nike was founded in January 1962 in Oregon, United States by Philip Knight and Bill Bowerman. Nike has somewhere around 700 or more retail outlets spread all over the world, and has approximately 45 offices outside the United States. And it employs 30,000 people all over the world. Nike had a revenue excess of $16 billion in 2007. Nike's factories are mostly located in Asian countries like Pakistan, India, Malaysia, China, Indonesia, Philippines, Taiwan, Vietnam and Thailand.

The primary stakeholders of the company would be the shareholders, business partners, the employees, and the customers/ consumers. What the shareholders and the investors want from the company is that the company achieves its profits, the employees of the expect work satisfaction, pay along with good supervision and the customers are concerned with quality, safety and availability of services when they require it. And when any primary stakeholder group is not satisfied the organisation's progress becomes questionable.

The secondary stakeholders of the company would be the community. Most companies like Nike exist under a charter or licenses and operate within the limits of safety laws, environmental protection and other laws and regulations. The socially responsible organisations like Nike should consider the effect of their actions upon all stakeholders. What all of these stakeholders want from the company is that the company is ethically and socially responsible and when this secondary stakeholder group becomes dis-satisfied, the reputation of the company gets tarnished (for example, the debate of sweatshops tarnished the reputation of Nike).

Issues faced by Nike:

- Child labor and the sweat shop problem;
- Workers given a very low wage, and overtime in countries like Vietnam, China and Indonesia under a subcontract;
- Poor working conditions, squalid working conditions and forced labor in the factories that manufacture their products;
- Environmental damage done to society by air and water pollution, noise, and change in the climate due to pollution. (Stockdale & Crosby, 2004)

There are different kinds of guiding principles that can prevent Nike type scandals, and this is what the company did:

PR campaign

Nike decided to use a PR campaign so that it was able to repair its social image due to the sweatshop debate. The PR campaign covered the following actions:

Employment Practices

The management of Nike took a look at its employment practices; they made sure that the company was following the policies on recruitment, training, health, safety and welfare. The management of the company also oversaw their environmental practices – to make sure that the company follows procedures that are responsible in terms of waste disposal and avoidance and energy inputs.

Training Plan

They conducted and designed a training program for the employees. The management remembered that training and development programs are not universal solutions to every need of the company. Effective job designs, selection, placement and other activities of the HR department are also very important.

Assessing Performance

They set targets and identified performance measure standards. If performance is to be rated accurately, the performance of the company would require the management to assess each and every relevant performance dimension.

Ethical Responsibility

The management of Nike understood that ethical responsibility is needed within the company because it is the obligation of organisation's management to make decisions and take actions that will grow the welfare and interest of the society and the organisation. It would include activities and commitments that are related to human rights, governance and ethics, development, working conditions of the employees, community involvement, customer satisfaction, relations with the company's suppliers and customers and lastly respect for diverse cultures and different people.

5 Case study – BP

BP plc is one of the largest oil and alternative energy companies in the world. It has set targets with regard to reducing its CO2 emissions and the development of alternative sources of energy such as solar power. However, in recent years BP's environmental image has been tarnished. Whether BP has acted unethically is considered to be ambiguous by some.

British Petroleum plc developed their image considerably; altering the meaning of BP to mean 'Beyond Petroleum' and aiming to 'reduce … greenhouse gas emissions by 10%' (Bulkin, 2010) between 1990 and 2010, which they did successfully; signalling their intent to either aid the environment in their business practices or simply to cultivate a 'greener' image to ensure the ever more environmentally aware public will favour their products, and to capture the developing market for alternative energy. BP's ethical stand point appears to consider the broader responsibilities contributing to their businesses' decisions and policies. However it is necessary to established whether ethical decisions and Corporate Social Responsibility (CSR) are based upon intentions, goals, outcomes; or, a mixture of each.

BP have adopted a 'progressive approach to environmental protection'; setting targets and producing reports on their environmental development progress. The 'Ethical Conduct Policy' considers factors such as adhering to Human Rights regulations; ensuring that all operations are fair and legal, and dismissing those who act unlawfully as they did in 2006; zero tolerance of bribery or gifts as facilitation payments. These factors are demonstrated by the management in decisions, policies and actions. Moreover, pledging its name to the United Nations Global Compact (UNGC) and partnering the Red Cross's appeal for financial support; all demonstrate BP's commitment to being a ethically astute corporate citizen. Therefore, can it be argued that BP is an ethical company? Or can it be seen that these actions are simply the mask of an organisation whose only responsibility is to its shareholders and top management?

Many of BP's actions have, contrastingly, been regarded as extremely unethical. The Alaskan oil spills, Texas City refinery fire, treatment of Colombian farmers and the explosion in the Gulf of Mexico. Decisions were made, which ultimately lead to destructive consequences for many stakeholder groups. The complex ethical dilemmas facing BP are thus: it must be decided how to weight emphasis on different stakeholders and to what extent the immediate mistakes and unethical practices are allowable in pursuit of a better, more sustainable future; and, to what extent is it ethical to publicise the firm's ethics and CSR for the predominant purposes of profit maximisation.

It could be argued that BP should: adopt riskier strategies that result in higher returns; cut safety costs; and exploit small minorities. The results could provide a benefit for a great number of people over time. Adopting this view, FDI host nations, customers and shareholders would benefit most, leading to greater levels of investment and higher revenues. Thus, more investment can be made by BP to developing alternative energy sources creating a more sustainable future. So exploitation of, and accidents regarding, small numbers of employees, the environment, and local communities can all be seen as blips, even calculated casualties, in the pursuit of a better world.

However, environmental destruction and human deaths would widely be considered unethical. This contradicts the human rights of the employees. Therefore, there should be short-term operational decisions, such as ensuring that safety standards are appropriate for employees; rather than pursuing additional profits and hiding behind a mask of public relations. Viewed from this perspective, 'calculated casualties' don't provide the greatest amount of good; it simply highlights an unethical and ruthless pursuit of profits. BP's employees could be seen to act unethically as the immediate results of some decisions induce suffering and detrimental effects to the environment, employees and local communities. The firm's "green-washing" of its CSR to gain public approval of its practises and generate profits, could be considered unethical.

An alternative view of BP's ethical behaviour suggests that those who are in charge of safety should ensure that their job has been completed thoroughly. BP should not view the employees or environment as factors of production used to maximise profits for shareholders; suggesting that any reduction of safety is acting unethically and irresponsibly. Some say that BP's CSR and sustainability image are a marketing gimmick.

Thus, it can be seen that one view provides a moral standpoint for BP; looking to the future as it attempt to pioneer alternative energy sources; aiming to please the greatest number of people. However, another view demonstrates that BP acts selfishly to maximise profits quickly. Another view can be used to show that BP's decisions makers employ unethical practise. They don't just fail to consider all stakeholders, but consciously exploit many in order to increase efficiency and cut costs, often at the expense of safety.

However, traditional ethical theories should not be viewed as completed 'rules', but as contributing to a wider ethical understanding for decision making. BP's business actions are complex and have implications for all stakeholders. Senior management will often squeeze deadlines which force decision makers to 'cut corners'. Hence, an variety of ethical perspectives are needed to conclude whether actions that lead to the Texas City Fire, the Gulf of Mexico explosion and other events, were a result of conscious unethical decision making or unexpected and unfortunate casualties of good business practise in the pursuit of future global improvements. However, it could conversely be argued, that BP is simply a collection of human beings who have limited insight into the full consequences of their actions and thus, are justified in pursuing their own self-interests, regardless of other human's demands. Therefore, Interpretation of BP's CSR and ethical policy is ambiguously subjective and open to conflicting perspectives.

6 Conflicts within employing organisation

- The syllabus makes specific reference to the importance of exercising ethical principles in conducting and reporting on internal reviews.
- There may be times, however, when a professional accountant's responsibilities to an employing organisation and their professional obligations to comply with the fundamental principles are in conflict.
- Ordinarily, a professional accountant in business should support the legitimate and ethical objectives established by the employer and the rules and procedures drawn up in support of those objectives.
- Nevertheless, where compliance with the fundamental principles is threatened, a professional accountant in business must consider a response to the circumstances.

Pressures that may be faced

A professional accountant may be put under pressure by managers, directors or other individuals to:

- act contrary to law or regulation
- act contrary to technical or professional standards
- facilitate unethical or illegal earnings management strategies
- lie to, or otherwise intentionally mislead (including misleading by remaining silent) others, in particular:
  - the auditors of the employing organisation
  - regulators
- Issue, or otherwise be associated with, a financial or non-financial report that materially misrepresents the facts, including statements in connection with, for example:
  - the financial statements
  - tax compliance
  - legal compliance
  - reports required by securities regulators.

Safeguards to be applied

The significance of threats arising from such pressures, such as intimidation threats, should be evaluated. If they are other than clearly insignificant, safeguards should be considered and applied as necessary to eliminate them or reduce them to an acceptable level. Such safeguards may include:

- obtaining advice where appropriate from within the employing organisation, an independent professional advisor or a relevant professional body.
- the existence of a formal dispute resolution process within the employing organisation.
- seeking legal advice.

7 Ethical budget setting

Conflicting objectives

Imagine you are a manager and you help upper management establish the master budget (the planning phase). Furthermore, you are evaluated based on achieving budgeted profit on a quarterly basis (the control phase). You will receive a $10,000 quarterly bonus, in addition to your basic salary, if you meet or exceed budgeted profit. There is an inherent conflict between the planning and control phases of this process. You are helping the company plan, but you also want to be sure budgeted profit is as low as possible so you can get the $10,000 bonus.

Establishing a sales and profit budget that is considerably lower than what is likely to happen causes problems for the entire organisation. Production may be short of materials and labour, causing inefficiencies in the production process. Selling and administrative support may be lacking due to underestimating sales. Customers will not be satisfied if they must wait for the product. The dilemma you face as a manager in this situation is whether to do what is best for you (set a low profit estimate to earn the bonus) or do what is best for the company (estimate accurately so the budget reflects true sales and production needs).

Organisations must recognize this conflict and have processes in place to ensure both the interests of individual employees and the interests of the organisation as a whole are served. For example, employees can be rewarded not just for meeting goals but also for providing accurate estimates. Perhaps a long-term share option incentive system would provide motivation to do what is best for the organisation. Whatever incentive system is implemented, organisations must promote honest employee input and be aware of fraudulent reporting to achieve financial targets.

Undue pressure

Imagine another ethical scenario – your manager is pressurising you to meet the budget. This could involve you and your staff working overtime that you don't want (and are not contracted) to do, through to 'window dressing' of the actual results by delaying or pulling forward costs and revenues in to the required time period to meet the budget.

You know that your manager will not be happy if you don't meet the budget. What should you do?

There are two main courses of action available to you:

You could do as you are told. This would keep your manager happy and probably make your life easier. It may enable you and your manager to earn a reward or bonus. However, if you lose the trust of your staff or effectively mislead higher management by lying as to the state of the budget then this is not good for you or the company. It is likely to become apparent in the near future and it is an unethical course of action.

You could work as hard as you can to meet the budget but if it doesn't work out, then take the wrath of your manager. This is probably the most ethical course of action, but it may make your job harder in the future. Your manager might be angry with you and make your future working life difficult. However, there are courses of action open to you. You could face your manager and state that he or she is being unreasonable, and unethical in their request. If this falls on deaf ears and your position becomes untenable, then you might escalate your concerns to a higher level of management, human resources or perhaps the audit committee. They should take your issue seriously and investigate the managers actions. He or she, if they are found to have exerted undue pressure on you, should be reprimanded and probably investigated further since their actions may not have been a 'one-off' incident. Their 'moral compass' may be questionable and at this point high level management should ask whether they want such a manager working for their company. However, in some cases, high level management may also agree with the manager 'pushing' to meet targets. At this point you should question whether you want to work for such an organisation. CIMA's code of ethics suggests that resignation may be your final option.

Test your understanding 11

CIMA's code of ethics identifies five categories of common threat. Which of the following are part of the five threats: (Select all that apply.)

A Self interest

B Self review

C Familiarity

D Confidentiality

E Advocacy

Test your understanding 12

When you form a close relationship with others so that your professional judgement becomes compromised this is considered to be the threat of:

A Self review

B Self interest

C Familiarity

D Advocacy

Test your understanding 13

Safeguards against ethical threats might include: (Select all that apply.)

A Intimidation

B Disciplinary actions

C Disclosure of confidential information

D Training

E Internal control systems

F Inducements

Test your understanding 14 – Private hospital (Case study)

Scenario

A private hospital has a canteen that provides staff and visitors with subsidised meals and refreshments. The canteen's selling prices are supposed to cover running costs, so that there is no net cost to the hospital. Over the past eighteen months the canteen has been reporting losses that have been increasing steadily despite monthly sales remaining constant. The cost of purchases has grown substantially for no apparent reason. The purchasing of supplies and the choice of suppliers is the sole responsibility of the Canteen Manager. The current Canteen Manager has been in post for almost two years.

Trigger

The hospital's Chief Executive asked the Head of Internal Audit to investigate why the canteen was making losses and a thorough investigation was conducted under the supervision of F, an experienced auditor and qualified accountant. The internal audit team discovered that the losses started shortly after the Canteen Manager changed suppliers. F compared the invoiced prices charged by the new supplier with those charged by the former supplier and discovered that the new supplier was significantly more expensive.

F interviewed the Canteen Manager, who claimed that he had changed suppliers because the new supplier was more reliable and provided higher quality products. F was suspicious and contacted a number of alternative suppliers. None of the potential suppliers whom F contacted would have charged as much as the canteen was paying for basic commodities such as rice and potatoes. Furthermore, the canteen's invoices showed that it was paying far more than the normal market price for branded goods, such as crisps and chocolate bars.

F was in the Canteen Manager's office one lunch time. He saw a laptop computer open at an email to the supplier and investigated further. The Canteen Manager had been using a personal email account to email the owner of the supplier on a daily basis. The emails revealed that:

- the owner had been inflating the selling prices of all goods sold to the hospital by 20%;
- the Canteen Manager passed these inflated invoices for payment; and
- the owner then paid half of the 20% that had been overcharged to the Canteen Manager in cash.

F confiscated the laptop, which was the Canteen Manager's personal property, and submitted it, along with a full report, to the Head of Internal Audit.

Two weeks later, F was asked to meet with the hospital's Chief Executive. The hospital's directors had discussed the report carefully and had interviewed the Canteen Manager and decided that they did not wish to refer the matter to the police. The Canteen Manager had been accompanied by a lawyer, who stated that the Canteen Manager denied all charges of fraud and pointed out that there was very little evidence to support F's accusations. F could have easily falsified the emails on the laptop and the owner of the food supplier had supplied the lawyer with a statement that no payments had been made to the Canteen Manager. The Chief Executive had agreed that the hospital would return the Canteen Manager's laptop and would make him a substantial payment in return for his agreement to resign quietly. The Chief Executive had also promised that the Canteen Manager would receive a positive reference. F was asked to destroy any remaining notes and documents relating to this investigation and to remain silent, not discussing the case with anyone either within the hospital or any third parties.

Task

(a) Critically evaluate the decision by the Chief Executive to pay the Canteen Manager to resign quietly.

(b) Advise F on the ethical issues arising from destroying his notes and maintaining silence on this investigation.

(30 minutes)

Test your understanding 15 – M mobile telephones (Case study)

Scenario

M is the leading retailer of mobile telephones in its home country. The company has almost 100 branches, with at least one branch in every major town and city. Some branches are located within walking distance of one another.

M has a highly aggressive management team. It views sales growth as the key to the company's continuing success. It believes that increasing their share of the retail market will enable M to negotiate large discounts from manufacturers and network providers. It also creates economies of scale in the advertising and promotion of the company and its services.

Two years ago the directors abandoned traditional budgeting and target setting. They decided that budgets did not necessarily give branch staff a sufficient incentive to maximise sales because they tended to work towards achieving but not surpassing sales targets. They introduced a new management control system with the following features:

- Shop sales are recorded using electronic point of sales (EPOS) cash registers that are linked to head office. Every sale indicates the branch and the member of staff responsible for the sale. These transactions are recorded in real time during the course of the day.
- A terminal in every shop lists a running total of that shop's sales for the day, analysed between each member of sales staff. The terminal also indicates the shop's ranking for the day relative to all of M's other shops.
- Every shop manager must be at work at least an hour before the shop opens. During that hour the manager receives a telephone call from the regional sales manager to discuss the previous day's sales and likely sales during the day ahead.
- Each shop manager is permitted considerable freedom to introduce special offers and promotions, subject to achieving an acceptable margin on each sale made.
- At the end of every week the manager and staff of the ten shops with the highest sales are given a substantial bonus. The manager and staff at the ten shops with the poorest sales are given one week's notice to improve or they face being moved to other shops or even dismissal.
- Sales have grown rapidly since this system was introduced, although the rate of growth has been declining recently.

The Director of Human Resources has investigated staff absenteeism and turnover and has discovered that many of M's branch managers and sales staff have been with the company for several years. They seem to thrive in the competitive environment and the company pays staff with good sales records a substantial salary compared with other retailers. M also suffers a high staff turnover every year and some members of staff are frequently absent for health reasons, with their doctors certifying them as ill due to stress-related conditions.

Trigger

M's Chief Accountant is concerned that the company's management accounting systems are unethical and she has provided the board with a copy of CIMA's Code of Professional Ethics.

Task

Write a letter to the Board advising on the ethical implications of their approach to personnel management.

(20 minutes)

Test your understanding 16 – Grove council (Case study)

Scenario

Grove Council is the local government authority responsible for the running of public services in a district of approximately 200 square miles and with a population of over 300,000. The Grove district comprises a mixture of towns, villages and rural areas.

The Council employs approximately 13,000 staff in a wide variety of occupations. The Council is responsible for the maintenance of the entire public infrastructure in its area of responsibility, including the roads and sewerage systems. The Council also manages education and care for vulnerable residents such as the elderly and infirm. The Council has a divisional structure, with divisions taking responsibility for specific matters such as education, roads and so on throughout the Grove district.

Employment law requires that every employer, including Grove Council, must maintain a register of all workplace injuries sustained by employees. There is no precise definition of a reportable injury, but Council guidelines indicate that anything that requires a dressing, such as a bandage or sticking plaster, must be reported as minor injuries. Injuries are classified as "serious" if they require the victim to be absent from work for more than three days and "severe" if they require admission to hospital or involve a fatality.

Trigger

The latest injury statistics show that there were 150 injuries during the last year, of which 20 were serious injuries and 3 were severe. The Council's Director of Operations is satisfied with these figures because the number of injuries is no worse than in previous years. He holds the view that such figures are to be expected given the diverse range of jobs, many of which are risky, throughout the Council. The Chief Executive of the Council does not share these views: he thinks that the Council should try to prevent all injuries by eliminating accidents in the workplace.

The Chief Executive asked Grove Council's internal audit department to review the systems for reporting injuries. As part of the response to that request a CIMA qualified member of internal audit was sent to investigate the repair depot that maintains the Council's fleet of vehicles. The depot employs a team of over 40 mechanics and is equipped with a full range of welding and lifting equipment.

The depot's injury register had only two entries for the year prior to the internal audit visit. Both injuries were severe and each involved an injury that required an ambulance to be called and an employee to be admitted to hospital.

On enquiry, several of the mechanics explained that the small number of reports is due to the depot manager refusing to record injuries unless they are either serious or severe. Several of the depot mechanics are trained in first aid and no records are kept of any injuries that they treat. All of the mechanics refused to put these allegations in writing for the internal auditor.

The internal auditor asked the Head of Internal Audit to send an urgent report to the Chief Executive, but the Head of Internal Audit refused to do so on the grounds that there was insufficient evidence of manipulation. The Head of Internal Audit threatened to suspend the internal auditor if she repeated these allegations to anyone else either inside or outside of the Council. The internal auditor is dissatisfied with the Head of Internal Audit's response and is considering whether to take the matter further.

Task

As the internal auditor prepare briefing notes, which may be used in a meeting with the Audit Committee, covering:

(a) An analysis of the ethical dilemma faced by the internal auditor.

(b) The recommended course of action that the internal auditor should take if she is unable to persuade the Head of Internal Audit to draw these allegations of under-reporting of injuries to the attention of the senior management of Grove Council.

(30 minutes)

Test your understanding 17 – SPQ (Integration)

As a CIMA member, you have recently been appointed as the Head of Internal Audit for SPQ, a multinational listed company that carries out a large volume of Internet sales to customers who place their orders using their home or work computers. You report to the Chief Executive although you work closely with the Finance Director. You have direct access to the Chair of the audit committee whenever you consider it necessary.

One of your internal audit teams has been conducting a review of IT security for a system which has been in operation for 18 months and which is integral to Internet sales. The audit was included in the internal audit plan following a request by the Chief Accountant. Sample testing by the internal audit team has revealed several transactions over the last three months which have raised concerns about possible hacking or fraudulent access to the customer/order database. Each of these transactions has disappeared from the database after deliveries have been made but without sales being recorded or funds collected from the customer. Each of the identified transactions was for a different customer and there seems to be no relationship between any of the transactions.

You have received the draft report from the internal audit manager responsible for this audit which suggests serious weaknesses in the design of the system. You have discussed this informally with senior managers who have told you that such a report will be politically very unpopular with the Chief Executive as he was significantly involved in the design and approval of the new system and insisted it be implemented earlier than the IT department considered was advisable. No post-implementation review of the system has taken place.

You have been informally advised by several senior managers to lessen the criticism and work with the IT department to correct any deficiencies within the system and to produce a report to the Audit Committee that is less critical and merely identifies the need for some improvement. They suggest that these actions would avoid criticism of the Chief Executive by the Board of SPQ.

Required:

Explain the ethical principles that you should apply as the Head of Internal Audit for SPQ when reporting the results of this internal review and how any ethical conflicts should be resolved.

(20 minutes)

Test your understanding 18 – Erasmus (Integration)

You are the newly-appointed financial controller of Erasmus, a fully owned subsidiary of the Think Group. The following matters have come to your attention:

(1) Your assistant, a newly-qualified Management Accountant, is heavily in debt to a junior member of the finance staff, who has a considerable amount of personal wealth in spite of his fairly junior position in the company.

(2) The CEO of the company was in the habit of making accounting adjustments to the financial statements prepared by the finance director in order to 'smooth out variances' if actual performance was not going to plan.

(3) A member of your department, another Management Accountant, recently made significant errors in completing the sales tax returns to the tax authorities, which resulted in a fine and interest charges for an underpayment of the sales tax liability.

Required:

Discuss how you would deal with each of these three problems in order to bring about an improvement in the ethical standards in the systems of management. Indicate any problems you might expect to arise when you attempt to bring about change.

(15 minutes)

Test your understanding 19 – Five ethical situations (Integration)

In all of the ethical situations below, the people involved are qualified members of CIMA.

- A applies for a job and enhances his CV by indicating he obtained first time passes in all his examinations, although he actually failed three exams at the first attempt.
- B is the management accountant in C Ltd. B is paid a bonus based on the profits of C Ltd. During accounts preparation B notices an error in the inventory calculation which has the effect of overstating profits. B decides to take no action as this would decrease the bonus payable.
- D is responsible for the purchase of computer equipment in E Ltd. Quotes from three suppliers have been received for installation of new hardware; one supplier, F Co, has promised a 10% discount payable to D if their quote is accepted.
- G is preparing the management accounts in H Ltd. Part of the information presented to him indicates that H Ltd entered into an illegal agreement with I Ltd to fix price increases in the goods H and I supply. H and I together supply 90% of the total market. The price setting enabled H and I to obtain higher than expected profits for their sales.
- J is preparing the management accounts for K Ltd. L, the senior management accountant, has instructed J to omit the negative overhead variance from the accounts on the grounds that they show an 'unacceptable loss' with the inclusion of the variance.

Required:

(a) Explain how professional codes of ethics address possible conflicts of interest facing accountants.

(15 minutes)

(b) For each of the situations above:

(i) Identify and explain the ethical threat to the accountant.

(ii) Discuss the ethical safeguards available to overcome that threat.

(30 minutes)

8 Chapter summary

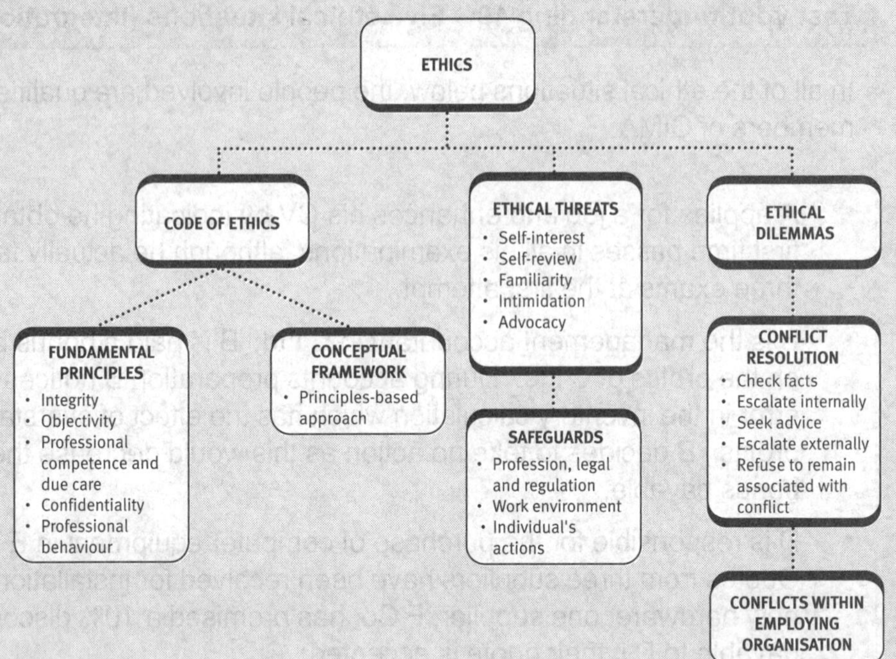

Test your understanding answers

Test your understanding 1

The correct answers are B, C and D – The fundamental principles are integrity, objectivity, professional competence and due care, professional behaviour and CONFIDENTIALITY (not communication).

Test your understanding 2

The correct answer is D – By definition.

Test your understanding 3

The correct answer is A – By definition.

Test your understanding 4

C

Allowing a part-qualified colleague to complete the work at home exposes the firm to a high risk that the work will be rushed and not up to the quality expected.

Test your understanding 5

A, B and E

- Option A – Integrity implies fair dealing and truthfulness. L would not be telling the truth if she provided the reference.
- Option B – L's objectivity is likely to be threatened anyway given she is a personal friend of the client.
- Option C – There is nothing to suggest L is compromising her duty to maintain her skills.
- Option D – The client is clearly giving L permission to contact the bank.
- Option E – Giving a misleading reference would discredit the accountancy profession if knowledge of it became public.

Test your understanding 6

A

John can benefit directly from any manipulation or questionable judgements he makes concerning the accounts.

Test your understanding 7

A and D

- Option A – Potential customers may see B's products as less safe as a result of the issue.
- Option B – Unlikely given B Company's risk assessment.
- Option C – As option 2 above.
- Option D – A recall is more ethical since, if successful, it will prevent injury completely.

Test your understanding 8

A and B

- Option A: The board has a fiduciary responsibility to its employees. It could be argued this responsibility is more important than ever when employees are vulnerable – for example in very poor countries.
- Option B: If it is no longer safe to mine R33, the communities are indeed under threat since the mining is their main source of funds.
- Option C: The board of D has a duty to set a suitable 'tone from the top' and a high level commitment to internal controls and risk management. They must conduct regular risk assessments and would be unable to ignore the findings of the report.
- Option D: The poorest nations are unlikely to have detailed employment laws with regards to safety.
- Option E: See Option C above.

Test your understanding 9

The correct answer is A – The correct order of events is to firstly check the facts. Then once you are sure of the facts to escalate internally. If the issue cannot be resolved internally then you should escalate it externally e.g. call CIMA. Finally if the ethical issue continues you should dissociate with the conflict i.e. possibly resign.

Test your understanding 10

B, D and F

- Option A: This is not appropriate since the employer's objectives are fraudulent.
- Option B: This is a reasonable course of action although it will cause upset.
- Option C: There are no other managers in D Co.
- Option D: This is a reasonable, although expensive course of action.
- Option E: D Co is a small, family-run business, which is unlikely to have a formal dispute resolution process.
- Option F: This is the most immediately practical although may not get results since the son may refuse to comply.

Test your understanding 11

The correct answers are A, B, C and E – The five ethical threats are self-interest, self review, advocacy, intimidation and familiarity.

Test your understanding 12

The correct answer is C – By definition.

Test your understanding 13

The correct answers are B, D and E – Training, disciplinary actions and internal control systems should help to safeguard against ethical threats.

Intimidation, inducements and disclosure of confidential information may cause ethical issues.

Test your understanding 14 – Private hospital (Case study)

(a) It would be unacceptable for the Chief Executive to make this arrangement in order to protect the reputations of the hospital's senior management. If the public becomes aware of the fraud then the fact that the senior management team had not detected it sooner could lead to criticism of the hospital's governance arrangements.

The Chief Executive may have been acting in the best interests of the hospital. Under the circumstances, it would have been necessary to have suspended the manager from duty on full pay until the allegations could be properly investigated. It would almost certainly have been impossible for this investigation to reach a satisfactory conclusion and so the suspension would have been prolonged and expensive. Paying the manager to leave made it possible to restrict the cost of the settlement to the agreed sum.

The hospital would also have been unable to appoint a replacement Canteen Manager while the investigation was still in progress. The payment will leave the post vacant and so a new appointment can be made to this important role. may be demotivated if they discover that the control system had broken down in this way and that a major fraud had been committed. Paying the manager to leave quietly will enable the directors to maintain the impression that the control environment is functioning.

The payment will, of course, come from funds that had been intended to treat patients. Even if the payment is justified as the least expensive resolution of this problem, it is undesirable for hospital resources to be spent in this way.

(b) Qualified accountants are generally subject to ethical codes that are almost identical to CIMA's Code of Ethics for Professional Accountants. That code applies within the company and to contact with third parties. Thus, F is subject to a formal duty to respect the confidence of the hospital and not divulge this arrangement to anybody else, either within the hospital or outside of it.

This duty of confidence does not necessarily apply in every case. F has a wider duty to the stakeholders involved and so society in general. F could breach this duty of confidence if doing so was in the public interest. F should consider that possibility, although it seems unlikely to be the case given the facts. The amounts stolen from the hospital are unlikely to be sufficiently large as to warrant breach of confidence. On the other hand, the fact that the manager will receive a positive reference could mean that he will be able to repeat the fraud, which could create some justification for F to report the matter to, say, the police.

F is obliged to act with integrity. It could be argued that F has already discharged his responsibility by reporting the suspected fraud to the head of internal audit, who has clearly reported the matter to senior management. It appears that the management team has reached a decision that is in the hospital's best interests and so there is no real need for F to take any further action.

Test your understanding 15 – M mobile telephones (Case study)

Address

Date

Dear Board of Directors,

Re: Ethical principles

CIMA's Code of Professional Ethics states that a professional accountant is required to comply with five fundamental principles.

Integrity

A person should be straightforward and honest in all professional and business relationships.

Objectivity

A person should not allow bias, conflict of interest or undue influence of others to override professional or business judgements.

Professional competence and due care

A person has a continuing duty to maintain professional knowledge and skill at the level required to ensure that an employer or customer receives a competent professional service.

Confidentiality

A person should respect the confidentiality of information acquired as a result of professional relationships and should not disclose any such information to third parties without proper authority.

Professional behaviour

A person should comply with relevant laws and regulations and should avoid any action that discredits the company. Not all of M's directors will be a professional accountant but the code of ethics will still be appropriate to a professional company such as M and its directors. The Director of Human Resources is concerned that M has a high staff turnover, linked to the high absence rate due to 'stress related conditions' at M. The highly competitive environment at M is being blamed for this.

Sales have grown rapidly although the rate is now slowing. It is possible that in the past sales staff have been adopting an aggressive sales technique which only works once with customers, since they are not pleased with their purchase and don't return to make another. This is a short-sighted sales technique, where sales growth will be high at first, but then fewer repeat purchases are made and sales staff struggle to meet their objectives in the future.

Staff will become very worried about the implications of failing to meet the sales objectives if they think that they have only a week to correct their actions, or face being moved to another shop or dismissed. Moving to another shop may be inconvenient for their home life, and dismissal would be worrying in that they may not be able to find another job quickly, becoming unable to provide for any family they may have.

If moving to another store is seen as a threat by staff then this is unethical, since professional staff and companies do not use threats to incentivise their staff.

The employer has a responsibility to treat information about their employees in confidence. If the staff's results are being published, anyone can identify under-performers, which breaches confidentiality.

The environment at M may suit certain individuals who thrive on competition, but for others it will be very stressful if they are not natural sales people and they have dependents that rely on their salary. From a director's point of view, working a member of staff so hard that they become ill is unethical.

Sales staff may be driven to 'hard-sell' products to customers, and may even tell un-truths to secure a sale. This goes against the principle of integrity stated in the code of ethics. M's reputation will become tarnished if it becomes public knowledge that their employees mislead customers in to buying a product that is not suitable for them.

Similarly rewarding a member of staff for high sales that may not have been ethically made will reflect badly on the management of M.

New staff members are unlikely to meet the sales growth objective straight away. They will be unfamiliar with some of the products and could misadvise a customer. They should be allowed a period of settling in. The new staff are possibly the major part of the high staff turnover at M.

The high absenteeism and staff turnover is not good for M as it is very costly to pay someone to be off work or to frequently recruit new members of staff.

New staff will learn sales techniques from the more established staff members, which may not always be ethical sales methods. The element of competition may lead them to lack objectivity in their sales dealings. Older sales staff should not have undue influence over the new staff, and the new staff should be encouraged to have their own ethical principles.

I hope this clarifies any queries you had. Should you require any further information, please do not hesitate to ask.

Yours sincerely,

A.N. Accountant

Test your understanding 16 – Grove council (Case study)

Briefing notes

To: Audit Committee

From: Internal auditor

Date: Today

Subject: Ethics

(a) The internal auditor has reason to believe that records are being falsified that could threaten the health and safety of staff at the depot. If members of staff stop reporting minor cuts and bruises then the Council will not be aware of risks that could result in a more serious accident, such as a safety issue with a particular machine. That could lead to avoidable accidents occurring because the need for repairs or modifications was not apparent. Remaining silent about these allegations could be viewed as a breach of the requirement to apply professional competence and due care.

Bypassing the Head of Internal Audit by reporting directly to the Chief Executive or another senior officer would breach the duty to demonstrate professional behaviour. She is subordinate to her head of department and he has ruled that the matter is to be taken no further. Any report that cannot be substantiated could lead to a waste of time and effort and could undermine the credibility of internal audit.

Any report to a third party would breach the internal auditor's duty of confidence. As an employee, she has a duty not to divulge any information to a third party. The fact that she is a CIMA member, as so bound by CIMA's Code of Ethics for Professional Accountants, makes that duty even more significant.

(b) The internal auditor should consider whether she has reason to believe that any inaction on her part is likely to lead to a serious risk to life or health. If the records that are being suppressed relate to trivial cuts and bruises and are unlikely to leave staff exposed to more serious risks then she should almost certainly do nothing further.

It would be possible for her to approach the depot manager and seek an explanation as to whether these allegations are true. If the manager makes a genuine commitment to report honestly then the problem will be resolved.

If her review of the facts suggests that the depot's reporting practices are significantly increasing the risk of severe injuries then she should take matters further. The depot had two out of only three severe injuries for the Council as a whole. Failing to act on such information could be viewed as criminal negligence on her part.

Any report should be made in the first instance to an appropriate senior Council officer, possibly addressed to the Chief Executive in the first instance. She should only report to a third party, such as the Health and Safety Executive, if the risk is high enough to justify the breach of confidence and the internal report is ignored.

If she does bypass her Head of Internal Audit then she may feel it necessary to resign.

Test your understanding 17 – SPQ (Integration)

The fundamental principles that relate to the work of accountants as internal auditors are integrity (acting honestly and avoiding misleading statements); objectivity (impartiality and freedom from conflicts of interest); professional competence and due care; confidentiality; professional behaviour and the avoidance of conduct that might bring discredit to CIMA; and technical competence (the presentation of information fully, honestly and professionally).

Most of these principles apply in the present case. If the evidence justifies it, integrity and objectivity require that it be brought to the audit committee's attention. However, professional and technical competence requires that the Head of Internal Audit be confident in the audit findings before doing so.

CIMA's Ethical Guidelines describe the process for resolving ethical conflicts. Accountants working in organisations may encounter situations which give rise to conflicts of interest, ranging from fraud and illegal activities to relatively minor situations. An ethical conflict is not the same as an honest difference of opinion.

CIMA members should be constantly conscious of, and be alert to factors which give rise to conflicts of interest. In the present case, the ethical conflict is the real or perceived pressure placed on the Head of Internal Audit not to embarrass the Chief Executive. There is also the question of divided loyalty to the Chief Executive, to the audit committee, and to the Head of Internal Audit's professional responsibilities as a CIMA member.

Although it has not been suggested to the Head of Internal Audit that the matter not be reported, there is a suggestion that the report be softened and that work carry on behind the scenes to improve the system.

However, it is important that a draft report be produced and submitted for comment before it is sent to the audit committee. This presents the opportunity for other views to be aired. One course of action may be to discuss the matter with the Finance Director to determine his/her view and with the Chief Executive to determine that person's reactions to the draft audit report.

When faced with ethical conflicts, members should:

- Follow the organisation's grievance procedure.
- Discuss the matter with the member's superior and successive levels of management, always with the member's superior's knowledge (unless that person is involved).

Discussion with an objective adviser or the professional body may be useful to clarify the issues involved and alternative courses of action that are available, without breaching any duty of confidentiality. Throughout, the member should maintain a detailed record of the problem and the steps taken to resolve it.

If an ethical conflict still exists after fully exhausting all levels of internal review, the member may have no recourse on significant matters other than to resign and report the matter to the organisation. Except when seeking advice from CIMA or when legally required to do so, communication of information regarding the problem to persons outside the employing organisation is not considered appropriate.

Test your understanding 18 – Erasmus (Integration)

(1) **Indebtedness of the assistant to the junior staff member**

This situation might call into question the independence and objectivity of the assistant in carrying out his work within the finance function. It could also threaten my own position, if it were generally known that a member of my staff is receiving financial assistance from a junior colleague.

The position of the assistant is difficult, because he is presumably unable to repay the debt immediately, and he might be unaware of the fact that he has put the internal audit section into an embarrassing position.

I should discuss the position with him, and explain the problem that it has caused. He should be reminded of CIMA's ethical guidelines about the need to maintain objectivity and independence. I should find out how quickly he plans to repay the debt. If this will not happen quickly, I should ask whether he might be able to obtain a loan to repay the debt. (The company might possibly be willing to provide a loan for such a purpose.)

If the assistant is unable to agree to my suggestion, I should have to consider recommending that he should be moved to another position where his independence and objectivity would not be compromised.

(2) **CEO's accounting adjustments**

It is my responsibility to provide the CEO with financial information that is competently and accurately prepared. The CEO presumably shares the financial information with his board colleagues and the board of the parent company. I need to consider whether any adjustments made by the CEO to financial statements that I prepare will bring my integrity into question.

I should resist attempts by the CEO to amend financial results to make them seem better than they actually are. It would be particularly worrying if figures have been altered in order to improve the financial rewards for the CEO. On the other hand, some prudent adjustments to the figures might be justifiable.

I should discuss the situation with the finance director and the CEO, and establish whether the CEO intends to continue altering financial statements in the future, and his reasons for doing so. If the situation cannot be resolved, I should have to consider my position within the company. I should not remain in a position where I know that my integrity is being compromised.

(3) **Errors in the sales tax returns**

CIMA members have an ethical duty to carry out their work with professional competence. Technical competence means that the staff in my department should understand the necessary rules in relation to the tax work they do. Ignorance is no excuse for mistakes, and a repetition of the errors – and the fine – must be avoided.

I need to ensure that the staff who carry out specialist tasks are competent to carry them out. Training should be provided if required. Suitable instructions and guidance should also be available for reference.

Test your understanding 19 – Five ethical situations (Integration)

(a) There are a number of possible threats to fundamental ethical principles which lead to conflicts of interest affecting accountants in their work. Professional codes of ethics aim to enable the accountant to understand how to resolve these conflicts of interest.

Conflicts of interest and their resolution are explained in the conceptual framework to the code of ethics. A framework is needed because it is impossible to define every situation where threats to fundamental principles may occur or the mitigating action required. Different assignments may also create different threats and mitigating actions – again it is not possible to detail all the assignments an accountant undertakes. The framework helps to identify threats – using the fundamental ethical principles as guidance. This approach is preferable to following a set of rules which may not be applicable in a particular case.

Once a material threat has been identified, mitigating activities will be performed to ensure that compliance with fundamental principles is not compromised.

Where conflicts arise in the application of fundamental principles, the code of ethics provides guidance on how to resolve the conflict.

The conceptual framework:

- provides an initial set of assumptions, values and definitions which are agreed upon and shared by all those subject to the framework.
- is stated in relatively general terms so it is easy to understand and communicate.
- recognises that ethical issues may have no 'correct' answer.
- provides the generalised guidelines and principles to apply to any situation.

(b) **Situation 1**

Ethical threat – dishonesty

Accountants need to be honest in stating their level of expertise – and not mislead employers by implying they have more expertise than they actually possess. In this situation, A is implying he was better at studying for his exams than his actual exam success rate. This may make the potential employer view A more favourably, or enable A to meet a recruitment criteria of 'first time passes only' for success in obtaining the job.

Ethical safeguards

It is difficult to stop provision of incorrect information in this instance. However, A should be following the fundamental ethical principle of integrity in applying for the job. Alternatively, the potential employer could ask all applicants to confirm that information provided is accurate as a condition of employment. Any errors or omissions found later could act as initial grounds for disciplinary action.

Situation 2

Ethical threat – overstatement of profits and salary

B's bonus is determined by the same accounts that B is working on. The threat is that B will overstate profits in some way to ensure that the bonus payable is as high as possible. Again, accountants should act with integrity and honestly, although these ideals conflict in this case with B's remuneration.

Ethical safeguards

The main safeguard will be to ensure that someone other than B determines the amount of B's bonus (and checks the accounts produced) – or that the bonus is not linked to the accounts that B is preparing. This removes the conflict of interest.

Situation 3

Ethical threat – receipt of bribes/gifts

D stands to gain 10% of a contract price by accepting the quote from F rather than another company. This means D's objectivity may be breached because he will be favourably impressed by the quote from F. There is also an issue of confidentiality because presumably D will want to keep the payment 'secret' from E Ltd so his employer does not know of the inducement.

Ethical safeguard

From D's point-of-view, the obvious ethical safeguard is not to accept the bribe. This removes the objectivity issue leaving D free to choose the best system rather than the one with the most financial advantage to him. Alternatively, D can inform the senior management and/or board of E Ltd, provide the relevant information on the three quotes, and let the board make the final decision. Should the board choose F then again D should not accept the bribe.

Situation 4

Ethical threat – price fixing

In most situations, G would keep the affairs of his client confidential, and would be acting with integrity in taking this action. However, there is a conflict as H and I appear to have been acting illegally; increasing their profits at the expense of their customers. G can either choose to keep quiet about the situation or disclose the information to relevant third parties, effectively 'blowing the whistle' on H and I.

Ethical safeguards

G could report to the ethics committee or audit committee in H, should the company have either of these committees. As long as some appropriate action was taken, then this relieves G from external reporting obligations. External disclosure should only be made after taking into account various issues such as the gravity of the matter, the number of people affected and the likelihood of repetition. As many people are affected and repetition seems likely then external disclosure is likely to be appropriate.

Situation 5

Ethical threat – incorrect financial information

Accountants need to be able to prepare information honestly and with objectivity. However, in this situation, J is being pressured into producing information which will be incorrect, simply to show K Ltd in a better light. The instruction provides a conflict with J's integrity because he wants to follow the instructions of L but may not be able to do so because this would be dishonest.

Ethical safeguards

J needs to consult with other people apart from L in an attempt to determine the correct course of action. J can consult with any committee charged with governance (e.g. the audit committee or ethics committee) or if necessary take advice from his professional body. If after these discussions, the situation cannot be resolved, J may have to consider resignation.

Situation 4

Ethical threat – wrongdoing

In most situations, G would keep the affairs of his client confidential and would be acting with integrity in this action. However, there is a conflict as H and I appear to have been acting illegally in order to boost their profits at the expense of their customers. G can either choose to take no action about the situation or disclose the information to relevant third parties, effectively 'blowing the whistle' on H and I.

Ethical safeguards

G should report to the ethics committee/audit committee in H, should the company have either of these committees. As long as some appropriate action is taken, then this relieves G from external reporting obligations. External disclosure should only be made after taking into account various factors such as the gravity of the matter, the number of people affected and the likelihood of repetition. As many people are affected and repetition seems likely then external disclosure is likely to be appropriate.

Situation 5

Ethical threat – incorrect financial information

Accountants need to be able to present information honestly and with objectivity. However, in this situation, J is being pressured into producing information which will be incorrect, simply to show K Ltd in a better light. The instruction provides a conflict with J's integrity because he wants to follow the instructions of K but may not be able to do so because this would be dishonest.

Ethical safeguards

J needs to consult with other people apart from K in an attempt to determine the correct course of action. These could include the committee charged with governance (e.g. the audit committee or ethics committee) or the relevant ethics advice from J's professional body. If after these discussions the situation cannot be resolved, J may have to consider resignation.

hapter

9

Corporate governance

Chapter learning objectives

Lead	**Component**
B3. Evaluate the risks associated with corporate governance.	(a) Evaluate the risks associated with poor governance structures.

Indicative syllabus content

- The separation of the roles of CEO and Chairman.
- The role of Non-Executive Directors.
- The roles of Audit Committee, Remuneration Committee, Risk Committee and Nominations Committee.
- Directors' remuneration.
- The agency implications of salaries, bonuses, performance-related pay, executive share options and benefits in kind.

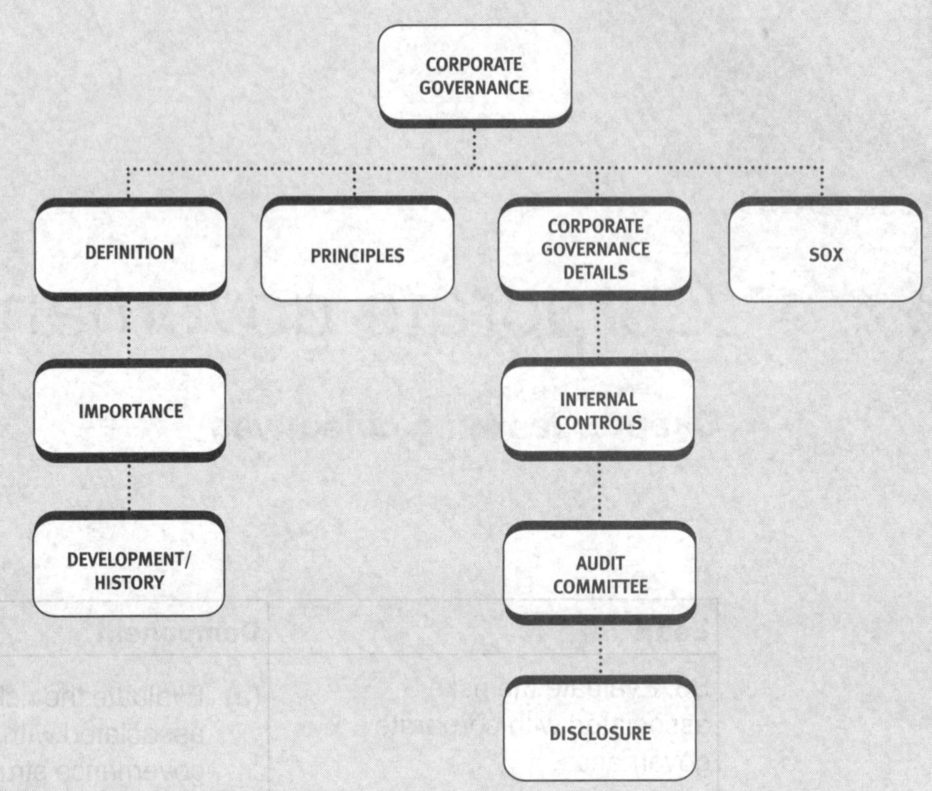

1 What is corporate governance?

Corporate governance has been defined in many different ways, but generally it can be described as:

'the system by which companies are directed and controlled in the interest of shareholders and other stakeholders'.

There are different codes and practices around the world but they tend to cover similar areas:

- The role of the board of directors.
- The reliability of financial reports and the relationship between the company and its auditors.
- The interest of the company's shareholders in the company.

Importance of corporate governance

- In most developed countries, listed companies are required to operate systems of corporate governance laid down either by statute or by professional organisations (such as the Securities and Exchange Commission (SEC) in the US or the Financial Services Authority (FSA) in the UK).
- The requirements are often given the support of the stock exchanges, in that they are built into listing rules.

- The development of corporate governance codes is closely associated with the UK, hence this is a model to discuss best practice.
- The UK Corporate Governance Code follows a principles-based approach (see next section), and is endorsed by the London Stock Exchange. The US system has been much more legislative with the introduction of the Sarbanes-Oxley Act of 2002 (to be discussed later in this chapter).
- It should be appreciated that corporate governance has links to risks and internal controls. Whilst good corporate governance cannot stop company failure or prevent companies failing to achieve their objectives, it is a major help, and well-run companies tend to achieve their objectives in a less risky way. As a result it is part of risk reduction.

Development of corporate governance

- Governance regulations have developed largely as a result of a series of corporate failures in the 1980s and early 1990s.
- The corporate governance themes that began to emerge from these collapses were:
  - poorly-run companies, especially companies with a board of directors dominated by a single chairman/chief executive figure, and companies with 'greedy' or 'fat cat' directors (demonstrating the agency problem of a company failing to operate in the best interests of its shareholders)
  - poor financial reporting, raising questions about auditing and internal control systems, and
  - an apparent lack of interest by the major investment institutions in the performance of the companies in which they invested.
- More recently the UK Corporate Governance Code has been developed further in accordance with the 2008–09 global financial crisis.

Company collapses

Several issues or problems appear to emerge when there is a corporate governance 'scandal' and a company has collapsed.

- The company has not been well-run by its board of directors.
- In many cases, there has been an individual who has dominated the board and exerted excessive influence on decision-making by the board. In many cases, this individual held the positions of both chairman of the board and chief executive officer.
- A board of directors might have lacked sufficient breadth of knowledge and experience to appreciate the problems the company was in and the risks it faced.

- Companies were being run in the interests of the executive directors, who received high remuneration packages and generous bonuses, but the rewards were not being given for the achievement of objectives that were in the best interests of the shareholders. The interests of the directors were not properly aligned with those of the shareholders.
- Financial reporting was unreliable and the published accounts did not seem to give any indication of the true financial position of the company. In some cases there was a suspicion that the auditors were not sufficiently independent of the company and so not fulfilling their responsibilities adequately. Alternatively, the auditors were accused of doing their job badly or of being misled by the company's directors and management. (In 2002 audit firm Arthur Andersen collapsed from the consequences of its involvement in the Enron scandal.)
- Whenever a company collapsed unexpectedly, there have been suspicions that the internal control system was ineffective. There usually appears to have been inadequate risk management generally.
- Questions have also been asked about major institutional shareholders, and whether they could have done more to identify problems in companies and persuade or force the directors to make improvements.

Maxwell Communications Corporation

Robert Maxwell was born in to extreme poverty in Czechoslovakia in 1923. By the time of his death (accident or murder was never established) in 1991 he was a media mogul, having built a publishing empire that spanned the world. In the weeks that followed his death however, news emerged of the state of his company's finances.

After the Second World War he set up Pergamon Press publishing scientific journals. It became very profitable and he turned his attention to politics, later becoming a Member of Parliament for the Labour Party. His relationship with the Party was an uneasy one since anyone who criticised him was confronted in the courts. This was when signs emerged of his dishonesty.

In 1969, Maxwell agreed a takeover bid for Pergamon by Leasco (an American financial and data processing group). The profits of Pergamon were questioned by Leasco and eventually talks fell apart as a Department of Trade and Industry (DTI) enquiry ensued. Inspectors found that the profits depended on transactions with Maxwell family private companies. The DTI concluded that Maxwell 'is not a person... who can be relied upon to exercise proper stewardship of a publicly quoted company'.

In 1980 Maxwell took over the troubled British Printing Corporation renaming it Maxwell Communications Corporation. In 1984 he bought Mirror Group Newspapers (MGN) and Macmillan publishers, which put his company further into debt. In 1991 he floated MGN as a public company desperate to raise cash that would save the Group from bankruptcy (with debts over £2 billion). After Maxwell's death it transpired that he had taken money from the pension funds to keep the companies afloat and boost the share price.

Enron

In December 2001, US energy trader Enron collapsed. Enron was the largest bankruptcy in US history. Even though the United States was believed by many to be the most regulated financial market in the world, it was evident from Enron's collapse that investors were not properly informed about the significance of off-balance sheet transactions. US accounting rules may have contributed to this, in that they are concerned with the strict legal ownership of investment vehicles rather than with their control. By contrast, International Accounting Standards follow the principle of 'substance over form'. There were some indications that Enron may have actively lobbied against changing the treatment in US financial reporting of special purpose entities used in off-balance sheet financing. Overall, there was a clear need for greater transparency and trust in reporting.

The failure of Enron also highlighted the over-dependence of an auditor on one particular client, the employment of staff by Enron who had previously worked for the auditors, the process of audit appointments and re-appointments, the rotation of audit partners and how auditors are monitored and regulated.

As a consequence of the failure of Enron and WorldCom, the United States has introduced Sarbanes-Oxley legislation to address many of the criticisms of reporting and auditing practice. In their comments on the failure of Enron, the Association of Certified Chartered Accountants recommended the need for global financial markets to have a global set of principles-based financial reporting standards and a global code of corporate governance, arguing that legalistic, rules-based standards encourage creative, loophole-based practice.

Former chief executive Kenneth Lay died in 2006 before he could stand trial. Enron's former chief financial officer Andrew Fastow was sentenced in late 2006 to six years in prison for stealing from Enron and devising schemes to deceive investors about the energy company's true financial condition. Lawyers have to date won settlements totalling $US 7.3 billion from banks including JPMorgan Chase, Bank of America, Citigroup, etc.

Barings Bank

Barings Bank was Britain's oldest bank, having existed for 200 years before it collapsed as a result of uncontrolled derivatives trading by Nick Leeson in the bank's Singapore office.

The collapse of Barings Bank in 1995 was caused by Nick Leeson, a 26-year-old dealer who lost £800 million in unauthorised dealings in derivatives trading from his base in Singapore. Leeson suppressed information on account '88888' which he used for trading between 1992 and 1995, which management was unaware of. The losses wiped out the Bank's capital.

As only a small amount of money (a margin) is needed to establish a derivatives position, it is possible to face financial obligations beyond an organisation's ability to pay. Therefore, strict controls are needed. There are many risk management and control lessons to be learned from the failure of Barings.

Barings had placed Nick Leeson in charge of both the dealing desk and the back office. The back office records, confirms and settles trades made by the front office and provides the necessary checks to prevent unauthorised trading and minimise the potential for fraud and embezzlement. In this dual position, Leeson was able to relay false information back to London.

An internal audit report in August 1994 concluded that Leeson's dual responsibility for both the front and back office was an excessive concentration of powers and warned of the risk that Leeson could override controls. The internal auditors' responsibility was to make sure the directors were aware of the risk they were facing by not implementing the separation of duties. However, directors did not implement these recommendations. Their response was that there was insufficient work for a full-time treasury and risk manager. There was also a lack of supervision of Leeson by Barings' managers, either in Singapore or London.

Senior managers of Barings had a superficial knowledge of derivatives, did not understand the risks of the business, did not articulate the bank's risk appetite or implement strategies and control procedures appropriate to those risks.

When the Singapore exchange made margin demands on Barings, large amounts of cash had to be paid out but still no steps were taken by the London head office to investigate the matter. Eventually, the amounts required were so great that Barings were forced to call in receivers. The trading positions taken out by Leeson were unhedged and the cost of closing out the open contracts was US$1.4 billion.

The information in this case study comes from the Report of the Board of Banking Supervision (BoBS) Inquiry into the Circumstances of the Collapse of Barings.

Worldcom

WorldCom filed for bankruptcy protection in June 2002. It was the biggest corporate fraud in history, largely a result of treating operating expenses as capital expenditure.

WorldCom (now renamed MCI) admitted in March 2004 that the total amount by which it had misled investors over the previous 10 years was almost US$75 billion (£42 billion) and reduced its stated pre-tax profits for 2001 and 2002 by that amount.

WorldCom stock began falling in late 1999 as businesses slashed spending on telecom services and equipment. A series of debt downgrades had raised borrowing costs for the company, struggling with about US$32 billion in debt. WorldCom used accounting tricks to conceal a deteriorating financial condition and to inflate profits.

Former WorldCom chief executive Bernie Ebbers resigned in April 2002 amid questions about US$366 million in personal loans from the company and a federal probe of its accounting practices. Ebbers was subsequently charged with conspiracy to commit securities fraud, and filing misleading data with the Securities and Exchange Commission (SEC). Scott Sullivan, former chief financial officer, pleaded guilty to three criminal charges.

The SEC said WorldCom had committed 'accounting improprieties of unprecedented magnitude' – proof, it said, of the need for reform in the regulation of corporate accounting.

Parmalat

In December 2003, Italian dairy-foods group Parmalat, with 36,000 employees in 30 countries, went into bankruptcy protection with US$ 8–10 billion of vanished assets. The company was 51% owned by the Tanzi family.

Parmalat defaulted on a US$185 million bond payment that prompted auditors and banks to scrutinise company accounts. Thirty-eight per cent of Parmalat's assets were supposedly held in a bank account in the Cayman Islands but no such account ever existed. Letters received from the bank by auditors were forgeries.

Parmalat has been one of the largest financial frauds in history. The company falsified its accounts over a 15-year period. This was not identified by two firms of auditors, Grant Thornton and Deloitte Touche Tohmatsu. At least 20 people have been involved in the fraud, including members of the Tanzi family, the chief financial officer, board members and the company's lawyers. Calisto Tanzi the founder and chief executive was arrested on suspicion of fraud, embezzlement, false accounting and misleading investors.

Tanzi admitted that he knew the accounts were falsified to hide losses and the falsified balance sheet was used to enable Parmalat to continue borrowing. He also confessed to misappropriating US$620 million, although prosecutors believe it could be as much as US$1 billion.

Equitable Life

During the 1960s to 1980s the 242-year-old Equitable Life had sold thousands of policies with guaranteed returns, some as high as 12%. The company ran into problems in 2000 when it closed to new business after years of excessive returns to special policy holders had left the company with no money to absorb a deterior-ation in the value of its stock market investments. It had a 'black hole' in its finances estimated at £4.4 billion because it had been paying out more to policy holders than it held in reserves. Equitable lost a case in the House of Lords in 2000 that led to a further deterioration in its financial position of £1.5 billion.

A report by Lord Penrose published early in 2004 said that the former management was primarily culpable for Equitable's near collapse, aided by the failure of regulators to identify the mutual insurer's financial position. The autocratic former Chief Executive and chief actuary Roy Ranson was blamed for keeping regulators and the board of Equitable in the dark about the precarious state of Equitable's financial position throughout the 1990s. The Penrose report also said that there had been weaknesses in the way that insurance companies were supervised throughout that period. The 'light touch' approach to regulation had not been changed to meet the requirements of an increasingly sophisticated and risky investment industry.

The Penrose report said that management had been dominated by 'unaccountable' actuaries, a board of non-executives who had no idea what was going on at the company they were charged with overseeing and a regulator that failed to act as any kind of protector for policy holders.

Lord Penrose said, "The board at no stage got fully to grips with the financial situation faced by the Society. Information was too fragmented [and], their collective skills were inadequate for the task".

Test your understanding 1

The lack of knowledge and supervision by management, and the excessive concentration of power placed on one employee enabling the overriding of controls was prevalent at:

A Enron

B Maxwell Communications Corporation

C Barings Bank

D Worldcom

Test your understanding 2

Money secretly taken from the pension fund to keep the company afloat and boost the share price was the cause for concern at:

A Enron

B Maxwell Communications Corporation

C Barings Bank

D Worldcom

2 Principles of good corporate governance

The Listing Rules of the London Stock Exchange require each listed company to state in its annual report:

- How it has applied the principles of the UK Corporate Governance Code.
- Whether or not it has complied with the provisions of the Code throughout the accounting period.

Although there are some legal requirements relating to corporate governance, the main approach is that listed companies are required to 'comply or explain' with the provisions of the Code. This is referred to as a principles-based approach.

The principles of the UK Corporate Governance Code relate to the following areas:

- Leadership
- Effectiveness
- Accountability
- Remuneration
- Relations with shareholders.

Leadership

Every company should be headed by an effective board which is collectively responsible for the long-term success of the company. There should be a clear division of responsibilities and no one individual should have unfettered powers of decision (See Maxwell illustration earlier.). The chairman is responsible for leadership of the board and ensuring its effectiveness. Non-executive directors should constructively challenge and help develop proposals on strategy.

- There should be a clear division of responsibilities between running the board (the role of the chairman) and the executive responsibility for the running of the company's business (the role of the CEO).
- The roles of chairman of the board and CEO should not be held by the same individual.

This was not the case at Marks and Spencer plc in 2008 when they appointed Stuart Rose as CEO and Chairman. The company stated that it was a temporary role for 3 years until they identified a new CEO from within the company. Major shareholders – Legal and general, didn't agree with this and a heated debate ensued, not least due to the dual role going against the then called UK 'Combined Code' of corporate governance. Other investors – Schroders said that M&S were setting an 'appalling example' to other UK companies.

The Board eventually agreed to Stuart Rose being put up for re-election every year, and they appointed a new 'heavy weight' NED as senior independent director to 'keep an eye on him'.

Many smaller investors were very happy with the arrangement.

Stuart Rose remained CEO and Chair at M&S for over two years until Marc Bolland (formerly of Morrisons) took over as CEO and Robert Swannell took over as Chair (also chair of HMV).

Roles of Chairman and CEO

Chairman

The specific responsibilities of the chairman, inter alia, are to:

- provide leadership to the board, supplying vision and imagination, working closely with the CEO
- take a leading role in determining the composition and structure of the board which will involve regular assessment of the:
  - size of the board
  - balance between executive directors and NEDs
  - interaction, harmony and effectiveness of the directors
- set the board's agenda and plan board meetings
- chair all board meetings, directing debate toward consensus
- ensure the board receives appropriate, accurate, timely and clear information
- facilitate effective contribution from NEDs
- hold meetings with the NEDs, without the executive directors present
- chair the AGM and other shareholders' meetings, using these to provide effective dialogue with shareholders
- discuss governance and major strategy with the major shareholders
- ensure that the views of shareholders are communicated to the board as a whole.

CEO

The specific responsibilities of the CEO, inter alia, are to:

- develop and implement policies to execute the strategy established by the board
- assume full accountability to the board for all aspects of company operations, controls and performance
- manage financial and physical resources
- build and maintain an effective management team
- put adequate operational, financial, planning, risk and internal control systems in place
- closely monitor operations and financial results in accordance with plans and budgets
- interface between board and employees
- assist in selection and evaluation of board members
- represent the company to major suppliers, customers, professional associations, etc.

Test your understanding 3

One person has carried out the roles of CEO and chairman since BB Co was floated on the stock exchange 20 years ago. Recently, analysts have begun to criticise this policy explaining that since the CEO acts as his own boss because he has no chairman to report to, unchecked risk taking may result and although this can produce strong short-term results it can also ending up harming a company.

The board of BB Co however believes that a single Chairman/CEO may provide advantages in both leadership and oversight in light of his or her superior knowledge of the organisation.

Best practice dictates that the roles should be separated. Which of the following could be improved by splitting the roles of CEO and Chairman?

Select **all** that apply.

A Accountability.
B Transparency.
C Compliance.
D Speed of decision making.
E Unity of leadership.

Non-Executive Directors (NEDs)

Non-executive directors should scrutinise the performance of management in meeting agreed goals and objectives and monitor the reporting of performance. They should satisfy themselves on the integrity of financial information and that financial controls and systems of risk management are robust and defensible. They are responsible for determining appropriate levels of remuneration of executive directors and have a prime role in appointing and, where necessary, removing executive directors, and in succession planning.

These functions are, to some extent, carried out as part of their positions on key committees – remuneration committee, nominations committee and audit committee – as well as discussions as part of the main Board.

Further details on NEDs

Roles

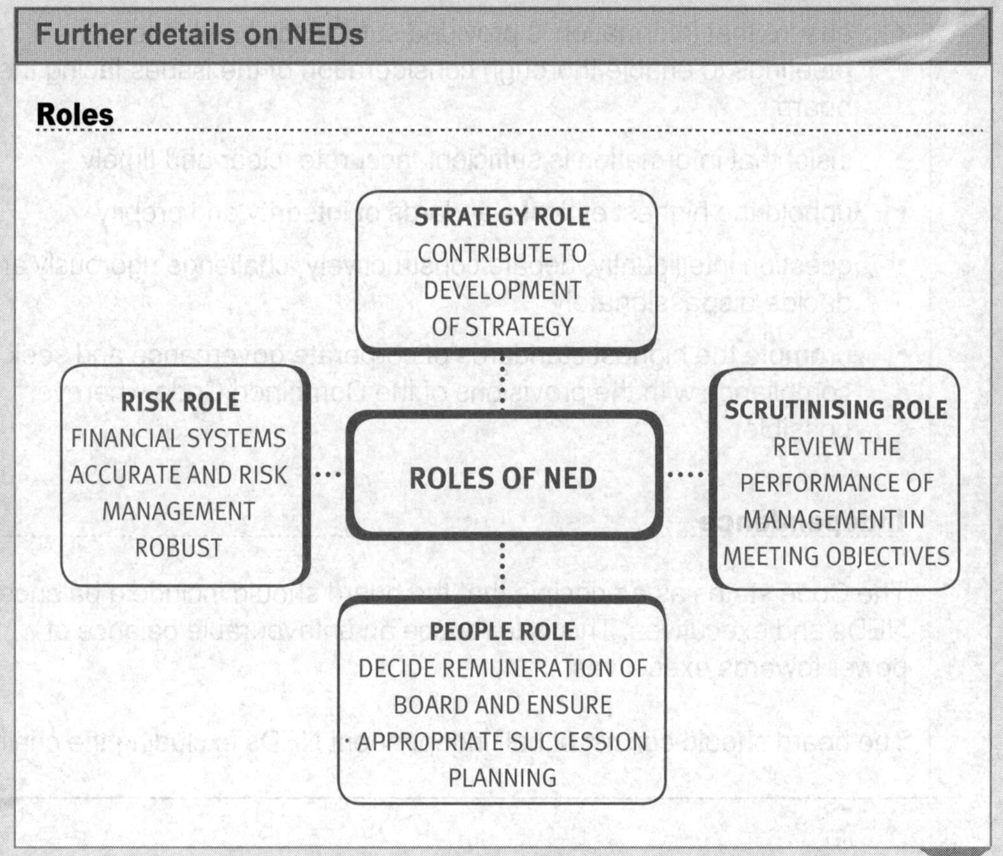

Strategy role: this recognises that NEDs have the right and responsibility to contribute to strategic success, challenging strategy and offering advice on direction.

Scrutinising role: NEDs are required to hold executive colleagues to account for decisions taken and results obtained.

Risk role: NEDs ensure the company has an adequate system of internal controls and systems of risk management in place.

People role: NEDs oversee a range of responsibilities with regard to the appointment and remuneration of executives and will be involved in contractual and disciplinary issues.

Effectiveness

To be effective, a NED needs to:

- build a recognition by executives of their contribution in order to promote openness and trust
- be well-informed about the company and the external environment in which it operates
- have a strong command of issues relevant to the business
- insist on a comprehensive, formal and tailored induction, continually develop and refresh their knowledge and skills to ensure that their contribution to the board remains informed and relevant
- ensure that information is provided sufficiently in advance of meetings to enable thorough consideration of the issues facing the board
- insist that information is sufficient, accurate, clear and timely
- uphold the highest ethical standards of integrity and probity
- question intelligently, debate constructively, challenge rigorously and decide dispassionately
- promote the highest standards of corporate governance and seek compliance with the provisions of the Combined Code wherever possible.

Independence

The Code states as a principle that the board should include a balance of NEDs and executives. This is to reduce an unfavourable balance of power towards executives.

The board should consist of half independent NEDs excluding the chair.

One NED should be the senior independent director who is directly available to shareholders if they have concerns which cannot or should not be dealt with through the appropriate channels of chairman, CEO or finance director.

The primary fiduciary duty that NEDs owe is to the company's shareholders. They must not allow themselves to be captured or unduly influenced by the vested interests of other members of the company such as executive directors, trade unions or middle management.

There are also concerns over the recruitment of NED's and the challenge that this may bring to independence.

Recruiting those with previous industry involvement can result in a higher technical knowledge, a network of contacts and an awareness of what the strategic issues are within the industry. While these might be of some benefit to a NED's contribution, they can make the NED less independent as prior industry involvement might also reduce the NED's ability to be objective and uncontaminated by previously held views.

Accordingly, it is sometimes easier to demonstrate independence when NEDs are appointed from outside the industry.

In practice, many companies employ a mix of NEDs, and it is often this blend of talents and areas of expertise that is what makes a non-executive board effective.

Reasons for NED independence

- To provide a detached and objective view of board decisions.
- To provide expertise and communicate effectively.
- To provide shareholders with an independent voice on the board.
- To provide confidence in corporate governance.
- To reduce accusations of self-interest in the behaviour of executives.

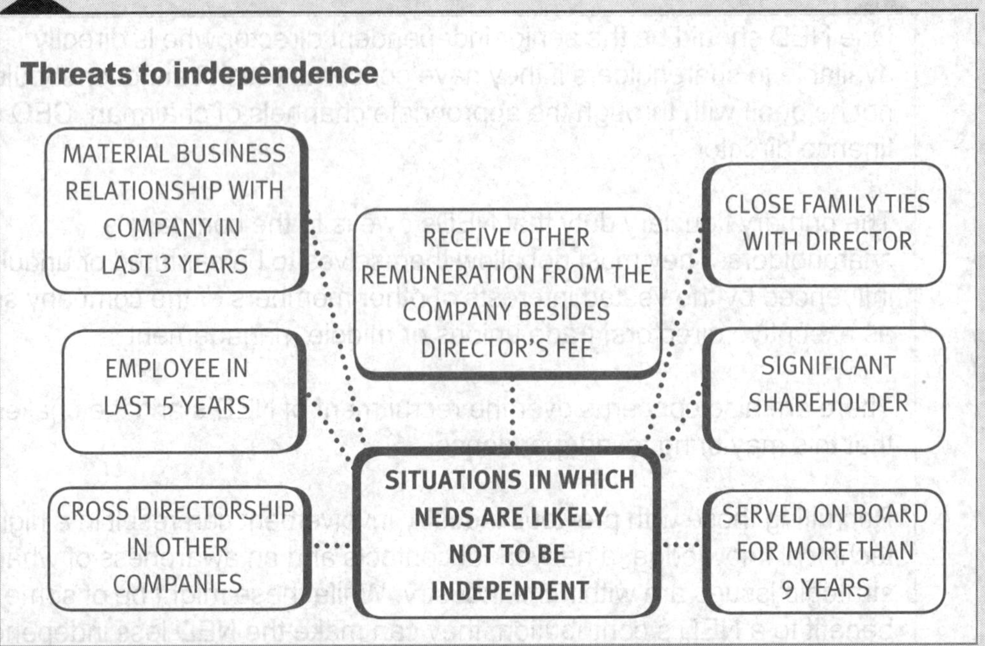

Test your understanding 4

A Company is a large retailer which operates supermarkets all over Country E. It has a board of 11 directors, 5 of whom are non-executive (NED). None of the directors have any experience of the grocery market in Country E and over half are newly appointed (within the last year).

Country E's industry is fast moving and dynamic. The executive directors are finding it time consuming to explain strategic decisions to the NED's and when they do, a perceived lack of understanding on the NED's part often leads them to disagree with the executive directors and delay things further.

The CEO has suggested that the executive directors meet without the NED's in order to make strategic decisions on a timely basis. These decisions could then be explained to the NED's at a later date.

Which of the following may be consequences of the NED's only finding out about strategic decisions after they are made?

Select all that apply.

A Management's performance in meeting objectives will not be assessed by the NED's.

B NED's will be unable to ensure risk management processes and systems are robust.

C Decisions will be more relevant to the business since they will be made by the most knowledgeable staff.

D Strategic decisions may not be made in the best interests of stakeholders.

E The NED's will be able to concentrate on other aspects of their role and improve their knowledge about A Company since time will be saved.

Effectiveness

The board and its committees should have the appropriate balance of skills, experience, independence and knowledge. There should be a formal procedure for the appointment of new directors to the board and all directors should be able to allocate sufficient time to the company to discharge their responsibilities effectively.

All directors should receive induction on joining the board and should regularly update and refresh their skills and knowledge, and all directors should be submitted for re-election at regular intervals, subject to continued satisfactory performance.

Nominations Committees

The need for nominations committee is identified in many codes of best practice.

As an example, the UK Corporate Governance Code (2010) requires that **there should be a formal, rigorous and transparent procedure for the appointments of new directors to the board.**

The main responsibilities and duties of the nominations committee are to:

- Review regularly the structure, size and composition of the board and make recommendations to the board.
- Consider the balance between executives and NEDs on the board of directors.
- Ensure appropriate management of diversity to board composition.

- Provide an appropriate balance of power to reduce domination in executive selection by the CEO/chairman.
- Regularly evaluate the balance of skills, knowledge and experience of the board.
- Give full consideration to succession planning for directors.
- Prepare a description of the role and capabilities required for any particular board appointment including that of the chairman.
- Identify and nominate for the approval by the board candidates to fill board vacancies as and when they arise.
- Make recommendations to the board concerning the standing for reappointment of directors.
- Be seen to operate independently for the benefit of shareholders.

Accountability

The board should present a balanced and understandable assessment of the company's position and prospects.

The board is responsible for determining the nature and extent of the significant risks it is willing to take in achieving its strategic objectives. The board should maintain sound risk management and internal control systems. The board should establish formal and transparent arrangements for considering how they should apply the corporate reporting and risk management and internal control principles and for maintaining an appropriate relationship with the company's auditor.

Audit committee

The board should establish an audit committee of at least three, or in the case of smaller companies two, independent non-executive directors. In smaller companies the company chairman may be a member of, but not chair, the committee in addition to the independent non-executive directors, provided he or she was considered independent on appointment as chairman. The board should satisfy itself that at least one member of the audit committee has recent and relevant financial experience.

The audit committee's role is:

- to monitor the integrity of the financial statements of the company and any formal announcements relating to the company's financial performance, reviewing significant financial reporting judgements contained in them;

- to review the company's internal financial controls and, unless expressly addressed by a separate board risk committee composed of independent directors, or by the board itself, to review the company's internal control and risk management systems;
- to monitor and review the effectiveness of the company's internal audit function;
- to make recommendations to the board, for it to put to the shareholders for their approval in general meeting, in relation to the appointment, re-appointment and removal of the external auditor and to approve the remuneration and terms of engagement of the external auditor;
- to review and monitor the external auditor's independence and objectivity and the effectiveness of the audit process, taking into consideration relevant UK professional and regulatory requirements;
- to develop and implement policy on the engagement of the external auditor to supply non-audit services, taking into account relevant ethical guidance regarding the provision of non-audit services by the external audit firm, and to report to the board, identifying any matters in respect of which it considers that action or improvement is needed and making recommendations as to the steps to be taken.

The terms of reference of the audit committee, including its role and the authority delegated to it by the board, should be made available. A separate section of the annual report should describe the work of the committee in discharging those responsibilities.

The audit committee should review arrangements by which staff of the company may, in confidence, raise concerns about possible improprieties in matters of financial reporting or other matters. The audit committee's objective should be to ensure that arrangements are in place for the proportionate and independent investigation of such matters and for appropriate follow-up action.

The audit committee should monitor and review the effectiveness of the internal audit activities. Where there is no internal audit function, the audit committee should consider annually whether there is a need for an internal audit function and make a recommendation to the board, and the reasons for the absence of such a function should be explained in the relevant section of the annual report.

The audit committee should have primary responsibility for making a recommendation on the appointment, re-appointment and removal of the external auditor. If the board does not accept the audit committee's recommendation, it should include in the annual report, and in any papers recommending appointment or re-appointment, a statement from the audit committee explaining the recommendation and should set out reasons why the board has taken a different position.

The annual report should explain to shareholders how, if the auditor provides non-audit services, auditor objectivity and independence is safeguarded.

Risk management and internal control

The board should, at least annually, conduct a review of the effectiveness of the company's risk management and internal control systems and should report to shareholders that they have done so. The review should cover all material controls, including financial, operational and compliance controls.

Remuneration

Levels of remuneration should be sufficient to attract, retain and motivate directors of the quality required to run the company successfully, but a company should avoid paying more than is necessary for this purpose. A significant proportion of executive directors' remuneration should be structured so as to link rewards to corporate and individual performance.

Remuneration Committees

The performance-related elements of executive directors' remuneration should be stretching and designed to promote the long-term success of the company.

The remuneration committee should judge where to position their company relative to other companies. But they should use such comparisons with caution in view of the risk of an upward ratchet of remuneration levels with no corresponding improvement in performance.

They should also be sensitive to pay and employment conditions elsewhere in the group, especially when determining annual salary increases.

Levels of remuneration for non-executive directors should reflect the time commitment and responsibilities of the role. Remuneration for non-executive directors should not include share options or other performance-related elements. If, exceptionally, options are granted, shareholder approval should be sought in advance and any shares acquired by exercise of the options should be held until at least one year after the non-executive director leaves the board. Holding of share options could be relevant to the determination of a non-executive director's independence.

The remuneration committee should carefully consider what compensation commitments (including pension contributions and all other elements) their directors' terms of appointment would entail in the event of early termination. The aim should be to avoid rewarding poor performance. They should take a robust line on reducing compensation to reflect departing directors' obligations to mitigate loss.

Notice or contract periods should be set at one year or less. If it is necessary to offer longer notice or contract periods to new directors recruited from outside, such periods should reduce to one year or less after the initial period.

The board should establish a remuneration committee of at least three, or in the case of smaller companies two, independent non-executive directors. In addition the company chairman may also be a member of, but not chair, the committee if he or she was considered independent on appointment as chairman. The remuneration committee should make available its terms of reference, explaining its role and the authority delegated to it by the board . Where remuneration consultants are appointed, a statement should be made available of whether they have any other connection with the company.

The remuneration committee should have delegated responsibility for setting remuneration for all executive directors and the chairman, including pension rights and any compensation payments. The committee should also recommend and monitor the level and structure of remuneration for senior management. The definition of 'senior management' for this purpose should be determined by the board but should normally include the first layer of management below board level.

The board itself or, where required by the Articles of Association, the shareholders should determine the remuneration of the non-executive directors within the limits set in the Articles of Association. Where permitted by the Articles, the board may, however, delegate this responsibility to a committee, which might include the chief executive.

Shareholders should be invited specifically to approve all new long-term incentive schemes (as defined in the Listing Rules) and significant changes to existing schemes, save in the circumstances permitted by the Listing Rules.

Test your understanding 5

PK is a large listed company. The remuneration committee consists of 4 Directors with the Finance Director chairing the committee. The other three members are NED's although only two of these have been assessed as independent by the nominations committee. The remuneration committee has responsibility for both executive and non-executive pay policy with these policies being put forward by approval at the AGM by shareholders.

What actions should PK take to comply with best practice corporate governance? Select ALL that apply.

A The Finance Director should resign from PK

B The remuneration committee should not have responsibility for NED remuneration

C The non-independent NED should resign from the remuneration committee

D The Finance director should resign from the remuneration committee

E All NEDs on the remuneration committee should be replaced

Remuneration policy – The Sage Group plc

The following is an extract of the Remuneration Report (2011) of The Sage Group plc:

'Remuneration Policy

The Remuneration Committee, in setting the remuneration policy, recognises the need to be competitive in an international market. The Committee's policy is to set remuneration levels which ensure that the executive directors are fairly and responsibly rewarded in return for high levels of performance. Remuneration policy is designed to support key business strategies and to create a strong, performance orientated environment. At the same time, the policy must attract, motivate and retain talent... The Remuneration Committee considers that a successful remuneration policy must ensure that a significant part of the remuneration package is linked to the achievement of stretching corporate performance targets... generating a strong alignment of interest with shareholders... Around 75% of each executive's total compensation value is delivered through performance-related incentives, and is therefore 'at risk' if stretching performance targets are not reached.

Performance Share Plan (PSP)

The Committee established the PSP as the Group's main long-term equity incentive to drive financial and market performance... The individual limit on award levels under the Plan is 300% of salary. PSP awards will normally have a maximum value of 210% of salary. This represents a 'core' award to the value of 140% of salary, which, if maximum EPS (earnings per share) growth is attained, and TSR (total shareholder return) performance is ranked upper quartile against the comparator group, could rise to 210% of salary...

A sliding scale based on EPS is used. 25% of the award vests at the end of the period if the increase in EPS exceeds RPI (retail prices index) by 9% over the period; 100% of the award vests at that time only if RPI is exceeded in that period by 27%...

Awards are also subject to a TSR 'multiplier' whereby the level of vesting based on EPS achievement is adjusted according to TSR performance over the same three year period compared with a group of international software and computer services companies.' (These include Adobe Systems, Cap Gemini, Microsoft, Oracle, SAP amongst others.)

The Report goes on to detail audited information including outstanding awards granted to each director under the PSP. For example, the Chief executive Officer's details were:

	Awarded 1 Oct 2010 number	Awarded during the year number	Vested during the year number	Lapsed during the year number	Awarded 30 Sept, 2011 number	Vesting date
G S Berruyer	361,647	–	(95,167)	(266,480)	–	3 March 2011
	745,649	–	–	–	745,649	3 March 2012
	507,280	–	–	–	507,280	4 March 2013
	–	737,795	–	–	737,795	10 March 2014
Total	1,614,576	737,795	(95,167)	(266,480)	1,990,724	

- 'The market price of a share on 10 March 2011, the date of the awards made in the year ended 30 September 2011 was 272.1p.
- The market price of a share on 3 March 2011, the date the above awards vested in the year ended 30 September 2011 was 280.8p. The market price of a share on 3 March 2008, the date on which these awards were granted was 202.25p.'

As you will be able to calculate from the illustration, the awards are well-worth receiving if company performance meets the targets set. The targets are reasonably straightforward, there being only two – EPS and TSR; however, the calculation of the award does become reasonably complicated.

The time period for tie-in is 3 years which is in line with the UK stock exchange listing rules/the UK Corporate Governance Code, whereby directors should get a reasonable time to prove themselves but not so long that the company cannot refresh the Board should it wish to.

3 Directors' remuneration

Remuneration is defined as payment or compensation received for services or employment and includes basic salary, bonuses and any other economic benefits.

Behavioural impact

Whatever remuneration package is determined, it is essential to ensure that the directors' objective is to do a good job for the stakeholders of the company.

The remuneration package should be motivational, not too small or too easily earned. The remuneration committee should design a package that attracts, retains and motivates the director. This should take in to account the market rate i.e. comparable companies remuneration packages.

Components of the directors' remuneration package

- Basic salary – covering the job itself, the skills required, the directors' performance, their contribution to company strategy and market rates;
- Performance-related pay – remuneration dependent on the achievement of some performance measure. This could be short-term e.g. a bonus paid to the director at the end of the accounting year for achieving a certain level of profit or earnings per share, or long-term e.g. executive stock options. Stock/share options are contracts that allow the director to buy shares at a fixed price. If the share price rises above the exercise price the director can sell the shares at a profit. This encourages the director to manage the company in such a way that the share price increases, therefore share options are believed to align the directors' goals with those of the shareholders. Problems arise when the directors' actions are solely focussed on the share price to the exclusion of other stakeholder objectives. Also, if the share price rises too much the director could be tempted to sell their shares and retire, which defeats the objective of trying to tie the director in to the company for the long-term.
- Pension contributions – the remuneration committee should consider the pension consequences of increases in basic salary;
- Benefits in kind – are various non-wage compensations e.g. a company car, or health insurance.

Share (stock) options

Bonuses to directors based on the current year's profit can lead to short termism, in that the directors will maximise the current year's profit by not investing in new products and not developing existing ones (these costs would reduce the current year's profit). Not investing in new products and not developing existing ones will adversely affect future profits and may threaten the long-term existence of the business.

It is argued that share options are an effective way of paying directors and of avoiding short-termism, as the value of a share should be a reflection of the long-term profitability of the company.

Until recently, there has been no charge in the company's profit and loss account for share options, so the shareholders are not aware of the value of the options granted to the directors. However, share options can be very valuable to directors. Excluding the cost of share options from the financial statements understates directors' remuneration.

The grant date is the date when the employee and employer enter into an agreement that will entitle the employee to receive an option on a future date, provided certain conditions are met.

The service date is the date or dates on which the employee performs the services necessary to become unconditionally entitled to the option.

The vesting date is the date when the employee, having satisfied all the conditions becomes unconditionally entitled to the option.

The exercise date is when the option is taken up.

Normally, the option is granted at the market price of the shares at the grant date (e.g. 250p a share). If, at the exercise date of, say, 30 June 2010, the value of the shares is 290p, the director will buy the shares from the company for £2,500,000 and immediately sell them in the market for £2,900,000, making a gain of £400,000. If the value of the shares is less than 250p on 30 June 2010, the director will not purchase the shares (as he/she would make a loss), so the director's gain on the option will be zero.

Interestingly, most directors of UK listed companies buy and sell the shares at the exercise date (30 June 2010 in this case). Only a small minority of directors buy the shares at the option price and continue to hold them.

Share options as a measure of long-term profitability

The 'theory' of share options is that the share price on 30 June 2010 will be based on the company's long term profitability, so if the company is doing well, the share price will be higher and the director's profit on buying the shares (and subsequently selling them) will be higher. So the director's gain on selling the shares will reflect the director's success in increasing the long-term profits and hence the share price of the company.

To a certain extent, this 'theory' is correct in that the share price tends to increase if the company's profitability increases. However, share price movements also depend on other factors, such as the general price movement of other shares and investors' views about the future profitability and growth in the particular type of trade the company is in. For instance, in late 1999 and early 2000 there was an enormous increase in the value of telecom and dot.com shares, yet many of these companies had never made a profit. Thus, the increase in the share price did not depend on the profitability of the companies, and it could be argued that the prices of these shares increased because this was a fashionable sector of the market in which to invest. At the same time as the increase in value of telecom and dot.com shares there was a substantial fall in the value of other shares, including well-known retailers. Sometimes, share prices were falling, despite the fact that the companies profits were increasing. So, it can be seen that the increase in the share price of a company may be more related to market conditions than its long-term profitability. Thus, awarding options on shares may not be a very effective way of paying directors, as the change in the share price may have little to do with profitability of the company and the directors' contribution to increasing those profits.

Regarded as a way of boosting productivity and employee retention, share options have become less popular since the economy turned bearish. Fuelled in the late 90s by dot com promises of untold future wealth, option holding employees had little or no prospect of realising any value. When the economy suffered, staff became more interested in staying in progressive, well-paid jobs with quantifiable packages, so there has been less reason to implement schemes. (Some employers had been accused of using share options for employees as a way to pay salaries of less than the market rate.)

Microsoft recently ended its own option scheme. It decided to grant shares instead (not options on shares), explaining this practice is recorded on balance sheets, giving analysts a better view of the company's financial state and workers a tangible incentive.

To compound matters, the International Accounting Standards Board proposes firms put the cost of share-based awards through the income statement.

Executive Share Options (ESOPs)

Executive share options (ESOPs) have been blamed for almost every business scandal that has made the headlines in the past decade.

An ESOP is part of a manager's remuneration package. The features generally involve the following:

- Each eligible manager is granted an allocation of options as part of his or her annual remuneration. The number of options will generally be decided by the remuneration committee, comprising non-executive directors.
- The options themselves will normally have a striking price that is equal to, or slightly higher than, the share price at the date the options are granted.
- There is usually a vesting period of a few years that must pass before the options can be exercised. If the manager resigns or leaves the company during that period then the options will lapse.
- The options can normally be exercised on a specific date at the end of the vesting period.

(The vesting period and the fact that the options must be exercised on a very specific date make them more difficult to value than the more typical traded options that can be bought and sold by third parties.)

There are two main reasons why shareholders might be keen to reward their directors with options.

- If the directors hold large numbers of options then they will have a financial incentive to maximise the share price. Provided the share price exceeds the exercise price at the relevant date the directors can exercise their options and buy shares for less than their market value. They will then either retain those shares as an investment (acquired at a bargain price, so providing an attractive return) or resell them at a guaranteed capital gain. If the share price does not rise during the vesting period then the directors will receive little or no value and so they will have a direct financial stake in delivering an increased share price.
- An investment opportunity that would be attractive to the shareholders because the potential returns are high might be unacceptable to the directors because they will be exposed to the risks of it going wrong and the loss of their jobs. For example, a new product that fails might have a very limited impact on shareholders' total investment portfolios but could end the careers of the directors who were responsible for recommending that it should proceed.

  Thus, if the shareholders really wish to align the directors' interests with their own they need to find some way to encourage the directors to accept the risks that they would choose to accept for themselves and ESOPs provide the answer.

If the directors hold large numbers of options then they will have an economic interest in accepting risky investment opportunities that they might otherwise be inclined to reject. If the investment succeeds and the share price rises then their options will be worth far more at the exercise date and they will not be exposed to any specific loss (at least on their options) if the investment fails and the share price plummets.

Thus, ESOPs give the shareholders the reassurance that the directors will wish to work hard to increase the share price and also accept realistic risks provided the potential return is high enough. They will also encourage the directors to take a long-term view and to remain with the company rather than move elsewhere and lose their options.

Directors should only be permitted to hold share options of any kind if they are honest and upright individuals. Clearly, many company directors are both but there will always be a few dishonest individuals in every walk of life. For example, in the past directors have purchased call options with their own money and then manipulated the share price by distorting the financial statements so that the options could be exercised at a massive profit. It was felt that company directors had too much of an incentive to cheat and manipulate when they held options and so it became illegal for them to own them.

In the late 1980s company directors were being accused of taking excessive salaries and bonuses and steps were taken to reduce the amounts being paid. In the USA a law was passed to restrict remuneration to $1m per annum. Shareholders were nervous that such a limit would give directors very little incentive to work hard and so ESOPs were used as a way round the restriction. It is extremely difficult to value the options granted under ESOPs and this meant that they were not accounted for in the total disclosed in the financial statements.

Major scandals such as Worldcom in the 1990s and the recent Credit Crunch have been blamed on the pressures created by the possibility of directors earning huge amounts from any manipulation of the share price, timed to coincide with the exercise date of ESOP options.

Test your understanding 6

Which of the following executive remuneration package elements will best align the interests of executive directors and shareholders?

A Cash bonus paid to director if company achieves profit growth targets

B Cash bonus paid if director achieves a range individual performance related targets

C Share option bonus scheme that is paid if company achieves profit growth targets

D Private Health insurance for director and immediate family

Relations with shareholders

The board as a whole has responsibility for ensuring that a satisfactory dialogue with shareholders takes place. The board should use the AGM to communicate with investors and to encourage their participation.

Relations with shareholders

The chairman should ensure that the views of shareholders are communicated to the board as a whole. The chairman should discuss governance and strategy with major shareholders. The senior independent director should attend sufficient meetings with a range of major shareholders to listen to their views in order to help develop a balanced understanding of the issues and concerns of major shareholders.

The chairman should arrange for the chairmen of the audit, remuneration and nomination committees to be available to answer questions at the AGM and for all directors to attend.

Test your understanding 7

Which of the following are principles of the UK Corporate Governance Code: (Select all that apply.)

A The role of chair and CEO should be separate

B Non-executive directors should be appointed

C The Board should meet once per month

D The Board is responsible for determining the nature and extent of the significant risks the company will face

4 Corporate governance and internal controls

The **board** is responsible for:

- maintaining a sound system of internal control,
- reviewing the effectiveness of internal controls, and
- reporting to shareholders that this review has been carried out.

It is the responsibility of **management** to:

- identify and evaluate the risks faced by the company, for consideration by the board
- design, operate and monitor a suitable system of internal control.

Turnbull Report

This is the most specific report regarding the requirements for internal control. (See Internal Control: Guidance for Directors on the Combined Code 1999 and revised 2005)

The Turnbull Report requires that internal controls should be established using a **risk-based approach**. Specifically a company should:

- Establish business objectives.
- Identify the associated key risks.
- Decide upon the controls to address the risks.

- Set up a system to implement the required controls, including regular feedback.

In establishing this structure the Turnbull Report summarises the way that businesses should be controlled (and also how this examination paper links the topics of risk and control).

In addition, the Turnbull Report addresses the responsibilities of directors and management in relation to risk and control, as discussed above.

Turnbull went on to suggest that directors should review internal controls under the five headings identified by COSO in 1992:

- Control environment.
- Risk assessment.
- Control activities.
- Information and communication.
- Monitoring.

The Turnbull Report went on to suggest that internal audit makes a significant and valuable contribution to a company.

Test your understanding 8

The Turnbull Report requires that:

A Internal controls should be established using a risk-based approach

B The CEO and chairperson are separate roles

C An audit committee is set up

D Director's remuneration is fully disclosed

Test your understanding 9

The principles of good corporate governance in the UK Corporate Governance Code include: (Select all that apply.)

A Leadership

B Efficiency

C Accountability

D Remuneration

E Relations with stakeholders

More on reviewing the effectiveness of internal controls

Management is accountable to the board for monitoring the system of internal control. The board has a responsibility for reviewing its effectiveness.

To review the effectiveness of the internal control system, the board should not rely on the existence of suitable embedded internal control processes. It should also receive regular reports on risks and controls, in addition to carrying out an annual assessment.

When reviewing reports on internal control, the board should:

- consider the significant risks and how they have been identified, evaluated and managed
- assess the effectiveness of the internal controls for managing each significant risk
- consider whether any controls are weak and action is necessary to strengthen them.

'Should the board become aware at any time of a significant failing or weakness in internal control, it should determine how the failing or weakness arose and re-assess the effectiveness of management's ongoing processes for designing, operating and monitoring the system of internal control' (Turnbull Report).

The annual assessment of the system of internal control should consider:

- the changes since the assessment carried out in the previous year
- the scope and quality of management's ongoing monitoring of risks and of the system of internal control
- the extent and frequency of the communication of the results of this monitoring to the board
- the extent and frequency of internal control weaknesses and failing that have been identified during the year
- the effectiveness of the company's public reporting processes.

More on board's statement on internal control

The annual report should provide sufficient meaningful and high-level information to enable the shareholders to understand the main features of the company's risk management processes and system of internal control.

At the very least, the board should disclose:

- that there is an ongoing process for identifying, evaluating and managing the significant risks faced by the company
- that this process has been in place throughout the year
- that the process is regularly reviewed by the board, and
- that it accords with the Turnbull Guidance.

The statement should include an acknowledgement by the board that it is responsible for the company's system of internal control and for reviewing its effectiveness.

The board should also summarise the process by which it reviewed the effectiveness of the control systems, whether that review was conducted directly or through, say, an audit committee.

5 Corporate governance and the audit committee

Audit committees were first required under the Cadbury Code (and are now required by the UK Corporate Governance Code) in response to criticisms of the relationship between the directors and the auditors.

It was felt that the auditors were not sufficiently independent of the board of directors and that, as a result, the auditors were not providing their monitoring and reporting role as they should be.

Particular criticisms of the relationship were about:

- Remuneration of the auditors – decided by the directors.
- Appointment of the auditors – at the discretion of the directors in practice.
- Reports of the auditors – received by the directors.
- The directors had the power to give other lucrative work to auditors.

To address these concerns, audit committees were to be established.

- Audit committees are made up of non-executive directors (at least one of which should have recent relevant financial experience) and have formal terms of reference.
- The audit committee should meet at least three times per year, and also at least once a year have a meeting with the auditors without the presence of any executive directors.

Responsibilities of an audit committee

The responsibilities of the audit committee would typically include:

- Review of the financial statements, and any interim reports produced.
- Review of the company's system of internal financial controls.
- Discussion with the auditors about any significant matters that arose on the audit.
- Review of the internal audit programme and significant findings of the internal auditors.
- Recommendations on the appointment and removal of the auditors.
- The setting of the audit fee in discussion with the auditors.
- Review of the audit report and any management letter provided by the external auditors.
- Review all the company's internal control and risk management systems (unless this is delegated to a separate risk committee).
- Ensure that a system is in place for whistleblowing.

Audit committee and financial reporting

The key roles of the audit committee are 'oversight', 'assessment' and 'review' of other functions and systems in the company.

The audit committee should review the significant financial reporting issues and judgements in connection with the preparation of the company's financial statements. Management is responsible for preparing the financial statements and the auditors are responsible for preparing the audit plan and carrying out the audit.

The audit committee needs to satisfy itself that the financial statements prepared by management and approved by the auditors are acceptable. It should consider:

- the significant accounting policies that have been used, and whether these are appropriate
- any significant estimates or judgements that have been made, and whether these are reasonable
- the method used to account for any significant or unusual transactions, where alternative accounting treatments are possible
- the clarity and completeness of the disclosures in the financial statements.

The committee should listen to the views of the auditors on these matters. If it is not satisfied with any aspect of the proposed financial reporting, it should inform the board.

Audit committee and internal control

In relation to internal controls, the audit committee should:

- review the company's internal **financial** controls
- review **all** the company's internal control and risk management systems, unless the task is taken on by a separate risk committee or the full board
- give its approval to the statements in the annual report relating to internal control and risk management
- receive reports from management about the effectiveness of the control systems it operates
- receive reports on the conclusions of any tests carried out on the controls by the internal or external auditors.

Audit committee and internal audit

The audit committee should monitor and review the effectiveness of the company's internal audit function. If the company does not have an internal audit function:

- the committee should consider annually whether there is a need for an internal audit function and make a recommendation to the board, and
- the reasons for the absence of an internal audit function should be explained in the relevant section of the annual report.

Where a company does have an internal audit function, the audit committee has an important role in preserving the independence of the internal audit function from pressure or interference.

The audit committee should:

- approve the appointment or termination of appointment of the head of internal audit
- ensure that the internal auditor has direct access to the board chairman and is accountable to the audit committee
- review and assess the annual internal audit work plan
- receive a report periodically about the work of the internal auditor
- review and monitor the response of management to the findings of the internal auditor
- monitor and assess the role and effectiveness of the internal audit function within the company's overall risk management system.

Audit committee and external auditors

The audit committee is responsible for oversight of the company's relations with its external auditors. The audit committee should:

- have the primary responsibility for making a recommendation to the board on the appointment, re-appointment or removal of the external auditors
- 'oversee' the selection process when new auditors are being considered
- approve (though not necessarily negotiate) the terms of engagement of the external auditors and the remuneration for their audit services
- have annual procedures for ensuring the independence and objectivity of the external auditors
- review the scope of the audit with the auditor, and satisfy itself that this is sufficient
- make sure that appropriate plans are in place for the audit at the start of each annual audit
- carry out a post-completion audit review.

Test your understanding 10

P Company follows a principles based code of corporate governance and has both an audit committee and a risk committee. Which of the following roles would be carried out by the audit committee?

Select **all** that apply

A Review of the financial statements, and any interim reports produced.

B Review of the company's system of internal financial controls.

C Discussion with the auditors about any significant matters that arose on the audit.

D Recommendations on the appointment and removal of the auditors.

E Act on any recommendations put forward by the auditors in the management letter.

F Review all the company's internal control and risk management systems.

Test your understanding 11

Within the UK Corporate Governance Code it states that the chairman should arrange for several stakeholder groups to attend the AGM. These include: (Select all that apply.)

A The audit, remuneration and nomination committees

B The directors

C The Chief Executive Officer

D The chairpersons of the audit, remuneration and nomination committees

E All non-executive directors

Test your understanding 12

Responsibilities of an audit committee include: (Select all that apply.)

A Review of the financial statements and any interim reports produced

B Review of the company's system of internal financial controls

C The detection of fraud

D Ensuring a system is in place for whistleblowing

6 International developments

Sarbanes-Oxley Act

The US financial world was rocked by a number of very serious financial scandals around 2000/2001, the most well known of which were Enron and Worldcom. The problems of Enron and Worldcom brought into question US accounting practices (for example, by exploiting loopholes in US accounting, Enron did not show its problems on its statement of financial position) and also the corporate governance exercised by directors. In order to restore confidence in the results of US companies the Sarbanes-Oxley Act was introduced.

- The SOX legislation is extremely detailed and carries the full force of the law behind it.
- The Act also includes requirements for the Securities and Exchange Commission (SEC) to issue certain rules on corporate governance.
- It is relevant to US companies, directors of subsidiaries of US listed businesses and auditors who are working on US listed businesses.

Differences to the UK Code

Overall the two main differences between SOX and the UK Code are:

(i) **Enforcement**

The UK Code is a series of voluntary codes (a '**principles-based** approach') whereas SOX takes a robust legislative approach which sets out clear personal responsibility for some company directors with a series of criminal offences that are punishable by fines (both company and its officers) or lengthy jail sentences (a '**rules-based** approach').

(ii) **Documentation**

SOX creates a much more rigorous demand for evidencing internal controls and having them audited.

Key points of SOX

SOX KEY POINTS
Auditor independence
Auditors are restricted in the additional services they can provide to an audit client.
Audit committee
Company must have an audit committee – will be disallowed from trading if it does not have one.
Internal control report
Annual report must include statements concerning the internal control systems in the company. (Section 404)
Certification of accuracy of financial statements
Must be vouched for by CEO and CFO.
Increased financial disclosures
Financial reports to detail off balance sheet financing.
Restrictions on dealing
Directors prohibited from dealing in shares at 'sensitive times'.
Audit partner
Senior partner must be changed every five years.

UK Code vs. SOX

Certification of accuracy the financial statements

SOX gives personal responsibility for the accuracy of the firm's financial statements to its principal executive officer (CEO) and the chief financial officer (Finance Director), who must provide a signed certificate to the Securities and Exchange Commission (SEC) vouching for the accuracy of the statements signed by the two officers above. It is a criminal offence to file defective financial statements.

The CEO and CFO must also hand back any bonuses for previous years if the financial statements need to be amended due to defective financial statements.

This is a far more specific requirement than the UK Code that only provides for a statement about the responsibility of the board for preparing financial statements and a going concern statement.

Increased financial disclosures

Whilst the UK Code focuses more on directors and their accountability to shareholders SOX includes a number of provisions for greater or more rapid disclosure of financial information:

- In its financial reports the company must disclose details about its off balance sheet transactions and their material effects.
- Material changes should be disclosed on a rapid and current basis i.e. new off balance sheet transactions, loss of a major customer or a one-off writing down charge.

Internal control report

Companies need to include a report on 'internal control over financial reporting' in their annual report. This must:

- Include a statement of management's responsibility for adequate control systems.
- Identify the framework to evaluate internal control.
- Provide an assessment of the effectiveness of internal control and any material weakness.

Again this follows the UK Code quite closely regarding the board's responsibilities and the role of the audit committee in reporting on the effectiveness of financial controls.

Audit committee

In the same way as the UK Code, SOX requires companies to comply with certain audit committee requirements. However, the US stock exchanges are prohibited from listing any firm that does not comply.

As per the Combined Code the committee should:

- Be independent (in the UK NEDs).
- Have responsibility for appointing and compensating auditors.
- Oversee the auditors.
- Establish whistleblower procedures regarding questionable accounting or audit matters.

Unlike the UK Code, however, SOX goes much further in restricting auditors and non-audit work. A number of specific non-audit activities are explicitly prohibited.

Whilst the UK Code discourages auditors carrying out non-audit work, an explanation of how companies safeguard auditor independence in the annual report is usually sufficient if additional work is carried out.

SOX also requires a compulsory rotation of the lead audit partner working on a corporate client.

Test your understanding 13

In the US, the accuracy of the financial statements is vouched for by: (Select all that apply.)

A The board of directors

B The audit committee only

C The chief financial officer

D The chairman only

E The chief executive officer

Test your understanding 14

The most heavily regulated corporate governance provisions are in:

A The UK

B The US

C Canada

D South Africa

The risk of no corporate governance

Imagine a poor country with no corporate governance at all. Should we trade with businesses within that country? Do we have a responsibility to encourage corporate governance?

In answer to the first question – should we trade with that country, the answer could be 'yes' or 'no'. Firstly – yes, the country is poor, prices might be low, the population might need employment. Our company could benefit from lower prices and benefit from good public relations by providing much needed jobs.

However, without corporate governance, businesses may not operate to the standards expected of our own country which could bring reputation risk. We might not be able to trust them.

So maybe the answer should be 'no'. The overseas company may be badly run by its management, with total disregard for the 'rules' we operate within our own country. The benefits to us now may be outweighed by any future costs in terms of lost reputation should an adverse event occur.

In answer to the second question – should we encourage corporate governance, then the answer should probably be 'yes'. Our richer countries success may be founded on operating within the guidelines of corporate governance – well-run companies following the 'rules'. The poorer country companies might learn from this and see that more profit can be made through trade with other countries that comply with corporate governance.

This will not happen overnight and is not costless. However, by asking those poorer companies to make small changes over time (such as having non-executive directors or not dealing using bribes) we would encourage trade with them, which in itself would bring monetary advantage which could be reinvested to improve their company in the future.

Test your understanding 15

Country N is a poor developing nation with no corporate governance structures in place. Several large international organisations have recently publicised decisions not to trade with Country N because its' government and business structures are seen as corrupt and its treatment of workers poor.

Company Q, one of the world's largest manufacturers has however decided to maintain its relationship with Country N from where it sources many of its components at competitive prices. Company Q has issued a media statement detailing how it intends to encourage the government and companies within Country N to adopt corporate governance 'best practice'.

Which of the following are reasons why Company Q might encourage Country N to adopt corporate governance principles rather than simply cease trading with them?

Select **all** that apply.

A If Country N follows best practice corporate governance this will attract trading partners and potentially increase the wealth of the nation.

B Company Q will be able to continue to source it's components from Country N without disruptions to supply whilst carrying out plans to encourage corporate governance best practice.

C Company Q is likely to satisfy stakeholders who are concerned about CSR through encouraging better working conditions in Country N.

D Company Q may be seen as ethical and progressive if it encourages better governance standards in Country N.

E If suppliers in Country N improve the way they are controlled, there are less likely to be problems with the components Company Q purchases.

The Harvard Law School in the US produced a report in 2013 considering the Board's responsibility towards managing it's stakeholders interests. It is reproduced, in part, below:

Companies today are being called upon by their stakeholders to not only boost their profits, but also to help address some of their country's most challenging problems, including those concerning economic development and the environment. Corporate stakeholders (which typically include shareholders, employees, customers, suppliers, the general public, governments and regulators) are demanding that companies recognise their responsibilities in addressing those problems. As a result, companies are increasingly working with stakeholders to understand their views and concerns on various environmental, social, corporate governance and economic issues and to incorporate and address those views and concerns in the company's strategic decision-making processes.

The Corporate Social Responsibility (CSR) report can be a key component of a company's stakeholder engagement strategy.

Why should the Board be responsible for managing stakeholders' interests?

Corporate Value. Stakeholder engagement includes the formal and informal ways a company stays connected to its stakeholders (the individuals or parties that have an actual or potential interest in or impact on the company, its operations and financial results). Stakeholders often have the ability to influence the success (or failure) of a company at various levels. A primary objective of corporate stakeholder engagement is to build relationships with stakeholders to better understand their perspectives and concerns on key issues (including CSR issues) and to integrate those perspectives and concerns (when and where feasible and prudent) into the company's corporate strategy. Companies tend to recognise certain value associated with stakeholder engagement, including:

- enabling informed board and management decision making;
- avoiding or reducing business risks due to better business intelligence;
- developing and expanding business opportunities, brand value and reputation; and
- bringing diverse perspectives together to facilitate innovation; all of which help drive long-term sustainability and shareholder value.

Rise in Shareholder Activism. Shareholder activism on CSR issues continues to rise, necessitating further engagement between companies and their shareholders and other stakeholders. Related stakeholder concerns can be proactively discussed and addressed, companies may be able to avert a potentially costly and prolonged proxy fight, and relationships between companies and their stakeholders may be nurtured.

Rise in Sustainable and Responsible Investing. Stakeholder engagement and understanding and addressing stakeholders' CSR concerns have become especially important as shareholders and potential investors are increasingly evaluating CSR issues when analyzing investment decisions. Under sustainable and responsible investing ("SRI") principles, investors apply various CSR criteria in their investment analysis. It has been reported that SRI grew by more than 22% to $3.74 trillion in managed assets during the period from 2010–2012. In 2011, the California Public Employees' Retirement System ("CalPERS"), for instance, as part of its "total fund" approach to investment, adopted three core themes for integrating CSR issues into its investment decisions: (1) corporate governance (including issues such as shareowner rights and executive compensation), (2) climate change (including issues related to water stress, carbon emissions, energy efficiency, clean technology and renewable energy) and (3) human capital (including issues of health and safety, responsible contracting and diversity).

Why CSR and the CSR Report?

CSR is defined many ways but generally refers to how a company addresses and manages its environmental, social, corporate governance and economic impacts and how such impacts may affect the company's stakeholders. CSR provides companies an opportunity to strengthen their business (through cost savings, risk mitigation and value enhancement) while contributing to society. CSR should focus on the important areas of interaction between the company and its key stakeholders and address value creation actions as part of the company's strategy.

A 2013 global consumer survey reported that CSR remains a powerful differentiator, influencing both consumer behavior and corporate reputation. Nearly all consumers in that survey noted that when companies engage in CSR, they have a more positive image of the company, would be more likely to trust that company and would be more loyal to that company. Consumer respondents added that it is acceptable if a company is not perfect, provided that the company is honest and transparent about its CSR efforts.

The CSR report, therefore, provides a company with an opportunity to communicate its CSR efforts to the company's stakeholders and to discuss (within the confines of a single document) certain company successes and challenges on a wide array of CSR issues, including corporate governance, climate change, employee and supplier diversity initiatives, and community investments and partnerships. The CSR report is also a medium for transparency (which often improves a company's reputation with certain stakeholders, particularly shareholders, employees, suppliers and communities within which the company operates) and may be used as an effective outreach tool as part of an ongoing shareholder relations campaign. In addition, the CSR report provides existing and potential investors with CSR information to assist in analysing investment decisions.

The CSR Report

Corporate CSR reports address issues most important to each of the company's key stakeholders, for example:

Shareholders – addressing the company's business model and corporate governance, including disclosing the role of the board in risk management, in sustainability reporting and in evaluating CSR performance.

Employees – addressing diversity, health and safety, training and mentoring, employee relations, and wages and benefits.

Customers – addressing customer service and privacy.

Suppliers – addressing labor standards and whether suppliers are required to implement their own CSR programs.

Communities – addressing corporate philanthropy and charitable contributions, community investment and partnerships, volunteerism and the environmental impact of operations.

Governments and Regulators – addressing lobbying, public policy and the effects of and compliance with environmental regulations.

Other Considerations

With respect to CSR, the CSR report and stakeholder engagement, a company and/or its board of directors may also want to consider the following:

CEO Responsibility and Board Oversight. The chief executive officer should ultimately be responsible for establishing effective communications with the company's stakeholders with CSR oversight by the board or board committee (or committees). Such oversight may include (1) review of CSR trends and impacts on the company's operations, financial results and stakeholders and (2) periodic updates from the chief executive officer/ management concerning the company's positions on and actions taken relating to relevant CSR issues and how such positions and actions have affected or may affect stakeholders.

Focus on Impact. Because management time and resources are limited, companies should focus on those CSR issues that may have the greatest impact on them and their operations and finances.

Stock Exchange Reporting Initiatives. Although the CSR report is not currently mandated by any federal law or regulation, there is a reported global effort by certain groups, including investors, to mobilize stock exchanges to adopt a listing requirement regarding sustainability (CSR) reporting. Regulators in the United Kingdom, for example, are requiring companies listed on the main market of the London Stock Exchange to publish full details of their greenhouse gas emissions for reporting years ending on or after September 30, 2013. While there currently is no mandatory sustainability (CSR) reporting requirement for companies listed on the New York Stock Exchange or NASDAQ, both exchanges have joined the United Nations' Sustainable Stock Exchanges initiative which aims to explore how exchanges can work together with investors, regulators and listed companies to enhance corporate transparency on CSR issues and encourage responsible long-term approaches to investment.

Identify Corporate Team. Companies should identify the corporate team that will be responsible for their CSR report and include, at a minimum, employees from their investor/public/community relations, legal, compliance, regulatory and human resources departments.

Other Components of Stakeholder Engagement. The CSR report is only one component of an effective stakeholder engagement strategy. Other components of such strategy may include supplemental reports (e.g., Carbon Disclosure Project reports), regulatory filings, the annual meeting of shareholders and direct dialogue with stakeholders (e.g., community town hall and employee as well as supplier meetings).

Test your understanding 16

Generally share options should not be awarded to non-executive directors. However, if they are awarded the non-executive director may sell them:

A Whenever he or she wants to

B When they leave the non-executive Board

C At nil profit

D One year after leaving the non-executive board

Test your understanding 17

Which of the following are usually staffed by non-executive directors? (Select all that apply.)

A The risk committee

B The nominations committee

C The audit committee

D The remuneration committee

Test your understanding 18 – H electronics (Integration)

H is a company that manufactures basic electronic components such as capacitors and printed circuit boards for the IT industry. The company has recently appointed K as a non-executive director. K was the founder and chief executive of a quoted executive recruitment consultancy and employment agency. She has stood down from that role and has accepted the position on H's board in order to seek fresh challenges.

H's board meets twice every year for a formal discussion of company strategy. These meetings tend to look back at H's performance for the previous half-year. This discussion mainly focuses on a report based on the monthly management accounts for the previous half year and then briefly considers the future impact of these. Monthly management accounts are presented to the board at their monthly board meetings.

K has attended two of the meetings relating to strategy. At the conclusion of the second meeting she expressed two concerns about the half-yearly board meetings. Firstly the meetings focus on feedback rather than feed forward. K argued that the board should be constantly forward looking and aiming to identify new opportunities. K believes that historical summaries of past performance distract from the need to plan for the future. Secondly, K believes that the half-yearly meetings focus on details associated with the existing business model rather than strategic direction. She believes that it would be a more productive use of the board's time at these meetings to work towards identifying strategic opportunities that might be pursued over the next three to five years. When she was chief executive of her employment agency the board met at least once per year and frequently more often to think about new strategies that might be pursued.

H's Production Director has complained that K has really misunderstood the board's responsibility for the management of H. The Production Director believes that her first argument is invalid because the distinction between feedback and feed forward control is more about day to day tactical management rather than strategic management. The Production Director believes that feed forward is more about fine tuning rather than strategic management. The Production Director also believes that K's comments about strategic direction demonstrate a very limited understanding of manufacturing electronics. H must respond and react to the requirements of the IT industry. H cannot really innovate. The life cycle of the company's products is such that changes to H's strategic direction happen infrequently. The Production Director has suggested that K should restrict her comments to the information prepared for consideration by the full board, especially as she has come from the service sector and has no real understanding of manufacturing.

Required:

(a) Evaluate the respective arguments put forward by K and by the Production Director concerning the need for H's full board to be forward looking rather than focussing on past performance.

(b) Evaluate K's argument that H's board should review the company's strategic direction at its half-yearly meetings.

(c) Evaluate the Production Director's argument that K should not comment on the manner in which H is run because of her background and lack of experience in a manufacturing company.

(45 minutes)

Test your understanding 19 – C consultancy (Case study)

Scenario

C is a partnership that offers a range of consultancy services involving structural engineering. The firm specialises in examining plans prepared by architects to ensure that the buildings being planned are structurally sound. This requires careful consideration of the design and the materials being used to ensure that the resulting building will be stable and can withstand the effects of the wind and other forces of nature. C specialises in major contracts and the firm often advises on complex designs that use innovative building techniques.

C has a reputation for having a competitive culture. The firm offers salaries that are much higher than the industry average. There is an "up or out" culture which means that qualified staff must demonstrate the potential to be promoted to the next level of seniority within a relatively short period or they will be encouraged to leave.

C has 45 partners, all of whom are qualified structural engineers, and approximately 400 professional staff. C's professional staff comprises engineers at different stages in their careers, ranging from team leaders to junior trainees. The team leaders are all experienced engineers who are eligible for promotion to partnership in the event that a vacancy arises. Selection for partnership depends on the ability to consistently complete assignments to a high standard and within budget.

Trainee engineers are appointed on a three year contract, during which time they are expected to pass their professional exams. C takes on approximately 50 trainees every year. Those trainees who demonstrate the necessary qualities to succeed in C are offered the opportunity to stay with the firm at the conclusion of their training contracts. Those who do not receive such an offer must leave.

Each partner is responsible for a portfolio of assignments, and each portfolio is accounted for as a profit centre. Partners are expected to be aware of the opportunities to bid for assignments and to win new business despite competition from other engineering firms. C has a reputation for bidding aggressively and accepting tight deadlines. Each partner is responsible for a portfolio of assignments, each of which will involve a team leader and several assistants. Professional staff time is charged to assignments on an absorption costing basis and the firm's time recording system calculates a notional profit for each assignment based on the cost of time charged against the fee generated.

At the end of every financial year each partner receives an equal share of the firm's annual profit, but it is a matter of pride for each partner to generate more profit for the firm than he or she receives from the annual profit share.

All partners enjoy equal seniority and major strategic decisions are decided by a simple majority vote of the partnership. The firm is managed on a day to day basis by a management committee which comprises three partners. Every partner is expected to take a turn as a member of the management committee at some stage in his or her career. One person joins the committee every year to take over from the committee member whose term of office has expired. The third year of service on the management committee is spent as the firm's managing partner. There is no additional reward for serving on the management committee, but during that year the committee members are not expected to be responsible for a full complement of assignments and the managing partner is not expected to be responsible for any assignments.

Task

As an external consultant, write a letter to the audit committee evaluating the strengths and weaknesses of C's governance arrangements with respect to the partnership and its management committee.

(20 minutes)

Test your understanding 20 – P chemicals (Case study)

Scenario

P is a major quoted company that manufactures industrial chemicals. The company's Board comprises a Chief Executive and five other executive directors, a non-executive chairman and four non-executive directors.

Trigger

Two of the non-executive directors have served on P's board for five years. The company has a policy of asking non-executive directors to stand down after six years and so the Chairman has established a Nominations Committee to start the process of selecting replacements.

Three replacements have been suggested to the Nominations Committee. The nominees are:

- S, who is on the main board of C Pensions, an investment institution which owns 5% of P's equity. S has worked for C Pensions for 20 years and has always worked in the management of the company's investments, initially as an analyst and more recently as director in charge of investments. Before working for C Pensions, S was an investment analyst with an insurance company for 15 years.
- T, who is a CIMA member, is about to retire from full-time work. T has had a varied career, completing the CIMA qualification while working as a trainee accountant with a food manufacturer, then as a management accountant with an engineering company and finally as a senior accountant with a commercial bank. T was promoted to the bank's board and has been Finance Director for eight years.
- U, who is a former politician. After a brief career as a journalist, U became a member of parliament at the age of 35. After spending 20 years as a politician, including several years as a government minister, U has recently retired from politics at the age of 55. U already holds two other non-executive directorships in companies that do not compete with and are not in any way connected to P.

The Chairman of P is keen to recruit more non-executive directors as a matter of priority because the Remuneration Committee faces a difficult task. The executive directors are presently remunerated with a combination of a salary and executive stock options. P's shareholders have expressed concern about the pressures created by these stock options and have asked that they be replaced by individual bonuses that reflect the personal contribution made by each of the executive directors.

The Chairman and the non-executive directors are discussing the level of bonus that should be awarded for the current year. This has been complicated because P made a loss for the first time. The Chief Executive has stated that it would not be appropriate to accept a bonus from a loss-making company, but the other executive directors claim that the loss was attributable to economic and industrial conditions and that their leadership minimised the loss. All of the executive directors other than the Chief Executive have asked for substantial bonuses to reflect their leadership in difficult times.

Task

Prepare a briefing note to the Chairman, in your capacity as a non-executive director, which:

(a) Evaluates the suitability of each of the three nominees.

(30 minutes)

(b) Discusses the problems associated with determining a suitable level of bonus for each of P's executive directors.

(20 minutes)

Test your understanding 21 – JKL (Case study)

Scenario

JKL is a profitable but small FTSE 500 company in a technology-related service industry with annual sales of £150 million. Its gearing is 50% of total assets, secured by a mortgage over its main site. The industry is highly competitive but there are major barriers for entry to new competitors and the long-term future of JKL is considered by industry analysts to be sound.

The Board comprises a non-executive chairman, a chief executive who has a large shareholding, an executive finance director, operations director and marketing director and a non-executive director with wide knowledge of the industry and who retired from the company 3 years ago. There is only one committee of the board. The audit committee consists of the chairman, non-executive director and finance director.

There is no internal audit function in JKL but the external auditors are relied on to report on any weaknesses in control and their letter of engagement authorises them to carry out work over and above the financial audit in relation to internal control. The external auditors have always given a 'clean' audit report to the company and have reported that internal controls within JKL are sound. There is no formal risk management process in place in JKL although board meetings routinely consider risk during their deliberations.

Trigger

The chairman and chief executive both believe that compliance with corporate governance reforms will not benefit JKL and is likely to be too costly. This is disclosed in JKL's Annual Report.

Task

Write a report to the Chairman

(a) evaluating the key reforms and best practice in:

- corporate governance
- risk management that have taken place over the last few years and which affect JKL;

(30 minutes)

and

(b) with reasons, which (if any) of those reforms should be adopted by the company.

(15 minutes)

Test your understanding 22 – HFD (Case study)

Scenario

HFD is a registered charity with 100 employees and 250 volunteers providing in-home care for elderly persons who are unable to fully take care of themselves. The company structure has no shareholders in a practical sense although a small number of issued shares are held by the sponsors who established the charity many years previously. HFD is governed by a seven-member Board of Directors. The Chief Executive Officer (CEO) chairs the board which comprises the chief financial officer (CFO) and five independent, unpaid non-executive directors who were appointed by the CEO based on past business relationships. You are one of the independent members of HFD's board.

The CEO/Chair sets the board agendas, distributes board papers in advance of meetings and briefs board members in relation to each agenda item. At each of its quarterly meetings the Board reviews the financial reports of the charity in some detail and the CFO answers questions. Other issues that regularly appear as agenda items include new government funding initiatives for the client group, and the results of proposals that have been submitted to funding agencies, of which about 25% are successful. There is rarely any discussion of operational matters relating to the charity as the CEO believes these are outside the directors' experience and the executive management team is more than capable of managing the delivery of the in-home care services.

The Board has no separate audit committee but relies on the annual management letter from the external auditors to provide assurance that financial controls are operating effectively. The external auditors were appointed by the CEO many years previously.

Trigger

HFD's Board believes that its corporate governance could be improved by following the principles applicable to listed companies.

Task

Prepare briefing notes for a meeting with the Board:

(a) Recommending how HFD's Board should be restructured to comply with the principles of good corporate governance.

(30 minutes)

(a) Explaining the aspects of CIMA's ethical principles and the conceptual framework underlying those principles which you would consider relevant to continuing in your role as an independent member of HFD's Board.

(20 minutes)

7 Chapter summary

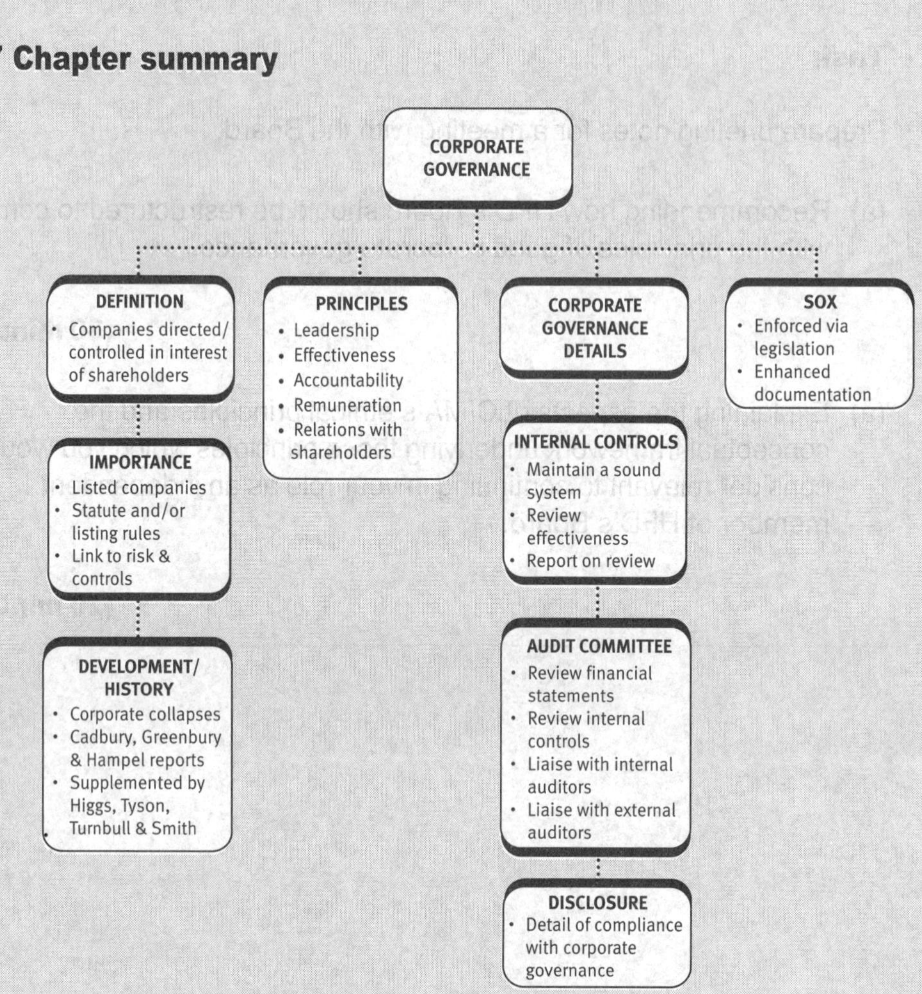
CORPORATE GOVERNANCE
DEFINITION
• Companies directed/controlled in interest of shareholders
IMPORTANCE
• Listed companies
• Statute and/or listing rules
• Link to risk & controls
DEVELOPMENT/ HISTORY
• Corporate collapses
• Cadbury, Greenbury & Hampel reports
• Supplemented by Higgs, Tyson, Turnbull & Smith
PRINCIPLES
• Leadership
• Effectiveness
• Accountability
• Remuneration
• Relations with shareholders
CORPORATE GOVERNANCE DETAILS
INTERNAL CONTROLS
• Maintain a sound system
• Review effectiveness
• Report on review
AUDIT COMMITTEE
• Review financial statements
• Review internal controls
• Liaise with internal auditors
• Liaise with external auditors
DISCLOSURE
• Detail of compliance with corporate governance
SOX
• Enforced via legislation
• Enhanced documentation

Test your understanding answers

Test your understanding 1

The correct answer is C – Nick Leeson had responsibility of both the back and front office dealings of Barings Bank, dealing with issues that none of his managers understood.

Test your understanding 2

The correct answer is B.

Test your understanding 3

A, B and C

- Option A: Yes because the CEO has a named person (The Chairman) in addition to the NED's to whom he or she must account for the company's performance and his or her own behaviour.
- Option B: Yes – It is clear that the CEO is directly involved in the management of the company and the chairman can adopt a more supervisory position.
- Option C: Yes – It is considered best practice because it provides a reassurance to the shareholders and ensures compliance with relevant codes.
- Option D: No – It could be argued that decision making is quicker with just one leader who does not need to seek the approval of the chairman.
- Option E: No – There is a danger than the leadership becomes fragmented, especially if the two most senior members of staff do not agree and cannot provide a united front. This can lead to a lack of goal congruence in an organisation.

Test your understanding 4

D and E

- Option A – The NED's will still be able to assess managements performance in meeting objectives, it is the objectives themselves they will not be involved in setting.
- Option B – provided the NED's are informed on a timely basis about strategic decisions they will be able to carry out their risk role.
- Option C – it appears that the ED's are no more knowledgeable than the NED's in this scenario.
- Option D – The role of the NED is to scrutinise decisions made by ED's and act on behalf of shareholders and other stakeholders. Without this involvement there is a risk decisions are made in the best interests of the executive directors. This is a key reason why NED's should be involved in strategic decision making.
- Option E – It cannot be disputed that time will be saved and the NED's could use it to carry out other duties. This does not make the proposal correct.

Test your understanding 5

B, C and D

The remuneration committee should consist of independent NED's and should not consider NED remuneration. This should be decided by the board as a whole and/or shareholders depending on the specific requirements in the company Articles of Association.

A – there is no need for the FD to resign from the company but they shouldn't be on the remuneration committee.

E – there is no need to replace all NEDs

Test your understanding 6

C

Whilst the best trigger for the awarding of a bonus would be the director achieving a range of individual performance targets, share options would best align remuneration to shareholder interests as both parties would want the company share price to rise to maximise their individual financial return.

Test your understanding 7

The correct answers are A, B and D – The Board should meet regularly, not necessarily monthly.

Test your understanding 8

The correct answer is A – By definition.

Test your understanding 9

The correct answers are A, C and D – Efficiency should read as effectiveness. Stakeholders should read as shareholders.

Test your understanding 10

A, B, C and D

- Option E the audit committee would review the management letter and actions taken by the board but not take action themselves.
- Option F would be carried out by the risk committee.

Test your understanding 11

The correct answers are B, C and D – Only the chairmen of each of these committees are suggested to attend.

Test your understanding 12

The correct answers are A, B and D – The detection of fraud is management's responsibility. The audit committee could advise on any fraud found.

Test your understanding 13

The correct answers are C and E – In the US, the accuracy of the financial statements is vouched for by the chief financial officer and the chief executive officer.

Test your understanding 14

The correct answer is B – The US has a 'rules-based' corporate governance provision. This has been prompted by the higher number and higher value of corporate scandals occurring there.

Test your understanding 15

B, C, D and E

- Option A – is a reason why good governance may benefit Country N. It is not specific to Company Q.
- Option B, C, D and E all relate to Company Q.

Test your understanding 16

The correct answer is D.

Test your understanding 17

The correct answer is B, C and D – A risk committee can be staffed by executive directors. The other committees are covered by corporate governance codes and are staffed by non-executive directors.

Test your understanding 18 – H electronics (Integration)

(a) K's basic argument is that the board ought to be forward looking, with a view to setting a strategic direction for H. That is a far more constructive approach to running the company than focussing on past performance. Part of her concern may be due to the fact that the half-yearly reports are really just an amalgamation of the monthly management accounts that have already been considered by the executive directors during their monthly meetings.

The Production Director's response is logical because the present arrangements appear to focus on looking at H's present position and reflecting on the effectiveness of its strategies. That is not as pointless nor is it as backward looking as K suggests. H's management team is aware that the board will be looking at performance on a half-yearly basis and so there will always be an incentive to perform well in terms of working towards the company's strategic objectives. Presumably the main board has agreed that six months is a suitable interval over which to review progress, although it is also clearly only a brief period in terms of the company's product life cycle.

The Production Director could be correct in the sense that feed forward control is largely about determining corrective action on the basis of predicted results. Strategic management should be largely about setting targets and developing tactics to achieve those results. Feed forward control is more appropriate to the monitoring of the effectiveness of tactics.

It is to be hoped that neither director is arguing too strongly for one approach to managing H. K is not necessarily asking that the board does not use historical information in order to inform its deliberations and the Production Director does not appear to be arguing for all board meetings to be backward thinking.

(b) It could be argued that the board ought to provide senior and middle management with a clear strategic direction. Strategies ought to have clear and specific objectives that give management something to work towards. For example, H's board may ask management to develop plans that will increase production capacity by 50% over the next three years.

Once a strategy has been put in place it should be kept under review and changed if necessary. However, changes should be kept to the minimum, otherwise management will become confused and may be demoralised. H's board should aim to motivate management by demonstrating commitment to the strategy rather than actively engaging in making changes to it. Otherwise, strategic management may be driven by day-to-day changes and circumstances and H will have no real direction.

H is a manufacturing company that requires complex and expensive technology. Many changes in strategy will prove expensive to implement. H exists to service demand for components from a wider industry. Many aspects of strategy will be set by H's customers and H will have to be responsive to the industry's demands. It would make considerable sense for H to consider progress towards implementing strategies on a half-yearly basis but it is unlikely that it will be feasible for the company to make meaningful changes of strategic direction twice per year.

On balance, it appears that K's arguments have been influenced by her experience in the service sector, where it is likely to be possible to be far more innovative because the costs of following different strategic directions are likely to be lower.

(c) The Production Director's arguments raise significant questions about the role of the non-executive director. It would make little sense for K to have a seat on the board if she was not judged capable of making a meaningful contribution to the board's work.

It could be argued that non-executive directors have a significant role to play in providing oversight of the workings of the board as a whole. To an extent, it would be desirable for the non-executives to maintain some distance from the active management of the company, even at the strategic level, because they will then be capable of being a little more impartial in their oversight. K's role could be more concerned with making sure that the executive directors have a clear and consistent direction in mind for the company, rather than in participating in developing a strategy herself.

It may be possible for the non-executive directors to offer some fresh insights that would not have occurred to their colleagues on the executive board, without compromising their independence. K comes from a completely different background and may be able to ask questions that would not be considered by the executive directors. From time to time it is healthy to challenge accepted norms and to ask whether things could be improved. K clearly has an entrepreneurial outlook and that could raise questions about whether H could identify new revenue streams or meet customer needs in a different way.

If the non-executives are to provide effective oversight then they should not be constrained by the executive directors. They should be permitted to raise questions about any aspect of the company's management. The executive directors should recognise that the search and appointment process should ensure that only competent and capable people are appointed to the board and should respect the non-executives accordingly.

Test your understanding 19 – C consultancy (Case study)

Address

Date

Dear Audit Committee,

It was a pleasure meeting with several of your colleagues at C recently. Further to those meetings regarding C's governance arrangements and the management committee, I write to inform you of my findings.

Strengths

The fact that there is no benefit in terms of salary or seniority means that the partners are not likely to be in competition for promotion to the management committee. That has the advantage of ensuring that they focus on winning business and supervising assignments. The management committee will be made up of practising engineers who fully understand the important issues in the running of the firm. The fact that the members will return to normal partnership within three years means that they will not introduce any radical developments that may be beneficial to themselves but harmful to the partnership as a whole.

The partnership will include a number of members who have served on the management committee, which will give them a better understanding of the firm's management.

Weaknesses

Partners may view the need to serve on the committee as an interruption of their professional activities as engineers. Their reduced commitment to assignments during the first two years and withdrawal from assignments in the third year could cost them contact with the architects and contractors on whom they rely for referrals.

Partners may be tempted to take on an excessive workload while serving on the committee and so the firm's leadership will suffer because it is not a top priority. Partners who are eligible for membership of the management committee may feel that it will interrupt their ongoing careers and so may start to lobby for exclusion. That will defeat the objective of every partner taking it in turn and may mean that only those partners who are willing, who may not be the best candidates, will participate.

The annual change of managing partner means that there will be no real continuity in that position, although each new incumbent will have spent the previous two years on the committee.

The fact that there is no room for professional management on the committee means that the administrative aspects of managing this engineering firm may not enjoy the prominence they deserve.

The fact that major strategic decisions are left to the partnership as a whole may mean that the management committee tends not to look beyond the immediate future.

Major strategic changes may be difficult to implement if it is necessary to obtain a majority of the votes from 45 partners.

Should you have any further queries, please do not hesitate to ask.

Yours sincerely

External consultant

Test your understanding 20 – P chemicals (Case study)

(a) **Briefing notes**

To: The Chairman

From: A non-executive director

Date: Today

Subject: Suitability of nominees and bonuses

Suitability of nominees

S is employed by a major shareholder, which is regarded as a problem for potential non-executives in terms of the guidance in the Combined Code. There is a risk that S will suffer a conflict of interest in that decisions that are good for P as a whole may not be ideal for C Pensions and vice versa. That problem could be overcome to an extent by recognising S's interest as and when it becomes an issue and making sure that there are sufficient independent directors to compensate. S has no skills or experience that would be directly relevant to the strategic management of a manufacturing company. Having said that, it could be that S will bring a fresh perspective to board meetings and so the lack of direct experience could be an advantage. S also has a great deal of experience of managing investment portfolios and that could be valuable in terms of presenting arguments to the board from the perspective of institutional investors. S's experience in that regard could be useful in areas such as financial reporting and so S may be a valuable member of the audit committee.

T is a qualified accountant and that will provide skills that will be directly relevant to the financial reporting and control aspects that are generally associated with non-executive directors. T has had a full and varied career and that will give a range of perspectives that may be valuable to P. T's experience includes the manufacturing sector and that may give insights into the management of capital intensive businesses such as P. T has a range of contacts in banking that will undoubtedly be useful when it comes to negotiating with potential lenders. T is about to retire and so should have sufficient time to devote to this position.

U has had very little experience that is directly relevant to the management of P. U's parliamentary career could, however, have provided skills that are of some value, such as assessing the interests of different stakeholders . That could be a major benefit in the management of a company that manufactures chemicals. U's political contacts could also prove valuable, partly in terms of evaluating proposals that could affect P's position and partly in terms of lobbying to ensure that any changes are not too damaging to the company. U's reputation as a former senior politician will give an incentive to act with integrity and that will enhance P's reputation for honest management. The fact that U appears keen to have a number of directorships is a worry because it implies that P will not necessarily have sufficient time and attention. Furthermore, lobbying for companies that have different issues may mean that U will not always be free to put P first when using former political contacts.

(b) **Bonuses**

One concern is that the bonus mechanism may encourage dysfunctional behaviour. The remuneration committee will have to determine bonuses in such a way that directors cannot improve their rewards by making decisions that are harmful to the company, such as cutting expenditure on discretionary areas such as training in order to improve short-term profit at the expense of the long-term.

Assessing the contribution of individual board members will be difficult because it may be difficult to identify the impact that an individual has had on the running of the company. Measuring contribution effectively requires speculation as to the performance that would have occurred in the director's absence. That would probably involve discussion with the director, who is hardly objective under these circumstances.

One problem with basing the bonus on the contribution of each individual director is that the executive board members may start to compete with one another for the sake of maximising their bonus. Individual directors may feel that it is in their personal interests to withhold information from the rest of the board and to avoid discussing ideas in case they do not receive full credit for their contribution.

The shareholders may feel that the system is a cynical attempt to extract more pay from the company. The remuneration committee members will have to ensure that they do everything they can to reassure the shareholders that any bonus payments are deserved otherwise the board as a whole may lose the shareholders' confidence.

There is even a danger that the shareholders may start to lose confidence in the ability of the non-executives to act in an independent manner in their contribution to the oversight of the company.

The directors will have to receive a realistic reward for their services; otherwise they may feel disillusioned and demotivated. It probably makes very little difference that they are well paid in relation to P's other managers and employees. They are likely to measure their rewards in relation to the directors of other quoted companies.

Test your understanding 21 – JKL (Case study)

Report

To: Chairman

From: A.N. Accountant

Date: Today

Subject: Corporate governance

Introduction

You have asked me to report on the key reforms in corporate governance and risk management that have taken place recently which affect JKL and to recommend (with reasons), which (if any) of those reforms should be adopted by JKL.

This report addresses the following issues: corporate governance, in particular non-executive directors and the audit committee; and risk management, internal control and internal audit. The recommendations are contained at the end of this report.

Corporate governance

Corporate governance in most of the western world is founded on the principle of enhancing shareholder value. Major corporate collapses have been a feature of recent business history in the United Kingdom and elsewhere, and the publicity surrounding these collapses and the actions of institutional investors have raised corporate governance to prominence. The emergence of corporate governance can be seen as a result of regulatory action in response to past failings; changing financial markets including the desire of institutional investors to be more active and the dependence of an ageing population on pensions and savings which have been affected by declining confidence in stock markets.

The main principles of corporate governance are in relation to directors, the remuneration of directors, accountability and audit, relations with shareholders, and in particular with institutional shareholders and disclosure. The 'comply or explain' approach requires listed companies to disclose how they have applied the principles in the Corporate Governance Code and to either comply with the Code or to explain any departure from it. Under the Code, board effectiveness can be summarised as the effective splitting of the roles of chairman and chief effective; the role of non-executive directors and the role of remuneration, nomination and audit committees of the board. In JKL, the roles of chairman and chief executive are split but JKL does not comply with recommendations in relation to non-executive directors or the audit committee. I shall deal with each of these in turn.

Non-executive directors

The board should include a balance of executive and non-executive directors, and in particular 'independent' non-executives. It is recommended that a smaller company (outside FTSE 350) should have at least two independent non-executive directors. The notion of independence precludes non-executives from having recently been an employee of, or in a material business relationship with the company; receiving performance-related pay or a pension; having family ties or cross directorships; representing a substantial shareholder, or having been a board member for an excessive period of time.

Non-executive directors should be independent in judgement and have an enquiring mind. They need to be accepted by management as able to make a contribution; to be well informed about the company and its environment and be able to have a command of the issues facing the business. Non-executives need to insist that information provided by management is sufficient, accurate, clear and timely.

There should be a formal, rigorous and transparent procedure for the appointment of new directors to the board. Levels of remuneration should be sufficient to attract, retain and motivate directors of the quality required to run the company successfully. All directors should receive induction on joining the board and should regularly update and refresh their skills and knowledge. The board should undertake a formal and rigorous annual evaluation of its own performance and that of its committees and individual directors.

Audit committee

The Code states that the board of smaller companies (below FTSE350) should establish an audit committee of at least two members, who should all be independent non-executive directors. At least one member of the audit committee should have recent and relevant financial experience.

The audit committee has a role to act independently of management to ensure that the interests of shareholders are properly protected in relation to financial reporting and internal control. The main role and responsibilities of the audit committee should include monitoring the integrity of the company's financial statements; reviewing the company's internal control and risk management systems; monitoring and reviewing the effectiveness of the internal audit function; making recommendations to the board for the appointment, re-appointment and removal of the external auditor and approving the terms of engagement and remuneration of the external auditor, including the supply of any non-audit services; reviewing and monitoring the external auditor's independence and objectivity and the effectiveness of the audit process.

There should be no less than three audit committee meetings each year held to coincide with key dates in the financial reporting and audit cycle as well as main board meetings. JKL's audit committees should have, as part of its terms of reference, the responsibility to assess risk management and internal control within JKL. Each of these is considered in turn.

Risk management

Risk management is the process by which organisations systematically identify, evaluate, treat and report risk with the goal of achieving organisational objectives. Risk management increases the probability of success, reduces both the probability of failure and the uncertainty of achieving the organisation's objectives.

A risk management strategy should include the risk profile of the organisation, that is the level of risk it finds acceptable; the risk assessment and evaluation processes the organisation practices; the preferred options for risk treatment; the responsibility for risk management and the reporting and monitoring processes that are required. Resources (money, experience and information, etc.) need to be allocated to risk management.

The benefits of effective risk management include being seen as profitable and successful with fewer surprises, predictable results without profit warnings or reporting major exceptional items. Being seen to have a system of risk management is also likely to be reflected in reputation and credit rating.

JKL has no clear risk management system in place and while the board considers risk, it does not do so systematically. Consequently, there may be risks faced by JKL that it has not recognised.

Internal control

The Code incorporates what is known as the Turnbull Guidance, which recommends the adoption by a company's board of a risk-based approach to establishing a sound system of internal control and reviewing its effectiveness.

The board should acknowledge that it is responsible for the company's system of internal control and for reviewing its effectiveness. It should also explain that the system is designed to manage rather than eliminate the risk of failure to achieve business objectives, and can only provide reasonable but not absolute assurance against material mis-statement or loss. The board's statement on internal control should disclose that there is an ongoing process for identifying, evaluating and managing the significant risks faced by the company, that it has been in place for the year and up to the date of approval of the annual report and accounts, and that it has been regularly reviewed by the board and conforms to the Turnbull Guidance.

Reviewing the effectiveness of internal control is one of the board's responsibilities, which needs to be carried out on a continuous basis. The Board should regularly review reports on internal control – both financial and non-financial – for the purpose of making its public statement on internal control. When reviewing management reports on internal control, the board should consider the significant risks and assess how they have been identified, evaluated and managed; assess the effectiveness of internal controls in managing the significant risks, having regard to any significant weaknesses in internal control; consider whether necessary actions are being taken promptly to remedy any weaknesses and consider whether the findings indicate a need for more exhaustive monitoring of the system of internal control.

For risk management and for the board's assessment of the adequacy or otherwise of internal control, an internal audit function should be considered.

Internal audit

Internal audit is an independent appraisal function established within an organisation to examine and evaluate its activities and designed to add value and improve an organisation's operations. The main role of internal audit is to provide assurance that the main business risks are being managed and that internal controls are operating effectively.

The need for an internal audit function will depend on the scale, diversity and complexity of business activities and a comparison of costs and benefits of an internal audit function. Companies that do not have an internal audit function should review the need for one on an annual basis. Changes in the external environment, organisational restructuring or adverse trends evident from monitoring internal control systems should be considered as part of this review. An internal audit may be carried out by staff employed by the company or be outsourced to a third party.

In the absence of an internal audit function, management needs to apply other monitoring processes in order to assure itself and the board that the system of internal control is functioning effectively. The board will need to assess whether those processes provide sufficient and objective assurance.

Recommendations

JKL's single non-executive director is not, under the Code, considered to be independent. It is recommended that JKL appoint two independent non-executive directors to the board.

In JKL, the audit committee currently consists of the chairman, non-executive director and finance director. It is recommended that the two newly appointed independent non-executives (recommended above) be appointed and that both the chairman and the finance director attend, but not be members of the audit committee.

The audit committee should review JKL's risk management system and put in place an appropriate policy and system that reflects the risks faced.

JKL's internal controls appear to be adequate based on the external auditor's report; however, it is recommended that JKL's board specifically consider the adequacy of the external audit report in reviewing the effectiveness of internal control in JKL.

The audit committee should also consider the outcomes of the recommended risk management system before accepting the adequacy of internal controls.

This report does not recommend the appointment of internal auditors separate to the external audit function. However, once the board has implemented a risk management system and assessed the adequacy of internal controls, the value of internal audit function should be reassessed.

Test your understanding 22 – HFD (Case study)

Briefing notes

To: The Board

From: A.N. Accountant

Date: Today

Subject: Corporate governance and ethics

(a) Good corporate governance requires that a company be headed by an effective board with a clear division of responsibilities between running the board and running the company /charity with no individual having unfettered decision-making power. There should be a balance of executive and non-executive directors so that no individual or group can dominate the board. There should be a formal and rigorous process for the appointment of directors who should receive induction training. Information should be supplied in a timely manner to board members so that the board can discharge its duties. The board should then evaluate its performance both individually and collectively each year.

These principles do not seem to be applied for HFD as it is dominated by the chief executive who also acts as chair and appears to dominate the board through his appointment of non-executive directors and his control over the agenda. To meet the principles of good corporate governance, HFD should:

– Separate the roles of chief executive and chairman with the chairman being a non-executive director.

– Ensure that all directors are independent of influence by the chief executive. Positions should be advertised with interviews being conducted, perhaps initially by an independent person. Appointments should be for a defined period, after which directors should stand for re-election.

– Provide induction training to new board members in the goals and operations of the charity.

– Annually evaluate the performance of each director and the board as a whole.

- Accountability and audit principles of good corporate governance require that a board should be able to present a balanced and understandable assessment of the company's position and prospects, should maintain a sound system of internal control and maintain an appropriate relationship with the company's auditors.
- HFD's Board does not seem to be able to make a balanced and understandable assessment of the company's position and prospects, given the narrow confines of what the CEO/Chair allows it. The CEOs relationship with the external auditors is not appropriate.
- To meet the principles of good corporate governance, HFD should:
  - Set an agenda for board meetings that encompasses a wide variety of strategic matters including the charity's strategy, operations, risk management, internal controls and not be limited to financial reports and proposals for funding.
  - Consider meeting more frequently than quarterly.
  - Obtain an independent assessment of the company's internal controls by appointing a firm to act as (outsourced) internal auditor.
  - Affirm the reporting relationship of the external auditors to the board as a whole, and not to the CEO. The external auditors may need to be changed if they are unwilling to accept this changed relationship.

Although it is good practice, it is not necessary to have a separate audit committee, but if not, the functions of the audit committee should be carried out by the full board itself.

The disclosure principle requires that a company's annual report contains a high level statement of how the board operates and the decisions taken by the board and management, details of board members, meetings, performance evaluation, etc. HFD should provide adequate disclosure of board functioning in its annual report to make this aspect of the charity transparent.

(b) CIMA's Code of Ethics for Professional Accountants makes clear that an accountant's responsibility is more than satisfying the needs of a client, he/she must also act in the public interest. It is irrelevant whether or not the CIMA member is paid for his/her services, which are still expected to comply with the ethical principles.

There are 5 fundamental principles in the Code of Ethics: integrity, objectivity, professional competence and due care, confidentiality and professional behaviour.

Of particular relevance to HFD are objectivity, and professional competence and due care. Objectivity may be impeded due to bias because of his/her appointment by the CEO or the influence of the CEO or other persons on the board who may align themselves with the CEO.

The demands of professional competence and due care means that the accountant must look beyond the narrow agenda set by the CEO to a broader perspective than financial statements to non-financial risks (mainly in relation to the charities operation) and the adequacy of internal controls (as it is insufficient to rely wholly on the external auditor's annual management letter).

The conceptual framework underlying CIMA's ethical principles requires accountants to risk manage their own position in relation to the work they are performing and in so doing to identify, evaluate and mitigate any risks they face. The main risks faced by an accountant include those relating to self-interested behaviour, self-review, advocacy, familiarity and intimidation.

The major threats faced in relation to HFD are familiarity and intimidation. The accountant has been appointed to the board as a result of some prior business relationship which may affect his/her objectivity. The CEO/Chair of HFD also appears to be a dominating individual and the accountant may be intimidated by this individual, resulting in the accountant's views not being presented accurately and/or forcefully.

The accountant as board member needs to identify and evaluate the risks of familiarity and/or intimidation that s/he faces, and ensure that s/he takes appropriate action (ultimately resignation from the board) to maintain his/her independence and objectivity.

(b) CIMA's Code of Ethics for Professional Accountants states that an accountant's responsibility is more than satisfying the needs of the client, but the must also act in the public interest. Irrespective of whether or not the CIMA member is a qualified member, he/she/they are still expected to comply with its ethical principles.

There are 5 fundamental principles in the Code of Ethics: integrity, objectivity, professional competence and due care, confidentiality and professional behaviour.

Of particular relevance to HFD are objectivity and professional competence and due care. Objectivity may be impeded due to bias because of his/her appointment by the CEO or the influence of the CEO or other persons on the board who may align themselves with the CEO.

The demands of professional competence and due care mean that the accountant must look beyond the narrow remit set by the CEO to a broader perspective than financial statements to include financial risks (mainly in relation to the charities operation) and the adequacy of internal controls as it is insufficient to rely wholly on the external auditor's annual management letter.

The conceptual framework underlying CIMA's ethical principles requires accountants to ask manage their own position in relation to the work they are performing and in so doing to identify, evaluate and mitigate any risks they face. The main risks faced by an accountant include those relating to self-interested behaviour, self-review, advocacy, familiarity and intimidation.

The major threats faced in relation to HFD are familiarity and intimidation. The accountant has been appointed to the board as a result of some prior business relationship which may affect his/her objectivity. The CEO/Chair of HFD also appears to be a dominating individual and the accountant may be intimidated by this individual resulting in the accountant's views not being presented effectively and/or forcefully.

The accountant as board member needs to identify and evaluate the risks of familiarity and/or intimidation that s/he faces, and ensure that s/he takes appropriate action (ultimately resignation from the board) to maintain his/her independence and objectivity.

hapter

10

Audit

Chapter learning objectives

Lead	Component
C2. Evaluate risk management strategies and internal controls.	(a) Evaluate the essential features of internal control systems for identifying, assessing and managing risks.
C3. Evaluate the purposes and process of audit in the context of internal control systems.	(a) Evaluate the effective planning and management of internal audit and internal audit investigations.

Indicative syllabus content

- The risk manager role as district from that of internal auditor.
- Forms of internal audit: compliance audit, value for money audit/management audit, social and environmental audit.
- Operation of internal audit, the assessment of audit risk and the process of analytical review, including different types of benchmarking, their use and limitations.
- Effective internal audit: independence, staffing and resourcing and organisational remit.
- The preparation and interpretation of the internal audit report.

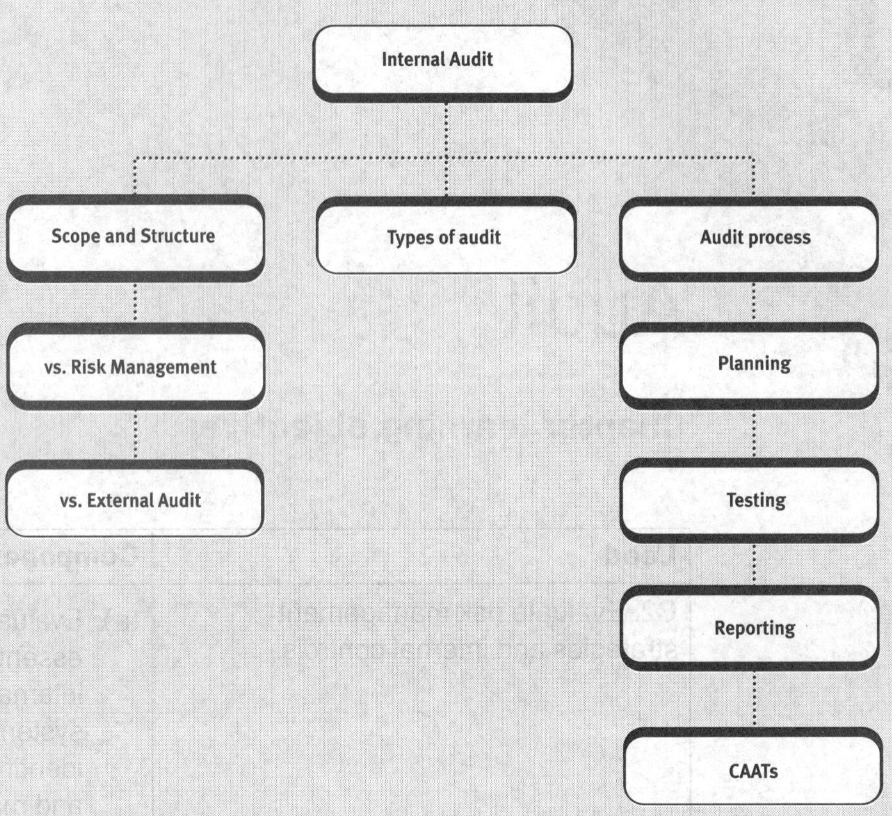

1 Management review of controls

The UK's Turnbull committee says that a review of internal controls should be an integral part of management's role. The board or committees should actively consider reports on control issues. In particular they should consider:

- The identification, evaluation and management of all key risks facing the organisation;
- The effectiveness of internal control – financial, operational, compliance and risk management controls;
- Communication to employees of risk objectives with targets and performance indicators;
- The action taken if any weakness is found.

The report goes on to recommend that the board should consider:

- The nature and extent of the risks which face the organisation;
- The threat of those risks occurring;
- The organisation's ability to reduce the probability and consequences of the risk, and to adapt to any changing risks;
- The costs and benefits of any controls implemented.

An effective internal control system should keep management properly informed about the progress of the organisation (or lack of it) towards the achievement of its objectives. Management and supervisors have a responsibility for monitoring controls in the area of operations for which they are responsible. Internal control might also be monitored by an internal audit function.

What is internal audit ?

Internal auditing is an independent and objective assurance activity designed to add value and improve an organisation's operations. It helps an organisation accomplish its objectives by bringing a systematic approach to evaluating and improving the effectiveness of risk management, control, and governance processes. Internal auditing improves an organisation's effectiveness and efficiency by providing recommendations based on analyses and assessments of data and business processes.

Internal auditing provides value to governing bodies and senior management as an objective source of independent advice.

The scope of internal auditing within an organisation is broad and may involve topics such as the efficacy of operations, the reliability of financial reporting, deterring and investigating fraud, safeguarding assets, and compliance with laws and regulations.

Internal auditing frequently involves measuring compliance with the entity's policies and procedures. However, internal auditors are not responsible for the execution of company activities; they advise management and the Board of Directors (or similar oversight body) regarding how to better execute their responsibilities.

An internal audit function therefore acts as an internal control, to ensure that the internal control system is operating effectively.

Risk management vs. internal audit

Risk management

- A risk management team would be considered to own the entire risk management process.
- They would be ultimately responsible for all aspects of this process including identification and maintenance of the company's risk register, assessment, prioritisation, treatment of risks and establishment of controls to manage these risks.

- The team would lead the company in developing a risk response strategy and would act in an advisory capacity supporting all areas of the business.
- Provision of training and development by risk staff would facilitate operational managers' ability to identify risks in their area of work and devise controls by which to manage them.

Internal audit

- The role of internal audit is that of monitoring and reviewing the effectiveness of the controls implemented by operational managers.
- In the context of risk management their key activity is in the testing and evaluation of the risk controls (hence ensuring that **those who design controls should not test them**).
- In a wider context the internal audit department can carry out special investigations as directed by management, and can assist the organisation in review of the efficient use of resources.
- Internal audit teams can provide support and assistance to senior management in a range of projects, some of which may fall outside the risk management arena.
- They are often able to contribute to the work of operational teams in identifying risks due to their extensive knowledge of the business, but this is not their primary responsibility.

In summary, risk management identify risks or problems, management devise controls which they think will prevent the risk or problem and the auditors check that the control works. If it doesn't, then it is still a problem and management will implement further or different controls which audit will check again. And so the process goes on until the risk or problem is minimised to the satisfaction of management i.e. it is within the companies attitude to risk.

There are three different parties involved in the process review – risk management, managers and auditors, to ensure independence and the best solution for the company.

Factors affecting the need for internal audit

There are a number of factors that affect the need for an internal audit department:

Factor	Comment
The scale, diversity and complexity of the company's activities	The larger, the more diverse and the more complex a range of activities is, the more there is to monitor (and the more opportunity there is for certain things to go wrong).
The number of employees	As a proxy for size, the number of employees signifies that larger organisations are more likely to need internal audit to underpin investor confidence than smaller concerns.
Cost/benefit considerations	Management must be certain of the benefits that will result from establishing internal audit and they must obviously be seen to outweigh the costs of the audit.
Changes in the organisational structures, reporting processes or underlying information systems	Any internal (or external) modification is capable of changing the complexity of operations and, accordingly, the risk.
Changes in key risks could be internal or external in nature	The introduction of a new product, entering a new market, a change in any of the PEST/PESTEL factors or changes in the industry might trigger the need for internal audit.
Problems with existing internal control systems.	Any problems with existing systems clearly signify the need for a tightening of systems and increased monitoring.
An increased number of unexplained or unacceptable events.	System failures or similar events are a clear demonstration of internal control weakness.

Where there is no internal audit department management needs to apply other monitoring processes in order to assure itself and the board that the system of internal control is functioning as intended. In these circumstances, the board will need to assess whether such procedures provide sufficient and objective assurance.

Test your understanding 1

Teddy plc is a small UK-based family run company selling traditional wooden toys from a small chain of shops. The firm has seen rapid sales growth since engaging in e-commerce via a website and selling via large third party online retailers.

The newly appointed Finance Director is the first board member from outside the family and has suggested it would be a good idea for Teddy plc to consider establishing an internal audit department as he has already noticed a large inventory discrepancy.

Which THREE of the following factors are the main reasons for the need for an internal audit at Teddy plc?

A If a company is listed on the stock exchange it must have an internal audit

B The growing scale and diversity for Teddy plc. Suggests there is more to monitor

C Potential internal control issues are starting to arise at Teddy plc.

D The introduction of e-commerce at Teddy plc

E The fact the board has majority family members

F The wish of the shareholders at Teddy plc.

Test your understanding 2

Z is the head of the risk management team at P Co, a large listed manufacturer. P Co also has a well-established internal audit team which is run completely independently of any operational functions within the company in accordance with best practice.

Each year P Co takes on around 20 graduate trainees and in their first month of employment they undergo a detailed induction. As part of this training they listen to presentations on the role of several departments within P Co including internal audit. This year, the board of P Co has decided to ask Z to speak to the graduates about the role of the risk management team and how it differs from that of internal audit.

Z is preparing her presentation. Which of the following will she include and explain as roles of the risk management team?

Select all that apply.

A The maintenance of P Co's risk register

B The establishment of controls to manage risks

C The evaluation and testing of risk controls

D The provision of training and development to operational staff to help them to identify risk

E Review of the efficient use of resources across the organisation

F Overall responsibility for risk management within P Co

2 Scope and standard of internal audit work

Scope of internal audit work

The internal audit department will typically have the following scope and objectives as prescribed by the management of the business:

(Do not treat this as a comprehensive list of all the areas that the internal auditor considers, as management may prescribe different functions to meet the needs of their company).

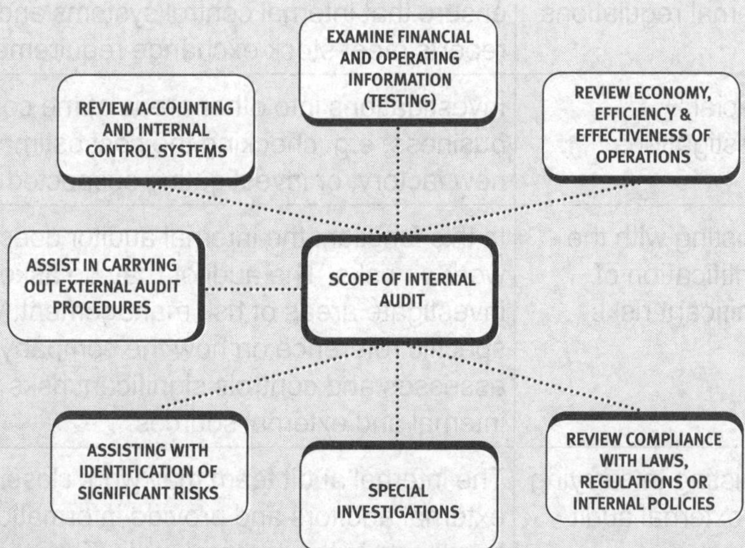

More on scope of internal audit work

Work area	**Comment**
Reviewing accounting and internal control systems (financial audit)	This is the traditional view of internal audit. The internal auditor checks the financial controls in the company, possibly assisting or sharing work with the external auditor. The internal auditor would comment on whether appropriate controls exist as well as whether they are working correctly. In this work, the internal auditor does not manage risk, but simply reports on controls.
Examining financial and operating information	Internal auditors ensure that reporting of financial information is made on a timely basis and that the information in the reports is factually accurate.
Reviewing the economy, efficiency and effectiveness of operations	This is also called a value for money (VFM) audit (see more later in this chapter). The auditor checks whether a particular activity is cost-effective (economical), uses the minimum inputs for a given output (efficient) and meets its stated objectives (effective).
Reviewing compliance with laws and other external regulations	This objective is particularly relevant under corporate governance codes where the internal auditor will be carrying out detailed work to ensure that internal control systems and financial reports meet stock exchange requirements.
Special investigations	Investigations into other areas of the company's business, e.g. checking the cost estimates for a new factory, or investigating suspected fraud.
Assisting with the identification of significant risks	In this function, the internal auditor does start to work on risks. The auditor may be asked to investigate areas of risk management, with specific reference on how the company identifies, assesses and controls significant risks from both internal and external sources.
Assisting in carrying out external audit procedures	The internal audit team may work closely with the external auditors and provide information that can be utilised in the external audit. There is an obvious benefit to the company from this in the form of a reduction in the audit fee.

Standard of internal audit work

The internal audit function would be expected to carry out their work to a high professional standard. To achieve this the audit function should be well managed and have clear and appropriate procedures for carrying out its work.

It would be expected that:

- There is a formal plan of all audit work that is reviewed by the head of audit and the board/audit committee.
- The audit plans should be reviewed at least annually.
- Each engagement should be conducted appropriately:
  - Planning should be performed.
  - Objectives should be set for the engagement.
  - The work should be documented, reviewed and supervised.
  - The results should be communicated to management.
  - Recommendations for action should be made.
- The progress of the audit should be monitored by the head of internal audit, and if recommendations that the head feels are appropriate are not acted on, the matters should be brought to the attention of the board.

Standards of internal audit work

Internal auditors can follow the same standards as external auditors. However, there are also International Standards for Internal Audit issued by the Internal Auditing Standards Board (IASB) of the Institute of Internal Auditors.

- **Attribute standards** deal with the characteristics of organisations and the parties performing internal auditing activities.
- **Performance standards** describe the nature of internal auditing activities and provide quality criteria for evaluating internal auditing services.

Attribute standards for internal audit

Objective of standard	Explanation
Independence	The internal audit activity should be independent, and the head of internal audit should report to a level within the organisation that allows the internal audit activity to fulfil its responsibilities. It should be free from interference when deciding on the scope of its assurance work, when carrying out the work and when communicating its opinions.
Objectivity	Internal auditors should be objective in carrying out their work. They should have an impartial attitude, and should avoid any conflicts of interest. For example, an internal auditor should not provide assurance services for an operation for which he or she has had management responsibility within the previous year.
Professional care	Internal auditors should exercise due professional care and should have the competence to perform their tasks. They should have some knowledge of the key IT risks and controls, and computer-assisted audit techniques.

Performance standards for internal audit

Area of work	Explanation
Managing internal audit	• The head of internal audit should manage the internal audit activity to ensure that it adds value to the organisation. • The head of internal audit should establish risk-based plans to decide the priorities for internal audit work, consistent with the organisation's objectives. • The internal audit plan should be reviewed at least annually. • The head of internal audit should submit the plan of work to senior management and the board for approval. Independence is maintained by the internal auditor/audit committee being able to decide the scope of internal audit work without being influenced by the board/senior management.
Risk management	• The internal audit department should identify and evaluate significant risk exposures and contribute to the improvement of risk management and control systems. It should evaluate risk exposures relating to governance, operations and information systems, and the reliability and integrity of financial and operating information, the effectiveness and efficiency of operations, safeguarding of assets, compliance with laws, regulations and contracts. Independence is maintained by the internal auditor being given access to information on all these areas and being able to report freely on any errors or omissions found.
Control	• The internal audit department should help to maintain the organisation's control system by evaluating the effectiveness and efficiency of controls, and by promoting continuous improvement. Independence is again maintained by ensuring full provision of information and independent reporting lines (via the audit committee).

Governance	• The internal audit department should assess the corporate governance process and make recommendations where appropriate for improvements in achieving the objectives of corporate governance. Independence is maintained by the internal auditor being able to report breaches of corporate governance code without fear of dismissal.
Internal audit work	• Internal auditors should identify, analyse, evaluate and record sufficient information to achieve the objectives of the engagement. • The information identified should be reliable, relevant and useful with regard to the objectives of the engagement. • The auditors' conclusions should be based on suitable analysis and evaluation. • Information to support the conclusions of the auditors should be recorded. Independence is maintained by the internal auditor being able to show that normal standards of internal audit work have been followed; there has been no pressure to 'cut corners' either from senior management or because the internal auditor decided to carry out the work to a lower standard.
Communicating results	• Internal auditors should communicate the results of their engagement, including conclusions, recommendations and action plans. • The results should be communicated to the appropriate persons. Independence is maintained by the internal auditor being able to communicate to a committee or person separate from the board who also has the power to take appropriate action on the internal auditors' reports.

3 Structure, independence and effectiveness of internal audit

Structure and independence of internal audit

To ensure that the internal audit function provides an objective assessment of control systems and their weaknesses, there should be measures in place to protect the independence of the internal audit department.

- The internal auditors should be independent of executive management (but have direct access to the highest level of management if required) and should not have any involvement in the activities or systems that they audit (free from operational responsibility).
- The head of internal audit should report directly to a senior director.
- In addition, however, the head of internal audit should have direct access to the chairman of the board of directors, and to the audit committee, and should be accountable to the audit committee.
- The audit committee should approve the appointment and termination of appointment of the head of internal audit.
- In large organisations the internal audit function will be a separate department.
- In a small company it might be the responsibility of individuals to perform specific tasks even though there will not be a full-time position.
- Some companies outsource their internal audit function, often to one of the large accountancy firms.
- The internal auditor will review the accounting and control systems, perform testing of transactions and balances, review the 3E's, implementation of corporate policies, carry out special investigations, and assist the external auditors where necessary.
- They should be technically competent and exercise due professional care by planning, supervising and reviewing any work performed. Documentation should be kept, results communicated to management and recommendations made.

Test your understanding 3

The Board of NN, a large drinks manufacturer, decided to set up an internal audit function. The proposal was appoint an internal auditor at mid-management level who would report directly to the Finance Director.

NN had recently expanded its product range and this had created the need for greater control over internal activities. The need was highlighted by a recent event where internal quality checks were not carried out and thousands of units of production were wasted as a result.

The board discussed whether to promote internally or appoint the new internal auditor from outside the company and they also expressed concerns over the level of authority the internal auditor may expect. Although they recognised the post as important, they believed too much authority might compromise the operational effectiveness of other departments.

Which of the following statements are likely to be correct with respect to the board's deliberations? Select all that apply.

A Reporting to the Finance Director is a clear threat to the independence of the internal auditor.

B Recruiting an internal auditor from outside the organisation may help with independence and objectivity.

C Appointment of an internal auditor will ensure events such as the loss of production due to poor quality control do not re-occur.

D The internal auditor will not be involved with the work of other departments and so the fears of the board over operational effectiveness are groundless.

E Internal auditors must operate as a separate department within NN and so a single appointment will not be adequate.

Outsourcing internal audit

In common with other areas of a company's operations, the directors may consider that outsourcing the internal audit function represents better value than an in-house provision. Local government authorities are under particular pressure to ensure that all their services represent 'best value' and this may prompt them to decide to adopt a competitive tender approach.

Advantages of outsourcing internal audit

- Greater focus on cost and efficiency of the internal audit function.
- Staff may be drawn from a broader range of expertise.
- Risk of staff turnover is passed to the outsourcing firm.
- Specialist skills may be more readily available.
- Costs of employing permanent staff are avoided.
- May improve independence.
- Access to new market place technologies, e.g. audit methodology software without associated costs.
- Reduced management time in administering an in-house department.

Disadvantages of outsourcing internal audit

- Possible conflict of interest if provided by the external auditors.
- Pressure on the independence of the outsourced function due to, for example, a threat by management not to renew contract.
- Risk of lack of knowledge and understanding of the organisation's objectives, culture or business.
- The decision may be based on cost with the effectiveness of the function being reduced.
- Flexibility and availability may not be as high as with an in-house function.
- Lack of control over standard of service.
- Risk of blurring of roles between internal and external audit, losing credibility for both.

Minimising these risks

Some general procedures to minimise risks associated with outsourcing the internal audit function will include:

- Controls over acceptance of internal audit contracts to ensure no impact on independence or ethical issues.
- Regular reviews of the quality of audit work performed.
- Separate departments covering internal and external audit.
- Clearly agreed scope, responsibilities and reporting lines.
- Performance measures, management information and risk reporting
- Procedure manuals for internal audit.

Test your understanding 4

X plc is a financial services company. Shares in X have recently been listed on the UK stock exchange.

You are a Management Accountant of X, and have been talking to your CEO about the need to implement a system of internal controls in order to comply with corporate governance requirements. X already has an Internal Audit function, which reports direct to the CEO. The CEO believes that Internal Audit should be outsourced to one of the many audit firms offering such services, but NOT the company's external auditor.

Advise the CEO which THREE of the following are ADVANTAGES of doing this.

A Specialist skills may be more readily available

B Risk of staff turnover is passed to the outsourcing firm

C Better understanding of the organisation's objectives and culture

D May improve independence

E Decisions relating to Internal Audit can be based solely on cost

Ethical threats to independence

Situations could occasionally arise in which an auditor, especially an internal auditor, might be asked to behave (or might be tempted to behave) in a way that conflicts with ethical standards and guidelines.

Conflicts of interest could relate to unimportant matters, but they might also involve fraud or some other illegal activity.

Examples of such ethical conflicts of interest are as follows:

Threat	Example
There could be pressure from an overbearing supervisor, manager or director, adversely affecting the accountant's integrity.	The auditor is asked not to report adverse findings. The threat could be made more personal, e.g. by indicating that the auditor's employment will be terminated if disclosure is made.
An auditor might mislead his employer as to the amount of experience or expertise he has, when in reality the expert advice of someone else should be sought.	The auditor wants to retain his position within the internal audit department or gain respect because of the apparent experience that they have.
An auditor might be asked to act contrary to a technical or professional standard. Divided loyalty between the auditor's superior and the required professional standards of conduct could arise.	An auditor is told to ignore the incorrect application of an accounting standard or the incorrect reporting of directors' remuneration.

Resolution of ethical conflicts of interest

Conflict resolution has been covered earlier.

Effectiveness and efficiency of internal audit

The work of an internal audit department should be monitored to assess effectiveness in the broader context of the company's risk management systems.

The internal audit process must provide benefits in excess of its cost.

- The **efficiency** of internal audit can be assessed by comparing actual costs and output against a target, such as:

- the cost per internal audit day
- the cost per audit report
- the number of audit reports produced.

- The **effectiveness** of internal audit needs to be measured in a way that indicates the extent to which it provides assurance to management, the audit committee and the board about the effectiveness of the system of internal control.
  - This can be done by identifying evidence of improvements in internal control.

An internal audit report can be prepared for many company activities or systems. E.g. payroll.

If an internal audit was to be performed it might consider the following:

(1) At the front of the report there would usually be an **executive summary**. This would cover the main objectives and scope of the audit, the work performed in brief, the results found and recommendations made.

(2) The **scope of the assignment** would be elaborated on in the next section. This would detail the methodology used e.g. observation, questionnaires, etc, and the areas covered e.g. joiners, leavers, etc.

(3) The next section might be **observations and recommendations** i.e. what the auditor observed during his testing, whether the system was working as it was designed to, and whether any recommendations should be implemented. It should also say who is responsible for any implementations and by when they should be undertaken. The number of recommendations could range from none i.e. the system is working perfectly, to many. This is probably the most practical and most useful part of the report for management.

(4) The recommendations may be **graded by importance**. For example a Level 1 recommendation may need to be implemented immediately since it poses a significant risk to the company, whereas a Level 5 recommendation, say, might be desirable but not necessarily life-threatening so can be implemented later.

(5) Finally there will be a **statement of responsibility** from the internal auditor. This will detail any Auditing Standards (standard tests or rules an auditor should follow) used during the course of the work and any limitations that the audit work was performed under. To a cynic, this is the auditors 'get out' clause i.e. some might read it as 'we performed the audit work to the best of our ability, but we can't test everything, so if we missed something, we are sorry but it wasn't our fault'! The auditor will finally **sign** the report.

The internal audit report is often seen as a **'trigger for risk management'** both in the real world and in the CIMA P3 case study exam.

4 Internal and external audit

To a large extent, the work of internal auditors and external auditors is similar, and overlaps. It is therefore important that their efforts should complement each other, rather than duplicate each other.

Comparison of internal to external audit

	External audit	**Internal audit**
Role required by:	Statute, for limited companies.	Directors and shareholders, usually in larger organisations.
Appointed by:	Shareholders or directors.	Directors, via the Chief Internal Auditor (CIA).
Reports to:	Shareholder (primary duty) and management (professional responsibility).	Directors, via the CIA.
Reports on:	Financial statements.	Internal controls mainly.
Forms opinions on:	True and fair view and proper presentation.	Adequacy of ICS as a contribution to the economic, efficient and effective use of resources.
Scope of assignment:	Unlimited, to fulfil statutory obligation.	Prescribed by directors.

Relationship of internal audit to external audit

The audit plan of the external auditors should be drawn up taking into consideration the work of internal audit, and the extent to which the external auditors can rely on the findings of the internal auditors in reaching their audit opinion.

Factors that the external auditor should consider include:

- the status of internal audit within the organisation
- the scope of the internal audit function
- whether management act on the recommendations of the internal auditor
- the technical competence of the internal auditors
- whether the objectives of the internal audit work are aligned with that of the external auditor
- whether the work of the internal audit function appears to have been planned, supervised, reviewed and documented with due professional care.

Note that there is no particular expectation that the external auditor will be able to rely on the work done by internal audit. The duties of both sets of auditors will differ and hence the work of internal audit may be of very little relevance to the external auditor.

However, in some instances, the external auditors do rely on the internal auditors work if areas of the external auditors audit program have been covered (and the factors mentioned above can be met). Providing the testing performed meets the scope and quality level that the external auditor requires, then the external auditor will place 'some' reliance on the work already performed by internal audit, and consequently reduce the amount of further testing required in order to state an opinion.

However, the external auditors would not place 'total' reliance on the internal auditors work. (They would effectively need to audit the internal auditors work by testing it in part before they could rely on it.)

For example, internal audit might know that during the annual external audit purchase compliance tests are performed to ensure that, say, all purchases are backed up by an order, the order is authorised, etc. The sample normally taken by the external auditor might be, say, 20 transactions. Internal audit could choose to perform this work during the course of the year and present their findings to the external auditor when they arrive to perform the annual audit. The external auditors would then check the internal auditors work by re-performing the compliance tests on a few transactions, say, 3 of the 20. Providing no errors were found, the external auditors would then perform their own, new compliance tests on a reduced number of, say, 5 transactions.

More testing will have been performed since both internal and external audit have been involved, giving a higher assurance level (or lower risk).

Also, this 'sharing' of work can lead to a reduced external audit fee, because some of the testing has been done internally at a reduced cost.

Management letter

In addition to an internal or external audit report, the auditor will usually produce a 'management letter'. This letter usually includes a list of 'issues' that the auditor came across during the course of his audit work.

The letter usually includes a table of:

- issues concerning the auditor (usually a control that could be improved);
- recommendations to implement or improve the controls.

The auditor would usually state a time frame by which the new controls should be implemented and then re-visit the department to ensure that the implementation had taken place.

The management are at liberty to reply to the auditor. They may state that the recommended control has been implemented, or why it hasn't been, perhaps because it was too costly, or is on-going.

Test your understanding 5

In a large company which complies with the UK Corporate Governance Code, the head of internal audit should report directly to:

A A senior director

B The external auditor

C The audit committee

D The risk manager

Test your understanding 6

The primary scope of an internal auditor's work includes: (Select all that apply.)

A Examining financial and operating information

B Reviewing compliance with laws and regulations

C Identifying risk

D Assisting with external audit procedures

Test your understanding 7

Internal audit can be outsourced. A disadvantage of this might be:

A Cost

B Skill

C Independence

D Control

Differing perspectives on fraud

The **external auditor** is responsible for identifying material misstatements in the financial statements in order to ensure that they give a true and fair view. By definition then, the external auditor is responsible for detecting any **material** fraud that may have occurred. However, they have no specific responsibility with regard to immaterial fraud. If they identify them they will be reported to those charged with governance, but there is no duty to identify them.

Internal auditors may be given an assignment:

- to assess the likelihood of fraud, or if a fraud has been discovered,
- to assess its consequences and
- to make recommendations for prevention in the future.

Fraud investigation

Fraud investigation can be carried out by an auditor. It is **not their primary objective** when carrying out an audit, but they are **duty bound to report a fraud if during the course of their work they identify fraudulent activities**.

It is the company directors who are responsible for identifying fraud.

A fraud investigation should cover the following steps:

(1) Ascertaining the facts of the fraudulent activity.

(2) Gathering evidence of the crime – documentary, interviews with witnesses, observational, etc.

(3) Corroborating the evidence.

(4) Consider whether you have the right of access to the evidence you require. Many cases have been thrown out of court because evidence has been improperly obtained.

(5) Maintaining confidentiality so that the perpetrator doesn't realise they are being investigated.

(6) Consider the cost of the investigation versus the value of the fraud, although ethically all frauds should be stopped.

(7) Ascertain the value of the fraud.

(8) Consider the loss of reputation if the fraud becomes public.

Test your understanding 8 – SHD (Integration)

SHD is a property development company involved in multiple development projects across the country. In the last year a member of the finance department has established an expenses fraud through the use of a false supplier. Invoices are raised in the name of this supplier on a monthly basis for miscellaneous materials to the various development sites. These invoices are paid directly via the accounts payable system without going to the site project managers.

This fraud has increased the variable costs of construction projects by 15% in the last year, a point which has been identified by the external auditors in their recent audit. The auditors approached the management accountant for further information on the cost increase.

Required:

Discuss the differing views of external auditors and internal auditors to this increase in variable costs.

Test your understanding 9 – Z (Case study)

Scenario

Z is a government agency that is responsible for promoting road safety.

Trigger

Z needs to buy a fleet of 24 buses that have been converted into mobile exhibition spaces so that they can be driven around to educate community groups about the importance of safe road use.

The management board of Z has decided to use a sealed bid system to tender for this fleet of buses. The sealed bid system is as follows:

- Suppliers who wish to bid for the contract to supply and modify 24 buses should submit a sealed bid to Z's chief buyer.
- The bid should be submitted in a plain envelope with a typed label stating "Bus Bid". There should be no other writing on the envelope.
- The bid should identify:

  (1) The supplier

  (2) The type of bus to be modified

  (3) Details of all the modifications to be undertaken

  (4) The price of supplying 24 modified buses

- On receipt of the sealed envelope the chief buyer of Z will sign across the flap of the envelope and place the bid in the safe.

Z's chief executive contacted the head of internal audit immediately before the end of the bidding process and requested that the internal audit department attend the meeting at which the envelopes would be opened. A senior member of the internal audit department was assigned to the task. In addition, the meeting would be attended by the chief buyer, the head of operations and the departmental manager who would be responsible for managing the exhibitions.

At the meeting the chief buyer announced that four bids had been received. The envelopes were opened in random order by the internal auditor.

The contents were:

Envelope 1: a bid of GBP 2.8 million from supplier L
Envelope 2: a bid of GBP 3.0 million from supplier K and a letter to withdraw a previously submitted bid of GBP 2.0 million
Envelope 3: a bid of GBP 3.2 million from supplier M
Envelope 4: a bid of GBP 2.0 million from supplier K

The details of the bids in envelopes 2 and 4 from supplier K were identical except for the price.

Supplier L's bid of GBP 2.8million was rejected immediately because the bidder was planning to use a slightly smaller model of bus than the others and planned to use poor quality materials for the modifications. It was, therefore, agreed that the winning bid would be the revised offer to supply the buses for GBP 3.0 million from supplier K. The head of internal audit was concerned that there could be some irregularities in this bidding process and asked the chief executive to postpone placing an order for the buses until the internal audit department had undertaken an investigation.

Task

(a) Explain THREE factors that could have caused the head of internal audit to be concerned about the bidding process for the buses.

(10 minutes)

(b) Recommend, with reasons, the work that the internal auditor should undertake if the bidding process for the buses is investigated.

(20 minutes)

(c) Write a note to the chief executive which recommends TWO advantages and TWO disadvantages of the internal auditor being actively involved in the investigation of suspected fraud.

(15 minutes)

5 Types of audit work

As there are many risks and many controls within a business, there will be many different types of audit that can be performed. All types will essentially ensure the same thing – that the companies processes are being adhered to.

Some different types of audit work are discussed below, but the list is not exhaustive.

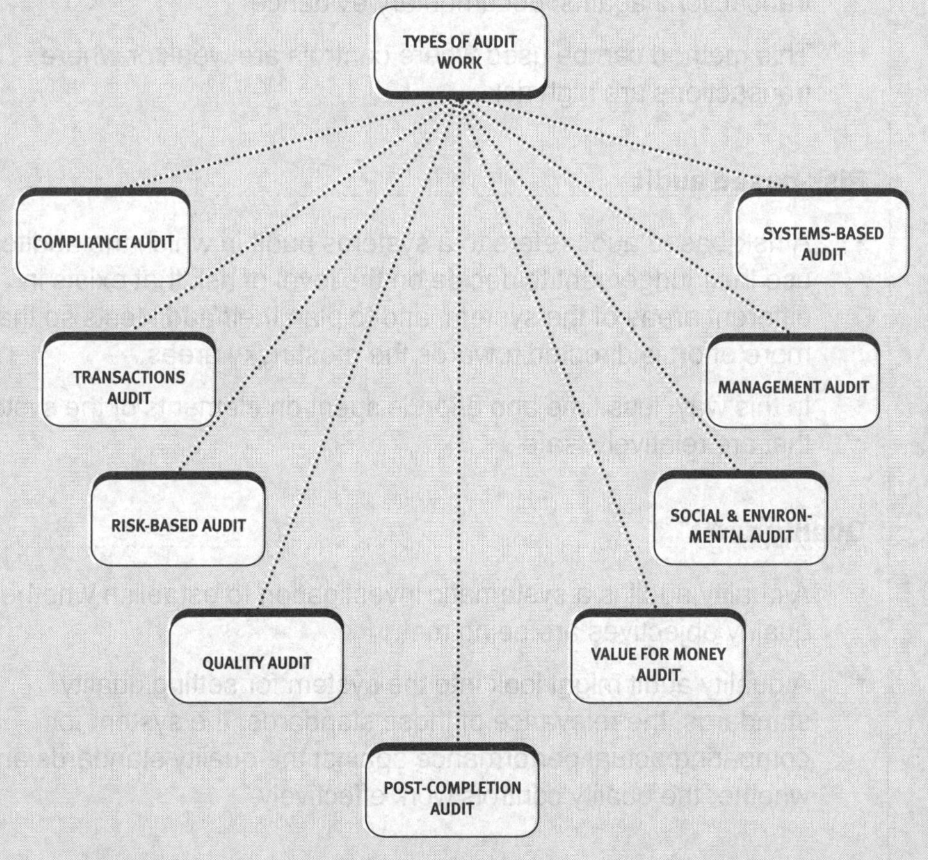

More on audit types

Compliance audit

- Compliance audits check the implementation of written rules, regulations and procedures.
- They were used originally for financial transactions, because the government (tax authorities) needed assurance that the financial figures were correct.
- The concept of compliance has been extended to other areas, such as regulatory inspections and quality audits, where there is a requirement to verify that activities are being performed in strict compliance with approved standards and procedures.

Transactions audit

- A transactions audit involves the checking of a sample of transactions against documentary evidence.
- This method can be used where controls are weak or where transactions are high risk.

Risk-based audit

- A risk-based audit refers to a systems audit in which the auditors use their judgement to decide on the level of risk that exists in different areas of the system, and to plan their audit tests so that more effort is directed towards the most risky areas.
- In this way, less time and effort is spent on elements of the system that are relatively 'safe'.

Quality audit

- A quality audit is a systematic investigation to establish whether quality objectives are being met.
- A quality audit might look into the system for setting quality standards, the relevance of those standards, the system for comparing actual performance against the quality standards and whether the quality controls work effectively.

Post-completion audit (or post-completion review)

- A post-completion audit is an objective and independent appraisal of the measure of success of a project.
- It should cover the project throughout its lifecycle from the planning and implementation stages through to performance after commissioning.
- The review should take place at some time after the project or process has been completed or is being used. Review should not be too soon, where the project or process hasn't been given a chance to 'bed in'. But it should also not be too late where important feedback and learning has not been applied on later projects.
- Its objective is to provide feedback as to the success of a project or otherwise, and acts as a learning tool for future projects.
- Projects are often assessed on three criteria: time, cost and quality. Was the project implemented on time? Did the project come in on budget? Was the project delivered at the expected quality level, or more commonly, did it solve the original issue that prompted the project?
- Post-completion audits are often performed by internal audit, as long as they are not involved in the original design of the project itself. The auditor will source the documentation which stated the original objectives of the project, and then follow the process carried out to ensure that all activities led to the successful completion of these objectives – in an economical, efficient and effective way. If the objectives were not met, why not? And what should be done about it?

The latter four types of audit work will now be considered in more detail.

Value for money audit

An area that internal auditors have been getting increasingly involved in is value for money audits. These have been replaced in terminology more recently by 'best value' audits, but many of the principles remain the same.

In a value for money (VFM) audit the auditor assesses three main areas.

Economy

- The economy of a business is assessed by looking at the inputs to the business (or process), and deciding whether these are the most economical that are available at an acceptable quality level.

Efficiency

- The efficiency of an operation is assessed by considering how well the operation converts inputs to outputs.

Effectiveness

- The effectiveness of an organisation is assessed by examining whether the organisation is achieving its objectives. To assess effectiveness there must be clear objectives for the organisation that can be examined.

More on VFM audit

A VFM audit is 'an investigation into whether proper arrangements have been made for securing economy, efficiency and effectiveness in the use of resources'. It is an audit into the '3 Es' in an item or operation.

- **Economy** means obtaining the required resources at the lowest cost. There would be a lack of economy, for example, if there was overstaffing in a particular department or if an excessive price was paid for materials of the required quality. It is important to remember that economy does not mean achieving the lowest cost possible: it means keeping costs within acceptable limits for obtaining resources of the desired quality.
- **Efficiency** means using the minimum quantity of resources to achieve a given quantity and quality of output. Efficiency can be measured either in terms of:
  - maximising the output for a given quantity of input, such as the maximum quantity of services provided per employee or per £1 spent, or
  - achieving a given quantity of output with the minimum resources possible.
- **Effectiveness** exists when the output from a system achieves its intended aims and objectives.

Managers are responsible for achieving economy, efficiency and effectiveness in the operations for which they are responsible. A VFM audit provides a check to confirm that management is fulfilling this responsibility properly.

VFM audits have commonly been associated with auditing in the public sector, but they are applicable in any type of organisation, in the public or private sectors.

Problems with VFM audits

There are several problems with conducting a VFM audit.

- It might be **difficult to measure outputs**, particularly in government services. For example, the output from an education system can be measured in many different ways, both in terms of the numbers educated and the quality of education. In the health service, outputs might be measured in terms of the numbers of patients treated; on the other hand, successful preventive medicine would be measured in terms of reductions in the numbers of patients treated for particular conditions.
- The **objectives of the activity might be difficult to establish**, particularly in the public sector. For example, what are the objectives of the police service? If an activity has several different objectives, the problem is then how to decide their priorities. For example, the objective of the police force might be to maintain public order, arrest criminals, deter criminals, and so on.
- **The focus must be EITHER on economy and efficiency OR on effectiveness**. It is difficult to report on both issues simultaneously because costs can almost always be reduced by cutting back on the quality of service, while outputs can almost always be improved by spending more.
- **Quality might be ignored when economy and efficiency are measured**. For example, a government might succeed in reducing the costs of secondary education, but only by making schools overcrowded and by lowering the standards of the education provided. VFM tends to focus more on economy and efficiency because those are much easier to measure than effectiveness.

Test your understanding 10 – Seatown (case study)

Scenario

Seatown is located on the coast. The town's main industry is tourism with an emphasis on family holidays and consequently the cleanliness of the town's beaches is a major factor in the town's success.

The town council, which is the local government authority, has a cleaning department that is responsible for keeping the beaches clean and tidy. Early every morning, as soon as the tide has gone out, the beaches are swept using equipment that is towed behind tractors. This equipment skims the top layer of sand and runs it through a filter to remove any litter before returning the cleaned sand to the beach. Most litter takes the form of paper and plastic packaging, but it can include glass bottles and aluminium cans.

To try to prevent litter being left on the beach the town council also places bins on the beaches above the high water mark. Litter bins need to be emptied regularly otherwise holidaymakers pile their rubbish beside the bins and that leads to litter being spread by the wind or by seabirds scavenging for food scraps.

The cost of cleaning the beaches is a major expense for the town council.

Trigger

The management team of the town council has asked the internal audit department to investigate whether the town is getting good "value for money" from this expenditure. The head of internal audit has sought clarification from the town managers on whether the audit should focus on the economy and efficiency of the cleaning operations or their effectiveness. Economy and efficiency audits generally focus on whether cost can be reduced for the same level of service and effectiveness audits ask whether better service can be achieved for the same cost.

Task

Prepare a letter addressed to the town council's internal audit department:

(a) Recommending, giving reasons, the matters that they should study in order to evaluate the economy and efficiency of the beach cleaning activities.

Your answer should include advice on how to obtain the necessary data and information.

(20 minutes)

(b) Recommending, giving reasons, the matters that they should study in order to evaluate the effectiveness of the beach cleaning activities.

Your answer should include advice on how to obtain the necessary data and information.

(20 minutes)

(c) Explaining why it is easier to investigate the economy and efficiency rather than the effectiveness of the cleaning activities.

(10 minutes)

Social and environmental audit

Environmental audit

An environmental audit is defined as:

'A management tool comprising a systematic, documented, periodic and objective evaluation of how well organisations, management, and equipment are performing, with the aim of contributing to safeguarding the environment by facilitating management control of environmental practices, and assessing compliance with company policies, which would include meeting regulatory requirements and standards applicable.'

It is possible that an 'accounting' trained auditor could be asked to perform one of these audits but it is unlikely that they would be able to perform the task with the proper competence. The auditor is unlikely to have the necessary skills and therefore it would be professionally wrong to accept the assignment.

Social audit

The social audit would look at the company's contribution to society and the community. The contributions made could be through:

- Donations.
- Sponsorship.
- Employment practices.
- Education.
- Health and safety.
- Ethical investments, etc.

A social audit could either confirm statements made by the directors, or make recommendations for social policies that the company should perform.

Environmental reporting

The environmental report that is included in the annual report by many companies is sometimes accompanied by an 'auditors' statement'.

The environmental report produced by companies will normally contain information about:

- Sustainability.
- Targets achieved.

- Compliance with regulations.
- Emissions.
- Industrial legacies.·
- Obtaining ISO 14001 (environmental management systems).

Many companies conduct an internal audit on these matters, and then have the audit verified by external assessors. It is possible that the external auditor could be asked to be an external assessor, however, it is more likely with environmental matters that the person will be an appropriately qualified environmental assessor.

Management audit

A management audit is sometimes called an **operational audit.**

A management audit is defined by CIMA as 'an objective and independent appraisal of the effectiveness of managers and the corporate structure in the achievement of the entities' objectives and policies'.

- Its aim is to identify existing and potential management weakness and recommend ways to rectify them.'
- This type of audit would require the use of very experienced staff who understand the nature of the business.

More on management audit

The **objectives of a management audit** might be:

- re-focusing resources towards 'mission-critical' objectives
- improving efficiency (improving work flows, eliminating unnecessary activities, eliminating duplicated activities, etc)
- improving the effectiveness of management support tools (such as improvements in controls, automated system support etc)
- assessing the appropriate levels of service for an activity or operation
- identifying cost savings
- identifying opportunities to enhance revenue
- improvements in governance.

The **elements of a management audit** might include:

- a review of policies and procedures
- a general review of workloads, work methods and work flows
- an evaluation of systems and processes
- a review of management practices
- a review of resource utilisation
- a detailed cost analysis.

The **findings of a management audit** might focus not so much on compliance with policies and procedures, but on:

- a lack of technical competence or knowledge of the business amongst managers, and insufficient management training
- an unwillingness to delegate
- regular failure to achieve standards or targets
- inadequate management information systems
- poor communications within or between departments
- poor management/staff relationships
- an absence of clear leadership
- a failure by management to make good decisions.

Systems-based audit

A systems-based audit is an audit of internal controls within an organisation. Although the term refers to any type of system, it is often associated with the audit of accounting systems, such as the sales ledger system, purchase ledger system, receipts and payments, fixed asset records, stock records and so on.

The aim of such an audit is to identify weaknesses in the system (weaknesses in either the controls or in the application of controls, such that there is a risk of material inaccuracy in financial records and statements, or a risk of fraud). More will be seen of systems-based audit in the next chapter.

A systems-based audit would take the following steps:

- Identify the objectives of each system
- Identify the procedures
- Identify why the system might not meet its objectives
- Identify ways to manage the above
- Identify if current controls are adequate
- Report on the above.

Test your understanding 11

Checking a sample of transactions against documentary evidence is an example of:

A A transactions audit

B A compliance audit

C A value for money audit

D A risk based audit

Test your understanding 12

An objective and independent measure of the success of a project is known as:

A A quality audit

B A compliance audit

C A value for money audit

D A post completion audit

6 The audit process

Introduction

This chapter looks at a typical audit process as it would be carried out by the internal auditor to audit a company's systems or processes. A key point to consider when going through this process is the problems that might be encountered when attempting to audit these different areas.

The audit process

The audit process can be summarised in the following diagram:

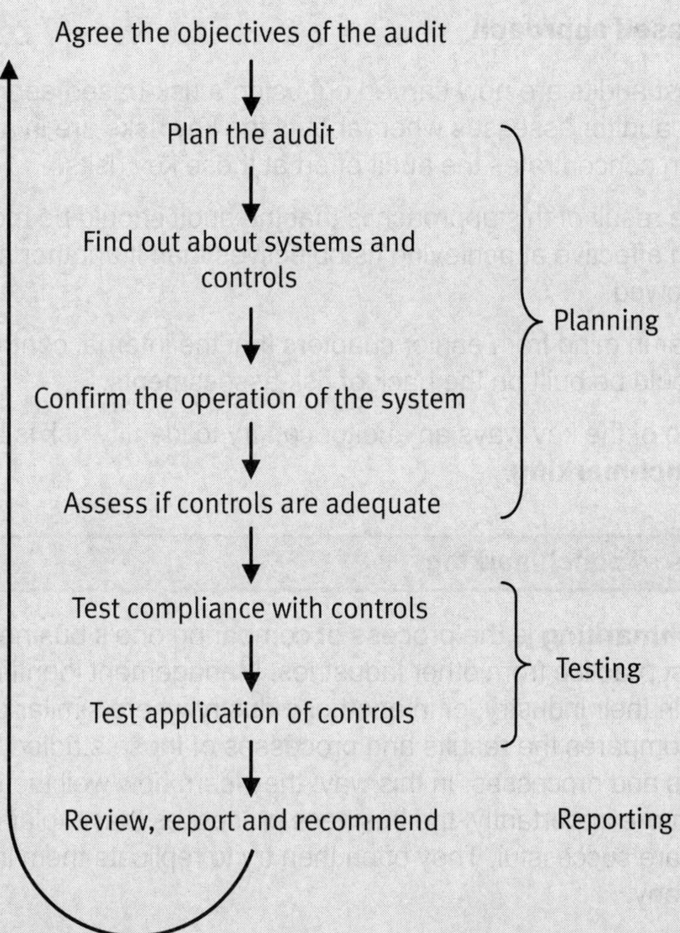

7 Audit planning

Audits should be planned. There should be an audit programme for each financial year, in which the internal auditors set out which activities or operations they will audit, and what the purpose of the audit will be in each case.

- **Objectives of the audit**
  - For example, to check whether the internal controls within a particular operation are adequate and are applied properly.
- **Conduct of the audit**
  - The auditors need to decide what information they need and what investigations they need to carry out.
  - Decisions have to be made about:
    - how to collect and record evidence, and
    - how much evidence to collect

- **Resources and timing**
  - The auditors should assess how much time and effort will be required to carry out the audit, and schedule the work accordingly.

Risk-based approach

- Most audits are now carried out using a risk-based approach, whereby the auditor assesses whereabouts the key risks are in a system, and then concentrates the audit effort at those key risks.
- The result of this approach is that the audit should be more efficient and effective at achieving its objectives than if another approach were followed.
- Bear in mind from earlier chapters that the internal control system should be built on the back of risk assessments.
- One of the key ways an auditor can try to identify risk is by **benchmarking**.

Types of benchmarking

Benchmarking is the process of comparing one's business processes to best practice from other industries. Management identifies the best firms in their industry, or in another industry where similar processes exist, and compares the results and processes of those studied to one's own results and processes. In this way, they learn how well the targets perform and, more importantly, the business processes that explain why these firms are successful. They often then try to replicate them in their own company.

There are many different types of benchmarking, since it is simply the comparison of one thing to another, but some examples include:

Process benchmarking – the company focuses its observation and investigation on business processes with a goal of identifying and observing the best practices from one or more benchmarked firms. Process analysis is required where the objective is usually to benchmark cost and efficiency. This is increasingly applied to back-office processes where outsourcing may be a consideration.

Product benchmarking – the process of designing new products or upgrades to current ones. This process can sometimes involve reverse engineering which is taking apart competitors products to find strengths and weaknesses.

Functional benchmarking – a company will focus its benchmarking on a single function e.g. Production, to improve the operation of that particular function. Complex functions such as Human Resources, Finance and Information Technology are unlikely to be directly comparable in cost and efficiency terms and may need to be disaggregated into processes to make valid comparison.

Competitor benchmarking – involves studying the leading competitor or the company that best carries out a specific function.

Environmental benchmarking – This is the process of collecting, analysing and relating environmental performance data of comparable activities with the purpose of evaluating and comparing performance between or within the entities. Entities can include processes, buildings or companies. Benchmarking may be internal within a single organisation, or – subject to confidentiality restrictions – external between competing entities.

Environmental benchmarking

Environmental and sustainability benchmarking is a tool for comparing the environmental and sustainability performance of different organisations. This form of benchmarking is becoming increasingly important as these issues gain prominence within businesses.

A major retailing company in the UK produces an annual report on their environmentalism and sustainability. It covers many angles, including their targets for:

- recycling and waste management;
- information about their 'green stores' which are built and run using environmental techniques such as using hemp walls, biomass heating systems and rainwater recycling;
- carbon emissions including their investment in their aerodynamic road transport fleet;
- staff shopping where employees and customers are encouraged to donate or swap clothing, etc to manufacture new garments, donate clothing to charities or to reduce waste;
- sustainable supplies including Fairtrade, recycled and organic products;

The company publishes 20 different targets, some with many sub-targets, and gives information on whether they have been achieved, are 'on plan', are 'behind plan' or have been cancelled (and if so, why).

Competitor firms will use this information to generate their own targets, to compare (benchmark) and to learn.

Using the financial statements to benchmark

During the planning stage of any audit , internal or external, the auditor must identify the key risks a company faces. One of the ways an auditor can do this is by using the financial statements or management accounts over several periods or years.

Performing ratio analysis, such as calculating the gross profit margin, net profit margin, receivable, payable and inventory turnover days will enable the auditor to compare the results with previous years, or their expectations. This may, in turn, help them to identify 'anomalies' or risks that the financial statements are incorrect in certain areas.

For example, imagine a company has had a gross profit margin of 40% and a net profit of 20% for several years. This year the auditor calculates the gross profit margin to be 40% but the net profit margin to have fallen to 15%. This may indicate that certain expenses have inflated or that there may be errors within the expenses (but not sales or cost of sales as this would have affected the gross profit margin also). So the auditor has narrowed down the problem to being somewhere within expenses. They could now calculate each expense as a percentage of sales and compare them to previous years. Let us imagine that the auditor identifies that 'repairs and renewals' has increased dramatically compared to previous years. They would then investigate this account and might identify that several items of expenditure that should have been capitalised (to appear on the statement of financial position) have inadvertently been posted to repairs and renewals. A simple journal correcting this can now be performed. i.e. credit repairs and renewals, debit non-current assets. (Depreciation will need to be recalculated too.)

The auditor would then reperform their ratio analysis, recalculating the net profit margin which should now be in line with the expected 20% of previous years.

On the other hand, there may have been good reason why the net profit margin had fallen. It may be that, say, rent had increased due to their landlord increasing their rental charges. This would not be a financial statement error, but could be ascertained through discussions with the finance department/finance director. In this case, it may be that the financial statements are in fact correct and that in the future the net profit margin is expected to be 15%.

The key point is that the auditor spotted an 'anomaly' or risk, investigated it and resolved to their satisfaction whether there was a risk that the financial statements were incorrect.

Annual audit plan and risk analysis

When preparing an audit plan for the year, the internal auditors should try to focus on those areas of operation where the potential risk to the business is greatest.

One way of assessing risk is to consider, for the operations or procedures subject to audit:

- the inherent risk, and
- the quality of control.

Inherent risk is the risk in the activity or operation, ignoring the controls in the system. For example, a cash based business such as a market stall or a taxi business is inherently risky due to possible theft or mis-declaration of tax payable.

Inherent risk relates both to the severity and the incidence of the risk, i.e.:

- the potential loss if an adverse situation or event arises, and the probability that an adverse situation or event will arise.

The size of the inherent risk will depend on a variety of factors, such as:

- the size of the operations unit, or the size of the expenditure budget
- the nature of the assets used or handled (e.g. systems involving the handling of cash or payments to suppliers have high inherent risk, due to the opportunities for fraud or loss)
- the extent to which procedures are computerised.

The **quality of control** is the perceived quality of the existing controls for the activity. Confidence in the quality of control will be affected by:

- the apparent effectiveness of management and supervision
- pressures on management to achieve targets
- changes in the system activities and procedures
- changes in key personnel
- a high staff turnover
- a rapid expansion in operations and the volume of transactions handled

- the length of time since the last audit of the activity was carried out. Confidence in the quality of controls will diminish over time without fresh reassurance from another audit that the controls are still effective.

The activities which should be given priority for audit are those where the inherent risk is high and the quality of control is low.

Audit risk

This is the risk that the auditors might give an inappropriate opinion on something which they tested i.e. they say that a process is well controlled when in fact it is out of control. Using the example of auditing the financial statements, audit risk has three components elements:

Inherent risk. This is the risk that an amount in the financial statements (for an asset or liability, or a transaction) might be stated as a materially incorrect amount, ignoring the existence of existing internal controls.

Control risk. This is the risk that the existing controls are not sufficient to prevent or detect a material mis-statement of a value in the financial statements.

Detection risk. This is the risk that the auditors' substantive tests will not reveal a materially incorrect amount in the financial statements, if such an error exists.

Materiality

The term 'materiality' is often used in the context of financial reporting. An item in the financial statements is material if its omission or a misstatement of its value would be likely to influence a user of the financial statements. However, materiality cannot be specified mathematically, because it has a qualitative as well as a quantitative aspect.

Materiality should also be considered in relative terms. For example, the risk of valuing an asset incorrectly by $100,000 would be material in the context of a company with assets of $1 million, but far less material in the context of a company with assets of $100 million.

Test your understanding 13

CC is a house builder in Country Y which specialises in developing large sites with many hundreds of houses across all regions of the country. It has an internal audit team who are currently preparing an audit plan for the year ahead focussing on areas of operation where the potential risk to the business is greatest.

Which of the following are inherent risks for CC?

Select **all** that apply.

A The risk that the economic downturn will encourage management to overstate progress on certain housing developments.

B The risk that expensive inventory is stolen from sites which are not secured properly overnight.

C The risk that the internal audit plan omits a particular area of risk which could have significant implications for CC.

D The risk that government regulations over house building will change and CC will be in breach of new rules.

E The risk that sites for developments, once work has begun are found to be unsuitable and must be abandoned.

8 Systems investigation and documentation

The auditors should document the system or operation subject to audit, and document their findings or judgements. They will need to ascertain what the system is and also the controls that operate over the system.

Ascertaining systems

The auditor could use the following sources and methods to ascertain how the systems operate:

Flowcharts	These could be examined or created from discussions with staff who use and operate systems.
Interviews/ Questionnaires	The staff who operate the system can describe how they use it. This has the advantage over other existing system documentation as it identifies how the staff use the system even if this is out of line with the proper procedures.

Systems documentation The auditor can research the documentation of the system when it was produced to identify how the system operates. Documentation tends to be best for computerised systems as they will have gone through a proper systems development approach and also they tend to be least well understood by users.

Observation The operation of the system can be observed.

Ascertaining controls

To specifically assess the controls in systems an auditor could use standard control questionnaires. These documents are structured so as to identify all key internal controls and also enable the auditor to assess the quality of the controls.

More on audit tools

Flowcharts

Flowcharts might be used to record:

- the sequence of activities and checks within an operation or procedure
- which individuals carry out each procedure or check.

The advantages of flowcharting the stages in an operation are that:

- a flowchart is more often effective at presenting information in an understandable form than a narrative description
- if there are weaknesses in the controls within an operation, these might be easier to identify by studying a flowchart.

Questionnaires

A questionnaire is a list of questions for which the auditor needs to finds answers in order to gather the information or evidence he needs. The questions should be specific, and should ideally call for a 'Yes' or 'No' answer, although room should be left on the form for additional comments to be added if required.

The answers to the questions help the auditor both to:

- establish the facts, and
- identify potential control weaknesses.

9 Control assessment

Once auditors have ascertained what the controls are they need to make an assessment of the internal controls and whether they will achieve their objectives.

Example of controls

A company has a small accounting department, in which the same individual is made responsible for accounts payable and also for carrying out the bank reconciliation checks. Ideally, these tasks should be segregated, because there is a risk that the individual might be making out cheques to his or her personal bank account, and the fraud would not be identified by the bank reconciliation process.

To overcome this weakness in the control system, a number of controls might be applied, such as:

- requiring that all cheques are signed by hand by a senior manager in the company, instead of signed automatically
- a review by the individual's supervisor of all bank reconciliations
- a periodic listing from the company's bank of all the payments out of the company's bank account in the period, for review by a senior manager.

10 Audit testing

Having made an assessment of the existing controls and identified the areas of greatest risk the auditor will move onto the testing.

Auditors need to carry out tests, to ensure that procedures are performed correctly, and that controls to prevent or detect errors are adequate and applied effectively.

Types of testing

Compliance testing (test of controls):

The test of controls should be carried out to ensure that the controls identified at the planning stage operate as they should.

If the controls are not being complied with then there will be a material weakness in the control system and the result could be serious errors or fraud and the business objectives may not be achieved.

The results of the compliance testing should indicate whether:

- the controls are effective, or
- the controls are ineffective in practice, even though they appeared adequate 'on paper'.

Substantive testing (test of balances or transactions):

Substantive testing, on the other hand, does not look at the controls in the system – it rather concentrates on the output and ensuring that the output is as expected.

Substantive testing is normally associated with financial systems but can also be used for non-financial systems.

The purpose of the substantive tests is either to:

- confirm that the controls are effective
- where the controls are ineffective, to establish the apparent consequences.

For example, an audit of a quality control system would give the following types of testing:

Substantive test	Monitor the number of quality control failures as a proportion of good output.
Compliance test	Observe the functioning of the quality control staff to ensure they are checking output.

In the exam, students should for options with words like **reconcile, analyse, observe, monitor or sample** at the beginning of a sentence that recommends an audit test. Try to avoid options with the word 'check' since that can be construed as vague, unless it explains fully what they would be checking for and why.

Test your understanding 14

Which of the following is a substantive audit test?

A Observing the functioning of the quality control staff to ensure that they are checking output

B Matching customer orders to invoices

C Monitoring the number of quality control failures as a percentage of output

D Observing staff clocking in and out to ensure that productive time is recorded accurately

Test your understanding 15 – Compliance testing (Integration)

Company X has recently employed John. John went through the company's interview process – after submitting his curriculum vitae and filling in the standard application form, he attended two interviews (one individual and one group). He was then offered the job and asked to start the following Monday.

John has been at X for a month now and his manager is not happy with his work. He is frequently late in to the office, and he frequently makes mistakes in the tasks he is given.

His manager has heard a rumour that the qualification he stated on his application form is false, which could explain his poor work.

Required:

Discuss the problem at X and suggest controls that should be in place to prevent this occurrence.

Detail appropriate compliance tests the internal auditor should perform on the recruitment process to ensure that this does not happen in the future.

Test your understanding 16 – Audit testing (Integration)

Recommend some compliance and substantive tests that could be undertaken by an auditor to check whether errors are occurring in payroll processing. Staff are paid weekly in cash. The objective of the audit is to ensure that:

(i) payments are only made to genuine employees.

(ii) all deductions from pay are calculated correctly.

(iii) employees are paid only for hours worked.

(iv) deductions are paid over to the appropriate authorities.

11 Sampling

With any audit testing it will probably be necessary to undertake some form of sampling.

Sampling is testing a proportion of a population to gain assurance about the population as a whole.

Audit sampling

The application of audit procedures to less than 100% of the items within an account balance or class of transactions to obtain and evaluate evidence about some characteristic of the items selected in order to form a conclusion on the population.

Risks that occur with sampling

As soon as an auditor decides to sample a population, there are risks that are brought into the audit:

Sampling risk	This is the risk that the auditor's conclusion, based on the results of the sample, may be different from the result that would have been obtained had all items in the population been tested. (This risk can never be removed if sampling is done.)
Non-sampling risk	This is the risk that the auditor may use inappropriate procedures, or misinterpret evidence that the test results give. As a result the auditor would fail to recognise an error. (This risk is avoidable if auditors use the appropriate procedures.)

Test your understanding 17

The risk that an amount in the financial statements might be stated as materially incorrect (ignoring the existence of current internal controls) is called:

A Detection risk

B Control risk

C Inherent risk

D Sampling risk

12 Analytical review

Analytical review is arguably the most important test available to the auditor as they can be used in the audit of most items – both financial and non-financial – and can be used at various points in the audit process.

Definition

Analytical review is the examination of ratios, trends and changes in the business from one period to the next, to obtain a broad understanding of the results of operations, and to identify any items requiring further investigation.

When the results appear abnormal the auditors will investigate more closely to find out the cause(s) by performing further work.

Ratios

During the audit of any part of the financial statements, analytical review often involves the calculation of ratios, such as:

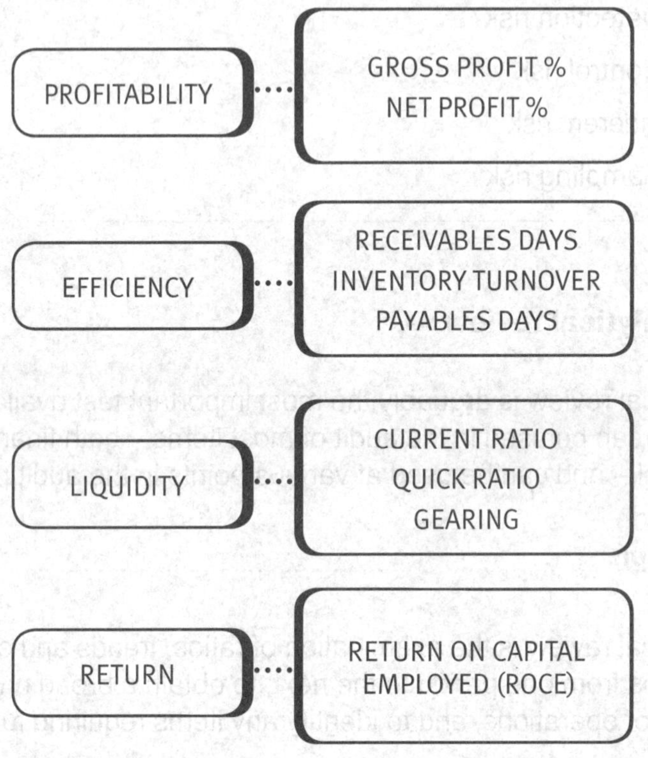

Nature of analytical review

Comparisons of information could be with:

	Examples		
• Prior periods/anticipated results	20X1	20X1	20X0
	Actual	Budget	Actual
Number of new products launched	9	11	10

- Predictive estimates — Depreciation for year = 15% × y/e cost
- Similar industry info — Staff turnover v industry average

Uses of analytical review

Analytical review will be used at all stages of the audit.

Planning	They will be used to identify risks, and therefore help in deciding the level of testing, and its nature and timing.
Substantive testing	Analytical review is a very important substantive procedure that can provide sufficient audit evidence in some areas. In practice in the audit of financial information, expenses in the income statement, accruals and prepayments are all audited by substantive analytical procedures.
Overall review	The procedures are used to conclude whether the area being tested is consistent with the auditors' knowledge of the business entity and the expected results.

Test your understanding 18 – Car dealership (Integration)

You are an internal auditor for a car dealership with a number of branches. You have responsibility for looking at where efficiency gains could be made. From the following information, recommend, with reasons, which region you would look at first.

	North	**South**	**East**	**West**
Number of salesmen	16	12	10	24
Total sales value in the last month (£000)	2,700	2,520	2,320	2,400
Number of sales orders	180	156	160	190
Number of sales discussions	660	364	432	740

More on analytical review

In order to use analytical procedures effectively you need to be able to create an expectation. It will be difficult to create an expectation if operations are significantly different from last year, more so if the changes haven't been planned for. If the changes were planned, we can compare the actual with the forecast. It will also be difficult to use analytical procedures if there have been lots of one-off events in the year as there will be nothing to compare them with.

Test your understanding 19 – D courier company (Case study)

Scenario

F is a member of the internal audit department of D, a courier company. F has recently completed a compliance audit of the extent to which the company's delivery vans are being maintained in accordance with the company's policy.

Each of D's depots has a full-time mechanic. The company's policy is that the depot mechanic is required to check each van's fluid levels and give a road test on a monthly basis. The Depot Manager is responsible for ensuring that every van has been checked in this manner.

Trigger

One of D's delivery drivers was recently involved in a road traffic accident. The police report relating to this accident indicates that the van's brakes had failed because of a leak in the brake pipe. The delivery driver has been charged by the police with an offence because it is illegal to drive a vehicle with defective brakes.

D's Transport Manager has reviewed the van's maintenance log. The log shows that the depot mechanic had not inspected the van during the six weeks before the accident. The Head of Internal Audit has reviewed F's report and has noticed that although F had visited the depot shortly before the accident occurred he had reported that policies were being adhered to.

The Head of Internal Audit has asked F to explain why he gave a positive report when records prove that policies had not been adhered to. F explained that the Depot Manager had admitted that the vans had not been inspected as frequently as company policy required because the depot mechanic had been absent for two weeks because of ill health. There were no other qualified mechanics available to carry out these inspections and the depot's repair budget was insufficient to pay for the vans to be inspected by a third party. The Depot Manager had asked F not to note this omission in the audit report because it would lead to disciplinary action, which would harm the Depot Manager's career. F agreed not to report the missed inspections provided that the Depot Manager promised that all of the vans would be inspected as soon as possible when the depot mechanic returned to work.

The Head of Internal Audit was dissatisfied with F's behaviour alleging F had not acted in an independent manner. F denies that accusation because he has no connection to the Depot Manager or any of the depot's other staff. Additionally, F has pointed out that the Depot Manager could easily have falsified the maintenance records to conceal the fact that the vans had not all been inspected on schedule and a negative internal audit report would simply encourage Depot Managers to falsify their records in future.

Task

(a) Evaluate the Head of Internal Audit's assertion that F had not behaved in an independent manner.

(b) Discuss the implications of F's behaviour for the governance of D. The Head of Internal Audit wishes to conduct a thorough investigation into the level and frequency of the inspection of the company's delivery vans.

(c) Prepare a briefing note from the Head of Internal Audit to the internal audit department recommending the tests that could be conducted to ensure that the depot mechanics are inspecting vehicles in accordance with company policy. You should explain the purpose of the tests that you have recommended.

(45 minutes)

13 Audit reporting

Audit report

The final stage of an audit is the audit report. In an internal audit assignment the audit report does not have a strict structure, however, it would be expected to feature a number of different parts:

- The objectives of the audit work.
- A summary of the process undertaken by the auditor.
- The results of tests carried out.
- The audit opinion (if an opinion is required).
- Recommendations for action.

When giving recommendations auditors must always ensure that the recommendations are practical and cost-effective.

The auditor will need to consider whether the residual risk will be reduced by the recommendation. If it will not, the recommendation is not worthwhile.

- The internal auditor should have a process of post-implementation review to ensure that recommendations have been actioned by management.

Test your understanding 20

The audit process is made up of the following steps:

A Plan the audit; document systems and controls; test compliance with controls; report to board

B Plan the audit; report to the board; document systems and controls; test compliance with controls

C Document systems and controls; test compliance with controls; report to board; test application of controls

D Document systems and controls; test application of controls; test compliance with controls; report to board

Test your understanding 21

H is the internal auditor of S Co and has been carrying out work on the purchases cycle to assess the internal controls in place and make recommendations for improvements. He is due to present his findings to the audit committee and has been asked to prepare a report.

Which of the following are sections to be included in the report? Select all that apply

A Executive Summary

B Observations and work done

C A signed opinion

D Recommendations

E A statement of compliance with the relevant laws

14 Audit of computer systems

In the case of computer systems, audits are carried out:

- to check whether the system is achieving its intended objectives, and
- in the case of accounting systems, to check that the information produced by the system is reliable.

Problems of auditing computer systems

Auditing computer systems gives some different problems and some new opportunities to auditors to test systems. There are several problems for the auditor of computer systems that do not occur with 'manual' systems, including:

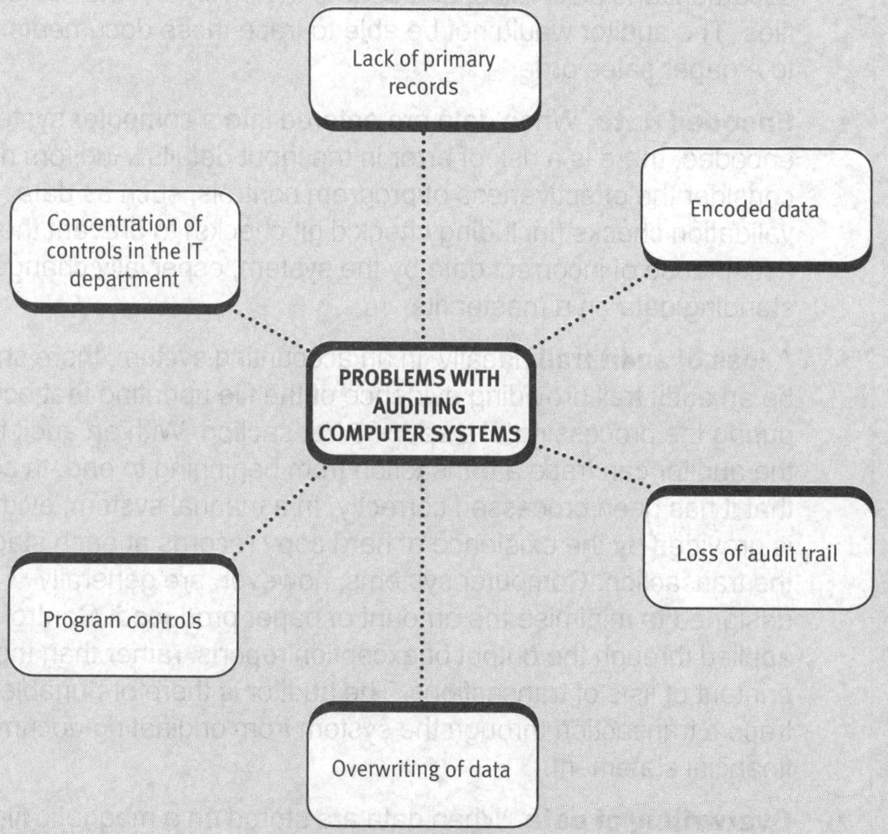

More on problems with auditing computer systems

There are several problems for the auditor with computer systems that do not occur with 'manual' systems. These include:

- **Concentration of controls** in the IT department. In large computer systems, many of the controls over data are concentrated in the central IT department. This can be a potential weakness in the control system, because of the risk of an accidental or deliberate corruption of data or programs, of which the user departments are not aware.
- A **lack of primary records.** In some computer systems, a document originating a transaction might not be created. For example, in an on-line system a customer order received by telephone might be keyed into the system. The system might then generate a despatch document and an invoice, and update the inventory and customer files. The auditor would not be able to trace these documents back to a paper sales order.
- **Encoded data.** When data are entered into a computer system and encoded, there is a risk of error in the input details. Auditors need to consider the effectiveness of program controls, such as data validation checks (including check digit checks) to prevent the acceptance of incorrect data by the system, especially changes to standing data on a master file.
- A **loss of audit trail.** Ideally, in an accounting system, there should be an audit trail providing evidence of the file updating that occurs during the processing of a specific transaction. With an audit trail, the auditor can trace a transaction from beginning to end, to confirm that it has been processed correctly. In a manual system, evidence is provided by the existence of hard copy records at each stage of the transaction. Computer systems, however, are generally designed to minimise the amount of paper produced. Control is applied through the output of exception reports, rather than the printout of lists of transactions. The auditor is therefore unable to trace a transaction through the system from originating document to financial statement.
- **Overwriting of data.** When data are stored on a magnetic file, it will eventually be overwritten with new data. If the auditor needs some of this data to carry out audit tests, it will be necessary to take steps to make the data available. The auditor might therefore need to take copies of data files during the course of the year, and retain them for audit purposes.
- **Program controls.** The auditor has to test the controls in the computer system on which he intends to rely. This means that he must test the controls written into the computer programs. To do this, it will be necessary to use computer-assisted audit techniques.

Errors

Additionally, when auditors audit computer systems they need to be aware of the types of errors that occur in the systems. The characteristics of errors are:

- No one-off errors unless deliberate amendment of individual items.
- Systematic errors which repeat across all transactions.
- Higher danger that input errors will not be detected.

Audit approach

The audit approach for computer auditing is often summarised in one of two ways:

- through the computer; or
- round the computer.

Round the computer

Under this approach the auditor does not attempt to understand the operation of the computer system, but rather treats it as a 'black box'. To audit the system, the auditor matches up inputs to predicted outputs to ensure that the outputs are being processed correctly.

The approach is good in that it does not require a high level of expertise of IT in the audit teams, but it is only suitable if the following conditions are met:

- Computer processing is relatively simple
- Audit trail is clearly visible
- A substantial amount of up-to-date documentation exists about how the system works.

Problems with auditing round the computer include:

- Computer files and programs are not tested, hence there is no direct evidence that program is working as documented
- If errors are found it may be impossible to determine why they have happened
- All discrepancies between predicted and actual results must be fully resolved and documented no matter how small (this is because controls are being tested).

Through the computer

This approach actually interrogates the computer files and computer controls and relies much more on the processes that the computer uses.

The auditor follows the audit trail through the internal computer operations and attempts to verify that the processing controls are functioning correctly. The computer controls are directly tested and the accuracy of computer-based processing of input data is verified.

To audit through the computer requires more expertise and a longer set-up time; however, the results can be of very good quality.

This approach utilises different computer-assisted audit techniques (CAATs) such as test data and audit software, discussed below.

15 Computer-assisted audit techniques (CAATs)

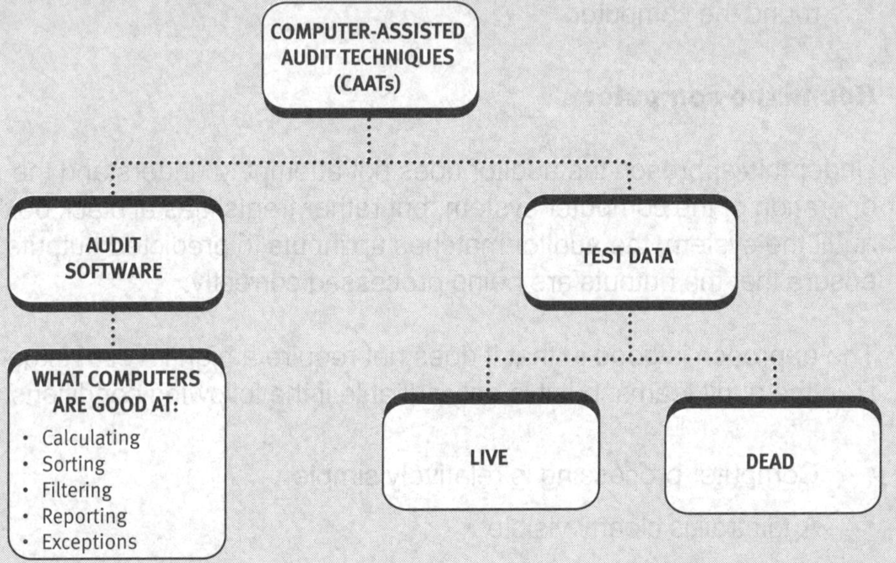

Computer-assisted audit techniques are methods of using a computer to carry out an audit of a computer system. There are two main categories of CAAT:

- audit software, such as audit interrogation software
- test data.

Audit interrogation software

Audit software consists of computer programs used by auditors to interrogate the files of a client. Normally the client's data files are input into the audit software program on the auditor's computer, and the auditor can then test those files. Examples of what audit software can do include:

- Extract a sample according to specified criteria
  - Random
  - Over a certain amount
  - Below a certain amount
  - At certain dates
- Calculate ratios and select those outside the criteria
- Check calculations (for example, additions)
- Prepare reports (budget vs. actual)
- Produce letters to send out to customers suppliers
- Follow items through a computerised system
- Search for underlying relationships and check for fraud.

Packages are generally designed to:

- read computer files
- select information
- perform calculations
- create data files, and
- print reports in a format specified by the auditor.

Audit software enables large volumes of data to be processed very quickly and accurately. The main drawback of audit software is that it can take a long time to set up the systems with the client data, and it will require expertise.

CAATs and fraud detection

Audit software includes a variety of routines for identifying transactions where there could be a suspicion of fraud, such as:

- comparing the home addresses of employees with the addresses of suppliers, to identify employees who are also suppliers
- searching for duplicate cheque numbers
- analysing the sequence of transactions to identify missing invoices or cheques
- identifying suppliers with more than one supplier code or more than one mailing address
- finding several suppliers all with the same address
- listing payments for transactions that fall just within the spending authorisation limit of the individual who has authorised the payment.

Benefits and weaknesses of CAATs

Benefits of CAATs	**Examples**
CAAT's force the auditor to rely on programmed controls during the audit. Sometimes it may be the only way to test controls within a computer system, therefore enables the auditor to test program controls.	Credit limits within a system can only be changed by the accountant. A computer assisted check will test that this is the case.
Large number of items can be tested quickly and accurately.	Checking the depreciation charged on each asset would be quicker with a computer assisted program than manually.
CAAT's test original documentation instead of print outs, therefore the authenticity of the document is more valid this way.	Actual wages will be tested instead of paper copies.

After initial set-up costs, using CAATs are likely to be cost-effective, as the same audit software can be used each year as long as the system doesn't change.	Examples of use or audit tests (1) Calculation checks (2) Reviewing lists of old or outstanding items and investing those specifically (3) Detecting for unreasonable items (4) Detecting violation of the system rules (5) New analysis (6) Completeness checks (7) Selects samples (8) Identifying exception reporting facilities.
Allow the results from using CAATs to be compared with 'traditional' testing.	If the two sources of evidence agree then this too will increase the overall audit confidence.

Weaknesses of CAATs	**Recommendations**
CAAT's will be limited depending on how well the computer system is integrated. The more integrated the better the use of CAAT's. For example, the invoices should be computer generated and then processed through the accounts system to feed in to the financial statements.	Ensure understanding of the system to assess whether audit software will be relevant for the company. Need to assess whether there is a need for the audit software.
It takes time to design CAATs tests therefore, may not be cost-effective if the auditor is dealing with a bespoke system, as there may be a lot of set-up costs. The reason for this is it takes time to write specific test data or to program the audit software to the needs of the client.	A cost-benefit analysis from the audit point of view should be carried out prior to deciding to use the audit software.

If the company you are auditing cannot confirm all system documentation is available, then the auditors will be unable to do the tests effectively due to lack of understanding.	Do not use audit software until these have been identified.
If there is a change in the accounting year, or from the previous year, then the audit software will have to be reset and designed, therefore may be costly.	A cost-benefit analysis from the audit point of view should be carried out prior to deciding to use the audit software.

Test your understanding 22 – Audit software (Integration)

Recommend how audit software could be used in the audit of a mail order company concerned that deliveries are not being invoiced and that stock files are not being updated.

Embedded audit facilities

Embedded audit facilities might be written into a program, particularly in on-line/real-time systems. These facilities can carry out automatic checks or provide information for subsequent audit, such as:

- extracting and storing information for subsequent audit review, with sufficient details to give the auditor a proper audit trail
- identifying and recording items that are of some particular audit interest, as specified by the auditor.

Test data

Test data can be used by inputting the data into the system and checking whether it is processed correctly. The expected results can be calculated in advance, and checked against the actual output from the system. The auditors might include some invalid data in the tests, which the system should reject.

It will only be used if the auditor is intending to do a 'test of controls' audit, and it must be considered cost effective.

Live data = test data are processed during a normal production run.

Dead data = test data are processed outside the normal cycle.

The stages involved in using test data are:

(1) Gain a thorough understanding of how the system being tested is supposed to work and the controls that are included in it.

(2) Devise the test data set. This should be a set of data containing both valid and invalid items. The controls in the system should identify the invalid items.

(3) Run the test data. This can be 'live' (within the normal processing at the client), or 'dead' (outside the normal processing). Live runs give more reliable results but are more risky to operate.

(4) Evaluate the results. It is important that the auditor fully evaluates the results of the test data and does further work if unexpected results occur.

Risks with test data

Risks	**Controls**
Damage to the system as the system is tested to its limits.	Ensure auditors understand the system and have software support.
Corruption of the systems data if test data are not properly removed.	Ensure process for data removal.
System down time if 'dead' data used.	Establish when system can be used with minimum disruption to the business.

Examples of test data

Tests	**Reason for the test**
Revenue	
Input an order into the client's system that would cause a customer to exceed their credit limit	The order should not be accepted, or should raise a query whether you are sure you wish to proceed. If this happens then the auditors will have confidence the system is working properly
Input a negative number of items on an order	Ensures only positive quantities are accepted
Input incomplete customer details	The system should not process the order unless all information is completed
Input an excessive amount	There are reasonable checks in the system to identify possible input errors. A warning should appear on the screen confirming the number

Purchases	
Raise an order from a supplier not on the preferred supplier list	A query should be raised as to whether you want to proceed with this transaction
Process an order with an unauthorised staff ID	The system should reject the process altogether or send the request through to an appropriate person for authorisation
Try and make changes to the supplier standing data using the ID of someone who is not authorised to do so	The system should reject the process altogether or send the request through to an appropriate person for authorisation
Payroll	
Try and set up a new employee up on the payroll system using an unauthorised ID	The system should reject the process altogether or send the request through to an appropriate person for authorisation
Try and make employee changes of detail using an unauthorised ID	The system should reject the process altogether or send the request through to an appropriate person for authorisation
Make an excess change, for example increase someone's salary by $1,000,000 by someone authorised	The system should have parameters in place to question this amount, and maybe reject it due to it being outside the normal range

Test your understanding 23

E Company administers payments to home owners to enable them to insulate their homes, or up-grade their heating system. E is in receipt of a central government grant which it must only distribute to home owners whose income is below a certain level or who fall into a 'vulnerable' category, as stipulated by the government guidelines.

E Company must not administer payments twice to the same address, or breach a maximum award amount. E company must also receive proof (in the form of an invoice) that the money awarded has been used for the intended items. E Company maintains computerised records of all payments awarded with inbuilt controls to ensure they do not breach government guidelines.

The internal auditors of E Company are using 'test data' to perform checks on whether the computer controls over awarding payments are working correctly. They are using 'dead data' to test the system.

Which of the following issues is the test data unlikely to detect?

Select **all** that apply.

A Whether the system will allow a payment which breaches the upper limit to be processed.

B Whether the system works consistently in the same way

C Whether the system will allow a payment to be made to the same address twice.

D Whether the system will allow a payment to be made to an individual not classed as vulnerable or on a low income.

E Whether an address which has received a grant is valid.

F Whether 'spot checks' at addresses were carried out correctly.

Test your understanding 24

Factors affecting the need for an audit include: (Select all that apply.)

A The number of directors

B Turnover

C The diversity of the company's activities

D A change in organisational structure

E Net assets

Test your understanding 25

The testing and evaluation of controls is usually performed firstly by which one of the following?

A Risk management

B External audit

C Internal audit

D Management

Test your understanding 26 – G Manufacturing (Case study)

Scenario

G is a manufacturing company that employs 800 production staff and 90 administrative staff. The company operates from a single site.

Trigger

A new Chief Executive was appointed in July 2013. She was recruited from a much larger manufacturing company that is an indirect competitor of G, where she was the Marketing Director.

Since her appointment the Chief Executive has focussed on learning as much as she possibly can about the company's culture. She spent the whole of August meeting representatives from all levels of staff from within the company and other stakeholders such as customers and suppliers. She has called a board meeting to discuss her findings. Her findings are as follows:

- The company manufactures high quality products that are popular with customers. All members of G's staff are proud to be associated with the manufacture of the products.
- G's managers and supervisors take a very relaxed approach when working with subordinates. Staff are empowered to make decisions on their own without consulting their superiors if they are confident that they are acting in the company's best interests.
- The relaxed management style has harmed the control environment immensely. Only a minority of the company's staff take the budgetary control system seriously and hardly any of them pay serious attention to variance reports. In contrast to all other departments, morale in the accounts department is very low because the members of the accounts staff feel that they waste a significant amount of time every month chasing heads of departments for reports and for other important information.
- These attitudes are echoed by external stakeholders. Customers are delighted with the quality of G's products, but often find that G's invoices and monthly statements contain errors. Suppliers claim that invoices submitted to G are settled very promptly 90% of the time, but the remainder have to be chased because G's accounts staff do not always receive accurate and complete records of orders placed and goods received.

The Chief Executive has warned the board that the control environment must be improved as a matter of priority. She proposes to send an email to all staff congratulating them on their achievements on product quality, but stating that the rather lax attitude towards management and record keeping will have to stop. Over time, she plans to impose disciplinary measures on staff who are responsible for bookkeeping errors or delays. She also proposes that G should create an internal audit department to monitor compliance with formal processes and procedures.

The Production Director has argued that the Chief Executive's proposals are counter-productive and that most of the delays and omissions are due to employees giving priority to the creation of an excellent product.

Task

Write a briefing note to the Chief Executive recommending, stating reasons, the steps that he should take in order to create an effective internal audit department.

(30 minutes)

Test your understanding 27 – Multinational car manufacturer

Scenario

M is a multinational car manufacturer. M sells six models of car around the world. Each model has its own assembly factory. Each of the factories is located in a different country and each factory is incorporated as a company. Car assembly is heavily automated, using robots to assemble and weld, and so final assembly is generally in a country that is chosen for its proximity to major markets.

M has many other factories that make components. For example, one factory manufactures all of the music systems for every car sold by M and another manufactures all of the windscreens. These factories can be located in countries that offer low labour costs. For example, the music systems are built using unskilled labour in a developing country.

Each country in which M sells cars has its own M subsidiary that deals with distribution. All sales are to car dealerships and each dealership buys cars directly from its local M subsidiary.

National governments are keen to ensure that intra-group transfers are at arm's length prices and are set so that M will not pay too little tax. Therefore the transfer pricing policy in M is that transfers should be at "market price". Consequently the transfer prices that are used by M do not necessarily reflect the manufacturing costs and so some group members report very small profits. The company's reward system for its senior managers and directors is linked to the profits that are reported by their subsidiary.

M's transfer pricing arrangements take up a great deal of management time. In many cases, arm's length market prices are difficult to identify because there are no direct comparisons available. For example, the subsidiary that manufactures music systems does not sell its products to anyone other than the six assembly companies. Even if similar products can be found that are traded openly by other manufacturers, there are very specific problems with determining an objective market price. For example, there are transport costs and questions over the discounts that are granted for bulk sales. There is an even greater problem with finished cars because M sells its cars at higher prices in more prosperous markets.

Trigger

M's main board is concerned that the company may be investigated by the tax authorities in one or more of the countries where it does business. The Head of Group Internal Audit has been asked to assist the board by conducting an internal investigation in order to establish whether M should change any of its transfer pricing practices.

Task

Write a briefing note to the Board advising on the matters that it should cover when briefing the Head of Group Internal Audit in order to be certain that its requirements are met by the internal audit investigation into M's transfer pricing practices.

Write a note to the Head of Group Internal Audit discussing four factors that they should consider when assessing the possibility that a subsidiary could be investigated by its local tax authority.

(30 minutes)

16 Chapter summary

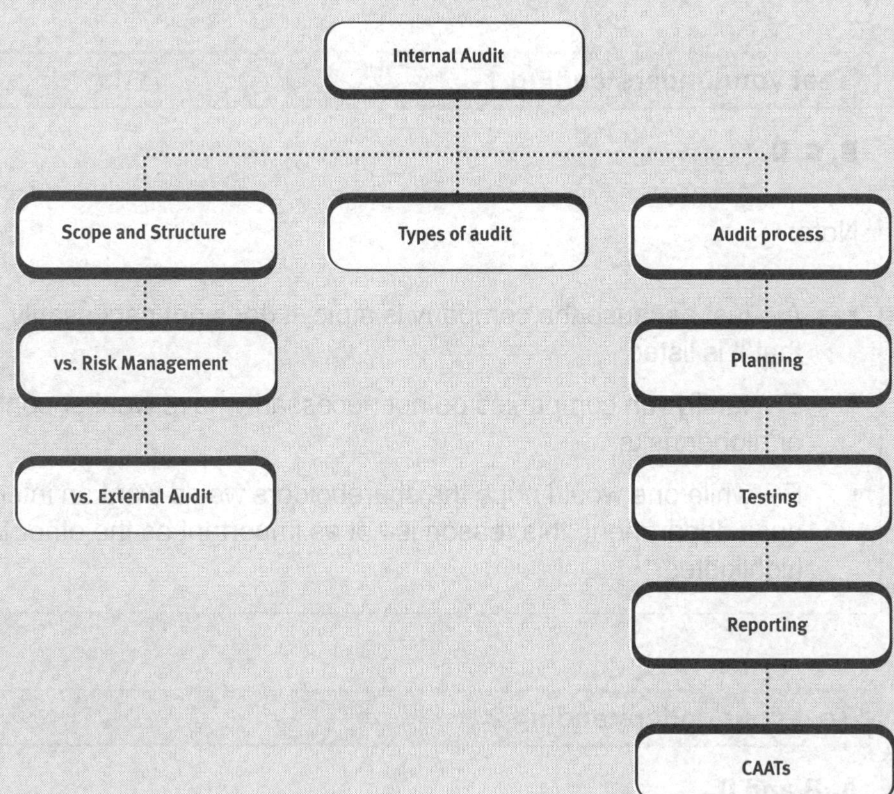

Test your understanding answers

Test your understanding 1

B, C, D

Note:

- A – just because the company is a plc, it does not necessarily follow that it is listed
- E – family run companies do not necessarily have weaker controls or higher risks
- F – while one would hope the shareholders would want an internal audit department, this reason is not as important as the other factors highlighted.

Test your understanding 2

A, B and D

- Option C: This is an internal audit role. The risk management team cannot establish controls and then test them objectively.
- Option E: This is a role that internal audit may carry out.
- Option F: This is a responsibility of the board.

Test your understanding 3

A and B only

- Option A: True – The internal auditor cannot report to a director who might be the subject of an internal audit.
- Option B: True – Since objectivity is the key attribute of an internal auditor, an outside appointment, without any personal grievances or conflicts, within NN will be more independent than an internal promotion.
- Option C: False – The internal auditor could review controls over quality control for adequacy but not directly prevent the re-occurrence of any events.
- Option D: False – In carrying out their work, the internal auditors will need to question operational staff and observe them carrying out their roles. This will inevitably take time. However, improvements suggested by internal audit should outweigh any short term loss of efficiency.
- Option E: False – Many organisations have a single internal auditor. Whilst a team and a separate department are ideal, they are not compulsory.

Test your understanding 4

A, B, D

Note:

- C – Internal staff are more likely to have a better understanding of the organisation's objectives and culture
- E – the decision should be based on a range of factors including cost, quality, skills, etc

Test your understanding 5

The correct answer is A – Reporting should be to a senior director. They should also have access to the chairman, and be accountable to the audit committee.

Test your understanding 6

The correct answers are A, B and D – Identifying risk is the role of risk management. Internal audit test the controls in place to prevent or detect risk. However, if in the course of internal audit work a risk is identified then it will be reported to risk management (which is a secondary role for audit).

Test your understanding 7

The correct answer is D – By outsourcing the internal audit function control may be lost.

Test your understanding 8 – SHD (Integration)

External audit perspective

External auditors form an opinion on whether the financial statements show a true and fair view. This means they will seek explanations for any unusual items, areas of expenditure, etc so they can form their opinion.

The fact that variable overheads have increased means that they will require evidence (such as approved invoices) to verify these expenses .

They will need to ensure that expenditure is bona fide to the business. If it appears difficult to determine why these expenses have been incurred, then the issue of legitimate business expense is raised.

At the extreme there is the possibility of reporting under the Proceeds of Crime Act of 2002 that the business may have been involved in fraud or money laundering.

Internal audit perspective

The lack of apparent reason for incurring the additional overhead expenses also appears to be a weakness in the internal control systems. Segregation of duties is poor and this has allowed someone to set up a supplier and process invoices for payment to that supplier.

The internal auditors will be concerned by such weaknesses in control and seek to rectify the situation.

They may also notice the increase in expenditure and question the efficient use of resources on the development projects.

Test your understanding 9 – Z (Case study)

(a) The whole point of this type of tendering process is to ensure that each bidder has an incentive to tender at the lowest possible acceptable price. Doing that requires that the bidding parties know as little as possible about one another and that the bids themselves are kept secure.

There are a number of areas of concern in this case: The winning bidder withdrew what would have been the lowest offer and replaced it with a higher bid. There could be an innocent explanation for that, but it is a matter of some concern that the bid was replaced because it could indicate a knowledge of the other bidders' tenders. If that is the case then there could have been some collusion between the bidder and a member of staff in Z's buying department. Alternatively, the bidder could have colluded with the other companies that were most likely to have placed bids for this contract.

The winning bid was not the lowest one submitted. That could simply some favouritism on the part of the selection committee. There may be a perfectly valid justification for rejecting a lower bid, but it seems strange that a bidder for a major contract would submit a tender for a product that is not fit for purpose. The process was not particularly secure. The bids themselves were addressed to a relatively junior manager and were not stored under conditions of great secrecy. The chief buyer could easily have opened incoming bids and put them in replacement blank envelopes without that being obvious to anybody. The internal auditor was not involved until very late in the process and most of those present at the opening were directly involved in the project. The internal audit department could have taken a more active role in the whole process of safeguarding bids and in opening them under secure conditions.

(b) The internal auditor should attempt to establish who had access to the sealed bids after they had been received. It would be an easy matter for anybody who had access to the safe to type a label and put the bid in a new envelope. It would not be particularly difficult to forge a colleague's signature (or for the chief buyer to sign the envelope).

The easiest way for the auditor to determine who had access would be to visit the buying department and to note the location of the safe and the occupants of the office in which it is located. The auditor should use indirect, open-ended questions to determine whether the safe is normally kept locked when the is occupied and who has access to the key or combination.

The opened envelopes, which should have been retained, should be examined and the chief buyer asked to confirm that all of the signatures were genuine. That would effectively mean that the chief buyer was accepting personal responsibility for the bids that were considered. The internal auditor should attempt to establish whether there is any form of relationship between any member of the buying department and the winning bidder. Even those who could not access the safe would possibly know who had bid from the covering letters, which were kept separately, and that could have permitted the winner to gather information that led to submitting a higher winning bid. The purchase ledger should be checked to determine whether Z had any previous dealings with the winning bidder.

The reasons for the rejection of the cheaper bid should be investigated. The fact that the bus was slightly smaller could be a reason for rejection as could the specification for the modifications, but these might not be material to the selection. If the buses were large enough and within the parameters of the tender document and the materials were of an acceptable specification then the cheapest bid should have been accepted.

(c) **Note**

To: The Chief Executive

From: A.N. Accountant

Date: Today

Subject: The advantages and disadvantages of the internal auditor being actively involved in the investigation of suspected fraud.

Dear Sir,

The advantages include:

The internal auditor should be independent of those who are being investigated. It would be difficult to identify anybody else outside of the buying department with the necessary understanding of the process.

The internal auditor will have the necessary skills to undertake the investigation and also knows and understands the entity's culture and systems. An external auditor could undertake the investigation, but would not have this insight. The entity can be assured of the internal auditor's discretion and so there should be very little risk of the facts leaking out without the board's permission. Internal audit staff are generally professionally qualified and are also trained to be discreet.

The disadvantages include:

Using the internal audit department in this way could make it more difficult for the internal auditors to maintain a good working relationship with those under audit. Internal auditors are generally reluctant to investigate potential fraud because it may undermine their relationship with line staff.

The audit could be very time consuming and could be a major distraction from the ongoing schedule of internal audit activities. The internal audit department's time is a valuable resource and it will generally be allocated to specific tasks as part of a plan. The fact that the evidence has been gathered by the company's own staff could undermine its credibility if, say, the company seeks compensation as a result of the investigation or pursues criminal charges. If there has been any staff fraud then the police will require a clear and unambiguous chain of evidence and the fact that colleagues have been involved in the initial investigation may interfere with their ability to build a criminal case. If you have any further queries please do not hesitate to ask.

Best wishes

A.N. Accountant

Test your understanding 10 – Seatown (case study)

Address

Date

Dear Sirs,

Re: The economy, efficiency and effectiveness of beach cleaning activities

(a) The total cost of all activities should be measured against budget and previous years. That cost should be broken down according to whether it relates to sweeping or emptying bins and by the nature of the expense within that (e.g. labour or vehicle running costs) so that any costs can be identified and managed.

The breakdown of the total should be linked to the cost drivers in order to measure trends or spot anomalies. For example, the cost of running tractors should be divided by the number of tractors or the number of kilometres travelled to determine the cost per vehicle or vehicle-kilometre. Much of this information should be readily available from existing management accounting records maintained by the town.

It may be possible to break costs down to reflect the cost of cleaning specific beaches or stretches of beach. If so, that might indicate whether a particular stretch is costing a disproportionate amount of time and money because of issues over location or problems such as rocks or soft sand. It may be possible to reduce costs by closing such beaches to the public during quieter parts of the holiday season to reduce costs. Analysing costs in this way will almost certainly require staff to maintain logs for a period in order to show how time and resources are being applied.

Any deviations from budget should be investigated, as should any fluctuations in the measures over time.

Comparable statistics should be obtained from other towns in order to determine whether there is scope to benchmark. There is no reason for other towns to withhold that information because the nature of any competition is unlikely to be affected by expenditure on cleaning services.

For the purpose of any comparison the total cost should be related to the number of beaches being cleaned and the length of the beaches in order to adjust for the scale of the operation.

(b) The quantity of refuse collected by each means (sweeping v emptying bins) should be measured in order to reflect the output from the service.

The number of complaints lodged by holidaymakers and residents should be monitored. Those relating to the cleanliness of the beach should be highlighted as an indicator of public perceptions.

The town council should conduct market research to ask beach users what they think about the amenities provided and the questions should include some discussion of the cleanliness of the beach. That should be repeated regularly throughout the holiday season, partly because the problem may change in response to peaks and troughs in the number of users and partly because the use of the beach may change depending on whether families are using it for play during the summer holidays or older couples are simply walking on the beach when the weather is cooler at the beginning and end of the holiday season.

The number of incidents attended by the beach first aiders should be analysed to highlight injuries such as cuts caused by broken glass.

The town council should conduct detailed audits of the beach itself by inspecting areas immediately after the sweeping operation and also during the day. That will require setting a standard for the audit, such as deciding what constitutes a piece of litter (for example, should a small shred of paper that would be difficult to filter out of the sand be counted in the same manner as, say, an empty soft drinks can?)

Compliance with the town council's standards should be monitored. For example, there should be a check to ensure that the bins are actually emptied according to the schedule. Any deviation should be investigated to establish whether that is due to staff failure or because the schedule is impractical.

(c) In general, effectiveness audits are more difficult than economy and efficiency audits.

Economy and efficiency is a matter of cost accounting. The cost of providing the cleaning services is largely a matter of using traditional accounting techniques to analyse data that would be collected for financial reporting and management accounting purposes anyway. There are some subjective decisions that may have an impact, such as identifying relevant costs, but even those problems are largely questions of definition.

Effectiveness involves making some difficult decisions about measuring performance. Surrogates, such as the quantity of litter uplifted, can lead to dysfunctional behaviour because that could encourage more frequent emptying of bins at the expense of sweeping. Sweeping will not necessarily collect a huge quantity of material but it might remove dangerous objects such as broken glass.

It may also be necessary to set targets for the end result of the cleaning activities and that could be difficult. What is an acceptable level of litter? What matters more, perceptions of litter or actual cleanliness? The two could differ because many users may not be aware of litter on the beach.

Should you have any further queries, please do not hesitate to ask.

Yours Faithfully

A.N. Accountant

Test your understanding 11

The correct answer is A – By definition.

Test your understanding 12

The correct answer is D – By definition.

Test your understanding 13

A and D.

- Option A is an inherent risk which exists regardless of internal controls.
- Option B is a control risk.
- Option C is a detection risk.
- Option D is an inherent risk which exists regardless of internal controls.
- Option E is a control risk.

Test your understanding 14

The correct answer is C Substantive tests concentrate on output (the end result) ensuring that it is as expected.

A, B and D are compliance tests (on the process) to test that controls are operating as they were designed to.

Test your understanding 15 – Compliance testing (Integration)

Company X appears to have a recruitment 'process' – application forms and interviews, although this may not have taken the process far enough.

Once a candidate has been selected their application form should be verified, usually by checking their qualifications to actual certificates (not copies) and taking up references (usually two – one work and one personal). There is no mention of this happening at X and may be the reason that John cannot perform the job to any satisfaction. The rumour may be true.

John's start date appears to be too soon to enable the aforementioned controls to be implemented. There should be a sufficient period between interview and any start date to enable all claims made on the application form to be verified.

Personnel/human resources should be the department to verify the application form, which they may not have done. Therefore the internal auditor should visit the department, ascertain the recruitment process and test that the process is adhered to.

Compliance tests might include:

- Select a sample of employee files and test to see whether the application form is present.
- From the application forms, trace the references taken up.
- Check that the references were positive i.e. that previous employers found the staff punctual, trustworthy, etc.
- From the application forms, trace the copies of certificates (taken from the originals) which back up any qualifications stated.
- Qualifications could be further tested by contacting the relevant body to ascertain whether they have record of said employee.

The controls at X appear to be ineffective since the process does not cover these vital activities. Alternatively these activities might be part of X's personnel process, and the personnel staff have not followed them. Either way the personnel staff need to be reprimanded and further controls implemented to prevent future occurrences.

Test your understanding 16 – Audit testing (Integration)

Compliance tests

- Look for evidence of the approval of new workers, such as a formal instruction to the payroll department.
- Check that the timesheets are all approved by a supervisor.
- Check that all overtime has been approved.
- Observe the wages payout to ensure:
  - wages are only collected by the person being paid;
  - all staff sign for their wages.
- Ensure that a PAYE/NIC control account is reconciled and reviewed each month by an appropriate manager.

Substantive tests

- Take a sample of timesheets and re-calculate wages and deductions.
- Perform a reconciliation of total hours worked to gross pay and compare month by month.
- Check a sample of payments to the pay rate records to ensure they are being used correctly.
- Re-perform the PAYE/NIC control account for a month to ensure it has been done correctly.

Test your understanding 17

The correct answer is C – Detection risk is the risk that the auditor's tests do not reveal a materially incorrect amount.

Control risk is the risk that the existing controls are not sufficient to prevent or detect a material mis-statement.

Test your understanding 18 – Car dealership (Integration)

A number of performance ratios could be calculated across the different regions to compare performance:

	North	South	East	West
Sales value per salesman (£)	168,750	210,000	232,000	100,000
Sales discussions per salesman	41	30	43	31
Average orders per discussion	0.27	0.43	0.37	0.26
Average value per order (£)	15,000	16,200	14,500	12,600

From the above performance measures it can be seen that the West region is the most inefficient. In all measures this region is at or very near the bottom performance criteria which indicates there should be room for efficiencies. This region should be selected for audit.

Test your understanding 19 – D courier company (Case study)

(a) An independent auditor would report honestly, without any bias or conflict. Independence is an attitude of mind that involves making a truthful report regardless of the consequences. In this case, F appears to have identified with the Depot Manager, despite there being no particular reason for doing so. F has been sympathetic to the Depot Manager's position and that sympathy has resulted in a distorted internal audit report. F's duty was to investigate compliance with a specific rule concerning maintenance and to report the results to senior management. It was not part of F's duty to consider whether a truthful report would harm the Depot Manager's career. The responsibility for deciding whether to take action against the Depot Manager lay with D's board and F should have provided a full report on the circumstances. That report could have included a summary of the Depot Manager's predicament arising because of the absence of the mechanic.

F should not accept responsibility for the impact of a truthful report on the Depot Manager's career. The Depot Manager could have dealt with the fact that there was inadequate cover when the mechanic was absent by reporting the situation to head office. The Depot Manager should not have asked F to deal with this omission retrospectively by lying in the internal audit report.

(b) The internal audit department is a vital element of the control environment in any large entity. The directors rely on internal audit to ensure that formal control processes and procedures are operating as they should. The directors cannot observe the workings of these systems for themselves unless the entity is very small and so the internal audit department provides vital feedback.

If the directors cannot trust the internal audit department to report honestly and accurately then they will have no way of knowing whether their policies and instructions are being carried out. That is a major issue in terms of good corporate governance because the shareholders hold the directors responsible for the governance arrangements and expect them to run the company an effective manner. Cases where problems have arisen because of compliance failures by managers and staff have tended to reflect badly on the board.

F's behaviour is also sending a very clear signal to D's staff. If breaches are not reported and acted upon then staff may decide not to comply. If the internal audit department, whose very existence is to report compliance failures, does not act then the staff will start to become demotivated and lazy. If D's board does not act quickly and decisively then its ability to manage the company effectively will be seriously compromised by this audit failure.

(c) The first thing would be to review the records maintained by the depot. These should indicate that the inspections were carried out and the mechanic should have signed as proof. This test will not actually prove that the tests took place because the mechanic could have signed the documents recklessly, but the signature does at least prove that the staff are willing to accept responsibility for the inspections having been carried out. Internal audit could review the records relating to repairs and breakdowns for each depot. This would be a useful analytical review exercise that could identify any depots that were at a higher risk of not carrying out adequate inspections. Ideally, the cost of repairs should be separated from the cost of routine maintenance.

During branch visits the internal audit staff should be aware of the work being done by the depot mechanics. The depot staff may behave differently during an audit visit, but it would be reassuring to see whether the mechanics were inspecting vehicles. The auditor could supplement these observations by asking the mechanics and the drivers to explain the maintenance procedures in order to establish indirectly whether they volunteered information about the regular fluid checks.

The internal auditor could conduct a spot check on the fluid levels of a sample of vehicles at the depot. These should focus on vans that have recently been checked. If the fluid levels are low then there is a strong likelihood that the checks were not carried out.

A sample of claims should be checked to ensure that:

- each claim is supported by receipts
- the total of the claim has been added up correctly
- the amount actually paid was the same as the total amount of the claim.

(a) **Briefing note**

To: Internal auditors

From: Head of internal audit

Date; Today

Subject: Audit tests

Substantive tests

In the case of audits of financial systems and activities, substantive tests seek to provide audit evidence about the completeness, accuracy and validity of the transactions, and the amounts relating to those transactions that are included in the accounting records and financial statements.

Here, substantive tests might take the form of:

Analytical review. Comparing total salesmen's expenses in previous years, both in total and as a percentage of sales revenue, to check whether the total amount of expenses in the current year appears to be consistent with previous years.

Detailed tests of transactions, such as:

- verifying that the salesmen are all legitimate employees of the company
- taking a sample of claims and checking whether specific items of expense are valid, for example that the salesman's claims for hotel accommodation and subsistence were incurred in his sales area

– taking a sample of claims and checking whether the claims for petrol/mileage are consistent with the total number of miles travelled by the car, as evidenced by car service records.

Test your understanding 20

The correct answer is A The correct order of events is to: Plan the audit; document systems and controls; test compliance with controls; test application of controls; report to board

Test your understanding 21

A, B and D

- Options A, B and D are typical of an internal audit report on internal controls.
- Options C and E are more in keeping with an **external** audit report.

Test your understanding 22 – Audit software (Integration)

Possible use of audit software:

- Sequence checks on delivery note file and invoice file.
- Computer can check that every delivery results in an amendment to the invoice file and the stock file (with list produced of every exception).
- Exception reports generated of zero value invoices and non-invoiced deliveries.
- Calculation checks on all invoices to ensure in line with price lists. Check on agreement of deliveries against order files.

Test your understanding 23

B, D, E and F

- Option A: The internal auditor can attempt to process payments which both breach and do not breach the upper limit .Those that do breach it should be rejected.
- Option B: Dead data means test data are processed outside the normal cycle. It is not possible to conclude with certainty that the 'live' system would work in the same way.
- Option C: Same address payments should be rejected.
- Option D: The test data will check computer controls, not whether proof of income etcetera has actually been seen.
- Option E: As long as an address has not been awarded a payment before it should be accepted by the system. This does not mean it is a valid address, only that it has not been recorded before.
- Option F: The test data will check computer controls, not the work of staff performing spot checks.

Test your understanding 24

The correct answers are B, C, D and E The number of employees (not directors) may affect the need for an audit – the more employees, the higher the risk that supervision may not be an effective control.

Test your understanding 25

The correct answer is C – This is internal audits key activity, hence ensuring that those who design the controls do not test them.

Test your understanding 26 – G Manufacturing (Case study)

Briefing note

To: Chief Executive

From: A.N. Accountant

Date: Today

Subject: Creating an effective internal audit department

Dear Sir,

Firstly, the board should decide the level of commitment that it is going to make to internal audit. A half-hearted attempt will lead to an under resourced and ineffective department. A realistic staffing level should be decided before anything further is done and the associated costs should be budgeted for.

The terms of reference should be decided. Those will include the powers that will be enjoyed by internal audit and the internal auditor's access to the board. It will be easier to recruit an experienced Head of Internal Audit if it can be shown how the department will be viewed within the organisation as a whole.

The Board should recruit the Head of Internal Audit before interviewing for the other audit staff. That will enable G to offer the Head of Internal Audit the opportunity to have some say in recruitment to ensure that suitable staff are taken on. G should use a recruitment agency to identify suitable candidates because agencies are likely to have access to lists of potential applicants who are interested in moving on to new challenges.

The remainder of the audit team should be recruited, perhaps using an agency, under the Head of Internal Audit's overall supervision. The team members should have appropriate skills and qualifications, including membership of a professional body, or be working towards a qualification if they are to be employed in a junior role.

The department should be based in a suitable location, with realistic provision for administrative support such as secretarial support. If internal audit is not shown to be adequately resourced then its credibility will suffer in the eyes of the other staff.

The Board should provide internal audit with a statement of the department's powers to request information and documents. Giving internal audit a formal charter within the organisation will help to ensure the department's credibility and its freedom to conduct meaningful investigations.

The initial reports submitted by internal audit will have to be seen to receive the Board's endorsement in order to underpin the directors' support. That could involve requesting a follow-up to deal with any weaknesses or compliance failures. The Board should not take disproportionate action, otherwise the internal audit department will be viewed as a threat, but it should be clear to all staff that the internal audit reports will be read and taken seriously.

Should you have any further queries, please do not hesitate to ask.

Best wishes

A.N. Accountant

Test your understanding 27 – Multinational car manufacturer

(a) **Briefing note**

To: The Board

From: A.N. Accountant

Date: Today

Subject: Investigation into transfer pricing

The board has to provide the Head of Internal Audit with a very clear objective for this audit. This is a very specific task that could prevent the company from being tied up in a number of investigations around the world. The board should identify the problem areas that are likely to prompt a tax investigation in one or more of the subsidiaries and brief the internal auditor accordingly so that the group is aware of the "worst possible case".

The Head of Internal Audit should be briefed on the extent to which evidence should be gathered. This could be a desk-based audit carried out from head office or it could involve local teams visiting subsidiaries. The Head of Internal Audit should be given a detailed budget of the time and resources that are to be invested in this study.

If the audit team is to visit subsidiaries and engage with local management then the audit staff will have to know how much they are permitted to reveal about the investigation. Transfer pricing is clearly a very controversial matter for M and local managers may be unsettled by any suggestion that pricing policies may be changed.

The timetable should be established. If the board requires the findings quickly then it will either have to accept a less detailed investigation or it will have to reallocate internal audit resources from other areas.

(b) **Note**

To: Head of Group Internal Audit

From: A.N. Accountant

Date: Today

Subject: Tax investigation

Dear Sir,

I attach some notes regarding factors that should be considered when assessing the possibility that a subsidiary could be investigated by the local tax authority.

National tax rates

The countries that are most likely to investigate transfer prices are those that have the highest tax rates. Ranking tax rates and import tariffs will provide the internal audit team with an indication of the subsidiaries that are at greatest risk of being the subject of an investigation.

Credibility of tax charge

The manipulation of transfer pricing is associated with the underpayment of tax. The internal audit team should calculate the tax paid by each subsidiary as a percentage of accounting profit. A subsidiary with a very low effective rate of tax is more likely to be investigated for the distortion of transfer prices. Alternatively, the authorities may relate the tax charge to other statistics. For example, a company that has a healthy reported revenue and a very small tax liability may be suspected of manipulation

History of tax investigations

The history of individual countries may also be relevant. For example, the UK government was concerned about the potential underpayment of tax by some multinational companies and so any UK subsidiaries may be more at risk of an investigation by the tax authorities.

Visible market prices

The nature of the products being supplied may also affect the risk of an investigation. For generic items such as nuts and bolts or spark plugs, there will be a readily observable market that is visible to the tax authorities. If M's transfer prices are close to the observable market prices for such items then there is very little risk that a tax investigation will occur and so there is less point in conducting an audit investigation. If the pricing implications are complicated because there is no meaningful comparison then any tax investigation will be more disruptive and it could be useful to pre-empt that with an audit investigation so that M has its defence ready.

hapter

11

Financial risk

Chapter learning objectives

Lead	Component
D1. Evaluate financial risks facing an organisation.	(a) Evaluate financial risks facing an organisation.
D2. Evaluate alternative risk management tools.	(b) Evaluate appropriate methods for identification and management of financial risks associated with international operations.

Indicative syllabus content

- Sources of financial risk associated with international operations.
- Transaction, translation, economic and political risk.
- Exposure to interest rates.
- Minimising political risk.
- Responses to economic risk, translation and transaction risks.

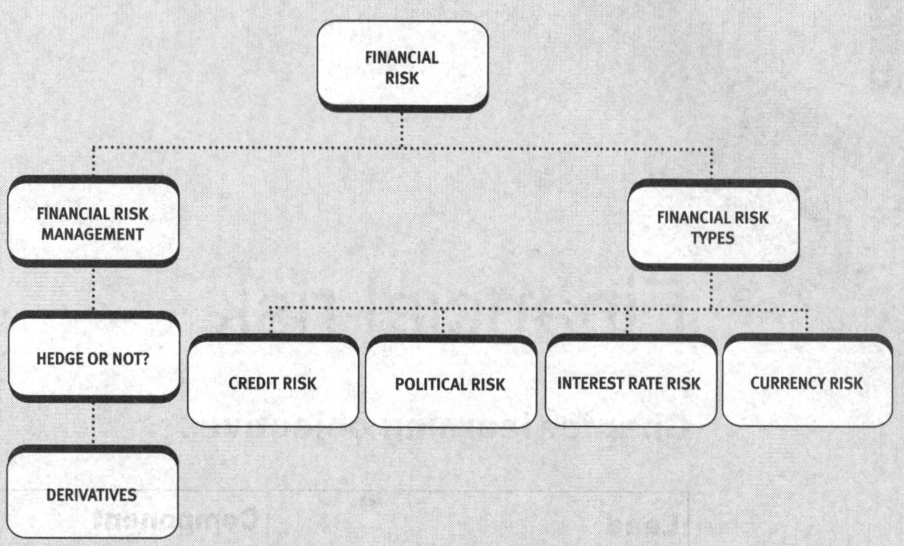

1 Overview of financial risk

Financial risk is *'a risk of a change in a financial condition such as an exchange rate, interest rate, credit rating of a customer, or price of a good'*.

Types of financial risk

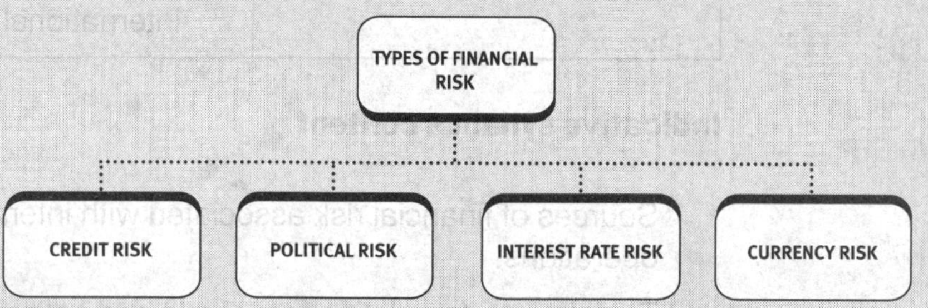

Political risk is not necessarily a financial risk but is included here because often financial risk is from the perspective of foreign business activities. Political risk is essentially to do with the wider risks of foreign direct investment.

2 Credit risk

Credit risk is the risk of non-payment or late payment of receivables. Credit risk will always exist in businesses that make credit sales and therefore it needs to be managed.

Management of credit risk

The most common methods used to manage and control credit risk are:

- Strong **credit control procedures**, including:
  - policies regarding credit checks
  - credit limits and terms
  - debt collection activities such as aged debtor analysis, statements and reminders.
- **Insuring** against the risk – it is possible to take out credit risk guarantees to act as insurance against debtor default.
- **Debt factoring without recourse** – the debts can be sold to a factoring business but without the obligation to buy back those debts in the event of default.

Test your understanding 1

X is a financial institution, lending to consumers for the purchase of consumer durables. X currently has a total of £120 million lent to customers, and currently has 200,000 loans outstanding to customers. The management accountant of X has calculated that the likelihood of a customer defaulting on a loan is 2%. What is the 'credit risk exposure' of X, on its consumer lending?

Express your answer in £, rounded to the nearest million.

3 Political risk

Political risk is the risk faced by an overseas investor, that the host country government take adverse action against, after the company has invested.

It can take different forms and the threats (financial and non-financial) can include:

- Risk of confiscation or destruction of overseas assets
- Commercial risks because foreign governments discriminate against overseas firms e.g. quotas, tariffs, other taxes
- Restricted access to local borrowings
- Insisting on resident investors or a joint venture with a local company
- Restrictions on repatriating cash (capital or dividends)
- Restrictions on conversion of the currency
- Rationing the supply of foreign currency

- Exchange rate volatility due to political actions
- A minimum number of local nationals to be employed
- Price fixing by the government
- Minimum percentage of local components to be used
- Invalidating patents
- Claiming compensation for past actions

More on sources of political risk

Whilst governments want to encourage development and growth they are also anxious to prevent the exploitation of their countries by multinationals.

Whilst at one extreme, assets might be destroyed as the result of war or expropriation, the most likely problems concern changes to the rules on the remittance of cash out of the host country to the holding company.

Exchange control regulations, which are generally more restrictive in less developed countries. For example:

- rationing the supply of foreign currencies which restricts residents from buying goods abroad
- banning the payment of dividends to foreign shareholders such as holding companies in multinationals, who will then have the problem of blocked funds.

Import quotas to limit the quantity of goods that subsidiaries can buy from its holding company to sell in its domestic market.

Import tariffs could make imports (from the holding company) more expensive than domestically produced goods.

Insist on a minimum shareholding, i.e. that some equity in the company is offered to resident investors.

Company structure may be dictated by the host government – requiring, for example, all investments to be in the form of joint ventures with host country companies.

Discriminatory actions

- **Supertaxes** imposed on foreign firms, set higher than those imposed on local businesses with the aim of giving local firms an advantage. They may even be deliberately set at such a high level as to prevent the business from being profitable.
- **Restricted access to local borrowings** by restricting or even barring foreign owned enterprises from the cheapest forms of finance from local banks and development funds. Some countries ration all access for foreign investments to local sources of funds, to force the company to import foreign currency into the country.
- **Expropriating assets** whereby the host country government seizes foreign property in the national interest. It is recognised in international law as the right of sovereign states provided that *prompt consideration at fair market value in a convertible currency* is given. Problems arise over the exact meaning of the terms prompt and fair, the choice of currency, and the action available to a company not happy with the compensation offered.

Management of political risk

Companies cannot prevent political risk, but they should seek to minimise it whenever the risk appears significant.

Before undertaking a foreign direct investment, a company needs to assess its exposure to political risk by:

- Using political ranking tables such as Euromoney magazine tables;
- Evaluating the country's macro-economic situation – balance of payments, unemployment levels, per capita income, inflation, exchange rate policy, rate of economic growth;
- Evaluating the current government's popularity, stability and attitude to foreign investment, together with the attitude of opposition parties;
- Looking at the historical stability of the political system;
- Looking at changing religious and cultural attitudes;
- Taking advice from the company's bank (if there is a representative office in the overseas country), the British embassy in the overseas country, and the Department of Trade and Industry (DTI).

Some methods of minimising risks are as follows:

- Prior negotiation (concession agreements and planned divestment)
- Structuring investment (local sourcing of materials and labour)
- Entering into foreign joint ventures
- Obtaining agreements and contracts with overseas government
- Using local financing
- Plans for eventual ownership/part-ownership by foreign country's investors.

More on managing political risk

Joint ventures. A company might go into a joint venture with one or more partners. A joint venture can reduce risk because:

- if each joint venture partner contributes a share of the funding for the venture, the investment at risk for each partner is restricted to their share of the total investment (although, the upside is reduced because each party has less invested in this potentially lucrative venture)
- if a local company is selected as a joint venture partner, the likelihood of winning major contracts in the country might be much greater. Some governments have made the involvement of a local company in a joint venture a condition of awarding contracts to consortia involving a foreign company
- the local venture partner has a better understanding of the local political risks and can manage them more effectively than a foreigner would be able to. Also the government might be less inclined to act against the interests of the local venture partner.

Pre-trading agreements. Prior to making the investment, agreements should be secured if possible with the local government regarding rights, remittance of funds and local equity investments and (where appropriate) the award of government contracts to businesses.

Gaining government funding. In some situations, it might be possible to gain government funding for a project or contract, with the government being either a customer, a backer or a partner for the deal. If government funding can be obtained:

- the government will have an interest in the transaction reaching a successful conclusion
- there should be little or no risk of exchange control regulations preventing the withdrawal of profits from the country.

Local finance. A company might try to obtain local finance for an investment in a particular country. The availability of local finance might depend on the state of the banking and capital markets in the country concerned. The major advantage of local finance is that it creates liabilities in the foreign currency, and so reduces:

- translation exposures: assets in the foreign currency can be offset against liabilities in the same currency
- transaction exposures, in the sense that interest costs will be payable in the foreign currency and can be paid from income in the same currency.

Raising finance locally might also help to maintain the interest of the local government in the success of the business, and there is less risk that the assets will be confiscated.

Planning for the eventual part-ownership or full ownership of the business by locals. Target dates might be set in advance of making the investment for the eventual part-ownership or full ownership of the business by local people. The transfer of ownership should be extended over a long-term, partly to ensure that a satisfactory return on investment is obtained but also to encourage the local government to understand the long-term benefits of foreign investment.

Test your understanding 2 – Political risk (Integration)

A UK company is planning to build and operate a factory in West Africa.

Required:

Discuss the potential political risks that may arise and recommend risk mitigation strategies that could be implemented to bring these risks to a satisfactory level.

(20 minutes)

4 Interest rate risk

Interest rate risk is the risk of gains or losses on assets and liabilities due to changes in interest rates. It will occur for any organisation which has assets or liabilities on which interest is payable or receivable.

Interest rates and LIBOR

Non-financial organisations normally have many more interest-bearing liabilities than interest-bearing assets. These include bank loans and overdrafts, and issues of bonds or debentures. As a general rule:

- interest on bank loans and overdrafts is payable at a **variable rate** or **floating rate**, with the interest set at a margin above a benchmark rate such as the base rate or the London Inter Bank Offer Rate (LIBOR)
- interest on most bonds, debentures or loan stock is at a **fixed rate**.

When interest is at a floating rate, the amount of interest payable in each period is set by reference to the benchmark interest rate on a specific date, such as the starting date for the interest period. For example, suppose that a company has a bank loan on which it pays interest every six months at 50 basis points above LIBOR. (100 basis points = 1%, therefore 50 basis points = 0.50%.) At the start of an interest period, the six-month LIBOR rate might be, say, 4.75%: if so, the company would pay interest at the end of the six months at 5.25% for the six-month period. If LIBOR moves up or down, the interest rate payable every six months will go up or down accordingly.

(**Note:** LIBOR is the London Interbank Offered Rate. It is a money market rate at which top-rated banks are able to borrow short-term in the London sterling or eurocurrency markets. There are LIBOR rates for major traded currencies, including the US dollar, euro and yen, as well as sterling.)

Exposure to interest rate risk

The exposure to interest risk will depend on the amount of interest bearing assets or liabilities that it holds and the type that these are (floating or fixed rate).

Types of interest rate risk exposure

- **Floating rate loans:** If a company has floating rate loans, changes in interest rates alter the amount of interest payable or receivable. This directly affects cash flows and profits and the risk therefore is quite obvious.
- **Fixed rate loans:** If a company has fixed rate loans interest rate risk still exists. Even though interest charges themselves will not change, a fixed rate can make a company uncompetitive if its costs are higher than those with a floating rate and interest rates fall. (Remember interest rate risk can be about assets or liabilities – an asset that pays a fixed rate of interest will be worth less if interest rates rise.)

More on fixed rate exposure

Companies with fixed rate borrowings are also exposed to interest rate risk, because by paying a fixed rate of interest on its liabilities, a company runs the risk that:

- if interest rates fall, it will be unable to benefit from the lower rates available in the market, because it is committed to paying fixed rates, and
- competitor organisations might have floating rate liabilities, and so will benefit from lower interest costs, and so improve their profitability and competitive strength.

The same, of course, is true in reverse for a company that has fixed or floating rate deposits/investments.

Measuring exposure to interest rate risk

Floating rate loans

Interest risk exposure is the *total amount of floating rate assets and liabilities*. The higher the value of loans the greater the exposure to changes in interest rates.

Fixed rate loans

This is measured by the *total amount of fixed rate assets or liabilities together with average time to maturity and average interest rate*. Longer periods of tie-in at fixed rates could be beneficial, or more costly, to businesses depending on what market rates are and also what the future expectations of interest rate changes are. It is expectations that determine risks.

Illustration of interest rate risk exposure

Block has the following liabilities at 1 January Year 1:

- Bank loans £400 million, interest at LIBOR + 50 basis points
- £50 million floating rate bonds, interest at LIBOR + 25 basis points
- £200 million 6.5% bonds, redeemable 30 June Year 3
- £350 million 6% bonds, redeemable 30 September Year 4

Interest rate exposure:

The company has floating rate liabilities of £450 million and fixed rate liabilities of £550 million.

Average interest rate of fixed rate liabilities:

£200m × 6.5%	£13m
£350m × 6%	£21m
£550m of loans with	£34m of interest = 6.18% average rate

The average interest rate would be compared to other companies in the same industry to ascertain whether it was higher or lower, whilst bearing in mind the general expectation of movement in the base rate. For example, if Block's average rate is higher than the competitors and the base rate is expected to fall, then it will be deemed more risky because Block will pay more interest in the future compared to its competitors.

Average time to maturity of fixed rate liabilities:

£200m × 2.50 years	500.00
£350m × 3.75 years	1,312.50
	1,812.50
1, 812.50/£550m	3.30 years average remaining life

Time to maturity creates a separate measure of exposure. Again Block's average time to maturity will be compared to its competitors. If the time to maturity is longer than the competitors and rates are expected to fall then Block is more risky since it has tied itself in to longer term fixed rate borrowings, paying out too much interest and possibly incurring a redemption penalty if it tried to restructure its debt.

Refinancing

Refinancing risk is associated with interest risk because it looks at the risk that loans will not be refinanced or will not be refinanced at the same rates.

The reasons for this could include:

- Lenders are unwilling to lend or only prepared to lend at higher rates.
- The credit rating of the company has reduced making them a more unattractive lending option.
- The company may need to refinance quickly and therefore have difficulty in obtaining the best rates.

5 Currency risk

Currency risk is the risk that arises from possible future movements in an exchange rate. It is a two-way risk, since exchange rates can move either adversely or favourably.

Currency risk affects any organisation with:

- assets and/or liabilities in a foreign currency
- regular income and/or expenditures in a foreign currency
- no assets, liabilities or transactions that are denominated in a foreign currency. Even if a company does not deal in any currencies, it will still face economic risk since its competitors may be faring better due to favourable exchange rates on its transactions.

Currency risk can be categorised into three types: economic, transaction and translation exposure.

Economic risk

Economic risk is any change in the economy, home or abroad, which can affect the value of a transaction before a commitment is made i.e. payment or receipt.

A company may not have any transactions in a foreign currency i.e. it buys and sells in its home currency, but it is still affected by economic risk.

This can be due to several factors:

- Competitive position – even if a company trades wholly in its own currency, other companies can cause it to lose money in the form of reduced sales. For example, if a competitor company trades (either buys or sells) abroad where the currency is more favourable – cheaper for supplies, or allows a higher price for sales, then the competitor will be more profitable. Conversely, if the exchange rates are adverse for the competitor, they would be less profitable.
- Elasticity of demand – exchange rates can make a company's products more or less expensive. When an exchange rate makes the product more expensive, say, the demand for that product will probably fall. However, if the product is available at a lower price from another company, who perhaps trades in a different currency which enables the product to be made and sold more cheaply, then demand does not fall but transfers to that other company. Therefore the home company has lost sales, is less profitable and shareholder returns will fall.

- Pricing – competitor's product prices will affect a company's ability to raise their prices and affect their competitive position. For example, Scottish sheep farmers are exposed to economic risk when New Zealand lamb comes onto the market more cheaply in October/November. (Lambing in the UK occurs around March). The Scottish sheep farmers have to reduce their prices through October/November to maintain their volume of sales.

In effect, economic risk is the variation in the value of the business (i.e. the present value of future cash flows) due to unexpected changes in the economy.

Management of economic risk

One way the risk can be reduced is to diversify globally, meaning that a company can reduce its risk by having operations located all over the world or by doing business with other companies located in other parts of the world. This is portfolio theory – the idea of reducing risk by 'not having all your eggs in one basket'. This can be broken down into:

Diversification of production and sales

If a firm manufactures all its products in one country and that country's exchange rate strengthens, then the firm will find it increasingly difficult to export to the rest of the world. Its future cash flows and therefore its present value would diminish. However, if it had established production plants worldwide and bought its components worldwide (a policy which is practised by many multinationals, e.g. Ford) it is unlikely that the currencies of all its operations would revalue at the same time. It would therefore find that, although it was losing on exports from some of its manufacturing locations, this would not be the case in all of them. Also if it had arranged to buy its raw materials worldwide it would find that a strengthening home currency would result in a fall in its input costs and this would compensate for lost sales.

Diversification of suppliers and customers

Similarly a company could diversify its supplier and customer base so that if the currency of, say, one supplier strengthens, purchasing could be switched to a cheaper supplier.

Diversification of financing

When borrowing internationally, firms must be aware of foreign exchange risk. When, for example, a firm borrows in Swiss francs it must pay back in the same currency. If the Swiss franc then strengthens against the home currency this can make interest and principal repayments far more expensive. However, if borrowing is spread across many currencies it is unlikely they will all strengthen at the same time and therefore risks can be reduced.

Borrowing in foreign currency is only truly justified if returns will then be earned in that currency to finance repayment and interest. International borrowing can also be used to hedge the adverse economic effects of local currency devaluations. If a firm expects to lose from devaluations of the currencies in which its subsidiaries operate it can hedge this exposure by arranging to borrow in the weakening currency. Any losses on operations will then be offset by cheaper financing costs.

Note that diversification (of any type) will not necessarily help in extreme circumstances e.g. during a global recession.

Marketing

A way of managing economic risk is quite simply to have a very good marketing ploy that enables you to convince your customers that your product is the one to buy despite it being more expensive!

More on economic risk

Economic risk is the possibility that the value of the company (the present value of all future post tax cash flows) will change due to unexpected changes in future economies (which includes exchange rates). The size of the risk is difficult to measure as economies can change significantly and unexpectedly. Such changes can affect firms in many ways:

- Imagine a UK company had an investment in South East Asia during the late 1990s. They would have suffered some economic risk due to the economic downturn in that part of the world at that time. An economic downturn can reduce trade and have an impact on foreign currency exchange rates. This means that the UK company's investment might be worth less upon first glance. However, the wider implications might include the fact that the factory makes goods for export. Then the downturn might reduce costs. Meanwhile if the competition are manufacturing in the 'booming' West and costs are higher (material and wage inflation) then the Asian subsidiary may have the competitive advantage. Therefore, the economic downturn may not be wholly downside risk.

- Suppose a UK company invests in a subsidiary in Africa. The currency of the African country depreciates each year for several years. The cash flows remitted to the UK are worth less in sterling terms each year, causing a reduction in the investment value.
- A French company buys raw materials that are priced in US dollars. It converts the raw materials into a finished product which it exports to Japan. Over several years the euro appreciates against the dollar but depreciates against the yen. The euro value of the French company's income increases while the US dollar cost of its materials decreases, resulting in an increase in value of the company's cash flows.
- Insisting on dealing in only the home currency may affect the foreign demand for its products if the pound appreciates or their relationship with suppliers if the pound weakens.
- Consider a UK company exporting goods or services to Spain, in competition with (say) US companies. In this case, if the US dollar weakens relative to the euro (even if the pound remains unchanged against the euro), it will become cheaper for the Spanish customers to import those goods and services from the US supplier if the order is denominated in the foreign currency. Even if the order is denominated in euros (the Spanish currency) the euro price from the US supplier might not convert into enough sterling to make it worthwhile for the UK company.
- Deciding to acquire resources, say equipment in Italy, with a view to supplying goods or services to the UK market. In this case the company's costs are in euros with expected revenues in sterling. If sterling were to weaken against the euro, the costs of the operation could become uneconomic.

However, many of the above examples are not as straightforward as they might first seem, due to the compensating actions of economic forces. For example, if the exchange rate of a South American country depreciates significantly, it is probably due to high inflation. If the South American subsidiary of a UK company increases its prices in line with inflation in South America, its cash flows in the local currency will increase. However, these will be converted at a depreciating exchange rate to produce (theoretically) a constant sterling value of cash flows. Alternatively, if the subsidiary does not increase its prices, it may increase its sales volume by selling at a lower price. Therefore the subsidiary / group has not 'lost out'.

Measurement of economic exposure

Although economic exposure is difficult to measure it is of vital importance to firms as it concerns their long-run viability. Economic exposure cannot be ignored as it could lead to reductions in the firm's future cash flows or an increase in the systematic risk of the firm, resulting in a fall in shareholder wealth.

There are a very limited number of factors that can be observed to attempt to quantify economic exposure, which include the price elasticity of demand for products. For example, as prices rise demand usually falls, but the rate at which it falls and the resulting cashflows will impact on the value of a company. The price rise could be due to a change in the exchange rate.

Economic risk

Imagine a fictitious airport, XL, in country X with the £ as its currency.

XL services passengers that live in its own country (20%) and passengers that travel from other countries (80%).

90% of the travellers passing through XL are holiday makers while the other 10% travel for business purposes.

The fuel bought by the airlines passing through XL is mainly bought in the US where the currency is the $.

Why is the company exposed to currency risk?

Passenger numbers will be affected by the strength of the £:

- Only 20% of passengers live in the UK and travel within the country on internal flights. The other 80% will be exposed to foreign currency movements making their trips more or less expensive. For example, a holiday maker from the UK will find a holiday in the US more expensive if the £ weakens against the $ and may choose not to travel. Similarly passengers from outside the UK may choose other destinations if the £ strengthens against their home currency.
- Most passengers are travelling on holiday so they have a much wider choice of destinations than business travellers. A business person may have to go to a particular country because that is where the customer or supplier is based. In theory, 90% of XL's customers could change their travel plans and that could reduce demand for XL's routes.

- Movements in the value of the £ could affect interest rates and that may also prevent holiday makers from travelling due to the increase in the cost of their mortgage.
- If the £ weakens against the $, say, then fuel, for example, may become more expensive. This could force the airlines to raise prices which might reduce passenger numbers or the number of flights.

How can the risks you have identified be managed?

The first step is to always consider whether there are any natural hedges. For example, a strong £ would give holiday makers from country X more spending money when they travel abroad. However, that will also increase the airlines' costs when converted to their home currency and so fares may increase. These factors might offset each other.

Once the airport has established the overall impact of the strengthening or weakening of the £ the next step would be to hedge that risk. For example, if the strengthening was discovered to be bad then the airport might borrow in $ to create a hedge.

It would also be worth diversifying the routes covered by the airlines. It might be worth offering airlines that travel to popular destinations a discount for flying from XL. The cost of the discount could be viewed as an investment in managing currency risk.

Test your understanding 3

Which of the following can reduce economic risk?

A Diversifying activities across the UK

B Diversifying production and sales

C Diversifying suppliers and customers

D Diversification of financing

Transaction risk

This is the risk related to buying or selling on credit in foreign currencies. There is a danger that, between the time of the transaction and the date of the cash flow, exchange rates will have moved adversely. This risk, unlike the translation risk, actually affects the cash flows of the business.

Illustration of transaction risk

A UK company purchases goods on six months' credit from a US supplier for US$150,000. At the time of the transaction, the exchange rate was £1/US$1.8000 and the expected payment for the purchase was £83,333 (US$150,000/1.8000).

However, suppose that the exchange rate changes in the next six months, and the dollar strengthens in value to £1/US$1.5000. The company must acquire the US$150,000 to make the payment, and if it buys this dollar currency at the exchange rate when the date of the payment is due, the actual cost will be £100,000. This is £16,667 more than originally expected. The UK company has been exposed to a transaction liability in US dollars for six months, and as a result of the dollar increasing in value during that time, an unexpected 'loss' of £16,667 arose.

The exchange rate might have moved the other way. If the exchange rate when the payment was due had changed to £1/US$2.0000, with the dollar falling in value, it would cost only £75,000 to acquire the dollars to make the payment. This is £8,333 less than originally expected, therefore there would be a 'profit' of £8,333 on the favourable exchange rate movement.

Test your understanding 4

A UK company has just despatched a shipment of goods to Sweden. The sale will be invoiced in Swedish kroner, and payment is to be made in three months' time.

Neither the UK exporter nor the Swedish importer uses the forward foreign exchange market to cover exchange risk.

If the pound sterling were to weaken substantially against the Swedish kroner, what would be the foreign exchange gain or loss effects upon the UK exporter and the Swedish importer?

A UK exporter: Gain/Swedish importer: No effect

B UK exporter: No effect/Swedish importer: Gain

C UK exporter: Loss/Swedish importer: No effect

D UK exporter: Gain/Swedish importer: Gain

Test your understanding 5 – H plc (Integration)

H plc (a UK company) expects to make the following transaction in six months' time:

- US$100,000 purchases from US suppliers.

Exchange rates are as follows:

Dollar rate today	US$1/£0.5556
Dollar rate in six months	US$1/£0.5420

Required:

Calculate the payment required in sterling if H plc makes the payment now or in six months time.

Management of transaction risk

This will be covered in detail in the next chapter.

Translation risk

This arises when a company has assets or liabilities denominated in foreign currencies. The risk is that exchange rate volatility will cause the value of assets to fall or liabilities to increase resulting in losses to the company.

More on translation risk

The financial statements of overseas subsidiaries are usually translated into the home currency in order that they can be consolidated into the group's financial statements. Note that this is purely a paper-based exercise – it is the translation not the conversion of real money from one currency to another.

Settled transactions

When a company enters into a transaction denominated in a currency other than its functional currency (which could be the home currency or that of its parent), that transaction must be translated into the functional currency before it is recorded. The transaction will initially be recorded by applying the spot rate. However when cash settlement occurs the settled amount will be translated using the spot rate on the settlement date. If this amount differs from that used when the transaction occurred, there will be an exchange difference which is taken to the income statement in the period in which it arises.

Unsettled transactions

The treatment of any 'foreign' items remaining on the statement of financial position at the year end will depend on whether they are classified as monetary or non-monetary.

Monetary items include cash, receivables, payables and loans, and they are re-translated at the closing rate (year-end spot).

Non-monetary items include non-current assets, inventory and investments, and are not re-translated but left at historic cost.

For example, if a company has a foreign subsidiary which includes property, plant and equipment this will be valued at the date it was acquired (or revalued). However, if these assets were acquired using a loan, then the loan is translated at the closing rate (current spot) which could be very different to the spot when the assets were bought. This gives rise to currency risk because the assets and liabilities no longer offset each other. (This is covered by the 'temporal method' in International Accounting Standard (IAS) 21.)

The reported performance of an overseas subsidiary in home-based currency terms can be severely distorted if there has been a significant foreign exchange movement.

Any foreign exchange gains or losses are recorded in equity. They are unrealised and will only become realised when the subsidiary is sold.

Unless managers believe that the company's share price will fall as a result of showing a translation exposure loss in the company's accounts, translation exposure should not normally be hedged. (The company's share price, in an efficient market, should only react to exposure that is likely to have an impact on cash flows.)

However, research shows that company directors do spend (in some people's opinion – waste) money hedging translation risk. The management of translation risk is often considered to be dysfunctional behaviour.

Management of translation risk

Any change in parity will affect reported profits (and hence earnings per share), total assets, borrowings, net worth (and hence gearing) but – to repeat – it will not have affected the measured cash flow in the period being reported on.

Academic theory argues that translation risk, of itself, need not concern financial managers, but in practice, there are two strong arguments in favour of the relevance of translation risk:

(1) Although it does not affect the value of the entity as a whole, it can affect the attribution of that value between the different stakeholders. Higher gearing may lead to higher interest rates being charged on bank loans, either directly in accordance with clauses in borrowing agreements or indirectly as a result of the company's credit rating being reduced. The banks benefit at the expense of the equity investors in the business. If the treasurer is pursuing an objective of maximising shareholder wealth, he will want to manage this risk.

(2) If the accounts are being used 'beyond their design specification', for example as the basis for calculating bonus payments for directors and senior managers, then there is a temptation to protect the current year's figures, even though it is known that doing so has a long-term cost. This is comparable to pulling profit into the current year, knowing that it will both reduce next year's profit and result in tax being paid earlier than necessary.

The former is a good reason, the latter is often the real reason for managing translation risk.

Test your understanding 6

The risk that exchange rates will cause assets to fall in value, or liabilities to increase in value, resulting in losses to a company is called:

A Transaction risk

B Translation risk

C Economic risk

D Currency risk

Test your understanding 7

Debt collection activities such as aged debtor analysis, statements and reminders are controls to overcome:

A Interest rate risk

B Foreign exchange risk

C Political risk

D Credit risk

6 Using financing packages to split risks

As you will be aware, different finance options carry differing levels of risk and return for the investors concerned. The two extremes are:

- Equity (ordinary share capital) usually carries the highest risk (unsecured, uncertain dividend, share price may fall, last in line in the event of a liquidation) but potentially the highest return.
- Loan capital is usually lower risk (secured, specified interest) but has a lower typical return.

In between these extremes are a wide range of alternatives with differing risk/return profiles.

For example, venture capitalists often like to invest in unquoted companies via convertible loan stock to skew their risk exposure:

- If the company concerned performs moderately then the risk exposure effectively amounts to getting interest paid and the loan redeemed at some future point (usually within 5 years).
- If the investment performs badly then the downside exposure is limited to getting some interest paid and perhaps their investment back in the event of a winding up.
- If the investment performs well, then the company is usually prepared for flotation when the VC will convert the debt into equity to sell a large number of shares at a high profit.

Any financing package can be assessed by how it shares risks and returns out between different investors.

Test your understanding 8 – MacDonald Farm (Case study)

Context

The entire share capital of MacDonald Farm Ltd is owned by Ken MacDonald and his wife, Jane. Its business is owning and running a 1,200 acre farm, growing a range of fruit and vegetables.

External Trigger and Response

Due to changes in farm subsidies and increasing customer pressure from large supermarket chains, MacDonald Farm Ltd faces a sharp decline in its annual trading profits, which in recent years have averaged $180,000.

Ken MacDonald is therefore investigating using 200 acres to set up a new exclusive 18-hole golf course. Preliminary research suggest that planning permission will be forthcoming and demand projections are encouraging, given that membership waiting lists at the two existing golf clubs in the area exceed 350. If the project goes ahead, the new golf club is expected to be much better appointed than the two existing courses nearby.

Further information

The golf club company

It is proposed that MacDonald Farm Ltd will sign a 100-year lease with a new company, Calum Golf Club Ltd, which will pay an annual rent of $50,000 to MacDonald Farm Ltd for use of the land.

The issued capital of the golf club company will be two $1 shares, owned by Mr and Mrs MacDonald, and the remainder of its initial funding will be $2 million in the form of 15% per annum irredeemable loan stock. Fifty local business men, including Mr MacDonald, have each agreed to purchase $40,000 of this stock. The terms of the debenture loan stock issue prohibit a dividend being paid on the two ordinary shares so that any surplus is applied for the benefit of the club and its members.

Of the funds thus raised, $450,000 will be spent on converting the arable land to become a landscaped golf course. A further $50,000 will provide working capital.

The club house company

The remaining $150,000 will be used to purchase a 25% stake in a separate company, Tarpon Club House Ltd, that will develop and operate a club house. This will have conference facilities, a sports hall, two bars and a restaurant. A local property company will subscribe the other 75% of the share capital of Tarpon Club House Ltd.

Calum Golf Club Ltd will pay an annual rent of $50,000 for the use of the club house, but Tarpon Club House Ltd will manage and run all facilities offered there, taking the profits that will be earned.

When ready to commence business in January 20X6, the new golf club will be much better appointed than the two existing Norbridge courses, and the only serious competition for comparable leisure facilities will come from three hotels in Norbridge itself and a country house four miles away.

Costs and revenues

Annual operating expenses of Calum Golf Club Ltd are budgeted at $900,000.

On the revenue side, Calum Golf Club Ltd's share of profits on the investment in Tarpon Club House Ltd is expected to total $200,000 in 20X6, the first year of operations. Green fees, chargeable to non-members using the golf course, are expected to amount to an additional $100,000 a year.

On the assumption that target membership levels are achieved, annual subscriptions are initially to be set at $1,000 for each member. This will be $200 less than for full membership at the two rival golf clubs in the area. In addition, no joining fees will be payable in the first year of operation, but thereafter (as with the other two clubs) they will be equal to one year's subscription.

Breakeven analysis

Based on the above data the break-even point for Calum Golf Club Ltd has been estimated at 600 members:

Expected fixed costs	$900,000
Income from Club House	$200,000
Green Fees Income	$100,000
Net costs to be covered	$600,000
Membership fee	$1,000
Break-even membership	600

Task (time allowed 30 minutes)

Write a brief report to Mr and Mrs MacDonald regarding the proposed golf club explaining their risk/return profile under different possible scenarios.

Test your understanding 9 – RED (Case study)

Scenario

RED is a successful company manufacturing electronic equipment. Until recently, most of its sales were to customers in its domestic market, with just a few export sales. Recently, however, the board of directors of RED have approved a new export-led strategy for growth. The company is planning to grow sales and profits substantially by targeting new markets in other countries.

The targeted markets are:

- the US and countries in Western Europe;
- countries with developing economies.

Trigger

The finance director of RED is concerned about the large amount of working capital required to finance the increase in trade. He has estimated that for every $1 of working capital needed to finance domestic sales, the company will need $2.50 to finance the same volume of export sales. He has also expressed concerns about the lack of experience of the credit assessment team in the accounts department in carrying out credit assessments on customers in other countries. He believes that credit risks will be much higher with customers in the new markets.

The risk management committee of RED will consider various risks associated with export sales at its next meeting, and as management accountant you have been asked to provide a discussion paper for the meeting.

Task

Prepare a discussion paper for the meeting in which you:

(a) explain why credit risks might be higher with export sales;

(15 minutes)

(b) recommend methods of reducing these credit risks;

(15 minutes)

(c) discuss other risks associated with an export sales strategy, that the company should evaluate, control and monitor

(15 minutes)

Test your understanding 10 – Equip (Integration)

Equip plc is a major exporter of agricultural equipment to Australia, New Zealand and throughout Europe. All production facilities are in the United Kingdom. The majority of raw materials and tools are also sourced in the United Kingdom, with a few imports from Eire, priced in sterling. Major competitors are based in the United States and Germany. There are plans to set up a manufacturing subsidiary in Australia, funded in part by an Australian dollar loan to be taken out by Equip plc. The new manufacturing facility would be used to source the Australian and New Zealand markets.

Required:

(a) Describe the potential currency exposures faced by this company before setting up the manufacturing subsidiary. (10 minutes)

(b) Consider the effects of setting up the new manufacturing subsidiary in Australia with respect to the following:

(i) Will any of the exposures identified in (a) above be reduced?

(ii) What new currency exposures will the group face? 15 minutes)

Test your understanding 11 – Economic risk (Case study)

Scenario

R is a large retail organisation that imports goods from Australia for sale in its home market, where the currency is the R$. The directors of R are aware that the company is subject to significant economic exposure to movements on the AUS $ because any appreciation of the AUS $ will increase the cost of goods for resale. R has attempted to create a partial hedge against this by placing all of its cash reserves in a AUS $ bank account. That way the losses associated with any increase in cost prices will be partially offset by a gain on the bank account.

Trigger

The directors are concerned that the translation gains and losses on the AUS$ bank balance are visible to shareholders, whereas the offsetting of economic exposure is not and so their hedging policy may be misunderstood. The AUS bank account has a balance of AUS$30m. The exchange rate is presently R$3 to AUS$1.

Task

(a) Prepare a briefing note advising the directors on the matters that they would have to consider in order to determine the extent of R's economic exposure.

(10 minutes)

(a) Evaluate the validity of the directors' concern that "the translation gains and losses on the AUS$ bank balance are visible to shareholders, whereas the offsetting of economic exposure is not and so their hedging policy may be misunderstood".

(15 minutes)

7 Chapter summary

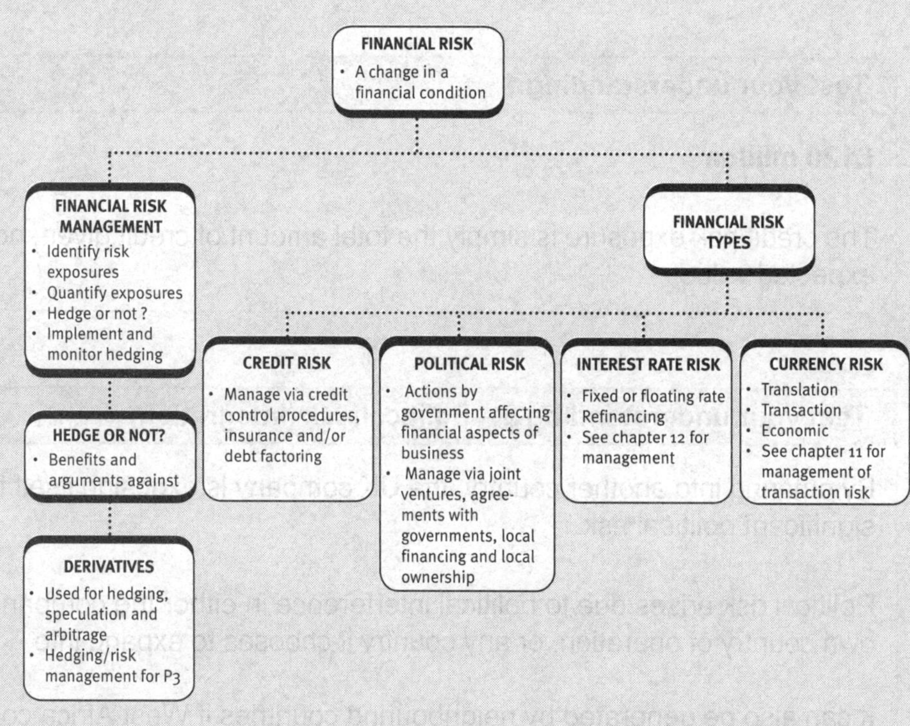

Test your understanding answers

Test your understanding 1

£120 million

The credit risk exposure is simply the total amount of credit given, not an expected value

Test your understanding 2 – Political risk (Integration)

By entering into another country, the UK company is exposing itself to significant political risk.

Political risk arises due to political interference in either the company's own country of operation, or any country it chooses to expand into.

It can also be generated by neighbouring countries if West Africa could be affected. If, for example, the UK company intends to ship goods from WA then these ships may become a target by the pirates with a cost in the form of lost goods in transit and delays in production.

West Africa's political risk can be viewed from different levels of government:

Local government

Local political risk arises from the influence of local councils or state governments. It manifests itself in the decisions made by local government that may negatively affect the factory (such as business rates increases, or indirect taxation). Ideally, the UK company should try to source a representative from the local government on to the factory project.

National government

Government decisions will also impact upon the factory. For example, the National government may have offered tax incentives for the first few years of the project but might increase taxes or even introduce new streams of taxation such as green taxes in later years. They may also take punitive measures such as penalising businesses they see as operating incorrectly (e.g. low wages), or businesses operating at odds with their specified aims and objectives.

International government

International bodies such as the UN can also be a source of political risk for businesses if they find out about activities of which they disagree e.g. low wages.

Although the new factory might serve both parties aims and objectives now, there may come a point in time in the future where the respective governments of the UK & West Africa disagree on an issue, which could have serious repercussions for the UK company in the long run.

In addition, if West Africa had a relatively new government this would also be a concern, insofar that if their term in office was short any future government may reverse the decisions taken by their predecessors.

Political risk also covers legal and compliance risk to an extent. The UK company should ascertain whether there are any additional laws in West Africa of which they should be aware. The use of local lawyers should help.

Mitigation strategies

Mitigating political risk is never easy, as governments tend to be far more powerful than individual companies. However, there are some methods of reducing the risk. One such method would be for the UK company to invite locals (employees, local government) to become part owners in the factory.

Another option is for it to provide the foreign government with details of an eventual exit strategy that will leave the business in the hands of locals.

Neither of these strategies may be acceptable to the UK company.

Test your understanding 3

The correct answers are B, C and D – Diversifying globally would be better than diversifying across the UK. Having operations across the world will reduce risk – portfolio theory.

Test your understanding 4

A

- The Swedish importer is unaffected as he is invoiced in his local currency
- The UK exporter will gain as the kroner received can be converted into more pounds.

Test your understanding 5 – H plc (Integration)

Value of transaction at original rates

	£
US$100,000 purchases @ 0.5556	55,560 payment

Value of transaction at future rates

US$100,000 purchases @ 0.5420	54,200 payment

The amount saved by paying in six months time is £1,360. This saving arises due to the exchange rate moving in your favour.

Do not forget that you would have had approximately £55,000 in the bank for six months longer, earning interest which makes this an even better option.

Test your understanding 6

The correct answer is B – Transaction risk is the risk of buying or selling on credit.

Economic risk is any change in the economy, home or abroad, which can affect the value of a transaction before a commitment is made.

Currency risk is the risk that arises from possible future movements in an exchange rate.

Test your understanding 7

The correct answer is D – Credit control procedures will help to alleviate credit risk.

Test your understanding 8 – MacDonald Farm (Case study)

Report

To: Mr and Mrs MacDonald

From: An advisor

Date: Today

The risk/return profile of the proposed golf club investment

Introduction

This report has been prepared to analyse the risk/return profile of Mr and Mrs MacDonald if they undertake the proposed development of Calum Golf Club.

Risk appetite/objectives

Given increasing pressure on farm income we have assumed that the primary objective with the golf club investment is to provide a low risk source of income to compensate for anticpated falls in profit.

Risk exposure

We have analysed your risk exposure under the following scenarios:

Scenario 1: the golf club is extremely successful:

- You will receive an annual rent of $50,000 and interest of $6,000 on the debentures.
- No dividends can be paid on profits.
- Presumably you will also have a 100% share in a successful golf company, although no information has been given as to the possibility of selling this. Also the value of the shares will be limited by the restriction on dividends.

Scenario 2: the golf club just hits its BEP of 600 members:

- You will receive an annual rent of $50,000 and interest of $6,000 on the debentures.
- No dividends can be paid on profits.

Scenario 3: the golf club fails to hit its BEP

- In the short term the club could borrow funds if required to be able to meet its cost commitments so it is likely that you will still receive an annual rent of $50,000 and interest of $6,000 on the debentures.
- Given your investment via limited shares, you will not face any further liability for club losses.
- However, if faced with the prospect of making an ongoing loss, the golf club may decide to start trying to cut costs. The choices are not attractive – it could cut salary and maintenance costs but this would undermine its competitive strategy of differentiation, making the situation worse.

Scenario 4: the golf club cannot pay interest on the debentures

- If the interest is not paid, then the debenture holders may insist on the appointment of a receiver to liquidate their investment.
- In such a scenario it is unlikely that any rent will be paid. If this occurs, then it is not clear if the farm can reclaim the land and sell the club house, perhaps even returning the land to arable use.

Conclusion and preliminary recommendations

Unless the golf club does very badly, you should receive a steady income of $56,000 per annum, equating to around $280 per acre, considerably higher than the $150 per acre earned on arable land historically. The investment gives a higher return than arable farming and at a lower risk, and is thus recommended on financial grounds.

However, before proceeding, we recommend that you seek to clarify/address the following risk areas:

- What is the legal position concerning the land and club house should rent not be paid?
- What assets are the debentures secured on, if any, as this will affect possible outcomes should interest not be paid?

Test your understanding 9 – RED (Case study)

Key answer tips

Part (a) requires you to consider the risk / return trade-off; a business will be willing to take higher risks as long as it obtains a higher return. Export sales are more risky, and you will need to give examples here of why this is the case.

In answering part (b) ensure that you explain your recommendations clearly and show how they will reduce the risks established in part (a). You may find it helpful to plan your answers to parts (a) and (b) together since this will ensure you generate as many ideas as possible.

Part (c) is quite open, allowing you to use some common sense as opposed to text-book knowledge.

(a) Credit risks can be higher with export sales than with domestic sales, for several reasons.

It might be more difficult to obtain information about customers in other countries in order to check their credit status. Information should be easier to obtain from European countries, where the services of a credit reference agency can be used, than from developing countries. When credit information is not available, decisions about granting credit are likely to involve an acceptance of greater-than-usual risk.

When customers are in countries where economic conditions are difficult, perhaps in developing countries, customers might have financial difficulties. They would therefore be a higher credit risk.

There can be problems with late payment, when goods are delayed in shipment. Customers are usually reluctant to pay for goods until they have been delivered or at least are in transit. Delays in shipment are therefore likely to result in delays in payment.

Many customers need to be 'chased' for payment. It is easier to chase customers in the same country than it is to chase customers in other countries, due to difficulties with language and time differences.

When a customer refuses to pay, there could be problems with taking legal action. If a customer is in another country, the difficulties will include a lack of knowledge of the local legislative system.

(b) Since credit risks can be higher with export sales, it is important to take measures to restrict the risk and keep it within acceptable limits.

RED might consider the following options:

For sales to countries where credit reference agencies operate, the services of a credit reference agency might be used to obtain information on the credit status of potential customers. In developing countries, the trade section of the embassy might be able to provide assistance in obtaining information about credit conditions in the country.

The company should develop clear policies and procedures on granting credit and collecting payments. The staff involved in granting credit and in chasing customers for payment should be given training in how to apply these policies and procedures. The policies and procedures, and the internal controls that are applied to credit checking and debt collection, should be reviewed and re-assessed regularly, and adjusted where weaknesses are identified

It might be possible to agree to a secure method of settlement of debts for exports to developing countries. With export trade to many countries, documentary credits are a commonly-used method of payment. The exporter is required to deliver a specified set of documents to a bank representing the importer: these documents typically include shipping documents, insurance documents, an invoice and a letter of credit. If the documents are all in order, the buyer agrees to make the payment, usually by means of a term bill of exchange drawn on the buyer's bank that gives the buyer a suitable period of credit. The bill of exchange, since it is a bank bill (and which might be confirmed by a second bank in the exporter's country), should be a fairly low credit risk. It is a promise by the bank to make the payment on the due date. If the exporter needs earlier payment, the bill can be discounted.

Letters of credit are much less common for sales to countries with an advanced economy. For sales to customers in Western Europe, RED might be required to give credit on normal trade terms. The credit risk might be reduced if RED used the services of an export factor. The factor would undertake to collect debts on behalf of RED. If the service is a without-recourse factoring service, the factor would also make the credit checks on the customer, and would effectively insure RED against the credit risk.

RED might consider the possibility of export credit insurance, although the premiums can be expensive.

(c) There are significant business risks in an export-led sales growth strategy.

Due to cultural differences, customers in other countries might have different needs and requirements from the products they buy. RED would therefore need to consider whether its products need to be adapted and altered to meet country-specific needs.

Similarly, due to cultural differences there could be difficulties in adapting to the business practices of the targeted countries.

Other business risks include the potential difficulties in building up good relationships with customers in distant countries. It might be necessary to negotiate agreements with a local agent or 'partner' for the storage and distribution of products locally. These will need to be managed carefully, and operational difficulties are likely to arise.

Inevitably, there will be risks of loss or damage to goods during shipment, but it is standard business practice to insure the goods against loss and damage (with either the seller or the buyer paying the insurance cost).

If RED agrees to invoice customers in their domestic currency, or in another foreign currency (such as US dollars or euros) foreign exchange risk would arise on transactions. However, these risks could be hedged using forward foreign exchange contracts.

In some developing countries, there might possibly be political risks. A government might take action, for example, to restrict foreign currency payments by residents to foreign suppliers.

A developing country might experience severe economic difficulties for a time: this has been the experience in the past, for example, of several countries in South and Central America. For a company exporting to such countries, there will be a risk that an economic downturn could disrupt export sales.

Test your understanding 10 – Equip (Integration)

(a) *Transaction risk:*

Sales revenue denominated in Australian dollars, New Zealand dollars euros, other.

Economic risk:

Purchase costs denominated in sterling but sourced from Eire.

Price pressure from competitors in the United States and Germany (this will be affected by the currency cost base of these companies).

Translation risk:

Minor as Equip Plc has no foreign subsidiaries – just retranslation of year-end currency debtors.

Overall assessment:

Mismatch of sterling cost base versus exposed sales revenue.

(b) (i) Reduction in exposure:

- Australian dollar transaction risk.
- Australian dollar economic risk.
- Exposure from competitors is not eliminated.

(ii) New exposures, to the extent that they do not net out:

- Translation risk from incorporating subsidiary accounts.
- Translation risk arising from the Australian dollar debt.
- Transaction risk as a result of the Australian dollar dividend payments to the UK.

The end result will depend on the success of the Australian operation, the actual figures involved and any increase in local sales that may naturally result from a greater presence in Australia. For example, exposure to New Zealand dollars could increase if sales to New Zealand were to increase.

Test your understanding 11 – Economic risk (Case study)

(a) **Briefing note**

To: The Board

From: A.N. Accountant

Date: Today

Subject: Determining the extent of R's economic exposure

Dear Sirs,

Economic exposure is generally difficult to measure, but an understanding can be obtained by identifying the factors that will lead to economic exposure. Generally, these boil down to identifying the effects of changes to cost prices and selling prices, both for the entity itself and for its competitors. R's purchase prices may be affected by movements in the AUS$. The actual effects may not be linear because R's Australian suppliers may not pass on the full effects of the currency movement. The suppliers may believe that the market for these products is sensitive to price rises and so the suppliers may choose to absorb some of the increased cost themselves. The likelihood of that happening will be determined in part by the availability of similar goods from economies that are not bound by the AUS$.

Currency movements may force R to raise its selling prices to customers. That makes the elasticity of demand for R's products important. It may be that prices are inelastic and that consumers are willing to buy just as much even if the price rises slightly. R's competitors may also buy products priced in AUS$ and that will reduce R's problem to an extent because all competing products will be affected in the same manner.

(b) The financial statements will show the gains and losses arising on R's currency holdings. The shareholders may be concerned that the company's assets are exposed in this way and that they are risking a serious loss if the AUS$ declines against the R$. The economic exposure that is being hedged will be apparent from the fact that the company will generate less revenue and make less profit when the AUS$ is high. This will not appear anywhere as a single, visible item or disclosure in the financial statements.

The shareholders could be forgiven for believing that the only exposure is with respect to the AUS$ balance. There is nothing to prevent the directors from explaining their strategy to the shareholders. It does not matter that there is a lack of symmetry in accounting for the different currency exposures provided the shareholders accept this explanation. This is, however, a complicated area and it would be legitimate for the directors to worry that the shareholders will misunderstand. If the shareholders believe that the directors' policy is misguided then it could undermine their confidence in the board. Technically, the directors are supposed to pursue the maximisation of shareholder wealth and so they should always act in accordance with the shareholders" best interests. It would be dishonest to leave the company exposed to a manageable risk for no good reason simply because the shareholders may misinterpret the directors' behaviour.

chapter

12

Currency risk management

Chapter learning objectives

Lead	Component
D2. Evaluate alternative risk management tools.	(a) Advise on the effects of economic factors that affect future cash flows from international operations. (b) Evaluate appropriate methods for the identification and management of financial risks associated with international operations.

Indicative syllabus content

- Exchange rate theory and the impact of differential inflation rates on forecast exchange rates.
- Theory and forecasting of exchange rates (e.g. interest rate parity, purchasing power parity and the Fisher effect).
- Internal hedging techniques.
- Operation and features of the more common instruments for managing currency risk: swaps, forward contracts, money market hedges, futures and options.
- Note: The Black Scholes option pricing model will not be tested numerically. However, an understanding of the variables which will influence the value of an option will be assumed.

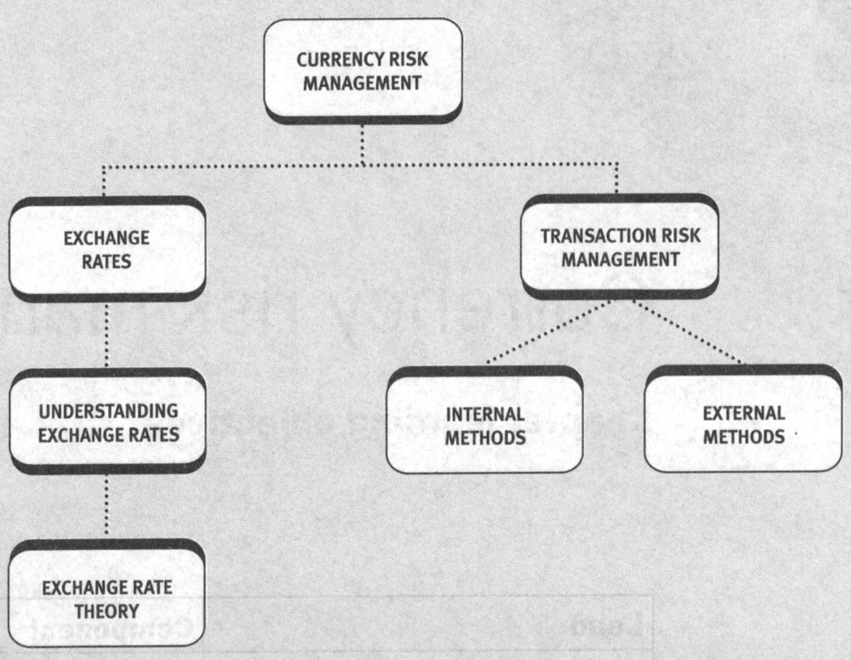

1 Understanding exchange rates

The foreign exchange, or forex, market is an international market in national currencies. It is highly competitive and virtually no difference exists between the prices in one market (e.g. New York) and another (e.g. London).

Exchange rates

An exchange rate is expressed in terms of the quantity of one currency that can be exchanged for one unit of the other currency – it can be thought of as the price of a currency. For example:

1 USD = 0.6667 GBP

This means that 0.6667 GBP will buy 1 USD, i.e. the price of a USD is 0.6667 GBP. Hence:

- to convert from USDs to GBPs you must multiply by 0.6667
- to convert from GBPs to USDs you must divide by 0.6667.

(**Note:** This could also be stated as US$1 = £0.6667, or US$1: £0.6667. You may see any of these expressions in exam questions. By convention exchange rates are expressed (and rounded) to four decimal places, though this may not always be the case for information provided in questions.)

Spot rate

This is the rate given for a transaction with immediate delivery. In practice this means it will be settled within two working days.

Inverting exchange rates

Exchange rates may also be expressed the other way round, i.e. the USDs are expressed in terms of GBPs instead of vice versa.

e.g. the above spot rate 1 USD = 0.6667 GBP

may be expressed in terms of USDs to GBPs by dividing the rate into 1,

i.e. 1 ÷ 0.6667 = 1.5000

Therefore an equivalent illustration of the rate is:

1 GBP = 1.5000 USD

Spread

Banks do not operate wholly for the greater good; in fact they wish to make a profit out of the deal. This means that they need to earn a **margin** or **spread** on the deal, as well as commission and fees.

e.g. 1 GBP = 1.5500 – 1.4500 USD

- the rate at which the bank will sell the variable currency (USDs) in exchange for the base currency (GBPs) is 1.4500 USD. (i.e. the rate at which it will buy GBPs).
- the rate at which the bank will buy USDs in exchange for GBPs is $1.5500 USD. (i.e. the rate at which it will sell GBPs).

The key to understanding our (the company's) position is to identify that the bank always wins, hence in the example above the bank buys GBP LOW and sells GBP HIGH.

Illustration of spread prices

The rate quoted is 1 GBP = 1.4330 – 1.4325 USD.

- Company A wants to buy 100,000 USD in exchange for GBP.
- Company B wants to sell 200,000 USD in exchange for GBP.

What rate will the bank offer each company?

Company A wants to buy USD100,000 in exchange for GBP (so that the bank will be selling USDs and buying GBPs):

- If we used the lower rate of 1.4325, the bank would sell dollars for GBP69,808
- If we used the higher rate of 1.4330, the bank would sell dollars for GBP69,784.

Clearly the bank would be better off selling dollars (and buying sterling) at the lower rate of 1.4325.

Company B wants to sell USD200,000 in exchange for sterling (so the bank would be buying USDs and selling GBPs):

- If we used the lower rate of 1.4325, the bank would buy dollars for GBP139,616
- If we used the higher rate of 1.4330, the bank would buy dollars for GBP139,567

The bank will make more money buying dollars (and selling sterling) at the higher rate of 1.4330.

Test your understanding 1 – Spread (Integration)

Assume that the spread is GBP 1 = USD 1.5500 – 1.4500. Consider the situations of three UK-based companies:

(a) A Ltd imports goods from Texas to the value of USD100,000. Payment is cash on delivery; what is the cost in sterling of this purchase?

(b) B plc exports goods to California valued at USD50,000. Receipt of payment is immediate on delivery of the goods; what is the value of GBP received?

(c) C Ltd wishes to buy a product from US that is for sale in the UK at GBP12 each; at what dollar price must it purchase the product?

Cross rates

You may not be given the exchange rate you need for a particular currency, but instead be given the relationship it has with a different currency. You will then need to calculate a **cross rate**.

For example, if you have a rate in GBP1/USD and a rate in GBP1/EUR, you can derive a cross rate for EUR1/USD by dividing the GBP1/USD rate by the GBP1/EUR rate.

Illustration of cross rate calculation

A French company is to purchase materials costing USD100,000. You have the following information:

GBP1/USD	1.9000
GBP1/EUR	1.4500

What is the value of the purchase in euros?

Solution

The solution could be calculated in two stages:

(1) Convert the purchase into sterling:

USD100,000/1.9000 = GBP52,632

(2) Convert the sterling value into euros

GBP52,632 × 1.4500 = EUR76,316

However, an easier alternative, particularly if there are a number of transactions to convert, is to calculate a cross rate:

The EUR1/USD rate will be 1.9000/1.4500 = 1.3103

The value of the transaction is therefore:

USD100,000/1.3103 = EUR76,318

Test your understanding 2

The exchange rate for USD/GBP is USD1.4417/GBP1 and the exchange rate for EUR/GBP is 1.1250.

How many dollars are there to the Euro?

Test your understanding 3 – Cross rates (Integration)

A US company has to pay EUR100,000 for a machine. You have the following information:

GBP1/EUR1.5300

GBP1/USD1.8700

Required:

What is the cost of the machine in dollars?

2 Exchange rate theory

Forecasting exchange rates

A company may wish to forecast exchange rates for a number of short-term and long-term reasons. These may include:

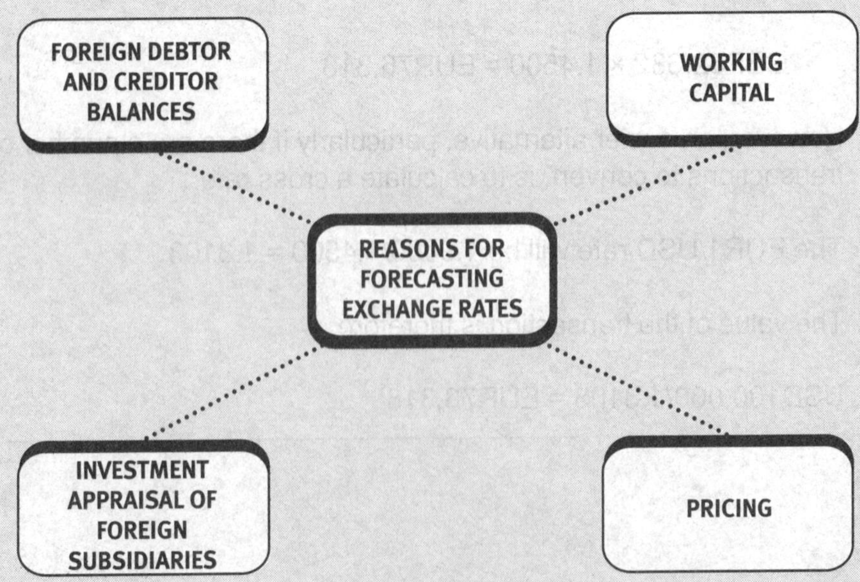

More on forecasting exchange rates

- **Foreign debtor and creditor balances** – Our balances in other currencies may change dramatically over the short-term in terms of sterling. If we are unable to forecast with some degree of certainty we open ourselves up to potentially very damaging exchange rate losses.
- **Working capital** – For a company with subsidiaries overseas it is important to be able to forecast movements in exchange rates over the medium-term to better facilitate the funding of those balances.
- **Pricing** – Movements in exchange rates may force the company to revise its pricing strategy in an individual country. This may be in response to a movement in the exchange rates between the country of manufacture and that of sale. Alternatively it is possible that an exchange rate movement favouring a competitor may also lead to a revision of prices.
- **Investment appraisal of foreign subsidiaries** – A longer-term forecast of exchange rate movements will be needed to identify the impact on a NPV analysis of the economic risks of a project.

- In the short-term rates may fluctuate due to market sentiment and **speculation** which are not easily explained theoretically, over the longer-term more fundamental factors take effect.
- If we could forecast exchange rates with some degree of accuracy this would reduce the transaction risk faced by a company, and may allow it to minimise hedging costs.

Why exchange rates fluctuate

Changes in exchange rates result from changes in the demand for and supply of the currency. These changes may occur for a variety of reasons including:

Speculation

Speculators enter into foreign exchange transactions with a view to making a profit from their expectations of the currency's future movements. If they expect a currency to devalue, they will short sell the currency with the hope of buying it back cheaply at a future date.

Balance of payments

Since currencies are required to finance international trade, changes in trade may lead to changes in exchange rates. In principle:

- demand for imports in the US represents a demand for foreign currency or a supply of dollars
- overseas demand for US exports represents a demand for dollars or a supply of the currency.

Thus a country with a current account deficit where imports exceed exports may expect to see its exchange rate depreciate, since the supply of the currency (imports) will exceed the demand for the currency (exports).

Any factors which are likely to alter the state of the current account of the balance of payments may ultimately affect the exchange rate.

Government policy

Governments may wish to change the value of their currency. This can be achieved directly by devaluation / revaluation, or via the foreign exchange markets (buying of selling their currency onto the markets).

Capital movements between economies

There are also **capital movements between economies.** These transactions are effectively switching bank deposits from one currency to another. These flows are now more important than the volume of trade in goods and services.

Thus supply/demand for a currency may reflect events on the capital account. Several factors may lead to inflows or outflows of capital:

- changes in *interest rates*: rising (falling) interest rates will attract a capital inflow (outflow) and a demand (supply) for the currency
- *inflation rates*: asset holders will not wish to hold financial assets in a currency whose value is falling because of inflation.

These forces which affect the demand and supply of currencies, and hence exchange rates, have been incorporated into a number of formal models.

We shall consider three related theories that together should give some insight into exchange rate movements:

(1) Purchasing power parity theory (PPPT)

(2) Interest rate parity theory (IRPT)

(3) The International Fisher Effect

Purchasing power parity theory (PPPT)

This theory suggests the rate of exchange will be directly determined by the relative rates of inflation suffered by each currency. If one country suffers a greater rate of inflation than another its currency should be worth less in comparative terms.

The basis of PPPT is the *'Law of One Price'*:

- identical goods must cost the same regardless of the currency in which they are sold.
- if this is not the case then **arbitrage** (buying at the lower price, selling at the higher price) will take place until a single price is charged. Remember this is where a commodity that appears cheap is bought by many traders. The sellers then realise that they can put up their price due to the commodities popularity. Demand will then fall at this higher price and potential profits have been competed away. However, imagine that this commodity has to cross a countries border – it would be easy to cross the border from, say Switzerland to France to buy cheaper groceries. If many Swiss did this it might affect the Swiss Franc/Euro exchange rate. However it is much more difficult to make the same saving if you live in the UK even if you believe that the GBP/Euro is out of line.

PPPT

A company is going to buy a non-current asset at a cost of USD30 million. If the current rate is GBP1/USD1.5000 this would mean that in sterling terms it would cost **GBP20 million.**

What would be the prices in one year in each country given that the inflation rate in the US is 8% and in the UK is 5%?

	The US market		**The UK market**
Year 0 (now)	USD30m	(GBP1/USD1.5000)	GBP20m
Inflation	8%		5%
Year 1	USD32.4m		GBP21m

What is the effective exchange rate in one year's time?

We can divide the US price by the UK price to calculate the revised exchange rate:

$$\text{Rate} = \frac{32.4}{21.0} = 1.5429$$

Rule: The country with the higher inflation will suffer a fall (depreciation) in their currency.

The PPPT formula gives:

$$\text{Future spot rate} = \text{Current spot rate} \times \frac{1 + i_f}{1 + i_h}$$

i_f rate of inflation in the foreign country

i_h rate of inflation in the home country

spot rate in terms of 1 unit of home currency/foreign currency (e.g. £1/US$)

In the above illustration, the future spot rate would be calculated by

$$1.5000 \times \frac{1.08}{1.05} = 1.5429$$

Test your understanding 4

The USD and GBP are currently trading at GBP1/USD1.7200.

Inflation in the US is expected to grow at 3% pa, but at 4% pa in the UK.

What is the future spot rate in a year's time? (Give your answer to 4dp)

Problems with PPPT in practice

- Is the law of one price justified? In many markets it is apparent that the suppliers or manufacturers charge what the market will bear, this differing from one market to another.
- The costs of physically moving some products from one place to another mean that there will always be a premium in some markets in relation to another.
- Differing taxation regimes may dramatically affect the costs of a product in one market to that in another.
- Manufacturers may be able to successfully differentiate products in each market to limit the amount of arbitrage that occurs.

Is PPPT a good predictor of future spot rate?

PPPT certainly does explain the reasoning behind much of the movements in exchange rates but is not a very good predictor of exchange rates in the short- to medium-term.

Reasons for this include:

- Future inflation rates are only an estimate and often cannot be relied upon to be accurate.
- The market is dominated by speculation and currency investment rather than trade in physical goods.
- Government intervention in both direct (e.g. management of exchange rates) and indirect ways (e.g. taxation policies) can nullify the impact of PPPT.

Interest rate parity theory (IRPT)

This theory is based on very similar principles to that of PPPT.

The IRPT claims that the difference between the spot and the forward exchange rates is equal to the differential between interest rates available in the two currencies.

The **forward rate** is a future exchange rate, agreed now, for buying or selling an amount of currency on an agreed future date.

IRPT

An investor has USD 5 million to invest over one year in either dollars (USD) or sterling (GBP). His options are to:

- Invest in dollars at the prevailing dollar interest rate of 10.16% or,
- Convert the dollars to sterling at the prevailing spot rate (GBP1/USD1.5000) and invest in sterling at 7.1%.

The one-year forward rate is GBP1/USD1.5429.

Analysing the options open to this investor:

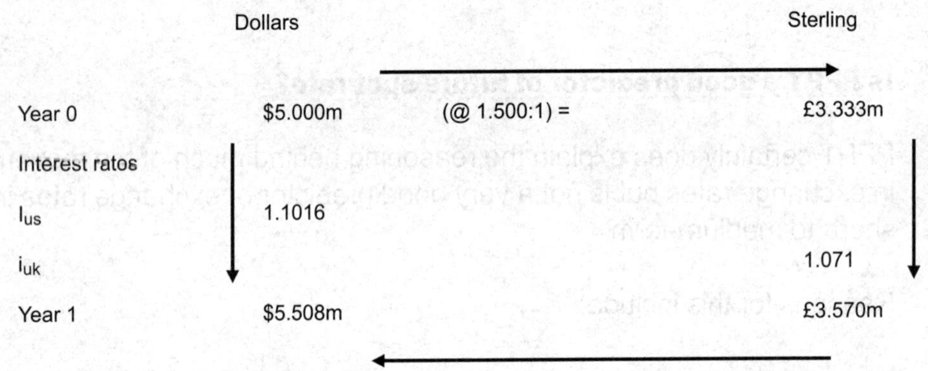

In one year USD 5.508 million must equate to GBP 3.570 million, so what you gain in extra interest you lose in an adverse movement in exchange rates. The effective exchange rate is

$$\text{Exchange rate} = \frac{5.508}{3.570} = 1.5429$$

which equals the forward rate for one year. The forward rate moves to bring about interest rate parity between the currencies.

Rule: IRPT predicts that the country with the higher interest rate will see the forward rate for its currency subject to a depreciation.

The IRPT formula gives:

$$\text{Forward rate} = \text{Current spot rate} \times \frac{1 + ints_f}{1 + ints}$$

Where

$ints_f$ money risk-free rate of interest for the foreign currency
$ints_h$ money risk-free rate of interest for the home currency
spot rate in terms of 1 unit of home currency/foreign currency (e.g. GBP1/USD)

Test your understanding 5

A treasurer can borrow in Swiss francs (CHF) at a rate of 3% pa or in the UK at a rate of 7% p.a. The current rate of exchange is GBP1/10CHF.

What is the likely rate of exchange in a year's time? (Give your answer to 4 dp)

More on IRPT

The interest rate parity model shows that it may be possible to predict exchange rate movements by referring to differences in nominal exchange rates. If the forward exchange rate for sterling against the dollar was no higher than the spot rate but US nominal interest rates were higher, the following would happen:

- UK investors would shift funds to the US in order to secure the higher interest rates, since they would suffer no exchange losses when they converted USD back into GBP.
- The flow of capital from the UK to the US would raise UK interest rates and force up the spot rate for the USD.

The IRP theory holds because of **arbitrage** (discussed earlier). Arbitrageurs actively seek out anomalies in the exchange rate market. They buy and sell currency to make a profit (buy at a low price and sell at a high price, as with any commodity). If many arbitrageurs do this, the exchange rate alters (differences in supply and demand will alter the price), the exchange rate moves and the anomaly then disappears. Nick Leeson at Barings Bank used to be an unsuccessful arbitrageur!

Is IRPT applicable to determining forward rates?

The only limitation on the universal applicability of this relationship will be due to government intervention. These may arise in a number of ways including the following:

- **Controls on capital markets** – The government may limit the range and type of markets within their financial services system.
- **Controls on currency trading** – These may be in the form of a limit on the amount of currency that may be taken out of a country or the use of an 'official' exchange rate that does not bear any relation to the 'effective' rate at which the markets wish to trade.
- **Government intervention in the market** – The government may attempt to control or manipulate the exchange rate by buying or selling their own currency.

The International Fisher Effect

The International Fisher Effect claims that the interest rate differentials between two countries provide an unbiased predictor of future changes in the spot rate of exchange.

- The International Fisher Effect assumes that all countries will have the same real interest rate, although nominal or money rates may differ due to expected inflation rates.
- Thus the interest rate differential between two countries should be equal to the expected inflation differential.
- Therefore, countries with higher expected inflation rates will have higher nominal interest rates, and vice versa.

The Fisher effect

As seen in your earlier studies, the Fisher effect looks at the relationship between interest rates and inflation. Inflation is the difference between the real return on investment (real interest) and the nominal return (nominal interest rate). The relationship between the nominal rate of interest, the real rate of interest and inflation can be expressed by the formula:

[1 + nominal rate] = [1 + real rate] × [1 + inflation rate]

Example

One-year money market interest rates in the UK are 5.06%. Inflation in the UK is currently running at 3% per annum.

The real one-year interest rate in the UK can be calculated as follows:

[1.0506] = [1 + real rate] × [1.03]
[1 + real rate] = 1.0506/1.03 = 1.02
Real rate = 0.02 or 2% per year.

The nominal or market interest rates in any country must be sufficient to reward investors with a suitable real return plus an additional return to allow for the effects of inflation.

Test your understanding 6

If the interest rate on USD deposits is 8%, the interest rate on EUR deposits is 5%, and the spot rate is USD/EUR0.9200, what is the one year forward rate predicted to be if interest rate parity holds?

A USD/EUR0.9463

B USD/EUR1.0567

C USD/EUR0.8944

D USD/EUR1.1180

Test your understanding 7 – Parity relationships (Integration)

Spot USD1/EUR0.9050

Interest rates p.a. on short-term government securities

US treasury	6.0%
Eurozone	4.5%

Inflation rates

US	2.0%
Eurozone	1.3%

Required:

Calculate using the parity relationships (PPPT and IRPT) the theoretically correct forward rates. Determine the reasons for a difference between the two, if one arises.

Test your understanding 8 – L (Integration/Case study)

L manufactures specialised paper products for sale in its home country, Country B. The market is very price sensitive. Some of L's competitors are based in its home country and others export to Country B.

The manufacturing process is not particularly skilled, but it is very labour intensive. L's largest costs are for wages and flax fibre (the basic raw material used in manufacturing L's products). Almost 60% of L's total manufacturing cost is for wages.

L's directors are considering moving production offshore to Country R, a developing country that has low wage rates. The products will then be transferred to Country B for sale.

L's home currency is the BND. Country R's currency is the RTD. At present, the exchange rate is 1.00 BND = 2.50 RTD.

L presently pays an hourly rate of 6.00 BND to its production staff. Workers with comparable skill levels would be paid 2.75 RTD per hour in Country R.

Flax fibre is sold as a commodity on the global markets. It is priced in US Dollars (USD). All of L's purchases of flax fibre are imported.

Shipping flax fibre to the new factory would be much cheaper than shipping it to L's home country. Those savings would pay for the cost of shipping the finished products to L's home country for sale.

L's directors are currently asking for information that will help them with an appraisal of the financial viability of the new factory. L's Chief Economist has reported that there are no credible long-term economic forecasts available. She has, however, obtained some basic economic indicators that could be used to predict future wage rates:

	Country B	Country R
Interest rates per annum	5.00%	9.00%
General inflation per annum	2.00%	4.70%

Required:

(a) (i) Produce a forecast of the hourly rate in BND that will be paid to employees in Country R in five years' time. You must explain the assumptions that you have made at each stage of your calculations.

(15 minutes)

(ii) Evaluate the assumptions that were made and explained in (a) (i),explaining why reality could differ from what you assumed.

(10 minutes)

(b) Discuss the Production Director's statement that the price of flax fibre is irrelevant to the decision to move production to Country R because flax fibre is priced in terms of USD

(10 minutes)

(c) Advise L's board of the political risks that L will be taking in its home country if it proceeds with this project.

(10 minutes)

Test your understanding 9 – G clothing (Case study)

Background

G is a major clothing retailer, specialising in fashionable clothes for young people. G has shops in every major town and city in its home country. G's customers are extremely conscious of brand names and G must stock the latest products from the biggest and most popular manufacturers in order to remain competitive.

Most of G's most popular brands are imported from the USA. The clothes are expensive to import because the Government in G's country imposes a tariff, which requires G (and all other importers) to pay a tax on all clothing imports. The Government's reason for imposing this tariff is to protect local manufacturers from foreign competition. G is located in a relatively prosperous country and wages are fairly high.

G has been losing sales to a major competitor, which is based in G's home country and has shops in the same towns and cities as G, which sells the same range of clothing but at a lower price. G attempted to compete on price, but stopped doing so when it became apparent that the competitor could undercut any price that G set.

G has investigated the competitor's trading strategy. It appears that the competitor is able to exploit anomalies in the market by buying its inventory in a neighbouring country and bringing it across the border. Two of the countries that adjoin G's home country are not particularly prosperous. Many foreign suppliers, including G's suppliers, supply goods to distributers (and also directly to retailers) in those countries at lower prices than they do in G's home country because they are aware that the final consumers there have low incomes and are not able to pay high prices for brand name clothing. Furthermore, those neighbouring countries do not charge tariffs on clothing imports.

Trigger

G's home country is part of a trading bloc which includes the neighbouring country from which the competitor is suspected of buying its inventory. There are no physical barriers to regulate the borders between countries within that bloc. Legally, any goods imported from a neighbouring country are subject to tariffs, but G suspects that the competitor has not been declaring these imports to the Government department responsible for collecting tax and so the competitor has benefitted from both cheaper purchase prices and the evasion of the tariff.

Some of G's senior managers have recommended that G should copy its competitor by cancelling all contracts with the major US manufacturers and buying all goods from intermediaries in a neighbouring country. Others recommend reporting their suspicions to the manufacturers and to the Government.

Task

As G's management accountant, prepare a briefing note for the Board:

(a) Discussing the argument that purchasing power parity theory should prevent exporters from charging different prices in different countries.

(b) Discussing the potential risks and benefits to G of buying its inventory from intermediaries in the neighbouring countries.

(c) Recommending actions that the Government in G's home country could take in order to determine whether G's competitor had been evading the tariff on imported clothing.

(45 minutes)

Arbitrage

Arbitrage is the simultaneous purchase and sale of a security in different markets with the aim of making a risk-free profit through the exploitation of any price differences between the two markets. (CIMA Official Terminology)

(The purchase and sale does not necessarily have to be a security. It could be as simple as buying apples in one market and selling them in another at a higher price.)

Arbitrage is mainly used by **speculators** rather than as a hedging tool.

Arbitrage differences are short-term. When other traders see differences in the price of a commodity they will exploit them and the prices will converge. The differences will disappear as equilibrium is reached.

Some kinds of arbitrage are completely risk-free – this is pure arbitrage. For instance, if Euros are available more cheaply in London than in New York, arbitrageurs can make a risk-free profit by buying euros in London and selling an identical amount in New York. Opportunities for pure arbitrage have become rare in recent years, partly because of the globalisation of financial markets and immediate access to information via the use of the internet. This enables almost anyone (who understands what they are doing) to trade and potentially make a profit.

More on arbitrage

For example, imagine you bought and sold fruit and vegetables on a market stall. One day asks for a kilo of apples. You don't have any apples but you know where you can get some. Having ascertained that the customer will pay up to GBP1 per kilo, you contact a friend who has apples on another market stall. They are selling at GBP0.90 per kilo. You offer to buy the kilo of apples at GBP0.90, collect them from the other market stall, and sell them for GBP1 making GBP0.10 profit. If enough customers ask for apples, eventually the friend will realise that there is an increased demand for apples, which appear to be in short supply, and they will increase their price. This effectively eliminates the opportunity for arbitrage profits.

The same principle can be applied to any commodity but is commonly used by 'day-traders' with exchange rates. They look for an apparently 'cheap' currency and then sell it quickly, at a profit, to someone who needs it.

Margaret is a day-trader (based in the UK) looking for arbitrage opportunities on the currency market. On 1st June she thinks she has spotted a difference in the market for USD.

She can buy USD 2 for EUR1.50. She can buy one euro for GBP0.80. She can sell dollars for USD 1.50/GBP1. She has GBP100,000 available to invest for the purpose of making a profit.

Margaret converts her GBP in to EUR: GBP100,000/0.80 = EUR125,000

Margaret then converts her EUR into USD: (EUR125,000/1.5) × 2 = USD166,667

Margaret now sells the USD: USD166,667/1.50 = GBP111,111

Margaret has made a risk-free profit of GBP11,111.

Test your understanding 10

A speculator can buy USD2 for GBP1, sell one EUR for GBP0.80 and can sell USD for USD1.50/EUR1. There is GBP1,000,000 available to invest for the purpose of making a profit.

What is the possible profit using arbitrage opportunities? (Give your answer in GBP to the nearest £100).

Test your understanding 11 – U company (Integration/Case study)

U is an administrative assistant in the treasury department of a multinational company. U was checking some current market valuations when she noticed an anomaly in the rates associated with the USD/GBP exchange rates.

The spot rate for converting GBP to USD was 1.556 USD to the GBP. The three month forward rate for converting USD back to GBP was 1.499 USD to the GBP.

U's bank was prepared to lend GBP at a fixed rate of 5.08% per annum. The bank was also prepared to offer a fixed rate for USD deposits of 5.12%.

U printed these figures out and spoke to the company treasurer because she believed that there was an arbitrage opportunity. The treasurer agreed that U's figures indicated that an opportunity existed, but said that the opportunity would have disappeared in the time that it had taken her to walk across the office.

U asked why the multinational company did not pay greater attention to the possibility of arbitrage opportunities. The treasurer replied that "Arbitrage is a full-time occupation and it is a rather risky commercial venture. I am happy to leave the potential profits to the arbitrageurs who have made it their business to trade in that way". The treasurer also stated that the company's treasury department is a cost centre and that he had no desire to make it into a profit centre.

Required

(a) Calculate the potential gain that could have been made by the company if it had borrowed GBP 10m in order to exploit the anomaly that she had identified.

(b) (i) Evaluate U's argument that the company could profit from this opportunity.

(ii) Evaluate the treasurer's argument that arbitrage is a risky commercial venture.

(c) Evaluate the treasurer's view that it is better for the company's treasury department to operate as a cost centre rather than as a profit centre.

(45 minutes)

3 Financial risk management

The stages in the financial risk management process are essentially the same as in any risk management process:

(1) identify risk exposures

(2) quantify exposures

(3) decide whether or not to hedge

(4) implement and monitor hedging program.

Stage 1 and 2 was covered in chapter 3.

Hedge or not ?

Hedging can involve the reduction or elimination of financial risk by passing that risk onto someone else. Or internal hedging techniques involve reducing risk by creating an offsetting position that has a tendency to cancel any risks.

Benefits of hedging

- hedging can provide certainty of cash flows which will assist in the budgeting process
- risk will be reduced, and hence management may be more inclined to undertake investment projects
- reduction in the probability of financial collapse (bankruptcy)
- managers are often risk-averse since their job is at risk. If a company has a policy of hedging it may be perceived as a more attractive employer to risk-averse managers.

Arguments against hedging

- shareholders have diversified their own portfolio, thus further hedging by the business may harm shareholders' interests
- transaction costs associated with hedging can be significant
- lack of expertise within the business, particularly with regards to use of derivative instruments
- complexity of accounting and tax issues associated with the use of derivatives.

Derivatives

A derivative is a financial instrument whose value depends on the price of some other financial asset or underlying factor (such as oil, gold, interest rates or currencies).

The directors of an organisation will decide how to use derivatives to meet their goals and to align with their risk appetite.

Derivatives have the following uses:

- **Hedging:** used as a risk management tool to reduce / eliminate financial risk.
- **Speculation:** used to make a profit from predicting market movements.

- **Arbitrage:** used to exploit price differences between markets. (This will be short-term only. If a commodity appears to be cheap, demand will increase which will push up the price. Hence the price differential, where a gain could be made in the past, has now closed.)

For the purposes of this subject we are interested in the hedging use of derivatives.

Treasury function

The treasury function exists in every business, though in a small business it may be absorbed into the accounting or company secretarial work.

The **main functions** of treasury are:

- managing relationships with the banks – regarding the investment of surplus cash or making arrangements to allow deficits of cash, or to arrange hedging.
- working capital and liquidity management – to ensure that sufficient but not excessive amounts of cash are available on a daily basis to fund inventory, payables and receivables.
- long-term funding management – providing cash for longer term investments such as non-current assets or arranging mortgages / debentures.
- currency management – dealing with all currencies which will entail both internal and external hedging techniques, sourcing currencies, managing foreign currency bank accounts.

More on the treasury function

Organisational structure

The treasurer has the capacity to make large gains or losses in a short period of time, particularly when trading in financial derivatives. As a result it is important to define and carefully monitor the responsibility and authority associated with treasury.

There are a number of differing structures for the treasury activity within a business. The two key debates are discussed below.

Profit centre or cost centre

Should the treasury activities be accounted for simply as a cost centre, or as a profit centre in its own right (making profit out of trading activities)?

Advantages of operating as a profit centre, as opposed to cost centre include:

- a market rate is charged to business units throughout the entity, making operating costs realistic
- the treasurer is motivated to provide services as efficiently and economically as possible.

The main disadvantages are:

- the profit concept brings the temptation to speculate and take excessive risk
- management time can be wasted on discussions about internal charges for the treasury activities
- additional administrative costs will be incurred.

Centralised or decentralised

Many large companies operate a centralised treasury function, which has merits and limitations.

Risks associated with centralised treasury include:

- a lack of motivation towards managing cash in the subsidiaries, since any cash that is received is swept up to head office to be managed from the group's perspective.
- the risk that, should head office commit some error in their treasury operations, the financial health of the whole group could be placed in jeopardy.

Risks associated with decentralised activity are:

- that one company might pay large overdraft interest costs, while another has cash balances in hand earning low interest rates.
- the risk of not generating the profits for the group that would be earned if the group funds were actively managed by a treasury operation seeking profits rather than individual executives just seeking to minimise costs.

Corporate treasury policies

A UK retailer

A well-known UK retailer 'operates a centralised treasury function to manage the Group's funding requirements and financial risks in line with the Board approved treasury policies and procedures, and delegated authorities. … Group Treasury also enters into derivative transactions, principally interest rate and currency swaps and forward currency contracts. The purpose of these transactions is to manage the interest-rate and currency risks arising from the Group's operations and financing. It remains Group policy not to hold or issue financial instruments for trading purposes, except where financial constraints necessitate the need to liquidate any outstanding investments. The treasury function is managed as a cost centre and does not engage in speculative trading. The principal risks faced by the Group are liquidity/funding, interest rate, foreign currency risks and counterparty risks.

(a) **Liquidity/funding risk**

The risk that the Group could be unable to settle or meet its obligations as they fall due at a reasonable price.

The Group's funding strategy ensures a mix of funding sources offering flexibility and cost effectiveness to match the requirements.

(b) **Counterparty risk**

Counterparty risk exists where the Group can suffer financial loss through default or non-performance by financial institutions.

Exposures are managed through Group treasury policy which limits the value that can be placed with each approved counterparty to minimise the risk of loss. The counterparties are limited to the approved institutions with secure long-term credit ratings A+/A1 or better assigned by Moody's and Standard & Poor's respectively, unless approved on an exception basis by a Board director. Limits are reviewed regularly by senior management.

(c) **Foreign currency risk**

Transactional foreign currency exposures arise from both the export of goods from the UK to overseas subsidiaries, and from the import of materials and goods directly sourced from overseas suppliers.

Group treasury hedge these exposures principally using forward foreign exchange contracts progressively covering up to 100% out to 18 months. Where appropriate hedge cover can be taken out longer than 18 months, with Board approval. The Group is primarily exposed to foreign exchange risk in relation to GBP against movements in USD and EUR.

(d) **Interest rate risk**

The Group is exposed to interest rate risk in relation to the GBP, USD, EUR and Hong Kong dollar (HKD) variable rate financial assets and liabilities.

The Group's policy is to use derivative contracts where necessary to maintain a mix of fixed and floating rate borrowings to manage this risk. The structure and maturity of these derivatives correspond to the underlying borrowings and are accounted for as fair value or cash flow hedges as appropriate.

Capital policy

The Group's objectives when managing capital are to safeguard its ability to continue as a going concern in order to provide optimal returns for shareholders and to maintain an efficient capital structure to reduce the cost of capital.

In doing so the Group's strategy is to maintain a capital structure commensurate with an investment grade credit rating and to retain appropriate levels of liquidity headroom to ensure financial stability and flexibility. To achieve this strategy the Group regularly monitors key credit metrics such as the gearing ratio, cash flow to net debt see (note 29) and fixed charge cover to maintain this position. In addition the Group ensures a combination of appropriate committed short-term liquidity headroom with a diverse and smooth long-term debt maturity profile.

During the year the Group maintained an investment grade credit rating of Baa3 (stable) with Moody's and BBB-(stable) with Standard & Poor's, and through the successful tender of GBP200m of existing short-dated bonds in conjunction with a new GBP400m 10 year bond issue extended the average fixed debt maturity by one year to ten years and increased short-term liquidity by GBP200m.

In order to maintain or re-align the capital structure, the Group may adjust the number of dividends paid to shareholders, return capital to shareholders, issue new shares or sell assets to reduce debt.

Test your understanding 12 – J electronics (Case study)

Scenario

J manufactures specialised electronic equipment in the UK.

All of J's directors come from an electronic engineering background and the small administrative staff provides basic clerical and book-keeping support.

Trigger

The company has just won its first export order and will receive payment of USD 15 million in three months. J's Chief Executive is concerned that the USD may decline against the GBP during the three months and has asked the company's bank to offer a guaranteed price for the currency when it is received.

The bank has offered to enter into a forward contract with J at a rate of GBP1 = USD 1.65.

J's Chief Executive is unhappy with this offer because the present exchange rate is GBP1 = USD 1.60. Given the size of the transaction, this constitutes a major additional cost that J had not budgeted for when setting its selling price. J's Chief Executive would rather wait until the payment is received in the hope that the spot rate at that time is better than the GBP1 = USD 1.65 offered by the bank.

J's Chief Executive is concerned that the differential rate being charged by the bank is unfair. He believes that global economics are so complicated that it is impossible to forecast exchange rate movements and the movements in the exchange rate are just as likely to be favourable as unfavourable to J over the next three months.

J's bank manager has pointed out that the rate offered is in line with market expectations and that it is unrealistic for the Chief Executive to ask the bank to commit itself to guaranteeing that today's exchange rate can be obtained on a transaction that will occur in three months.

The bank manager has recommended that J appoints a full-time corporate treasurer to take on the responsibility of the treasury function and relieve the Chief Executive of that burden.

Task

Write a briefing note to the Board:

(a) Evaluating the bank manager's recommendation to appoint a corporate treasurer.

(b) Recommending, stating reasons, the steps that the directors of J should take in the selection of a suitable person for the role of corporate treasurer.

(30 minutes)

4 Currency risk management

There are several methods of managing exposure to currency risk. As a general rule the simplest and most convenient methods are used by any business.

The methods can be split as follows:

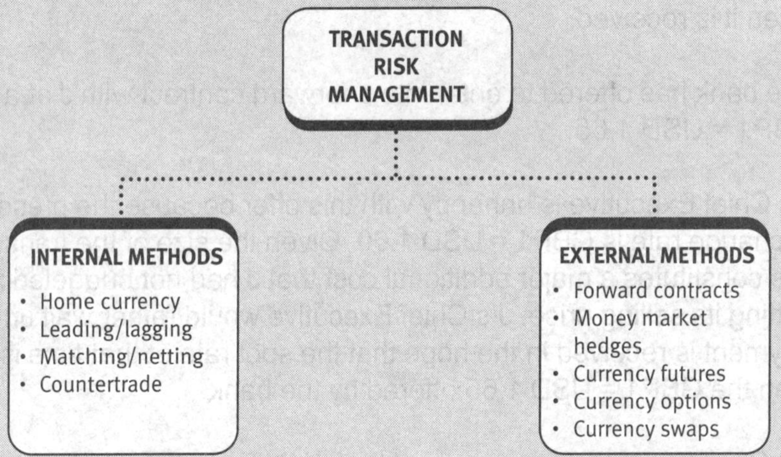

The differences between internal and external hedging can be very significant:

- Internal hedging is often more effective for dealing with economic risk;
- Internal hedging is often cheaper and simpler to understand;
- External hedging is popular with treasury departments because of the excitement of setting up any transactions.

5 Internal hedging

If a company wants to remove transaction risk, it is possible to hedge this internally in a number of ways, including:

- Invoice in home currency.
- Leading and lagging payments.
- Offsetting – matching, netting and pooling.
- Countertrade.

More on internal hedging techniques

Invoice in home currency

If a UK business invoices in GBP and only accepts invoices from suppliers in GBP then it partly removes currency risk. The currency risk is transferred to the customer or supplier. However economic risk is not removed – the value of the business will still fall if the overseas competition are 'winning' with their overseas trade in foreign currencies.

This method does give some very practical business issues:

- The customers and suppliers may not be prepared to accept all the currency risk and therefore they will not trade with the business.
- The other parties may not be prepared to accept the same prices and will require discounts on sales or premiums on purchases.
- There are other ways of hedging risks that mean that the risk of transacting in foreign currency is acceptable.

Leading and lagging

This is a method of trying to makes gains on foreign currency payments.

Leading is making a payment before it is due, and lagging is delaying a payment for as long as possible. This is effective if the company has a strong view about the future movements in the exchange rate.

For example, a company has to make a USD100,000 payment to a US supplier. The payment is due in two months' time but could be paid immediately or delayed until three months' time. Sterling is expected to depreciate in value against the US dollar over the next three months. In this case the company would want to pay as early as possible and therefore lead. To check this, consider that if the rate went from USD:GBP 2.0000 to USD:GBP 1.5000, the payment in GBP would go from GBP50,000 to GBP66,667. The company would obviously want to only pay GBP50,000.

Problems with leading and lagging include:

- Early payment will cost a company in interest foregone on the funds that have been disbursed early;
- The payee will not be happy that payment may become overdue, especially if the currency is expected to fall;
- It requires the company to take a view on exchange rates i.e. speculate. There is a risk that the company will be wrong.

Offsetting

Matching

This technique involves matching assets and liabilities in the same currency. Financing a foreign investment with a foreign loan would reduce the exposure to exchange risk since as the rate changes favourably on one it would move adversely on the other.

Netting

Netting normally involves the use of foreign currency bank accounts. If a company knows it will be both receiving and paying in foreign currency, it can reduce exchange risk by using the foreign receipts to cover the foreign payments. The netting will work best if the dates of the receipt and payment are as near together as possible.

In a group, netting can be done across the group by a treasury function. This would mean that if one subsidiary is making foreign payments and another subsidiary is taking foreign receipts, the group can net the two off.

Pooling

Pooling is a system of managing cash. When a business has several bank accounts in the same currency, it might be able to arrange a system with its bank(s) whereby the balances on each bank account in the same currency are swept up into a central account at the end of each day, leaving a zero balance on every account except the central account. Overdraft balances and positive cash balances are all swept up into the central account maximising interest earned and minimising any bank charges or interest payable.

This does not provide a system for hedging against FX risk, but can be an efficient system for cash management. It avoids overdraft costs on individual bank accounts, and it enables the treasury department to make more efficient use of any cash surpluses.

For an efficient system of cash pooling, there needs to be a centralised cash management system. The current organisation allows each subsidiary to operate their own cash management system. Pooling can be organised by each subsidiary. However, it might be even more efficient if subsidiaries operating in the same currencies shared the same pooling system, hence it is best operated by a central treasury function.

Countertrade

This involves parties exchanging goods and services of equivalent value. It is the old fashioned bartering and avoids any type of currency exchanges. However the tax authorities do not like this method – if cash does not change hands it is difficult to establish the value of the transaction and any related sales tax payable. For this reason, countertrade is not very common since it can lead to disputes with the tax authorities and take up management time.

Matching

A company wishes to fund a USD1m investment and uses a USD1m loan. The exchange rate is USD1.8:GBP1 on the date the investment is made, but sterling strengthens to USD2:GBP1 six months later.

The company has matched its assets and liabilities:

Investment (asset)

At acquisition (USD1m/1.8) = GBP555.6k

Six months later (USD1m/2) = GBP500k

Loan (liability)

At acquisition (USD1m/1.8) = GBP555.6k

Six months later (USD1m/2) = GBP500k

Whether at acquisition or six months later, the asset and the loan are worth the same as each other.

Netting

Division A is due to receive USD1m on Friday. Division B has a payable of USD700,000 due on the same day.

Because the receipt is at the same time as the payment, the company should use the receipt of USD1m to pay their supplier USD700,000. This would minimise any transaction costs arising from buying USD700,000 from the bank.

The USD300,000 left could be kept in a USD bank account for later USD payments, saving on further transaction costs in later months, or it could be converted into the home currency (now, or at some time in the future when rates are more favourable).

6 External hedging

If a company wants to remove transaction risk it is also possible to hedge this externally in a number of ways including:

- Netting centres;
- Forward contracts;
- Money market hedges;
- Futures;
- Options;
- Swaps.

7 Netting centres

Multilateral netting is a treasury management technique used by large companies to manage their intercompany payment processes, usually involving many currencies. Netting can yield significant savings from reduced foreign exchange trading.

A netting centre collates batches of cashflows between a defined set of companies and offsets them against each other so that just a single cashflow to or from each company takes place to settle the net result of all cashflows.

The netting process takes place on a cyclical basis, typically monthly, and is managed by a central entity called the netting centre.

Although netting centres are occasionally used to net off cashflows in just one currency, it is more usual for a netting centre to manage cashflows in several currencies. In a multiple currency netting system, each company's cashflows are converted to an equivalent amount in the company's base currency, so that the company still has only a single net position to settle in that currency.

A netting centre is typically used by a multinational company that has many production and sales divisions in a number of countries. Direct billing in many currencies by each company can lead to excessive foreign exchange trading, in which individual companies may be both buying and selling the same currencies many times over. The objective of using a netting centre is to reduce the overall foreign exchange volume traded and thereby cut the amount of foreign exchange spread paid by the company to manage all the currency conversions.

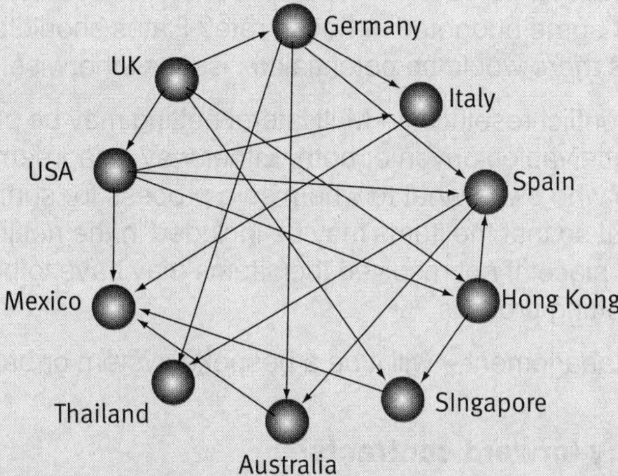

Without netting, each company settles its receipts and payments directly and individually with each of the other companies.

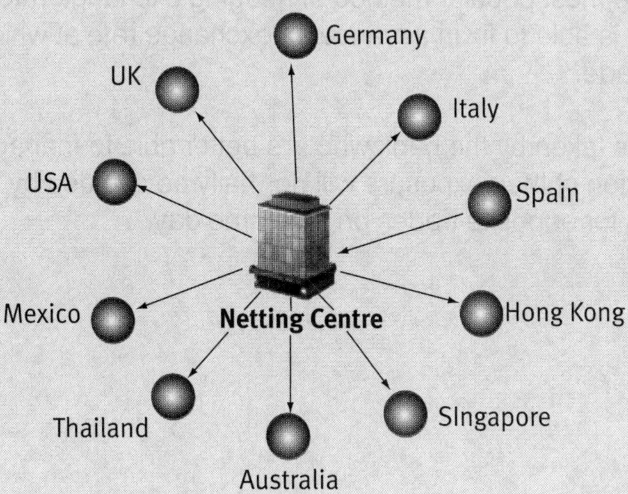

After using a netting centre, each company pays or receives a single local currency balance to or from the netting centre.

For netting to be successful participants must agree on a number of issues such as:

- Currencies – Which currencies will be used for invoicing? They may be the buyer's, the seller's or a third currency.
- Credit period – Ideally all participants should have the same credit periods but there may be variations for those participants who are long or short of funds.
- Settlement dates – The netting settlement dates and the netting cycle timetable must be known by all the participants and adhered to. Netting periods must also be decided e.g. weekly, monthly etc.
- Exchange rates – The exchange rates to be used in the netting must be agreed. Will it be spot or forward rates, mid at 11-00 am or some budgeted in-house rate? Rates should be 'arms length' as there would be potential tax issues otherwise.
- Conflict resolution – Multilateral netting may be payment driven, receivables driven or both. Either way disagreements will arise as to who owes what to whom so a process for sorting these issues out so that the items may be included in the netting will need to be in place. If not resolved then items may have to be pulled from the netting process.
- Management – will it be a bespoke system or bank managed.

8 Currency forward contracts

A forward contract is an agreement to buy or sell a specific amount of foreign currency at a given future date using an agreed forward rate.

This is the most popular method of hedging exchange rate risk. The company is able to fix in advance an exchange rate at which a transaction will be made.

The risk is taken by the bank who are better able to manage their exposure. A proportion of their exposure will normally be avoided by writing forward contracts for opposite trades on the same day.

Illustration of currency forward contract

It is now 1 January and Y plc will receive USD10 million on 30 April.

It enters into a forward exchange contract to sell this amount on the forward date at a rate of GBP1/USD1.6000. On 30 April the company is guaranteed GBP6.25 million (USD10 million/1.6000).

The transaction risk has been removed (if the receipt arrives on time).

Features and operation

Forward contracts are a commitment, and as a result they have to be honoured even if the rate in the contract is worse than the rate in the market.

Forward contract rates are often quoted at a **premium** or **discount** to the current spot rate.

- A discount means that the currency being quoted (the dollar) is expected to fall in value in relation to the other currency (sterling). If a currency falls in value then you need more of that currency to buy a single unit of the other, i.e. we need more dollars to buy a single pound.
- A discount is often to referred to as 'dis', a premium as 'prem'.
- These can be quoted in cents (i.e. USD0.01) and shown as 'c' in the quote.

In most exam questions you can use the following rule for obtaining a forward rate from the spot rate:

- add a forward discount to the spot rate ('**add:dis**')
- subtract a forward premium from the spot rate.

(**Note:** This rule is only applicable where the exchange rate is quoted as 'amount of foreign currency to a home currency unit'.)

(Also note that discounts and premiums derive from the interest rate parity formula, in theory.)

Remember that you will need to be aware of whether the premium or discount is quoted in, say, dollars or cents. It would usually be cents. There are 100 cents in a dollar. (Similarly there are 100 cents in a euro.) This affects how you add or deduct the discount or premium in terms of decimal places.

For example, if the dollar was currently 1.5000 and there was a premium of 0.5 c (c means cents, and there are 100 cents in a dollar so this is half a cent) this makes the forward rate 1.4950 (1.5000 – 0.0050).

Test your understanding 13 – Forward contract (Integration)

Calculate the forward contract bid and offer prices in the following situation:

(i)	The current spot rate is	GBP1=USD1.5500 – 1.4500
	and, one month forward rate is quoted at	0.55 – 0.50 c dis
(ii)	The current spot rate is	GBP1= EUR1.7150 – 1.6450
	and, one month forward rate is quoted at	0.68 – 0.75 c pm

Test your understanding 14 – EEFS (Integration)

EEFS Ltd (a UK company) sold goods to the value of USD2.0 million. Receipt is due in 90 days.

The current spot rate is GBP1 = USD 1.5430 – 1.5150.

There is a three-month discount forward of 2.5 cents – 1.5 cents.

What is the amount of sterling that EEFS Ltd will receive under the forward contract? Give your answer in GBP to the nearest £100.

Advantages and disadvantages

The advantages of forward contracts are that they:

- Are simple, and so have low transaction costs;
- Can be purchased from a high street bank;
- Fix the exchange rate;
- Are tailored, so are flexible to amount and delivery period.

The disadvantages are that there is:

- A potential credit risk since the company is contractually bound to sell a currency, which it may not have received from its customer;
- No upside potential.

More on disadvantages of forward contracts

There are two key disadvantages of forward contracts:

It is a **contractual commitment** which must be completed on the due date.

This means that if a payment from the overseas customer is late, the company receiving the payment and wishing to convert it using its forward exchange contract will have a problem. The existing forward exchange contract must be settled, although the bank will arrange a new forward exchange contract for the new date when the currency cash flow is due.

To help overcome this problem an **'option date' forward exchange contract** can be arranged. This is a forward exchange contract that allows the company to settle a forward contract at an agreed fixed rate of exchange, but at any time between two specified dates. If the currency cash flow occurs between these two dates, the forward exchange contract can be settled at the agreed fixed rate.

It is **inflexible.** It eliminates the downside risk of an adverse movement in the spot rate, but also prevents any participation in upside potential of any favourable movement in the spot rate. Whatever happens to the actual exchange rate, the forward contract must be honoured, even if it would be beneficial to exchange currencies at the spot rate prevailing at that time.

Test your understanding 15

The spot rate for Swiss francs is GBP1/CHF 1.6734 – 1.6802.

The three month forward premium is 0.0200 – 0.0250.

If you wanted to sell your CHF forward what exchange rate would you receive from the bank?

A 1.6552

B 1.6534

C 1.6934

D 1.7052

Test your understanding 16 – J electronics (Case study)

J manufactures specialised electronic equipment in the UK. The company has just won its first export order and will receive payment of USD 15 million in three months. J's Chief Executive is concerned that the USD may decline against the GBP during the three months and has asked the company's bank to offer a guaranteed price for the currency when it is received.

The bank has offered to enter into a forward contract with J at a rate of GBP1 = USD 1.65.

J's Chief Executive is unhappy with this offer because the present exchange rate is GBP1 = USD 1.60. Given the size of the transaction, this constitutes a major additional cost that J had not budgeted for when setting its selling price. J's Chief Executive would rather wait until the payment is received in the hope that the spot rate at that time is better than the GBP1 = USD 1.65 offered by the bank.

J's Chief Executive is concerned that the differential rate being charged by the bank is unfair. He believes that global economics are so complicated that it is impossible to forecast exchange rate movements and the movements in the exchange rate are just as likely to be favourable as unfavourable to J over the next three months.

J's bank manager has pointed out that the rate offered is in line with market expectations and that it is unrealistic for the Chief Executive to ask the bank to commit itself to guaranteeing that today's exchange rate can be obtained on a transaction that will occur in three months.

The bank manager has recommended that J appoints a full-time corporate treasurer to take on the responsibility of the treasury function and relieve the Chief Executive of that burden.

All of J's directors come from an electronic engineering background and the small administrative staff provides basic clerical and book-keeping support.

Required:

Prepare a note to your finance director evaluating the respective arguments of J's Chief Executive and the bank manager about the rate offered by the bank on the forward contract.

(15 minutes)

9 Money market hedges (MMH)

The money markets are markets for wholesale (large-scale) lending and borrowing, or trading in short-term financial instruments. Many companies are able to borrow or deposit funds through their bank in the money markets.

Instead of hedging a currency exposure with a forward contract, a company could use the money markets to lend or borrow, and achieve a similar result.

Since forward exchange rates are derived from spot rates and money market interest rates (see IRPT earlier in this chapter), the end result from hedging should be roughly the same by either method.

Features and operation

The basic idea of an MMH is to create assets and liabilities that 'mirror' the future assets and liabilities.

Rule: The money required for the transaction is exchanged at today's spot rate, and is then deposited/borrowed on the money market to accrue to the amount required for the transaction in the future.

Note: Interest rates are used for the depositing / borrowing. The rates are usually quoted per annum. If you require a six monthly rate then you simply divide by 2. If you require a quarterly rate, then divide by 4.

Money market interest rates

Money market interest rates are available for any length of borrowing or deposit period, up to about one year. Banks quote rates for standard periods, such as overnight, one week, one month, three months, six months and one year.

Two rates are quoted:

- The **higher** rate is the interest rate that the bank will **charge on loans**.
- The **lower** rate is the interest rate that the bank will **pay on deposits**.

All rates are quoted on an annual basis.

Example

A London bank quotes the following interest rates on US dollars:

	1 month
USD LIBOR	3¼ – 3 ⅛

In the above example, suppose that a company wanted to borrow US dollars for one month. The bank would charge 3¼% per annum.

For the purpose of your examination, you can assume that the rate for one month is one-twelfth of the rate for one year; therefore in this example, the actual interest for one month would be 3¼%/12 = 0.270833%. If the company borrowed, say, US$1 million for one month, it would repay the loan plus interest of USD2,708.33 at the end of the loan period.

Characteristics

- The basic idea is to avoid future exchange rate uncertainty by making the exchange at today's spot rate instead.
- This is achieved by depositing/borrowing the foreign currency until the actual commercial transaction cash flows occur:

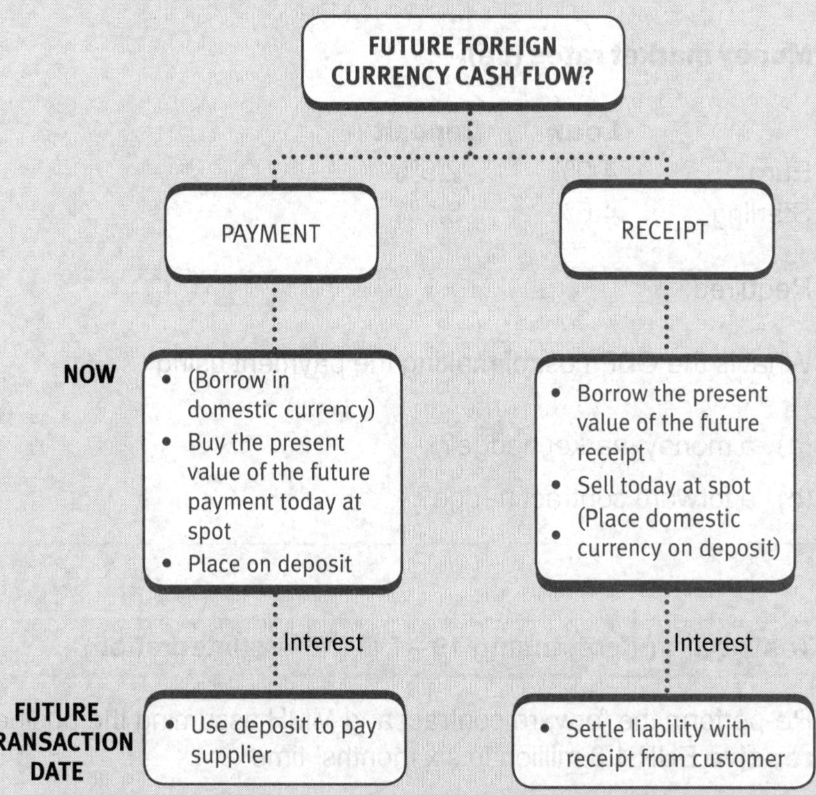

Test your understanding 17

A UK company is due to receive USD12,000 in 6 months time from a customer.

The USD/GBP forward rate is 1.9550 – 1.9600 and the spot rate is 1.9960 – 1.9990.

Interest rates in the US to borrow are 12% and to lend are 11%. In the UK interest rate to borrow are 11% and to lend are 10%.

If the company chooses to use a money market hedge, how much will they receive in GBPs in 6 months time?

Test your understanding 18 – DD Ltd – 1 (Integration)

DD Ltd (a UK company) is required to make a **payment** of EUR1.3 million in six months' time. The company treasurer has established the following rates going forward:

Spot rate	GBP1 = EUR1.5095 – 1.5050
Six month	GBP1 = EUR1.5162 – 1.4895

Money market rates (pa):

	Loan	Deposit
Euro	4.0%	2.5%
Sterling	4.6%	3.1%

Required:

What is the GBP cost of making the payment using

(a) a money market hedge?

(b) a forward contract hedge?

Test your understanding 19 – DD Ltd – 2 (Integration)

Re-perform the forward contract and MMH assuming the business will **receive** EUR 1.3 million in six months' time.

Advantages and disadvantages

The advantages of money market hedges are that they:

- Ensure there is no currency risk because exchange takes place today.
- Have fairly low transaction costs.
- Offer flexibility (especially if customer delays payment).

The disadvantages are that:

- They are complex.
- It may be difficult to get an overseas loan in the case of a foreign currency receipt.

Further comments

- Interest rate parity implies that a money market hedge should give the same result as a forward contract.
- This approach has obvious cash flow implications which may prevent a company from using this method, e.g. if a company has a considerable overdraft it may be impossible for it to borrow funds now.

10 Currency futures

In essence this form of hedging is very similar to the use of a forward contract. The critical difference is that, whereas using a forward contract requires the preparation of a special financial instrument 'tailor-made' for the transaction, currency futures are standardised contracts for fixed amounts of money for a limited range of future dates.

Features and operation

Futures are derivatives contracts and as such can be traded on futures exchanges. The contract which guarantees the price (known as the futures contract) is separated from the transaction itself, allowing the contracts to be easily traded.

Denomination

Futures contracts are limited to a small range of currencies and are typically denominated in terms of dollars (USD). There are also markets in euro (EUR) denominated futures contracts but this is relatively new and much less common.

Given USD denominated currency futures, we would simply know them in terms of the other currency, i.e. the GBP1/USD future will be known as GBP contracts or EUR1/USD futures are known as EUR contracts.

Futures are standardised contracts for standardised amounts. For example, the Chicago Mercantile Exchange (CME) trades sterling futures contracts with a standard size of GBP62,500. Only whole number multiples of this amount can be bought or sold hence they rarely cover the exact foreign currency exposure.

Process

There is a three step process which can be followed to answer a futures question:

Step 1: Set up

Set up the hedge by addressing 3 key questions:

- Do we initially buy or sell futures?

To decide whether to buy or sell futures, the simplest way is to follow this rule: identify the currency of the futures contract (e.g. GBP) and then do the same to the futures that you intend to do to that currency (e.g. buy or sell).

- Which expiry date should be chosen?

Settlement takes place in three-monthly cycles (March, June, September or December). It is normal to choose the first contract to expiry after the required conversion date.

- How many contracts?

Step 2: Contact exchange

Pay the initial margin. Then wait until the transaction/settlement date.

Margin: The futures exchange requires all buyers and sellers of futures to pay a deposit to the exchange when they buy or sell. This deposit is called an initial margin. This margin is returned when the position is closed out.

Step 3: Closing out

At the end of the contract's term the position is *closed out*. This means that on expiry of the contract the trading position is automatically reversed. Any profit or loss is computed and cleared, and the underlying commodity is retained by the trader.

The margin is refunded by the exchange.

The value of the transaction is calculated using the spot rate on the transaction date.

Concept

In essence we are hedging or speculating on the movement of the exchange rate on the futures market.

More on futures contracts

When a futures contact is bought or sold, the buyer or seller must deposit an **initial margin** with the exchange. If losses are incurred, the buyer or seller may be called on to deposit additional funds (**variation margin**) with the exchange. Equally, profits are credited to the margin account on a daily basis as the contract is 'marked to market'.

Most futures contracts are closed out before their settlement dates by undertaking the opposite transaction to the initial futures transaction, i.e. if buying currency futures was the initial transaction, it is closed out by selling currency futures.

Effectively a future works like a bet. If a company expects a USD receipt in 3 month's time, it will lose out if the USD depreciates relative to sterling. Using a futures contract, the company 'bets' that the USD will depreciate. If it does, the win on the bet cancels out the loss on the transaction. If the USD strengthens, the gain on the transaction covers the loss on the bet.

Ultimately futures ensure a virtual no win/no loss position.

Futures calculation illustration

It is 15 October and a treasurer has identified the need to convert euros into dollars to pay a US supplier USD12 million on 20 November. The treasurer has decided to use December euro futures contracts to hedge with the following details:

- Contract size EUR 200,000.
- Prices given in USD per EUR (i.e. EUR1 = …).
- Tick size USD 0.0001 or USD 20 per contract.

He opens a position on 15 October and closes it on 20 November. Spot and relevant futures prices are as follows:

Date	Spot	Futures price
15 October	1.3300	1.3350
20 November	1.3190	1.3240

Calculate the financial position using the hedge described.

Solution

Step 1	(1) Buy or sell initially? (2) Which expiry date? (3) How many contracts?	(1) We need to sell EUR (to buy USD), so sell futures now. (2) Transaction date is 20 November, so choose December futures (the first to expire after the transaction date). (3) Cover USD 12m/1.3350 = EUR 8.99 million, using EUR 200,000 contracts, hence 8.99m/0.2m = 44.9, which we will round to 45 contracts.
Step 2	Contact the exchange – state the hedge	Sell 45 December futures (at a futures price of EUR1/USD 1.3350)
Step 3	Calculate profit/loss in futures market by closing out the position.	Initially: Sell at 1.3350 Close out: Buy at 1.3240 Difference is USD0.011 per EUR1 profit 45 × EUR200,000 covered, so total profit is 0.011 × 45 × 200,000 = USD99,000
Step 3 continued	Transaction at spot rate on 20 November: Need to pay US$12m less profit = USD11.901m, needed at spot rate of EUR1/USD1.3190	Cost in EUR is EUR 9,022,744

Ticks

A tick is the minimum price movement for a futures contract.

Take for example a sterling futures contract for a standard amount of GBP 62,500 in sterling. The contracts are priced at the exchange rate, in US dollars, and the tick size (minimum price movement) is USD0.0001.

If the price of a sterling futures contract changes from, say, USD 1.7105 to USD 1.7120, the price has risen USD 0.0015 or 15 ticks.

The significance of a tick for futures trading is that every one tick movement in price has the same money value.

Take for example a sterling futures contract for a standard amount of GBP 62,500: every movement in the price of the contract by one tick is worth USD6.25, which is GBP 62,500 at USD0.0001 per GBP1.

Basis and basis risk

The current futures price is usually different from the current 'cash market' price of the underlying item. In the case of currency futures, the current market price of a currency future and the current spot rate will be different, and will only start to converge when the final settlement date for the futures contract approaches. This difference is known as the **'basis'**.

At final settlement date for the contract (in March, June, September or December) the futures price and the market price of the underlying item ought to be the same; otherwise speculators would be able to make an instant profit by trading between the futures market and the spot 'cash' market.

Most futures positions are closed out before the contract reaches final settlement. When this happens, there will inevitably be a difference between the futures price at close-out and the current spot market price of the underlying item. In other words, there will still be some basis.

Because basis exists, an estimate can be made when a hedge is created with futures about what the size of the basis will be when the futures position is closed.

Example

In February, a UK company wishes to hedge a currency exposure arising from a US dollar payment that will have to be made in May, in three months' time. The current spot exchange rate is USD1.5670 and the current June futures price is USD1.5530. The basis is therefore 140 points in February.

If it is assumed that the basis will decline from 140 points in February to 0 in June when the contract reaches final settlement (say four months later), we can predict that the basis will fall from 140 in February by 105 points (140 × 3 months/4 months) to 35 points in May, when it is intended to close the futures position.

Basis risk is the risk that when a hedge is constructed, the size of the basis when the futures position is closed out is different from the expectation, when the hedge was created, of what the basis ought to be.

In the example, when the futures position is closed in May, the actual basis might be, say 50 points, which is 15 points higher than expected when the hedge was constructed.

Advantages and disadvantages

The advantages of currency futures contracts are that they:

- Offer an effective 'fixing' of exchange rate;
- Have no transaction costs;
- Are tradable.

The disadvantages are that:

- A foreign futures market must be used for GBP futures;
- They require up front margin payments;
- They are not usually for the precise tailored amounts that are required.

Test your understanding 20

A UK company sells goods to a US company to the value of $2,650,000 in August. It is now June and spot is $1.9800/£. A June futures contract is quoted as $1.9790. A September futures contract is quoted as $1.9000. Sterling futures are traded in contracts of £62,500. The UK company always buys the minimum number of contracts, being prepared to leave un-hedged any small residual amount.

How many contracts should be bought?

Test your understanding 21 – S (Integration/Case study)

S has been studying some of the fundamental economic data relating to both the USA and the Eurozone. She believes that her understanding of economics gives her an advantage over many other market participants. She believes that she has spotted an anomaly in the pricing of futures for the EUR to USD exchange rate.

The contract value is USD 125,000.

The tick size is 0.0001, which gives a tick value of USD 12.50.

The current spot markets value 1 EUR = USD 1.3036.

The rate offered by the futures markets is USD 1.3004 for delivery in three months.

The interest rates offered on deposits are 3.000% per annum on EUR deposits and 2.000% per annum on USD deposits.

S notes that the markets expect the USD to strengthen against the EUR. However, S's own personal analysis of various economic and political indicators suggests that the USD will actually weaken to 1 EUR = USD 1.350. She intends to exploit this different view by entering into a futures contract that will require her to deliver USD in three months.

S has discussed this arrangement with a broker, who has advised her that it will be possible for her to enter into a contract which meets her requirements, but that she will have to make an initial margin payment of 15% of the EUR value of the future. In addition, she may be required to deposit further margin during the life of the contract. The broker will not pay any interest on the margin deposits.

S has personal savings of EUR 100,000 that she can use to invest in this venture. She does not believe that she will ever be asked to provide additional margin and so she intends to use as much of her funds as possible to invest in the initial margin.

Required:

(a) Calculate the gain S will make writing a futures contract, assuming that she invests the maximum possible amount that she can afford in the initial margin and that her expectations turn out to be accurate.

(b) Discuss the risks that S will be taking if she enters into this contract.

(c) Explain why S chose to use a futures contract as the basis for her speculation in the market.

(45 minutes)

11 Currency options

A currency option is a right, but not an obligation, to buy or sell a currency at an exercise price on a future date.

If there is a favourable movement in rates the company will allow the option to **lapse**, to take advantage of the favourable movement. The right will only be **exercised** to protect against an adverse movement, i.e. the worst-case scenario.

Features and operation

As a result of this, options could look great, BUT they have a cost. Because options limit downside risk but allow the holder to benefit from upside risk, the writer of the option will charge a non-refundable **premium** for writing the option.

It is possible for the holder of the option to calculate the gains and losses on using options:

The gain if the option is exercised: this is the difference between the exercise price (option strike price) and the market price of the underlying item	X
Less: The premium paid to purchase the option	(X)
	X

There are two types of option:

- A **call** option gives the holder the right to **buy** the underlying currency.
- A **put** option gives the holder the right to **sell** the underlying currency.

Test your understanding 22 – UK exporter (Integration)

A UK exporter is due to receive USD 25 million in 3 months' time. Its bank offers a 3 month dollar put option on USD 25 million at an exercise price of GBP1/USD1.5000 at a premium cost of GBP 300,000.

Required:

Show the net GBP receipt if the future spot is either USD 1.6000 or USD 1.4000

Illustration of currency options

A typical pricing schedule for the EUR currency option on the Philadelphia (US) exchange is as follows.

Strike price	CALLS			PUTS		
	Jun	Sept	Dec	Jun	Sept	Dec
115.00	1.99	2.25	2.47	0.64	1.32	2.12
116.00	1.39	2.03	2.28	1.00	1.56	–
117.00	0.87	1.55	1.81	1.43	2.22	–
118.00	0.54	1.08	1.30	–	–	–

- Here, the options are for a contract size of EUR 125,000 and prices (both strike price and premia) are quoted in USD (cents) per EUR 1.
- So to buy a call option on EUR 125,000 with an expiry date of September and at a strike price of EUR 1 = USD 1.1700 would cost 1.55 cents per euro, or USD 1,937.50.
- Similarly, the premium on a June put at a strike price of 115.00 (EUR 1 = USD 1.1500) would cost 0.64 cents per euro, or USD 800.

The decision as to which exercise price to choose will depend on cost, risk exposure and expectations.

- In the exam it is unlikely that you will be given such a wide range of values – it is more likely to have just one call and one put option price.

Test your understanding 23 - Option costs and premiums

Pricing schedule for Sterling currency options on the Philadelphia (US) exchange.

The contract size is £31,250, all figures are quoted in USD (cents).

Strike price	CALLS			PUTS		
	Mar	Jun	Sept	Mar	June	Sept
145.00	1.41	2.57	3.62	–	0.42	0.87
146.00	1.21	2.34	3.41	0.15	0.81	1.27

A company wants to buy a call option at a strike price of 1.4600 with an expiry date of March; another company wants to set up a put option with a strike price of 1.4500 expiring in June.

Which of the following is correct?

A The cost of each contract for the call option is $378.125

B The cost of each contract for the call option is £378.125

C The cost of each contract for the call option is $131.25

D The cost of each contract for the call option is £131.25

E The premium for each put option contract is $131.25

F The premium for each put option contract is £131.25

G The premium for each put option contract is £378.125

Options hedging calculations

Step 1: Set up the hedge by addressing 4 key questions:

- Do we need call or put options?
- Which expiry date should be chosen?

- What is the strike price?
- How many contracts?

Step 2: Contact the exchange. Pay the up-front premium. Then wait until the transaction/settlement date.

Step 3: On the transaction date, compare the option price with the prevailing spot rate to determine whether the option should be exercised or allowed to lapse.

Step 4: Calculate the net cash flows – beware that if the number of contracts needed rounding, there will be some exchange at the prevailing spot rate even if the option is exercised.

In- and out-of the money options

The strike price for an option might be higher or lower than the current market price of the underlying item.

For example, a call option might give its holder the right to buy GBP 125,000 in exchange for USD at USD 1.7900, and the current spot rate could be higher than USD 1.7900, below USD 1.7900 or possibly USD 1.7900 exactly.

- If the exercise price for an option is more favourable to the option holder than the current 'spot' market price, the option is said to be **in-the-money**.
- If the exercise price for an option is less favourable to the option holder than the current 'spot' market price, the option is said to be **out-of-the-money**.
- If the exercise price for the option is exactly the same as the current 'spot' market price, it is said to be **at-the-money**.

An option holder is not obliged to exercise the option, and will never do so if the option is out-of-the-money. **An option will only ever be exercised if it is in-the-money**.

However, when an option is first purchased, or during the period before the expiry date, an option might be out-of-the-money.

Options that start out-of-the-money might become in-the-money if the market price of the underlying item changes. On the other hand, an option that starts out-of-the-money might stay out-of-the-money until expiry, and so will lapse without being exercised.

Advantages and disadvantages

The advantages of currency options are that:

- They offer the perfect hedge (downside risk covered, can participate in upside potential).
- There are many choices of strike price, dates, premiums, etc.
- The option can be allowed to lapse if the future transaction does not arise.

The disadvantages are that:

- Traded sterling currency options are only available in foreign markets.
- There are high up-front premium costs (non-refundable).

Test your understanding 24

A company is due to receive USD 3 million in 3 months' time.

The spot rate is USD 1.9500/GBP but the company is worried that the USD will weaken. They have been offered a three month put option on USD at USD 1.9700/GBP, costing USD 0.02 per GBP.

If the company chooses to buy and then exercise the option, what is its net receipt in GBP?

Test your understanding 25

Which of the following are characteristics of an 'over the counter option' as compared to an 'exchange traded option'?

A Can be customised to meet the customer's needs in terms of amount and duration.

B Settlement at maturity.

C Easy to liquidate the position.

D Potential to benefit from favourable exchange rate changes.

The Black-Scholes model

Writers of options have to decide what level of premium to set, and for this they use complex option pricing models. These models are also used to calculate the fair value of an option at any given date (useful for financial reporting purposes).

In the exam you will not be expected to calculate option values, but you are expected to be aware of the factors that affect the option price. The most common option pricing model used is the Black-Scholes model.

The basic principle of the Black-Scholes model is that the market value, or price, of a call option consists of two key elements:

- The intrinsic value of the option.
- The time value of the option.

Between these two elements there are five variables affecting the price of a call option.

Intrinsic value

This is the difference between the current price of the underlying asset and its option strike (exercise) price. For the market value of a call option to rise, one or both of the following variables must change:

(1) Current price of the underlying asset must increase.

(2) Strike price must fall (hence making it more likely that the option will be exercised, and so is worth something).

Time value

This reflects the uncertainty surrounding the intrinsic value, and is impacted by three variables:

(1) Standard deviation in the daily value of the underlying asset. The more variability that is demonstrated, the higher the chance that the option will be 'in the money' and so will be exercised.

(2) Time period to expiry of the option. A longer time period will increase the likelihood that the asset value increases and so the option is exercised.

(3) Risk free interest rates. Having a call option means that the purchase can be deferred, so owning a call option becomes more valuable when interest rates are high, since the money left in the bank will be generating a higher return.

Limitations of the Black-Scholes model

The basic form of the Black-Scholes model has been illustrated above. It is widely used by traders in option markets to give an estimate of option values, and more expensive scientific calculators include the model in their functions so that the calculations can be carried out very quickly.

However, the model in its basic form does suffer from a number of limitations:

- It assumes that the risk-free interest rate is known and is constant throughout the option's life.
- The standard deviation of returns from the underlying security must be accurately estimated and has to be constant throughout the option's life. In practice standard deviation will vary depending on the period over which it is calculated; unfortunately the model is very sensitive to its value.
- It assumes that there are no transaction costs or tax effects involved in buying or selling the option or the underlying item.

Certain of these limitations can be removed by more sophisticated versions of the model, but the basic model is complicated enough for the purposes of this text.

The discussion of the value of options does not just relate to currency options but is relevant to interest rate options and other assets or liabilities.

For example, a company may wish to purchase an option to buy a factory which is under construction. The company might pay a premium to the builder of the factory which entitles them to first option to buy the completed factory (not a commitment to buy). If in the following months the council, say, change the planning guidelines and no further developments can be constructed, then the option becomes very valuable if another company then wishes to build a factory in the same location because it could be sold on (subject to the builder's agreement) at a profit.

Test your understanding 26

Which of the following is not a factor upon which an option value depends:

A The current share price

B The standard deviation of return on underlying share

C The time to expiration of the option

D The number of shares in issue

Test your understanding 27

Which of the following would decrease the intrinsic value of a put option? (Select ALL that apply)

A An increase in the time to expiry

B A decrease in the market value of the share

C A decrease in the volatility value of the share

D A decrease in the strike price

Test your understanding 28

Which of the following will increase the value of a call option? (Select ALL that apply)

A An increase in the strike price

B An increase in the time to expiry

C A decrease in the volatility of the share

D A decrease in the market value of the share

Test your understanding 29 – R antiques (Case study)

R is a company that buys and sells antique furniture and paintings. The company has a buying team that travels extensively, both in its home country and abroad. R specialises in large and rare items that are bought and sold for considerable amounts of money.

R is based in a country whose currency is the T$.

R sold goods to the value of W$ 9.00 million to a collector in the Country W, where the currency is the W$. R will be paid for these goods in three months, immediately before the goods are shipped.

R recently purchased a painting from a wealthy individual in Country W for W$ 8.00 million. It has a buyer for the painting who is anxious to purchase it as soon as possible. The painting is one of the most famous pieces by Country W's most loved painter. The seller auctioned the painting, which had been previously on display in Country W's national gallery, in order to donate the proceeds to charity. The arrangements to obtain the necessary government licences and permits to take the painting from Country W mean that it will take six months to complete this transaction. R will have to pay the W$ 8.00 million that is owed for these goods in six months' time, otherwise the sale will not be completed and the transaction will be cancelled.

R's Chief Executive is concerned that the company is quite heavily exposed to currency transaction risk on these payments because the exchange rate between W$ and T$ can be very volatile. He has asked R's accountant to investigate the possibility of hedging the transactions.

The present exchange rates are as follows:

	Buy W$	Sell W$
Spot	W$ 1 = T$2.200	W$ 1 = TS2.280
Three months forward	W$ 1 = T$2.207	W$ 1 = T$2.287
Six months forward	W$ 1 = T$2.213	W$ 1 = T$2.293

Interest rates on deposits are presently 3.6% per year on W$ and 4.8% per year on T$.

A 3 month W$ put option to sell W$ 9 million at a strike rate of W$ 1 = T$ 2.207 and a premium of T$ 1 million payable immediately.

The premium on a call option to buy W$ 8million at a strike rate of W$ 1 = T$ 2.293 and a premium of T$ 1.10 million, payable immediately.

R's Chief Accountant has identified four possibilities:

- Leave the transactions unhedged. The proceeds of the sale could be converted to T$ and banked on receipt and the payment could be made by buying W$ on the spot market in six months.
- Use options. R could use options to cover both transactions.
- Sell and buy forward. R could sell W$ 9.00 million forward and buy W$ 8.00 million forward, with both transactions timed to coincide with the related receipt and payment.
- Lead the payment. R could pay the vendor in advance, as soon as the W$ 9.00 million is received. The remaining W$ 1.00 million could be converted to T$ on receipt.

Required:

Prepare a briefing note to the Finance Director:

(a) Evaluating, for each of the FOUR possible actions identified by R's Chief Accountant:

(i) The associated risks;

(ii) The cost (as far as it is possible to do so from the information provided).

(30 minutes)

(b) Discussing the risks to R associated with the need to obtain government licences and permits before the painting can be shipped from Country W (your answer should include how those risks can be reduced).

(15 minutes)

Test your understanding 30 – M (Case study/Integration)

M is a manufacturing company. M's home currency is the E$. M made a sale to a customer for goods to the value of E$10 million. The customer's currency is the U$ and the customer insisted on being invoiced in that currency.

The spot rate for exchange is E$4 = U$1. The customer is due to pay U$2.5 million in 30 days.

The exchange rate between these two currencies is volatile, with the daily volatility being 0.8%. There are no forward markets for this combination of currencies, but M has found two counterparties who are willing to enter into option arrangements:

Counterparty 1 is prepared to sell M a put option that will grant M the right to sell U$2.5 million for E$9 million on the expected date of receipt of the customer's payment. The option will cost M E$200,000.

Counterparty 2 is prepared to buy a call option from M that will give counterparty 2 the right to buy U$2.5 million for E $10.5 million. Counterparty 2 will pay M E$160,000 for this option.

Required:

(a) (i) Calculate the 30 day 95% value at risk on the U$ receivable.

(ii) Calculate the probability that either of the two options will be exercised.

(b) Evaluate the implications for M of each of the two option arrangements.

(c) Discuss the factors that M and the counterparties should take into account when negotiating the price of the options.

(45 minutes)

12 Forex swaps

Characteristics

In a forex swap, the parties agree to swap equivalent amounts of currency for a period and then reswap them at the end of the period at an agreed swap rate. The swap rate and amount of currency is agreed between the parties in advance. Thus it is called a 'fixed rate/fixed rate' swap.

The main objectives of a forex swap are:

- To hedge against forex risk, possibly for a longer period than is possible on the forward market.
- To access capital markets, in which it may be impossible to borrow directly.

Forex swaps are especially useful when dealing with countries that have exchange controls and/or volatile exchange rates.

Forex swap

Suppose that A plc, a UK construction company, wins a contract to construct a bridge in Argentina. The bridge will require an initial investment now, and will be sold to the Argentinean Government in one year's time. The Government will pay in pesos.

The problem is the company's exposure to currency risk. They know how much will be received in one year's time in pesos but not in sterling as the exchange rate changes daily.

Various possible hedging strategies:

(1) Decide to do nothing, i.e. accept the risk – win some, lose some.

(2) Lock into a forward contract for converting the amount receivable in one year's time into GBP, if a forward market exists.

(3) Undertake a money market hedge: take out a loan in pesos to cover the initial cost, and repay the loan from the disposal proceeds in a year's time. We would then only be exposed on the profit we make (if we make any).

(4) Enter into a forex swap. Instead of taking out a loan in pesos we:

(a) Swap GBP today for the pesos required to cover the initial investment, at an agreed swap rate.

(b) Take out a loan in GBP today to buy the pesos.

(c) In one year's time (in this example) arrange to swap back the pesos obtained in (a) for pounds at the same swap rate.

(d) Just like taking out a loan in pesos we are therefore only exposed on the profit that we make. We could of course use another hedging technique to hedge the profit element.

Say the bridge will require an initial investment of 100m pesos and is will be sold for 200m pesos in one year's time.

The currency spot rate is 20 pesos/GBP, and the government has offered a forex swap at 20 pesos/GBP. A plc cannot borrow pesos directly and there is no forward market available.

The estimated spot rate in one year is 40 pesos/GBP. The current UK borrowing rate is 10%.

Determine whether A plc should do nothing or hedge its exposure using the forex swap.

Solution

Without swap	0	1
Buy 100m pesos @ 20	(5)	
Sell 200m pesos @ 40		5.0
Interest on sterling loan (5 × 10%)		(0.5)
	(5.0)	**4.5**

With forex swap		
Buy 100m pesos @ 20	(5.0)	
Swap 100m pesos back @ 20		5.0
Sell 100m pesos @ 40		2.5
Interest on sterling loan (5 × 10%)		(0.5)
Net receipt of (£2.0 million)	**(5.0)**	**7.0**

A plc should use a forex swap.

(Key idea: The forex swap is used to hedge foreign exchange risk. We can see that in this basic exercise that the swap amount of 100m pesos is protected from any deprecation, as it is swapped at both the start and end of the year at the swap rate of 20, whilst in the spot market pesos have depreciated from a rate of 20 to 40 pesos per pound.)

A currency swap allows the two counterparties to swap interest rate commitments on borrowings in different currencies.

In effect a currency swap has two elements:

- An exchange of principal in different currencies, which are swapped back at the original spot rate – just like a forex swap.
- An exchange of interest rates – the timing of these depends on the i ndividual contract.

The swap of interest rates could be 'fixed for fixed' or 'fixed for variable'.

Currency swap

Warne Co is an Australian firm looking to expand in Germany and is thus looking to raise EUR 24 million. It can borrow at the following fixed rates:

A$ 7.0%

EUR 5.6%

Euroports Inc is a French company looking to acquire an Australian firm and is looking to borrow A$40 million. It can borrow at the following rates:

A$ 7.2%

EUR 5.5%

The current spot rate is A$1 = EUR0.6.

Required:

Show how a 'fixed for fixed' currency swap would work in the circumstances described, assuming the swap is only for one year and that interest is paid at the end of the year concerned.

Solution

Timing	**Warne Co**	**Euroports Inc**
Now – Borrow from bank	A$40m @ 7.0%	EUR 24m @ 5.5%
Exchange principals	Pay A$40m to Euroports	Pay €24m to Warne
	Receive EUR 24m	Receive A$40m
End of year – Pay interest to banks	Pay A$2.8m interest	Pay EUR 1.32m interest
	Pay EUR1.32m to Euroports	Receive EUR 1.32m
Exchange interest	Receive A$2.8m	Pay A$2.8m to Warne
Swap principals back	Pay EUR 24m to Warne	Pay A$40m to Euroports
	Receive A$40m	Receive EUR 24m
Interest costs:		
Without swap (24 × 5.6%) (40 × 7.2%)	EUR 1.344m	A$2.88m
	EUR 1.320m	A$2.80m
With swap	EUR 24,000	A$80,000
Saving		

Test your understanding 31

SW plc is a UK company looking to expand in to the USA. It wants to raise USD 20 million at a variable interest rate. It has been quoted the following:

USD LIBOR + 60 points

GBP 1.2%

AP Inc is an American company looking to refinance an existing loan of GBP 18 million at a fixed rate. It can borrow at the following rates:

USD LIBOR + 50 points

GBP 1.5%

The current spot rate is USD 1 = GBP 0.90.

Required:

Calculate the saving made by both companies if they enter into the currency swap.

Test your understanding 32

Which of the following is an external hedging technique? (Select all that apply.)

A A forward contract

B A money market hedge

C Pooling

D A futures contract

Test your understanding 33

A UK company has sold goods to a Danish company and will receive 300,000 Danish Kroner in 3 months time. Which of the following would hedge its position?

A Selling a call option on Danish Kroner

B Buying a put option on Danish Kroner

C Using the forward market to buy Kroner at the 3 month forward rate

D Buying Danish Kroner futures

Test your understanding 34 – Q (Case study/Integration)

Background

Q is a Sri Lankan company that manufactures machine parts. Q plans to establish a wholly-owned French subsidiary that will manufacture its range of products in France for distribution across the European Union (EU). Q has been established for many years, but it is not widely known outside of Sri Lanka despite the fact that its product range has a very good reputation.

Q's Finance Director visited Paris recently in order to discuss the financing arrangements for the subsidiary with a number of French banks. Q could easily borrow the funds at an attractive rate in Sri Lankan Rupees (LKR), but Q's board would prefer to borrow in Euros (EUR). Unfortunately, the French banks felt that they would be taking a risk if they were to back a foreign borrower who was unknown to them and so they either refused Q's loan application or they offered to lend at a high rate of interest.

Trigger

On the flight home the Finance Director entered into a conversation with P, the passenger in the next seat. P is the founder of a French design company that wishes to build a factory in Sri Lanka. All of Sri Lanka's banks have refused to lend to P. One French bank has agreed to make the loan, but at a high rate of interest. P would prefer to raise the finance in LKR and has decided to travel to Sri Lanka in the hope that a face to face meeting with the bank lending officers will be more successful than a negotiation by telephone and email.

When Q's Finance Director and P realised that they had complementary requirements they started to discuss the possibility of a currency swap that might be mutually beneficial.

They each require to borrow the equivalent of €20 million for six years to establish their respective businesses.

The current spot rate is LKR 155.0 to the EUR.

Q can borrow in LKR at an annual rate of 9% for six years or in EUR at an annual rate of 12%.

A French accountant has told Q that a similar French business would be able to borrow €20 million for six years at 6%.

P can borrow in EUR at a rate of 10% for six years.

All of the proposed loans would be repayable in one lump sum at the end of the borrowing period.

P proposes borrowing EUR 20 million from a French bank at 10%. Q would borrow LKR 3,100 million at 9% from the Sri Lankan bank. The two companies would swap these principal sums and would each pay the interest on the other's borrowings. P is confident that both parties will generate sufficient surpluses from their new foreign operations to raise the necessary currency to meet the interest payments and to accumulate sufficient funds to swap the principal sums back at the end of six years.

Task

(a) In a briefing note to the Board, explain THREE reasons why Q would wish to borrow in EUR in order to finance the proposed French subsidiary.

(b) Calculate an estimated LKR to EUR exchange rate at the date of repayment in six years. Note: Your answer should include an explanation of your method.

(20 minutes)

Test your understanding 35 – Marcus (Integration)

Marcus, based in France, has recently imported raw materials from the USA and has been invoiced for USD 240,000, payable in three months' time.

In addition, it has also exported finished goods to Japan and Australia.

The Japanese customer has been invoiced for USD 69,000, payable in three months' time, and the Australian customer has been invoiced for AUD 295,000, payable in four months' time.

Current spot and forward rates are as follows:

EUR1/USD

Spot:	0.9850 – 0.9830
Three months' forward:	0.9545 – 0.9520

AUD1/EUR

Spot:	1.8920 – 1.8890
Four months' forward:	1.9540 – 1.9510

Current money market rates (per annum) are as follows:

USD:	10.0% – 12.0%
AUD:	14.0% – 16.0%
EUR:	11.5% – 13.0%

Required:

Show how the company can hedge its exposure to FX risk using:

(i) the forward markets;

(ii) the money markets;

and in each case, determine which is the best hedging technique.

Test your understanding 36 – UK company (Integration)

A UK company will receive USD 2.5 million from an American customer in three months' time in February.

Currently:

Futures:	GBP contracts (GBP62,500)	December	GBP1/USD 1.5830
		March	GBP1/USD 1.5796

Margins are USD1,000 per contract.

GBP1/USD forward rates:	Spot	1.5851 – 1.5842
	One month	0.53 – 0.56 c pm
	Three month	1.64 – 1.72 c pm

28 February:

Assume that the spot rate moves to 1.6510 – 1.6490

March futures have a price of 1.6513

Required:

Calculate the GBP receipt using a forward contract and a future.

13 Chapter Summary

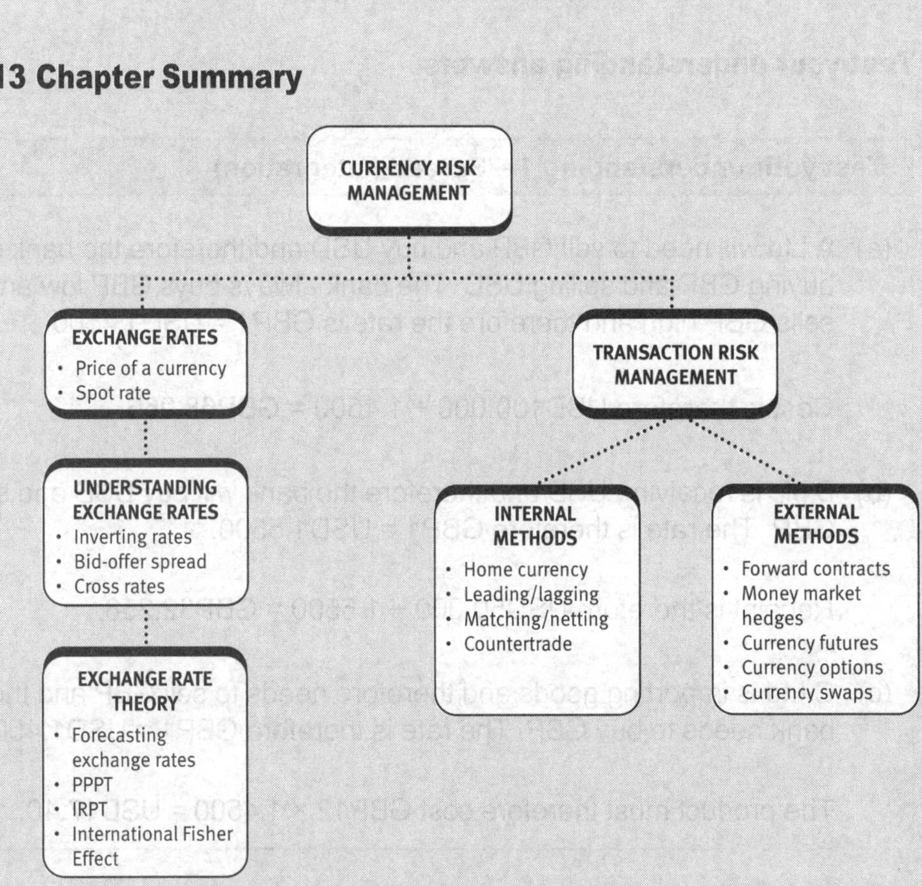

Test your understanding answers

Test your understanding 1 – Spread (Integration)

(a) A Ltd will need to sell GBP and buy USD and therefore the bank is buying GBP and selling USD. The bank always buys GBP low and sells GBP high and therefore the rate is GBP1 = USD1.4500.

Cost is therefore USD100,000 ÷ 1.4500 = GBP68,966.

(b) B plc is receiving USD and therefore the bank will buy USD and sell GBP. The rate is therefore GBP1 = USD1.5500.

Receipt is therefore USD50,000 ÷ 1.5500 = GBP32,258.

(c) C Ltd is importing goods and therefore needs to sell GBP and the bank needs to buy GBP. The rate is therefore GBP1 = USD1.4500.

The product must therefore cost GBP12 × 1.4500 = USD17.40.

Test your understanding 2

The implied cross rate is USD/GBP divided by EUR/GBP = 1.4417/1.1250 = 1.2815

Test your understanding 3 – Cross rates (Integration)

The USD1/EUR cross rate will be calculated as:

1.5300/1.8700 = 0.8182 i.e. USD1/EUR0.8182.

The cost of the machine is therefore:

EUR100,000/0.8182 = USD122,220

Test your understanding 4

$$1.7200 \times \frac{1.03}{1.04} = \text{USD}1.7035$$

Test your understanding 5

$$10 \times \frac{1.03}{1.07} = \textbf{CHF9.6262}$$

Test your understanding 6

The correct answer is C –

$(1 + r_{€})/(1 + r_{\$}) \times Spot_{€/\$} = Forward_{€/\$}$

$(1 + 0.05)/(1 + 0.08) \times 0.92 = 0.8944$

Test your understanding 7 – Parity relationships (Integration)

PPPT

$$\text{Future spot rate} = 0.9050 \times \frac{1 + 0.013}{1 + 0.02}$$

$$= \text{EUR } 0.8988$$

IRPT

$$\text{Forward rate} = 0.9050 \times \frac{1 + 0.045}{1 + 0.06}$$

$$= \text{EUR } 0.8922$$

The rates are similar, but not identical under the two different forecasting methods.

Using the Fisher Effect, the real rate of interest can be found in both US and Eurozone.

US:

(1 + m)	= (1 + r) (1 + i)
(1+ 0.06)	= (1 + r) (1 + 0.02)
Hence r	= 3.9%

Eurozone:

(1 + m) = (1 + r) (1 + i)
(1+ 0.045) = (1 + r) (1 + 0.013)
Hence r = 3.2%

For the PPPT and the IRPT to give identical predicted rates, the International Fisher Effect must hold, which states that real rates of interest are identical in all countries. This is apparently not the case.

Other factors that may affect the prediction of exchange rates include:

- Transaction costs of shifting money and making investments.
- Lack of mobility of capital and goods, and the costs associated with this.
- Political intervention.
- Cultural differences between different countries.
- Central bank action.
- Trader activity.
- Key commodity prices (e.g. oil is priced in US dollars).

Test your understanding 8 – L (Integration/Case study)

(a)

(i) The forecast hourly rate is assumed to grow in line with the rate of inflation in the proposed host country. We assume that the inflation rate will remain constant for five years.

Over five years, the inflation rate will compound by (1.047)5 = 25.8%. The forecast hourly rate is 2.75 RTD + 25.8% = 3.46 RTD.

We assume that the exchange rates will move in line with the differences in the interest rates. We assume that those rates will remain constant.

Over five years the rates will change as follows (1.09/1.05)5 = 1.21.

The exchange rate will be 1 BND = 2.50 × 1.21 = 3.025 RTD.

The hourly rate in BND = 3.46/3.025 = 1.14 BND.

(ii) The first assumption is that wages will move in line with inflation in the host country. Given that prices are rising it seems likely that L will have to pay more for wages. The actual rises that will be granted will vary in accordance with the bargaining power of the employees and so it is unlikely that the actual rises will closely match the rate of inflation.

Given that L is a multinational operating in a developing country, it may have to pay rises that exceed the rate of inflation in order to avoid claims of exploitation.

Interest rate parity suggests that the expected exchange rates will move very closely in line with the differential interest rates. That does not mean that the actual rates will turn out in accordance with expectations. The governments of either country may decide to manage their interest rates in order to strengthen or weaken their exchange rates.

(b) It could be argued that a kilo of fibre will cost a specific number of USD regardless of whether it is imported to the home country or the host. Basic costing suggests that the value is irrelevant, particularly when transportation does not affect pricing.

Unfortunately, things are more complicated because L will be importing finished paper, which contains flax fibre, rather than flax fibre itself. Transfer pricing arrangements will mean that the paper will have to be sold to L's trading subsidiary in the home country at the open market price for paper. Changes in the price of the underlying raw materials may not directly affect the market price in a linear manner and so the price of flax fibre could change the taxable profits in the two countries.

(c) The most immediate problem is that L will make its present employees redundant. That will undermine the company's reputation. Customers may buy their paper from other suppliers rather than be associated with L. The home government may also be concerned that L has exported jobs and may take sanctions against the company. It could, for example, grant contracts to other companies.

L will also come under suspicion for operating in a developing country. Activists in the home country may feel that L is exploiting badly paid workers in the developing country.

Even if such accusations are unfounded L may suffer responses ranging from negative press comment to demonstrations at its remaining locations.

Test your understanding 9 – G clothing (Case study)

Briefing note

To: The Board of G

From: Management accountant

Date: Today

Subject: Currency risk management

Dear Sirs,

Introduction

This briefing note covers three issues:

(a) The argument that purchasing power parity theory should prevent exporters from charging different prices in different countries.

(b) The potential risks and benefits to G of buying its inventory from intermediaries in the neighbouring countries.

(c) Recommends actions that the Government in G's home country could take in order to determine whether G's competitor had been evading the tariff on imported clothing.

(a) **Purchasing power parity theory (PPP)**

Purchasing power parity theory (PPP) suggests that a commodity will sell for the same amount across the world, regardless of the currency in which it is priced. That is because of arbitrage. It is illogical that customers will buy goods in their home country if they can buy them elsewhere and import them more cheaply.

There is considerable evidence that PPP does not hold in reality. There are some fairly obvious reasons for that. With very few exceptions, it is unlikely to be convenient to buy goods from across an international border. Travel and transportation costs will frequently exceed any savings.

There can be artificial factors, such as tariffs and differential pricing practices by suppliers.

(b) **The potential risks and benefits to G of buying its inventory from intermediaries in the neighbouring countries**

The only benefit is the obvious one that G will possibly be able to reduce its costs. Those savings will make it easier to compete with other retailers who are using the same sources.

The fact that this behaviour is illegal in G's home country means that the company may be open to prosecution. The staff who are responsible for making the arrangements may also be held personally responsible, which will harm G's reputation if any of them are prosecuted. Staff may refuse to act illegally, which could undermine discipline in G and could lead to problems in processing partially completed transactions.

G's contract will be with foreign intermediaries, who may offer a lower standard of service than the manufacturer. Any disputes over quality or delivery may lead to G being unable to obtain an adequate resolution. The intermediaries may not offer the full range of new designs and may not be able to meet all of G's requirements for volume.

The manufacturers may be unwilling to encourage G to buy from intermediaries because they will lose the benefits of differential pricing in the two markets. They may report G to the authorities or take G to court to prevent it from stocking or selling these "grey imports". The manufacturers may then refuse to sell goods to G in the future in order to deter other retailers from copying this practice.

(c) **Actions that the Government in G's home country could take**

The government can inspect the retailer's books to determine where it obtains its goods. Given that most of the fashion clothes appear to be imported, there ought to have been duty paid on virtually all of the retailer's purchases. The total duty paid should be roughly equivalent to the total purchases multiplied by the rate of duty.

The retailer is unlikely to record all transactions accurately in its bookkeeping records if it is defrauding the revenue authorities. The government should check that the purchase records are accurate by going back to basic records, such as sales recorded by individual shops. There should be a realistic relationship between the level of sales and the level of purchases. If the gross profit percentage is very high then that would suggest that purchases are being understated.

The customs authorities should conduct spot checks of vehicles crossing into the country as a matter of routine anyway. Customs officers should be instructed to look out for goods despatched to the competitor by anyone other than the original manufacturer. Any such goods should be seized and the relevant paperwork investigated to determine whether duty has been paid.

The revenue authorities can conduct spot inspections of goods being delivered to the competitor's premises. Again, the origin of the goods should be investigated for unpaid duty. The authorities can always levy an estimated charge on the competitor and force the competitor to prove that such a payment is not appropriate.

Test your understanding 10

GBP66,700

The speculator should

(1) Convert GBP into USD: 1,000,000 × 2 = USD2,000,000

(2) Convert USD into EUR: 2,000,000/1.50 = EUR1,333,333

(3) Now sell the EUR: 1,333,333 × 0.80 = GBP1,066,667

The speculator has made a risk-free profit of GBP66,667.

Test your understanding 11 – U company (Integration/Case study)

(a) Principle of borrowing, depositing and selling resulting balance forward

- Borrow GBP £10m
- Convert to USD at spot rate = GBP10m x 1.556 = USD 15.560m
- Deposit at 5.12% for three months. Interest = USD 15.560m × 5.12% × 3/12 = USD 0.1992m
- Total deposit by end of three months = USD 15.560m + 0.1992 = USD 15.7592m
- Sell USD forward = USD 15.7592m/1.499 = GBP 10.5131m
- Interest on GBP borrowings = GBP 10m × 5.08% × 3/12 = GBP 0.127m

– Total repayment = GBP 10.1270m

– Gain = GBP 10.5130 – 10.1271 = GBP 0.3861m

(i) U has clearly identified the possibility of an arbitrage profit that could be exploited without risk to the company. Interest rate parity suggests that if the USD is expected to strengthen against GBP then the interest rate offered for USD deposits should be lower than the rates on GBP. The fact that it wasn't made it possible to borrow in GBP, deposit in USD, sell the resulting USD forward, all in the knowledge that the resulting GBP balance would be more than enough to settle the GBP loan.

Any business opportunity that offers a positive return in absolute terms from zero investment with zero risk must be highly desirable. U has found such an opportunity through good luck. Simple economics suggest that markets will not offer positive returns to participants who do not invest anything and who do not take any risk and so such opportunities will either require great skill to identify or considerable good luck.

(ii) In practice, arbitrageurs draw attention to anomalies by moving funds to exploit them and the inconsistencies are quickly corrected to make further profits impossible. That explains why U's treasurer did not ask U to act on her discovery. Professional arbitrage companies use electronic trading to seek out these opportunities and exploit them. U discovered the opportunity by chance, but it is unlikely that she would have been able to put the various trades in place quickly enough to beat the professionals.

The very nature of arbitrage means that the trades themselves are risk free, but there are considerable costs associated with arbitrage operations. Arbitrageurs must pay a great deal for real-time market data, which is a substantial fixed cost. There is also substantial investment in the IT systems and other facilities. It is entirely possible that there will be too few opportunities offered by the market to generate an adequate return to cover those costs and provide a realistic return on investment.

The anomalies that arise tend to be far smaller than those discovered by U. Arbitrage requires very large transactions to generate sufficient profit in absolute terms to make the process worthwhile. Participants must be sufficiently liquid to meet margin requirements and to have the confidence of the institutions who have to accept the bids being made.

The financial institutions which create the markets have an incentive to avoid creating arbitrage opportunities and they are clearly going to use sophisticated systems of their own to avoid doing so. There will also be competition from other arbitrageurs, all of whom will be attempting to move more quickly than anybody else so that they enjoy all of the profit.

(c) Generally, the treasury department provides a service to the entity, by managing cash flows and dealing with banks and other sources of finance. The treasury aims to reduce the costs borne by the entity and the intention is that these savings will more than offset the cost of running the department.

The treasury can only become a profit centre if it develops a revenue stream. Normally that involves speculating in the financial markets in order to generate gains. There are two competing arguments relating to speculation:

One is that the treasury department has considerable expertise. Speculation is a zero sum game that involves being able to out-think the market and buy or sell mispriced financial instruments. The treasury department could use its natural advantage over other market participants, who have a lesser understanding and inferior data to trade at a profit.

The counter-argument is that active trading in the markets involves leaving positions exposed to loss and so there is a risk. Losses can arise when trades are unsuccessful. The entity would be bidding against counterparties who may be even more skilled and better informed.

It is generally difficult to make a consistent profit from speculation. Markets are generally efficient and most participants – even trained corporate treasurers – should accept that the market prices are correct. Active trading will increase costs and also increase risks for the entity.

Test your understanding 12 – J electronics (Case study)

Briefing note

To: The Board

From: A.N. Accountant

Date: Today

Subject: Appointment of a corporate treasurer

Dear Sirs,

(a) A corporate treasurer could strengthen J's management team. At present, there is nobody with any particular expertise in accountancy or finance in the company. The fact that J has secured an order of this magnitude suggests that the company is of a size where it requires more attention to be paid to financial management. The fact that the order was for export suggests that there is a need for support in this area, particularly given that the chief executive's discussion with the bank indicates a lack of understanding.

It could be argued that it would make more sense to appoint a qualified accountant to manage all aspects of the accounting function, including treasury matters. A qualified treasurer is trained in greater depth to manage the relationship with the bank and to manage receipts and payments. A professionally qualified accountant holding, say, the CIMA qualification should have sufficient skill in treasury matters to deal with the treasury needs of a medium-sized and growing company and should be able to contribute to other areas such as the development of management accounting and financial reporting.

There is a danger that the company's needs would not justify such an appointment and that the costs would outweigh the benefits. There is a danger that appointing an accountant or treasurer will prove a distraction from the basic business of manufacturing and selling electronics if the appointee feels it necessary to table reports and ask the board to fine-tune financial decisions.

It may be that J would be better advised to take on a part-time accountant rather than a full-time treasurer. That would strike a balance between the conflicting arguments for and against an appointment.

(b) The first step is to define the role clearly so that J can decide on the skills and experience that the treasurer will require.

It would be worth appointing a recruitment agency to assist with identifying suitable candidates. J's board has no experience to draw upon in identifying experts in this area and so it would make more sense for the company to ask a specialist agency to produce a shortlist.

The final interview should be conducted by J's directors. Even if the recruitment agency has shortlisted a suitable candidate it is important that the board is satisfied that it can work with this individual.

J should insist on seeing a detailed CV and checking up on all references. The board will not really be in a position to provide detailed oversight of this individual, which makes competence an issue, and the appointee will be in a significant position of trust with respect to J's bank balances, which makes honesty important too.

Test your understanding 13 – Forward contract (Integration)

(i) **Add** a **discount** to get the forward rate.

Spot rate	1.5500	–	1.4500
Add discount	0.0055		0.0050
Forward rate	1.5555	–	1.4550

(ii) **Subtract** a **premium** to get the forward rate.

Spot rate	1.7150	–	1.6450
Subtract premium	(0.0068)		(0.0075)
Forward rate	1.7082	–	1.6375

Test your understanding 14 – EEFS (Integration)

GBP 1,275,500 (rounded)

EEFS Ltd is expecting a receipt of USD, and therefore wishes to buy GBP from the bank. The bank will sell GBP high and therefore the rate is 1.5430 (current spot). The discount of 2.5c must be added to the rate thus giving a rate of 1.5680.

The sterling receipt is therefore USD2m ÷ 1.5680 GBP 1,275,510

Test your understanding 15

The correct answer is A

A bank buys high and sells low so the appropriate spot rate is 1.6802.

A premium should be deducted. 1.6802 – 0.0250 = 1.6552

Test your understanding 16 – J electronics (Case study)

Note

To: Finance Director

From: A.N. Accountant

Date: Today

Subject: Forward contract offer rate

Dear Finance Director,

The Chief Executive is correct in stating that changes in the exchange rate cannot be predicted with any certainty, but that does not mean that today's rate is the best forecast of the rate that will prevail in three months' time. The capital markets use differences in interest rates to establish the anticipated rate between two currencies, which suggests that there will be an observable difference in the interest rates available on GBP versus USD which will explain the forward rate on offer. The interest rate on USD is, presumably, higher at present, which implies that the USD is expected to weaken against GBP and so it is perfectly realistic for the bank to offer an inferior rate for three months compared to spot.

The bank manager's argument seems to take the question of the differential rates for granted. The fact that the offer is consistent with market sentiments suggests that there is a rational basis to expect the USD to decline. If the market rate was unrealistic then there would be arbitrage opportunities that would enable market participants to exploit the market's pricing error and that market error would be corrected very quickly.

The Chief Executive's argument that J should leave this position unhedged suggests that it is illogical to pay a premium in return for a reduction in risk. There is clearly a possibility that J will enjoy an upside if the position if left unhedged and the USD weakens by less than the amount anticipated by the bank's forward rate. The question is whether the associated possibility of a loss outweighs the potential gain.

The fact that J has not taken the possibility of changing exchange rates into account in pricing this sale is irrelevant. J is going to receive USD 15m regardless of the fact that a higher price should have been charged to reflect anticipated changes in the exchange rate.

Test your understanding 17

The company should borrow from the bank just enough to end up owing exactly USD12,000

- Amount borrowed = USD12,000/1.06 = USD 11,321.

They should convert this into GBP at spot

- Converted amount = 11,321/1.9990 = GBP 5,663.

They should then invest this for 6 months in the UK

- End up with 5,663 × 1.05 = GBP 5,946 (fixed, certain sum)

Test your understanding 18 – DD Ltd – 1 (Integration)

DD Ltd

(a) The money market hedge to pay EUR in six months' time requires DD Ltd to borrow in GBP, translate to EUR and deposit in EUR.

A payment of EUR1.3 million in six months (only 1.25% interest) will require a EUR deposit now of (EUR1,300,000 ÷ 1.0125) EUR1,283,951. This means that with a spot rate of 1.5050 the GBP loan will need to be GBP853,124.

The loan of GBP853,124 will increase over the six months to the date of repayment by 2.3% and will therefore be GBP872,746.

The cost is therefore GBP872,746.

(b) The forward contract will use the six-month forward rate of 1.4895 for buying EUR.

The cost is therefore (EUR1,300,000 ÷ 1.4895) GBP872,776

There is virtually no difference between the two methods. This is expected because any significant difference would mean that profit could be made simply by converting one currency into another.

Test your understanding 19 – DD Ltd – 2 (Integration)

Under an MMH the company would borrow EUR now, translate into GBP and deposit for six months.

The borrowing would be EUR1,300,000 ÷ 1.02	EUR 1,274,510
This would translate now into 1,274,510 ÷ 1.5095	GBP 844,326
By growth for interest for six months this becomes	GBP 857,413

Forward contract

The forward contract would give:

EUR 1,300,000 ÷ 1.5162	GBP 857,407

Test your understanding 20

22

$2,650,000/(1.9000 × £62,500) = 22.32 contracts rounded down to 22.

Test your understanding 21 – S (Integration/Case study)

(a) The margin requirement means that S can write forwards worth a maximum of EUR 100,000/15% = EUR 666,667.

The USD value = 666,667 × 1.3004 = USD 866,934.

S can write 866,934/125,000 = 6 contracts = USD 750,000.

S will have to pay a margin of USD 750,000/1.3004 × 15% = EUR 86,512.

If she deposited that sum for three months she would earn interest of EUR 86,512 × 3% /4 = EUR 649.

If her predictions prove accurate, the cost of closing out her position will be 750,000/1.350 = EUR 55 5,556 for the USD 750,000.

The counterparty's cost will be 750,000/1.3004 = EUR 576,746.

The overall position will be settled by a net payment of EUR 576,746 – 555,556 – 649 = EUR 20,541in favour of S.

(b) The most obvious risk is the upside risk that she will earn a significant return from her ability to identify an anomaly in the market. If she is confident then she must compare the possibility of a capital gain of EUR 576,746 – 555,556 = EUR 21,190 against the opportunity cost of interest foregone of EUR 649. This seems like a relatively small risk, provided S has not overstated the probability of success.

The downside risk is that the gain will not materialise and she will have tied up her finances needlessly. The market's expectation is that the spot rate will match the rate implied by her future contract. The currency markets for the USD and the EUR are both highly visible and are the subject of intense scrutiny. It would possibly be easier to develop better insights into smaller economies that do not attract the same degree of study. The financial loss is very limited in this case..

It is possible that the USD will strengthen further than the market's expectations, in which case she will be faced with the prospect of a loss when she closes out her position. For example, if the USD strengthens to 1.2 then closing out her position will cost a net EUR 576,746 – (750,000/1.2) = EUR 48,254. In theory, this speculative loss could be substantial. In practice, it is to be hoped that there will not be a massive movement of the EUR against the USD.

There could be a problem if the exchange rates move against her because S may be required to deposit additional margin. The fact that she could only write a whole contract would mean that she will have some of her EUR 100,000 left to meet such a contingency, but her position may be abandoned if she cannot keep up with margin requests.

The fact that the exchange requires margin deposits will indemnify S against any default by the counterparty.

(c) It would probably be difficult for S to exploit her expectations in any other way. She appears to be based in the eurozone. She could borrow USD in order to finance a EUR deposit, which would yield a profit when the USD loan was repaid using weakened currency. Doing so would almost certainly involve fairly disproportionate transaction costs.

Borrowing and investing directly would also limit her ability to profit from her insight. Using a derivative such as a future makes it possible to gear up her position. If she borrowed, say, EUR 100,000 worth of USD (to match her savings) then she would benefit from a position worth that amount. She can create a position with an exposure of USD 750,000 by investing only EUR 86,512 in margin.

Futures contracts make it possible for S to speculate via a regulated market, where the exchange will protect parties' interests. That would also make it relatively easy to close out her position in the event that she started to feel uneasy about the prospects of success.

Realistically, the downside is limited to the extent to which the USD could strengthen. If she invested in some other instruments, such as options, she could lose everything if the option expired out of the money

Test your understanding 22 – UK exporter (Integration)

Dividing by the smallest GBP1/USD rate gives the highest GBP receipt – the premium is paid no matter what so it should be ignored for the purposes of determining whether to exercise the option.

Future spot USD 1.6000

- Exercise the option.
- USD 25m/USD1.5000 = GBP 16.67m less GBP300,000 premium gives a net receipt of GBP 16.37m

Future spot USD 1.4000

- Abandon the option.
- USD 25m/USD 1.4000 = GBP 17.86m less GBP 300,000 premium gives a net receipt of GBP 17.56m

Test your understanding 23 - Option costs and premiums

Call:
£31,250 × $0.0121 = $378.125
Put:
£31,250 × $0.0042 = $131.25
Option 1 and 5 are correct.

Test your understanding 24

The GBP received upon exercise will be 3,000,000/1.9700 = GBP 1,522,843.

The cost of the option will be 0.02 × 1,522,843 = USD 30,457.

At spot this cost in GBP is 30,457/1.9500 = GBP 15,619.

Therefore the net receipt will be 1,522,843 – 15,619 = GBP 1,507,224

Test your understanding 25

The correct answers are A, B and D – Exchange traded options are easier to liquidate as there is an active, liquid secondary market.

Test your understanding 26

The correct answer is D – A, B and C are stated as factors affecting option prices in the Black – Scholes model.

Test your understanding 27

D

A and B would increase the value of the option.

C would decrease the value of the option – but would not affect its intrinsic value (difference between the MV and the strike price)

Test your understanding 28

B

All the others would reduce the value

Test your understanding 29 – R antiques (Case study)

Briefing note

To: The Finance Director

From: A.N. Accountant

Date: Today

Subject: Currency risk management

This briefing note evaluates, for each of the FOUR possible actions identified by R's Chief Accountant:

- The associated risks;
- The cost (as far as it is possible to do so from the information provided); and

It also discusses the risks to R associated with the need to obtain government licences and permits before the painting can be shipped from Country W

Evaluation of each of the FOUR possible actions identified by R's Chief Accountant

(1) **Leave the transactions unhedged**

Risks

There is a degree of natural hedging built into this approach. R's net exposure to gains and losses is on the W$1m difference between the receivable and payable for the first three months. Thereafter, R will be exposed to movements on the W$8m payable. Interest rates on W$ are lower and so the markets expect the T$ to weaken, which could mean that there will be a loss on the settlement of the payable.

Costs

There is no direct cost associated with leaving the separate balances unhedged.

(2) **Use options**

Risks

The options will leave R with no downside risk on either position, but there is an upside arising from the possibility that there is no need to exercise the options in the event that rates move in R's favour. The exercise prices are set at the expected rates according to the rates on forwards and so there is an expectation that R will have little or no incentive to exercise the options. The premiums are, however, quite significant and so it seems that the options' writers are seeking quite a significant amount of compensation for accepting this risk, which implies that there is a significant expectation that the rates will be volatile over the three and six month periods.

Costs

There will be a premium on each of the options, which will cost R a total of S$1.00m + 1.1m = S$2.1m. That sum is payable immediately, and so R will have to fund those payments for the lives of the options.

(3) **Sell and buy forward**

Risks

The forward contracts will virtually eliminate the transaction risks on the currencies. There could be a counterparty risk arising from the possibility that the counterparty to the transaction will default. These contracts also mean that R is committed to the purchase or sale of W$, which may be a problem if the underlying transactions fall through or are postponed for some reason.

Costs

Provided the transactions are completed on time, there will be no specific cost. It is possible that the counterparty will require some form of security or margin payment and that could involve some cost to finance that arrangement.

(4) **Lead the payment**

Risks

The only exposure to currency risk arises from the net amount of W$1m outstanding for the first three months. There will be no currency balance left outstanding thereafter. There is, however, the risk that R will have no means to force the auction house to hand over the painting because the funds will already have been paid.

Cost

Either of the following is acceptable.

R will suffer an opportunity cost because it will be paying W$8m three months early. The interest foregone = W$8m × 3.6% × 3/12 = W$72,000. For the sake of consistency, that payment will have a net present value of W$72,000/(1 + (0.036 × 6/12)) = W$70,727 or T$156,519

Or

R will suffer an opportunity cost because it will be paying W$8m three months early. The interest foregone = W$8m × 3.6% × 3/12 = W$72,000. For the sake of consistency, that payment will have a net present value of W$72,000/(1 + (0.036 × 3/12)) = W$71,356 or T$156,987

(b) **Obtaining government licences and permits**

Many countries regard the export of art as a serious matter because of the implications for national culture. The fact that R is paying millions of dollars to a wealthy individual means that the painting's sale may attract a great deal of attention. It may be that art lovers in W will regard this as a matter of national pride and will attempt to persuade the government to block the export.

If R cannot obtain an export licence then the painting's value may be reduced substantially. Essentially, the resale market for the painting will be restricted to buyers who are willing to leave it in W.

Ideally, R should have investigated the likely reaction of the government to this sale before bidding at the auction. That could have involved talking to the relevant government officials and also looking at any recent transactions involving significant pieces of art.

It may be possible to negotiate a clause that makes the sale conditional on the grant of an export licence. Unfortunately, that will have the effect of transferring the risk to the vendor and so that might prove unacceptable.

R should be ready to argue that the sale of the item will benefit the good cause that is the recipient of the previous owner's generosity. It may be possible to mount a public relations response to any attempt to delay the export of the painting.

Test your understanding 30 – M (Case study/Integration)

(a) (i) The value of the receivable is E$10m.

- The daily standard deviation = E$10m × 0.8% = E$80,000.
- At 95% the daily value at risk = E$80,000 × 1.645 = E$131,600.
- The 30 day 95% value at risk = E$131,600 × √30 = E$720,803.

(ii) The option will be exercised if the price falls below E$9m or rises above E$10.5m.

- A loss of E$1m (to take the price below E$9m) equates to a daily value at risk of E$1m/√30 = E$182,574.
- For that loss to occur E$80,000 × Z = E$182,574, so Z = 2.28. When Z = 2.28, probability = 0.5 – 0.4887 = 0.0113.
- A gain of E$0.5m equates to a daily value at risk of E$0.5m/√30 = E$91,287.
- For that gain to occur E$80,000 × Z = E$91,287, so Z = 1.14. When Z = 1.14, probability = 0.5 – 0.3729 = 0.1271.
- The overall probability of either option being exercised = 0.0113 + 0.1271 = 13.84%.

(b) M has hedged the receivable using a combination of two options.

The downside risk is limited to a potential loss of E$1m. If the value of the receivable declines to less than E$9m then M will exercise its put option and will sell the U$ to the counterparty.

The upside risk has also been limited to a potential gain of E$0.5m. In the event that the receivable is worth more than E$10.5m the counterparty will exercise the call option and will buy the U$ for the option price.

While it is not particularly desirable to limit the upside risk, M has effectively offset part of the cost of the put option by doing so. The put option will cost the company E$200,000 or 2% of the value of the receivable. Combining that with the sale of the call option will reduce the net cost of the hedge to only E$200,000 – 160,000 = E$40,000.

M will be taking the risk that Counterparty 1 will be in a position to honour its commitment in the event of a loss on the receivable. The options are both OTC arrangements and are not organised through a recognised exchange, so there are fewer safeguards concerning the solvency of the counterparties.

(c) Setting the price

The most immediate factor in setting a price would be the question of whether the options are in the money or out of the money. In this case, both options are out of the money and so neither will be exercised unless there is a fairly significant movement in the underlying currency.

The two factors that combine to create the remainder of the value is the volatility of the underlying currency and the time remaining until exercise. The more volatile the currency, the greater the possibility that there will be a movement big enough to make it viable to exercise the option. The longer the time remaining, the more chance of exercise.

It would also be worth considering any forecasts and the likelihood of a movement in a particular direction. If there is a strong reason to believe that the receivable will increase in value then the counterparty will have to charge less for the option in order to make it attractive.

Test your understanding 31

Timing	**SW**	**AP**
Now: Borrow from banks	GBP 18 m at 1.2%	USD 20 m at LIBOR + 0.5%
Exchange principals	Pay GBP 18 m to AP and receive USD 20 m	Pay USD 20 m to SW and receive GBP 18 m
End of the year:		
Pay interest to banks	Pay GBP 216,000 interest	Pay USD 20 m × (L + 0.5%) interest
Exchange interest based on swap terms	Pay AP USD 20 m × (L + 0.5%) and receive GBP 216,000	Receive USD 20 m × (L + 0.5%) and pay GBP 216,000 to SW
Swap back principals	Pay USD 20 m to AP and receive GBP 18 m	Pay GBP 18 m to SW and receive USD 20 m

Net result:

Interest costs		
Without swap	USD 20 m × (L + 0.6%)	GBP 18 m × 1.5% = GBP 270,000
With swap	USD 20 m × (L + 0.5%)	GBP 18 m × 1.2% = GBP 216,000
Saving	USD 20 m × 0.1% = $20,000	GBP 54,000

Test your understanding 32

The correct answers are A, B and D

Pooling is where the balances of all subsidiaries are kept together when considering interest rates and overdraft limits. It should reduce interest payable, increase interest earned and prevent overdraft limits being breached.

Test your understanding 33

B

C and D would be used to hedge a Kroner payment.

A (selling options) is not a hedging method.

Test your understanding 34 – Q (Case study/Integration)

Briefing note

To: The Board

From: A.N. Accountant

Date: Today

Subject: Borrowing in EUR

Dear Sirs,

(a) The French subsidiary will (hopefully) generate a surplus in EUR, so any weakening of the EUR against the LKR will reduce the value when converted to Q's home currency. If Q borrows in € then any decline in the exchange rate will reduce the value of the loan and so there will be a degree of hedging associated with the finance.

Even if it is a little more expensive to borrow in € than in LKR, the reduction in risk may justify any additional expense. Thus the EUR and LKR costs are not necessarily directly comparable.

Borrowing in France will give Q a little more flexibility in the event that the subsidiary fails. All of the assets and liabilities will be in France and Q will be in a strong position when it comes to negotiating a deal with the French bank because it could simply abandon its position altogether.

(b) A similar French business would pay an interest rate of 6% to borrow EUR. That rate is most directly comparable to the LKR rate of 9% that will be charged in Sri Lanka because those rates are effectively adjusted for the same degree of risk. In that case, the rule of interest rate parity could be used to show that the LKR is expected to decline against the EUR.

The present spot rate is LKR 155.0 = EUR 1.

The spot rate implied in six years = $(1.09/1.06)^6 \times 155.0$ = LKR 183.25/EUR1

Test your understanding 35 – Marcus (Integration)

US$ Exposure

As Marcus has a USD receipt (USD 69,000) and payment (USD 240,000) maturing at the same time (three months), it can match them against each other to leave a net liability of USD 171,000 to be hedged.

(i) **Forward market hedge**

Buy USD 171,000 three months' forward at a cost of:

USD 171,000/0.9520 = EUR179,622 payable in three months' time.

(ii) **Money market hedge**

The money market hedge to pay USD in three months' time requires Marcus to borrow in EUR, translate to USD and deposit in USD.

A payment of USD 171,000 in three months (only 2.5% interest) will require a USD deposit now of (171,000 ÷ 1.025) USD166,829. This means that with a spot rate of 0.9830 the EUR loan will need to be EUR 169,714.

The loan of EUR 169,714 will increase over the three months to the date of repayment by 3.25% and will therefore be EUR 175,230.

The cost is therefore EUR 175,230.

In this case the money market hedge is a cheaper option.

AUD Receipt

Converting exchange rates to home currency

EUR1/AUD

Spot:	0.5294 – 0.5285
Four months forward:	0.5126 – 0.5118

AUD 295,000 to be hedged.

(i) **Forward market hedge**

Sell AUD 295,000 four months' forward at a cost of:

AUD 295,000/0.5126 = EUR 575,497 receivable in four months' time.

(ii) **Money market hedge**

The money market hedge to receive AUD in four months' time requires Marcus to borrow in AUD, translate to EUR and deposit in EUR.

A receipt of AUD 295,000 in four months (only 5.33% interest) will be balanced with a AUD loan now of (295,000 ÷ 1.0533) AUD 280,072. This means that with a spot rate of 0.5294 the EUR deposit will need to be EUR 529,037.

The deposit of EUR 529,037 will increase over the four months to the date of repayment by 3.83% and will therefore be EUR 549,299. In this case, more will be received in euros under the forward hedge.

Test your understanding 36 – UK company (Integration)

Forward contract

$$\frac{2,500,000}{(1.5851 - 0.0164)} = \text{GBP } 1,593,676$$

Futures

Time line

	30/11	28/2	31/3
SPOT	\$1.5851	\$1.6510	
March Futures	\$1.5796	\$1.6513	

Step 1: Set up – 30/11

- Downside risk will be if GBP rises in value.
- Bet that GBP will rise on futures market.
- Buy March GBP futures
- No. of contracts =

$$\frac{\frac{\text{USD } 2.5\text{m}}{\text{USD } 1.5796}}{\text{GBP } 62{,}500} = 25$$

Step 2: Contact exchange

- Buy 25 March futures contracts @ USD 1.5796
- Deposit margin = $\frac{25 \times \text{USD } 1{,}000}{\text{USD } 1.5842}$ = (GBP 15,781)

Step 3: Close out – 28/2

- Futures profit:

Difference = 1.6513 – 1.5796 = 0.0717.

Profit = 0.0717 × 25 × 62,500 = USD 112,031

+ margin returned (USD 25,000) = USD 137,031

- Convert receipt & profit at spot = $\frac{\text{USD } 2.5\text{m} + \text{USD } 137{,}031}{\text{USD } 1.6510}$ = GBP 1,597,233

Net futures position (net of initial margin payment)

= GBP 1,597,233 – GBP 15,781

= GBP 1,581,452

With benefit of hindsight, the forward contract would have been a better choice.

chapter

13

Interest rate risk management

Chapter learning objectives

Lead	Component
D2. Evaluate alternative risk management tools.	(c) Evaluate appropriate methods for the identification and management of financial risks associated with debt finance.

Indicative syllabus content

- Operation and features of the more common instruments for managing interest rate risk: swaps, forward rate agreements, futures and options.
- Techniques for combining options in order to achieve a specific risk profile: caps, collars and floors.
- Internal hedging techniques.

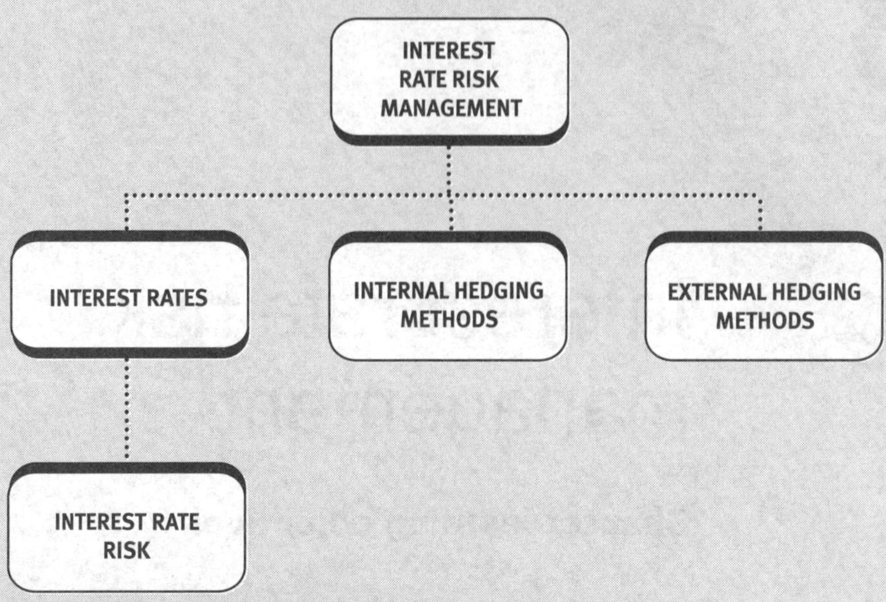

1 Interest rates

Lending and depositing rates

A bank will quote two interest rates to a customer – a lending rate and a depositing rate. The lending rate is always higher than the depositing rate because the bank wants to make a profit.

London Inter Bank Offer Rate (LIBOR)

This is the interest at which a major bank can borrow wholesale short-term funds from another bank in the London money markets.

- There are different LIBOR rates for different lengths of borrowing, typically from overnight to one year.
- Most variable rate loans are linked to LIBOR and therefore a loan at LIBOR + 2% (where LIBOR is 4.5%) would mean that the customer would pay interest at 6.5% on the loan.

LIBOR, LIBID and basis points

LIBOR

Each top bank has its own LIBOR rates, but an 'official' average of LIBOR rates is calculated each day by the British Bankers Association. The LIBOR rates that it publishes, the BBA LIBOR rates, are used as benchmark rates for some financial instruments, such as short-term interest rate futures.

LIBOR is important because London is the world's major money market centre. However, other financial centres have similar benchmark interest rates in their money market. For example, the banks of the eurozone produce an alternative benchmark rate of interest for the euro. This is called euribor, but it is similar in concept to euro LIBOR, with the only difference that the average rate is calculated daily from data submitted by a completely different panel of banks.

Most floating rate loans for companies are linked to LIBOR. For example, a company might borrow at 1.25% above LIBOR. In the language of the financial markets, 1% = 100 **basis points**, so a loan at 1.25% above LIBOR might be called a loan at LIBOR plus 125 basis points. If it pays interest every six months, the interest payable at the end of each period will be set with reference to the LIBOR rate at the beginning of the period.

LIBID

LIBID stands for the London Interbank Bid Rate. It is less important than LIBOR, but you might come across it. LIBID is the rate of interest that a top-rated London bank could obtain on short-term wholesale deposits with another bank in the London money markets. LIBID is always lower than LIBOR.

2 Interest rate risk and its management

The concept of interest rate risk is discussed in chapter 4. Along with the risk to cash flow and/or competitiveness, companies face the risk that interest rates might change in value (upside risk as well as downside risk), and between the point when the company identifies the need to borrow or invest and the actual date when they enter into the transaction. For example, a company might anticipate that they will need to borrow in the future but do not yet know exactly how much or when. If in the interim, interest rates rise the delayed decision will cause higher interest payments in the future.

Compared to exchange rates, interest rates are less volatile, but changes in them can still be substantial.

The term structure of interest rates provides an implicit forecast (according to market expectations) that is not guaranteed to be correct but is the most accurate forecast available.

Just like currency risk, interest rate risk management techniques can be split between internal and external methods.

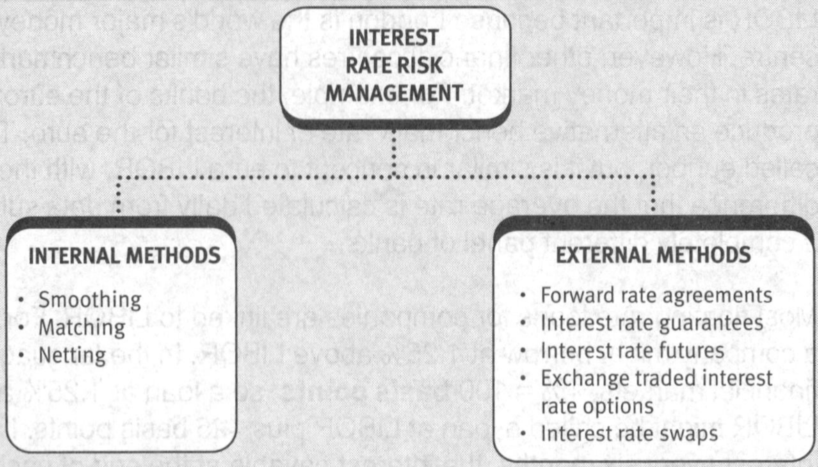

3 Internal hedging

Internal (or operating) hedging strategies for managing interest rate risk involve restructuring the company's assets and liabilities in a way that minimises interest rate exposure. These include:

- **Smoothing** – the company tries to maintain a certain balance between its fixed rate and floating rate borrowing. The portfolio of fixed and floating rate debts thus provide a natural hedge against changes in interest rates. There will be less exposure to the adverse effects of each but there will also be less exposure to an favourable movements in the interest rate.
- **Matching** – the company matches its assets and liabilities to have a common interest rate (i.e. loan and investment both have floating rates).
- **Netting** – the company aggregates all positions, both assets and liabilities, to determine its net exposure.

Marks and Spencer's funding and interest rate hedging policy

The Group's funding strategy is to ensure a mix of financing methods offering flexibility and cost effectiveness to match the requirements of the Group … Interest rate risk primarily occurs with the movement of sterling interest rates in relation to the Group's floating rate financial assets and liabilities. Group policy for interest rate management is to maintain a mix of fixed and floating rate borrowings. Interest rate risk in respect of debt on the balance sheet is reviewed on a regular basis against forecast interest costs and covenants. A number of interest rate swaps have been entered into redesignate fixed and floating debt.

4 External hedging

To manage the risk of interest rates moving before an agreed loan or deposit date, the following techniques can be used:

	Over-the-counter (OTC) instruments	**Exchange traded instruments**
'Fixing' instruments	Forward rate agreements (FRAs)	Interest rate futures
'Insurance' instruments	Interest rate guarantees (IRGs), (sometimes called caps/floors or options)	Interest rate options

'Fixing' instruments lock a company into a particular interest rate providing certainty as to the future cashflow, whilst 'insurance' instruments allow some upside flexibility in the interest rate i.e. the company can benefit from favourable movements but are protected from adverse movements.

OTC instruments are bespoke, tailored products that fit the companies needs exactly. Exchange traded instruments are ready-made and standardised.

These will be discussed in more detail in the following sections.

5 Forward rate agreements (FRAs)

An FRA is a forward contract on an interest rate for a future short-term loan or deposit. An FRA can therefore be used to fix the interest rate on a loan or deposit starting at a date in the future.

It is a contract relating to the level of a short-term interest rate, such as three-month LIBOR or six-month LIBOR. FRAs are normally for amounts greater than £1 million.

Features and operation

An important feature of an FRA is that the agreement is independent of the loan or deposit itself.

- It is about the rate of interest on a **notional** amount of principal (loan or deposit) starting at a future date.
- The FRA does not replace taking out the loan (deposit) but rather the **combination** of the loan (deposit) and the FRA result in a fixed effective interest rate.

Settlement of FRAs

When an FRA reaches its settlement date, the buyer and seller must settle the contract.

- If the fixed rate in the agreement (the FRA rate) is higher than the reference rate (LIBOR), the buyer of the FRA makes a cash payment to the seller. The payment is for the amount by which the FRA rate exceeds the reference rate.
- If the fixed rate in the agreement (the FRA rate) is lower than the reference rate (LIBOR), the seller of the FRA makes a cash payment to the buyer. The payment is for the amount by which the FRA rate is less than the reference rate.

Setting up the hedge

Hedging is achieved by a combination of an FRA with the 'normal' loan or deposit.

- **Borrowing** (hence concerned about interest rate rises)

  The firm will borrow the required sum on the target date and will thus contract at the market interest rate on that date.

  Previously the firm will have **bought** a matching FRA from a bank or other market maker and thus receive compensation if rates rise.

- **Depositing** (hence concerned about a fall in interest rates)

  The firm will deposit the required sum on the target date and will thus contract at the market interest rate on that date.

  Previously the firm will have **sold** a matching FRA to a bank or other market maker and thus receive compensation if rates fall.

In each case this combination effectively fixes the rate.

Terminology

In the terminology of the markets, an FRA on a notional three-month loan/deposit starting in five months time is called a '5–8 FRA' (or '5v8 FRA').

Pricing

FRA's will be priced according to the current bank base rate and future expectations of its movements. The bank will try to predict the interest rate at the date of inception of the borrowing and over its duration, and add on a profit margin. The bank will expect to make a profit for the risk they are taking in lending a company money and therefore any FRA will be priced at some amount above the base rate for a borrower. The amount above the base rate will depend on several factors including the banks attitude to their estimated interest rate (how sure they are in their prediction) and also the reputation of the company they are lending to.

Illustration of hedging using FRAs

A company wishes to borrow £10 million in six months' time for a three-month period. It can normally borrow from its bank at LIBOR + 0.50%. The current three-month LIBOR rate is 5.25%, but the company is worried about the risk of a sharp rise in interest rates in the near future.

A bank quotes FRA rates of:

3 v 9:	5.45	–	5.40 %
6 v 9:	5.30	–	5.25%

Required:

(a) How should the company establish a hedge against its interest rate risk using an FRA?

(b) Suppose that at settlement date for the FRA, the LIBOR reference rate is fixed at 6.50%. What will be the effective borrowing rate for the company?

Solution

(a) The company wants to fix a borrowing rate, so it should buy an FRA on a notional principal amount of £10 million. The FRA rate is for a 6 v 9 FRA, and the FRA rate is therefore 5.30% (you will have to buy from the bank at the higher rate – remember the bank always wins !).

(b) At settlement date interest rates have risen and the reference rate is higher than the FRA rate. The FRA will therefore be settled by a payment to the FRA buyer of 1.20% (6.50% – 5.30%).

	%
Actual interest rate on three-month loan (LIBOR + 0.50%)	(7.00)
Gain on FRA	1.20
Effective interest cost	(5.80)

This effective interest cost is the FRA rate of 5.30% plus the 0.50% margin above LIBOR that the company must pay on its borrowing.

Test your understanding 1

It is 30 June. A company needs a £10 million 6 month fixed rate loan from 1 October which it intends to hedge using a forward rate agreement (FRA). The relevant FRA rate is 6% on 30 June.

What will the net payment on the loan be if interest rates rose to 9% by October?

Test your understanding 2 – Cooper plc – 1 (Integration)

It is 31 October and Cooper plc is arranging a six-month £5 million loan commencing on 1 July, based on LIBOR. Cooper wants to hedge against an interest rate rise using an FRA. The current LIBOR is 8%.

(a) If LIBOR turned out to be 9% on 1 July, evaluate the use of the FRA.

(b) If LIBOR on 1 July was 5%, re-evaluate the FRA.

6 Interest rate guarantees (IRGs)

Interest rate guarantees are options on FRAs so the treasurer has the choice whether to exercise or not.

IRGs are sometimes referred to as **interest rate options** or **interest rate caps/floors.**

Features and operation

They are over-the-counter instruments arranged directly with a bank and have a maximum maturity of one year.

A company wishing to **borrow** in the future could hedge by **buying** an FRA so would need an IRG that provides a **call** option on FRAs.

A company wishing to **deposit** in the future could hedge by **selling** an FRA so would need an IRG that provides a **put** option on FRAs.

The company would only exercise the option to protect against an adverse interest rate movement.

Decision rules

If there is an adverse movement	If there is a favourable movement
↓	↓
Exercise the option to protect	Allow the option to lapse

IRGs are more expensive than the FRAs as one has to pay for the flexibility to be able to take advantage of a favourable movement.

Test your understanding 3 – Cooper plc – 2 (Integration)

It is 31 October and Cooper plc is arranging a six-month £5 million loan commencing on 1 July, based on LIBOR. Cooper wants to hedge against an interest rate rise using an IRG. The current LIBOR is 8%.

The IRG fee is 0.25% p.a. of the loan.

(a) If LIBOR turned out to be 9% on 1 July, evaluate the use of the IRG.

(b) If LIBOR on 1 July was 5%, re-evaluate the IRG.

7 Interest rate futures (IRFs)

IRFs are similar in principle to forward rate agreements in that they give a commitment to an interest rate for a set period.

They are tradable contracts and operate for set periods of three months, and terminate in March, June, September and December.

As with currency futures, the futures position will normally be closed out for cash and the gain or loss will be used to offset changes in interest rates.

There are two types of IRFs:

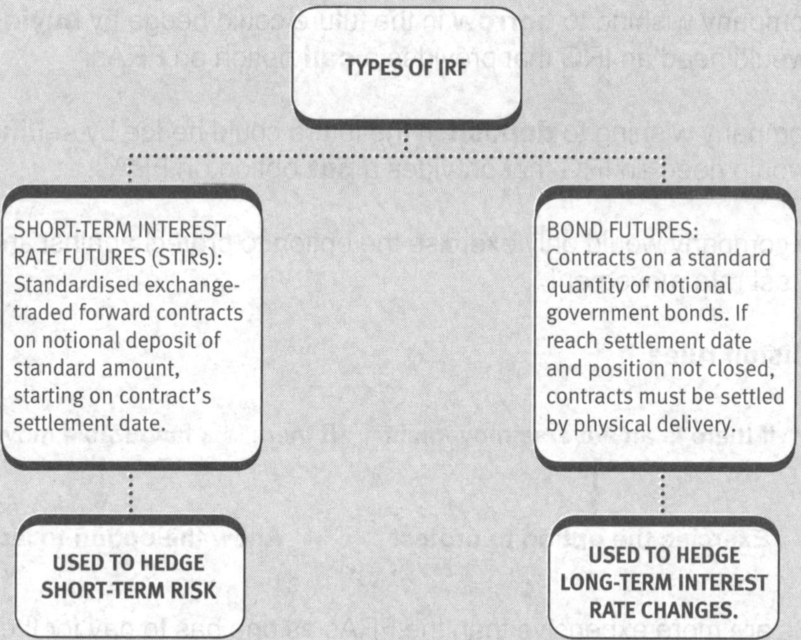
TYPES OF IRF
SHORT-TERM INTEREST RATE FUTURES (STIRs): Standardised exchange-traded forward contracts on notional deposit of standard amount, starting on contract's settlement date.
BOND FUTURES: Contracts on a standard quantity of notional government bonds. If reach settlement date and position not closed, contracts must be settled by physical delivery.
USED TO HEDGE SHORT-TERM RISK
USED TO HEDGE LONG-TERM INTEREST RATE CHANGES.

(**Note:** These notes concentrate on STIRs which are more common.)

Features and operation

The future operates by the customer making a commitment to effectively deposit or borrow a fixed amount of capital at a fixed interest rate. The notional sterling deposit/loan on the LIFFE (London futures exchange) is £500,000.

Pricing

The future is priced by deducting the interest rate from 100.

- if the interest rate is 5% the future will be priced at 95.00.
- the reason for this is that if interest rates increase, the value of the future will fall and vice versa if interest rates reduce.

Gains and losses on STIRs are calculated by reference to the interest rate at the date of close out. The difference between the futures price at inception and close will be the gain or loss.

Futures hedging calculations

Companies can hedge using futures by buying or selling a number of futures contracts that cover a loan period and value.

- Most companies use futures to hedge **borrowings** and therefore hedge against an increase in the interest rate.
- To do this the company **sells** futures.

IRFs are complicated by a number of factors including:

- Contract sizes and standard contract lengths (3 months).
- Margins/deposits payable at the start of the hedge.
- Speculators – who dominate the market.

More information on hedging with IRFs

Hedging against the risk of a rise in interest rates with STIRs

If a company plans to borrow short-term in the future and wants to create a hedge against the risk of a rise in interest rates before then:

- It should set up a position with futures that will give it a profit if interest rates go up. The profit from futures trading will offset the higher interest cost on the loan, when it is eventually taken out.
- On the other hand, if the interest rate goes down, the effect of the hedge will be to create a loss on the futures position, so that the benefit from borrowing at a lower interest rate on the actual loan, when it is taken out, will be offset by the loss on the futures position.

This hedge is created by **selling** short-term interest rate futures.

The **futures position should be closed** when the actual loan period begins, by buying an equal number of futures contracts for the same settlement date.

- **If interest rates have gone up, the market price of futures will have fallen.** A profit will be made from futures by having sold at one price to open the position and then buying at a lower price to close the position. The profit should offset the increased interest rate.

- **If interest rates have gone down, the price of futures will have risen.** A loss will be made from futures by having sold at one price to open the position and then buying at a higher price to close the position. The loss should offset the lower interest rate.

The company should have eliminated any downside or upside risk, and be paying the interest rate it wanted.

Imperfect hedge with IRFs

One problem is that futures are for a **standard size** of contract, whereas the amount of the loan or deposit to be hedged might not be an exact multiple of the amount of the future contract's notional deposit.

For example, suppose that a company wishes to hedge against the risk of a rise in the three-month LIBOR rate for a three-month loan of US$9,250,000. Futures could be sold to hedge the exposure, but the number of contracts sold would have to be either 9 or 10 (notional deposit = $1 million per contract). However, the unhedged amount is likely to be small (perhaps immaterial) in comparison to the hedged amount.

A second problem is the existence of **basis risk:** the future rate (as defined by the future prices) moves approximately but not precisely in line with the cash market rate.

The current futures price is usually different from the current 'cash market' price of the underlying item. In the case of interest rate futures, the current market price of an interest rate future and the current interest rate will be different, and will only start to converge when the final settlement date for the futures contract approaches. This difference is known as the **'basis'**.

At final settlement date for the contract (in March, June, September or December) the futures price and the market price of the underlying item ought to be the same; otherwise speculators would be able to make an instant profit by trading between the futures market and the spot 'cash' market (arbitrage).

Most futures positions are closed out before the contract reaches final settlement. When this happens, there will inevitably be a difference between the futures price at close-out and the current market price of the underlying item. In other words, there will still be some basis.

FRAs vs. STIRs

Short-term interest rate futures are an alternative method of hedging to FRAs. They have a number of similarities.

- Both are binding forward contracts on a short-term interest rate.
- Both are contracts on a notional amount of principal.
- Both are cash-settled at the start of the notional interest period.

FRAs have the advantage that they can be tailored to a company's exact requirements, in terms of amount of principal, length of notional interest period and settlement date.

However, futures are more flexible with regard to settlement, because a position can be closed quickly and easily at any time up to settlement date for the contract.

Given the efficiency of the financial markets, the difference between the two in terms of effective interest rate is unlikely to be large.

Hedging with bond futures

Bond futures might be used to hedge the risk of a change in the price of bonds over the next few months. They can be particularly useful to bond investors for hedging against the risk of a rise in long-term interest rates and a fall in bond prices.

Suppose that an investment institution has a quantity of UK government bonds and its financial year-end is approaching. It would like to secure the value of its bond portfolio and hedge against the risk of a rise in long-term interest rates and fall in bond prices over the next few months.

It can do this with bond futures. As with hedging with STIRs, a hedge is constructed so that if interest rates move adversely, an offsetting gain will be made on the bond futures position. For a bond investor, a hedge can be constructed whereby if interest rates go up and bond prices fall, there will be a loss on the bond portfolio but an offsetting gain on the bond futures position.

Bond futures fall in value when interest rates go up. **For a bond investor, the required hedge is therefore to sell bond futures.** If the interest rate goes up, both the bonds and the bond futures will fall in value. The futures position can be closed by buying futures at a lower price than the original sale price to open the position. The gain on the futures position should match the loss in the value of the bonds themselves.

Test your understanding 4

Borrowers will wish to hedge against an interest rate rise by:

A Selling futures now and selling futures on the day that the interest rate is fixed

B Selling futures now and buying futures on the day that the interest rate is fixed

C Buying futures now and selling futures on the day that the interest rate is fixed

D Buying futures now and buying futures on the day that the interest rate is fixed

Test your understanding 5

It is 24 May. A company needs to borrow £20 million for 9 months from 1 December and, to limit interest rate risk exposure, intends to hedge using short term interest rate futures (STIRs). The notional sterling deposit/loan for STIRs is £500,000.

Which of the following statements is/are true? (Select all that apply)

A The company will need 240 futures contracts

B The company will need 120 futures contracts

C The company will need 40 futures contracts

D The company will set up the hedge by buying futures

E The company will set up the hedge by selling futures

F The futures hedge will eliminate all interest rate risk for the company

8 Exchange traded interest rate options

The future and options market provides a product that can cap interest rates for borrowers like an IRG.

This option gives its buyer the right to buy or sell an interest rate future, at a specified future date at a fixed exercise rate, i.e. to effectively have the 'right to bet' on an interest rate increase as shown on the futures market.

Because they are an option as opposed to a commitment, they require the option holder to pay the writer of the option a **premium**.

Features and operation

The characteristics of an option are:

- They fix the interest on a notional amount of capital (either for borrowers where put options are used, or for lenders where call options are used).
- They are for a given interest period (e.g. six months) starting on or before a date in the future.

(**Note**: Interest rate options are only options on interest rates and not an option to take a loan. The loan is taken quite independently of the option.)

Given that these are options to buy or sell futures, all the futures information is still valid, for example:

- The standard size of the contracts, i.e. £500,000, $1,000,000, etc.
- The duration of the contract, i.e. 3 month contracts.
- Maturity dates end of March, June, September and December.

(Standard contracts are only for exchange traded options. It is possible to purchase a bespoke option – variable contract sizes and dates, provided a willing counterparty can be found.)

A **call** option gives the holder the right to **buy** the futures contract.

A **put** option gives the holder the right to **sell** the futures contract.

You always buy the option – buy the right to buy or buy the right to sell.

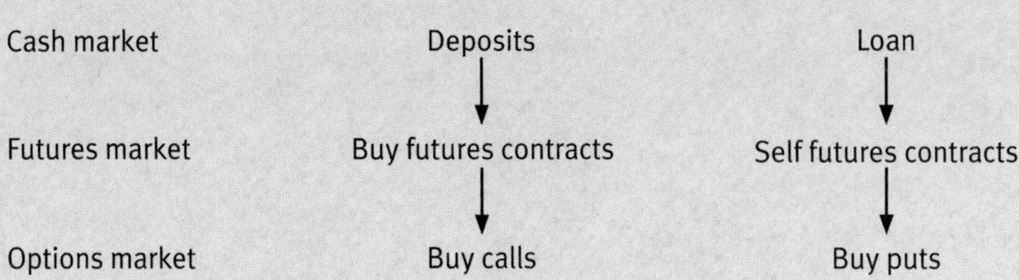

(Note: this is the opposite way round from IRGs, where borrowers needed call options and savers put options on FRAs)

Test your understanding 6

It is 4 July. A company needs to deposit £5 million for 6 months from 1 November and, to limit interest rate risk exposure, intends to hedge using options on short term interest rate futures (STIRs). The notional sterling deposit/loan for STIRs is £500,000.

Which of the following statements is/are true? (Select all that apply)

A The company will need 10 options contracts

B The company will need 20 options contracts

C The company will need 5 options contracts

D The company will need put options

E The company will need call options

Collars

- Premiums can be reduced by using a collar.
- Simultaneously buying a put and selling a call option creates a collar, hence a cap and floor is created but premium is saved.
- For example:

	%
Cap at 5.75%, pay a premium	(0.77)
Floor at 5.25%, receive a premium	0.16
Net cost	(0.61)

- The premium saved comes at the expense of giving up the benefits of any interest rate falls below the floor value.

More on collars

- A company buys an option to protect against an adverse movement whilst allowing it to take advantage of a favourable movement in interest rates. The option will be more expensive than a futures hedge. The company must pay for the flexibility to take advantage of a favourable movement.
- A collar is a way of achieving some flexibility at a lower cost than a straight option.
- Under a collar arrangement, the company limits its ability to take advantage of a favourable movement. It buys a cap (or ceiling) by buying the right to sell (a put option) as normal but also sells a floor (by selling the right to buy - a call option) on the same futures contract to a counterparty, but with a different exercise price.
- The floor sets a minimum cost for the company. The counterparty is willing to pay the company for this guarantee of a minimum income. Thus the company gets paid for limiting its ability to take advance of a favourable movement if the interest rate falls below the floor rate. The company does not benefit therefore the counterparty does.

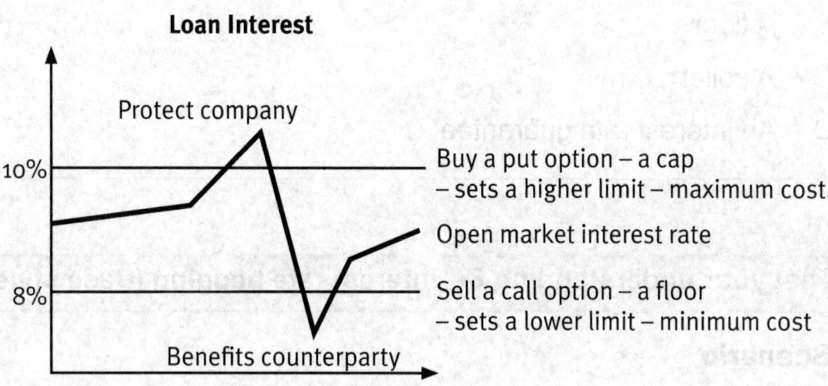

- It involves a company arranging both a minimum and a maximum limit on its interest rates payments or receipts. It enables a company to convert a floating rate of interest into a semi-fixed rate of interest.

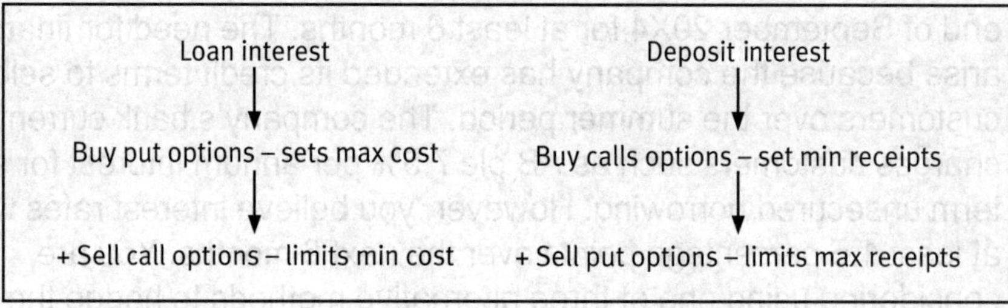

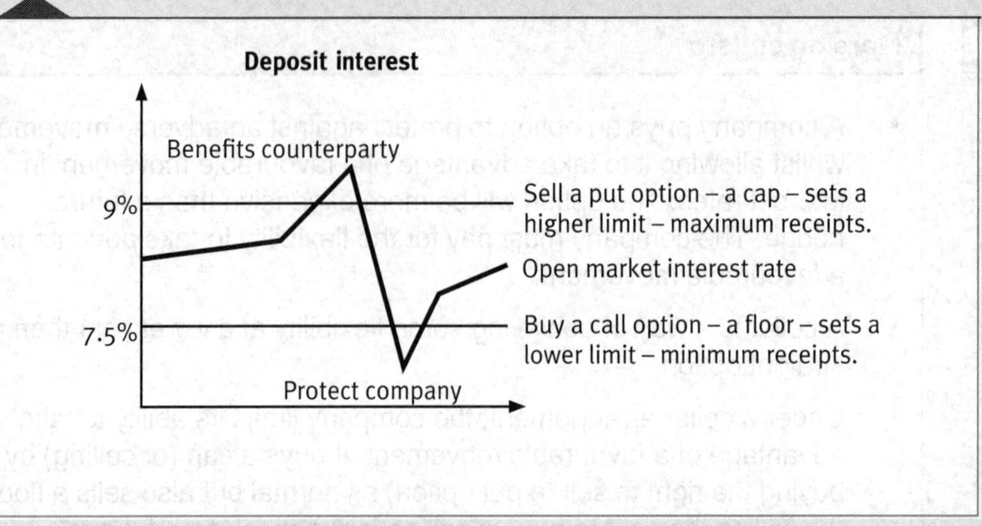

Test your understanding 7

An option whereby the lender sets a maximum and minimum interest rate simultaneously is called:

A A cap

B A floor

C A collar

D An interest rate guarantee

Test your understanding 8 – Interest rate hedging (Case style)

Scenario

Assume you are the Treasurer of AB, a large engineering company, and that it is now May 20X4.

Trigger

You have forecast that the company will need to borrow £2 million by the end of September 20X4 for at least 6 months. The need for finance will arise because the company has extended its credit terms to selected customers over the summer period. The company's bank currently charges customers such as AB plc 7.5% per annum interest for short-term unsecured borrowing. However, you believe interest rates will rise by at least 1.5 percentage points over the next 6 months. You are considering using one of three alternative methods to hedge the risk:

- forward rate agreements; or
- interest rate futures; or

- an interest rate guarantee (a borrower's option or short-term cap).

You can purchase an interest rate cap at 7% per annum for the duration of the loan to be guaranteed. You would have to pay a premium of 0.1% of the amount of the loan. As part of the arrangement, the company will agree to pay a 'floor' rate of 6% per annum.

Task

Prepare a briefing note to the Finance Director discussing the features of each of the three alternative methods of hedging the interest rate risk and advise on how each might be useful to AB, taking all relevant and known information into account.

(30 minutes)

Test your understanding 9 – Gymbob (Case study)

Scenario

Gymbob plc is a national chain of gyms listed on the UK Stock Market. It was set up nearly twenty years ago, and has 40 branches nationwide each having essentially the same facilities – a dry side including a gym with running machines, cross trainers, rowing machines and weights, and a wet side including a swimming pool, sauna, spa pool, and steam room. There are daily classes for both the wet and dry side activities, held by various full-time and freelance instructors.

Trigger

The directors of Gymbob have heard of a rival gym chain being put up for sale for £20 million. Gymbob would be very keen to acquire their competitor, since the gyms are well patronised and in locations that complement Gymbob's current portfolio. Gymbob would be able to raise most of the purchase price in cash or by liquidating investments, but would still need to borrow £5 million. It is anticipated that, all going well, they would need to borrow the £5 million in 3 months' time for only a one-year period. Current interest rates are 7% for this type of loan, and Gymbob's directors would not want to pay more than this since they have other commitments. They are considering the use of a forward rate agreement, interest rate future or an interest rate option.

Task

Prepare an email to the finance director explaining how each of the three interest rate hedging alternatives might be useful to Gymbob.

(20 minutes)

9 Interest rate swaps

An interest rate swap is an agreement whereby the parties agree to swap a floating stream of interest payments for a fixed stream of interest payments and vice versa. There is no exchange of principal.

Features and operation

- In practice interest rate swaps are probably the most common form of interest rate hedge used by companies because they can hedge loans of anywhere between a year and 30 years and therefore are used for long-term borrowings.
- In this chapter we only consider the 'plain vanilla' swap of fixed or floating rate (or vice versa) without any complications that can occur in practice.
- The companies involved in a swap can be termed 'counterparties'.
- Some banks specialise in swaps and therefore they have become a tradable instrument.
- In practice banks often act as counterparties and attempt to hedge their risk by having a large number of positions in the fixed and floating rate markets.

The following diagram summarises the operation of a swap:

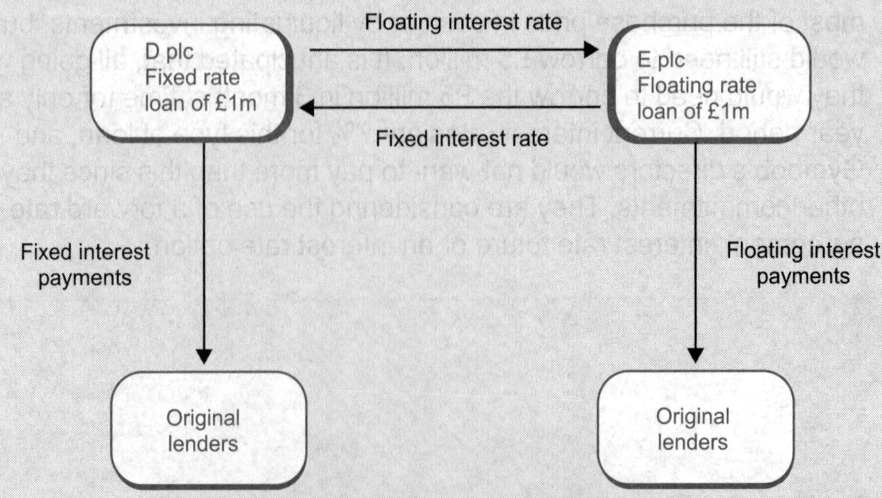

In practice the way the payments are made is that a net payment is made from D plc to E plc depending on the difference in the fixed and floating interest rates.

This type of swap will only work if one company wants a fixed rate whilst another company wants a variable rate.

Interest rate swap calculation

Company A wishes to raise $10 million and to pay interest at a floating rate, as it would like to be able to take advantage of any fall in interest rates. It can borrow for one year at a fixed rate of 10% or at a floating rate of 1% above LIBOR.

Company B also wishes to raise $10 million. They would prefer to issue fixed rate debt because they want certainty about their future interest payments, but can only borrow for one year at 13% fixed or LIBOR + 2% floating, as it has a lower credit rating than company A.

Calculate the effective swap rate for each company – assume savings are split equally.

Solution

(Note: Sometimes the question will tell you which company is currently borrowing which type of finance (fixed or variable). If this isn't given, you will need to use the first two steps to establish which company has the comparative advantage.)

Step 1: Identify the type of loan with the biggest difference in rates.

- Answer: Fixed (difference of 3% (13% vs. 10%) as opposed to just 1% for variable)

Step 2: Identify the party that can borrow this type of loan the cheapest.

- Answer: Company A
- Thus Company A should borrow fixed, company B variable, reflecting their **comparative advantages**.

(**Note:** All swap questions will start from step 3.)

Step 3: Interest difference

	A		*B*		*TOTAL*
Now:	10	+	LIBOR + 2	=	LIBOR + 12
Want:	LIBOR + 1	+	13	=	LIBOR + 14
			Difference		2

- 'Now' refers to the loan that the companies will take out.
- 'Want' refers to the type of interest payments that they desire to have, and the cost that they would have to pay if they arranged it themselves.
- The difference is shared equally between the companies.

Step 4: Possible swap

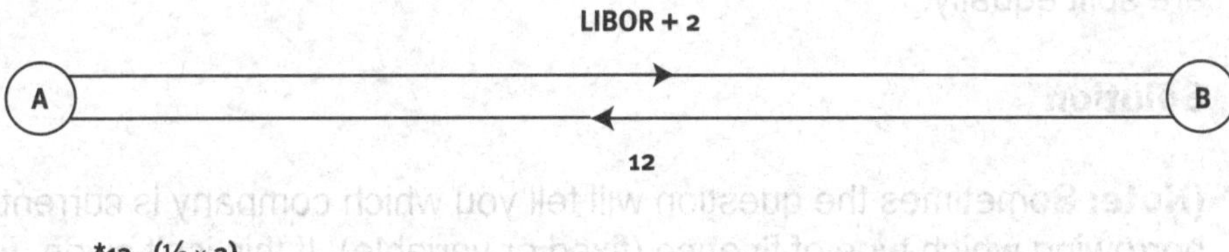

*13 - (½ x 2)

Note: there are many ways of setting up the terms of a swap to achieve the required results

- both companies get the type of interest they desire, and
- save their share of the difference calculated above.

The method used here is:

(1) company B pays off ALL of company A's variable rate interest (LIBOR + 2% in this case)

(2) company A then pays to B interest equivalent to its own fixed rate (13%) less share of the difference (½ × 2% = 1% in this case).

Step 5: Check

	A	B
	%	%
Pay own interest	(10.00)	(LIBOR + 2)
Receive	12.00	LIBOR + 2
Pay	(LIBOR + 2)	(12.00)
Net interest	(LIBOR)	(12.00)

Both companies achieved what they wanted, so the swap works.

Calculations involving quoted rates from intermediaries

In practice a bank normally arranges the swap and will quote the following:

- The 'ask rate' at which the bank is willing to receive a fixed interest cash flow stream in exchange for paying LIBOR.
- The 'bid rate' that they are willing to pay in exchange for receiving LIBOR.
- The difference between these gives the bank's profit margin and is usually at least 2 basis points.

Note: LIBOR is the most widely used benchmark or reference rate for short-term interest rates worldwide, although the swap could relate to Euribor, say.

The bank will usually set up the swap by identifying the potential swap partners and helping to set the terms of any legal agreement between the two parties. The bank will charge both companies a commission (profit margin) for doing this. From the companies point of view, the bank will probably know the potential swap partners credibility and therefore there should be less risk of default by one of the companies.

Interest rate swap with Intermediary

Co A currently has a 12-month loan at a fixed rate of 5% but would like to swap to variable. It can currently borrow at a variable rate of LIBOR + 12 basis points.

The bank is currently quoting 12-month swap rates of 4.90 (bid) and 4.95 (ask).

Show Co A's financial position if it enters the swap.

Solution

	Co A
Actual borrowing	(5.00%)
Payment to bank	(LIBOR)
Receipt from bank (bid)	4.90%
Net interest rate after swap	**(LIBOR + 0.10%)**
Open market cost – no swap	(LIBOR + 0.12%)
Saving	2 basis points

Note: the advantage of swaps with intermediaries in the exam is that you may not need to know anything about the counterparty, making calculations much simpler.

Test your understanding 10

Co B has a 12-month loan at a variable rate of LIBOR + 15 basis points but, due to fears over interest rate rises, would like to swap to a fixed rate. It can currently borrow at 5.12% fixed.

The bank is currently quoting 12-month swap rates of 4.90 (bid) and 4.95 (ask).

Required:

Show Co B's financial position if it enters the swap.

Further swap example

Company A has a 12 month loan at a variable rate of LIBOR + 50 basis points but, due to fears over interest rate rises, would like to swap to a fixed rate. It can currently borrow at 5.40% fixed.

Company B currently has a 12 month loan at a fixed rate of 4.85% but would like to swap to variable. It can currently borrow at a variable rate of LIBOR + 65 basis points.

The bank is currently quoting 12 month swap rates of 4.50 (bid) and 4.52 (ask).

Required:

Show how the swap via the intermediary would work.

Solution

- Co A already has a variable outflow so must receive LIBOR from the bank to convert this to fixed. It will pay the bank the ask rate.
- Similarly Co B must pay the bank variable and receive fixed at the bid rate.

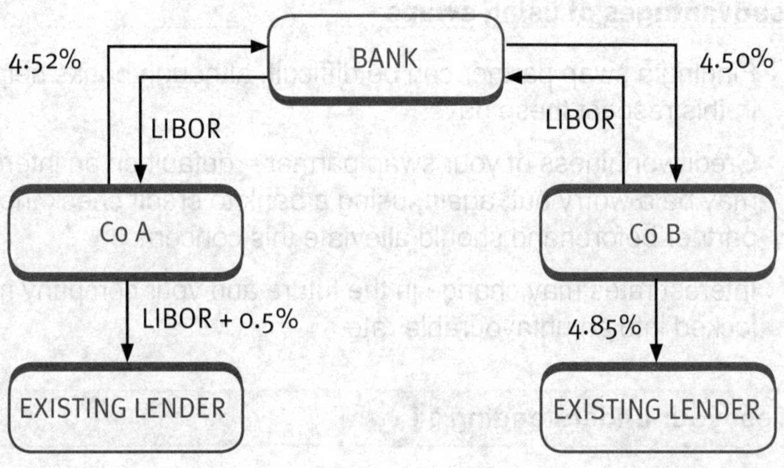

	A	B
Actual borrowing	(LIBOR + 0.5%)	(4.85%)
Payment to bank	(4.52%)	(LIBOR)
Receipt from bank	LIBOR	4.50%
Net interest rates after swap	**(5.02%)**	**(LIBOR + 0.35%)**
Open market cost – no swap	(5.40%)	(LIBOR + 0.65%)
Saving	38 basis points	30 basis points

Note: In this case A can borrow variable cheaper but B can get the best fixed rates. In this case the total potential saving = D fixed + D variable = 55 + 15 = 70 basis points.

Of this, 2 basis points have gone to the bank via the spread in quoted prices, leaving 68 to be shared between the two companies.

Advantages of using swaps

- As a way of managing fixed and floating rate debt profiles without having to change underlying borrowing.
- To take advantage of expected increases or decreases in interest rates.
- To hedge against variations in interest on floating rate debt, or conversely to protect the fair value of fixed rate debt instruments.
- A swap can be used to obtain cheaper finance. A swap should result in a company being able to borrow what they want at a better rate under a swap arrangement, than borrowing it directly themselves (this is known as the 'theory of **comparative advantage**').

Disadvantages of using swaps

- Finding a swap partner can be difficult, although banks help (for a fee) in this respect these days.
- Creditworthiness of your swap partner – default on an interest payment may be a worry but, again, using a bank to credit check the swap partner beforehand should alleviate this concern.
- Interest rates may change in the future and your company might be locked into an unfavourable rate.

Test your understanding 11

In a country which expects interest rates to rise, which type of debt would charge the highest rate of interest when issued?

A A fixed rate

B A floating rate

Test your understanding 12

Company A can borrow at 6% fixed or LIBOR + 0.2% variable and would like a variable rate. Company B can borrow at 6.5% fixed or LIBOR + 0.4% variable and would like a fixed rate. If the companies agree to share the differential equally, what is A's effective loan rate?

Test your understanding 13

L has a high credit rating and can borrow 10% fixed or LIBOR + 0.3% variable. It would like to borrow variable. T has a lower credit rating. It can borrow 11% fixed or LIBOR + 0.5% variable. It would like to borrow fixed. What is the quality spread differential?

Test your understanding 14

Which of the following is an internal hedging technique? (Select all that apply.)

A A forward contract

B Netting

C Smoothing

D Matching

Test your understanding 15

An interest rate derivative characterised by being available for any amount, redeemable on any date, payment on settlement and traded over the counter, is called?

A An interest rate swap

B A forward rate agreement

C An interest rate future

D An interest rate option

Test your understanding 16

In relation to interest rate hedging, which of the following statements is correct? (Select all that are relevant)

A The flexible nature of interest rate futures means that they can always be matched with a specific interest rate exposure

B Interest rate options carry an obligation to the holder to complete the contract at maturity

C Forward rate agreements are the interest rate equivalent of forward exchange contracts

D Matching is where a balance is maintained between fixed rate and floating rate debt

Test your understanding 17

When purchasing temporary investments, which of the following best describes the risk associated with the ability to sell the investment in a short time without significant price concessions?

A Liquidity risk.

B Investment risk.

C Interest rate risk.

D Purchasing power risk.

Test your understanding 18 – Q machine parts (Case study)

Scenario

Q is a Sri Lankan company that manufactures machine parts. Q plans to establish a wholly-owned French subsidiary that will manufacture its range of products in France for distribution across the European Union (EU). Q has been established for many years, but it is not widely known outside of Sri Lanka despite the fact that its product range has a very good reputation.

Trigger

Q's Finance Director visited Paris recently in order to discuss the financing arrangements for the subsidiary with a number of French banks. Q could easily borrow the funds at an attractive rate in Sri Lankan Rupees (LKR), but Q's board would prefer to borrow in Euros (EUR). Unfortunately, the French banks felt that they would be taking a risk if they were to back a foreign borrower who was unknown to them and so they either refused Q's loan application or they offered to lend at a high rate of interest.

On the flight home the Finance Director entered into a conversation with P, the passenger in the next seat. P is the founder of a French design company that wishes to build a factory in Sri Lanka. All of Sri Lanka's banks have refused to lend to P. One French bank has agreed to make the loan, but at a high rate of interest. P would prefer to raise the finance in LKR and has decided to travel to Sri Lanka in the hope that a face to face meeting with the bank lending officers will be more successful than a negotiation by telephone and email.

When Q's Finance Director and P realised that they had complementary requirements they started to discuss the possibility of a currency swap that might be mutually beneficial.

They each require to borrow the equivalent of €20 million for six years to establish their respective businesses.

The current spot rate is LKR 155.0 to the EUR.

Q can borrow in LKR at an annual rate of 9% for six years or in EUR at an annual rate of 12%.

A French accountant has told Q that a similar French business would be able to borrow €20 million for six years at 6%.

P can borrow in EUR at a rate of 10% for six years.

All of the proposed loans would be repayable in one lump sum at the end of the borrowing period.

P proposes borrowing EUR 20 million from a French bank at 10%. Q would borrow LKR 3,100 million at 9% from the Sri Lankan bank. The two companies would swap these principal sums and would each pay the interest on the other's borrowings. P is confident that both parties will generate sufficient surpluses from their new foreign operations to raise the necessary currency to meet the interest payments and to accumulate sufficient funds to swap the principal sums back at the end of six years.

Task

Prepare a note to Q's finance director evaluating the risks to Q from P's swap arrangement.

(15 minutes)

Test your understanding 19 – Z (Integration)

Z has an $8 million floating rate loan that has 14 years remaining before it is repaid. The loan was agreed one year ago. Z's directors now wish to use an interest rate swap to fix the rate for the remaining term of the loan, but Z's bank has not been able to find a counterparty whose needs precisely match Z's.

Z is paying 2% above LIBOR on the loan. If Z wished to take out a fixed rate loan then it would be possible to borrow at a rate of 6%.

Z's bank has identified a potential counterparty who can borrow at a fixed rate of 3% and requires a floating rate of LIBOR + 1%. The bank is prepared to act as an agent in return for 25% of the saving from the swap. The bank has warned Z's directors that it will have to give the counterparty the remainder of the net savings, after taking account of the bank's fee.

The counterparty intends to borrow for 10 years only and so this arrangement will not cover the whole of the remaining 14 years of Z's borrowing.

Z's bank has had a preliminary meeting with the counterparty, who has agreed in principle to this arrangement subject to making further investigations of Z. The bank has warned Z's board that it is unlikely that it will find an alternative counterparty in the foreseeable future. Furthermore, the bank is not willing to act as a counterparty to a swap with Z, although it will act as an agent between Z and a third party.

Required:

(a) Calculate the effective swap rates for both Z and the counterparty.

(15 minutes)

(b) Advise Z's board of the implications of entering into a 10 year swap in order to protect the cost of servicing a 14 year loan.

(15 minutes)

(c) Advise the counterparty on the risks associated with entering into the proposed swap with Z.

(15 minutes)

Test your understanding 20 – Swaps (Case study)

You are contacted by AB's bank and informed that another of the bank's clients, a smaller company in the same industry, is looking for a swap partner for a similar amount of borrowing for the same duration. The borrowing rates applicable to AB and RO are as follows:

	Floating	Fixed
AB	LIBOR + 0.3%	7.5%
RO	LIBOR + 0.5%	8.5%

Task

Prepare a briefing note to the finance director:

(a) Commenting briefly on why swaps may be used.

(15 minutes)

(b) Recommending how the two companies could co-operate in a swap arrangement to their mutual benefit, including the option of changing the type of loan normally preferred. Support your recommendation with appropriate calculations.

(15 minutes)

(c) Discussing the advantages and disadvantages of arranging a swap through a bank rather than negotiating directly with a counterparty.

(15 minutes)

Test your understanding 21 – QW (Case study)

Scenario

You are the treasurer of QW plc, a company with diversified, international interests. The company wishes to borrow £10 million for a period of three years. Your company's credit rating is good, and current market data suggests that you could borrow at a fixed rate of interest of 8% per annum or at a floating rate of LIBOR + 0.2% per annum. You believe that interest rates are likely to fall over the next three years, and favour borrowing at a floating rate.

Trigger

Your company's bankers are currently working on raising a three-year loan for another of their customers, ER plc. This company is smaller and less well known than QW plc, and its credit rating is not as high. ER plc could borrow at a fixed rate of 9.5% per annum or a floating rate of LIBOR + 0.5%. ER plc has indicated to the bank that it would prefer a fixed-rate loan. Your bankers have suggested you engage in a swap which might benefit both companies. The bank's commission would be 0.2% of the benefits to the two parties. Your counterpart in ER plc suggests that the commission fees and swap benefits should be shared equally.

Assume that interest is paid at the end of each twelve-month period of the loan's duration and that the principal is repaid on maturity (i.e. at the end of three years).

Task

Write a report to the board which:

(i) describes the characteristics and benefits of interest rate swaps compared with other forms of interest rate risk management, such as forward-rate agreements and interest rate futures.

(15 minutes)

(ii) explains the course of action necessary to implement the swap being considered with ER plc, and calculates and comments on the financial benefits to be gained from the operation.

(20 minutes)

10 Chapter summary

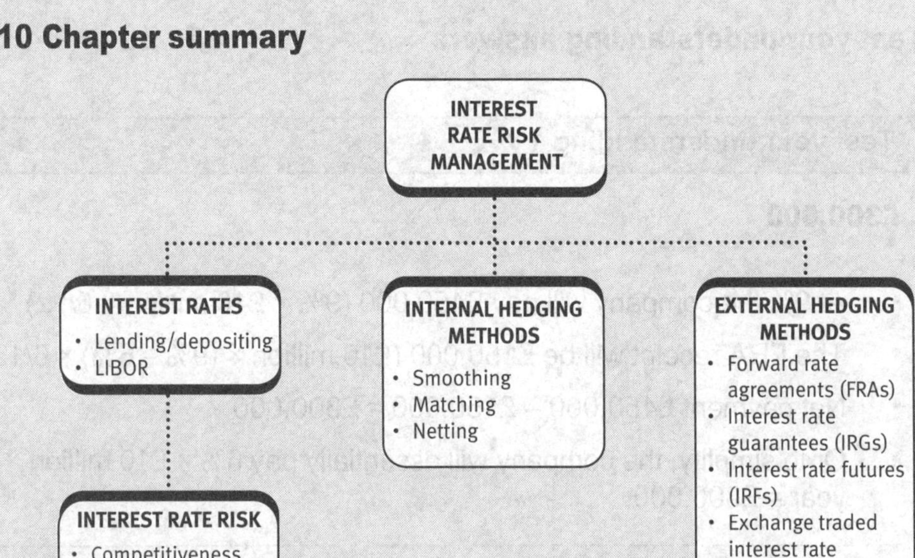

Test your understanding answers

Test your understanding 1

£300,000

- At 9% the company will pay £450,000 (9% × £10 million × 6/12).
- The FRA receipt will be £150,000 (£10 million × (9% – 6%) × 6/12)
- Net payment £450,000 – £150,000 = £300,000
- Or to simplify, the company will essentially pay 6% × £10 million × ½ year = £300,000.

Test your understanding 2 – Cooper plc – 1 (Integration)

31 October:

Cooper would purchase FRA $_{8–14}$ @ 8%

1 July:

(a)	**LIBOR = 9%**	% pa
	Cooper will pay loan interest	(9.00)
	Claim on FRA	1.00
	Net interest	(8.00)
(b)	**LIBOR = 5%**	% pa
	Pay loan interest	(5.00)
	Pay out on FRA	(3.00)
	Net interest	(8.00)

Remember that the point of an FRA is to manage future risk. In reality there is no point in looking at the past to see whether rates rose or fell. Perhaps the only worthwhile reason for doing this would be to measure the ability of the Treasury department in guessing what will happen to interest rates.

Test your understanding 3 – Cooper plc – 2 (Integration)

31 October:
Cooper would purchase $IRG_{8–14}$ @ 8%

1 July:

(a) **LIBOR = 9% (exercise option)**	% pa
Cooper will pay loan interest	(9.00)
Pay fee	(0.25)
Claim on IRG	1.00
Net interest	(8.25)

(b) **LIBOR = 5% (allow option to lapse)**	% pa
Pay loan interest	(5.00)
Pay fee	(0.25)
Net interest	(5.25)

Note: When LIBOR has fallen the IRG allows Cooper to take advantage of the lower interest rates. BUT the fee is still paid !

Remember again that the point of an IRG is to manage future risk. In reality there is no point in looking at the past to see whether rates rose or fell. Perhaps the only worthwhile reason for doing this would be to measure the ability of the Treasury department in guessing what will happen to interest rates.

Test your understanding 4

The correct answer is B – The interest rate risk arises between the present day and when the loan is taken out – the rate may rise and cost the borrower more. A borrower should sell an interest rate future now at a low interest rate (100 – r where r is, say, 5% = 95) and buy it later at the higher rate (100 – r where r is say 10% = 90). Buying at 90 and selling at 95 creates the profit you will need to offset the increased borrowing cost.

Test your understanding 5

B and E

STIRS are standardised for 3 month notional deposits or loans, so the number of contracts = (20 million/500,000) × (9 months/3 months) = **120**

The company wishes to borrow funds so would set up a hedge on the futures market by **selling** futures.

Statement F is incorrect – given the loan is needed to be taken out on the 1 December, the company would still be exposed to **basis risk**.

Test your understanding 6

B and E

STIRS are standardised for 3 month notional deposits or loans, so the number of contracts = (5 million/500,000) × (6 months/3 months) = **20**

The company wishes to deposit funds so would set up a hedge on the futures market by buying futures, so will need **call** options.

Test your understanding 7

The correct answer is C – A cap sets an interest rate ceiling.

A floor sets an interest rate lower limit.

A collar sets a maximum and a minimum interest rate.

An interest rate guarantee is an alternative name for an interest rate option.

Test your understanding 8 – Interest rate hedging (Case style)

Briefing note

To: The finance director

From: The treasurer

Date: Today

Subject: Interest rate risk hedging

Dear finance director,

With all three methods of hedging interest rate risk, a time limit has to be decided for the period of the hedge. With a Forward Rate Agreement (FRA) or an interest rate guarantee (option/cap), the time limit must be specific, with an agreed settlement date or expiry date, say six months exactly from the contract/transaction date. With futures, the hedge would be for six months from any date up to the settlement date for the futures, which in this question would probably be September.

It is assumed here that the required hedge is for exactly six months in all three cases.

FRA

An FRA is an over-the-counter instrument that can be arranged with a bank, fixing the interest rate on a notional principal amount for a given period of time, in this case six months. The notional six-month interest period would start from an agreed date in September, in four months' time, so the FRA would be a 4v10 FRA. FRAs are only available for quite large principal amounts (at least $1 million) and can be arranged up to about two years into the future.

A company wishing to fix an interest rate for borrowing should buy an FRA. Here, AB should buy a 4v10 FRA on a notional principal amount of £2 million. The bank would specify an interest rate for the FRA, which might be about 7.5% in this case.

The FRA is not an agreement to borrow the funds required. AB must arrange to borrow the £2 million separately. AB will borrow £2 million at the current market rate of interest in September, whatever this happens to be. The FRA would be settled by:

- a payment from the bank to AB if the benchmark interest rate (here probably the six-month LIBOR rate) is higher than the FRA rate; or
- a payment from AB to the bank if the benchmark rate is lower than the FRA rate.

The hedge works because the interest payment on the actual borrowing plus or minus the settlement amount for the FRA should fix the overall effective borrowing cost for AB. For example, if the interest rate does rise by 1.5 percentage points to 9% and AB borrows at this higher rate, it would receive a payment under the FRA agreement worth the equivalent of about 1.5%, thereby reducing the net borrowing cost to about 7.5% (depending on the actual rates that apply).

Interest rate futures

Short-term interest rate futures are exchange-traded instruments. A short sterling future is a notional three-month deposit of £500,000, traded on LIFFE.

A company wishing to fix a rate for borrowing should sell interest rate futures. Since AB wants to hedge the borrowing cost for £2 million for six months, it should sell 8 futures [(£2 million/£500,000) × (6 months/3 months)] and set up a 'short hedge'. It could sell either September or December futures, depending on when the interest period will begin, and when the September futures contract expires during the month.

The interest rate is in the price of the future. Prices are quoted at 100 minus the interest rate, so if AB were to sell September futures, say, at 92.50, this would 'fix' its borrowing rate at 7.5%. As the future approaches settlement date, if the interest rate has risen to 9%, the market price of September futures should have moved to about 91.00. AB could then close its position by buying 8 September futures, and making a profit of 1.50 (150 points) on each contract of its futures dealing. A profit of 150 points on 8 futures would be worth £15,000 (150 points × 8 × contracts £12.50 per point). This is equivalent to interest at 1.5% on £2 million for six months.

AB would borrow £2 million at the market rate. If this is 9%, the net borrowing cost would be 9% less the value of the profit on futures trading (1.5%) giving a net effective interest cost of 7.5%.

Since interest rate futures are only available in standardised amounts and dates, they are less flexible than FRAs, and so possibly less attractive to AB.

Interest rate guarantee

This is a type of borrower's option but with characteristics of an interest rate collar. Unlike an FRA or futures which are binding contracts on both parties, it is not a binding commitment on the option holder. If AB buys this instrument at a cap strike price of 7% (and a notional principal amount of £2 million for six months), for expiry in September, it will exercise its option if the interest rate at expiry is higher than 7%. It will then receive the interest value of the difference (on £2 million for six months) between the actual interest rate (six-month LIBOR) and the cap rate of 7%.

However, in this case, if the interest rate falls below 6%, the option counterparty (a bank) will exercise a floor option, and require AB to pay the difference between the actual interest rate and 6%.

As a result, AB is able to fix the benchmark interest rate between 6% and 7%. So if AB can borrow at, say, LIBOR + 0.50%, the interest rate guarantee would fix its actual borrowing cost between 6.5% and 7.5%, plus the cost of the guarantee.

Arranging this guarantee would cost £2,000 (0.1% of £2 million), which is equivalent to interest of 0.2% on £2 million for six months. The premiums payable on interest rate guarantees can be expensive and must be paid up-front, which can be compared to an FRA on which no premium is payable.

Usefulness of the instruments to AB

All three instruments can help AB to hedge against the risk of a rise in interest rates.

FRAs and futures are binding contracts, so that the hedge effectively fixes the borrowing cost. The interest rate guarantee is a form of option, so that AB can benefit from lower interest rates if they are between 6% and 7%. However, the guarantee has to be paid for.

All three instruments are arranged for a fixed amount and a fixed borrowing period, which means that a hedge might not be perfect. For example, if it turns out that AB needs to borrow £2.5 million for seven months starting in five months' time, none of the hedges would be perfect.

Test your understanding 9 – Gymbob (Case study)

Email

To: Finance director

From: A.N. Accountant

Date: Today

Subject: Interest rate risk management

Dear finance director,

Forward rate agreements offer Gymbob the facility to fix the future interest rate on borrowings for a specified period. For example, if Gymbob entered into an FRA with a bank in 3 months' time one year at a guaranteed 7%, then if the interest rate rose the bank would have to pay Gymbob the difference. On the other hand, if the interest rate fell, Gymbob would still have to pay the bank the difference. No matter which way the interest rate moved, Gymbob would pay 7%.

FRAs do not involve any actual lending of the principal sum of £5 million. This can be done with the same or a different bank, or other lender.

FRAs are usually for at least £1 million, and can be arranged for up to 2 or 3 years in the future, so FRAs appear to be a suitable way for Gymbob to manage interest rate exposure.

Interest rate futures are binding contracts between seller and buyer to take delivery of a specified interest rate commitment on an agreed date at an agreed price. They can be used to protect against interest rate rises and are available for a maximum of 1 – 2 years.

Futures contracts are sold now in the expectation that, as interest rates rise the contract value will fall, and they can then be purchased at a lower price, generating a profit on the futures deal. The profit compensates for the actual rises in interest rates experienced by companies that have borrowed funds from banks and elsewhere. If the interest rate moves in the opposite direction to that expected, a futures loss will occur, but this will be offset by cheaper interest costs in the market.

All contracts require a small initial deposit or margin.

Futures should allow Gymbob to hedge successfully against increases in the interest rate, although a perfect hedge is rare.

Interest rate options such as caps, floors and collars guarantee that the interest rate will not rise above, or fall below, an agreed fixed level during a specified time period commencing sometime in the future. The interest rate protection for Gymbob is similar to that given by an FRA.

However, options involve the payment of a premium to the seller of the option, whether or not the option is exercised. No premium is payable with an FRA.

Also, whilst protecting downside risk (an interest rate rise), Gymbob can take full advantage of favourable interest rate movements.

For example, if interest rates fall, the option is left to lapse and Gymbob will borrow the £5 million from the market at the lower rate. However, if rates rose, then Gymbob would exercise the option to guarantee a maximum cost of 7%.

However, the premium involved with an option can be prohibitively expensive. A way to lower this would be to take out a collar (a cap and a floor).

If you have any queries, please do not hesitate to ask.

Best wishes

A.N. Accountant

Test your understanding 10

	B
Actual borrowing	(LIBOR + 0.15%)
Payment to bank (ask)	(4.95%)
Receipt from bank	LIBOR
Net interest rates after swap	**(5.10%)**
Open market cost – no swap	(5.12%)
Saving	2 basis points

Test your understanding 11

The correct answer is A – Being able to fix the rate now, with the expectation of rates rising would save the company money and therefore the bank would charge a premium for this risk reduction.

Test your understanding 12

A will effectively pay LIBOR + 0.2% – 0.15% (spread differential) = LIBOR + 0.05%

Test your understanding 13

	L	T	Spread
Fixed rate %	10	11	1
Variable rate %	LIBOR + 0.3	LIBOR + 0.5	0.2
Quality spread differential %	0.8		

Test your understanding 14

The correct answers are B, C and D – Forward contracts require the use of a third party such as a bank.

Test your understanding 15

The correct answer is B – By definition the answer is an FRA. Futures are for specific amounts and dates. Options require a premium to be paid up front and not upon settlement. Swaps do not require payment on settlement.

Test your understanding 16

C

Note:

- A is false because interest rate futures have standardized sizes, which may not match the actual exposure
- B is false as options give the right but not the obligation
- D – in terms of interest rates matching involves ensuring assets and liabilities have a common type of interest rate (e.g. loan and investment both have floating rates)

Test your understanding 17

A

Note:

- Investment risk (B) relates to the investment, not the ability to sell an investment in a short period of time without significant price concessions.
- Interest rate risks (C) relates to the risk of interest rate changes affecting the value of the investments.
- Purchasing power risk (D) relates to the risk of changes in the value of the currency (e.g. due to inflation/deflation).

Test your understanding 18 – Q machine parts (Case study)

Note

To: Q finance director

From: A.N. Accountant

Date: Today

Subject: Currency swap with P

A currency swap involves the exchange of the actual sums borrowed (unlike an interest rate swap). That does not mean that Q will be accepting P's debts, though.

The worst possible outcome that might befall Q is that P defaults on its side of the swap. If that happens then Q will stop making the EUR payments to the French bank that provided P's loan. Q will then start to pay its own interest of the LKR loan. Q appears to be a solid and successful business and so it will not be difficult to generate the Rs required to meet the loan interest due to the Sri Lankan bank.

At the conclusion of the loan period Q will have to repay the LKR 3,100m rather than the €20m borrowed by P. Given the likely appreciation of the EUR that may actually be an advantage.

The only significant downside to P's default would be that Q would lose the potential hedge from the effective use of EUR debt to fund the French subsidiary. There would only be a risk associated with the actual currency swap if Q agreed to pay P's interest and principal irrespective of whether P met its counterparty obligations.

Test your understanding 19 – Z (Integration)

(a) The swap arrangements will be as follows:

	Z	Counterparty	Total
Now	LIBOR + 2%	3%	LIBOR + 5%
Wants	6%	LIBOR + 1%	LIBOR + 7%
Difference			2%
Paid to bank			0.5%
Saving		1.5%	

	Z	Counterparty
Pay own interest	(LIBOR + 2%)	(3%)
Receive	LIBOR + 2%	4.5%
Pay	4.5% to counterparty + 0.5% to bank	LIBOR + 2%
Net cost	5%	LIBOR + 0.5%

(b) Ideally, the swap would match the two parties' requirements exactly so that Z could have the protection that it wishes. In this case, Z will be faced with switching from an effective fixed rate under the swap to a variable rate at the end of year 10. The unprotected segment of the loan is in the distant future and so it is impossible to predict how variable rates may change during the next decade. Z could be faced with a hefty variable rate when the swap expires.

The corollary to the uncertainty is that the swap will hold for the next ten years and so the net present value of any future cash payments for the period from year 11 to year 14 will be relatively small. If that is a major concern, then Z could attempt to hedge the risk in some way. For example, putting funds on deposit at a variable rate over the next ten years will mean that the cash balance will increase more if interest rates increase and that will provide a means of offsetting any additional interest costs.

If Z does not enter into this swap arrangement then it may not find an alternative counterparty until it is too late. Interest rates may rise or the prospect of an increase may leave potential counterparties unwilling to swap a variable rate in return for a fixed rate loan. It would be far better to protect the company against interest rate risks for the next 10 years than to risk leaving the company exposed to risks for the whole of the remaining 14 years.

(c) The most important issue is that the worst possible case if Z defaults is that the counterparty will be left with the fixed rate liability that it was attempting to avoid through the swap arrangement. Presumably, the counterparty believes that interest rates are likely to fall and so wishes to obtain variable rate debt. If Z fails then the counterparty will have to pay interest at 6%. At that stage it may be possible to obtain a further swap with a different variable rate borrower, but that may be more expensive if the counterparty's expected fall in interest rates has occurred.

Z is a poorer credit risk than the counterparty, so there is some risk of default. The higher rates that Z has to pay and the fact that Z finds it necessary to offer the whole of the interest rate saving to attract a counterparty mean that Z is a poorer risk.

The fact that Z's directors did not consider the implications of interest rate movements when taking out a 14 year loan is a worry in itself. The counterparty would feel rather more confident if it was dealing with a management team that had a better understanding of financial management.

Banks frequently act as the counterparty rather than acting as the intermediaries between the two sides of a swap. The fact that Z's bank did not offer to take the arrangement on directly with Z and so enjoy the whole of the potential benefit rather than just 25% suggests that the bank does not wholly believe in Z's solvency.

Test your understanding 20 – Swaps (Case study)

Briefing note

To: The finance director

From: A.N. Accountant

Date: Today

Subject: Interest rate swaps

(a) Interest rate swaps can have several uses.

- They can be used by companies to arrange fixed rate borrowing, when direct access to fixed rate funding (the bond markets) is not possible, for example, if the company is too small or would not have a sufficiently good credit rating.
- Occasionally, they can be used to obtain lower cost borrowing, through interest rate arbitrage. This opportunity exists in the case of RO and AB.

- They can be used to alter the proportions of fixed and variable rate funding in a company's debt mix without the expense of redeeming existing debt and issuing new debt in its place, and so can be used to manage exposure to risk from possible future interest rate movements.

(b) AB is a larger company than RO, so we see that AB has cheaper borrowing rates in both the floating rate as well as the fixed rate market. However, while RO only has to pay 0.2% more in the floating rate market, it has to pay a full 1.0% more for fixed rate debt. This creates an opportunity to reduce their combined borrowing costs by 0.8% (1% – 0.2%).

AB has a comparative advantage in the fixed rate market, since it is cheaper by 1% than RO, compared to just 0.2% in the floating rate market. So, the companies could co-operate to their mutual benefit if:

- AB borrows at a fixed rate and swaps into floating rate; and
- RO borrows at a floating rate, where it can borrow comparatively more favourably than at a fixed rate (only 0.2% more), and swap into a fixed rate.

The opportunity for arbitrage is 0.8%, which means that if they share this equally, both will borrow 0.4% more cheaply than if they borrowed directly at a floating rate in the case of AB or at a fixed rate in the case of RO.

A swap could be arranged as follows:

- AB borrows in the fixed rate market at 7.5% and pays LIBOR to RO.
- RO borrows in the floating rate market at LIBOR + 0.5% and pays a fixed rate of 7.6% to AB.

The net effect is as follows:

AB pays 7.5% to the bank, receives 7.6% from RO and pays LIBOR to RO which equates to LIBOR – 0.1%.

RO pays LIBOR + 0.5% to the bank, receives LIBOR from AB, and pays 7.6% to AB which equates to a payment of 8.1%.

These net borrowing rates are each 0.4% less than AB could borrow at a floating rate or RO could borrow at a fixed rate.

(c) In practice, most swaps are arranged through banks that run a 'swaps book'. There are several advantages in dealing with a bank rather than directly with another company.

- In dealing with a bank, there is no problem about finding a swaps counterparty with an equal and opposite swapping requirement. The bank will arrange a swap to meet the specific requirements of each individual customer, as to amount and duration of the swap.
- In dealing with a bank, the credit risk is that the bank might default, whereas in dealing directly with another company, the credit risk is that the other company might default. Banks are usually a much lower credit risk than corporations.
- Banks are specialists in swaps, and are able to provide standard legal swaps agreements. The operation of the swap is likely to be administratively more straightforward.

The significant drawback to using a bank is that the bank will want to make a profit from its operations. In practice, it will generally do this by charging different swap rates for fixed rate payments and fixed rate receipts on different swaps. In terms of the RO and AB situation, where there is a credit arbitrage opportunity of 0.8%, if a swaps bank were to be used to arrange a separate swap with each company, it might take a profit of, say, 0.2%, leaving just 0.6% of benefit to be shared between RO and AB.

Test your understanding 21 – QW (Case study)

REPORT

To: The Board of QW plc

From: The Treasurer

Date: XX-XX-XX

Subject: Interest rate swaps

(i) A swap is an agreement between two parties to exchange the cash flows related to specific underlying obligations. In an interest rate swap, the cash flows are the interest payments arising on principal amounts. For example, company A might have outstanding borrowings of £1m with annual interest fixed at 10%, whilst company B has borrowings of £1m with annual interest paid at a floating rate of LIBOR + 1%.

If company A and company B agree on an interest rate swap, they agree to take on the other's interest obligations, so that company B will pay fixed annual interest of £100,000 pa, while company A will now pay floating interest of LIBOR + 1% on £1m. Such a swap might be entered into if company A thought that interest rates were going to fall, while company B thought they would rise.

A forward rate agreement (FRA) is a contract in which two parties agree on the interest rate to be paid for a period of time starting in the future, for example for a three-month period starting in six months' time. The contract is settled in cash; exposure is limited to the difference in interest rates between the FRA agreed rate and the actual rate, based on the notional agreed principal.

An interest rate futures contract is a standardised form of FRA traded on an investment exchange. Each contract is for a specified nominal amount of a specified financial instrument on a specified date.

The advantages of swaps compared to other forms of interest rate risk management are as follows:

- Swaps allow a company to restructure its capital profile without the expense of actually redeeming existing borrowings. Fixed borrowings can be changed to floating rate, or floating to fixed, without incurring the transaction costs and possible redemption penalties associated with actual redemption.
- Using the principle of comparative advantage, companies with different credit ratings can reduce their cost of borrowing, by borrowing at different costs in different markets.
- Swaps can offer access to capital markets for companies which would not normally be allowed to participate due to their low credit rating, by swapping borrowings with a company with a higher credit rating.

(ii) We (QW plc) could borrow at a fixed 8%, while ER plc borrows at a floating LIBOR + 0.5%, and then swap the interest obligations. Total interest paid by both parties is LIBOR + 8.5%.

The alternative is for us to borrow at a floating LIBOR + 0.2%, while ER plc borrows at a fixed 9.5%. Total interest then paid by both parties is LIBOR + 9.7%.

Clearly the swap is advantageous, since total interest is 1.2% less than the alternative. The bank's commission is 0.2%, leaving 1% (or £100,000) as the net benefit to be shared between the two companies. ER plc has opportunistically proposed that the net benefit should be shared equally between the two companies. Since our credit rating is better than ER's, it would be fairer for us to receive more than 50%, though this is a matter for negotiation.

As a final point, it should be noted that, if we are confident that interest rates are going to fall over the next three years, it will probably be better to take out floating rate borrowings from the start, rather than take out fixed rate borrowings and swap these for floating rate. We would not have to share the benefits of falling interest rates with any third party or pay the swap's commission payment to the bank. The decision therefore depends on how confident we are that interest rates will fall as expected. Please contact me again if I can be of any further help to you in this or any other matter.

hapter

14

Cost of capital and capital investment decisions

Chapter learning objectives

Lead	Component
E1: Evaluate the risks arising from changes in the environment for capital investment appraisal.	(a) evaluate investment projects.

Indicative syllabus content

- Cost of capital and risk.
- Recognising risk using the certainty equivalent method (when given a risk free rate and certainty equivalent values).
- Adjusted present value. (**Note:** The two step method may be tested for debt introduced permanently and debt in place for the duration of the project.)

1 Introduction

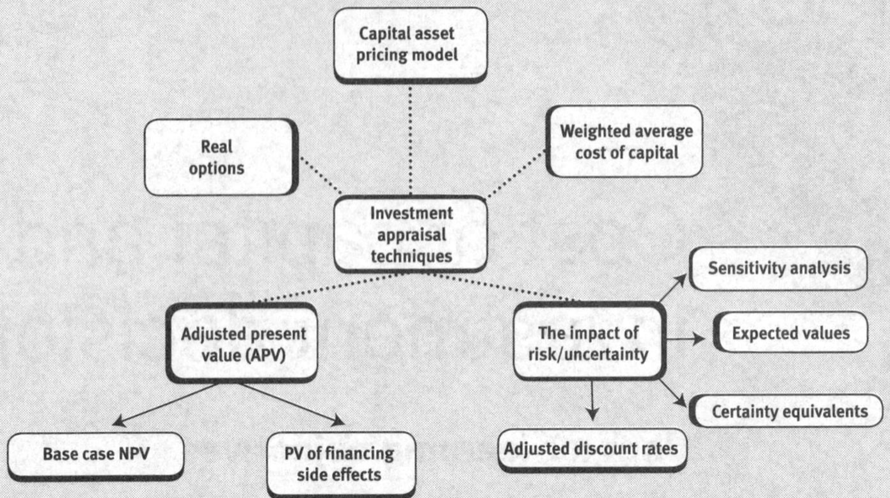

Introduction

In this chapter we consider how risk issues can be incorporated into investment appraisal decisions and will consider a range of different techniques with an emphasis on the following perspectives:

(a) How to measure and evaluate the different risks involved

(b) How each method incorporates risks into the decision making process

(c) How to decide on which investment appraisal technique to use, based on the risks involved

(d) How to implement the techniques specified.

Which types of risk to incorporate

When assessing a potential capital investment the following risks need to be considered:

- business risk
- financial or gearing risk

In each case we may need to consider both the risks of the project and the extent to which they are different to or impact the level of risk of the company. These risks can be incorporated by the choice of investment appraisal method used.

So, for example, if we are assessing the project by calculating a NPV, then the choice of discount rate should reflect both the project's business risk and gearing risk, both of which may be different from the company undertaking the investment.

In addition to the above, there is also a risk with investment decisions that the estimates used may not be completely reliable/certain/accurate. This aspect is generally dealt with via sensitivity analysis.

Real options

We will also look at the subject of real options, reflecting the fact that even discounted cash flow techniques may fail to deal fully with the implications, and value of uncertainty.

2 Recap of key investment appraisal techniques from earlier papers

Discounted cash flow techniques – the time value of money

A key principle underpining the use of discounted cash flow techniques is the "time value of money".

In simplistic terms this states that money received now is worth more than the expectation of the same amount being received at a later time in the future – the timing of a cash flow affects its perceived value to us. There are four reasons why this is the case:

- *Investment opportunities*

  Cash received sooner could be invested and earn a return

- *Cost of finance*

  Cash received sooner could be used to repay finance, thus saving interest

- *Inflation*

  Cash received sooner will buy more goods – inflation erodes the purchasing power of the money

- *Risk*

  The higher the level of risk, then the less certain the expectation of future cash flows become, thus making them less valuable to us when making a decision.

In P3 we are most concerned with the last of these. In particular we can state, for example, that

- higher risk projects should be assessed using higher discount rates

Later in this chapter we will consider the Capital Asset Pricing Model (CAPM), which has an equation that shows a very clear link between risk and required return.

Net Present Value (NPV)

A positive NPV indicates that the present value of inflows outweighs the present value of cash outflows, taking into account the time value of money factors above..

Thus, if risk has been incorporated into the discount rate, then we can state that

- a positive NPV should indicate that the project return is sufficiently high to compensate for the risks involved and still give the shareholders a gain.

The NPV approach can also be used to understand the potential benefits of risk management:

- Given the high correlation between corporate value and NPVs, a risk management policy can be seen to be beneficial if either it improves futures cash flows and/or reduces the cost of capital (discount rates) used.
- Cash flows can be improved by risk management in a number of ways:
  - Volatile profits may subject companies to higher tax rates in certain years than if profits had been more stable.
  - Costs of financial distress can be avoided. As well as facing higher financing costs, a company facing financial distress may find that, for example, customers may demand better warranty schemes or may be reluctant to buy a product due to concerns about the corporation's ability to fulfil its warranty; employees may demand higher salaries; senior management may ask for golden hellos before agreeing to work for the corporation; and suppliers may be unwilling to offer favourable credit terms
- Lower perceived risk should result in a reduced cost of equity and a lower cost of debt.

Internal rate of return (IRR)

Internal rate of return (IRR) has the following properties:

- the IRR of a project indicates the discount rate at which the NPV is zero.
- for most "normal" projects (i.e. cash outflow followed by inflows) the project NPV will be positive for discount rates < IRR and negative for discount rates > IRR

- the IRR can thus be viewed as a breakeven cost of capital

This makes the IRR very useful for performing sensitivity analysis on the discount rate.

For example:

- Suppose we estimate the cost of capital to be 12% and at this discount rate the project NPV is positive
- Before accepting the project we would then perform sensitivity analysis. Suppose we calculate the IRR to be 15%
- This means that as long as the discount rate is below 15% then the project is worth undertaking
- We can then revisit how we estimated the discount rate and re-evaluate any assumptions made to assess the risk of making a wrong decision.

Sensitivity analysis is recapped in more detail in the next section.

Discount rate considerations

In all the examples considered so far in this section on risk, a constant discount rate has been used, on the assumption that the cost of capital will remain the same over the life of the project. As the factors which influence the cost of capital, such as interest rates and inflation, can change considerably over a short period of time an organisation may wish to use different rates over the life of the project. Net present value and discounted present value allow this, but IRR and ARR present a uniform rate of return. Using NPV, for example, a different discount factor can be used for each year if so desired.

Perhaps, one of the major problems in using a discounted cash flow method is deciding on the correct discount rate to use.

It is difficult enough in year 1 but deciding on the rate for, say, year 4 may be very difficult because of changes in the economy, etc. If a very low rate is chosen almost all projects will be accepted, whereas if a very high discount rate is chosen very few projects will be accepted.

Looking back over the years, it would appear that the majority of managers have probably used too high a discount rate and have, as a consequence, not invested in projects that would have helped their organisation to grow in relation to their competitors. There are no prizes for being too conservative; it is just as much a failing as being too optimistic.

If there is any doubt over the correct discount rate to be used, sensitivity analysis can help.

More detail on adjusted discount rates

A useful scheme is to have a risk category schedule providing different risk gradings. For example, a "normal" project could be discounted at the usual cost of capital, with more risky projects being discounted at perhaps 2% more than this.

The difficulty with risk-adjusted discount rates lies mainly in the need for skillful management judgement as to the risk category, even though considerable product and market research may have been undertaken.

The capital asset pricing model (CAPM) is often used to calculate risk adjusted discount rates, as shown in the CIMA F3 syllabus.

Test your understanding 1

The lower risk of a project can be recognised by **increasing** which of the following?

Select ALL that apply.

A The cost of the initial investment of the project

B The estimates of future cash inflows from the project

C The internal rate of return of the project

D The required rate of return of the project

Test your understanding 2

A project has a net present value of $(543) when the discount rate is 20 per cent and $1,344 when it is 15 per cent.

Calculate the approximate internal rate of return (to the nearest whole per cent point) of this investment without calculating any further net present values.

Test your understanding 3

Which THREE of the following measures are of most use when evaluating the risk of a potential investment?

A Return on capital employed (ROCE)

B Residual income (RI)

C Beta factor

D Internal rate of return (IRR)

E Discounted payback period

F Discount rate

Probabilities and expected values

If forecasts are uncertain but probabilities can be attached to the possible outcomes, expected values (EV) can be calculated.

EV = (outcome 1 × probability 1) + (outcome 2 × probability 2) etc

Examples of expected values

Simple example

GH Co is trying to estimate sales in the coming year.

It has been predicted that there is a 30% chance of sales being $20,000, a 50% chance of sales being $30,000 and a 20% chance of sales being $40,000.

Required:

Calculate the expected sales in the coming year.

Solution:

Expected sales = (0.30 × 20,000) + (0.50 × 30,000) + (0.20 × 40,000) = $29,000

More complex example (dependent probabilities)

Following on from the example above, assume that the sales in year 2 are dependent on the level of sales achieved in the first year, as follows:

Sales in year 1 (as above)	Probability (as above)	Sales in year 2
$20,000	30%	Could be $20,000 (probability 70%) or $10,000 (probability 30%)
$30,000	50%	Will also be $30,000
$40,000	20%	Could be $40,000 (probability 60%) or $50,000 (probability 40%)

Required:

Calculate the expected sales in year 2.

Solution:

Expected sales in year 2

= 0.30 × [(0.70 × 20,000) + (0.30 × 10,000)]

+ 0.50 × 30,000

+ 0.20 × [(0.60 × 40,000) + (0.40 × 50,000)]

= $28,900

Test your understanding 4

The directors of GHY plc are considering a new project that is subject to considerable uncertainty.

The following costs and revenues have been estimated for the first year:

Cost	Probability	Revenue	Probability
100,000	0.1	120,000	0.2
150,000	0.2	150,000	0.3
200,000	0.4	180,000	0.4
250,000	0.3	200,000	0.1

Assuming that the costs and revenues are independent of each other, what is the probability of a loss occurring?

A 0.19

B 0.70

C 0.80

D 1.00

3 Sensitivity analysis

When undertaking an NPV analysis of a project, the accuracy of the NPV depends on the accuracy of the input factors in the calculation (e.g. estimates of cost of capital, sales, expenses, tax rates).

After computing the NPV of a project, sensitivity analysis can be used:

- to identify which of the input variables of the project could have the most adverse impact on the NPV of the project if they were to change.
- to assess the impact on the NPV of a certain change in a particular input factor.
- to consider by how much each input variable could change before the NPV of the project became zero (and hence the project became unacceptable).

Interpretation of sensitivity analysis results

A company has calculated the NPV of a project, and has subsequently identified the following sensitivities:

> Sales can fall by 10% or costs may rise by 20%, or the discount rate can increase by 1% before the NPV becomes zero.

In this case we would conclude that the project NPV is very sensitive to changes in discount rate (small percentage sensitivity) but not very sensitive to changes in costs. (Unless they changed by more than 20% the NPV would still be positive.)

Limitations of sensitivity analysis

The major problem is that we normally consider the impact of only one variable at a time. Management may be more interested in the risk of some key factors changing at the same time. For example, if the selling price changes, there is likely to be an impact on sales volume too. Sensitivity analysis can only deal with one of these variables changing at a time.

Also, sensitivity analysis does not include any assessment of the probability of certain variables changing.

It is therefore useful as an aid to decision making, rather than a decision rule in itself.

Two basic approaches to sensitivity analysis

(1) An analysis can be made of all the key input factors to ascertain by how much each factor must change before the NPV reaches zero, the indifference point.

(2) Alternatively specific changes can be calculated, such as the sales decreasing by 5%, in order to determine the effect on NPV.

Both approaches will be shown in the illustration below.

Definition of sensitivity analysis

Sensitivity analysis definition

A modelling and risk assessment procedure in which changes are made to significant variables in order to determine the effect of these changes on the planned outcome. Particular attention is thereafter paid to variables identified as being of special significance.

(CIMA Official Terminology, 2005)

Illustration 1 – Sensitivity

A project has an NPV of $1m. The PV of material costs (included in the NPV calculation) are $5m.

Sensitivity = (NPV/PV of cashflows affected by the estimate) × 100%

= 1m/5m = 0.2 (20%)

i.e. the material costs could rise by up to 20% and the project remains viable. A rise of greater than 20% will produce a negative NPV and the project would not be worthwhile.

Alternatively, sensitivity analysis could be used to assess the impact of a given percentage change in a variable.

To continue with the above example, if the material costs were to change by 10% (from a PV of $5m to $5.5m – a change of $0.5m) the NPV would reduce by $0.5m from $1m to $0.5m (a fall of 50%).

More detailed example of sensitivity analysis

AVI Co is evaluating a new investment project as follows:

$000	t_0	t_1	t_2	t_3	t_4
Sales		1,000	1,000	1,000	1,000
Costs		600	600	600	600
		400	400	400	400
Tax (30%)		(120)	(120)	(120)	(120)
Net		280	280	280	280
CapEx	(600)				
Tax relief on depreciation		45	45	45	45
(30% × 600/4)					
Net cash flow	(600)	325	325	325	325
DF @ 10%	1	0.909	0.826	0.751	0.683

NPV = $430,000

Sensitivity to sales (i.e. by how much could sales fall before NPV becomes zero)

= (NPV/PV of cashflows affected by the estimate of sales) × 100%

= [430/(1,000 × (1 – 0.30) × 3.170)] × 100%

= 19.4%

i.e. if sales were to fall by 19.4% (to $806,000 per annum) then the NPV would be zero.

Sensitivity to tax rate

= (NPV/PV of cashflows affected by the estimate of tax rate) × 100%

= [430/((45 – 120) × 3.170)] × 100%

= 181%

i.e. if the tax rate were to rise by 181% (from 30% to 30 × 2.82 = 84.6%) then the NPV would fall to zero.

Sensitivity to discount rate

This cannot be calculated in the same way. Instead the IRR of the project should be calculated and the difference between the existing cost of capital and the IRR then indicates the sensitivity to the discount rate.

Here the IRR is approximately 40%.

Interpretation of sensitivity calculations

AVI Co would initially be inclined to accept the project due to its positive NPV.

However, before making a final decision, the sensitivities would be considered. Any factors with small percentage sensitivities will have to be carefully assessed, because if the estimates of these factors turn out to be incorrect, the result may be a negative NPV.

In this example, the project NPV is not very sensitive to changes in the tax rate or the discount rate. The likelihood of sales falling by 19.4% would need to be assessed before making a final decision, but assuming that management decide that this is not a major risk, the project would be undertaken.

Test your understanding 5

A NPV calculation has been prepared for the following project based on latest best estimates of future cash flows:

Time	Narrative	CF $000	DF@10%	PV $000
0	Initial investment	(500)	1	(500)
1 – 5	Sales	400	3.791	1,516
1 – 5	Variable costs	(150)	3.791	(569)
1 – 5	Incremental fixed costs	(100)	3.791	(379)

NPV = + $68,000

Which ONE of the following estimates should be prioritised for further investigation on sensitivity grounds?

A Initial investment

B Selling price

C Sales volume

D Incremental fixed overheads

4 Certainty Equivalents

Certainty equivalents

As an alternative to using higher discount rates to incorporate risk, the certainty equivalents approach is as follows:

(1) The cash flows of the project are estimated / calculated as per normal

(2) These cash flows are then adjusted downwards by multiplying by a certainty equivalent factor. This in effect decreases the cash flow to reflect the level of uncertainty.

(3) The cash flows are then discounted at the risk-free rate. There is no need to include a risk premium in the discount rate as the cash flows have already been adjusted to take into account the risk and uncertainty.

In practice the major problem is that the use of certainty equivalents is subjective.

Definition of certainty equivalents

Certainty equivalent method – definition

An approach to dealing with risk in a capital budgeting context. It involves expressing risky future cash flows in terms of the certain cashflow which would be considered, by the decision maker, as their equivalent, that is the decision maker would be indifferent between the risky amount and the (lower) riskless amount considered to be its equivalent.

(CIMA Official Terminology, 2005)

Illustration 2 – Certainty equivalents

Year	*Cash flow*	*Certainty equivalent factor*	*Certainty equivalent cash flows*	*Discount factor at risk free rate (6%)*	*PV*
0	(1,000)	1.00	(1,000)	1.000	(1,000)
1	900	0.95	855	0.943	806
2	750	0.90	675	0.890	601

NPV = 407

More detail on certainty equivalents

The certainty equivalents method adjusts for risk by incorporating the decision maker's risk attitude into the investment decision by converting the expected cashflows of the project into equivalent riskless amounts.

The danger of using certainty equivalents lies in the high level of subjective judgement required from the decision-maker, while it could also be argued that risk-averse management might be better off using a higher discount rate.

Nevertheless, certainty equivalents do represent a useful tool in the investment appraisal armoury, especially in assessing cases where an apparently small change in a key variable can interact with others to create significant falls in inflows, with a possible cumulative effect over the life of the project.

Benefits of using certainty equivalents

- They are a very simple way of incorporating risk into an investment appraisal.
- They enable the decision maker to reduce the possible future cash flows to give a worst-possible scenario NPV.
- By using a risk-free rate for discounting, they avoid double counting the impact of risk, and they also avoid the need for the investor to estimate an appropriate discount rate which reflects the risk of the project cash flows.
- The certainty equivalent approach distinguishes between risk and time. A specific risk adjustment is applied to future time periods. The risk-adjusted discount rate approach treats risk quite differently. By building the risk adjustment into the discount rate, it takes greater account of risk in later time periods, effectively treating risk as if it increases exponentially over time. However, in some projects, project cash flows may not increase in risk over time at all and the risk-adjusted discount rate approach would not provide an appropriate adjustment for risk in such cases.

Drawbacks of using certainty equivalents

- They are very subjective. For example, it is very difficult to assess whether a 90% factor or an 85% factor should be applied.

Test your understanding 6

JK plc is undertaking a project which involves a £1million investment today which will generate cash savings of £350,000 per annum for 4 years. The relevant discount factor for the project is 7%.

Directors believe that the cash savings at the end of year 1 are 95% certain, in year 2 are 90% certain and for year 3 and 4 are only 75% certain.

Calculate the NPV of the project using certainty equivalents.

Test your understanding 7

LMN plc is undertaking a project which involves a £10million investment today and which will generate cash savings in perpetuity. The relevant discount factor for the project is 8%.

Directors believe that the cash savings (in perpetuity) at the end of each year are 95% certain.

Using certainty equivalents, the annual cash saving required for the project to break even is:

Test your understanding 8

DF plc is undertaking a project which involves a £4.5million investment today and which will generate cash savings of £400,000 in perpetuity. The relevant discount factor for the project is 8%.

Directors are worried as to the certainty of the future cash savings.

Using certainty equivalents, the certainty of the annual cash savings required for the project to break even is (expressed to 2 decimal places):

5 Real Options

Introduction to real options

Traditional approaches to investment appraisal tend to treat investments as one-off decisions which must be taken at a single point in time, with the opportunity otherwise being lost.

While this may typify some investment decisions, it certainly does not apply to them all.

In many situations it may be possible to delay and gain further valuable information, which could be influential in the viability or otherwise of the investment decision.

In such cases the opportunity to invest can be thought of as being very similar to a call option. It gives a right, but not an obligation, to a stream of cash flows associated with the project at some future date. When a company either decides to go ahead or completely rejects an investment proposal it effectively brings this option to an end.

While the option is open it has a value, and recent research would suggest that the NPV rule should be modified to take account of the value of this option.

Such options are called 'real options' because they are options on real physical assets, to distinguish them from financial options which are options on financial assets.

Real options

Terminology – call and put options

Before discussing investment decisions as options on future cash flows, it may be useful to identity the meaning of call and put options:

- a call option is an option to buy a specified asset at a specified exercise price on or before a specified exercise date;
- a put option is an option to sell a specified asset at a specified exercise price on or before a specified exercise date.

Application to investment appraisal

The NPV approach to investment appraisal makes two assumptions that may be questioned:

(1) a project is reversible;

(2) a project cannot be delayed.

The assumption that a project is reversible implies that if the project does not work out, the original investment can be recovered and applied to a new project. This is flawed, as in most significant projects the original investment will either be wholly or partly irreversible.

In some instances, it may not be possible to delay an investment decision, but in the majority of cases a delay is possible – although there may be costs associated with delay. If a project is irreversible to some degree, the ability to delay the investment decision in order to obtain new information is valuable. The additional costs associated with delay should be assessed against the benefits associated with that new information.

Investment projects can be related to financial call options, in that the project provides the right, but not the obligation, to purchase an asset (or commit to a series of cash flows) in the future. When an irreversible investment decision is made, the call option becomes exercised. The opportunity to delay an investment and keep the option alive has a value, which is not normally reflected in an NPV calculation.

The real options approach suggests that decisions that increase flexibility by creating and preserving options should be pursued. Decisions that reduce flexibility by exercising options and irreversibly committing resources should be valued at a lower figure than conventional NPV would suggest.

Categorisation of real options

In the context of investment decisions there are three options to be considered:

(1) The abandonment option (financial put option).

(2) Timing options (financial call option) – sometimes referred to as "wait and see options".

(3) Strategic investment options (financial call option) – sometimes referred to as "follow-on options".

Different types of real options

The abandonment option

Major investment decisions involve heavy capital commitments and are largely irreversible: once the initial capital expenditure is incurred, management cannot turn the clock back and act differently.

Because the management is committing large sums of money in pursuit of higher, but uncertain, payoffs, the ability to abandon, or 'bail out', should things look grim, can be valuable.

Timing options (or "wait and see options")

Management may view an investment as a 'now or never' opportunity, arguing that in highly competitive markets there is no scope for delay.

In effect, this amounts to viewing the decision as a call option which is about to expire. If a positive NPV is expected, the option will be exercised, otherwise the option lapses and no investment is made. However, delaying the decision by a year to gain valuable new information is likely to be a more valuable option.

This helps us to understand why entities sometimes do not take up apparently wealth-creating opportunities: the option to wait and gather new information is sufficiently valuable to warrant such delay.

Strategic investment options (or "follow-on options")

Certain investment decisions give rise to follow-on opportunities which are wealth-creating.

For example, new technology investment, involving large-scale research and development, is particularly difficult to evaluate, and many such projects would show negative NPVs as the uncertainty involved would demand the use of high discount rates. However, they offer the potential to access a large market in the future.

The negative NPV can be viewed as the option cost, or premium on the follow-on option. The value of the option is the value of the flexibility associated with the project.

Simple real options example

Cardiff Components Co is considering building a new plant to produce components for the nuclear defence industry.

Proposal A is to build a custom-designed plant using the latest technology, but applicable only to nuclear defence contracts.

A less profitable scheme, B, is to build a plant using standard machine tools, giving greater flexibility in application.

The outcome of a general election to be held one year hence has a major impact on the decision. If the current government is returned to office, their commitment to nuclear defence is likely to give rise to new orders, making proposal A the better choice. If, however, the current opposition party is elected, its commitment to run down the nuclear defence industry would make proposal B the better course of action.

Proposal B has, in effect, a put option attached to it, giving the flexibility to abandon the proposed operation in favour of some other activity.

(Illustration adapted from Pike and Neale)

Numerical illustration of real options

Initial scenario

A project, P, has expected cash flows as shown below:

Year 0	Year 1		Year 2		Year 3	
$	p	$	p	$	p	$
(3,500)	1/3	3,000	1/3	3,000	1/3	3,000
	1/3	2,000	1/3	2,000	1/3	2,000
	1/3	1,000	1/3	1,000	1/3	1,000
Expected values		2,000		2,000		2,000

Note that p = probability of each outcome.

The project's NPV at a discount rate of 10%, based on the expected value of its cashflows is:

Year	Cash flow ($)	DF 10%	PV ($)
0	(3,500)	1	(3,500)
1	2,000	0.909	1,818
2	2,000	0.826	1,653
3	2,000	0.751	1,503
			1,474

More details regarding the project

The initial investment of $3,500 in project P represents the purchase of a customised machine, the price of which is known with certainty.

Because it is a customised machine its resale value is low; it can only be sold for $2,000 up to 1 year after purchase. Thereafter, its resale value will be zero.

The option to abandon the project immediately

Once the machine is bought, the expected value of abandoning the project immediately would be $2,000 (1 × $2,000).

This must be compared with the expected value of continuing with the project, which is $4,974 ($1,818 + $1,653 + $1,503).

In this case, the expected benefits of continuing with the project far outweigh the returns from abandoning it immediately.

The option to abandon the project in 1 year's time

Once the machine has been in operation for a year, the first year's cashflow will be known with certainty.

Assume that in this scenario, the year 1 outcome determines the years 2 and 3 outcomes with certainty (i.e. if the outcome is $1,000 in year 1, it will also be $1,000 in year 2 and year 3, etc).

Note: if this were not to be the case, a decision tree could be used to identify all the potential combinations of outcomes.

Given that the machine can be sold for $2,000 at this point, the three possible outcomes if the project is abandoned in 1 year's time are:

Year	Cash flow ($)	DF 10%	PV ($)
New 0	2,000	1	2,000
1	(1,000)	0.909	(909)
2	(1,000)	0.826	(826)
			265

Year	Cash flow ($)	DF 10%	PV ($)
New 0	2,000	1	2,000
1	(2,000)	0.909	(1,818)
2	(2,000)	0.826	(1,652)
			(1,470)

Year	Cash flow ($)	DF 10%	PV ($)
New 0	2,000	1	2,000
1	(3,000)	0.909	(2,727)
2	(3,000)	0.826	(2,478)
			(3,205)

Note that in each case it has been assumed that the project has been abandoned, and therefore all the future cashflows have been foregone.

It can be seen that if the future cashflows are expected to be $2,000 per annum or $3,000 per annum, the project should not be abandoned in 1 year's time, since the value of the future cashflows foregone would be higher than the disposal value of $2,000.

However, if the future cashflows are expected to be $1,000, the project should be abandoned since the abandonment option has a positive NPV.

Assessing the value of the abandonment option

The fact that the project can be abandoned in 1 year's time if cashflows turn out to be at the low end of expectations ($1,000 per annum) gives an additional value to the overall project.

The value of this can be incorporated into the NPV of the project by recomputing the NPV based on the cashflows if the abandonment takes place, as follows:

Year 0	**Year 1**		**Year 2**		**Year 3**	
$	p	$	p	$	p	$
(3,500)	1/3	3,000	1/3	3,000	1/3	3,000
	1/3	2,000	1/3	2,000	1/3	2,000
	1/3	1,000+2,000	1/3	NIL	1/3	NIL
Expected values		2,667		1,667		1,667

The NPV of the project now becomes:

Year	**Cash flow ($)**	**DF 10%**	**PV ($)**
0	(3,500)	1	(3,500)
1	2,667	0.909	2,424
2	1,667	0.826	1,377
3	1,667	0.751	1,252
			1,553

i.e. the option to abandon the project in 1 year's time increases the NPV of the project by $79 ($1,553 – $1,474).

Valuing real options

Option valuation

Calculations on option pricing are not part of the syllabus, but it is worth noting that the Black-Scholes option pricing model can be used to value real options if the following five factors can be identified and entered into the model:

(1) present value of the future cash flows from the investment;

(2) initial outlay on the investment;

(3) time until the investment opportunity disappears, that is the length of time that an investment decision can be deferred without losing the opportunity to invest;

(4) variability of project returns;

(5) risk-free rate of interest.

In practice, however, the time to expiry and the variability of project returns may be difficult to measure.

Pricing an option using values for these factors will arguably provide more information about the value of a project than using NPV. However, quantifying these factors objectively is not straightforward.

6 The Capital Asset Pricing Model (CAPM)

The Capital Asset Pricing Model (CAPM) has two key elements:

- a methodology for measuring business risk
- an equation for determining what level of required return is needed to compensate for the measured level of risk.

It is often used as an alternative to the dividend valuation model when trying to calculate a cost of equity.

A key concept with CAPM is that it only considers "systematic risk".

Systematic and unsystematic risk

There are two elements that make up the business risk associated with a company:

- Unsystematic (or specific) risk

This is the risk of the company's cash flows due to specific factors such as strikes, R&D successes, systems failures, the actions of competitors, etc.

Such factors tend to net off across the whole of the stock market, so unsystematic risk factors do not move the market as a whole.

For example, if one supermarket develops a particularly effective advertising campaign, then it will see its profits rise and rivals' returns fall but the net effect on the stock market is zero. An investor who held (the right balance of) shares in each of the supermarkets concerned would not see a change in the overall value of their portfolio.

Unsystematic risk can thus be diversified away by having a wide enough share portfolio.

- Systematic (or market) risk

Systematic risk is the risk of the company's cash flows due to general macro-economic factors such as tax rates, oil prices, the position of the country in the economic cycle, unemployment, interest rates, etc.

Such factors typically affect the whole stock market and (in most cases) in the same way.

For example, in a recession all of the supermarkets mentioned above will suffer to some extent. The investor cannot diversify away the impact of a recession simply by buying shares in a wider range of companies.

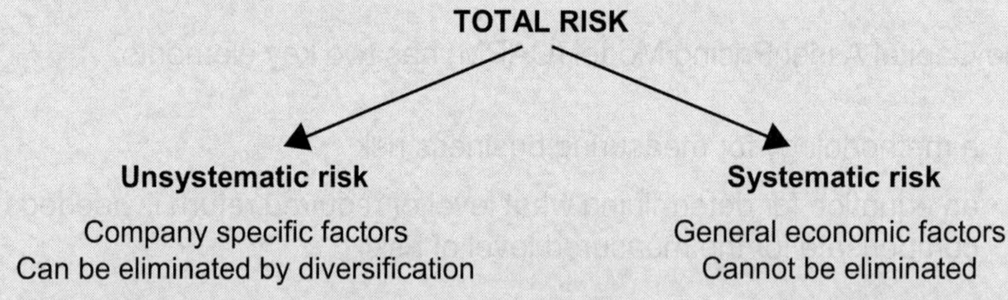

Diversification and the portfolio effect

By building a portfolio of investments, unsystematic risk can be reduced or diversified away. Systematic risk is not reduced in this way, so will be present in all portfolios.

For example, suppose an investor sets up a company making and selling ice cream (and has no other investments at this stage). The ice cream business will face both systematic risk (e.g. due to a recession) and also unsystematic risk due to potential changes in the weather – sunny weather producing good returns, cold weather poor returns. By itself the investment could be considered a high risk.

Suppose the investor is given the opportunity to buy a business that makes umbrellas. Viewed in isolation it could be argued that this is also a risky business, again due mainly to the weather but in the opposite way to ice cream. Thus, when the two entities are viewed as part of the same portfolio, then the return from the portfolio will have a much-reduced risk level. In good weather the returns from ice cream compensate for falls in umbrella sales and the opposite in poor weather.

This process is known as diversification, and when continued can reduce portfolio risk to a minimum. If an investor enlarges his portfolio to include approximately 25 shares the unsystematic risk is reduced to close to zero, the implication being that we may eliminate the unsystematic portion of overall risk by spreading investment over a sufficiently diversified portfolio.

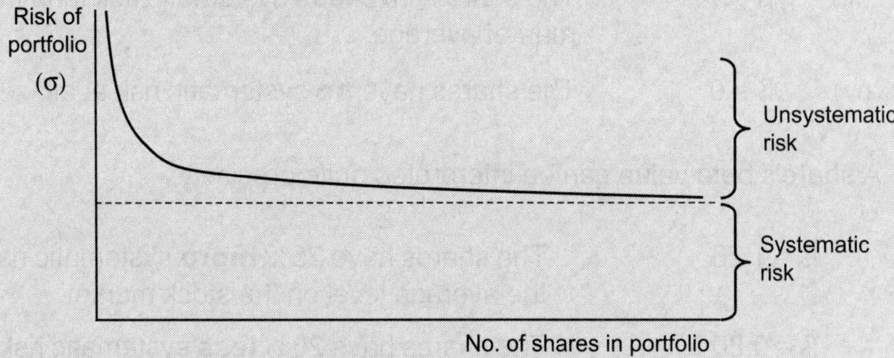

Perspective

Note that three different investors may have very different risk perspectives when considering an investment in the umbrella firm above:

- An investor with no other investments will consider all of the risks involved
- The owner of the ice cream business will be more interested in how their portfolio risk is reduced when the umbrella business is added to their existing investment.
- A well-diversified investor would only consider the systematic risk of the umbrella business as the unsystematic risk will be negated or absorbed in their portfolio (with perhaps a little tweaking).

CAPM assumes that we are dealing with the last of these three investors.

Note: we are NOT suggesting that the company carrying out the investment must be well-diversified. The key issue is whether or not the ultimate shareholders have a sufficiently diversified portfolio.

If we can measure the systematic risk of a company or investment, the CAPM will enable us to calculate the level of required return for a well-diversified investor who is not subject to unsystematic risk.

Measuring systematic risk – ß (beta) factors

Beta is a relative measure of systematic risk, comparing the systematic risk of the company or investment being considered with the average level of systematic risk in the stock market as a whole.

Beta values fall into four categories, with the following meanings:

(i)	ß > 1	The shares have **more** systematic risk than the stock market average.
(ii)	ß = 1	The shares have the **same** systematic risk as the stock market average.
(iii)	ß < 1	The shares have **less** systematic risk than the stock market average.
(iv)	ß = 0	The shares have **no** systematic risk at all.

A share's beta value can be interpreted quite precisely:

ß = 1.25	:	The shares have 25% **more** systematic risk than the average level on the stock market.
ß = 0.80	:	The shares have 20% **less** systematic risks than the average. (i.e. they only have 80% of the average level).

The security market line

The security market line (SML) shows the relationship between the level of systematic risk and the corresponding required return.

We know two points on the line:

(1) **The risk-free security**

This carries no risk and therefore no systematic risk and therefore has a **beta** of zero.

The required return would be the risk free interest rate in the economy.

(2) **The market portfolio**

This represents the market portfolio in total – the ultimate in diversification and therefore contains only systematic risk. It has a **beta** of 1.

The required return can be measured as the return on the market portfolio.

These two points may be plotted and then joined up with a straight line:

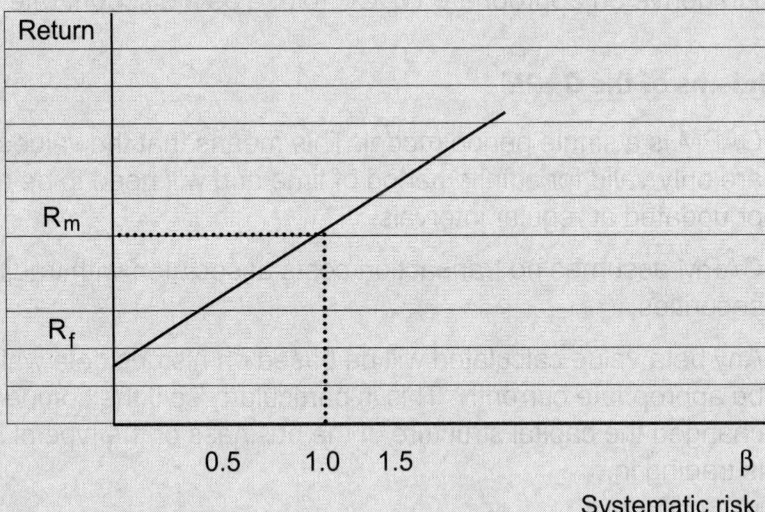

R_f is the point on the graph where the line intersects the axis, and then the higher the systematic risk, the higher the required rate of return.

The SML and the relationship between required return and risk can be shown using the following formula:

Formula

Required return = risk free rate + risk premium

$$k_e = R_f + [R_m - R_f]\,ß$$

where

k_e = required return from individual security

ß = Beta factor of individual security

R_f = risk-free rate of interest

R_m = return on market portfolio

Note: In exams, the question will sometimes refer to the market premium – this is the difference between R_m and R_f. It is the long term market premium that should be used in CAPM if this is different from current market rates.

The CAPM gives a required return for a given level of risk (measured by the beta factor). Therefore, if we can estimate the level of risk associated with a new investment project (the beta of the project), we can use CAPM to give a required return to shareholders.

Typically CAPM is used to determine the cost of equity which can then be used to derive an appropriate WACC to use as a discount rate.

Criticisms of the CAPM

(1) CAPM is a single period model. This means that the values calculated are only valid for a finite period of time and will need to be recalculated or updated at regular intervals.

(2) CAPM assumes no transaction costs associated with trading securities.

(3) Any beta value calculated will be based on historic data which may not be appropriate currently. This is particularly so if the company has changed the capital structure of the business or the type of business it is trading in.

(4) The risk free rate may change considerably over short periods of time.

(5) CAPM assumes an efficient investment market where it is possible to diversify away risk. This is not necessarily the case, meaning that some unsystematic risk may remain.

(6) Additionally, the idea that all unsystematic risk is diversified away will not hold true if stocks change in terms of volatility. As stocks change over time it is very likely that the portfolio becomes less than optimal.

(7) CAPM assumes all stocks relate to going concerns, this may not be the case.

Test your understanding 9

Which of the following are considered to be limitations when using the CAPM model to estimate a required return for a well-diversified investor?

Select ALL that apply.

A CAPM does not account for systematic risk

B CAPM does not account for total business risk

C CAPM ignores unsystematic risk

D CAPM is based on historical data and the variance surrounding the beta factor may be significant;

E CAPM does not look at the market return

F CAPM is a single period model, which is then used to calculate a discount rate for projects lasting many years

Test your understanding 10

You have been asked to evaluate the following three potential investments for a well-diversified client.

Investment	A	B	C
Expected return	12%	10%	6%
Beta	1.6	1.1	0.4

The market risk premium on the market portfolio is expected to be 6% and the risk-free rate 3%.

Which would you recommend buying?

Select ALL that apply.

A Project A

B Project B

C Project C

Test your understanding 11

A rational, risk-averse investor is considering investing in the following company shares:

Company	Risk	Expected Return
X	10%	15%
Y	6%	23%
Z	15%	30%

Which of the following statements are correct? (Select ALL that apply)

A Being risk averse, the investor will not invest in any of the risky shares shown.

B Being risk averse, the investor will choose Company Y as it has the lowest risk.

C The investor should definitely dismiss Company X as it gives a lower return for higher risk, compared to Company Y shares

D Being rational, the investor will see that Company Z is obviously best as the high return more than compensates for the risks involved.

E There is insufficient information given to make a decision as to which investment(s) is (are) to be preferred.

Risk and diversification (Case style question)

Scenario

You are the company accountant with a medium-sized, privately-owned company. The company has surplus funds which it does not believe it will be able to invest in company operations for at least five years. The majority shareholders are also the directors of the company and they do not wish the surplus funds to be distributed as dividends. A board meeting has therefore been called to discuss the proposal that the funds be invested in a portfolio of medium-to long-term securities.

Trigger

Three of the directors have recently attended a short course at the local university on *'Investment and the Management of Risk'*. They make the following comments at the meeting, based on their interpretations of what they have learnt on the course:

- 'If we hold a portfolio of stocks, we need only consider the systematic risk of the securities.'
- 'As a cautious investor we must always consider total risk.'
- 'We should not buy anything if the expected return is less than that on the market as a whole, and certainly not if it is below the return on the risk-free asset.'

Task

Prepare a memorandum to the Board that

(a) **explains to the members of the board the meaning of systematic, unsystematic and total risk and advise them, briefly, how all three types of risk can be measured, and**

(b) **discusses the directors' comments.**

(25 minutes)

7 Further aspects of CAPM – geared and ungeared betas

When using CAPM in practice one of the main issues lies in obtaining a suitable project beta.

- For quoted companies a beta can be estimated by comparing the company performance with the performance of the stock market as a whole. Betas of quoted companies are readily available online.
- For unquoted companies and projects the simplest way of obtaining a beta is to find a quoted company with similar business activities and then use its beta. So, for example, if a project involved fashion clothing, then a beta could be obtained by finding a listed fashion company and simply looking up its beta.

However, there is a complication here – there are two types of betas and you need to use the right one:

- "Ungeared" or "asset" betas – these only incorporate the (systematic) business risk
- "Geared" or "equity" betas – these incorporate both the (systematic) business risk and also the gearing risk of the company.

When betas are calculated for quoted companies, then an equity beta is obtained. However, if a project and listed company share the same business area, then they will have the same asset beta but not necessarily the same equity beta. Thus the equity beta will need to be degeared before it can be transferred to the project.

Beta revisited

Asset beta – reflects pure systematic business risk

Equity beta – reflects business and gearing risk

Betas can be geared and ungeared:

$$\beta \text{ asset} = \beta \text{ equity} \times \frac{V_e}{V_e + V_d(1-T)}$$

Degearing and regearing betas is in the F3 syllabus, so you should not expect to have to do this within the P3 exam. However, you do need to be aware of which beta is needed when in the different investment appraisal techniques covered in the rest of this chapter.

Test your understanding 12

Which of the following statements is/are true?

Select ALL that apply.

A If two companies operate in the same areas of business, then they will have the same asset betas

B Equity betas cannot be smaller than their corresponding asset betas

C If a company is all equity financed, then its equity and asset betas will be the same

D If using CAPM to calculate the cost of equity for a geared company, then the asset beta must be used.

8 Choice of investment appraisal method

In order to decide on the most appropriate investment appraisal method, you need to consider how the project (and its financing) will impact the risk of the company undertaking the investment.

Two key questions must be asked:

- Does the project have a different level of business risk to the company?
- Will the finance package chosen change the gearing level and hence the gearing risk of the company?

There are four possible outcomes:

Impact on financial gearing risk? \ Impact on business risk?	No change	Change
No change	The existing company WACC can be used to discount the project cash flows	A risk adjusted WACC must be calculated to reflect project business risk. This can then be used to discount project cash flows
Change	Adjusted present value (APV)	Adjusted present value (APV)

Using the company WACC as a discount rate

The company WACC is often used as a discount rate when using net present value or internal rate of return calculations. However, this is only appropriate if the following conditions are met:

(1) The capital structure is constant.

If the capital structure changes, the weightings in the WACC will also change.

(2) The new investment does not carry a different business risk profile to the existing company's operations.

If business risk is different, the CAPM would suggest that the required return of investors should be different.

Some firms get by the above restrictions by using the following arguments:

- The "small project" argument

  If we are only looking at a small investment then we would not expect any of k_e, k_d or the WACC to change materially. If the investment is substantial it will usually cause these values to change.

- The "gearing is constant in the long term" argument

  It may not be practical to use a mixture of debt and equity for every project. Suppose for this particular project we use debt – the above table states that we should be using APV as the gearing has changed. However, the firm could argue that next time it will use equity and that in the long run gearing will be kept constant. This argument may also be expressed as saying that rather than looking at the specific finance for the project, we should consider the firm having a "pool" of finance that gets topped up.

Using the company WACC is discussed in further detail below.

Using a risk adjusted WACC as a discount rate

Ideally we want a discount rate that reflects both the project's business risk and gearing risk.

In the previous case the company WACC was a suitable proxy as the company and project had both the same business risks and gearing risks - in essence the project looked like the company but in miniature. Now we consider what changes if the project business risk is different from that of the company:

- We can still use any data from the company regarding its gearing level and cost of debt as these will be the same for both the company and project
- However, we cannot use the company cost of equity but must use CAPM to get a project specific Ke
- Given this, we can then assemble a project WACC

This method is discussed further and illustrated in a later section.

Adjusted present value (APV)

Where the project finance results in a (significant) change in gearing then we need to use the APV technique. This is an entirely new technique at the strategic level and is covered in depth below.

Test your understanding 13

For each of the investment appraisal scenarios, match them to the most appropriate investment appraisal technique.

	Scenario		*Technique*
1	Collins plc, a car manufacturer, is currently financed by a mixture of debt and equity. It is looking at a project to build a new car. The project will be financed by issuing redeemable loan stock	A	Use the company WACC to calculate a NPV
2	Inglesi plc, a gun manufacturer, is currently financed by a mixture of debt and equity. It is looking at a project to design and sell designer clothing. The project will be financed to maintain the company's existing gearing ratio	B	Use a project-specific risk-adjusted WACC to calculate a NPV
3	Menace plc makes guitar effects units and is currently all-equity financed. It is considering a project to develop a new delay pedal. The project will be financed by cutting the forthcoming dividend.	C	Use Adjusted present value (APV)
4	Aspen plc runs a chain of restaurants and is currently financed by a mixture of debt and equity. It plans to open cinemas near its restaurants and plans to use a rights issue to finance the expansion.		

Test your understanding 14

YHG plc is a quoted ship building company. It is currently financed through a mixture of debt and equity and has a gearing ratio of 1:2 measured by the market value of debt to the market value of equity.

Select the appropriate investment appraisal technique for each of the investment scenarios given (Note: you can choose the same technique more than once if you wish).

Projects

A Build a new cruise liner. Finance by cutting the forthcoming dividend

B Starting a range of designer clothing. Finance to be raised to maintain the current gearing ratio

C Build a new warship for Country Z. The Government of Country Z has offered YHG a subsidized loan as part of the proposal

D Build a new oil tanker. Finance to be raised to maintain the current gearing ratio

Techniques

(1) Calculate a NPV using the existing company WACC as a discount rate

(2) Calculate a NPV using a risk-adjusted WACC derived from CAPM

(3) Adjusted Present Value (APV)

9 Using the company Weighted Average Cost of Capital (WACC)

The weighted average cost of capital (WACC) is the average of cost of the company's finance (equity, bonds, bank loans, and preference shares) weighted according to the proportion each element bears to the total pool of funds.

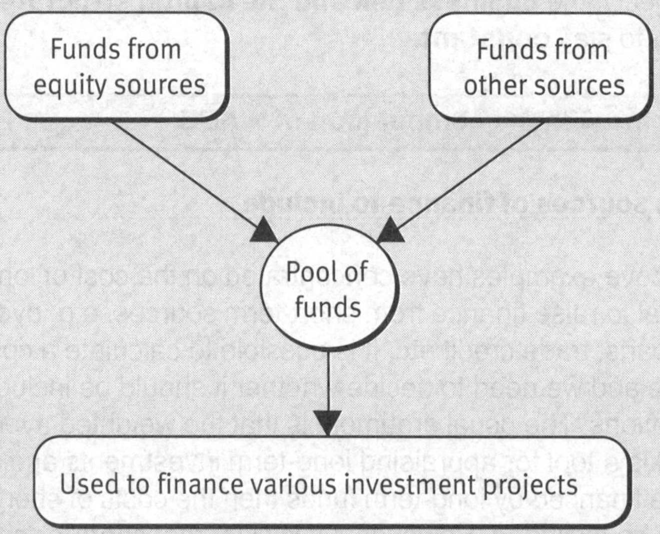

In order to provide a measure for evaluating these projects, the cost of the pool of funds is required. This is variously referred to as the combined or weighted average cost of capital (WACC).

The general approach is to calculate the cost of each source of finance, then to weight these according to their importance in the financing mix.

Procedure for calculating the WACC

The calculation involves a series of steps.

Step 1 Calculate weights for each source of capital.

Step 2 Estimate the cost of each source of capital.

Step 3 Multiply the proportion of the total of each source of capital by the cost of that source of capital.

Step 4 Sum the results of step 3 to give the weighted average cost of capital.

Formula

$$k_o = k_{eg}\left[\frac{V_E}{V_E + V_D}\right] + k_d\left[\frac{V_D}{V_E + V_D}\right]$$

The **existing WACC** of an entity should only be used as a discount rate for a new project if the **business risk and the capital structure** (financial risk) are likely to stay **constant**.

Problems with the computation of WACC

Which sources of finance to include

The above examples have concentrated on the cost of long-term finance. Firms also raise finance from short-term sources, e.g. overdrafts, short-term loans, trade credit etc. It is possible to calculate a cost for short-term finance and we need to decide whether it should be included in our calculations. The usual argument is that the weighted average cost of capital is a tool for appraising long-term investments and as these should only be financed by long-term funds then the costs of short-term funds should be excluded. However, if it is clear that short-term finance is being used to fund long-term projects, then it should be included.

Loans without market values

Bank loans do not have market values in the same way as bonds. All we can do in this case is to take the book value of loans as an approximation of market value.

Cost of capital for small companies

There are important factors which are relevant to the cost of capital of small companies:

- If the company is unquoted, then obtaining the cost of finance is much more difficult.
- The lack of liquidity offered by the company's securities, plus the smaller size of the company, tend to make finance more expensive.

10 Using a risk-adjusted WACC

The **existing WACC** of an entity should only be used as a discount rate for a new project if the **business risk and the capital structure** (financial risk) are likely to stay **constant**.

If the **business risk of the new project differs** from the entity's existing business risk, but gearing is held constant, then a risk-adjusted WACC should be calculated, by recalculating the cost of equity to reflect the business risk of the new project.

This will involve the following steps:

(1) Find a quoted company in the same business area as the project and find its equity beta

(2) Degear the equity beta to get an ungeared asset beta. This will also be the project's asset beta.

(3) Regear the project asset beta to reflect the project gearing (which is the same as the investing company's gearing)

(4) Put the project equity beta in the CAPM equation to get a project Ke

(5) Calculate the project WACC using the project Ke and the investing company's Kd and gearing ratio.

Test your understanding 15

G company makes lawnmowers and is considering a project to manufacture and sell outdoor table-tennis tables. The project will be financed to keep the gearing of G company constant.

T company is a listed company that makes and sells table-tennis tables.

The following information is available.

	G company	T Company
Equity beta	1.3	1.2
Gearing (debt/equity)	1/2	1/3

Which ONE of the following correct sets out the steps required for G Company to calculate a project cost of equity to use when calculating a risk-adjusted project WACC?

A Take the equity beta of 1.3, degear it to remove gearing of D/E = 1/2, regear to include gearing of 1/3 and then put into the CAPM equation

B Take the equity beta of 1.3, degear it to remove gearing of D/E = 1/3, regear to include gearing of 1/2 and then put into the CAPM equation

C Take the equity beta of 1.2, degear it to remove gearing of D/E = 1/2, regear to include gearing of 1/3 and then put into the CAPM equation

D Take the equity beta of 1.2, degear it to remove gearing of D/E = 1/3, regear to include gearing of 1/2 and then put into the CAPM equation

11 Adjusted Present Value (APV)

The **existing WACC** of an entity should only be used as a discount rate for a new project if the **business risk and the capital structure** (financial risk) are likely to stay **constant**.

A risk-adjusted WACC can be used when the business risk changes but gearing is unaltered.

Finally, if the capital structure is expected to **change significantly**, the **Adjusted Present Value** method of project appraisal should be used. This approach separates the investment element of the decision from the financing element and appraises them independently. APV is particularly recommended when there are complex funding arrangements (e.g. subsidised loans).

More details on when to use APV

It is not appropriate or necessary to use the APV method if there is just a simple change in the capital structure when a project is undertaken. In this case, it is simpler to recalculate the WACC based on the new capital structure and to use the risk adjusted WACC as a discount rate for the project cashflows.

APV should be used in the following circumstances:

(1) if the project is to be funded using a subsidised loan. The benefit of the subsidy can be separately identified in the APV calculations, so the APV method gives a more accurate assessment of the project and the associated financing;

(2) if there is to be a change in the debt capacity of the company. The APV method values separately the benefit to the company of the tax relief generated on the new finance.

(3) if the project is to be modelled under a number of capital structure options. A risk adjusted WACC could be recalculated for each potential capital structure position, but this would be a much more time consuming process than using APV.

Note that the calculation of APV usually takes the form of first calculating NPV as if the project financing was all by equity, and then incorporating adjustments to allow for the effects of the financing method to be actually used.

Bear in mind that difficulties in using APV may arise either in determining the costs involved in the financing method to be used, or in finding a suitable cost of equity for the basic NPV calculation. Nevertheless, APV often has the advantage of being a more positive approach than making an arbitrary adjustment to the entity's discount rate.

APV calculations

APV consists of two different elements:

APV = Investment element ('Base case NPV') + Financing element

(i.e. Value of a geared project = value of an all equity financed project + PV of financing side-effects)

Three step approach

APV takes a three-stage approach:

- **Stage One:** the project is evaluated as if it is all equity financed.
- **Stage Two:** the project's 'finance package' is evaluated
- **Stage Three:** Stages One and Two are combined to produce the APV.

Stage One

Stage One is a standard NPV analysis of the project, *except* for the discount rate used.

In APV, a special discount rate is used, to reflect the risk of an all equity financed company undertaking the new project (the 'base-case discount rate').

To determine such an "ungeared" cost of equity the project **asset** beta needs to be calculated and then substituted into the CAPM equation.

Note: when determining a risk-adjusted WACC, we found a similar quoted company, found its equity beta, degeared it and then regeared to incorporate project gearing. Here, once we have degeared the beta we can use it in the CAPM equation. There is no need to regear.

Stage Two

In Stage Two, the present value of the costs and benefits associated with the financing package is calculated.

The side-effects of financing can be numerous, and may include:

- tax relief on the interest paid on debt capital used;
- after tax issue costs of the finance needed for the project;
- tax relief of surplus debt capacity created by the project;
- government grants;
- tax relief on subsidised loans.

The discount rate to apply to the financing side-effects should reflect the systematic risk level involved for those side-effects identified above, it is usually assumed that the **pre-tax cost of debt** should be used.

This rate reflects the low risk nature of the tax benefits and avoids double-counting the tax relief on debt interest.

Stage Three

Having calculated the project's base-case net present value and also the present value of the financing side effects, these are then combined to find the project's Adjusted Present Value or APV.

e.g

Basic APV calculation

A project requires $1m capital investment, of which $400,000 will be raised using irredeemable loan stock. The project will save $220,000 per year after taxes into perpetuity.

Step 1: Base case NPV

Suppose that the business risk of the venture requires a 20% discount rate (based on a calculation of a suitable ungeared beta for the project).

Base case NPV = –1,000,000 + (220,000/0.2) = $100,000

Step 2: Financing side-effects

This project has one financial side-effect - the tax relief on the interest on the loan stock

Suppose that the pre-tax borrowing rate is 14% and the tax rate is 35%.

The interest tax shield = 0.35 × 0.14 × $400,000 = $19,600 per annum forever.

The PV of the tax shield = $19,600/0.14 = $140,000

Step 3: Project APV

APV = Base case NPV + PV of tax shield = $100,000 + $140,000 = $240,000

Given that this is positive, the project should be accepted.

Test your understanding 16

Company M makes motor cycles and is considering a project to manufacture and sell motorised wheelchairs. The project will be financed entirely by the issue of unsecured loan stock.

Company W is a listed company that makes and sells motorised wheelchairs.

The following information is available.

	M company	W Company
Equity beta	1.5	1.4
Asset beta	1.3	1.2

Which ONE of the following is the correct beta to use in the CAPM equation when determining a discount rate to use for calculating the "base case" NPV as part of a larger Adjusted Present Value (APV) calculation?

A 1.2

B 1.3

C 1.4

D 1.5

Test your understanding 17

AB plc is intending to invest in a new project and has calculated the following for the project:

- Base case NPV = £350,000
- Tax relief on debt interest = £5,000 per annum
- Present value of the tax shield = £50,000
- Issue costs = £100,000 after tax

The adjusted present value of the project is: ___________

Test your understanding 18

X plc needs to borrow £2 million for the purchase of a new machine. The directors expect the capital investment to provide annual cash flows of £300,000 net of taxation indefinitely.

At present the company is funded totally by equity. The discount rate it intends to use is 10% net. The current annual gross rate of interest required by the market on corporate undated debt of a similar risk is 8%. The after tax costs of issue will be £50,000. The marginal taxation rate is 30%.

Calculate the adjusted net present value of the investment in millions, to two decimal places.

Test your understanding 19

Y plc needs to borrow £1 million for the purchase of a new machine. The directors expect the capital investment to provide annual cash flows of £500,000 net of taxation for three years. The finance will be raised by the issue of 3 year 5% redeemable debentures at par.

At present the company is funded totally by equity and has a cost of equity of 12%. The current annual gross rate of interest required by the market on corporate 3 year debt of a similar risk is 5%. The after tax costs of issue will be £40,000. The marginal taxation rate is 30%.

Calculate the adjusted net present value of the investment in millions, to two decimal places.

Details of financing costs and benefits

Issue costs

Equity issue costs are not tax deductible but debt issue costs tend to be (however, the examiner will generally tell you what to assume here).

Sometimes the amount raised has to cover the issue costs. For example, if it says in a question that $480,000 of finance is needed for a project, net of issue costs of 4%, the total amount of finance raised will have to be 480,000 × (100/96) = $500,000 (hence the issue costs are $20,000).

PV of tax relief on interest payments = PV of tax shield

This is a calculation of an annuity, or a deferred annuity if tax relief is first received in year 2.

Annual tax relief = total loan × interest rate x tax rate

Subsidised/Cheap Loan

Like all loans, calculate the tax shield. In addition, you need to calculate the opportunity benefit of the cheap loan as follows:

PV of interest saved	X
Less PV of tax relief lost	(X)
PV of the cheap loan	X

Debt capacity

A project's debt capacity denotes its ability to act as security for a loan. It is the tax relief available on such a loan, which gives debt capacity its value.

When calculating the present value of the tax shield (tax relief on interest) one should base it on the project's theoretical debt capacity and not the actual amount of the debt used.

The company accrues a tax benefit from a project of each pound of debt finance that project can support, even if the debt is used on some other project. Therefore we use the theoretical debt capacity to match the tax benefit to the specific project.

This technique assumes that the theoretical debt capacity is fully utilised within the company as a whole.

Comprehensive APV illustration

Scrumpy is considering a project that requires an initial investment of $400,000 and is expected to generate annual net cash flows after tax of $175,000 over its 3 year life. The investment will have no residual value.

20% of the initial investment will be financed by equity. A further 40% of the initial investment will be financed by a subsidised loan at an interest rate of 5%. The balance will be met by a loan at the rate of 9% per annum. Issue costs for the equity are expected to be 3% of the amount raised, but can be assumed to be zero for the debt.

The project is in a sector which has an equity beta of 1.7 and an average debt:equity ratio of 1:3.

The risk free rate of return is 5% after tax and the market return is 13% after tax.

Corporate tax is at the rate of 30%. Assume that tax is paid at each year end without delay and there is no tax relief on capital expenditure or issue costs.

Required:

Evaluate the project using the APV approach.

Solution

Base-case NPV

$$\beta_{asset} = 1.70 \times \frac{3}{3 + 1(1 - 0.3)} = 1.38$$

Base-case discount rate = 5% + (13% – 5%) × 1.38 = 16%

Year	**Cash flow** ($)	**DF 16%**	**PV** ($)
0	(400,000)	1	(400,000)
1	175,000	0.862	150,850
2	175,000	0.743	130,025
3	175,000	0.641	112,175
			(6,950)

Financing side effects

PV of tax relief on debt interest

$400,000 × 0.4 × 0.09 × 0.3 × annuity factor years 1 – 3 @ 9% = $4,320 × 2.531 = $10,934

$400,000 × 0.4 × 0.05 × 0.3 × annuity factor years 1 – 3 @ 9% = $2,400 × 2.531 = $6,074

Total = $17,008

PV subsidised loan

Interest saving

= $400,000 × 0.4 × (0.09 – 0.05)(1 – 0.3) × Annuity factor years 1 – 3 @ 9%

= $4,480 × 2.531 = $11,338

Issue costs

$400,000 × 0.2 × 0.03 = $2,400

Adjusted present value

Base case NPV +/– PV of financing side effects

= –6,950 + 17,008 + 11,338 – 2,400 = $18,996

The project should be accepted as it has a positive APV of $18,996

Comparison of the APV method and the NPV method

APV can be used to appraise a project when there is a significant change in an entity's capital structure. However, following on from earlier chapters, we know that a project can also be appraised more directly by discounting its cashflows using an appropriate cost of capital.

The following worked example will compare the APV method with the standard NPV method.

Example

XX Co, a US based company, is considering diversifying its operations away from its main area of business (food manufacturing) by setting up a brand new plastics division.

Its first potential plastics project is an investment project which involves the purchase of a moulding machine which costs USD100,000. The project is expected to produce net post tax annual operating cash flows of USD15,000 into perpetuity.

The assets of the project will support debt finance of 40% of its initial cost. The loan will be irredeemable, and will carry an interest rate of 10% per annum. The balance of finance will be provided by a placing of new equity. Assume that there will be no issue costs associated with the new finance.

The plastics industry has an average geared (equity) beta of 1.368 and an average debt:equity ratio of 1:5 by market values. XX Co's current geared (equity) beta is 1.8 and 20% of its long-term capital is represented by debt which is generally regarded to be risk-free.

The risk-free rate is 10% p.a. and the expected return on an average market portfolio is 15%. Corporation tax is at a rate of 30%.

Evaluation of the project

Three approaches will be considered:

- Method 1: using the current WACC as a discount rate
- Method 2: using an adjusted WACC as a discount rate
- Method 3: adjusted present value (APV).

Method 1: Using the current WACC as a discount rate

The entity's current WACC would be:

[ke × 0.8] + [kd(1 – t) × 0.2]

= [(10% + 1.8 (15% – 10%)) × 0.8] + [(10% (1 – 0.30)) × 0.2]

= 16.6%

However, if this figure were used to discount the post tax operating cash flows of the project we would be making several errors:

- The current WACC is based upon XX Co's existing business risk (i.e. that of the food manufacturing industry). The plastics project involves considerably different business risk and should therefore be evaluated at a discount rate appropriate to its own business risk.
- The capital structure associated with the new plastics division is significantly different from XX Co's existing capital structure, so the weightings used in this WACC calculation are not relevant to the new investment.

In conclusion, it is not appropriate to use this WACC as a discount rate for the new project.

Before considering alternative Methods 2 and 3, let's consider the issues of business risk and capital structure separately.

Impact of a change in business risk

First, consider the issue of business risk.

The plastics project will have a different level of business risk from XX Co's existing operations, so we need to derive a suitable cost of equity for the plastics project, based on shareholders' expectations of the risk they are likely to face. Since no beta factor exists for the new project yet, we shall use a proxy beta factor based on the plastics industry to enable us to approximate the risk of the new project, and hence (using the CAPM model) the adjusted cost of equity.

The given plastics industry beta is a geared beta, so we first degear this to remove the impact of industry average gearing:

$$\text{Using: } ßu = ßg \times \frac{E}{E + D(1 - t)}$$

$$ßu = 1.368 \times \frac{5}{5 + 1(1 - 0.30)} = 1.2$$

So the ungeared beta for an entity in the plastics business = 1.2

Impact of a change in capital structure

Now, consider the issue of capital structure.

The assumption here is that the new project undertaken by XX Co effectively represents the setting up of a new division, whose future capital structure will be 40% debt : 60% equity (in common with the initial financing of the project). In this case, there are two options:

- the ungeared beta calculated above can be regeared to this new level of capital structure (40% debt:60% equity), and then used to find an adjusted WACC to be used for discounting – see Method 2 below.
- the Adjusted Present Value (APV) method can be used, where the ungeared beta is used to find an ungeared cost of equity, which is used for discounting the project cash flows before the impacts of financing are dealt with separately – see Method 3 below.

Method 2: Using an adjusted WACC as a discount rate

First, regear the ungeared beta (1.2) from above to reflect the 40% debt:60% equity gearing ratio associated with the new project.

Using: $$ßu = ßg \times \frac{E}{E + D(1 - t)}$$

$$1.2 = ßg \times \frac{0.6}{0.6 + 0.4 \times (1 - 0.30)}$$

$$1.2 = ßg \times 0.682$$

$$\frac{1.2}{0.682} = ßg = 1.76$$

Then, the CAPM model can be used to derive a risk adjusted cost of equity, and this cost of equity can be inserted into the WACC formula along with the new capital structure level (40% debt : 60% equity) to give a risk adjusted WACC for discounting as follows:

Cost of equity of 10% + 1.76 (15% – 10%) = 18.8% and a WACC for the plastics project is:

$$k_o = k_{eg}\left[\frac{V_E}{V_E + V_D}\right] + k_d\left[\frac{V_D}{V_E + V_D}\right]$$

i.e. (60/100) × 18.8% + (40/100) × 7% = 14.08%

Therefore the project NPV, at 14.08%, would be:

–USD100,000 + USD15,000/0.1408 = USD6,534

Note here that when discounting the project flows using the WACC, the post tax cash flows before financing charges are used, because financing charges are incorporated in the calculation of WACC, so deducting them as part of the cash flows would mean double counting their impact.

Method 3: Adjusted present value approach

As an alternative to adjusting the WACC as shown in Method 2 above, we sometimes use the Adjusted Present Value (APV) approach.

Step 1 Base case net present value

First compute a suitable (ungeared) cost of equity for the new project, based on the ungeared beta (1.2) derived above:

Required return of project = 10% + (15% – 10%) 1.2 = 16% p.a.

Then discount the project cash flows at 16%, to give a base case NPV of –USD100,000 + USD15,000/0.16 = –USD6,250 (negative figure).

Step 2 The financing side effects

In this case, the financing side effects comprise just the tax relief on the debt interest (benefit of financing). The present value of this element now needs to be computed as follows, using the pre tax cost of debt (10%) as a discount rate, since this rate accurately reflects the risk associated with the debt cashflows and hence the tax relief.

Debt interest = 10% × (40% × USD100,000) = USD4,000 per annum

Therefore tax relief = USD4,000 × 30% = USD1,200 per annum.

So PV of tax relief at 10% = USD1,200/0.10 = USD12,000

Adjusted present value

	USD
Base case NPV	(6,250)
Tax shield/relief on debt interest	12,000
APV	5,750

Comparison of Methods 2 and 3

Method 2 (discounting using a risk adjusted WACC) and Method 3 (APV) give slightly different results for the project appraisal (USD 6,534 and USD 5,750 respectively). This is because the amount of debt entered into the APV calculation in this case (USD40,000) represents 40% of the initial investment required, while the risk adjusted WACC calculation also incorporates the tax benefit on the additional debt capacity generated by the positive NPV of the project. If the APV calculation had used this higher level of debt capacity , the two methods would have given the same answer.

The two methods have the following relative advantages.

Advantages of the risk adjusted WACC method:

- the risk adjusted WACC method is conceptually easier to understand.
- it requires the calculation of a single hurdle rate which can be used for different projects, and to compare with other businesses.

Advantages of APV:

- APV can deal with other financing side effects such as subsidies on loans in a more transparent way than in a risk adjusted WACC calculation.
- using APV means less recalculating if assumptions regarding capital structure change. The base case NPV is calculated independently of any financing issues.

However, both methods share the following **limitations**:

- because the methods are both based on Modigliani and Miller's theories, they do not deal with the increased financial risk that comes with increasing gearing. Adjusting the beta for gearing simply recognises the impact of the change in capital structure on the cost of capital (because of the tax shield on debt). It does not deal with the "U-shaped" graph of WACC under the Traditional View of gearing which is more applicable in the real world.
- both methods assume that cost of capital stays constant into perpetuity, whereas in practice the various input components may well fluctuate as real world economic factors change.

Conclusion

Despite these limitations, both methods of investment appraisal can be used to give a useful insight into the viability or otherwise of a potential investment project.

As long as we are aware of the limitations, we can make sure that any marginal projects are evaluated using other methods too (such as payback period, modified internal rate of return, or non-quantitative methods) before a final decision is made.

Test your understanding 20

DT plc is a UK quoted company and all equity financed at present. It intends to spend £1.9million on new machinery. Expected cost savings are £300,000 per annum indefinitely (net of tax). The discount rate which should be applied to the project is 16%.

The new machinery purchase is to be financed by undated debt secured on DT's assets. The current relevant market rate on corporate debt is 9%, but half the loan will be subject to an interest rate of 3% under a Government subsidy scheme (in perpetuity).

The costs of issue, which are not tax deductible, are expected to be 5% of the gross issue proceeds.

The company's tax rate is 30%.

What is the base case NPV?

Test your understanding 21

DT plc is a UK quoted company and all equity financed at present. It intends to spend £1.9million on new machinery. Expected cost savings are £300,000 per annum indefinitely (net of tax). The discount rate which should be applied to the project is 16%.

The new machinery purchase is to be financed by undated debt secured on DT's assets. The current relevant market rate on corporate debt is 9%, but half the loan will be subject to an interest rate of 3% under a Government subsidy scheme (in perpetuity).

The costs of issue, which are not tax deductible, are expected to be 5% of the gross issue proceeds.

The company's tax rate is 30%.

What is the present value of the tax relief on the debt interest?

Test your understanding 22

DT plc is a UK quoted company and all equity financed at present. It intends to spend £1.9million on new machinery. Expected cost savings are £300,000 per annum indefinitely (net of tax). The discount rate which should be applied to the project is 16%.

The new machinery purchase is to be financed by undated debt secured on DT's assets. The current relevant market rate on corporate debt is 9%, but half the loan will be subject to an interest rate of 3% under a Government subsidy scheme (in perpetuity).

The costs of issue, which are not tax deductible, are expected to be 5% of the gross issue proceeds.

The company's tax rate is 30%.

What is the value of the subsidy?

Test your understanding 23

Pistachio Ltd is considering investing in a new project. The cost of the investment will be $2,500,000. The present value of the tax shield is $80,000 and the discount rate of the project is 12%.

What is the internal rate of return?

A 12%

B 11.6%

C 12.4%

D 11%

12 Chapter Summary

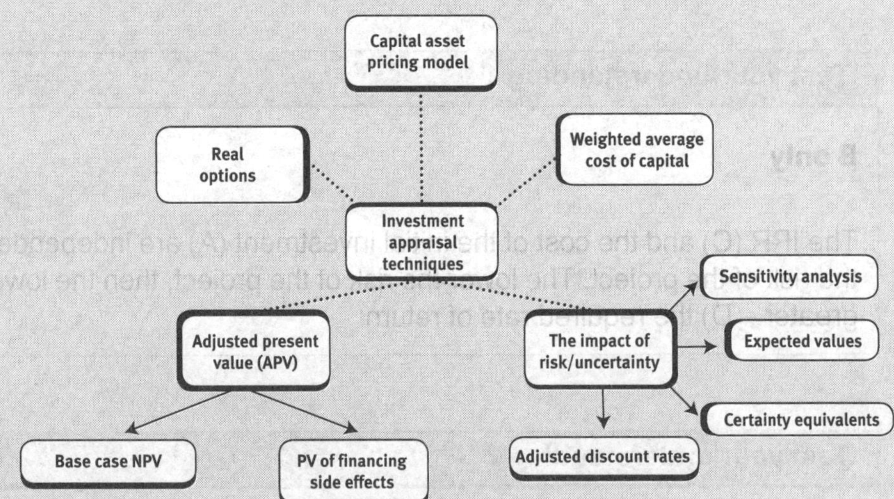

Test your understanding answers

Test your understanding 1

B only

The IRR (C) and the cost of the initial investment (A) are independent of the risk of the project. The lower the risk of the project, then the lower (not greater – D) the required rate of return

Test your understanding 2

At 15 per cent NPV is +1,344 and at 20 per cent it is – 543.

Using the formula (unlikely to be given in the exam, so make you learn it just in case)

- $IRR = R_1 + (R_2 - R_1) \times NPV_1/(NPV_1 - NPV_2)$
- IRR = 0.15 + (0.20 – 0.15) × 1,344/(1,344 + 543)
- IRR = 0.15 + 0.0356 = 0.1856 or 19% to the nearest per cent.

Using proportions (common sense approach)

- Discount rate increases by 5 per cent the NPV drops by 1,344 + 543 = 1,887.
- Starting at 15 per cent, the NPV must drop by 1,344 to reach zero. A $1,887 drop corresponds to a 5 per cent increase; a $1 drop corresponds to a 5/1,887 per cent increase; and so a $1,344 drop corresponds to a 1,344 × 5/1,887 = 3.56 per cent increase.
- Rounding to the nearest whole per cent point gives an IRR of 15 + 4 = 19 per cent.

Test your understanding 3

C, D and E

Comments:

- ROCE (A) and RI (B) are measures of return, not risk
- The beta factor (C) is a direct measure of systematic risk.
- The IRR (D) allows for sensitivity analysis on the estimated discount rate.
- Payback (E) can be used as an indicator of risk from the perspective of looking at potential liquidity problems.
- The choice of discount rate (F) **reflects** project risk rather than measuring it.

Test your understanding 4

B

Considering the four possible cost outcomes:

- If the cost is 100k (p = 0.1), then there is zero chance of a loss (p = 0)
- If the cost is 150k (p = 0.2), then a loss will occur if revenue is 120k (p = 0.2)
- If the cost is 200k (p = 0.4), then a loss will occur if revenue is 120k, 150k or 180k (p = 0.9)
- If the cost is 250k (p = 0.3), then a loss is certain (p = 1)

Overall probability of a loss = (0.1 × 0) + (0.2 × 0.2) + (0.4 × 0.9) + (0.3 × 1) = 0.7

Test your understanding 5

B – selling price

Sensitivity = (NPV/PV of CF affected) × 100%

A Initial investment: sensitivity = 68/500 = 13.6%

B Selling price: sensitivity = 68/1,516 = 4.5%

C Sales volume: sensitivity = 68/(1,516 - 569) = 7.2%

D Incremental fixed overheads: sensitivity = 68/379 = 17.9%

The estimate for the selling price has the lowest safety margin so should be re-assessed first.

Test your understanding 6

Time period and cashflow	Discount factor	Certainty equivalent	Present value £
0 (£1,000,000)	1.000	1.000	(1,000,000)
1 £350,000	0.935	0.95	310,888
2 £350,000	0.873	0.90	274,995
3 £350,000	0.816	0.75	214,200
4 £350,000	0.763	0.75	200,288

NPV = £371

Test your understanding 7

£10million = Cash saving/0.08 × 0.95

Cash saving = £10million × 0.08/0.95 = £842,105

Test your understanding 8

£4.5million = £400,000/0.08 × Certainty equivalent

Certainty equivalent = 0.90

Test your understanding 9

D and F only

Comments:

- Statement A is simply incorrect – CAPM **does** account for systematic risk
- Statements B and C are correct but not limitations. Given we are considering a well-diversified investor, we only need consider unsystematic risk, rather than total risk
- Statements D and F are limitations of CAPM
- Statement E is simply incorrect – CAPM **does** consider the market return in the CAPM equation

Test your understanding 10

B and C only

Assess the three potential investments by comparing the expected return with the required return (using CAPM):

Investment	A	B	C
Expected return	12%	10%	6%
Required return using CAPM	3 + 9.6 = 12.6%	3 + 6.6 = 9.6%	3 + 2.4 = 5.4%

Test your understanding 11

Only statement E is correct.

Statements A and B are incorrect – "risk aversion" simply means that the investor will only accept (higher) risks if there is the expectation of high enough returns to compensate.

Statement C is incorrect. Despite having an inferior risk:return profile the investor may choose Company X if either

- the investor already has a portfolio of shares and Company X has a particularly good fit with that portfolio – for example, having a negative correlation so it results in portfolio risks being reduced through diversification
- the investor is well diversified and X's expected return of 15% exceed the CAPM return calculated by putting X's beta in the CAPM equation. X may have very low systematic risk, thus making the return acceptable.

Statement D is incorrect. Being rational and risk averse would mean that the investor should consider both return and risk.

Statement E is correct – for example, we need to know the investor's existing portfolio (are they well diversified?) and the level of their risk aversion (for example, even if this is their only investment, it is not clear cut whether the extra return of Z compensates for the extra risk, when compared to Y) before a definite conclusion can be reached.

Risk and diversification (Case style question)

MEMORANDUM

To: The Board of Directors

From: The Company Accountant

Date: X June 20XX

Subject: Investing funds in a portfolio of securities

(a) This memorandum starts with some definitions:

Systematic risk is risk that cannot be eliminated by diversification.

Unsystematic risk is risk that can be eliminated by diversification.

Total risk is the sum of systematic and unsystematic risk.

These definitions can be explained as follows. There will be some uncertainty normally inherent in the future returns of any investment that is made. This uncertainty can be measured as the total risk of the investment by calculating the standard deviation of the investment's possible returns.

Some of this total risk can be diversified away by combining the investment with other different investments; this component of total risk is called unsystematic risk and relates to factors unique to the company itself or the business sector it is in.

The remainder of the total risk cannot be diversified away; this component of total risk is called systematic risk and relates to factors affecting the stock market as a whole e.g. the risk that interest rates rise.

Total risk is measured as the standard deviation of investment returns.

If future returns are unclear, the standard deviation of past returns over recent periods can be calculated as a measure of the investment's total risk.

Systematic risk is measured by looking at an investment's beta value. An investment with no systematic risk has a beta value of zero. An investment with the same systematic risk as the market as a whole has a beta of one. An investment with systematic risk twice that of the market as a whole has a beta of two, etc.

Unsystematic risk is normally measured as the difference between systematic risk and total risk i.e. as a balancing figure, although it is possible to calculate it separately.

(b) The expected return from any investment should compensate for its risk. If the investment is held alone, it is the total risk that is relevant. But if the investment is held as one unit in a widely diversified portfolio, the unsystematic risk will be eliminated, and it is only the systematic risk that is relevant.

Thus it is acceptable to buy investments with expected returns less than the expected return on the market as a whole, as long as those investments possess less risk than the market as a whole. It might be felt prudent, for example, to hold a proportion of a portfolio in cash on deposit, effectively as a risk-free asset, although the expected return will be lower than the return expected for investing in shares on the stock market.

It is even acceptable to buy investments with expected returns less than the risk-free rate of return, as long as those investments contribute sufficiently to the overall diversification of the portfolio held. Investments with negative beta values fall particularly into this category; their expected return is low but they offer substantial diversification opportunities.

Test your understanding 12

Statements A, B and C are true.

A If two companies operate in the same areas of business, then they will have the same asset betas – TRUE – asset betas only reflect business risk

B Equity betas cannot be smaller than their corresponding asset betas – TRUE – given that the equity beta reflects business risk and gearing risk, it must be greater than the asset beta as it reflects more risk. The two are only equal if there is no gearing risk.

C If a company is all equity financed, then its equity and asset betas will be the same – TRUE – see argument for statement B above.

D If using CAPM to calculate the cost of equity for a geared company, then the asset beta must be used – FALSE – the cost of equity will reflect all the risks faced by the equity shareholders, so should include both business risk and gearing risk, hence a geared (equity) beta is needed.

Test your understanding 13

The company WACC can only be used if both business risk and gearing remain unchanged by the project – this is the case with scenario 3

A risk adjusted WACC is used when the project has different business risk than the company but the gearing will remain unchanged – project – this is the case with scenario 2

APV must be used when there is a change in gearing project – this is the case with scenarios 1 and 4

Test your understanding 14

A3 – APV must be used when there is a change in gearing.

B2 – a risk adjusted WACC is used when the project has different business risk than the company but the gearing will remain unchanged.

C3 – APV must be used when there is a change in gearing.

D1 – the company WACC can only be used if both business risk and gearing remain unchanged by the project.

Test your understanding 15

Statement D is correct.

Calculating a risk adjusted WACC involves the following steps:

(1) Find a quoted company in the same business area as the project and find its equity beta – this is T company so we start with an equity beta of 1.2

(2) Degear the equity beta to get an ungeared asset beta – T company's gearing of 1/3 needs removing

(3) Regear the project asset beta to reflect the project gearing – G company's gearing of 1/2 needs putting in as this will also be the project gearing

(4) Put the project equity beta in the CAPM equation to get a project Ke.

(5) Calculate the project WACC using the project Ke and the investing company's Kd and gearing ratio.

Test your understanding 16

A

For the base case NPV the discount rate needs to reflect the project's business risk – here wheelchairs (hence we look at W company) – but should be an ungeared cost of equity (hence we need an asset beta).

Test your understanding 17

APV = £350,000 + £50,000 – £100,000 = £300,000

Test your understanding 18

Step 1: Base case NPV

Base case NPV = (£2m) + 300,000/0.10 = £1m

Step 2: Financing side-effects

- Costs of issue = (50,000)
- Tax shield on interest = £2m × 0.08 × 0.3 = £48,000, in perpetuity
- PV of tax shield = £48,000/0.08 = £600,000

Step 3: APV

APV = £1m – £50,000 + £600,000 = £1,550,000

Test your understanding 19

Step 1: Base case NPV

Base case NPV = (£1m) + 500,000 × 2 .402 (a 3 year discount factor @ 12%) = £201,000

Step 2: Financing side-effects

Costs of issue = (40,000)

Tax shield

- Annual tax relief on interest = 1m × 5% × 30% = 15,000 pa for three years
- PV of tax shield = 15,000 × 2.723 (a 3 year discount factor @ 5%) = 40,845

Step 3: APV

APV = 201,000 – 40,000 + 40,845 = £201,845 = £0.20 million to 2dp

Test your understanding 20

Base case NPV = £300,000/0.16 – £1,900,000 = (£25,000)

Test your understanding 21

Debt issued = £1,900,000/0.95 (issue costs) = £2million

Tax relief on interest = ((£1million × 0.09) + (1million × 0.03)) × 0.3 = £36,000

PV = £36,000/0.09 = £400,000

Test your understanding 22

9 – 3% = 6%

6% × £1million × (1 – 0.30) × 1/0.09 = £466,667

Test your understanding 23

The correct answer is B.

($2,500,000) + PV + $80,000 = 0
PV = $2,420,000
$2,420,000 × 0.12 = $290,400
290,400/2,500,000 = 0.11616

11.6%

hapter

15

Investment implementation and review

Chapter learning objectives

Lead	Component
E1: Evaluate the risks arising from changes in the environment for capital investment appraisal.	(b) evaluate conflicts that may arise from capital investment decisions. (c) evaluate the outcomes of projects post implementation and post completion.

Indicative syllabus content

- Managing conflicts between different stakeholder groups (profit maximisation versus wealth maximisation).
- Managing conflicts arising from performance indicators.
- Monitoring the implementation of plans.
- Post completion audit.

1 Objectives

Objectives of profit seeking organisations

Decisions to be made depend on the ultimate objectives of an organisation.

Academic studies have shown that organisations often have many, **sometimes conflicting,** objectives.

It is generally accepted that the primary strategic objective of a commercial company is the long-term goal of the **maximisation of the wealth of the shareholders**.

However, an organisation has many other stakeholders with both long- and short-term goals, such as:

- Equity investors (ordinary shareholders)
- The community at large
- Company employees
- Company managers/directors
- Customers
- Suppliers
- Finance providers
- The government

Definition of stakeholders

Stakeholders: Those persons and entities that have an interest in the strategy of an entity. Stakeholders normally include shareholders, customers, staff and the local community. (CIMA Official Terminology, 2005)

Examples of stakeholder objectives

Equity investors (ordinary shareholders) – Within any economic system, the equity investors provide the risk finance. There is a very strong argument for maximising the wealth of equity investors. In order to attract funds, the company has to compete with other risk-free investment opportunities, e.g. government securities. The shareholders require returns from the company in terms of dividends and increases in share prices.

The community at large – The goals of the community will be broad but will include such aspects as legal and social responsibilities, pollution control and employee welfare.

Company employees – Returns = wages or salaries. However, maximising the returns to employees does assume that risk finance can be raised purely on the basis of satisficing the returns to finance providers. The employees' other interests also include job security and good conditions of employment.

Company managers/directors – Such senior employees are in an ideal position to follow their own aims at the expense of other stakeholders. Their goals will be both long-term (defending against takeovers, sales maximisation) and short-term (profit margins leading to increased bonuses).

Customers – Satisfaction of customer needs will be achieved through the provision of value for money products and services.

Suppliers – Suppliers to the organisation will have short-term goals such as prompt payment terms alongside long-term requirements including contracts and regular business. The importance of the needs of suppliers will depend upon both their relative size and the number of suppliers.

Finance providers – Providers of loan finance (banks, loan creditors) will primarily be interested in the ability of the firm to repay the finance including interest. As a result it will be the firm's ability to generate cash both long and short term that will be the basis of the goals of these providers.

The government – The government will have political and financial interests in the firm. Politically it will wish to increase exports and decrease imports whilst monitoring companies via the Competition Commission. Financially it requires long-term profits to maximise taxation income.

Managing stakeholder interests

Part of managing any company involves dealing with any groups interested in the company, such as those mentioned above. (This list is not exhaustive.)

Dealing with customers and suppliers might be dealt with by lower level management, whereas dealing with shareholders and the bank are more likely to be dealt with by the Board. Customers and suppliers will need to be dealt with on a daily basis and there will probably be specialist departments within the company to do this, such as accounts receivable and accounts payable. Any marketing or public relations department may also be involved with customers.

Suppliers may be so numerous or large that the company has a 'procurement' department. Day to day issues will be managed by these specialist departments, however, should a major issue arise, such as a shortage in supply or a product harming a customer, then responsibility for corrective action may escalate up the chain of command as far as the Board.

Two stakeholders that are not mentioned on the list above are, for example, environmental groups and trade unions. The environmental stakeholder in many companies, for example, is often managed by exception in that a company will mainly deal with them only when a problem is brought to their attention. For example, environmentalists might suddenly protest outside the companies premises over the companies policy for waste management. Often the press arrive to cover the story and the company would need to deal with the unwelcome media attention which might harm their reputation. This could be to either admit fault (and hopefully to announce their corrective actions) or to deny it (and show evidence).

Some stakeholders, be they the bank, shareholders, environmental groups, or whoever may remain quiet and let the companies Board get on with managing the company. Others will show a constant interest in the company and need managing on a daily basis. Others will rear their heads now and again due to some action the company has taken. The time spent on the stakeholder and the level of action the Board will have to take will depend on the severity of the implications of the stakeholders concern.

For example, one day the companies bank overdraft may be exceeded and the finance director is called by the company's bank manager who demands immediate action for the problem to be rectified. At this point in time, the bank becomes a major stakeholder who needs managing. The next day a major shareholder hears of the bank overdraft being exceed and fears that their investment is at risk, so they contact the finance director and threaten to sell their shareholding. It may be that the overdraft issue was a 'blip' and has now been resolved and all stakeholders calm down. On the other hand, this could lead to the sale of the major shareholding causing a drop in the share price, other shareholders might sell, suppliers hearing about the cashflow problem might refuse to supply further goods, etc. A chain reaction has begun which management need to deal with.

Management need to realise the implications of their actions and the fact that there can be a large knock on effect caused by any of their decisions.

Test your understanding 1

Company M, a mining company, has won a contract with the Government of Country X to extract valuable minerals from virgin rain forest. The extraction is expected to boost earnings per share by 10% in the next year and create 1,000 jobs in Country X, although only 20% of these will go to local workers. Company M will sell the minerals to various global manufacturing companies.

As a member of Company M's senior management team, you have been tasked with analysing the likely stakeholder reaction to the new mining project. As part of your work, you looked at the experience of Company Q, an oil company. Company Q was recently criticised when its operations in Country X resulted in a major environmental incident and the loss of hundreds of lives. The subsequent investigation raised concerns over Country X's lax health and safety regulations and there were widespread allegations of government corruption and bribery. Company Q subsequently failed to win a lucrative new drilling contract in North America and the bad publicity from the Country X incident was cited as one of the reasons why.

Which of the following statements concerning stakeholders is/are correct? (Select ALL that apply)

A Company M's customers will not be concerned about the lax regulatory regime in Country X

B Company M's shareholders will be unanimously in favour of the expansion

C Country X's citizens are likely to see the potential damage to their environment as more important than job creation.

D Being a mining company, Company M is likely to have a poor reputation with environmental activists already, so the investment in Country X is unlikely to damage it any further.

Objectives and economic forces

When setting the company's strategy the financial manager is often constrained by both internal and external factors.

For example, significant expansion and an increase in dividends may not be feasible if the entity has a lack of skilled staff, and may become uneconomic if interest rates are set to rise (thus increasing the amount payable to banks and other debt finance providers).

The effect of interest rate and inflation changes

The effects of interest rate changes

Changes in interest rates affect the economy in many ways. The following consequences are the main effects of an increase in interest rates:

Spending falls – expenditure by consumers, both individual and business, will be reduced. This occurs because the higher interest rates raise the cost of credit and deter spending. If we take incomes as fairly stable in the short term, higher interest payments on credit cards/mortgages, etc., leave less income for spending on consumer goods and services. This fall in spending means less aggregate demand in the economy and thus unemployment results.

Asset values fall – the market value of financial assets will drop, because of the inverse relationship (between bonds and the rate of interest) explained earlier. This, in turn, will reduce many people's wealth. It is likely that they will react to maintain the value of their total wealth and so may save, thereby further reducing expenditure in the economy. This phenomenon seems to fit the UK recession of the early 1990s when the house-price slump deepened the economic gloom. For many consumers today a house, rather than bonds, is their main asset.

Foreign funds are attracted into the country – a rise in interest rates will encourage overseas financial speculators to deposit money in the country's banking institutions because the rate of return has increased relative to that in other countries. Such funds could be made available as loans to firms in that country by the banking sector.

The exchange rate rises – the inflow of foreign funds raises demand for the domestic currency and so pushes up the exchange rate. This has the benefit of lowering import prices and thereby bearing down on domestic inflation. However, it makes exports more expensive and possibly harder to sell. The longer-term effect on the balance of payments could be beneficial or harmful depending on the elasticity of demand and supply for traded goods.

Inflation falls – higher interest rates affect the rate of inflation in three ways. First, less demand in the economy may encourage producers to lower prices in order to sell. This could be achieved by squeezing profit margins and/or wage levels. Second, new borrowing is deferred by the high interest rates and so demand will fall. Third, the higher exchange rate will raise export prices and thereby threaten sales which in turn pressurises producers to cut costs, particularly wages. If workers are laid off then again total demand is reduced and inflation is likely to fall.

The effects of inflation

Inflation is defined simply as 'rising prices' and shows the cost of living in general terms.

If the rate of inflation is low, then the effects may be beneficial to an economy. Business people are encouraged by fairly stable prices and the prospect of higher profits. However, there is some argument about whether getting inflation below 3% to, say, zero, is worth the economic pain (of, say, higher unemployment). There is agreement, though, that inflation above 5% is harmful – worse still if it is accelerating. The main arguments are that such inflation:

Distorts consumer behaviour – people may bring forward purchases because they fear higher prices later. This can cause hoarding and so destabilise markets, creating unnecessary shortages.

Redistributes income – people on fixed incomes or those lacking bargaining power will become relatively worse off, as their purchasing power falls. This is unfair.

Affects wage bargainers – trades unionists on behalf of labour may submit higher claims at times of high inflation, particularly if previously they had underestimated the future rise in prices. If employers accept such claims this may precipitate a wage–price spiral which exacerbates the inflation problem.

Undermines business confidence – wide fluctuations in the inflation rate make it difficult for entrepreneurs to predict the economic future and accurately calculate prices and investment returns. This uncertainty handicaps planning and production.

Weakens the country's competitive position – if inflation in a country exceeds that in a competitor country, then it makes exports less attractive (assuming unchanged exchange rates) and imports more competitive. This could mean fewer sales of that country's goods at home and abroad and thus a bigger trade deficit. For example the decline of Britain's manufacturing industry can be partly attributed to the growth of cheap imports when they were experiencing high inflation in the period 1978–1983.

Redistributes wealth – if the rate of interest is below the rate of inflation, then borrowers are gaining at the expense of lenders. The real value of savings is being eroded. This wealth is being redistributed from savers to borrowers and from payables to receivables. As the government is the largest borrower, via the national debt, it gains most during inflationary times.

Internal and external constraints on strategy

Internal constraints on strategy

Key internal constraints on strategy include:

- a shortage of key skills;
- limited production capacity.

External constraints on strategy

Major external constraints include:

- The need to maintain good investor relations and provide a satisfactory return on investment
- Limited access to sources of finance, either due to weak credit worthiness or lack of liquidity in the banking sector and capital markets
- Gearing level. The main argument in favour of gearing is that introducing borrowings into the capital structure attracts tax relief on interest payments. The argument against borrowing is that it introduces financial risk into the entity. Financial managers have to formulate a policy that balances the effects of these opposing features.
- Debt covenants. These are clauses written into debt agreements which protect the lender's interests by requiring the borrower to satisfy certain criteria (e.g. a minimum level of interest cover)
- Government influence (see below)
- Regulatory bodies (see below)
- Major economic influences, such as interest rates, growth in GDP, inflation rates and exchange rates. The effects of interest rate and inflation changes on the economy are covered below.
- Accounting concepts. (Note: Detailed knowledge of accounting procedures will not be examined in this paper.)

Government influence

Governments often play a large part in influencing business activity. Some examples of the way in which governments can have an influence are as follows:

- Employment policy. Governments play a major role in attempting to stimulate employment. They can do this by funding vocational training programmes and funding employment programmes.
- Regional policy. Governments may make funds available to support regions of high unemployment and social deprivation.
- Inflation policy. Governments may use interest rates to control inflation. Increasing interest rates makes it more expensive for profit-making entities to borrow. It also makes borrowing more expensive for consumers, who then have less to spend. This will help to push prices down.
- Taxation policy. The government raises taxes on the profits generated by profit-making entities and on shareholders' dividends.
- International policy. Governments can promote trade, encourage experts or discourage imports.
- Legislation. Laws set out how people can and should behave towards one another, and particularly, how business should be conducted.

Developing strategy in the context of regulatory requirements

The financial manager must have a proper understanding of those aspects of legislation which impact upon entities. Such legislation will include the Companies Acts, health and safety regulations, laws relating to consumer protection and consumer rights, laws relating to contract and agency, employment law and laws relating to protection of the environment and promoting competition.

Listed companies also have to comply with Stock Exchange regulations, and entities which operate in some high profile industries will also find regulatory bodies monitoring their performance. For example, in the UK, Oftel (telecommunications), Ofcom (media) and Ofwat (water) have been set up by the government to monitor and regulate their respective industries.

Regulatory bodies

A clear set of objectives is required for each regulatory body. In general terms, a regulatory body will have the power to impose price controls or service controls (i.e. to dictate prices or the quality of service delivered).

The objectives may be classified under three headings:

(1) The protection of customers from monopoly power.

(2) The promotion of social and macroeconomic objectives.

(3) The promotion of competition.

(1) **Monopoly power**

Where market participants are judged to possess significant market power, and where there is no other protection for customers, controls on prices and on quality of service may be considered.

(2) **Social objectives**

Government objectives may include the availability and affordability of services in particular areas and to particular groups such as customers in remote rural areas.

(3) **Competition**

Where a market is not competitive, or is in the early stages of becoming so, there is a need for regulators whose role is to try to balance the interests of the various stakeholders.

Important issues for regulation are the prevention of 'cross-subsidy', that is the transferring or offloading of portions of overhead costs from lower- to higher-margin products, the limitation of non-price barriers affecting the entry of new competitors, and assuring reasonable quality of product in relation to price. Non-price barriers could include trade restrictions, or restricted access to supplies or distribution channels.

Stakeholder conflicts

Faced with a broad range of stakeholders, managers are likely to find they cannot simultaneously maximise the wealth of their shareholders and keep all the other stakeholders content.

In practice, the main strategic objective may be interpreted as achieving the maximum profit possible, consistent with balancing the needs of the various stakeholders in the entity.

Such a policy may imply achieving a satisfactory return for shareholders, whilst (for example) establishing competitive terms and conditions of service for the employees, and avoiding polluting the environment.

Conflicts of objectives between managers and shareholders

Agency theory

A possible conflict can arise when ownership is separated from the day-to-day management of an entity. In larger entities, the ordinary shares are likely to be diversely held, and so the actions of shareholders are likely to be restricted in practical terms. The responsibility of running the entity will be with the board of directors, who may only own a small percentage of the shares in issue.

The managers of an entity are essentially agents for the shareholders, being tasked with running the entity in the shareholders' best interests. The shareholders, however, have little opportunity to assess whether the managers are acting in the shareholders' best interests.

Agency theory: Hypothesis that attempts to explain elements of organisational behaviour through an understanding of the relationships between principals (such as shareholders) and agents (such as company managers and accountants). A conflict may exist between the actions undertaken by agents in furtherance of their own self-interest, and those required to promote the interests of the principals. (CIMA Official Terminology, 2005)

Investor relations

Where ownership is separated from the day-to-day management of an entity, managers may be motivated to behave in ways that are not optimal to the shareholders of the entity:

- Shareholders can spread their risk by investing in a number of entities. Managers have personal and financial capital invested in the entity and so may be averse to investing in a risky investment.
- Shareholder wealth will be maximised by investing in projects with positive net present values. Managers may be more interested in short-term payback than net present value as the investment criterion, in order to help further their own promotion prospects.
- Managers of entities that are subject to a takeover bid often put up a defence to repel the predator. While arguing this action is in the shareholders' best interests, shareholders of acquired entities often receive large gains in the value of their shares. The managers of the acquired entity often lose their jobs or status.
- Managers may be motivated to award themselves and staff better terms and conditions of service. This will incur costs and reduce profits. If equity investors are losing too much as a consequence, they may sell their shares and the market value of the entity will fall.

Goal congruence

Goal congruence: In a control system, the state which leads the individuals or groups to take actions which are in their self-interest and also in the best interest of the entity. (CIMA Official Terminology, 2005)

It is evident that an important element within profit-making entities is the extent to which all members of the management team and their staff work together to achieve the strategic objectives of that entity. An aspect of agency theory aims to demonstrate that while various kinds of contract exist, formal and informal (such as job descriptions, departmental responsibilities and office and factory rules), these can only be effective in helping to make an entity successful if there is general acceptance of them in practice, and a concerted effort by all concerned to strive in the same direction, that is, to achieve genuine goal congruence.

Performance and progress indicators (PIs)

In order to achieve the overall objective companies should set specific targets, financial and non-financial, in order to both communicate direction and measure performance, for example:

Financial

Profitability – e.g. annual 10% improvement in earnings, or earnings per share.

Cash generation – e.g. annual 10% improvement in operating cashflow.

Non-financial

Market share – e.g. four products out of six are dominant in the market.

Customer satisfaction – e.g. complaints to reduce from 5% to 2%.

These targets can be used to direct managers' attention towards key stakeholder requirements, to ensure that the organisation balances the needs of its different stakeholders and minimises the conflict between the different stakeholder groups.

More on financial and non financial objectives

Traditionally, managers have focused on financial measures of performance and progress. Increasingly, entities in both the private and public sectors are using non-financial indicators to assess success across a range of criteria, which need to be chosen to help an entity meet its objectives.

We discuss a number of common financial and non-financial indicators below.

Financial performance indicators

Return to investors. The return from ownership of shares in a profit-making entity can be measured by the formula:

$$\text{Annual return to investors} = \frac{(P_1 - P_0) + \text{Dividend}}{P_0}$$

This is the capital appreciation on the shares (the difference between P_1 and P_0 – the share price at the end and the start of the year respectively), plus dividends received during the year.

Cash generation. Poor liquidity is a greater threat to the survival of an entity than is poor profitability. Unless the entity is prepared to fund growth with high levels of borrowings, cash generation is vital to ensure investment in future profitable ventures. In the private sector the alternative to cash via retained earnings is borrowing. In the public sector this choice has not been available in the past, and all growth has been funded by government. However, in the face of government-imposed cash limits, local authorities and other public-sector entities are beginning to raise debt on the capital markets, and are therefore beginning to be faced with the same choices as profit-making entities.

Value added. This is primarily a measure of performance. It is usually defined as revenues less the cost of purchased materials and services. It represents the value added to an entity's products by its own efforts. A problem here is comparability with other industries – or even with other entities in the same industry. It is less common in the public sector, although the situation is changing and many public sector entities – for example those in the health service – are now publishing information on their own value added.

Nevertheless, it is a well-known and accepted measure which, once the input has been defined, is readily understood. Provided the input is consistent across entities and time periods, it also provides a useful comparative measure. Although the concept of profit in its true sense is absent from most of the public sector, profitability may be used to relate inputs to outputs if a different measure of output is used – for example: surplus after all costs, to capital investment.

Profitability. Profitability may be defined as the rate at which profits are generated. It is often expressed as profit per unit of input (e.g. investment). However, profitability limits an entity's focus to one output measure – profit. It overlooks quality, and this limitation must be kept in mind when using profitability as a measure of success. Profitability as a measure of decision-making has been criticised because:

- it fails to provide a systematic explanation as to why one business sector has more favourable prospects than another;
- it does not provide enough insight into the dynamics and balance of an entity's individual business units, and the balance between them;
- it is remote from the actions that create value, and cannot therefore be managed directly in any but the smallest entities;
- the input to the measure may vary substantially between entities.

Return on assets (RoA). This is an accounting measure, calculated by dividing annual profits by the average net book value of assets. It is therefore subject to the distortions inevitable when profit, rather than cash flows, is used to determine performance. Distorting factors for interpretation and comparison purposes include depreciation policy, inventory revaluations, write-off of intangibles such as goodwill, etc. A further defect is that RoA ignores the time value of money, although this may be of minor concern when inflation is very low.

RoA may not adequately reflect how efficiently assets were utilised: in a commercial context, taking account of profits but not the assets used in their making, for whatever reason, would overstate an entity's performance. In the public sector, the concept of profit is absent, but it is still not unrealistic to expect entities to use donated assets with maximum efficiency. If depreciation on such assets were to be charged against income, this would depress the amount of surplus income over expenditure.

Other points which may affect interpretation of RoA in the public sector are:

- difficulty in determining value;
- there may be no resale value;
- are for use by community at large;
- charge for depreciation may have the effect of 'double taxation' on the taxpayer.

Non-financial performance indicators

Market share. A performance indicator that could conceivably be included in the list of financial measures, market share is often seen as an objective for an entity in its own right. However, it must be judged in the context of other measures such as profitability and shareholder value. Market share, unlike many other measures, can take quality into account – it must be assumed that if customers do not get the quality they want or expect, then the entity will lose market share.

Gaining market share must be seen as a long-term goal of entities to ensure outlets for their products and services, and to minimise competition. However, market share can be acquired only within limits if a monopoly situation is to be avoided.

It is a measure that is becoming increasingly relevant to the public sector – for example universities and health provision. Health providers must now 'sell' their services to trusts established to 'buy' from them. Those providers which are seen to fail their customers will lose market share as the trusts will buy from elsewhere (within certain limits).

Customer satisfaction. This can be linked to market share. If customers are not satisfied they will take their business elsewhere and the entity will lose market share and go into liquidation. Measuring customer satisfaction is difficult to do formally, as the inputs and outputs are not readily defined or measurable. Surveys and questionnaires may be used but these methods have known flaws, mainly as a result of respondent bias. It can of course be measured indirectly by the level of sales and increase in market share.

Competitive position. The performance of an entity must be compared with that of its competitors to establish a strategic perspective. A number of models and frameworks have been suggested by organisational theorists as to how competitive position may be determined and improved. A manager needing to make decisions must know by whom, by how much, and why he is gaining ground or being beaten by competitors. Conventional measures, such as accounting data, are useful but no one measure is sufficient. Instead, an array of measures is needed to establish competitive position. The most difficult problem to overcome in using competitive position as a success factor is in collecting and acquiring data from competitors.

The public sector is increasingly in competition with other providers of a similar service both in the private and public sectors. For example hospitals now have to compete for the funds of health trusts. Their advantage is that it is easier to gain access to data from such competitors than it is in the private sector.

Risk exposure. Risk can be measured according to finance theory. Some risks – for example exchange-rate risk and interest-rate risk – can be managed by the use of hedging mechanisms. Shareholders and entities can therefore choose how much risk they wish to be exposed to for a given level of return. However, risk can take many forms, and the theory does not deal with risk exposure to matters such as recruitment of senior personnel or competitor activity.

Public sector entities tend to be risk averse because of the political repercussions of failure and the fact that taxpayers, unlike shareholders, do not have the option to invest their money in less (or more) risky ventures.

Test your understanding 2

Company F, a house building company, has won a contract with the Government of Country Y to build 10,000 new homes on a site of outstanding national beauty, consisting of farms and woodland, an hour's drive away from Y's capital city.

However, the opposition part in Country Y has protested that the plan will simply "reward big business" and "do little to meet the needs of the poor" or "protect the environment". As a result, the Government has stipulated a range of conditions on the building contract.

Which one of the following is most likely to help "meet the needs of the poor"?

A At least 50 of the homes should be classed as "affordable" and contribute towards the Government targets for "affordable housing" in the area

B All houses should have triple glazing and solar panels to reduce energy usage

C Company F would also build additional local schools, community centres and contribute towards the costs of new road building

D At least 40% of the workforce used in construction should consist of local residents and half of those should be people currently registered as unemployed

Objectives of not-for-profit organisations

Organisations such as charities, trade unions and associations (such as accountancy bodies) are not run to make profits but to benefit prescribed groups of people. For example, the primary objective of a charity is to pursue whatever charitable objectives it was set up for.

Since the services provided are limited primarily by the funds available, secondary objectives are to raise the maximum possible funds each year (net of fund-raising expenses), and to use the funds efficiently to maximise the benefit generated.

Financial objectives in the public sector

Financial objectives in public corporations

This category of organisation includes such bodies as nationalised industries and local government organisations. They represent a significant part of many countries' economies and sound financial management is essential if their affairs are to be conducted efficiently. The major problem here lies in obtaining a measurable objective.

For a stock market listed company we can take the maximisation of shareholder wealth as a working objective and know that the achievement of this objective can be monitored with reference to share price and dividend payments. For a public corporation the situation is more complex.

The entity's mission statement will lay out its key objectives. However, generally such organisations are run in the interests of society as a whole and therefore we should seek to attain the position where the gap between the benefits they provide to society and the costs of their operation is the widest (in positive terms).

The cost is relatively easily measured in accounting terms. However, many of the benefits are intangible. For example, the benefits of such bodies as the National Health Service or Local Education Authorities are almost impossible to quantify.

Such government organisations tend to use a low discount rate in investment appraisals (to take account of "time preference") and have complex methods of quantifying non-financial benefits in a standard NPV analysis.

Economists have tried to evaluate many public sector investments through the use of cost benefit analysis, with varying degrees of success. Problems are usually encountered in evaluating all the benefits. Value for money audits can be conducted in the public sector but these concentrate on monetary costs rather than benefits.

Note: A value for money audit is defined as an "investigation into whether proper arrangements have been made for securing economy, efficiency and effectiveness in the use of resources." (CIMA Official Terminology 2005)

Regulation

It is worth remembering that organisations that have had a public sector history or are themselves natural monopolies are often regulated in order to ensure the public are not the victims of the monopoly power these companies enjoy. This regulation can take many forms but can include the capping of the selling process, the taxing of super profits or simply a limit on the profits these organisations are allowed to make.

Performance and progress indicators – Public sector

Public sector entities are often appraised according to the "value for money" (VFM) that they generate.

Value for money may be defined as "performance of an activity in such a way as to simultaneously achieve economy, efficiency and effectiveness." (CIMA Official Terminology 2005)

This means maximising benefits for the lowest cost and has three constituent elements:

Economy is a measure of inputs to achieve a certain service or level of service.

Effectiveness is a measure of outputs, i.e. services/facilities.

Efficiency is the optimum of economy and effectiveness, i.e. the measure of outputs over inputs.

More detail on VFM

Measurement of VFM

In practice, value for money is difficult to measure, and it is a relative rather than an absolute measure. There will often be different views of what the objectives of a not-for-profit entity should be, and therefore, whether appropriate objectives have been achieved. What value does one put on curing an illness, or saving a life? Should the success of a hospital be measured by shorter waiting lists? These are societal matters, the discomfort being one of the reasons they are placed firmly in the public sector, rather than being left to the 'survival of the fittest' philosophy associated with the competitive markets.

A public sector college will measure the number of students, the number of courses, the ratio of lecturers to students, and so on. It will also seek its customers' assessments of the standard of, for example its lecturing and catering, and compare them with preset targets. In the language of strategic financial management, these are answers to the question 'How well did we do what we chose to do?'. You should also be aware, by now, of the dangers of concentrating on what can be measured. Note, for example that it is possible to measure crime detection, but it is not possible to measure crime prevention; it is possible to measure the extent to which the sick are cured, but not the extent to which sickness is prevented. People can be rewarded on the basis of measurables, but it should come as no surprise if they then skimp on the immeasurables: you get what you measure. Measuring performance is only a part of monitoring progress.

Test your understanding 3

Which of the following is an 'efficiency' target that a not for profit organisation might put in place?

A Negotiation of bulk discounts

B Pay rates for staff of appropriate levels of qualification

C Staff utilisation

D Customer satisfaction ratings

Test your understanding 4

Value for money is an important objective for not-for-profit organisations.

Which of the following actions is consistent with increasing value for money?

A Using a cheaper source of goods and thereby decreasing the quality of not-for-profit organisation services

B Searching for ways to diversify the finances of the not-for-profit organisation

C Decreasing waste in the provision of a service by the not-for-profit organisation

D Focusing on meeting the financial objectives of the not-for-profit organisation

Managing conflict arising from performance indicators can be difficult because performance indicators can be in conflict with each other.

For example a company may have several objectives, two of which might be to increase net profit, and at the same time to improve customer service. Improving customer service should increase sales which will increase net profit. However, it will probably also involve staff training which is an expense, thereby decreasing net profit. How is this conflict managed?

The ultimate objective of a profit-making company is usually to increase shareholder wealth, so with respect to improving customer service, a typical accountant would perform a cost-benefit analysis to establish the increase in sales (and therefore net profit) compared to the increase in training costs (and therefore the decrease in net profit). Whichever strategy added the most value to the company – improved customer service or not, then that strategy would be undertaken.

However, there are many other implications of either strategy. For example, it might be considered for how long customer satisfaction was improved before a competitor met or exceeded our high standards and therefore the estimated future value was reduced. It might also be considered whether the improved customer service might lead to other positive aspects for the company, such as increased reputation, international sales, etc which could also add value way beyond the staff training cost.

Unless management use their crystal ball, who knows how this might affect a company's future. Because of this unknown, often management and the Board do not necessarily adopt a 'maximise shareholder wealth' strategy, but instead they try to guess what the future holds, guess what the competition might do, keep their options open, and adopt a **satisficing strategy**, rather than shareholder wealth maximising strategy. This means that they try to keep everyone happy most of the time.

So this might mean that no performance indicator is maximised, but instead many are satisfied.

Another example of this could include whether to invest in a new non-current asset which would improve production efficiency in a particular department.

Imagine the manager of this department is awarded a bonus based upon meeting a particular Return on Capital Employed (ROCE). ROCE is calculated using profit divided by capital employed. By buying the new asset, efficiency should increase and therefore so should profit (providing everything made can be sold). But non-current assets will also rise within the capital employed figure, and probably by a much larger amount than the increased profit (at least initially). This means that the ROCE will fall and the manager would be reluctant to buy the new asset in the first place, despite it probably being a good thing for the company in the longer term.

Due to this conflict of objectives between the company and the manager, Residual Income (RI = Profit – (% × Capital employed)) has been used as a performance target instead, which may give the manager the desired bonus each year.

Using both ROCE and RI often gives conflicting results. The manager will believe that his hard work should be rewarded using the RI indicator, while others might prefer the ROCE indicator. Again a satisficing strategy may be required e.g. awarding the bonus based on meeting both indicators, perhaps by reducing the managers target, by amending the indicators in some way, or by using different performance indicators altogether. The decision is a tough one, but probably the best thing to do when any conflict arises is to discuss the issue with all relevant stakeholders and come up with a happy medium. i.e. satisfice. Otherwise, the company may never meet its targets, which becomes very demotivational, and good managers may leave.

2 Which investment appraisal method should be used?

To some extent, the decision as to which investment appraisal methods to use depends on the circumstances.

For example, if the company has short term liquidity problems, the payback period may well provide useful information. Alternatively, if a manager is being appraised based on the ROCE generated, he may decide to use the ARR method as an important investment appraisal method.

However, in most cases, the NPV method is considered to be the best investment appraisal method, because it measures the absolute gain in shareholders' wealth if a project is undertaken. This links to the primary financial objective of all companies – to maximise the wealth of the shareholders.

The IRR is useful as a follow up to NPV when trying to assess the sensitivity of the project to changes in input factors.

Financial and strategic considerations in investment appraisal

Financial methods of evaluation are by no means the only factors to be taken into account in investment appraisal.

Maximising shareholder wealth

We might define investment appraisal as being concerned with maximising shareholder wealth, but we must be careful to qualify this concept by making it subject to constraints associated with issues of social responsibility, such as effective controls over pollution.

Stakeholder considerations

Shareholders' wealth in this context needs to be linked with the wider view of stakeholder theory which is within the CIMA F3 syllabus.

The key point here is that many other interested parties apart from shareholders – for example, suppliers, lenders, employees, managers, as well as the general public – need to be taken into account in assessing a project's viability.

For example, a project with a large positive NPV would normally be considered to be acceptable. However, if undertaking the project would lead to job losses within the entity, or would increase pollution levels, the decision is not so clear cut.

In situations such as this, the competing needs of stakeholders would need to be assessed and compared.

Although it may seem to go against the key "maximise shareholder wealth" objective to reject a project with a positive NPV, it is worth considering that a project which fails to achieve the objectives of the other stakeholders might ultimately undermine the entity's position and may lead to negative publicity which might adversely impact shareholder wealth in the future.

Strategic considerations

The financial appraisal of a project must also be balanced against its strategic benefits to the entity.

For example, if a project has been appraised which has a small positive (or negative) NPV, usually the project would be rejected. However, if the project would help to consolidate the entity's competitive position, or give it the opportunity to expand into a new, attractive market, the decision is not so clear cut.

In this case, management would have to try to balance the financial requirements of the entity against the long-term strategic requirements.

If it is felt that undertaking a project now would improve the entity's prospects and likely shareholder wealth in the future, a project with a small positive (or negative) NPV might sometimes be accepted.

Note: Real options theory is one way of trying to formalise the process, by assigning values to strategic factors so that they can be incorporated more easily in the decision making process.

3 System development life cycle

The System Development Life Cycle (SDLC), or sometimes called the System Project Life Cycle (SPLC), has six main stages:

- Planning;
- Analysis
- Design;
- Development;
- Implementation;
- Review.

These stages were covered in lower level CIMA papers. For CIMA P3 the risks and controls of each stage should be considered.

Planning

The planning stage involved undertaking a feasibility study which looked at whether the project or development was actually possible, how much it might cost and whether the company could raise the funds, whether there were sufficient skills available, etc.

The risks at this stage might cover whether a feasibility study was carried out, and whether all parts were covered adequately. Management should not continue any further, thereby wasting time and money, unless the feasibility study demonstrates that the future project is feasible.

Controls to ensure this might include setting up a specific committee (with expertise) to ensure sufficient planning was conducted prior to any later stages, and whether all parts of the feasibility study were adequately researched, concluded and authorised.

Analysis

This stage involves the consideration of any current system and the problems with it. It may be too expensive, have errors in it, users don't like it, etc. Research and questionnaires will be used to ascertain what the real problem is.

Risks at this stage are that the actual problem is mis-diagnosed and consequently the incorrect solution is developed.

Controls will include sufficient budget and time to get to the root of the problem, and the consultation of all interested parties. Money and time spent at this stage should save waste later in the stages developing the incorrect solution.

Design

Once the problem is ascertained experts should now design the new, improved system. This might involve flowcharts showing information flows, initial computer coding, etc. A prototype might be developed to give the end users an idea of what is being developed. This will give the end user a chance to overcome any problems they envisage.

Controls should involve all users being consulted when the 'prototype' or design has been generated. Budget over run can be a problem at this stage – generating a perfect solution that is too costly (the costs outweighing the benefits). The finance department should be consulted to check that the solution comes within budget.

Development

Development takes the prototype a stage further and starts to build the full new system or project. This is usually in the hands of computer programmers these days, since many systems used in business are computerised.

The risks arising at this stage are that as the developer gets deeper into their solution they amend the design, or that they have insufficient expertise or time to develop a good solution.

To control this, management should receive constant feedback on the projects progress, and there should be an 'expert' overseeing the developers activities to ensure that they are developing what was agreed.

Implementation

During the implementation stage there are several activities such as file conversion, changeover, testing and training.

Changeover (direct, parallel, phased and pilot) was covered in your lower level CIMA papers, and risks included the system not working at all, cost over runs, errors or bugs in the system, etc. A lack of staff training would mean that further errors could be made, staff inefficiency and low morale/resignations if they became frustrated with the system. Ultimately the system could be rejected by staff if it is not implemented correctly.

Controls should involve plenty of time and a budget for staff training, and the correct method of changeover i.e. if the system is a critical business activity then direct changeover is unlikely to be acceptable as it would be too high risk to switch from one system to another simultaneously, unless significant testing had taken place.

Review

The last stage in the SDLC is review. This stage considers the success of the project some time after it was implemented. It is meant to consider improvements to the current project and to be a learning tool, so that future projects and their management run more smoothly.

Risks here might be that management don't care or have time to review a project and therefore never learn or improve in the future.

Criteria that are usually covered include time (did the project meet its deadline?), cost (did the project complete within budget?) and quality (did it meet the users expectations/solve the problem?)

The review stage often includes a review **after** the event, called a **post completion review** or **post completion audit** (see later in this chapter).

4 Project implementation and control

Introduction to stages of project implementation and control

In order for a project to succeed, it will need to have a clearly defined objective, a competent project manager and sufficient resources allocated to it.

At each stage of the project implementation and control process, the project manager will have to satisfy himself that the project will achieve its own objective, and in turn help to achieve the overall objectives of the entity.

There are several stages in the project implementation and control process, starting with conceptual stage and running through to control.

Conceptual stage

The conceptual stage is the first stage in the implementation of a new project. It is where the project team is brought together, under the control of the project manager. The team members will be allocated specific roles and responsibilities depending on their skills.

The conceptual stage is where the new product, service or process which is the focus of the project is worked on specifically.

For example, management might commission some market research to assess the key design features which customers require. Then (if the project is to involve the introduction of a new product) a product design will be created, and a trial product produced.

The aim of the conceptual stage is to finalise the design of the new product, service or process before high costs are incurred in the development and construction stages.

Development stage

Once the concept of the product, service or process has been well defined, the development stage is where the project team needs to check that the concept meets customer requirements.

This can be achieved by trial product testing and subsequent consumer feedback.

Any problems noted at this stage of the process can be addressed and the design can once again be amended before further costs are incurred.

Construction and initial manufacturing/operating stage

When the product, service or process has been developed, and any design problems have been addressed, the next stage is where the new product, service or process is launched.

For a product, this stage will be where the large scale production begins, making items based on the designs which were finalised during the development stage.

For a service or process, this is where the new service or process is implemented.

In the initial manufacturing/operating stage of the project, it will be critical for the project team to control the new product, service or process by continual product testing and product refinement (for products) or test runs and parallel running (for services or processes).

Control stage

Control is exercised by the project team all the way through the project.

It is however important that control continues even after the initial manufacturing/operating stage has ended.

The project team should continue monitoring the project, and comparing the actual results against the original budget (time and cost). It will be the job of the project team at the control stage to keep considering whether the project is likely to achieve its original objectives.

Any cost or time over runs should be communicated to management, and to the workers involved in the project at regular intervals. This feedback will help to prevent the project from deviating too far from its original budget and objectives.

Control by capital expenditure committee

Strict control of large projects must be maintained and the accountant must submit periodic reports to top management on progress and cost. A typical report would include data such as the following:

- Budgeted cost of the project, date started and scheduled completion date.
- Cost and over or under expenditure to date.
- Estimated cost to completion, and estimated final over or under expenditure.
- Estimated completion date and details of penalties, if any.

The capital expenditure committee will seek explanations for any overspending that may have arisen. Where projects are incomplete and actual expenditure exceeds the authorisation, additional authority must be sought to complete the project. In so doing, the committee must consider the value of the project as it then stands and the additional value that will be gained by completing it, compared with the additional expenditure to completion.

5 Post-completion audit of capital projects

Definition

A post-completion audit (PCA) can be defined as an "objective independent assessment of the success of a capital project in relation to a plan. It covers the whole life of a project and provides feedback to managers to aid the implementation and control of future projects."

(CIMA Official Terminology 2005)

Overview of a PCA

The PCA reviews the cashflows from the project after the project has finished, or sometimes during the life of the project. The aim is to identify any variances from the original budget and particularly to discover the causes of those variances.

A project's PCA provides the mechanism whereby experience of past projects can be fed into the entity's decision-making processes as an aid to the improvement of future projects.

Anecdotal evidence also suggests that the growing interest in PCA has arisen from a realisation that past investments have frequently failed to live up to expectations, and firms are keen to avoid repetition of the same mistakes.

Organisation of a PCA

Scope and purpose of a PCA

A good PCA report does not set out to identify the costs and benefits of a project in precise detail, but rather seeks to identify general lessons to be learned from a project. It is not a policing exercise, and, if it is to be effective, should not be seen as such. A PCA will nevertheless encourage honesty in facing problems at all levels of the organisation, as attempts to ignore or hide realities are unlikely to remain uncovered.

The task is often carried out by small teams, typically consisting of an accountant and an engineer who have had some involvement in the project. Surprising though it may seem, it is not common to find PCA as the responsibility of the internal audit department.

A PCA reviews all aspects of a completed project, to assess whether it lived up to initial expectations in terms of revenues and costs, and analyses the causes of deviations from planned results.

The key thing is that management will try to identify the causes of any variances from budget, and the lessons which can be learned to help with future project implementation.

Causes of variances could include poor management decisions, lack of controls over expenditure, poor application of the process, or problems with the process itself. For example, if it can be identified that there were insufficient controls over the costs at a particular stage of the project implementation, this will show management where resources should be targeted during the next project implementation.

Its main purpose is to enable the experiences – good or bad – gained during the life of one project to be made available for the benefit of future projects. The role of a PCA is thus essentially a forward-looking one; it seeks to establish lessons from the past for the future benefit of the organisation.

Communication of the PCA findings

The formal mechanism for transmitting the information to management is the final post-audit report, which provides a history of the project from inception to completion.

In the case of successful ventures, the reports will distinguish between projects which have a good outcome due to effective planning and management, and projects whose good outcome is the result of luck; in the case of unsuccessful ventures, the causes will be fully disclosed.

It is at the planning stage that project control is most important and effective, and past experience provides an invaluable input into the process.

Benefits and limitations of PCAs

Benefits of post-completion auditing

Six potential benefits from the operation of a PCA system have been identified, and these are listed below in the order in which they appear in Management Accounting Guide 9: Post Completion Auditing (CIMA, 1993):

(1) It improves the quality of decision-making by providing a mechanism whereby past experience can be made readily available to decision-makers.

(2) It encourages greater realism in project appraisal by providing a mechanism whereby past inaccuracies in forecasts are made public.

(3) It provides a means of improving control mechanisms by formally highlighting areas where weaknesses have caused problems.

(4) It enables speedy modification of under-performing/over-performing projects by identifying the reasons for the under- or over-performance.

(5) It increases the frequency of project termination for 'bad projects'.

(6) It highlights reasons for successful projects which may be important in achieving greater benefits from future projects.

Mills and Kennedy reclassified these benefits into three types:

- Type (a) – those which relate to the performance of the current project, i.e. the project under review.
- Type (b) – those which relate to the investment system itself.
- Type (c) – those which relate to the choice and performance of future projects.

Using this subdivision, the benefits listed in the Guide are grouped under the three categories, as follows:

Type	**Guide benefit**
(a)	4,5
(b)	3
(c)	1,2, 6

The authors reported that all the surveyed entities that had an operational PCA system at the time of their research gained type (b) benefits from their system, and almost 40% sought type (c) benefits. Only 20% of the entities sought type (a) benefits, which may be considered surprising.

However, it is pointed out that control of the current project during its life may be effectively gained through other procedures, such as routine project monitoring.

Limitations of post-completion auditing

The main limitations of post-completion auditing are;

- the process can be costly and time consuming;
- it requires good data collection systems to be in place;
- it is not a panacea for all the business's problems;
- it can be used to blame rather than learn from past mistakes.

Test your understanding 5

The primary reasons why companies undertake a post-completion audit of a capital project are: (Select all that apply.)

A To identify any variances and to discover the cause of them

B To improve future projects by avoiding past mistakes

C To identify the exact costs and benefits of a project

D To identify who to blame for past mistakes

Test your understanding 6

A typical capital expenditure progress report would include data on: (Select all that apply.)

A The date the project started

B Details of any penalties

C Estimated costs to completion

D Who was to blame for any overspends

Test your understanding 7

The directors of AB have commissioned some market research to assess the key design features of a potential new product which they think customers require.

This activity would take place within which stage:

A The conceptual stage

B The development stage

C The control stage

D The operating stage

Test your understanding 8 – Games plc (Case study)

Scenario

The Games is an international multi-sport event that is held within a region of the world every four years. It attracts competitors from 10 different countries within the region and is held at a different time from the Olympic Games. The Games are held in each of the countries in turn within the region. The next Games are scheduled to take place in Country C in October 2015. There are 25 sports included within the Games ranging from archery through to weightlifting. The Games were first held in 1979 and this is the first time that Country C has hosted them.

The Games Park is a major undertaking that is being built with two objectives in mind. The first is the creation of a suitable venue for the Games. The second is to leave a number of permanent facilities that will be useful to the local community for leisure purposes and as venues for more serious sporting competition at the national level in Country C.

The swimming pool was the first major construction activity to be completed. Swimming is a popular spectator sport and so the pool was designed to accommodate large numbers of seated spectators. The architects who designed the building knew that most of the spectator seating would be unnecessary once the Games were over and designed it so that it would be easy to remove the seating along one side of the pool when the Games finish. The intention was that the space that this would create could be converted for use as a hall which would be suitable for local clubs and youth groups to play a range of sports such as basketball and badminton.

The swimming pool was built by a construction company, working to GAMESCO's architect's plans. The contract allowed for up to an additional 10% to be charged in the event of agreed contingencies, such as problems with the site. In fact, the whole of this 10% was charged because of the discovery that the soil structure on which the swimming pool was to be built was unstable and had to be reinforced with concrete pilings.

The swimming pool was finished on time, despite the initial delays in preparing the site. When the building was formally handed over to GAMESCO it was discovered that much of the ducting for air conditioning, electrical supplies and so on had been routed under the seating that was scheduled to be removed after the Games. The contractor claimed that this was necessary because the original plan to route the ducting through the building's foundations would have been too expensive because of the additional work on the site and also because the foundations themselves had been redesigned by GAMESCO's architect to cope with the addition of the concrete pilings.

Trigger

The Mayor of the city that will take possession of the swimming pool after the Games has asked for a post completion audit of the swimming pool project. The city will be unable to adapt the seating area to provide the additional facility of a sports hall and the seating capacity will have no value. The project manager responsible for the swimming pool has argued that such an audit will serve no purpose.

Task

As the Head of Internal Audit, prepare an email to the project manager:

(i) Discussing the advantages and disadvantages to GAMESCO of conducting a post completion audit of the swimming pool project.

(15 minutes)

(ii) Recommending, stating reasons, the major issues that should be investigated during the post completion audit of the swimming pool project.

(15 minutes)

Test your understanding 9 – Stakeholders (Case study)

Quotation 1

'The directors of all businesses must consider the wishes of all potential stakeholders for whose support they are competing – not just owners but employees, suppliers, customers, lenders, regulators and the community in which their business operates.'

Quotation 2

'Stakeholder theory is incompatible with business and its objectives and should be firmly resisted.'

Task

Discuss the opposing arguments in the two quotations given above, and explain how these views might be reconciled.

Test your understanding 10 – Public v private sector objectives

Public sector organisations do not have the requirement to produce 'profit' in the same sense as the private sector. However, they are expected to work within budgets and recognise aspects of financial management familiar to the private sector.

The following are three examples of differences between the public and private sector:

(1) A company that operates a chain of private hospitals uses a discount rate of 16% to evaluate its investment decisions and generally expects an accounting rate of return of 25%. A government-funded hospital trust is required to achieve a return of only 6% on assets.

(2) Private sector companies are moving towards a more flexible approach to budgeting. Organisations in the public sector are moving in the opposite direction i.e. towards a more rigid approach to budgeting, enforced by the Treasury (up to three years).

(3) Public sector pay is subject to government controls and has for many years failed to keep pace with inflation. Market forces determine wages and salaries in the private sector.

Required:

Discuss the causes and consequences of the three scenarios outlined above, using examples to illustrate your answer where appropriate.

Note: Overseas candidates may use examples of organisations in their own country.

Test your understanding 11 – KAL (Case study)

Scenario

KAL is a large, listed entity based in a country in the eurozone. Its principal activity is the manufacture and distribution of electrical consumer goods. Manufacturing operations are located in the home country but goods are sold to wholesalers worldwide, priced in the customer's local currency. The group has experienced rapid growth in recent years and many of its IS/IT systems need upgrading to handle larger volumes and increased complexity.

Group treasury is centralised at the head office and its key responsibilities include arranging sufficient long-term and short-term liquidity resources for the group and hedging foreign exchange exposures.

Trigger

One of the first projects is a replacement treasury management system (TMS) to provide an integrated IS/IT system. The new integrated TMS will record all treasury transactions and provide information for the management and control of the treasury operations. It replaces the current system which consists of a series of spreadsheets for each part of the treasury operations.

Task

(a) Evaluate the benefits that might result from the introduction of the new TMS. Include in your evaluation some reference to the control factors that need to be considered during the implementation stage.

(10 minutes)

(b) Prepare a report advising the directors on the following:

- The main purpose of a post-completion audit (PCA):
- What should be covered in a PCA of the TMS project;
- The importance and limitations of a PCA to KAL in the context of the TMS project.

(15 minutes)

6 Chapter Summary

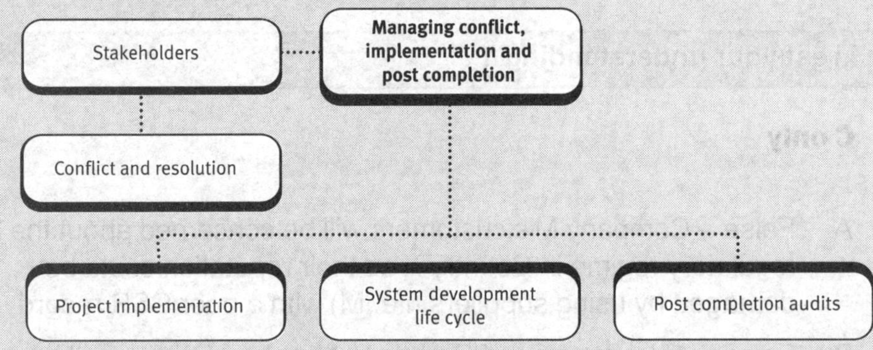

Test your understanding answers

Test your understanding 1

C only

A False – Company M's customers will be concerned about the lax regulatory regime in Country X as their reputation could be damaged by using suppliers (i.e. M) with a poor CSR record

B False – At least some of Company M's shareholders will be worried that any poor publicity received in operations in Country X could impact M's ability to win future contracts, in the same way that Company Q has suffered.

C True – only 200 jobs are being created in Country X at the experience of virgin rain forest.

D False – while Company M may (or may not) already have a poor reputation with environmental activists, the investment in Country X could damage it further, especially given the risk of incidents due to poor controls.

Test your understanding 2

D

A will create more affordable housing but only 50 houses have been suggested and many poor people will not be able to afford to buy them.

B is more concerned with protecting the environment but will have little impact on "the poor"

C will reduce the profits of big business but will have little impact on "the poor"

D is likely to have the greatest impact as, hopefully, many unemployed people will be able to get work on the construction site.

Test your understanding 3

C

A and B are economy measures, while D looks at effectiveness

Test your understanding 4

C

Test your understanding 5

The correct answers are A and B – The exact costs and benefits should already be known before a post-completion audit takes place.

Blame is not a primary reason for a post-completion audit. Learning from mistakes and consequent training are reasons why post-completion audits take place.

Test your understanding 6

The correct answers are A, B and C – Blame is not normally apportioned in the capital expenditure progress report, although it may be discussed and logged in the minutes of a progress meeting.

Test your understanding 7

The correct answer is A – The conceptual stage is the first stage in the implementation of a new project. Market research would take place now to prevent unnecessary expenditure later in the development and operating stages.

Test your understanding 8 – Games plc (Case study)

Email

To: Project Manager

From: Head of Internal Audit

Date: Today

Subject: Post completion audit

Dear Project Manager,

(i) This project requires a post-completion audit since at first sight this project appears to have been poorly managed. The costs were liable to overrun and the contractor responded by not working to the plan. There could be similar issues arising from other projects that are presently under way and that might be subject to the same difficulties. The issues with the stability of the site could affect a wider area than just the swimming pool and it would be desirable to prevent a recurrence.

It may be possible for GAMESCO to recover some of the cost of the swimming pool project if the post completion audit can determine who is to blame for the revised building plan. If it can be demonstrated that the builder had not properly consulted the project manager then the decision to deliver a completed project that is not to the correct specification could be grounds for liability.

A clear understanding of the issues may be useful to GAMESCO's senior management because mismanagement of such projects is often commented on in the press.

It may be too late for an audit to deal with similar problems elsewhere because the other major projects are likely to be well under way. It may be too late to change the direction of a project once the basic structure of a building has been put in place and so the audit might prove a waste of time and effort.

The fact that an audit is being commissioned could disrupt the relationship between GAMESCO and the builders, possibly delaying the completion of the Games Park. Regardless of the outcome of the audit the swimming pool was completed on time and within the 10% overrun on cost that was permitted. The builder appears to have acted in good faith in removing a secondary facility from the building because it would otherwise have been impossible to complete at an acceptable cost. An audit may provoke a defensive response from the building teams on other projects that are under way.

(ii) It seems likely that the issue that will be material in this audit is the fact that the completed building has not been built to plan. The auditor should start with a detailed study of all of the correspondence between the builder and GAMESCO's project manager, starting from the discovery of the problems with the foundation. The crucial issue is the question of how changes to the plan were dealt with after the problem with the soil structure was discovered. If the builder brought this to the project manager's attention and received permission to reroute the ducting then that makes GAMESCO responsible for the failure to meet the plan.
The auditor needs to fully understand the manner in which the setback with the foundation was managed. The discovery of the problem with the site suggests that the plan and the contract should have been revisited. The potential for a 10% overrun on costs seems to have been put in place for dealing with much less serious problems. It seems somewhat reckless to have spent the whole of this contingency reserve (and more) on foundations, leaving insufficient in the budget to complete the building to plan.

The auditor should obtain the formal plans or blueprints that were used by the contractor who fitted the ducting. The authorship of those plans should be indicated on the document and the plans themselves can be checked back to determine who signed them off as acceptable. These plans will almost certainly establish who made the final decision on the routing of the ducts.

The auditor should also review the schedule of site visits by the project manager and any other independent reviewers to establish whether there were problems with the oversight at that level. This is an important compliance test because it will establish the extent to which the project management team was supervising the build on GAMESCO's behalf. If these reviews were ineffective then the builders could almost be excused for taking shortcuts.

The auditor should also review the contract. If the completion of the work to plan was the responsibility of the builder, without any consideration of the fact that unforeseen problems had arisen, then the builder may still be responsible for the costs of rectifying this problem.

If you have any queries, please do not hesitate to contact me.

Best wishes

Head of Internal Audit

Test your understanding 9 – Stakeholders (Case study)

A sensible starting point is to list the various stakeholders and show how their interests may conflict, before reconciling the two statements.

A firm is a collection of contributors, all of whom have a stake in its ongoing success and survival. In a narrow sense, their respective interests are bound to conflict if pushed to the limit.

- Owners – want maximum dividends and share price.
- Lenders – want maximum security for their investment.
- Managers – want maximum pay and other forms of remuneration.
- Other employees – want maximum pay for minimum effort plus optimal health and safety standards.
- Customers – want maximum quality at minimum price plus maximum credit.
- Suppliers – want minimum settlement delay.
- Government – wants maximum tax take.
- Society – wants maximum environmental safeguards, contributions to charity and local community projects.

If pushed to the limit, most of these aims are likely to bankrupt the business. If shareholders' aims are pursued neglecting all else, it requires screwing down wages and conditions to minimal levels, racking up prices to take maximum advantage of short-term opportunities, never paying suppliers until threatened with legal action, and so on.

Such behaviour is not just anti-social, it is anti-survival. It will attract critical attention from the government and other bodies, resulting in penalties, fines and ongoing scrutiny which will damage the firm's reputation and market position irretrievably.

The SWM aim is not a short-term profit maximising aim. It aims to create sustainable and permanent value for owners. It is thoroughly consistent with treating customers and employees well and building up an image as a respected contributor to society.

It is thus easy to reconcile the two statements – firms that treat their stakeholders badly are unlikely to survive into the long term. To 'consider the wishes of all potential stakeholders' does not require *maximising* everyone's particular interests but striking a balance between them to the ultimate and ongoing benefit of all. This is simply good business.

Test your understanding 10 – Public v private sector objectives

(1) **Rates of return**

The private sector company has a higher required rate of return, and uses more measures of financial success than the public sector entity.

Causes

The private sector entity has a primary objective to increase shareholder wealth, so it has to measure financial performance carefully.

Its required rate of return is higher because the investors in the private entity perceive risk to be high. Public sector entities face lower risk since they are supported by governments.

The cost of finance for the public sector entity (provided by the government) will be lower, since the government can usually borrow money very cheaply. This means that the required return can be lower.

Consequences

The public sector entity will be more inclined to undertake relatively low return projects which the private sector entity will reject. Therefore, "unprofitable" treatments will still be undertaken in the public sector.

The private sector entity will perform a narrow range of treatments very efficiently. The public sector entity will offer a much broader range of treatments.

The lower required return in the public sector will give less incentive to reduce costs, so the public sector entity may be less efficient than the private sector.

(2) **Budgets**

Private sector entities have more flexible budgeting procedures than public sector entities.

Causes

Public sector entities tend to be larger, and have more bureaucratic structures. Hence, public sector budgeting can be a much more complex process.

The public sector is expected to look further into the future (3 years) whereas a private sector budget may only last for 1 year.

Private sector entities have a flexible approach to financing (effectively any project can be undertaken if the finance can be found). Public sector entities are allocated finance by government and therefore have an objective to work within this imposed constraint. Flexibility is therefore less important in a public sector entity.

The government likes to be able to compare performance of different public sector entities, so often a standard, rigid method of budgeting is proposed to enable comparisons to be made easily.

Consequences

Private sector entities find it easier to adapt quickly to real world factors which impact them.

Private sector entities tend to have a more flexible, "can-do" culture.

Public sector budgets tend to contain more budgetary slack, because the budget has often been set well in advance and then not amended to reflect new factors which come to light.

(3) **Pay**

Public sector pay lags behind that in the private sector.

Causes

Public sector job security tends to be better, so pay is not the only attraction of holding a public sector job.

Also, public sector pensions tend to be government funded, final salary schemes. In the private sector, final salary schemes are becoming less prevalent as firms struggle to afford them.

The government often tries to control inflation by keeping public sector pay rises under control. A low pay rise for public sector workers can be used as a signal of financial prudence.

Public sector staff are paid relatively little as a bonus or incentive payment. Most of the pay tends to be a basic salary determined by a very detailed pay scale.

Consequences

Public sector morale and motivation is often lower than in the private sector.

Good quality staff are often attracted to private sector roles where the staff are better rewarded.

The lack of bonuses in the public sector sometimes stifles creativity and discourages the use of initiative.

Test your understanding 11 – KAL (Case study)

(a) **Key points**

- The primary benefit is that one integrated system will replace a number of apparently disparate legacy systems. It is not clear if the new system will be an "off-the-shelf" system or will be bespoke for the entity. An off-the-shelf system may not match perfectly the requirements of the entity and may require changes to the capture and processing of data. On the other hand, a bespoke system may prove difficult to implement and maintain. Upgrades to the system may be more difficult to manage.
- Greater security of data should be achieved by having all the data in one system, rather than being copied from one spreadsheet to another.
- More flexibility of operations – information needs change and require different solutions. The new TMS system can be designed to include extra treasury functions which KAL might need in the future (for example interest rate hedging techniques).
- The new integrated system takes advantage of technological developments.
- May provide benefits that are cost-reducing or even income generating. For example, the move to a single integrated system should lead to operational efficiencies and potential staff savings. New management information may be available from the system that the existing systems are not able to provide. Maintenance costs for the new system should be lower than for the existing systems.

– Does the new system assist KAL meet its corporate objectives in any way? Have the objectives of introducing a new system been clearly defined? – if not, how can success be measured? (see further comments in part (b)).

– Can the system be adapted to decentralised function if KAL chooses to change its treasury policy on centralisation?

Control

In the implementation stage of the project, it will be critical for the project team to control the new product, service or process by test runs and parallel running.

The project team should continue monitoring the project, and comparing the actual results against the original budget (time and cost). They should keep considering whether the project is likely to achieve its original objectives.

Any cost or time over runs should be communicated to management, and to the workers involved in the project at regular intervals. This feedback will help to prevent the project from deviating too far from its original budget and objectives.

(b) **Report**

To: The directors

From: A.N. Accountant

Date: Today

Subject: Post-completion audit (PCA)

Introduction

A PCA reviews the cashflows from a project after the project has finished, or sometimes during the life of the project. The aim is to identify any variances from the original budget and particularly to discover the causes of those variances.

A project's PCA provides the mechanism whereby experience of past projects can be fed into the entity's decision-making processes as an aid to the improvement of future projects.

What should be covered?

In a PCA of the TMS project, the following areas should be covered:

- analysis of costs incurred, compared to budget
- analysis of time spent on the project, compared to budget
- analysis of the results of TMS system tests and parallel runs
- discussions with users – to identify whether there are any training needs
- discussions with management – to identify whether the new TMS system is helping to provide better management and control information as expected.

The key factors of importance of a PCA to KAL

- It enables a check to be made on whether the performance of the TMS corresponds with the expected results. If this is not the case, the reasons should be sought. This could form the basis for improvements in development of the system.
- It generates information, which allows an appraisal to be made of the managers who took the decision to upgrade the system. Managers will therefore tend to arrive at more realistic estimates of the advantages and disadvantages of the proposed investments.
- It can provide for better project planning in the future. If, in the evaluation, it is found that the planning of the investment programme was poor, provision can be made to ensure that it is better for future acquisitions.

Limitations

Sufficient resources are often not allocated to the task of completing PCAs so often are not undertaken. They can be time consuming and costly to complete. They are sometimes seen as tools for apportioning blame, so even where undertaken the lessons are often not disseminated and are not then embedded in future projects. If undertaken by the managers of the project, they may claim credit for all that went well and blame external factors for everything that didn't.

Conclusion

The main purpose of a PCA is as a learning tool – se we don't make the same mistakes again. This can save us from wasting resources (finance) in the future. However, PCAs can be costly and cause negative feeling when activities went badly.

Overall, PCAs are accepted as a worthwhile activity by most companies.

Index

3Es.....577, 911

A

Ability to bear risk.....90
Accepting risk (TARA).....79
Access logging.....215
Adjusted present value (APV).....857, 859, 864
Advance fee fraud.....395
Agency theory.....903
Analytical review.....597
Appraisal costs.....342
Arbitrage.....685, 689, 695
Assurance map.....69
Audit.....551
  analytical review.....597
  CAATs.....606
  committees.....492, 507
  computer systems.....603
  environmental.....581
  external.....568
  internal.....554
  management.....582
  planning.....585
  processes.....584
  report.....601
  risk.....586, 589
  sampling.....596
  social.....581
  systems-based auditing.....583
  testing.....593
  trail.....215
  types.....575
  Value for money.....577
Avoiding risk (TARA).....78

B

Backward integration.....76
Balanced scorecard.....362
Basis risk.....723, 786
Benchmarking.....586
Beta factors.....850
Beyond budgeting.....338
Big data.....284
Black-Scholes.....731, 847
Bribery Act.....165
Business continuity.....216
Business risk.....9, 857

C

Capital Asset Pricing Model (CAPM).....847, 855
Certainty equivalents.....837
Chief executive officer (CEO).....486
Chairman.....485
Changeover methods.....229
CIMA risk management cycle.....6
Cloud.....276
Code of ethics.....428
Committee of Sponsoring Organisations (COSO).....46, 144, 147
Committees:
  audit.....492, 507
  nominations.....491
  remuneration.....494
Commodity price risk.....9
Competitive risk *see* Economic risk
Compliance:
  risk.....8
  tests.....593
Computer assisted audit techniques (CAATs).....606
Computer Misuse Act.....224
Computer systems.....208
Conceptual framework (ethics).....433
Confidentiality.....430
Constraints on strategy.....900
Contingency controls.....213
Continuous improvement (kaizen).....341
Contractual inadequacy risk.....10
Controllable risks.....145
Controls:
  activities.....145, 148
  application.....218
  environment.....144, 147
  facility.....215
  management review of.....552
  personnel.....156, 214
  physical.....144
  physical access.....215
Corporate governance.....475
  definition.....476
  development.....477
  principles.....484
Corporate reputation risk.....22
COSO model.....144, 147
Costs of quality
  appraisal.....342
  external failure.....342
  internal failure.....342
  prevention.....342
Countertrade.....707
Credit crunch.....13
Credit risk.....18, 25, 640
Criminal records.....232
Critical success factors (CSF).....260

Index

Cross rates.....681
Culture risk.....25
Currency:
- forwards.....710
- futures.....719
- management.....358, 699
- money market hedge.....715
- options.....726
- risk.....18, 649
- risk hedging.....698
- swaps.....737

D

Data encryption.....221
Data mining.....282
Data Protection legislation.....209, 222
Data warehousing.....281
Decision support systems (DSS).....273
Debt capacity.....870
Directors:
- non-executive.....487
- remuneration.....498

Disaster recovery.....216
Diversification.....75, 650, 848
Downside risk.....2, 45
DSS *see* Decision support systems (DSS)

E

Economic risk.....12, 649
Economic Value Added (EVA™).....348
EIS *see* Executive information systems (EIS)
Embedded audit facilities.....610
Employee malfeasance risk.....24
Enterprise resource planning (ERP) systems.....273
Enterprise risk management (ERM).....46
Environmental:
- audit.....581
- benchmarking.....587
- reporting.....581
- risk.....20

ERP *see* Enterprise resource planning (ERP) systems
Ethics.....427
- budget setting.....447
- code of.....428
- conflict resolution.....437
- dilemmas.....437
- fundamental principles.....429
- risk.....435
- safeguards.....435
- threats.....433

EVA *see* Economic Value Added (EVA™)
Exchange rates.....678
Executive information systems (EIS).....273
Executive share options (ESOPs).....501
Executive Support Systems (ESS).....273
Expected values.....59, 831
Expert systems.....273
External audit.....568
External failure costs.....342

F

Facility controls.....215
Financial risk.....18, 26, 640
Firewalls.....221
Fisher effect.....690
Foreign currency *see* Currency
Forex swaps.....737
Forward contracts.....710
Forward integration.....76
Forward-rate agreements (FRAs).....779
FRAs *see* Forward-rate agreements (FRAs)
Fraud.....391
- detection.....407
- definition.....392
- investigation.....412, 572
- policy statements.....400
- prerequisites.....398
- prevention.....149, 400
- response.....409
- risk.....10, 22
- risk indictors.....397
- risk management strategy.....399
- types.....393
- whistle blowing.....408

Futures:
- foreign currency.....719
- interest rate.....784

G

Geared betas.....855
Gearing risk.....18
Governance.....476
Gross risk.....89

H

Hacking.....210
Hedging.....698
- benefits.....698
- external techniques.....704, 708, 779
- internal techniques.....704, 778
- risks.....78

Home currency invoicing.....705
Horizontal integration.....76

Index

I

Information:
- characteristics of.....270
- cost.....274
- good.....268
- security.....209
- strategy.....258, 262
- systems (IS).....213
- technology (IT).....278
- value of.....274

Inherent risk.....589
Input controls.....219
Integrity.....429
Integrity controls.....213
Interest rates:
- collars.....790
- forward-rate agreement.....779
- futures.....784
- guarantees.....783
- options.....788
- parity.....687
- risk.....18, 645, 777
- swaps.....794

Internal audit:
- definition.....553
- effectiveness.....567
- independence.....567
- outsourcing.....565
- scope.....557
- standards.....559
- structure.....563

Internal controls:
- COSO model.....144, 147
- environment.....144, 147
- governance.....504
- operational features.....151
- systems.....140
- Turnbull report.....142, 152, 504

Internal failure costs.....342
Internal hedging techniques:
- foreign exchange.....704
- interest rate.....778

Internal rate of return (IRR).....828
International:
- Fisher effect.....690
- risk.....25

Internet.....212
Intranets.....212
Investment appraisal.....827
Invoicing home currency.....705
IT *see* Information technology (IT)

J

Just in Time (JIT) methods.....340

K

Kaizen (continuous improvement).....341

L

Lagging.....705
Leadership.....484
Leading.....705
Lean management accounting.....367
Legal/litigation risk.....8, 25, 414
LIBID.....777
LIBOR.....646, 776
Logical access controls.....214

M

Management audit.....582
Management accounting controls.....332
Management control systems.....321, 331
Management information systems (MIS).....273
Matching.....706, 778
Materiality.....590
MIS *see* Management information systems (MIS)
Modern manufacturing methods.....339
Money market hedging.....715

N

Net present value (NPV).....828
Net risk.....89
Netting.....706, 778
Netting centres.....708
Network controls.....220
Nominations committee.....491
Non-executive directors (NEDs).....487
Non-financial performance measures.....361, 905
Normal distribution.....61
Not-for-profit organisations (NFPs, NPOs).....909

O

Objectives.....894
Objectivity.....270, 430
One tail test.....65
Operational risk.....9
Options:
- foreign currency.....726
- interest rate.....788
- real.....840

Organisational structure.....145, 334, 699
Output controls.....219

Index

P

Parity:
- interest rates.....687
- purchasing power.....685

Passwords.....214
Performance indicators.....261, 361, 905
Personnel controls.....156, 214
Physical access controls.....215
Physical controls.....154
Political risk.....8, 18, 641
Pooling.....75, 706
Post-completion audit.....918
Post implementation review.....231
Prerequisites for fraud.....398
Prevention costs.....342
Probabilities.....58, 831
Processing controls.....219
Product reputation risk.....9
Product risk.....9
Professional behaviour.....431
Professional competence and due care.....430
Project implementation and control.....918
Protected disclosure.....408
Purchasing power parity (PPPT).....685
Pure risk.....3
Pyramid schemes.....394

Q

Qualifying disclosure.....408
Quality costs.....342

R

Real options.....830
Regression analysis.....58, 63
Regulatory risk.....8
Remuneration:
- committees.....486
- directors.....490

Reputation risk.....414
- corporate.....22

Residual income.....335
Residual risk.....51, 81, 89
Responsibility accounting.....335
Return on investment.....335
Risk:
- appetite.....51
- assessment.....48, 54, 145, 148
- attitude.....51
- benefits.....5
- capacity.....51
- categories.....8
- committee.....54, 95
- controllable.....145
- cube.....81
- currency.....18, 649
- definitions.....2
- downside.....2, 45
- foreign exchange.....701
- gross.....89
- identification.....54
- interest rate.....645
- manager.....96
- mapping.....69
- net.....89
- political.....8, 18, 641
- pure.....3
- quantification.....58
- reduction (TARA).....78, 79
- register.....54
- reporting.....54, 84
- residual.....51, 81, 89
- response.....74
- roles.....94
- sharing.....78
- sources.....7
- speculative.....3
- strategy.....74, 91
- systematic.....847
- treatment.....54, 74
- two-way.....3
- types.....7
- uncontrollable.....145
- unsystematic.....847
- upside.....2, 45

Risk-adjusted discount rate.....830, 858, 863

S

Sampling.....596
Sarbanes-Oxley (SOX) legislation.....512
Security controls.....213
Security Market Line (SML).....850
SDLC *see* Systems Development Life Cycle (SDLC)
Segregation of duties.....153
Sensitivity analysis.....833
Shareholder value.....49
Share options.....499
Simulation analysis.....58, 68
SMA *see* Strategic management accounting (SMA)
SMART objectives.....261
Smoothing.....778
Social audit.....581
Software controls.....220
Sources of risk.....7

Spot rate.....679
Spread.....679
Speculative risk.....3
Standard deviation.....59
Steering committee.....278
STIRs.....784
Strategic enterprise management (SEM).....274
Strategic management accounting (SMA).....366
Strategic risk.....9
Substantive tests.....594
Swaps:
  currency.....737
  interest rate.....793
Systematic risk.....847
System backup.....217
Systems development.....226
Systems-based auditing.....583
Systems Development Life Cycle (SDLC).....226, 916
Systems investigation.....591
Systems theory.....324

T

TARA.....78
Technology risk.....19
Test data.....610
Ticks.....723
Total quality management (TQM).....342
Transferring risk (TARA).....74, 78
Transaction processing systems (TPS).....272
Transaction risk.....654
Transfer pricing.....349
Translation risk.....654
Treasury.....699
Turnbull report.....142, 152, 504
Two tail test.....65
Two-way risk.....3

U

Ungeared betas.....855
Unsystematic risk.....847
Upside risk.....2, 45
Uncertainty.....3

V

Value analysis.....343
Value at risk (VaR).....58, 60, 64
Value for money (VFM).....577, 911
VaR *see* Value at risk (VaR)
Value of information.....274
Vertical integration (forward/backward).....76
Viruses.....211, 221
Volatility.....58, 60

W

Weighted average cost of capital (WACC).....857, 861
Whistle blowing.....408

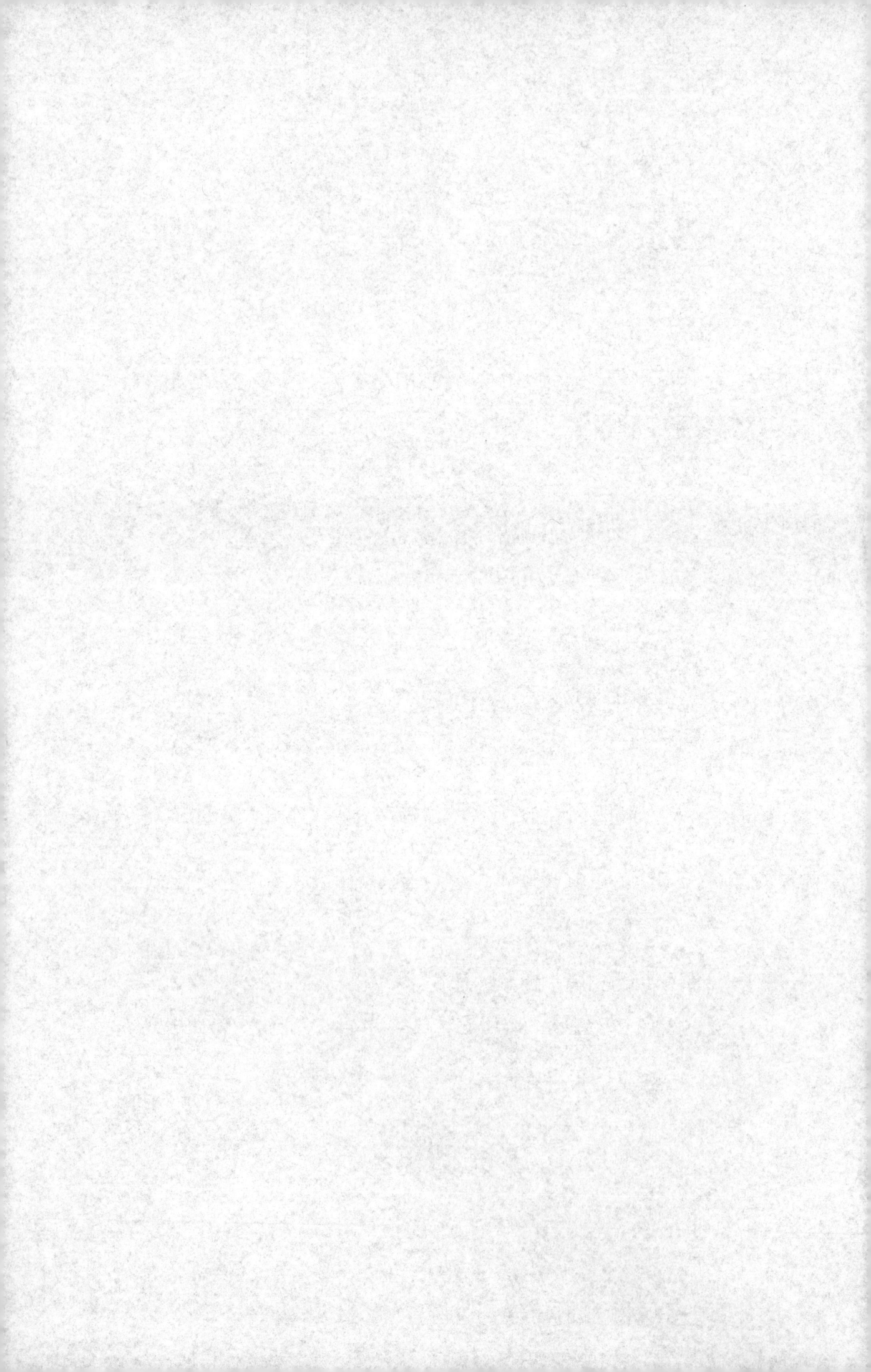